HONDA

ACCORD/PRELUDE
1996-00 REPAIR MANUAL

CHILTON'S

CEO	Rick Van Dalen
President	Dean F. Morgantini, S.A.E.
Vice President–Finance	Barry L. Beck
Vice President–Sales	Glenn D. Potere
Executive Editor	Kevin M. G. Maher, A.S.E.
Manager–Consumer Automotive	Richard Schwartz, A.S.E.
Manager–Professional Automotive	Richard J. Rivele
Manager–Marine/Recreation	James R. Marotta, A.S.E.
Production Specialists	Brian Hollingsworth, Melinda Possinger
Project Managers	Thomas A. Mellon, A.S.E., S.A.E., Eric Michael Mihalyi, A.S.E., S.T.S., S.A.E., Christine L. Sheeky, S.A.E., Richard T. Smith, Ron Webb
Schematics Editors	Christopher ... S.A.E., S.T.S., Stephanie A. S...
Editor	Paul T. DeSanto, A.S.E.

CHILTON *Automotive Books*

PUBLISHED BY W. G. NICHOLS, INC.

Manufactured in USA
© 2000 W. G. Nichols, Inc.
1025 Andrew Drive
West Chester, PA 19380
ISBN 0-8019-9118-8
Library of Congress Catalog Card No. 00-132211
1234567890 9876543210

www.chiltononline.com

Contents

Contents

SAFETY NOTICE

Proper service and repair procedures are vital to the safe, reliable operation of all motor vehicles, as well as the personal safety of those performing repairs. This manual outlines procedures for servicing and repairing vehicles using safe, effective methods. The procedures contain many NOTES, CAUTIONS and WARNINGS which should be followed, along with standard procedures to eliminate the possibility of personal injury or improper service which could damage the vehicle or compromise its safety.

It is important to note that repair procedures and techniques, tools and parts for servicing motor vehicles, as well as the skill and experience of the individual performing the work vary widely. It is not possible to anticipate all of the conceivable ways or conditions under which vehicles may be serviced, or to provide cautions as to all possible hazards that may result. Standard and accepted safety precautions and equipment should be used when handling toxic or flammable fluids, and safety goggles or other protection should be used during cutting, grinding, chiseling, prying, or any other process that can cause material removal or projectiles.

Some procedures require the use of tools specially designed for a specific purpose. Before substituting another tool or procedure, you must be completely satisfied that neither your personal safety, nor the performance of the vehicle will be endangered.

Although information in this manual is based on industry sources and is complete as possible at the time of publication, the possibility exists that some car manufacturers made later changes which could not be included here. While striving for total accuracy, Nichols Publishing cannot assume responsibility for any errors, changes or omissions that may occur in the compilation of this data.

PART NUMBERS

Part numbers listed in this reference are not recommendations by Nichols Publishing for any product brand name. They are references that can be used with interchange manuals and aftermarket supplier catalogs to locate each brand supplier's discrete part number.

SPECIAL TOOLS

Special tools are recommended by the vehicle manufacturer to perform their specific job. Use has been kept to a minimum, but where absolutely necessary, they are referred to in the text by the part number of the tool manufacturer. These tools can be purchased, under the appropriate part number, from your local dealer or regional distributor, or an equivalent tool can be purchased locally from a tool supplier or parts outlet. Before substituting any tool for the one recommended, read the SAFETY NOTICE at the top of this page.

ACKNOWLEDGMENTS

Nichols Publishing expresses appreciation to Honda Motor Co. Ltd., for their generous assistance. Nichols Publishing would also like to thank Scott Honda of West Chester, PA, for the use of their Honda Accord which is pictured on the cover of this manual.

Nichols Publishing would like to express thanks to all of the fine companies who participate in the production of our books:
- Hand tools supplied by Craftsman are used during all phases of our vehicle teardown and photography.
- Many of the fine specialty tools used in our procedures were provided courtesy of Lisle Corporation.
- Lincoln Automotive Products (1 Lincoln Way, St. Louis, MO 63120) has provided their industrial shop equipment, including jacks (engine, transmission and floor), engine stands, fluid and lubrication tools, as well as shop presses.
- Rotary Lifts (1-800-640-5438 or www.Rotary-Lift.com), the largest automobile lift manufacturer in the world, offering the biggest variety of surface and in-ground lifts available, has fulfilled our shop's lift needs.
- Much of our shop's electronic testing equipment was supplied by Universal Enterprises Inc. (UEI).
- Safety-Kleen Systems Inc. has provided parts cleaning stations and assistance with environmentally sound disposal of residual wastes.
- United Gilsonite Laboratories (UGL), manufacturer of Drylok® concrete floor paint, has provided materials and expertise for the coating and protection of our shop floor.

1

GENERAL INFORMATION AND MAINTENANCE

HOW TO USE THIS BOOK

Chilton's Total Car Care manual for the Honda Accord and Prelude is intended to help you learn more about the inner workings of your vehicle while saving you money on its upkeep and operation.

The beginning of the book will likely be referred to the most, since that is where you will find information for maintenance and tune-up. The other sections deal with the more complex systems of your vehicle. Operating systems from engine through brakes are covered to the extent that the average do-it-yourselfer becomes mechanically involved. This book will not explain such things as rebuilding a differential for the simple reason that the expertise required and the investment in special tools make this task uneconomical. It will, however, give you detailed instructions to help you change your own brake pads and shoes, replace spark plugs, and perform many more jobs that can save you money, give you personal satisfaction and help you avoid expensive problems.

A secondary purpose of this book is a reference for owners who want to understand their vehicle and/or their mechanics. In this case, no tools at all are required.

Where to Begin

Before removing any bolts, read through the entire procedure. This will give you the overall view of what tools and supplies will be required. There is nothing more frustrating than having to walk to the bus stop on Monday morning because you were short one bolt on Sunday afternoon. So read ahead and plan ahead. Each operation should be approached logically and all procedures thoroughly understood before attempting any work.

All sections contain adjustments, maintenance, removal and installation procedures, and in some cases, repair or overhaul procedures. When repair is not considered practical, we tell you how to remove the part and then how to install the new or rebuilt replacement. In this way, you at least save labor costs. "Backyard" repair of some components is just not practical.

Avoiding Trouble

Many procedures in this book require you to "label and disconnect . . ." a group of lines, hoses or wires. Don't be lulled into thinking you can remember where everything goes—you won't. If you hook up vacuum or fuel lines incorrectly, the vehicle may run poorly, if at all. If you hook up electrical wiring incorrectly, you may instantly learn a very expensive lesson.

You don't need to know the official or engineering name for each hose or line. A piece of masking tape on the hose and a piece on its fitting will allow you

to assign your own label such as the letter A or a short name. As long as you remember your own code, the lines can be reconnected by matching similar letters or names. Do remember that tape will dissolve in gasoline or other fluids; if a component is to be washed or cleaned, use another method of identification. A permanent felt-tipped marker or a metal scribe can be very handy for marking metal parts. Remove any tape or paper labels after assembly.

Maintenance or Repair?

It's necessary to mention the difference between maintenance and repair. Maintenance includes routine inspections, adjustments, and replacement of parts which show signs of normal wear. Maintenance compensates for wear or deterioration. Repair implies that something has broken or is not working. A need for repair is often caused by lack of maintenance. Example: draining and refilling the automatic transmission fluid is maintenance recommended by the manufacturer at specific mileage intervals. Failure to do this can shorten the life of the transmission/transaxle, requiring very expensive repairs. While no maintenance program can prevent items from breaking or wearing out, a general rule can be stated: MAINTENANCE IS CHEAPER THAN REPAIR.

Two basic mechanic's rules should be mentioned here. First, whenever the left side of the vehicle or engine is referred to, it is meant to specify the driver's side. Conversely, the right side of the vehicle means the passenger's side. Second, screws and bolts are removed by turning counterclockwise, and tightened by turning clockwise unless specifically noted.

Safety is always the most important rule. Constantly be aware of the dangers involved in working on an automobile and take the proper precautions. See the information in this section regarding SERVICING YOUR VEHICLE SAFELY and the SAFETY NOTICE on the acknowledgment page.

Avoiding the Most Common Mistakes

Pay attention to the instructions provided. There are 3 common mistakes in mechanical work:

1. Incorrect order of assembly, disassembly or adjustment. When taking something apart or putting it together, performing steps in the wrong order usually just costs you extra time; however, it CAN break something. Read the entire procedure before beginning disassembly. Perform everything in the order in which the instructions say you should, even if you can't immediately see a reason for it. When you're taking apart something that is very intricate, you might want to draw a picture of how it looks when assembled at one point in order to make sure you get everything back in its proper

position. We will supply exploded views whenever possible. When making adjustments, perform them in the proper order. One adjustment possibly will affect another.

2. Overtorquing (or undertorquing). While it is more common for overtorquing to cause damage, undertorquing may allow a fastener to vibrate loose causing serious damage. Especially when dealing with aluminum parts, pay attention to torque specifications and utilize a torque wrench in assembly. If a torque figure is not available, remember that if you are using the right tool to perform the job, you will probably not have to strain yourself to get a fastener tight enough. The pitch of most threads is so slight that the tension you put on the wrench will be multiplied many times in actual force on what you are tightening. A good example of how critical torque is can be seen in the case of spark plug installation, especially where you are putting the plug into an aluminum cylinder head. Too little torque can fail to crush the gasket, causing leakage of combustion gases and consequent overheating of the plug and engine parts. Too much torque can damage the threads or distort the plug, changing the spark gap.

There are many commercial products available for ensuring that fasteners won't come loose, even if they are not torqued just right (a very common brand is Loctite®). If you're worried about getting something together tight enough to hold, but loose enough to avoid mechanical damage during assembly, one of these products might offer substantial insurance. Before choosing a threadlocking compound, read the label on the package and make sure the product is compatible with the materials, fluids, etc. involved.

3. Crossthreading. This occurs when a part such as a bolt is screwed into a nut or casting at the wrong angle and forced. Crossthreading is more likely to occur if access is difficult. It helps to clean and lubricate fasteners, then to start threading the bolt, spark plug, etc. with your fingers. If you encounter resistance, unscrew the part and start over again at a different angle until it can be inserted and turned several times without much effort. Keep in mind that many parts, especially spark plugs, have tapered threads, so that gentle turning will automatically bring the part you're threading to the proper angle. Don't put a wrench on the part until it's been tightened a couple of turns by hand. If you suddenly encounter resistance, and the part has not seated fully, don't force it. Pull it back out to make sure it's clean and threading properly.

Be sure to take your time and be patient, and always plan ahead. Allow yourself ample time to perform repairs and maintenance. You may find maintaining your car a satisfying and enjoyable experience.

TOOLS AND EQUIPMENT

▶ **See Figures 1 thru 15**

Naturally, without the proper tools and equipment it is impossible to properly service your vehicle. It would also be virtually impossible to catalog every tool that you would need to perform all of the operations in this book. Of course, it would

be unwise for the amateur to rush out and buy an expensive set of tools on the theory that he/she may need one or more of them at some time.

The best approach is to proceed slowly, gathering a good quality set of those tools that are used most frequently. Don't be misled by the low cost of

bargain tools. It is far better to spend a little more for better quality. Forged wrenches, 6 or 12-point sockets and fine tooth ratchets are by far preferable to their less expensive counterparts. As any good mechanic can tell you, there are few worse experiences than trying to work on a vehicle with bad tools. Your monetary savings will be far outweighed by frustration and mangled knuckles.

Begin accumulating those tools that are used most frequently: those associated with routine maintenance and tune-up. In addition to the normal assortment of screwdrivers and pliers, you should have the following tools:

- Wrenches/sockets and combination open end/box end wrenches in sizes from ⅛–¾ in. or 3–19mm, as well as a ¹³⁄₁₆ in. or ⅝ in. spark plug socket (depending on plug type).

➡**If possible, buy various length socket drive extensions. Universal-joint and wobble extensions can be extremely useful, but be careful when using them, as they can change the amount of torque applied to the socket.**

- Jackstands for support.
- Oil filter wrench.
- Spout or funnel for pouring fluids.
- Grease gun for chassis lubrication (unless your vehicle is not equipped with any grease fittings—for details, please refer to information on Fluids and Lubricants, later in this section).
- Hydrometer for checking the battery (unless equipped with a sealed, maintenance-free battery).
- A container for draining oil and other fluids.
- Rags for wiping up the inevitable mess.

In addition to the above items there are several others that are not absolutely necessary, but handy to have around. These include Oil Dry((or an equivalent oil absorbent gravel—such as cat litter) and the usual supply of lubricants, antifreeze and

fluids, although these can be purchased as needed. This is a basic list for routine maintenance, but only your personal needs and desire can accurately determine your list of tools.

After performing a few projects on the vehicle, you'll be amazed at the other tools and non-tools on your workbench. Some useful household items are: a large turkey baster or siphon, empty coffee cans and ice trays (to store parts), ball of twine, electrical tape for wiring, small rolls of colored tape for tagging lines or hoses, markers and pens, a note pad, golf tees (for plugging vacuum lines), metal coat hangers or a roll of mechanic's wire (to hold things out of the way), dental pick or similar long, pointed probe, a strong magnet, and a small mirror (to see into recesses and under manifolds).

TCCS1200

Fig. 1 All but the most basic procedures will require an assortment of ratchets and sockets

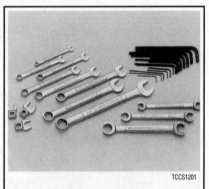

TCCS1201

Fig. 2 In addition to ratchets, a good set of wrenches and hex keys will be necessary

TCCS1202

Fig. 3 A hydraulic floor jack and a set of jackstands are essential for lifting and supporting the vehicle

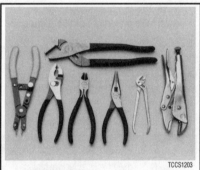

TCCS1203

Fig. 4 An assortment of pliers, grippers and cutters will be handy for old rusted parts and stripped bolt heads

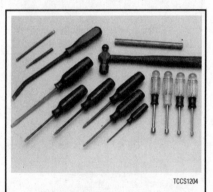

TCCS1204

Fig. 5 Various drivers, chisels and prybars are great tools to have in your toolbox

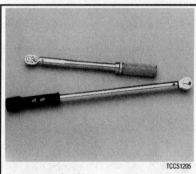

TCCS1205

Fig. 6 Many repairs will require the use of a torque wrench to assure the components are properly fastened

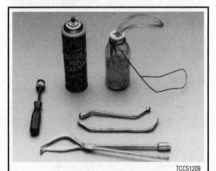

TCCS1209

Fig. 7 Although not always necessary, using specialized brake tools will save time

TCCS1210

Fig. 8 A few inexpensive lubrication tools will make maintenance easier

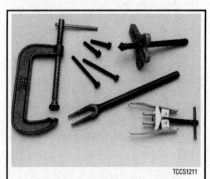

TCCS1211

Fig. 9 Various pullers, clamps and separator tools are needed for many larger, more complicated repairs

Fig. 10 A variety of tools and gauges should be used for spark plug gapping and installation

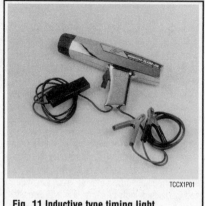

Fig. 11 Inductive type timing light

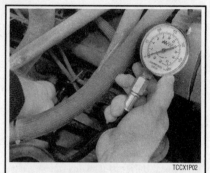

Fig. 12 A screw-in type compression gauge is recommended for compression testing

Fig. 13 A vacuum/pressure tester is necessary for many testing procedures

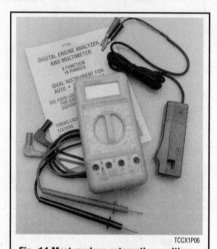

Fig. 14 Most modern automotive multimeters incorporate many helpful features

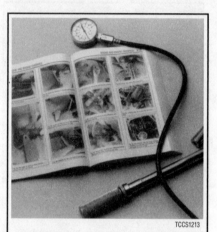

Fig. 15 Proper information is vital, so always have a Chilton Total Car Care manual handy

A more advanced set of tools, suitable for tune-up work, can be drawn up easily. While the tools are slightly more sophisticated, they need not be outrageously expensive. There are several inexpensive tach/dwell meters on the market that are every bit as good for the average mechanic as a professional model. Just be sure that it goes to a least 1200–1500 rpm on the tach scale and that it works on 4, 6 and 8-cylinder engines. The key to these purchases is to make them with an eye towards adaptability and wide range. A basic list of tune-up tools could include:

• Tach/dwell meter.
• Spark plug wrench and gapping tool.
• Feeler gauges for valve adjustment.
• Timing light.

The choice of a timing light should be made carefully. A light which works on the DC current supplied by the vehicle's battery is the best choice; it should have a xenon tube for brightness. On any vehicle with an electronic ignition system, a timing light with an inductive pickup that clamps around the No. 1 spark plug cable is preferred.

In addition to these basic tools, there are several other tools and gauges you may find useful. These include:

• Compression gauge. The screw-in type is slower to use, but eliminates the possibility of a faulty reading due to escaping pressure.
• Manifold vacuum gauge.
• 12V test light.
• A combination volt/ohmmeter
• Induction Ammeter. This is used for determining whether or not there is current in a wire. These are handy for use if a wire is broken somewhere in a wiring harness.

As a final note, you will probably find a torque wrench necessary for all but the most basic work. The beam type models are perfectly adequate, although the newer click types (breakaway) are easier to use. The click type torque wrenches tend to be more expensive. Also keep in mind that all types of torque wrenches should be periodically checked and/or recalibrated. You will have to decide for yourself which better fits your pocketbook, and purpose.

Special Tools

Normally, the use of special factory tools is avoided for repair procedures, since these are not readily available for the do-it-yourself mechanic. When it is possible to perform the job with more commonly available tools, it will be pointed out, but occasionally, a special tool was designed to perform a specific function and should be used. Before substituting another tool, you should be convinced that neither your safety nor the performance of the vehicle will be compromised.

Special tools can usually be purchased from an automotive parts store or from your dealer. In some cases special tools may be available directly from the tool manufacturer.

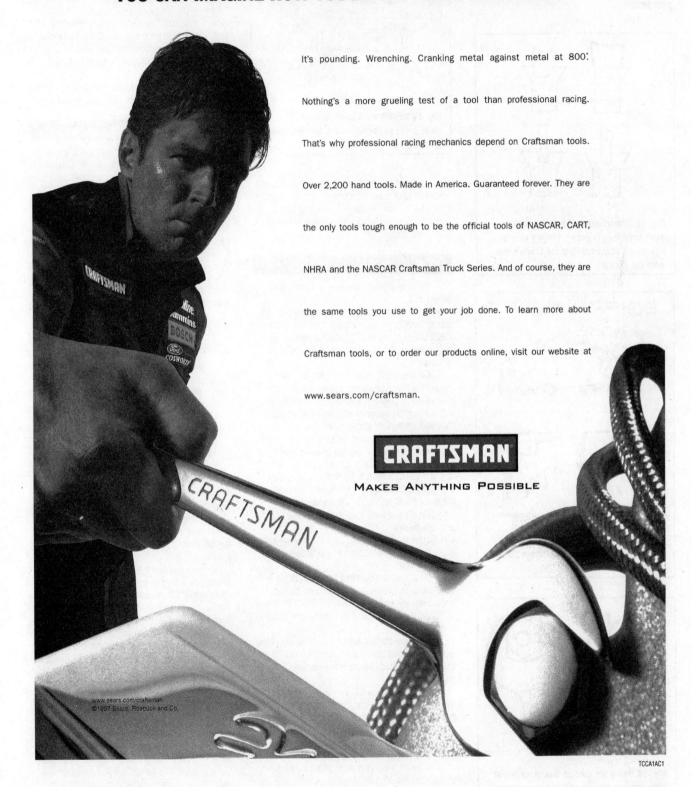
TCCA1AC1

SERVICING YOUR VEHICLE SAFELY

♦ **See Figures 16, 17, 18 and 19**

It is virtually impossible to anticipate all of the hazards involved with automotive maintenance and service, but care and common sense will prevent most accidents.

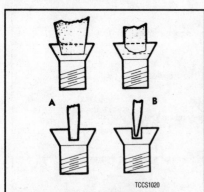

Fig. 16 Screwdrivers should be kept in good condition to prevent injury or damage which could result if the blade slips from the screw

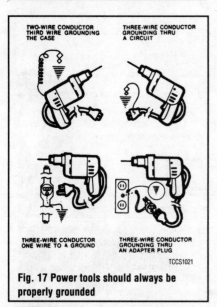

Fig. 17 Power tools should always be properly grounded

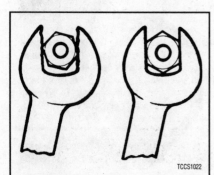

Fig. 18 Using the correct size wrench will help prevent the possibility of rounding off a nut

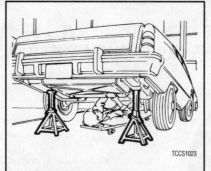

Fig. 19 NEVER work under a vehicle unless it is supported using safety stands (jackstands)

The rules of safety for mechanics range from "don't smoke around gasoline," to "use the proper tool(s) for the job." The trick to avoiding injuries is to develop safe work habits and to take every possible precaution.

Do's

• Do keep a fire extinguisher and first aid kit handy.

• Do wear safety glasses or goggles when cutting, drilling, grinding or prying, even if you have 20/20 vision. If you wear glasses for the sake of vision, wear safety goggles over your regular glasses.

• Do shield your eyes whenever you work around the battery. Batteries contain sulfuric acid. In case of contact with the eyes or skin, flush the area with water or a mixture of water and baking soda, then seek immediate medical attention.

• Do use safety stands (jackstands) for any undervehicle service. Jacks are for raising vehicles; jackstands are for making sure the vehicle stays raised until you want it to come down. Whenever the vehicle is raised, block the wheels remaining on the ground and set the parking brake.

• Do use adequate ventilation when working with any chemicals or hazardous materials. Like carbon monoxide, the asbestos dust resulting from some brake lining wear can be hazardous in sufficient quantities.

• Do disconnect the negative battery cable when working on the electrical system. The secondary ignition system contains EXTREMELY HIGH VOLTAGE. In some cases it can even exceed 50,000 volts.

• Do follow manufacturer's directions whenever working with potentially hazardous materials. Most chemicals and fluids are poisonous if taken internally.

• Do properly maintain your tools. Loose hammerheads, mushroomed punches and chisels, frayed or poorly grounded electrical cords, excessively worn screwdrivers, spread wrenches (open end), cracked sockets, slipping ratchets, or faulty droplight sockets can cause accidents.

• Likewise, keep your tools clean; a greasy wrench can slip off a bolt head, ruining the bolt and often harming your knuckles in the process.

• Do use the proper size and type of tool for the job at hand. Do select a wrench or socket that fits the nut or bolt. The wrench or socket should sit straight, not cocked.

• Do, when possible, pull on a wrench handle rather than push on it, and adjust your stance to prevent a fall.

• Do be sure that adjustable wrenches are tightly closed on the nut or bolt and pulled so that the force is on the side of the fixed jaw.

• Do strike squarely with a hammer; avoid glancing blows.

• Do set the parking brake and block the drive wheels if the work requires a running engine.

Don'ts

• Don't run the engine in a garage or anywhere else without proper ventilation—EVER! Carbon monoxide is poisonous; it takes a long time to leave the human body and you can build up a deadly supply of it in your system by simply breathing in a little every day. You may not realize you are slowly poisoning yourself. Always use power vents, windows, fans and/or open the garage door.

• Don't work around moving parts while wearing loose clothing. Short sleeves are much safer than long, loose sleeves. Hard-toed shoes with neoprene soles protect your toes and give a better grip on slippery surfaces. Jewelry such as watches, fancy belt buckles, beads or body adornment of any kind is not safe working around a vehicle. Long hair should be tied back under a hat or cap.

• Don't use pockets for toolboxes. A fall or bump can drive a screwdriver deep into your body. Even a rag hanging from your back pocket can wrap around a spinning shaft or fan.

• Don't smoke when working around gasoline, cleaning solvent or other flammable material.

• Don't smoke when working around the battery. When the battery is being charged, it gives off explosive hydrogen gas.

• Don't use gasoline to wash your hands; there are excellent soaps available. Gasoline contains dangerous additives which can enter the body through a cut or through your pores. Gasoline also removes all the natural oils from the skin so that bone dry hands will suck up oil and grease.

• Don't service the air conditioning system unless you are equipped with the necessary tools and training. When liquid or compressed gas refrigerant is released to atmospheric pressure it will absorb heat from whatever it contacts. This will chill or freeze anything it touches.

• Don't use screwdrivers for anything other than driving screws! A screwdriver used as an prying tool can snap when you least expect it, causing injuries. At the very least, you'll ruin a good screwdriver.

• Don't use an emergency jack (that little ratchet, scissors, or pantograph jack supplied with the vehicle) for anything other than changing a flat! These jacks are only intended for emergency use out on the road; they are NOT designed as a maintenance tool. If you are serious about maintaining your vehicle yourself, invest in a hydraulic floor jack of at least a 1½ ton capacity, and at least two sturdy jackstands.

FASTENERS, MEASUREMENTS AND CONVERSIONS

Bolts, Nuts and Other Threaded Retainers

▶ See Figures 20, 21, 22 and 23

Although there are a great variety of fasteners found in the modern car or truck, the most commonly used retainer is the threaded fastener (nuts, bolts, screws, studs, etc.). Most threaded retainers may be reused, provided that they are not damaged in use or during the repair. Some retainers (such as stretch bolts or torque prevailing nuts) are designed to deform when tightened or in use and should not be reinstalled.

Whenever possible, we will note any special retainers which should be replaced during a procedure. But you should always inspect the condition of a retainer when it is removed and replace any that show signs of damage. Check all threads for rust or corrosion which can increase the torque necessary to achieve the desired clamp load for which that fastener was originally selected. Additionally, be sure that the driver surface of the fastener has not been compromised by rounding or other damage. In some cases a driver surface may become only partially rounded, allowing the driver to catch in only one direction. In many of these occurrences, a fastener may be installed and tightened, but the driver would not be able to grip and loosen the fastener again. (This could lead to frustration down the line should that component ever need to be disassembled again).

If you must replace a fastener, whether due to design or damage, you must ALWAYS be sure to use the proper replacement. In all cases, a retainer of the same design, material and strength should be used. Markings on the heads of most bolts will help determine the proper strength of the fastener. The same material, thread and pitch must be selected to assure proper installation and safe operation of the vehicle afterwards.

Thread gauges are available to help measure a bolt or stud's thread. Most automotive and hardware stores keep gauges available to help you select the proper size. In a pinch, you can use another nut or bolt for a thread gauge. If the bolt you are replacing is not too badly damaged, you can select a match by finding another bolt which will thread in its place. If you find a nut which threads properly onto the damaged bolt, then use that nut to help select the

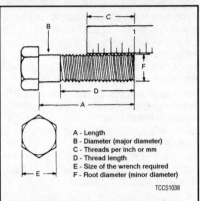

A - Length
B - Diameter (major diameter)
C - Threads per inch or mm
D - Thread length
E - Size of the wrench required
F - Root diameter (minor diameter)

TCCS1038

Fig. 22 Threaded retainer sizes are determined using these measurements

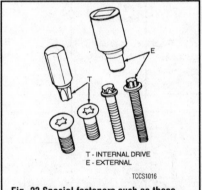

T - INTERNAL DRIVE
E - EXTERNAL

TCCS1016

Fig. 23 Special fasteners such as these Torx® head bolts are used by manufacturers to discourage people from working on vehicles without the proper tools

replacement bolt. If however, the bolt you are replacing is so badly damaged (broken or drilled out) that its threads cannot be used as a gauge, you might start by looking for another bolt (from the same assembly or a similar location on your vehicle) which will thread into the damaged bolt's mounting. If so, the other bolt can be used to select a nut; the nut can then be used to select the replacement bolt.

In all cases, be absolutely sure you have selected the proper replacement. Don't be shy, you can always ask the store clerk for help.

❄❄ WARNING

Be aware that when you find a bolt with damaged threads, you may also find the nut or drilled hole it was threaded into has also been damaged. If this is the case, you may have to drill and tap the hole, replace the nut or otherwise repair the threads. NEVER try to force a replacement bolt to fit into the damaged threads.

Torque

Torque is defined as the measurement of resistance to turning or rotating. It tends to twist a body about an axis of rotation. A common example of this would be tightening a threaded retainer such as

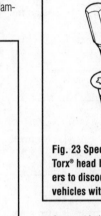

POZIDRIVE PHILLIPS RECESS TORX® CLUTCH RECESS

INDENTED HEXAGON HEXAGON TRIMMED HEXAGON WASHER HEAD

TCCS1037

Fig. 20 Here are a few of the most common screw/bolt driver styles

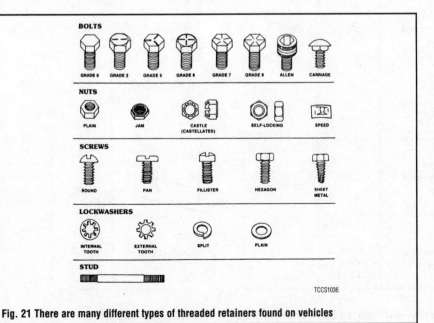

BOLTS
GRADE 0 GRADE 2 GRADE 5 GRADE 6 GRADE 7 GRADE 8 ALLEN CARRIAGE

NUTS
PLAIN JAM CASTLE (CASTELLATED) SELF-LOCKING SPEED

SCREWS
ROUND PAN FILLISTER HEXAGON SHEET METAL

LOCKWASHERS
INTERNAL TOOTH EXTERNAL TOOTH SPLIT PLAIN

STUD

TCCS1036

Fig. 21 There are many different types of threaded retainers found on vehicles

a nut, bolt or screw. Measuring torque is one of the most common ways to help assure that a threaded retainer has been properly fastened.

When tightening a threaded fastener, torque is applied in three distinct areas, the head, the bearing surface and the clamp load. About 50 percent of the measured torque is used in overcoming bearing friction. This is the friction between the bearing surface of the bolt head, screw head or nut face and the base material or washer (the surface on which the fastener is rotating). Approximately 40 percent of the applied torque is used in overcoming thread friction. This leaves only about 10 percent of the applied torque to develop a useful clamp load (the force which holds a joint together). This means that friction can account for as much as 90 percent of the applied torque on a fastener.

TORQUE WRENCHES

♦ See Figures 24, 25 and 26

In most applications, a torque wrench can be used to assure proper installation of a fastener. Torque wrenches come in various designs and most automotive supply stores will carry a variety to suit your needs. A torque wrench should be used any time we supply a specific torque value for a fastener. A torque wrench can also be used if you are following the general guidelines in the accompanying charts. Keep in mind that because there is no worldwide standardization of fasteners, the charts are a general guideline and should be used with caution. Again, the general rule of "if you are using the right tool for the job, you should not have to strain to tighten a fastener" applies here.

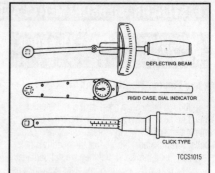

Fig. 24 Various styles of torque wrenches are usually available at your local automotive supply store

	Mark	Class		Mark	Class
Hexagon head bolt	Bolt head No. 4 4— 5— 6— 7— 8— 9— 10— 11—	4T 5T 6T 7T 8T 9T 10T 11T	Stud bolt	No mark	4T
	No mark	4T		Grooved	6T
Hexagon flange bolt w/ washer hexagon bolt	No mark	4T			
Hexagon head bolt	Two protruding lines	5T			
Hexagon flange bolt w/ washer hexagon bolt	Two protruding lines	6T	Welded bolt		4T
Hexagon head bolt	Three protruding lines	7T			
Hexagon head bolt	Four protruding lines	8T			

Fig. 25 Determining bolt strength of metric fasteners—NOTE: this is a typical bolt marking system, but there is not a worldwide standard

Class	Diameter mm	Pitch mm	Hexagon head bolt			Hexagon flange bolt		
			N·m	kgf·cm	ft·lbf	N·m	kgf·cm	ft·lbf
4T	6	1	5	55	48 in.·lbf	6	60	52 in.·lbf
	8	1.25	12.5	130	9	14	145	10
	10	1.25	26	260	19	29	290	21
	12	1.25	47	480	35	53	540	39
	14	1.5	74	760	55	84	850	61
	16	1.5	115	1,150	83	—	—	—
5T	6	1	6.5	65	56 in.·lbf	7.5	75	65 in.·lbf
	8	1.25	15.5	160	12	17.5	175	13
	10	1.25	32	330	24	36	360	26
	12	1.25	59	600	43	65	670	48
	14	1.5	91	930	67	100	1,050	76
	16	1.5	140	1,400	101	—	—	—
6T	6	1	8	80	69 in.·lbf	9	90	78 in.·lbf
	8	1.25	19	195	14	21	210	15
	10	1.25	39	400	29	44	440	32
	12	1.25	71	730	53	80	810	59
	14	1.5	110	1,100	80	125	1,250	90
	16	1.5	170	1,750	127	—	—	—
7T	6	1	10.5	110	8	12	120	9
	8	1.25	25	260	19	28	290	21
	10	1.25	52	530	38	58	590	43
	12	1.25	95	970	70	105	1,050	76
	14	1.5	145	1,500	108	165	1,700	123
	16	1.5	230	2,300	166	—	—	—
8T	8	1.25	29	300	22	33	330	24
	10	1.25	61	620	45	68	690	50
	12	1.25	110	1,100	80	120	1,250	90
9T	8	1.25	34	340	25	37	380	27
	10	1.25	70	710	51	78	790	57
	12	1.25	125	1,300	94	140	1,450	105
10T	8	1.25	38	390	28	42	430	31
	10	1.25	78	800	58	88	890	64
	12	1.25	140	1,450	105	155	1,600	116
11T	8	1.25	42	430	31	47	480	35
	10	1.25	87	890	64	97	990	72
	12	1.25	155	1,600	116	175	1,800	130

TCCS1241

Fig. 26 Typical bolt torques for metric fasteners—WARNING: use only as a guide

Beam Type

♦ See Figure 27

The beam type torque wrench is one of the most popular types. It consists of a pointer attached to the head that runs the length of the flexible beam (shaft) to a scale located near the handle. As the wrench is pulled, the beam bends and the pointer indicates the torque using the scale.

Click (Breakaway) Type

♦ See Figure 28

Another popular design of torque wrench is the click type. To use the click type wrench you pre-

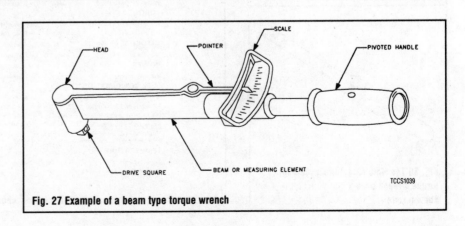

Fig. 27 Example of a beam type torque wrench

TCCS1039

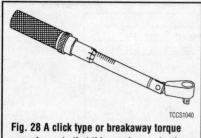

Fig. 28 A click type or breakaway torque wrench—note that this one has a pivoting head

adjust it to a torque setting. Once the torque is reached, the wrench has a reflex signaling feature that causes a momentary breakaway of the torque wrench body, sending an impulse to the operator's hand.

Pivot Head Type

▶ **See Figures 28 and 29**

Some torque wrenches (usually of the click type) may be equipped with a pivot head which can allow it to be used in areas of limited access. BUT, it must be used properly. To hold a pivot head wrench, grasp the handle lightly, and as you pull on the handle, it should be floated on the pivot point. If the handle comes in contact with the yoke extension during the process of pulling, there is a very good chance the torque readings will be inaccurate because this could alter the wrench loading point. The design of the handle is usually such as to make it inconvenient to deliberately misuse the wrench.

➡ It should be mentioned that the use of any U-joint, wobble or extension will have an effect on the torque readings, no matter what type of

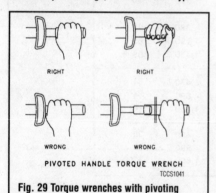

Fig. 29 Torque wrenches with pivoting heads must be grasped and used properly to prevent an incorrect reading

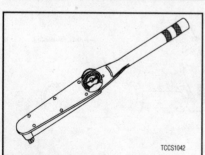

Fig. 30 The rigid case (direct reading) torque wrench uses a dial indicator to show torque

wrench you are using. For the most accurate readings, install the socket directly on the wrench driver. If necessary, straight extensions (which hold a socket directly under the wrench driver) will have the least effect on the torque reading. Avoid any extension that alters the length of the wrench from the handle to the head/driving point (such as a crow's foot). U-joint or wobble extensions can greatly affect the readings; avoid their use at all times.

Rigid Case (Direct Reading)

▶ **See Figure 30**

A rigid case or direct reading torque wrench is equipped with a dial indicator to show torque values. One advantage of these wrenches is that they can be held at any position on the wrench without affecting accuracy. These wrenches are often preferred because they tend to be compact, easy to read and have a great degree of accuracy.

TORQUE ANGLE METERS

▶ **See Figure 31**

Because the frictional characteristics of each fastener or threaded hole will vary, clamp loads which are based strictly on torque will vary as well. In most applications, this variance is not significant enough to cause worry. But, in certain applications, a manufacturer's engineers may determine that more precise clamp loads are necessary (such is the case with many aluminum cylinder heads). In these cases, a

Fig. 31 Some specifications require the use of a torque angle meter (mechanical protractor)

torque angle method of installation would be specified. When installing fasteners which are torque angle tightened, a predetermined seating torque and standard torque wrench are usually used first to remove any compliance from the joint. The fastener is then tightened the specified additional portion of a turn measured in degrees. A torque angle gauge (mechanical protractor) is used for these applications.

Standard and Metric Measurements

▶ **See Figure 32**

Throughout this manual, specifications are given to help you determine the condition of various com-

CONVERSION FACTORS

LENGTH–DISTANCE

Inches (in.)	x 25.4	= Millimeters (mm)	x .0394	= Inches
Feet (ft.)	x .305	= Meters (m)	x 3.281	= Feet
Miles	x 1.609	= Kilometers (km)	x .0621	= Miles

VOLUME

Cubic Inches (in3)	x 16.387	= Cubic Centimeters	x .061	= in3
IMP Pints (IMP pt.)	x .568	= Liters (L)	x 1.76	= IMP pt.
IMP Quarts (IMP qt.)	x 1.137	= Liters (L)	x .88	= IMP qt.
IMP Gallons (IMP gal.)	x 4.546	= Liters (L)	x .22	= IMP gal.
IMP Quarts (IMP qt.)	x 1.201	= US Quarts (US qt.)	x .833	= IMP qt.
IMP Gallons (IMP gal.)	x 1.201	= US Gallons (US gal.)	x .833	= IMP gal.
Fl. Ounces	x 29.573	= Milliliters	x .034	= Ounces
US Pints (US pt.)	x .473	= Liters (L)	x 2.113	= Pints
US Quarts (US qt.)	x .946	= Liters (L)	x 1.057	= Quarts
US Gallons (US gal.)	x 3.785	= Liters (L)	x .264	= Gallons

MASS–WEIGHT

Ounces (oz.)	x 28.35	= Grams (g)	x .035	= Ounces
Pounds (lb.)	x .454	= Kilograms (kg)	x 2.205	= Pounds

PRESSURE

Pounds Per Sq. In. (psi)	x 6.895	= Kilopascals (kPa)	x .145	= psi
Inches of Mercury (Hg)	x .4912	= psi	x 2.036	= Hg
Inches of Mercury (Hg)	x 3.377	= Kilopascals (kPa)	x .2961	= Hg
Inches of Water (H₂O)	x .07355	= Inches of Mercury	x 13.783	= H₂O
Inches of Water (H₂O)	x .03613	= psi	x 27.684	= H₂O
Inches of Water (H₂O)	x .248	= Kilopascals (kPa)	x 4.026	= H₂O

TORQUE

Pounds–Force Inches (in–lb)	x .113	= Newton Meters (N·m)	x 8.85	= in–lb
Pounds–Force Feet (ft–lb)	x 1.356	= Newton Meters (N·m)	x .738	= ft–lb

VELOCITY

Miles Per Hour (MPH)	x 1.609	= Kilometers Per Hour (KPH)	x .621	= MPH

POWER

Horsepower (Hp)	x .745	= Kilowatts	x 1.34	= Horsepower

FUEL CONSUMPTION*

Miles Per Gallon IMP (MPG)	x .354	= Kilometers Per Liter (Km/L)	
Kilometers Per Liter (Km/L)	x 2.352	= IMP MPG	
Miles Per Gallon US (MPG)	x .425	= Kilometers Per Liter (Km/L)	
Kilometers Per Liter (Km/L)	x 2.352	= US MPG	

*It is common to covert from miles per gallon (mpg) to liters/100 kilometers (1/100 km), where mpg (IMP) x 1/100 km = 282 and mpg (US) x 1/100 km = 235.

TEMPERATURE

Degree Fahrenheit (°F)	= (°C x 1.8) + 32
Degree Celsius (°C)	= (°F – 32) x .56

Fig. 32 Standard and metric conversion factors chart

ponents on your vehicle, or to assist you in their installation. Some of the most common measurements include length (in. or cm/mm), torque (ft. lbs., inch lbs. or Nm) and pressure (psi, in. Hg, kPa or mm Hg). In most cases, we strive to provide the proper measurement as determined by the manufacturer's engineers.

Though, in some cases, that value may not be conveniently measured with what is available in your toolbox. Luckily, many of the measuring

devices which are available today will have two scales so the Standard or Metric measurements may easily be taken. If any of the various measuring tools which are available to you do not contain the same scale as listed in the specifications, use the accompanying conversion factors to determine the proper value.

The conversion factor chart is used by taking the given specification and multiplying it by the necessary conversion factor. For instance, looking

at the first line, if you have a measurement in inches such as "free-play should be 2 in." but your ruler reads only in millimeters, multiply 2 in. by the conversion factor of 25.4 to get the metric equivalent of 50.8mm. Likewise, if the specification was given only in a Metric measurement, for example in Newton Meters (Nm), then look at the center column first. If the measurement is 100 Nm, multiply it by the conversion factor of 0.738 to get 73.8 ft. lbs.

SERIAL NUMBER IDENTIFICATION

Vehicle Identification Number (VIN)

▶ See Figures 33 and 34

The Vehicle Identification Number (VIN), which is a 17-digit code, can be found in three locations. It is stamped into the body on the top, center portion of the firewall, on a stamped plate attached to the left front top of the dashboard, and on a label located on the driver's door jam near the door latch. The VIN on the dashboard is the easiest to see, as it is close to the windshield on the driver's side of the vehicle and visible by looking through the windshield near the tip of the left side wiper blade.

93131P01

Fig. 33 To find the VIN, look through the left lower corner of the windshield. The number is stamped on a plate and attached to the dash

The 17-character label contains the following information:
- Digits 1, 2 and 3: Manufacturer, Make and Type of Vehicle
- Digits 4, 5 and 6: Line, Body and Engine Type
- Digit 7: Body and Transmission Type
- Digit 8: Vehicle Grade (Series)
- Digit 9: Check digit

```
1HG CG3 1 4 * W A 000001
       | |||||  | |
 a   b  cdef g h
```

a. **Manufacturer, Make and Type of Vehicle**
   1HG: HONDA OF AMERICA MFG., INC., U.S.A.
   HONDA, Passenger vehicle
b. **Line, Body and Engine Type**
   CG3: ACCORD COUPE/F23A1, F23A4
c. **Body Type and Transmission Type**
   1: 2-door Coupe/5-speed Manual
   2: 2-door Coupe/4-speed Automatic
d. **Vehicle Grade (Series)**
   4: LX
   5: EX
   7: EX-ULEV
e. **Check Digit**
f. **Model Year**
   W: 1998
g. **Factory Code**
   A: Marysville, Ohio Factory in U.S.A.
h. **Serial Number**

91181G06

Fig. 34 Typical Vehicle Identification Number (VIN) breakdown

- Digit 10: Vehicle model year
- Digit 11: Factory Code
- Digits 12 through 17: Serial Number

Engine

▶ See Figures 35 and 36

The installed engine type is part of the Line, Body, and Engine type three character code found in serial number positions 4, 5 and 6. This three-character code represents the basic body (or platform) type, and engine type installed for each particular model year. Sometimes this code will remain the same from one year to another although the installed engine type could change. Although the code describes which engine type is installed as original equipment for a particular model year, this code is not a portion of the five character engine type and serial number stamped on the engine block. The engine type and serial number are found near the front of the vehicle, stamped on the engine block where the transaxle housing and engine block join one another.

The engine type is a five-character code, which is followed by and separated from the engine serial number by a hyphen. This code is used the by the manufacturer to designate the engine type and the charts in this Total Car Care manual use the engine type to provide engine specifications which may vary from engine to engine. Locate the engine code stamped in the engine block and determine the

ENGINE AND VEHICLE IDENTIFACTION

Code ①	Liters (cc)	Cu. In.	Cyl.	Fuel Sys.	Engine Type	Eng. Mfg.
C27A4	2.7 (2675)	157	6	PGM-FI	SOHC	Honda
F22A1	2.2 (2156)	132	4	PGM-FI	DOHC	Honda
F22B1	2.2 (2156)	132	4	PGM-FI	SOHC	Honda
F22B2	2.2 (2156)	132	4	PGM-FI	SOHC	Honda
F23A1	2.3 (2254)	137	4	PGM-FI	SOHC	Honda
F23A4	2.3 (2254)	137	4	PGM-FI	SOHC	Honda
F23A5	2.3 (2254)	137	4	PGM-FI	SOHC	Honda
H22A1	2.2 (2157)	132	4	PGM-FI	SOHC	Honda
H22A4	2.2 (2157)	132	4	PGM-FI	DOHC	Honda
H23A1	2.3 (2259)	132	4	PGM-FI	DOHC	Honda
J30A1	3.0 (2997)	183	6	PGM-FI	SOHC	Honda

Code ②	Year
T	1996
V	1997
W	1998
X	1999
Y	2000

PGM-FI - Programmed Fuel Injection

① Stamped on engine

② 10 th digit of the VIN

91181C01

GENERAL ENGINE SPECIFICATIONS

Year	Model	Engine Displacement Liters (cc)	Engine ID/VIN	Fuel System Type	Net Horsepower @ rpm	Net Torque @ rpm (ft. lbs.)	Bore x Stroke (in.)	Com-pression Ratio	Oil Pressure @ rpm
1996	Accord DX/LX	2.2 (2156)	F22A1	PGM-FI	135@5200	142@4000	3.35x3.74	8.8:1	50@3000
	Accord EX	2.2 (2156)	F22B1	PGM-FI	145@5500	147@4500	3.35x3.74	8.8:1	50@3000
	Prelude S	2.2 (2156)	F22B2	PGM-FI	130@5300	139@4200	3.35x3.74	8.8:1	50@3000
	Prelude Si VTEC	2.2 (2157)	H22A1	PGM-FI	190@6800	158@5500	3.43x3.57	10.0:1	50@3000
	Prelude Si	2.3 (2259)	H23A1	PGM-FI	160@5800	156@4500	3.43x3.74	9.8:1	50@3000
	Accord V-6	2.7 (2675)	C27A4	PGM-FI	170@5600	165@4500	3.43x2.95	9.0:1	63@3000
1997	Accord Coupe	2.2 (2156)	F22B1	PGM-FI	145@5500	147@4500	3.35x3.74	8.8:1	50@3000
	Accord Coupe	2.2 (2156)	F22B2	PGM-FI	130@5300	139@4200	3.35x3.74	8.8:1	50@3000
	Accord Sedan	2.2 (2156)	F22B1	PGM-FI	145@5500	147@4500	3.35x3.74	8.8:1	50@3000
	Accord Sedan	2.2 (2156)	F22B2	PGM-FI	130@5300	139@4200	3.35x3.74	8.8:1	50@3000
	Accord Wagon	2.2 (2156)	F22B1	PGM-FI	145@5500	147@4500	3.35x3.74	8.8:1	50@3000
	Accord Wagon	2.2 (2156)	F22B2	PGM-FI	130@5300	139@4200	3.35x3.74	8.8:1	50@3000
	Prelude	2.2 (2157)	H22A4	PGM-FI	190@6800	158@5500	3.43x3.57	10.0:1	50@3000
	Prelude SH	2.2 (2157)	H22A4	PGM-FI	190@6800	158@5500	3.43x3.57	10.0:1	50@3000
	Accord Sedan	2.7 (2675)	C27A4	PGM-FI	170@5600	165@4500	3.43x2.95	9.0:1	63@3000
1998	Prelude	2.2 (2157)	H22A4	PGM-FI	①	158@5500	3.43x3.57	10.0:1	50@3000
	Prelude SH	2.2 (2157)	H22A4	PGM-FI	①	158@5500	3.43x3.57	10.0:1	50@3000
	Accord Coupe (EX, LX)	2.3 (2254)	F23A1	PGM-FI	150@5700	152@4900	3.39x3.82	9.3:1	50@3000
	Accord Coupe (EX, LX)	2.3 (2254)	F23A4	PGM-FI	150@5700	152@4900	3.39x3.82	9.3:1	50@3000
	Accord Sedan (DX)	2.3 (2254)	F23A5	PGM-FI	150@5700	152@4900	3.39x3.82	9.3:1	50@3000
	Accord Sedan (EX, LX)	2.3 (2254)	F23A1	PGM-FI	150@5700	152@4900	3.39x3.82	9.3:1	50@3000
	Accord Sedan (EX, LX)	2.3 (2254)	F23A4	PGM-FI	150@5700	152@4900	3.39x3.82	9.3:1	50@3000
	Accord Coupe (EX, LX)	3.0 (2997)	J30A1	PGM-FI	200@5500	195@4700	3.39x3.39	9.4:1	50@3000
	Accord Sedan (EX, LX)	3.0 (2997)	J30A1	PGM-FI	200@5500	195@4700	3.39x3.39	9.4:1	50@3000
1999	Prelude	2.2 (2157)	H22A4	PGM-FI	①	158@5500	3.43x3.57	10.0:1	50@3000
	Prelude SH	2.2 (2157)	H22A4	PGM-FI	①	158@5500	3.43x3.57	10.0:1	50@3000
	Accord Coupe (EX, LX)	2.3 (2254)	F23A1	PGM-FI	150@5700	152@4900	3.39x3.82	9.3:1	50@3000
	Accord Coupe (EX, LX)	2.3 (2254)	F23A4	PGM-FI	150@5700	152@4900	3.39x3.82	9.3:1	50@3000
	Accord Sedan (DX)	2.3 (2254)	F23A5	PGM-FI	150@5700	152@4900	3.39x3.82	9.3:1	50@3000
	Accord Sedan (EX, LX)	2.3 (2254)	F23A1	PGM-FI	150@5700	152@4900	3.39x3.82	9.3:1	50@3000
	Accord Sedan (EX, LX)	2.3 (2254)	F23A4	PGM-FI	150@5700	152@4900	3.39x3.82	9.3:1	50@3000
	Accord Coupe (EX, LX)	3.0 (2997)	J30A1	PGM-FI	200@5500	195@4700	3.39x3.39	9.4:1	50@3000
	Accord Sedan (EX, LX)	3.0 (2997)	J30A1	PGM-FI	200@5500	195@4700	3.39x3.39	9.4:1	50@3000
2000	Prelude	2.2 (2157)	H22A4	PGM-FI	①	158@5500	3.43x3.57	10.0:1	50@3000
	Prelude SH	2.2 (2157)	H22A4	PGM-FI	①	158@5500	3.43x3.57	10.0:1	50@3000
	Accord Coupe (EX, LX)	2.3 (2254)	F23A1	PGM-FI	150@5700	152@4900	3.39x3.82	9.3:1	50@3000
	Accord Coupe (EX, LX)	2.3 (2254)	F23A4	PGM-FI	150@5700	152@4900	3.39x3.82	9.3:1	50@3000
	Accord Sedan (DX)	2.3 (2254)	F23A5	PGM-FI	150@5700	152@4900	3.39x3.82	9.3:1	50@3000
	Accord Sedan (EX, LX)	2.3 (2254)	F23A1	PGM-FI	150@5700	152@4900	3.39x3.82	9.3:1	50@3000
	Accord Sedan (EX, LX)	2.3 (2254)	F23A4	PGM-FI	150@5700	152@4900	3.39x3.82	9.3:1	50@3000
	Accord Coupe (EX, LX)	3.0 (2997)	J30A1	PGM-FI	200@5500	195@4700	3.39x3.39	9.4:1	50@3000
	Accord Sedan (EX, LX)	3.0 (2997)	J30A1	PGM-FI	200@5500	195@4700	3.39x3.39	9.4:1	50@3000

PGM-FI: Programmed Fuel Injection

① Manual transaxle: 195@7000
  Automatic transaxle: 190@6600

91181C02

Fig. 35 The engine number is the number on the right that is stamped directly onto the engine block. The VIN number plate on the left is riveted onto the transaxle assembly

```
F23A1 - 1000001
      |         |
      a         b
```

a. Engine Type
  F23A1: 2.3 ℓ SOHC VTEC Sequential Multiport
  Fuel-injected engine (L4)
  F23A4: 2.3 ℓ SOHC VTEC Sequential Multiport
  Fuel-injected engine (L4)
b. Serial Number

91181G07

Fig. 36 Typical engine number breakdown

engine type before attempting to service the vehicle. Write the engine code and the engine type along with the complete VIN number of the vehicle on the inside cover of this Total Car Care manual. Knowing the engine type and vehicle serial number will not only help with obtaining the correct service information, this information will assist the local parts vendors when shopping for replacement parts. Bring the manual along when shopping for parts. Having the manual handy can help to properly identify a needed part. If a part has to be ordered, it's far better to order it correctly the first time and/or avoid having a vehicle completely disassembled only to find out the part needed is not in stock. On rare occasions, a part may be back-ordered, meaning the part is temporarily unavailable. In a situation such as this, it may be wise to wait until the part is available before starting on the repair or maintenance about to be undertaken, if the vehicle can be operated in a safe and reliable manner.

Transaxle

▶ See Figure 37

The seventh position of the vehicle VIN number represents the installed transmission type and body type. This single digit represents the body (or platform) type, and transmission type installed for each particular model year. Sometimes this code will remain the same from one year to another and from one model to another although the installed transmission type could be different. Although the code describes which transmission type is installed as original equipment for a particular model year, this code is not a portion of the four-character transmis-

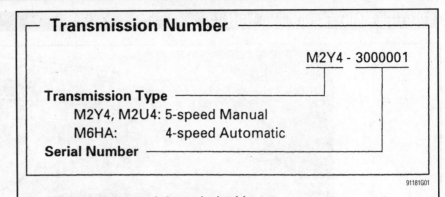

Transmission Number

M2Y4 - 3000001

Transmission Type
  M2Y4, M2U4: 5-speed Manual
  M6HA: 4-speed Automatic
Serial Number

91181G01

Fig. 37 Example of the transmission number breakdown

sion type and serial number stamped on the transmission casing.

The transmission type and serial numbers are stamped into the transmission casing facing up and near the starter motor assembly. The transmission type is a four-character code, which is followed by and separated from the transmission serial number by a hyphen. This code is used the by the manufacturer to designate the transmission type and the transmission specifications may vary from transmission to transmission.

Vehicle Emission Control Information (VECI) Label

▶ See Figure 38

The Vehicle Emission Control Information (VECI) label is located on the underside of the hood on Accord and Prelude models. This label is extremely important when performing maintenance, emissions inspection or ordering engine and engine management related parts.

Sometimes during production of the vehicle the manufacturer may institute updates that require a different component and/or specification. An example of this might be a change in the recommended spark plug and spark plug gap or ignition timing and valve adjustment specifications.

The label also reflects the emissions group that is installed on the vehicle. There are 3 possible emission groups and as a result the emissions equipment installed on the vehicle and the related maintenance specification could differ. The 3 possibilities are:
- 50ST (50 States)
- 49ST (49 States/Federal)
- CAL (California)

Another important emissions related notice is located directly below the VECI specifications. This notice pertains to the emissions test procedures that can be performed safely to the vehicle. Many states now perform a dynamic emissions inspection where the drive wheels are placed on a set of rollers. The emissions can be tested and a load applied to the driven wheels to simulate actual driving conditions.

If your vehicle is involved in a front end collision and the hood is replaced, make sure the repair shop either transfers or replaces the labels with the correct ones. The label part number often times appears on the label.

Federal Motor Vehicle Safety Standard Certification

The Federal Motor Vehicle Safety Standard Certification label located on the driver's side door jamb. The label lists the installed safety equipment such as air bags and safety restraints such as seat belts.

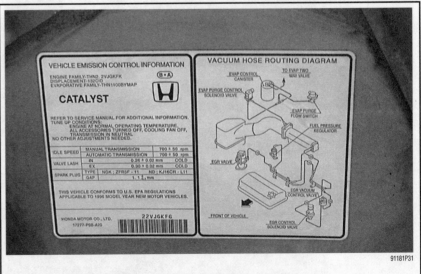

Fig. 38 The VECI label contains important information about your vehicle

ROUTINE MAINTENANCE AND TUNE-UP

UNDERHOOD MAINTENANCE COMPONENT LOCATIONS—2.2L ENGINES

1. Engine compartment fuse box
2. Air cleaner assembly
3. Battery
4. Coolant recovery tank
5. Spark plug wires
6. Distributor cap

7. Radiator cap
8. Engine oil fill cap
9. Spark plugs (4 located under the cover)
10. PCV valve
11. Brake master cylinder reservoir
12. Clutch master cylinder reservoir

13. Engine oil dipstick
14. Drive belt
15. Power steering pump reservoir
16. Windshield washer solvent reservoir

91181PE4

UNDERHOOD MAINTENANCE COMPONENT LOCATIONS—2.3L ULEV ENGINE

1. Air cleaner assembly
2. Engine compartment fuse box
3. Spark plug wires
4. Distributor cap
5. Spark plugs (recessed in the cylinder head)
6. Battery
7. Coolant recovery tank
8. Radiator cap
9. Brake master cylinder reservoir
10. Engine oil fill cap
11. Power steering pump reservoir
12. Engine oil dipstick
13. Drive belt
14. Windshield washer solvent reservoir
15. PCV valve

UNDERHOOD MAINTENANCE COMPONENT LOCATIONS—2.7L ENGINE

1. Engine compartment fuse box
2. Drive belt
3. Windshield washer solvent reservoir
4. Power steering pump reservoir
5. Engine oil dipstick
6. Engine oil fill cap
7. Spark plugs (3 in each bank of cylinders)
8. PCV valve
9. Distributor cap
10. Transmission fluid dipstick
11. Spark plug wires
12. Battery
13. Radiator cap
14. Coolant recovery tank
15. Brake master cylinder reservoir
16. Air cleaner assembly

Proper maintenance and tune-up is the key to long and trouble-free vehicle life, and the work can yield its own rewards. Studies have shown that a properly tuned and maintained vehicle can achieve better gas mileage than an out-of-tune vehicle. As a conscientious owner and driver, set aside a Saturday morning, say once a month, to check or replace items which could cause major problems later. Keep your own personal log to jot down which services you performed, how much the parts cost you, the date, and the exact odometer reading at the time. Keep all receipts for such items as engine oil and filters, so that they may be referred to in case of related problems or to determine operating expenses. As a do-it-yourselfer, these receipts are the only proof you have that the required maintenance was performed. In the event of a warranty problem, these receipts will be invaluable.

The literature provided with your vehicle when it was originally delivered includes the factory recommended maintenance schedule. If you no longer have this literature, replacement copies are usually available from the dealer. A maintenance schedule is provided later in this section, in case you do not have the factory literature.

Air Cleaner (Element)

REMOVAL & INSTALLATION

▶ **See Figures 39, 40, 41, 42 and 43**

1. Disconnect the negative battery cable.
2. Loosen the air cleaner cover screws/retaining clips.
3. Move the air cleaner cover out of the way.

Fig. 39 Unfasten the air filter cover retaining screws . . .

Fig. 40 . . . then remove the filter cover by lifting it off

Fig. 41 Pull the air filter cover and intake out of the way

Fig. 42 Lift the air filter out of the housing and replace if necessary

Fig. 43 Anytime you replace the air cleaner element (filter), make sure to wipe out the air cleaner housing assembly

4. Lift out the air cleaner element.
5. Wipe out the air box.
To install:
6. Place a new air filter element into the air box making sure it is fully seated.
7. Install the air box cover and tighten the retaining screws or secure the clips.
8. Connect the negative battery cable.

Fuel Filter

REMOVAL & INSTALLATION

Except 1998–00 Accord

▶ **See Figure 44**

1. If applicable, write down the anti-theft code for the radio.

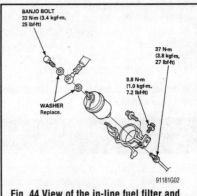

Fig. 44 View of the in-line fuel filter and banjo bolt tightening specifications

2. Disconnect the negative battery cable.
3. Cover the fuel filter fitting with a shop towel.
4. Properly relieve the fuel system pressure. For more details, please refer to Section 5 of this manual.
5. Remove the power steering feed hose clamp.
6. Detach the engine wiring harness bracket.
7. While holding the fuel filter with a back-up wrench, remove the banjo bolt from the fuel feed pipe.
8. Remove the fuel filter clamp.
9. Once all the necessary fuel lines, fittings, and fasteners have been detached, remove the fuel filter.
10. Installation is the reverse of removal.

➡**Always use new washers when reassembling the fuel filter.**

1998–00 Accord

▶ **See Figure 45**

1. Release the fuel system pressure by loosening the fuel pulsation dampener which is located on the top of the fuel rail. For more information, please refer to Section 5 of this manual.
2. If applicable, write down the anti-theft code for the radio.

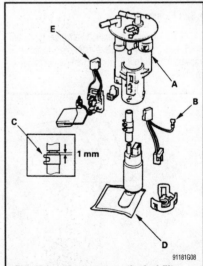

Fig. 45 In order to remove the fuel filter (A) on 1998–00 Accord models, you must first remove the fuel pump assembly

3. Disconnect the negative battery cable.
4. Remove the fuel fill cap.
5. Remove the fuel pump, as outlined in Section 5 of this manual.
6. Detach the fuel filter from the fuel pump.
7. Installation is the reverse of removal.

➡️**When installing a new fuel filter, always use a new base gasket.**

Positive Crankcase Ventilation (PCV) Valve

The Positive Crankcase Ventilation (PCV) valve is part of a system, which is designed to protect the atmosphere from harmful engine blow-by gas vapors. Blow-by gas from the crankcase, as well as fumes from crankcase oil, are diverted into the combustion chamber where they are burned during engine operation. Proper operation of this system is necessary for optimal engine performance, and decreases the amount of harmful vapors released into the atmosphere.

All Honda Accord and Prelude models are equipped with a Positive Crankcase Ventilation (PCV) system in which blow-by gas is returned to the combustion chamber through the air intake system.

➡️**For more information on the PCV system, please refer to Section 4 of this manual.**

The PCV valve should be checked according to the manufacturer's recommendations. On 1996 models with the 2.2L engine, Honda recommends checking the valve every 60,000 miles (96,000 km) or 4 years, whichever occurs first. Although there is not an official manufacturer's recommendation for the remaining model years, checking the PCV valve is a simple task, and most professionals would recommend checking the valve during tune-ups. Two consequences of a failed PCV valve are the possibility of an intake vacuum leak which could cause erratic engine running conditions, or the inability of the crankcase to adequately vent combustion blow-by gases causing potential oil leaks.

REMOVAL & INSTALLATION

▶ **See Figure 46**

The PCV valve is mounted in a rubber grommet, which is seated in the intake manifold and has a hose connected to it from the crankcase breather chamber.

1. Before removing the valve, thoroughly clean the area surrounding the valve.
2. Remove the valve by carefully lifting the valve away from the sealing grommet and the manifold.
3. Once the valve is removed check for loose, disconnected or deteriorated lines or hoses and replace if necessary. Make sure the hoses are clean and free of debris. Clean them with a suitable solvent, if necessary.

To install:
4. To install the PCV valve, coat the mounting grommet with a light coating of engine oil, then press the valve into the grommet.
5. Reinstall the vacuum line and clamp.

Evaporative Canister

The charcoal canister is part of the Evaporative Emission Control System. This system is designed to prevent the gasoline vapors of the fuel tank and intake manifold from being discharged into the atmosphere. Vapor absorption is accomplished with a charcoal canister, which stores the vapors until they can be purged and burned in the combustion process. The charcoal canister is designed to absorb fuel vapors under certain conditions, and is a coffee can-sized cylinder located in the engine compartment.

➡️**Because the evaporative canister temporarily stores and prevents unburned fuel vapors from entering the atmosphere, if when refueling, the vehicle's fuel tank is severely overfilled, it is possible to create a temporary condition of a raw fuel odor and possible sluggish performance until the vehicle is driven a distance of about 20 miles to purge the charcoal canister.**

SERVICING

▶ **See Figure 47**

➡️**For more information on the Evaporative Emission system, please refer to Section 4 of this manual.**

The charcoal canister does not require periodic replacement. However, periodically inspect the canister and attached hoses for wear, cracks and/or other damage and replace components as necessary.

Battery

PRECAUTIONS

Always use caution when working on or near the battery. Never allow a tool to bridge the gap between the negative and positive battery terminals. Also, be careful not to allow a tool to provide a ground between the positive cable/terminal and any metal component on the vehicle. Either of these conditions will cause a short circuit, leading to sparks and possible personal injury.

Do not smoke, have an open flame or create sparks near a battery; the gases contained in the battery are very explosive and, if ignited, could cause severe injury or death.

All batteries, regardless of type, should be carefully secured by a battery hold-down device. If this is not done, the battery terminals or casing may crack from stress applied to the battery during vehicle operation. A battery which is not secured may allow acid to leak out, making it discharge faster; such leaking corrosive acid can also eat away at components under the hood.

Always visually inspect the battery case for cracks, leakage and corrosion. A white corrosive substance on the battery case or on nearby components would indicate a leaking or cracked battery. If the battery is cracked, it should be replaced immediately.

GENERAL MAINTENANCE

▶ **See Figure 48**

A battery that is not sealed must be checked periodically for electrolyte level. You cannot add water to a sealed maintenance-free battery (though not all maintenance-free batteries are sealed); how-

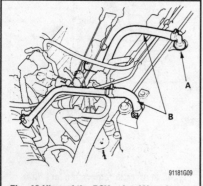

Fig. 46 View of the PCV valve (A) and related hoses (B)

91181G09

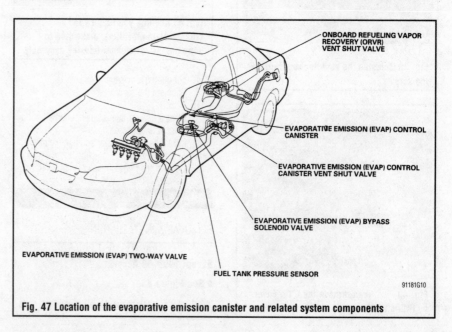

ONBOARD REFUELING VAPOR RECOVERY (ORVR) VENT SHUT VALVE

EVAPORATIVE EMISSION (EVAP) CONTROL CANISTER

EVAPORATIVE EMISSION (EVAP) CONTROL CANISTER VENT SHUT VALVE

EVAPORATIVE EMISSION (EVAP) BYPASS SOLENOID VALVE

FUEL TANK PRESSURE SENSOR

EVAPORATIVE EMISSION (EVAP) TWO-WAY VALVE

91181G10

Fig. 47 Location of the evaporative emission canister and related system components

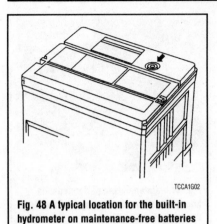

Fig. 48 A typical location for the built-in hydrometer on maintenance-free batteries

ever, a sealed battery must also be checked for proper electrolyte level, as indicated by the color of the built-in hydrometer "eye."

Always keep the battery cables and terminals free of corrosion. Check these components about once a year. Refer to the removal, installation and cleaning procedures outlined in this section.

Keep the top of the battery clean, as a film of dirt can help completely discharge a battery that is not used for long periods. A solution of baking soda and water may be used for cleaning, but be careful to flush this off with clear water. DO NOT let any of the solution into the filler holes. Baking soda neutralizes battery acid and will de-activate a battery cell.

Batteries in vehicles which are not operated on a regular basis can fall victim to parasitic loads (small current drains which are constantly drawing current from the battery). Normal parasitic loads may drain a battery on a vehicle that is in storage and not used for 6–8 weeks. Vehicles that have additional accessories such as a cellular phone, an alarm system or other devices that increase parasitic load may discharge a battery sooner. If the vehicle is to be stored for 6–8 weeks in a secure area and the alarm system, if present, is not necessary, the negative battery cable should be disconnected at the onset of storage to protect the battery charge.

Remember that constantly discharging and recharging will shorten battery life. Take care not to allow a battery to be needlessly discharged.

BATTERY FLUID

Check the battery electrolyte level at least once a month, or more often in hot weather or during periods of extended vehicle operation. On non-sealed batteries, the level can be checked either through the case on translucent batteries or by removing the cell caps on opaque-cased types. The electrolyte level in each cell should be kept filled to the split ring inside each cell, or the line marked on the outside of the case.

If the level is low, add only distilled water through the opening until the level is correct. Each cell is separate from the others, so each must be checked and filled individually. Distilled water should be used, because the chemicals and minerals found in most drinking water are harmful to the battery and could significantly shorten its life.

If water is added in freezing weather, the vehicle should be driven several miles to allow the water to mix with the electrolyte. Otherwise, the battery could freeze.

Although some maintenance-free batteries have removable cell caps for access to the electrolyte, the electrolyte condition and level on all sealed maintenance-free batteries must be checked using the built-in hydrometer "eye." The exact type of eye varies between battery manufacturers, but most apply a sticker to the battery itself explaining the possible readings. When in doubt, refer to the battery manufacturer's instructions to interpret battery condition using the built-in hydrometer.

➡Although the readings from built-in hydrometers found in sealed batteries may vary, a green eye usually indicates a properly charged battery with sufficient fluid level. A dark eye is normally an indicator of a battery with sufficient fluid, but one which may be low in charge. And a light or yellow eye is usually an indication that electrolyte supply has dropped below the necessary level for battery (and hydrometer) operation. In this last case, sealed batteries with an insufficient electrolyte level must usually be discarded.

Checking the Specific Gravity

▶ See Figures 49, 50 and 51

A hydrometer is required to check the specific gravity on all batteries that are not maintenance-free. On batteries that are maintenance-free, the specific gravity is checked by observing the built-in hydrometer "eye" on the top of the battery case. Check with your battery's manufacturer for proper interpretation of its built-in hydrometer readings.

✲✲ CAUTION

Battery electrolyte contains sulfuric acid. If you should splash any on your skin or in your eyes, flush the affected area with plenty of clear water. If it lands in your eyes, get medical help immediately.

The fluid (sulfuric acid solution) contained in the battery cells will tell you many things about the condition of the battery. Because the cell plates must be kept submerged below the fluid level in order to operate, maintaining the fluid level is extremely important. And, because the specific gravity of the acid is an indication of electrical charge, testing the fluid can be an aid in determining if the battery must be replaced. A battery in a vehicle with a properly operating charging system should require little maintenance, but careful, periodic inspection should reveal problems before they leave you stranded.

As stated earlier, the specific gravity of a battery's electrolyte level can be used as an indication of battery charge. At least once a year, check the specific gravity of the battery. It should be between 1.20 and 1.26 on the gravity scale. Most auto supply stores carry a variety of inexpensive battery testing hydrometers. These can be used on any non-sealed battery to test the specific gravity in each cell.

The battery testing hydrometer has a squeeze bulb at one end and a nozzle at the other. Battery electrolyte is sucked into the hydrometer until the float is lifted from its seat. The specific gravity is then read by noting the position of the float. If gravity is low in one or more cells, the battery should be slowly charged and checked again to see if the gravity has come up. Generally, if after charging, the specific gravity between any two cells varies more than 50 points (0.50), the battery should be replaced, as it can no longer produce sufficient voltage to guarantee proper operation.

CABLES

▶ See Figures 52 thru 58

Once a year (or as necessary), the battery terminals and the cable clamps should be cleaned. Loosen the clamps and remove the cables, negative cable first. On batteries with posts on top, the use of a puller specially made for this purpose is recommended. These are inexpensive and available in most auto parts stores. Side terminal battery cables are secured with a small bolt.

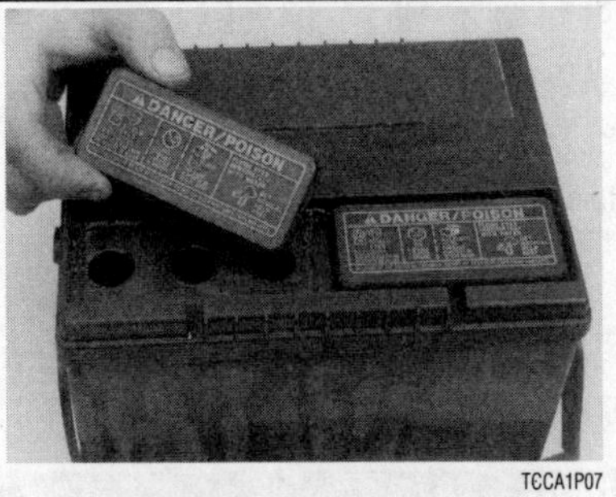

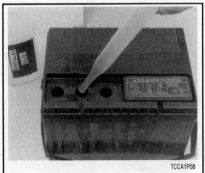

Fig. 49 On non-maintenance-free batteries, the fluid level can be checked through the case on translucent models; the cell caps must be removed on other models

Fig. 50 If the fluid level is low, add only distilled water through the opening until the level is correct

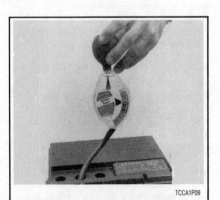

Fig. 51 Check the specific gravity of the battery's electrolyte with a hydrometer

Fig. 52 You can conduct a voltage drop test to help find poor connections

Fig. 53 Always disconnect the negative battery cable first, before disconnecting the positive cable

Fig. 54 Maintenance is performed with household items and with special tools like this post cleaner

Fig. 55 The underside of this special battery tool has a wire brush to clean post terminals

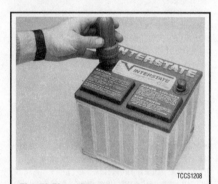

Fig. 56 Place the tool over the battery posts and twist to clean until the metal is shiny

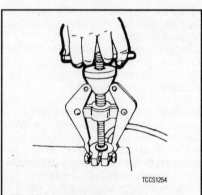

Fig. 57 A special tool is available to pull the clamp from the post

Fig. 58 The cable ends should be cleaned as well

Clean the cable clamps and the battery terminal with a wire brush, until all corrosion, grease, etc., is removed and the metal is shiny. It is especially important to clean the inside of the clamp thoroughly (an old knife is useful here), since a small deposit of foreign material or oxidation there will prevent a sound electrical connection and inhibit either starting or charging. Special tools are available for cleaning these parts, one type for conventional top post batteries and another type for side terminal batteries. It is also a good idea to apply some dielectric grease to the terminal, as this will aid in the prevention of corrosion.

After the clamps and terminals are clean, reinstall the cables, negative cable last; DO NOT hammer the clamps onto battery posts. Tighten the

clamps securely, but do not distort them. Give the clamps and terminals a thin external coating of grease after installation, to retard corrosion.

Check the cables at the same time that the terminals are cleaned. If the cable insulation is cracked or broken, or if the ends are frayed, the cable should be replaced with a new cable of the same length and gauge.

CHARGING

▶ See Figure 59

❋❋ CAUTION

The chemical reaction which takes place in all batteries generates explosive hydrogen

Fig. 59 You can use a digital multimeter to check a battery's state of charge

gas. A spark can cause the battery to explode and splash acid. To avoid serious personal injury, be sure there is proper ventilation and take appropriate fire safety precautions when connecting, disconnecting, or charging a battery and when using jumper cables.

A battery should be charged at a slow rate to keep the plates inside from getting too hot. However, if some maintenance-free batteries are allowed to discharge until they are almost "dead," they may have to be charged at a high rate to bring them back to "life." Always follow the charger manufacturer's instructions on charging the battery.

REPLACEMENT

▶ See Figures 60, 61, 62 and 63

When it becomes necessary to replace the battery, select one with an amperage rating equal to or greater than the battery originally installed. Deterioration and just plain aging of the battery cables, starter motor, and associated wires makes the battery's job harder in successive years. The slow increase in electrical resistance over time makes it prudent to install a new battery with a greater capacity than the old.

Belts

Accessory drive belts used on the Accord and Prelude models include two basic types: the flat multi-ribbed V-belt and serpentine belt. The flat

Fig. 60 Disconnect the negative battery first, then . . .

Fig. 61 . . . disconnect the positive cable

Fig. 62 Use a battery carrier as shown to minimize contact with battery acid

Fig. 63 Keep the battery level at all times to prevent a spill

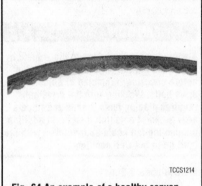

Fig. 64 An example of a healthy conventional "V" belt

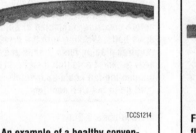

Fig. 65 Deep cracks in a belt will cause flex, building up heat that will eventually lead to belt failure

multi-ribbed V-belt actually resembles a serpentine belt, however, unlike a serpentine belt, only the ribbed inner surface of the belt makes contact with the components' pulleys. Rarely, does the back of a multi-ribbed belt ride against an idler or tensioner pulley.

Multi-ribbed V-belts typically operate one or two accessories per belt, whereas a single serpentine belt can often times drive multiple the accessories. The flat multi-ribbed V-belts used on both the Accord and Prelude models require periodic inspection and adjustment because the belts wear with age, are under tension and stretch over time. The serpentine belt is tensioned by a spring loaded tensioner assembly that keeps a constant tension on the belt at all times. As a serpentine belt wears and stretches over time, within a specified range, the tensioner automatically compensates for the wear and belt stretch.

INSPECTION

▶ See Figures 64 thru 69

The maintenance intervals suggested by the manufacturer vary by time, operating conditions (normal or severe), and mileage. A good rule of thumb is to inspect the drive belts every 15,000 miles (24,000 km) or 12 months (whichever occurs first). On manually adjusted multi-ribbed V-belts, measure the belt tension at a point halfway between the pulleys by pulling or pressing on the belt with a known force and measuring how far the belt moves, referred to as the amount of deflection. Note that "deflection" is not free-play, but the ability of the

belt, under actual tension, to stretch slightly and give. The specification for measuring belt tension includes the amount of force applied to the belt, and the amount of defection (movement) the belt should have when the force is applied. The amount of deflection varies depending on whether the belt is new or used. Although the manufacturer markets a specific tool for measuring belt deflection, a fisherman's spring scale capable of measuring a 22 lb. (98 N) pull and a small ruler can be substituted for this tool.

Inspect the belts for the following signs of damage or wear: glazing, cracking, fraying, crumbling or missing chunks. A glazed belt will be slightly brittle and perfectly smooth from slipping, and may exhibit a screeching noise when the engine is suddenly accelerated or first started. A good belt will have a slight texture of fabric visible and the surface should be soft and flexible. Cracks will usually start at the inner edge of a belt and run outward. A belt that is fraying will have the fabric backing de-laminating itself from the belt. A belt that is crumbling or missing chunks will have missing pieces in the cross-section of the belt, some times these chunks will be stuck in the pulley groove and not easily seen. All worn or damaged drive belts should be replaced immediately. It is best to replace all drive belts at one time, as a preventive maintenance measure.

Although it is generally easier on a component to have the belt too loose than too tight, a loose belt may place a high impact load on a bearing due to the whipping or snapping action of the belt. A belt that is slightly loose may slip, especially when

component loads are high. This slippage may be hard to identify. For example, the generator belt may run okay during the day, and then slip at night when headlights are turned on. Slipping belts wear quickly not only due to the direct effect of slippage but also because of the heat a slipping belt generates. Extreme slippage may even cause a belt to burn. A very smooth, glazed appearance on the belt's sides, as opposed to the obvious pattern of a fabric cover, indicates that the belt has been slipping.

Both multi-ribbed V-belts and serpentine belts can be checked for wear by inspecting the physical condition of the belt. To check belt stretch on multi-ribbed V-belts, look at the amount of adjustment that remains on the sliding portion of the adjustment bracket, or the threaded portion of the adjustment screw. If the adjustment range has is at its fully extended portion, the belt should be replaced.

Serpentine drive belts should be inspected for rib chunking (pieces of the ribs breaking off), severe glazing, frayed cords or other visible damage. Any belt which is missing sections of 2 or more adjacent ribs which are ½ in. (13mm) or longer must be replaced. You might want to note that serpentine belts do tend to form small cracks across the backing. If the only wear you find is in the form of one or more cracks are across the backing and NOT parallel to the ribs, the belt is still good and does not need to be replaced.

To check belt stretch on a serpentine belt, look at the range indicator on the tensioner assembly. The tensioner arm has a pointer that is compared to a small rectangular reference block on the tensioner

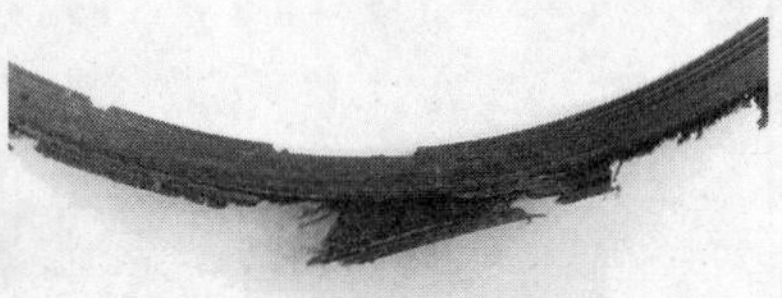

TCCS1217

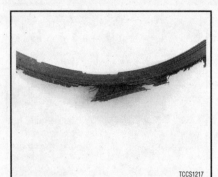

Fig. 66 The cover of this belt is worn, exposing the critical reinforcing cords to excessive wear

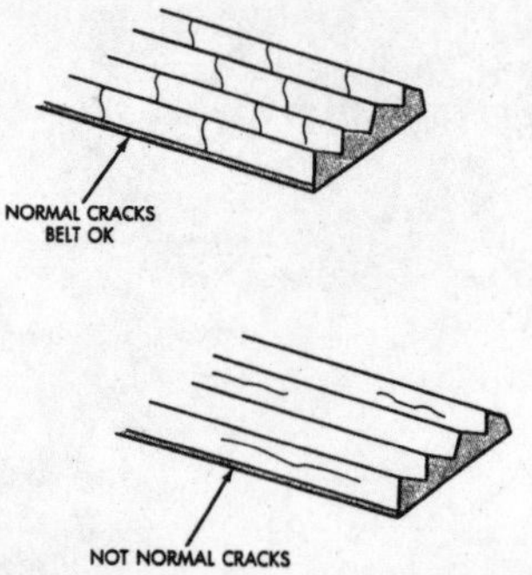

79244G63

Fig. 67 Typical wear patterns for a serpentine drive belt

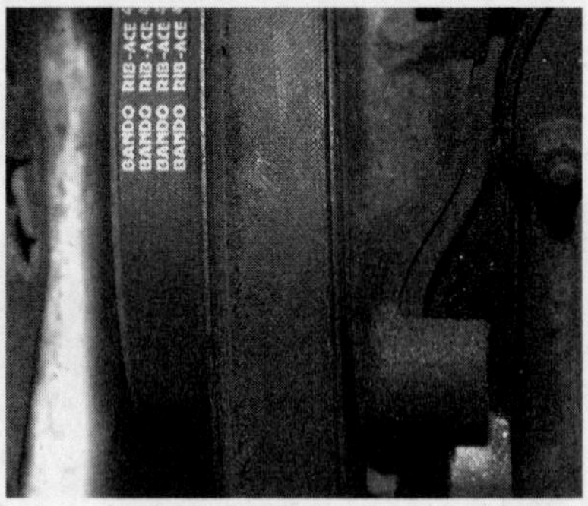

91181P08

Fig. 68 View of damaged ribbed belt as it sits on a pulley

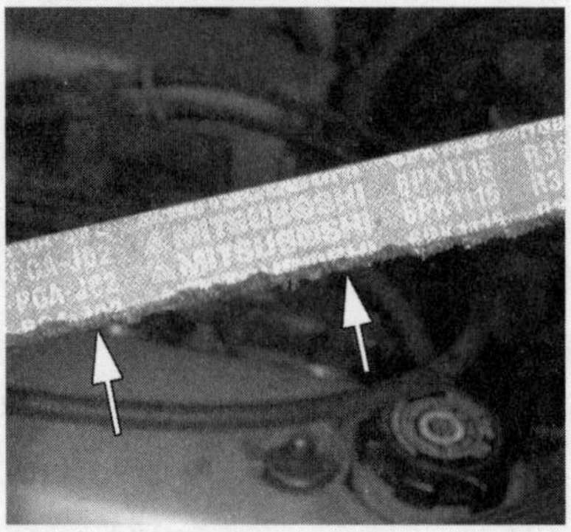

91181P34

Fig. 69 Look for frayed edges of the belt

mounting bracket. If the tensioner pointer has reached or is beyond the edge of the inspection block, the belt has stretched beyond its wear limits and should be replaced.

CHECKING BELT TENSION

See Figure 70

A damaged drive belt can cause problems should it give way while the vehicle is in operation. However, improper length belts (too short or long), as well as excessively worn belts, can also cause problems. Loose accessory drive belts can lead to poor engine cooling and diminished output from the alternator, air conditioning compressor or power steering pump. A belt that is too tight places a severe strain on the driven unit and can wear out bearings quickly.

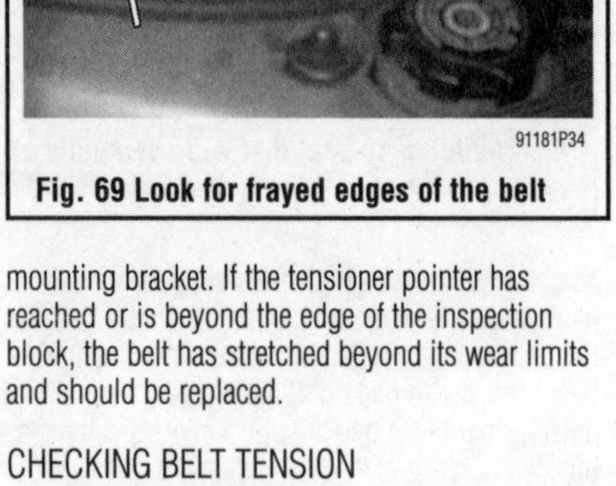

91182P33

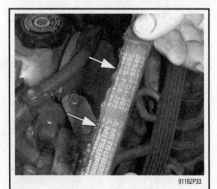

Fig. 70 Over-tensioning a belt may cause it to wear unevenly, as shown here

CAUTION

Always disable the power to the vehicle by disconnecting the negative battery cable before checking, replacing or adjusting the drive belts. Working with the drive belts requires placing tools, hands and fingers near areas of potential danger. In addition, the cooling fan could engage even with the ignition in the OFF position.

Multi-Ribbed V-Belts

To accurately check the belt tension of the multi-ribbed V-belts used on Honda products requires putting a known force on the belt midway between the longest straight distance between belt pulleys and measuring the belt's deflection. The specification varies depending on whether the belt is new or used. The manufacturer does have a belt tension gauge designed for this specific purpose, however a fisherman's spring scale capable of measuring 22 lbs. (98 N) and a small ruler can be easily substituted. To use the fisherman's spring scale to pull on the belt requires that a small flat shaped hook be made to wrap around the belt and the small hook of the spring scale. A sturdy metal coat hanger is a good source for the needed hook. Use the spring scale to apply a force at a 90° angle to the belt via the metal hook and measure the amount of belt movement (deflection) with the ruler. To measure the belt deflection of a flat multi-ribbed V-belt proceed as follows:

1. Note the radio security code and disconnect the negative battery cable.
2. Inspect the belt and determine the longest straight distance between two of the pulleys.
3. Determine the center point of the belt between the two pulleys of the longest straight distance between the two pulleys.
4. Attach one end the hook made for the spring scale to the center point of the belt and the other end to the spring scale and pull the spring scale at a 90° angle from the belt just enough to remove any slack in the hook.
5. Using a small ruler, place the ruler at a 90° angle to the belt, with the base of the rule aligned with, but not touching the non-ribbed side of the belt.
6. While holding the ruler stationary, pull the spring scale at a 90° angle from the belt, until the scale registers 22 lbs. (98 N) while using the ruler to note the distance the belt has moved. This movement is the belt's deflection.
7. Compare the measurement with the following specifications to determine if the belt is properly adjusted. The following belt deflection information is a guide to proper belt adjustment and is measured while applying a 22 lb. force to the belt:
   - Air conditioner/alternator belt, new: 3/16–1/4 in. (4.5–6.5mm)
   - Air conditioner/alternator belt, used: 5/16–3/8 in. (8.0–10.5mm)
   - Power steering belt, new: 7/16–1/2 in. (11.0–12.5mm)
   - Power steering belt, used: 1/2–5/8 in. (13.0–16.0mm)
8. Once the proper adjustment of the belt is achieved, remove the self-made hook, spring scale and ruler.
9. Reconnect the negative battery cable and enter the radio security code.

Serpentine Belts

The serpentine belt tension and tensioner can be checked but they cannot be adjusted. An automatic spring-loaded tensioner assembly is used with these belts to maintain proper adjustment at all times. The tensioner also serves as a wear indicator. When the belt is properly tensioned, the arrow on the tensioner arm must point within the small rectangular reference area on the tensioner's housing. If the arrow falls outside the range, either an improper belt has been installed or the belt has stretched beyond its wear limit. In either case, a new belt must be installed immediately to assure proper engine operation and to prevent possible accessory damage.

To check the serpentine belt tensioner assembly, look at the tension indicator on the tensioner assembly with the engine running. If the tensioner arm pointer moves excessively when the engine is running, the belt condition and the tensioner spring strength should be checked.

To check the tensioner spring strength proceed as follows:

1. Remove the serpentine belt. Refer to this section for specific details.
2. Remove the mounting bolts that secure the tensioner assembly to the engine.
3. Place two 6mm bolts through the tensioner assembly mounting holes and clamp the two bolts into a suitable vise. **Do not** clamp the tensioner assembly itself.

4. Using a beam type torque wrench, measure the amount of torque required to move the tensioner in a counterclockwise direction. If the torque required to move the tensioner is less than 17 ft. lbs. (23 Nm), replace the tensioner assembly.

ADJUSTMENT

➡The 3.0L engine uses a serpentine drive belt. Serpentine drive belts can not be adjusted.

✳✳ CAUTION

Always disable the power to the vehicle by disconnecting the negative battery cable before checking, replacing or adjusting the drive belts. Working with the drive belts requires placing tools, hands and fingers near areas of potential danger. In addition, the cooling fan could engage even with the ignition in the OFF position.

Belt tension on multi-ribbed V-belts can be checked by applying a force on the belt at the center point of its longest straight span. The belt movement (deflection) is then measured to determine if the belt is properly tensioned. If the belt is loose, it will slip, whereas if the belt is too tight it will damage the bearings in the driven unit.

To tension a multi-ribbed V-belt there are generally three types of mounting and adjustment methods for the various components driven by the drive belt. These types of mounting and adjustment methods are as follows:

• A pivoting component without an adjuster. This method, referred to as pivoting type without adjuster, is designed such that the component is secured by at least 2 bolts. One of the bolts is a pivoting bolt and the other is the lockbolt. When both bolts are loosened so that the component may move, the component pivots on the pivoting bolt. The lockbolt passes through the component and a slotted bracket, so that when the lockbolt's nut is tightened, the component is held in that position. The component must be moved by hand, or by carefully leveraging it with a properly placed object such as a hardwood handle or suitable prytool.

• A pivoting component with an adjuster. This method of component mounting, referred to as pivoting type with adjuster, is designed such that the component is secured by at least 2 bolts, with one of the bolts serving as a pivoting bolt and the other a lockbolt. When the mounting bolts are loosened so that the component may move, the component is moved by turning an adjustment bolt. The adjuster is composed of a bracket attached to the component and a threaded adjusting bolt. After loosening the pivoting and lockbolts, the adjusting bolt can be tightened or loosened to increase or decrease the drive belt's tension. With this type of mounting, the component does not have to be held in a tensioned position while tightening the pivoting and lockbolts, because the adjusting bolt applies the tension to the belt.

• A stationary mounted component with an adjustable idler pulley. This type of component mounting is referred to as the stationary type, because the component(s) is (are) mounted in a stationary position without the use of pivoting or lockbolts. The drive belt tension is adjusted by moving the position of an idler pulley.

➡When checking or adjusting the multi-ribbed V-belts, note that the belt deflection specification varies from component to component, and changes if the belt is new or used. Note, the amount of force applied to the belts when checking belt deflection is 22 lbs. (98 N), however the amount of deflection varies depending on belt type and whether new or used. Refer to the following information for each model to properly check and adjust the multi-ribbed drive belts.

2.2L, 2.3L and 2.7L Engines

These engines utilize two multi-ribbed V-belts. One belt is used to drive both the alternator and air conditioner compressor and a separate belt is used for the power steering pump.

✳✳ CAUTION

Always disable the power to the vehicle by disconnecting the negative battery cable before checking, replacing or adjusting the drive belts. Working with the drive belts requires placing tools, hands and fingers near areas of potential danger. In addition, the cooling fan could engage even with the ignition in the OFF position.

ALTERNATOR & AIR CONDITIONER BELT

The air conditioner compressor is mounted to the engine and cannot be moved, thus the belt is tensioned by moving the alternator which has two fasteners securing it to a bracket mounted on the engine. The lower lock nut and fastener are installed through a slotted bracket and the upper fastener allows the alternator to pivot.

To adjust the belt, perform the following:

1. Note the radio security code and disconnect the negative battery cable.
2. Loosen the upper pivot nut and lower locknut.
3. Move the alternator by turning the adjustment bolt on the lower bracket. Turning the adjustment bolt clockwise increases the belt tension, conversely, turning the adjustment bolt counterclockwise will decrease the belt tension.
4. Tighten the upper pivot bolt and lower locknut and then check the belt tension. If the belt tension is not within specification, repeat the previous procedures until the proper belt tension is achieved.
5. Reconnect the negative battery cable and enter the radio security code.

POWER STEERING PUMP BELT

The power steering pump has two fasteners securing it to a bracket mounted on the engine. The upper lock nut and fastener are installed through a slotted bracket and the lower fastener allows the pump to pivot.

To adjust the belt, perform the following:

1. Note the radio security code and disconnect the negative battery cable.
2. Loosen the upper locknut and lower pivot nut.
3. Move the pump by turning the adjustment bolt on the upper bracket. Turning the adjustment bolt clockwise increases the belt tension, conversely, turning the adjustment bolt counterclockwise will decrease the belt tension.
4. Tighten the upper locknut, lower pivot bolt, and then check the belt tension. If the belt tension is not within specification, repeat the previous procedures until the proper belt tension is achieved.

5. Reconnect the negative battery cable and enter the radio security code.

REMOVAL & INSTALLATION

✳✳ CAUTION

Always disable the power to the vehicle by disconnecting the negative battery cable before checking, replacing or adjusting the drive belts. Working with the drive belts requires placing tools, hands and fingers near areas of potential danger. In addition, the cooling fan could engage even with the ignition in the OFF position.

V-Belts

♦ See Figures 71, 72 and 73

If a belt must be replaced, the driven unit or idler pulley must be loosened and moved to its extreme loosest position, generally by moving it toward the center of the engine. After removing the old belt, check the pulleys for dirt or built-up material, which could affect belt contact. Carefully install the new

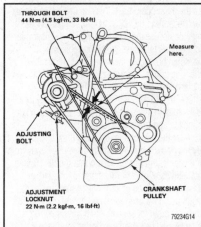

Fig. 71 Accessory drive belt routing—2.2L and 2.3L engines without A/C

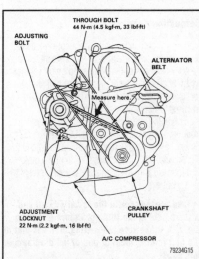

Fig. 72 Accessory drive belt routing—2.2L and 2.3L engines with A/C

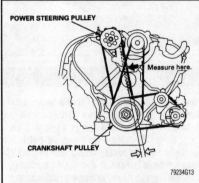

Fig. 73 Accessory drive belt routing—2.7L engines

belt, remembering that it is new and unused; it may appear to be just a little too small to fit over the pulley flanges. Fit the belt over the largest pulley (usually the crankshaft pulley at the bottom center of the engine) first, then work on the smaller one(s). Gentle pressure in the direction of rotation is helpful. Some belts run around a third, or idler pulley, which acts as an additional pivot in the belt's path. It may be possible to loosen the idler pulley as well as the main component, making the job much easier. Depending on which belt(s) being changed, it may be necessary to loosen or remove other interfering belts to access the being replaced.

When buying replacement belts, remember that the fit is critical according to the length of the belt ("diameter") and the width of the belt. The belt shape should match the shape of the pulley exactly. Belts that are not an exact match can cause noise, slippage and premature failure.

After the new belt is installed, draw tension on it by moving the driven unit or idler pulley away from the engine and tighten its mounting bolts. This is sometimes a three or four-handed job; and an assistant could be helpful. Make sure that all the bolts that have been loosened are retightened and that any other loosened belts have the correct tension. A new belt can be expected to stretch a bit after installation, so be prepared to readjust the new belt, if needed, within the first two hundred miles of use.

Serpentine Belts

Because serpentine belts use a spring loaded tensioner for adjustment, belt replacement tends to be somewhat easier than it used to be on engines where accessories were pivoted and bolted in place for tension adjustment. All the belt replacement involves is to pivot the tensioner to loosen the belt, then slide the belt off the pulleys. The two most important points are to pay CLOSE attention to the proper belt routing (since serpentine belts tend to be "snaked" all different ways through the pulleys) and to make sure the V-ribs are properly seated in all the pulleys.

➡Take a good look at the installed belt and make a note of the routing. Before removing the belt, make sure the routing matches that of the belt routing label or one of the diagrams in this book.

1. Note the radio presets and disconnect the negative battery cable.

2. If necessary, remove the power steering belt.
3. Use the proper-sized socket and breaker bar (or a large handled wrench) on the tensioner idler pulley center bolt to pivot the tensioner away from the belt. This will loosen the belt sufficiently that it can be pulled off one or more of the pulleys. It is usually easiest to carefully pull the belt out from underneath the tensioner pulley itself.
4. Once the belt is off one of the pulleys, gently pivot the tensioner back into position. DO NOT allow the tensioner to snap back, as this could damage the tensioner's internal parts.
5. Remove the belt from the other pulleys and remove it from the engine.

To install:

6. Begin to route the belt over the pulleys, leaving whichever pulley the belt was first released from during removal for last.
7. Once the belt is mostly in place, carefully pivot the tensioner and position the belt over the final pulley. Carefully release the pressure on the tensioner and it to contact with the belt, making sure the belt is properly seated in the ribs. If not, release the tension and seat the belt.
8. Once the belt is installed, take another look at all the pulleys to double check the installation.
9. Install and properly tension the power steering belt.
10. Connect the negative battery cable, enter the radio presets, then start and run the engine to check belt operation.
11. Once the engine has reached normal operating temperature, turn the ignition **OFF** and check that the belt tensioner arrow is within the proper adjustment range.

Timing Belt

SERVICING

▶ **See Figures 74 and 75**

Timing belts are typically only used on overhead camshaft engines. Timing belts are used to synchronize the crankshaft with the camshaft, at an exact 2 to 1 ratio, similar to a timing chain used on other overhead camshaft and overhead valve (pushrod) engines. Unlike a timing belt, a timing chain is not considered a maintenance item, as many timing chains can last the life of the engine without needing service or replacement. To maintain a constant 2 to 1 ratio, timing belts use raised teeth to mesh with the crankshaft and camshaft sprockets to operate the valve train of an overhead camshaft engine.

✳✳ WARNING

Timing belt maintenance is extremely important! These models utilize an interference-type, non-free-wheeling engine. If the timing belt breaks, the valves in the cylinder head may strike the pistons, causing potentially serious (also time-consuming and expensive) engine damage. The recommended replacement interval for the timing belt, under normal conditions, is every 84 months or 105,000 (168,000 km), miles whichever occurs first. For vehicles driven in severely hot (over 90°F or 32°C) or severely cold conditions (below -20°F or -29°C), the belt should be replaced every

60,000 miles (96,000 km), or every 84 months whichever occurs first. Refer to Section 3 for information on replacing the timing belt.

If the vehicle has been purchased used with an unknown service history, refer to the maintenance charts provided in this manual to compare the vehicle age and mileage to the recommended maintenance intervals.

➡**Maintenance intervals differ depending on the type of use and operating conditions the vehicle is subjected to. Maintenance intervals have been included in this manual for vehicles meeting the requirements for both normal and severe use.**

Engines can be classified as either free-running or interference engines, depending on what would happen if the piston-to-valve timing were disrupted, which would occur should a timing belt fail. A free-running engine is designed with enough clearance between the pistons and valves to allow the crankshaft to continue to rotate (pistons still moving) while the camshaft stays in one position (several valves fully open). If no other engine related failure occurs, it is likely no further internal engine damage will result. In an interference engine, should the timing belt fail, there is not enough clearance between the pistons and valves to allow the crankshaft to continue to rotate with the camshaft in one position, and the pistons will contact the valves causing internal damage. When this type of failure occurs, the engine will need to be disassembled and evaluated for repair or possibly replaced. Either

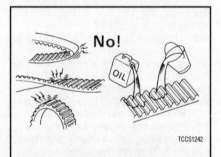

Fig. 74 Never bend or twist a timing belt excessively, and do not allow solvents, antifreeze, gasoline, acid or oil to come into contact with the belt

Fig. 75 Clean the timing belt before inspection so that imperfections or defects are easier to recognize

choice is an expensive one, many times that of replacing the timing belt.

All of the Honda engines covered by this manual utilize timing belts to drive the camshaft from the crankshaft's turning motion and to maintain proper valve timing. In addition to the belt driven camshafts, the 4-cylinder engines also have belt driven balance shafts. This belt is similar to the timing belt that drives the camshaft, though it is a separate belt and follows the same maintenance intervals as the camshaft drive belt.

The belt should be checked periodically to make sure it has not become damaged or worn. A severely worn belt may cause engine performance to drop dramatically, but a damaged belt (which could fail suddenly) may not give as much warning. In general, any time the engine timing cover(s) is (are) removed, inspect the belt for premature parting, severe cracks or missing teeth

❊❊ WARNING

Never allow antifreeze, oil or solvents to come into with a timing belt. If this occurs immediately wash the solution from the timing belt. Also, never excessive bend or twist the timing belt; this can damage the belt so that its lifetime is severely shortened.

Inspect both sides of the timing belt. Replace the belt with a new one if any of the following conditions exist:
• Hardening of the rubber-back side is glossy without resilience and leaves no indentation when pressed with a fingernail
• Cracks on the rubber backing
• Cracks or peeling of the canvas backing
• Cracks on rib root
• Cracks on belt sides
• Missing teeth or chunks of teeth
• Abnormal wear of belt sides—the sides are normal if they are sharp, as if cut by a knife.

Hoses

INSPECTION

▶ **See Figures 76, 77, 78 and 79**

The upper and lower radiator hoses, and the heater hoses, should be checked for deterioration, bulging, damage, leaks and loose hose clamps during every oil change, or once a year, or every

15,000 miles (24,000 km) whichever occurs first. Because the engine's cooling system operates under moderate heat and pressure, a pinhole-sized leak could allow enough coolant to escape quickly enough to render the vehicle inoperable. Operating an engine low on coolant, even for a short period of time, could cause very expensive internal damage. It is also wise to check the hoses periodically in early spring and at the beginning of the fall or winter when performing other preventative maintenance. A quick visual inspection could discover a weakened hose, which could have failed, and left the vehicle stranded at the side of the road, if it had remained unrepaired.

Whenever checking the hoses, make sure the engine and cooling system are cold. Visually inspect for cracking, rotting or collapsed hoses, and replace as necessary. Feel along the length of the hose. If a weak or swollen spot is noted when squeezing the hose wall, the hose should be replaced.

REMOVAL & INSTALLATION

▶ **See Figure 80**

❊❊ CAUTION

Never remove the radiator pressure cap from a hot engine, or when the engine is running, as personal injury from scalding, hot coolant or steam may result. The cooling system operates under moderate pressure as the engine temperature increases. Any attempt to remove the radiator pressure cap while the system is hot may cause the cap to be forced off by the cooling system pressure. Always wait until the engine has cooled before removing the pressure cap.

1. Before proceeding, make sure the engine is cool. Carefully feel the engine's valve cover, and upper and lower radiator hoses to ensure the engine and coolant temperature is cool enough to proceed.
2. Remove the radiator pressure cap.
3. Position a clean container under the radiator and/or engine draincock or plug, then open the drain and allow the cooling system to drain to an appropriate level. For most upper radiator hoses, only a small amount of coolant must be drained. To remove hoses positioned lower on the engine, such as a lower radiator hose, the entire cooling system must be drained.

❊❊ CAUTION

When draining the coolant, keep in mind that small animals are attracted to ethylene glycol antifreeze. Because animals are attracted to the sweet odor and taste of engine coolant, they may attempt to drink any that is left in an uncovered container or in puddles on the ground. This will prove fatal in sufficient quantity. Always drain coolant into a sealable container. Coolant may be reused unless it is contaminated or several years old.

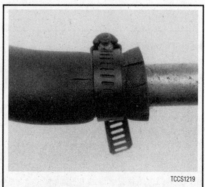

Fig. 76 The cracks developing along this hose are a result of age-related hardening

Fig. 77 A hose clamp that is too tight can cause older hoses to separate and tear on either side of the clamp

Fig. 78 A soft spongy hose (identifiable by the swollen section) will eventually burst and should be replaced

Fig. 79 Hoses are likely to deteriorate from the inside if the cooling system is not periodically flushed

Fig. 80 Using a pair of pliers, squeeze the tabs of the hose clamp to relieve the clamp tension, then remove the clamp

4. Loosen the hose clamps at each end of the hose requiring replacement. Clamps are usually either of the spring tension type (which require a pliers to squeeze the tabs and loosen) or of the screw tension type (which require screw or a hex driver to loosen). Slide the clamps back on the hose away from the connection once loosened.

5. Twist, pull and slide the hose off the fitting, taking care not to damage the neck of the component from which the hose is being removed.

→ If the hose is stuck at the connection, do not try to insert a screwdriver or other sharp tool under the hose end in an effort to free it, as the connection and/or hose may become damaged. Heater connections especially, may be easily damaged by such a procedure. Sometimes a cotter key removal tool can be used with a suitable penetrating lubricant spray to loosen a hose if it must be reused. Make sure the tool is free of nicks and burrs that might damage the hose. If the hose is to be replaced, use a single-edged razor blade to carefully make a slice along the portion of the hose that is stuck on the connection, perpendicular to the end of the hose. Do not cut too deep to prevent damaging the connection. The hose can then be peeled from the connection and discarded.

6. Clean both hose mounting connections. Inspect the condition of the hose clamps and replace them, if necessary.

To install:

7. Dip the ends of the new hose into clean engine coolant to ease installation.

Fig. 81 CV-boots must be inspected periodically for damage

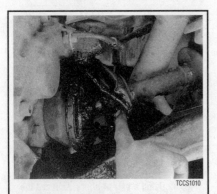

Fig. 82 A torn boot should be replaced immediately

8. Slide the clamps over the replacement hose, then slide the hose ends over the connections into position.

9. Position and secure the clamps at least ¼ in. (6.35mm) from the ends of the hose. Make sure they are located on the connection beyond the raised bead of the connector.

10. Locate the air bleed valves and open the valves one full turn.

11. Close the radiator or engine drains and properly refill the cooling system with the clean drained engine coolant or a suitable mixture of ethylene glycol coolant and water.

12. Close the air bleed valve once the fluid flowing from the valve is free of any air bubbles.

13. If available, install a pressure tester and check for leaks. If a pressure tester is not available, run the engine until normal operating temperature is reached (allowing the system to naturally pressurize), then check for leaks.

14. Once the engine cools, open the radiator cap and recheck the fluid level and top off as necessary.

✳✳ CAUTION

If checking for leaks with the system at normal operating temperature, BE EXTREMELY CAREFUL not to touch any moving or hot engine parts. Once temperature has been reached, shut the engine OFF, and check for leaks around the hose fittings and connections that were removed or replaced.

CV-Boots

INSPECTION

♦ See Figures 81 and 82

The CV (Constant Velocity) boots should be checked for damage each time the oil is changed and any other time the vehicle is raised for service. These boots keep water, grime, dirt and other damaging matter from entering the CV-joints. Any of these could cause early CV-joint failure which can be expensive to repair. Heavy grease thrown around the inside of the front wheel(s) and on the brake caliper/drum can be an indication of a torn boot. Thoroughly check the boots for missing clamps and tears. If the boot is damaged, it should be replaced immediately. Please refer to Section 7 for procedures.

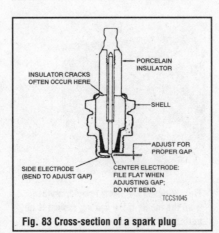

Fig. 83 Cross-section of a spark plug

Spark Plugs

♦ See Figure 83

A typical spark plug consists of a metal shell surrounding a ceramic insulator. A metal electrode extends downward through the center of the insulator and protrudes a small distance. Located at the end of the plug and attached to the side of the outer metal shell is the side electrode. The side electrode bends in at a 90° angle so that its tip is just past and parallel to the tip of the center electrode. The distance between these two electrodes (measured in thousandths of an inch or hundredths of a millimeter) is called the spark plug gap.

The spark plug does not produce a spark, but instead provides a gap across which the current can arc. The coil produces anywhere from 20,000 to 50,000 volts (depending on the type and application) which travels through the wires to the spark plugs. The current passes along the center electrode and jumps the gap to the side electrode, and in doing so, ignites the air/fuel mixture in the combustion chamber.

SPARK PLUG HEAT RANGE

♦ See Figure 84

Spark plug heat range is the ability of the plug to dissipate heat. The longer the insulator (or the farther it extends into the engine), the hotter the plug will operate; the shorter the insulator (the closer the electrode is to the block's cooling passages) the cooler it will operate. A plug that absorbs little heat and remains too cool will quickly accumulate deposits of oil and carbon since it is not hot enough to burn them off. This leads to plug fouling and consequently to misfiring. A plug that absorbs too much heat will have no deposits but, due to the excessive heat, the electrodes will burn away quickly and might possibly lead to preignition or other ignition problems. Preignition takes place when plug tips get so hot that they glow sufficiently to ignite the air/fuel mixture before the actual spark occurs. This early ignition will usually cause a pinging during low speeds and heavy loads.

The general rule of thumb for choosing the correct heat range when picking a spark plug is: if most of your driving is long distance, high speed travel, use a colder plug; if most of your driving is stop and go, use a hotter plug. Original equipment plugs are

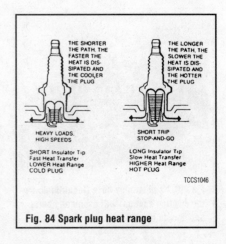

Fig. 84 Spark plug heat range

generally a good compromise between the 2 styles and most people never have the need to change their plugs from the factory-recommended heat range.

REMOVAL & INSTALLATION

▶ See Figures 85, 86, 87, 88 and 89

A set of spark plugs usually requires replacement after about 20,000–30,000 miles (32,000–48,000 km), depending on your style of driving. In normal operation plug gap increases about 0.001 in. (0.025mm) for every 2,500 miles (4,000 km). As the gap increases, the plug's voltage requirement also increases. It requires a greater voltage to jump the wider gap and about two to three times as much voltage to fire the plug at high speeds than at idle. The improved air/fuel ratio control of modern fuel injection combined with the higher voltage output of modern ignition systems will often allow an engine to run significantly longer on a set of standard spark plugs, but keep in mind that efficiency will drop as the gap widens (along with fuel economy and power).

When you're removing spark plugs, work on one at a time. Don't start by removing the plug wires all at once, because, unless you number them, they may become mixed up. Take a minute before you begin and number the wires with tape.

✳✳ WARNING

To prevent possible cylinder head damage, only attempt spark plug removal when the engine is completely cool.

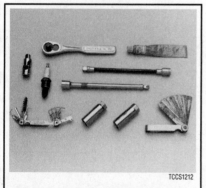

Fig. 85 A variety of tools and gauges are needed for spark plug service

TCCS1212

Fig. 87 Use the ratchet and extension to loosen the spark plug

91181P65

While the spark plugs on 4-cylinder Honda models are easily accessed from underhood, the rear bank of cylinders on the V6 models can be more challenging. You may find that just opening the hood will not be sufficient to give you access to the plugs on these models. If necessary, raise the front end of the vehicle on jackstands and try for access to the rear bank from underneath.

➡**On models with distributorless ignition, the ignition coils are located directly on top of each spark plug. The coils must be removed before the spark plugs. If necessary, refer to the ignition coil removal and installation procedure in**

1. If equipped, release the fasteners and remove the engine cover(s), as necessary for access to the spark plugs.
2. If necessary on some V6 vehicles, raise and support the front end of the vehicle safely using jackstands.
3. If equipped with distributor ignition, place a piece of masking tape around each spark plug wire and number it according to its corresponding cylinder.

➡**Don't remove all of the spark plug wires or ignition coils at once unless you label them first. It is too easy to get them confused during installation, resulting in an improper firing order and a no start condition.**

4. Carefully twist the spark plug wire boot to loosen it, then pull upward and remove the boot from the plug. Be sure to pull on the boot and not on the wire, otherwise the connector located inside the boot may become separated.

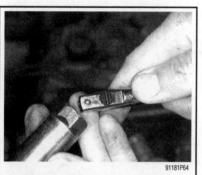

Fig. 86 A locking extension and deep spark plug socket are required for plug removal

91181P64

Fig. 88 Carefully withdraw the spark plug from the cylinder head

91181P66

5. Using compressed air, blow any water or debris from the spark plug well to assure that no harmful contaminants are allowed to enter the combustion chamber when the spark plug is removed. If compressed air is not available, use a rag or a brush to clean the area.

➡**Avoid spark plug removal while the engine is hot. Since the cylinder head spark plug threads are aluminum, the spark plug becomes tight due to the different coefficients of heat expansion. If a plug is too tight to be removed even while the engine is cold, apply a solvent around the plug followed with an application of oil once the solvent has penetrated the threads. Do this only when the engine is Cold.**

✳✳ WARNING

Be sure not to use a flexible extension on the socket. Use of a flexible extension may allow a shear force to be applied to the plug. A shear force could break the plug off in the cylinder head, leading to costly and frustrating repairs.

6. Using a ⅝ in. spark plug socket equipped with a rubber insert to properly hold the plug, turn the spark plug counterclockwise to loosen and remove the spark plug from the bore. When the plug has been loosened a few turns, stop to clean any material from around the spark plug holes; compressed air is preferred. If air is not available, simply use a rag to clean the area.

✳✳ WARNING

In no case should foreign matter be allowed to enter the cylinders. Severe engine damage could result.

To install:
7. Inspect the spark plug boot for tears or damage. If a damaged boot is found, the spark plug wire must be replaced.
8. Using a wire feeler gauge, check and adjust the spark plug gap. When using a gauge, the proper size should pass between the electrodes with a slight drag. The next larger size should not be able to pass while the next smaller size should pass freely.

➡**It's a good idea to apply an anti-seize compound on the threads of the spark plugs before**

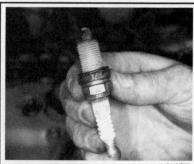

Fig. 89 Always use a replacement spark plug that meets or exceeds the manufacturer's recommendations

91184P08

installing them. Do not over-tighten the spark plugs, as this could damage the aluminum cylinder heads.

9. Carefully thread the plug into the bore by hand. If resistance is felt before the plug is almost completely threaded, back the plug out and begin threading again. In small, hard to reach areas, an old spark plug wire and boot could be used as a threading tool. The boot will hold the plug while you twist the end of the wire and the wire is supple enough to twist before it would allow the plug to crossthread.

❊❊ WARNING

Do not use the spark plug socket to thread the plugs. Always carefully thread the plug by hand or by using an old plug wire to pre-

vent the possibility of crossthreading and damaging the cylinder head bore.

10. Once the plug is threaded, use a torque wrench to tighten the plug to 13 ft. lbs. (18 Nm).

11. Apply a small amount of silicone dielectric compound to the end of the spark plug lead or inside the spark plug boot to prevent sticking, then install the boot to the spark plug and push until it clicks into place. The click may be felt or heard, then gently pull back on the boot to assure proper contact.

INSPECTION & GAPPING

♦ **See Figures 90, 91, 92, 93 and 94**

Check the plugs for deposits and wear. If they are not going to be replaced, clean the plugs thor-

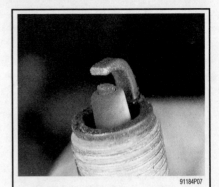
91184P07

Fig. 90 This spark plug has a worn center electrode

A **normally worn** spark plug should have light tan or gray deposits on the firing tip.

A **carbon fouled** plug, identified by soft, sooty, black deposits, may indicate an improperly tuned vehicle. Check the air cleaner, ignition components and engine control system.

This spark plug has been **left in the engine too long,** as evidenced by the extreme gap- Plugs with such an extreme gap can cause misfiring and stumbling accompanied by a noticeable lack of power.

An **oil fouled** spark plug indicates an engine with worn poston rings and/or bad valve seals allowing excessive oil to enter the chamber.

A **physically damaged** spark plug may be evidence of severe detonation in that cylinder. Watch that cylinder carefully between services, as a continued detonation will not only damage the plug, but could also damage the engine.

A **bridged or almost bridged** spark plug, identified by a build-up between the electrodes caused by excessive carbon or oil build-up on the plug.

TCCA1P40

Fig. 91 Inspect the spark plug to determine engine running conditions

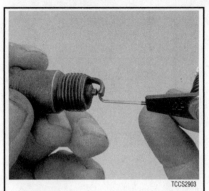

Fig. 92 Checking the spark plug gap with a feeler gauge

Fig. 93 Adjusting the spark plug gap

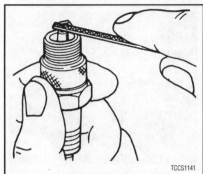

Fig. 94 If the standard plug is in good condition, the electrode may be filed flat— WARNING: do not file platinum plugs

oughly. Remember that any kind of deposit will decrease the efficiency of the plug. Plugs can be cleaned on a spark plug cleaning machine, which can sometimes be found in service stations, or you can do an acceptable job of cleaning with a stiff brush. If the plugs are cleaned, the electrodes must be filed flat. Use an ignition points file, not an emery board or the like, which will leave deposits. The electrodes must be filed perfectly flat with sharp edges; rounded edges reduce the spark plug voltage by as much as 50%.

Check spark plug gap before installation. The ground electrode (the L-shaped one connected to the body of the plug) must be parallel to the center electrode and the specified size wire gauge (please refer to the Tune-Up Specifications chart for details) must pass between the electrodes with a slight drag.

➡ NEVER adjust the gap on a used platinum type spark plug.

Always check the gap on new plugs as they are not always set correctly at the factory. Do not use a flat feeler gauge when measuring the gap on a used plug, because the reading may be inaccurate. A round-wire type gapping tool is the best way to check the gap. The correct gauge should pass through the electrode gap with a slight drag. If you're in doubt, try one size smaller and one larger. The smaller gauge should go through easily, while the larger one shouldn't go through at all. Wire gapping tools usually have a bending tool attached. Use that to adjust the side electrode until the proper distance is obtained. Absolutely never attempt to bend the center electrode. Also, be careful not to bend the side electrode too far or too often as it

may weaken and break off within the engine, requiring removal of the cylinder head to retrieve it.

Spark Plug Wires

TESTING

▶ See Figure 95

During every tune-up/inspection, visually check the spark plug cables for fluid contamination, burns, chaffing, cuts, or breaks in the insulation. Check the boots and the nipples on the ignition coil or distributor, if equipped. Replace any damaged wiring.

Every 60,000 miles (96,000 km) or 48 months, the resistance of the wires should be checked with an ohmmeter. Wires with excessive resistance will cause misfiring, and may cause the engine to be difficult to start in damp weather. Ignition wire resistance should not be greater than 25 kilohms.

To check resistance, remove the spark plug wire from the plug and ignition coil or distributor. Using an ohmmeter, measure the resistance of the wire by placing one lead of the ohmmeter at one end of the ignition wire, and the other ohmmeter lead at the other end of the ignition wire.

If the measured resistance is above the specifications, the ignition wire must be replaced.

REMOVAL & INSTALLATION

▶ See Figures 96 and 97

➡ The spark plug wires must be routed and connected properly. If the wires must be com-

pletely disconnected from the spark plugs and from the distributor cap or ignition coil at the same time, label the wires to assure proper reconnection.

When installing a new set of spark plug wires, replace the wires one at a time to avoid mixing them up. Start by replacing the longest cable first. Twist the boot of the spark plug wire ½ turn in each direction before pulling it off. Install the boot firmly over the spark plug. Route the wire exactly the same as the original. Insert the nipple firmly onto the tower of the distributor cap, if equipped. Use a silicone dielectric compound on the spark plug wire boots and distributor cap connectors prior to installation.

Distributor Cap and Rotor

REMOVAL & INSTALLATION

▶ See Figures 98 thru 104

1. If necessary, record the radio security code.
2. Disconnect the negative battery cable.
3. If the distributor cap is to be replaced, mark the ignition wires for identification and remove them from the distributor cap.
4. On 2.2L and 2.3L engines remove the two rear air filter housing bolts, using a 10mm socket, extension and ratchet, and move the housing to the left to allow enough clearance to remove the distributor cap.
5. Completely loosen the distributor cap mounting fasteners using an 8mm socket, extension and ratchet or a Phillips screwdriver.

Fig. 95 Checking individual plug wire resistance with a digital ohmmeter

Fig. 96 Remove the spark plug wire by first twisting it . . .

Fig. 97 . . . and then pulling up on the boot, not the wire itself, to remove it

Fig. 98 Always label the installed position of the wires to the distributor cap before removal

Fig. 99 Loosen the distributor cap retaining bolts using a wrench or a Phillips head screwdriver

Fig. 100 When removing the cap from the distributor . . .

Fig. 101 . . . be careful not to damage the ignition rotor, which is located beneath the cap

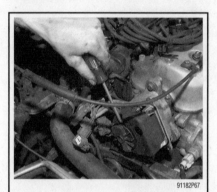

Fig. 102 Unfasten the rotor retaining screw, using a Phillips head screwdriver

Fig. 103 Remove the screw from the distributor rotor, then . . .

Fig. 104 . . . once the screw is removed, pull the rotor straight off of the distributor shaft

6. Carefully remove the distributor cap, taking care not to damage the cap seal or rotor, then position the cap aside.

7. Locate the threaded fastener that secures the ignition rotor to the shaft of the distributor, which is positioned opposite the rotor contact on the lower portion of the rotor, and remove the fastener.

8. Carefully lift the rotor off the distributor shaft.

➡Inspect the distributor cap to housing seal for damage and/or cracks. Replace if cracks are detected.

To install:

9. Install the rotor onto the distributor shaft and tighten the rotor mounting fastener.

10. Position the distributor cap seal on the distributor housing, then position the distributor cap on the housing.

11. Install the distributor cap by tightening the mounting fasteners in a crisscross pattern. Use care to not over-tighten the fasteners.

12. Reconnect the spark plug wires, making sure to install them exactly in the same position from which they were removed.

13. Reconnect the negative battery cable and enter the radio security code.

INSPECTION

1. Inspect the distributor cap for cracks and burned or worn electrodes. Inspect the center contact of the cap to make sure it will make a good connection with the rotor once installed. Replace the cap if it is cracked, or the contacts appear grooved, or if the center contact is worn.

2. Inspect the rotor for cracks and a worn or burned electrode. Replace the rotor if the contact surface is eroded or uneven.

3. Prior to reinstalling the distributor cap and rotor, thoroughly clean them with an electrical contact cleaner.

✳✳ WARNING

Because the distributor cap and rotor transmit a high-energy ignition voltage, avoid using any type of solvent, spray or lubricate on the inside or outside of the cap or on the rotor. When cleaning them, use only an electrical contact cleaner intended specifically for electrical circuits.

Ignition Timing

GENERAL INFORMATION

The ignition timing is a specification that is used to describe when a spark plug receives a high-energy voltage relative to the position of the piston. A piston that is at the top of its stroke is referred to as being at Top Dead Center (TDC). The piston in an internal combustion engine simply moves up and down in the cylinder bore of the engine block, and is attached to the crankshaft via the connecting rod. If the crankshaft is rotated one complete revolution, the piston will move two strokes, one downward stroke and one upward stroke. During the upward stroke of the piston, its position, relative to the top of its stroke is referred to as being Before Top Dead Center (BTDC). One complete revolution of the crankshaft is the equivalent to 360° of rotation. When a piston is at TDC, this position is referred to as the 0° position. If the crankshaft is rotated ½ a revolution, it has been rotated 180° and the piston would be at the bottom of its stroke.

Because the piston moves up or down as the crankshaft is rotated, the piston's location relative to TDC can be measured using the number of degrees of crankshaft rotation **before** the piston reaches TDC. The upward movement of the piston as it approaches TDC is referred to as Before Top Dead Center (BTDC).

The ignition timing specifications provided by the manufacturer and used in this manual are provided in degrees Before Top Dead Center (°BTDC).

When the spark plug receives the high-energy voltage, the intensity of this voltage is enough that the voltage jumps the gap of the spark plug, creating a spark. This spark is used to ignite the fuel air-mixture in the combustion chamber. As the fuel burns, it expands, creating energy and pressurizing the combustion chamber. This pressure presses on the top of the piston, pressing it downward on a power stroke, which transmits the energy through the connecting rod to the crankshaft.

For an engine to run properly and efficiently, the correct ignition timing is essential. If the ignition spark occurs too late during the piston's upward stroke, the ignition timing is referred to as being retarded. If the ignition spark occurs too early in the piston's upward stroke, the ignition timing is referred to as being advanced.

The engine's timing requirements change as the engine speed increases and as throttle position varies. The Honda products covered in this manual use an electronic ignition system, which monitors the engine's operating conditions, and changes the ignition timing accordingly. These engines use a distributor to provide the high-energy ignition voltage to the spark plugs. On these models, the ignition timing advance is controlled by the engine control units, however the idle speed ignition timing (base ignition timing) can be adjusted by placing the engine control unit in an adjust mode moving the distributor.

If the ignition timing is set too far advanced (BTDC), the ignition and expansion of the fuel in the cylinder will occur too soon and tend to force the piston down while it is still traveling up. This condition may causes engine detonation or ping. If the ignition timing is too far retarded After Top Dead Center, (ATDC), the piston will have already passed TDC and started on its way down when the fuel is ignited. This will cause the piston to be forced down for only a portion of its travel. This will result in poor engine performance and lack of power.

On vehicles with distributors, the ignition timing should be checked during a tune-up. Usually, once the timing is set it is not likely to change. On vehicles with distributorless ignition systems, the ignition timing can only be checked using expensive, specialized diagnostic equipment. Due to its cost and complexity, the use of such equipment is beyond the scope of this manual. The ignition timing on the distributorless ignition system cannot be adjusted and the system requires no maintenance aside from replacing spark plugs. The ignition timing will remain correct as long as the sensors and control unit function properly.

The ignition timing marks on both the Accord and Prelude are small notches located on the perimeter of the drive belt pulleys mounted on the engine's crankshaft. The engine cover above the pulleys has a pointer that is used to align with the timing notches. The 2.2L and 2.3L engines run in a counterclockwise direction when facing the drive pulleys. Two of the notches in the crankshaft pulley are painted. The notch that is painted **white** is TDC, (0° mark). The notch that is painted **red** is the idle speed ignition timing mark. On models where the crankshaft rotates in a counterclockwise direction, while facing the drive pulleys, the red idle speed ignition timing mark is located to the left of the white TDC mark. The painted red ignition timing notch also has notches

on either side of it. These notches, on either side of the red notch, represent 2° increments. As long as the idle speed ignition timing occurs somewhere between these two notches, the ignition timing is within specification. For example, the idle speed ignition timing for the 2.3L is 16° BTDC plus or minus 2°. The notches on either side of the red notch on the crankshaft pulley would indicate the following information. The notch to the right of the red notch would be 16° minus 2°, or 14°. The notch to the left of the red notch would be 16° plus 2°, or 18°. As long as the idle speed ignition timing for this example, occurs between these two marks (14°–18°), the idle speed ignition timing is considered to be within the recommended specification.

There are three basic types of timing lights available. The first is a simple neon bulb with two wire connections. One wire connects to the spark plug terminal and the other plugs into the end of the spark plug wire for the No. 1 cylinder, thus connecting the light in series with the spark plug. This type of light is dim and must be held very closely to the timing marks to be seen. Sometimes a dark corner has to be sought out to see the flash at all. This type of light is very inexpensive. The second type is powered by the vehicle's battery, by correctly connecting two alligator clips to the battery terminals. These timing lights are available with or without an inductive pickup. If the timing light does not have an inductive pickup, a wire must make physical contact with the ignition wire for the No. 1 spark plug. Using this type of arrangement usually requires the use of an adapter either at the spark plug or distributor cap connection. This tends to render this type of arrangement to be awkward, less convenient and time consuming to use.

A timing light with an inductive pickup is much easier to use. Simply connect the lead properly at the vehicle's battery and then clamp the inductive pickup around the ignition wire for the No. 1 spark plug. This type is a bit more expensive, but it provides a nice bright flash that can be easily seen, even in bright sunlight. It is easy to use, and the type most often seen in professional shops. The third type replaces the battery power source with 115-volt current. They work well, but are much less portable and convenient to use.

Some timing lights may have other features built into them, such as ignition advance checking devices, dwell meters, or tachometers. These are convenient, in that they reduce the tangle of wires under the hood, but may duplicate the functions of other tools and the features add to the expense of the tool. A timing light with an inductive pickup should always be used on Honda ignition systems when checking/adjusting ignition timing.

ADJUSTMENT

2.2L and 2.3L Engines

▶ See Figures 105 and 106

1. If equipped with an automatic transaxle, place the shifter in Park or Neutral. If equipped with a manual transaxle place the shifter in Neutral. Make sure to apply the parking brake and block the drive wheels.
2. With the heater off and in the full cold position, start the engine and hold the engine speed at 3000 rpm, until the radiator fan comes on at least one time. To check the ignition timing, the engine must be at idle speed and at normal operating temperature.

Fig. 105 To check the ignition timing with an inductive style timing light, simply connect the inductive lead around the plug wire and follow the manufacturer's instructions

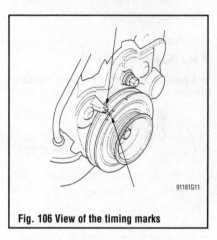

Fig. 106 View of the timing marks

Make sure all electrical consumers (defroster, radio, air conditioning, lights, etc.,) are turned OFF.

3. Locate the blue plastic Service Check (SCS) Connector, which can be found centrally located on the passenger side, under the dash.
4. Attach the SCS service connector tool number 07PAZ-0010100 or equivalent to the service connector.

➡A paper clip can be substituted for the tool by forming a "U" shaped bend in the paper clip and carefully inserting it into the back side of the SCS service connector terminals. The purpose of the tool is simply to connect the two wires together temporarily.

5. Connect a timing light to No. 1 ignition wire and point the light toward the pointer on the timing belt cover.
6. Check the idle speed and adjust if necessary.
7. The red mark on the crankshaft pulley should be aligned with the pointer on the timing belt cover.

➡The white mark on the crank pulley is Top Dead Center (TDC).

8. Adjust the ignition timing by loosening the distributor mounting bolts and rotating the distributor housing to adjust the timing. The timing should be set at 13–17° BTDC at 650–750 rpm
9. Tighten the distributor bolts to 17 ft. lbs. (24 Nm) and recheck the timing.
10. Remove the SCS service connector or the substituted paper clip from the SCS service plug.

2.7L Engine

▶ **See Figures 105 and 106**

1. Start and hold engine speed at 3000 rpms (no load) until the radiator fan comes on.

2. Access the service check connector from behind the dashboard and attach the SCS service connector's tool number 07PAZ-0010100 or equivalent, GRN/BLU and RED terminals with the SCS connector.

3. Check and adjust the idle speed to the manufacturers specifications.

4. Connect a timing light's inductive pickup to the No. 1 ignition wire and point it to the marks on the timing cover.

5. The timing should be set, as follows:
   • 1996–1997 models: 13–17° BTDC (Red timing mark) at 700–800 with the gear selector in Park or Neutral and all electrical accessories off.

3.0L Engine

▶ **See Figures 105 and 106**

➡**A Honda PGM diagnostic tester is needed to perform a proper check of the timing.**

1. Check and adjust the idle speed if it is out of the manufacturers specifications.

2. Connect the Honda PGM tester to the data link connector and follow the PGM tester operator manuals directions.

3. Start the engine and hold the engine at 3000 rpm's (engine under no load), with the gear selector in Park or Neutral.

4. Once the radiator fan comes on, let the engine idle.

5. Connect the timing light to the No. 1 spark plug wire and aim it at the pointer on the timing belt cover.

➡**The ignition timing must be checked under no load, and all electrical accessories OFF.**

6. The ignition timing should be between 8–14° BTDC (using the RED mark on the crankshaft as your reference) while idling in Park or Neutral.

Valve Lash

ADJUSTMENT

▶ **See Figures 107, 108 and 109**

➡**The radio may contain a coded anti-theft circuit. Obtain the security code before disconnecting the battery.**

1. Disconnect the negative battery cable.

2. The valves should be checked and adjusted when the engine is cold. If the engine has been run, allow it to cool to below 100°F (38°C) before beginning adjustments.

3. The valves must be checked or adjusted for each cylinder with the cylinder in the TDC position of the compression stroke.

4. Remove the cylinder head cover and the upper timing belt cover. For more information, please refer to Section 3.

5. Rotate the crankshaft in a counterclockwise direction until the painted white notch Top Dead Center (TDC) mark on the crankshaft pulley is aligned with the pointer on the engine cover, and the **UP** mark on the camshaft sprocket is facing up. The No. 1 cylinder is at TDC/compression stroke in this position.

6. With the cylinder at TDC on the compression stroke, check the valve clearance by inserting the correct size feeler gauge between the rocker and the valve tip of the valves for that cylinder.

7. Hold the rocker arm against the camshaft and use a feeler gauge to check the clearance at the valve stem; intake valve clearance should be 0.010 in. (0.26mm), exhaust valve clearance should be 0.012 in. (0.30mm). The service limit for both intake and exhaust valves is plus or minus 0.0008 in. (0.02mm).

8. To check the intake valves proceed as follows:
   a. Using a 0.009 in. (0.24mm) feeler gauge, see if the gauge will slide between the valve tip and the rocker.
   b. If the 0.009 in. (0.24mm) feeler gauge does not fit between the rocker and the valve tip, then adjust the valve. If the feeler gauge did fit, then try inserting a 0.011 in. (0.28mm) feeler gauge.
   c. If the 0.011 in. (.28mm) feeler gauge can be inserted between the rocker and the valve tip, then adjust the valve. If the feeler gauge cannot be inserted, then the valve adjustment for that valve is within the range specified.

9. The valve adjustment specification for the intake valve is 0.010 in. (0.26mm). To adjust an intake valve, proceed as follows:
   a. Loosen the locknut and turn the adjusting screw counterclockwise to loosen the adjustment screw.
   b. Hold the rocker arm against the camshaft and insert a 0.010 in. (0.26mm) feeler gauge between the rocker and the valve tip.
   c. Hold the locknut and turn the adjusting screw until a very light resistance is felt. The feeler gauge should be able to be moved with a slight amount of drag.
   d. While holding the adjustment screw in place, tighten the locknut and then recheck the clearance.

10. To check the exhaust valve clearance proceed as follows:
   a. Using a 0.011 in. (0.28mm) feeler gauge, see if the gauge will slide between the valve tip and the rocker.
   b. If the 0.011in. (0.28mm) feeler gauge does not fit between the rocker and the valve tip, then adjust the valve. If the feeler gauge did fit, then try inserting a 0.013 in. (0.33mm) feeler gauge.
   c. If the 0.013 in. (0.33mm) feeler gauge can be inserted between the rocker and the valve tip, then adjust the valve. If the feeler gauge cannot be inserted, then the valve adjustment for that valve is within the range specified.

Intake: 0.26 mm (0.010 in.) ± 0.02 mm (0.0008 in.)
Exhaust: 0.30 mm (0.012 in.) ± 0.02 mm (0.0008 in.)

Valve Adjusting Screw Locations

INTAKE

No. 4　No. 3　No. 2　No. 1

No. 4　No. 3　No. 2　No. 1

EXHAUST

91181G03

Fig. 107 Valve adjustment specifications—Accord with 2.2L and 2.3L engines

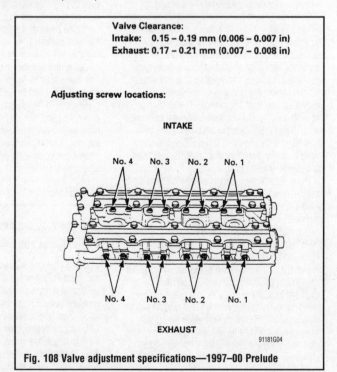

Valve Clearance:
Intake: 0.15 – 0.19 mm (0.006 – 0.007 in)
Exhaust: 0.17 – 0.21 mm (0.007 – 0.008 in)

Adjusting screw locations:

INTAKE

No. 4　No. 3　No. 2　No. 1

No. 4　No. 3　No. 2　No. 1

EXHAUST

91181G04

Fig. 108 Valve adjustment specifications—1997–00 Prelude

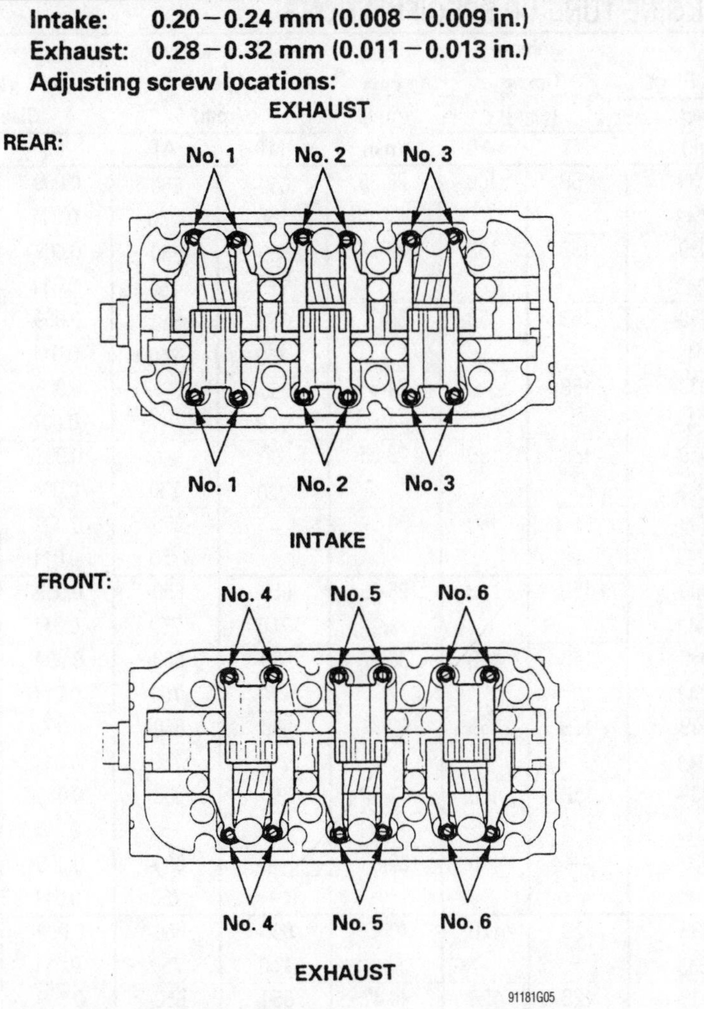

Intake: 0.20−0.24 mm (0.008−0.009 in.)
Exhaust: 0.28−0.32 mm (0.011−0.013 in.)
Adjusting screw locations:

EXHAUST

REAR:

No. 1   No. 2   No. 3

No. 1   No. 2   No. 3

INTAKE

FRONT:

No. 4   No. 5   No. 6

No. 4   No. 5   No. 6

EXHAUST

91181G05

Fig. 109 Valve adjustment specifications—V6 Accords

11. The valve adjustment specification for the exhaust valve is 0.012 in. (0.30mm). To adjust an exhaust valve, proceed as follows:

a. Loosen the locknut and turn the adjusting screw counterclockwise to loosen the adjustment screw.

b. Hold the rocker arm against the camshaft and insert a 0.012 in. (0.30mm) feeler gauge between the rocker and the valve tip.

c. Hold the locknut and turn the adjusting screw until a very light resistance is felt. The feeler gauge should be able to be moved with a slight amount of drag.

d. While holding the adjustment screw in place, tighten the locknut and then recheck the clearance.

12. Repeat the checking procedure for each valve and adjust the clearance for any valve found to be out of adjustment.

13. Once all of the valves for a cylinder have been checked, the crankshaft must be rotated counterclockwise to check the valves of another cylinder.

14. When rotating the crankshaft counterclockwise, the adjustment order is cylinder No. 1, cylinder No. 3, cylinder No. 4, cylinder No. 2.

15. Rotate the crankshaft counterclockwise 180° to bring the next cylinder to the TDC/compression position.

16. Refer to the following information to verify the cylinder to be checked is in the TDC/compression position:

• At TDC/compression for the No. 1 cylinder, the camshaft sprocket **UP** mark should be pointed straight up, and the TDC marks align with the edge of the cylinder head.

• At TDC/compression for the No. 3 cylinder, the camshaft sprocket **UP** mark should be horizontal, and pointed to the left.

• At TDC/compression for the No. 4 cylinder, the camshaft sprocket **UP** mark should be pointed straight down, and the TDC mark should align with the edge of the cylinder head.

• At TDC/compression for the No. 2 cylinder, the camshaft sprocket **UP** mark should be horizontal, and pointed to the right.

17. After checking the valves, check and if necessary, retighten the crankshaft pulley bolt in a clockwise direction to 181 ft. lbs. (245 Nm).

18. Thoroughly clean the cylinder head cover gasket and make sure it is fully seated into the head cover. Apply a liquid gasket sealant to the corners of the half circle portions of the gasket.

19. Install the cylinder head and timing belt covers, tightening the fasteners evenly to 86 inch pounds (9.8 Nm).

20. Reconnect the negative battery cable. Enter the radio security code.

Idle Speed and Mixture Adjustment

Idle speed and mixture for all engines covered by this manual are electronically controlled by a computerized fuel injection system. The only adjustment possible is the warm idle engine speed. No other adjustments are possible.

WARM IDLE SPEED ADJUSTMENT

Before setting the warm idle speed, the following items must be checked or verified:
• The Malfunction Indicator Light (MIL) light has not been on or flashing
• Ignition timing is within specification
• Spark plug condition is within specification
• Air cleaner condition is acceptable
• Positive Crankcase Ventilation (PCV) system is functioning properly

➡On Canadian vehicles, the parking brake must be applied before proceeding with any adjustments.

1. Make sure the heater is in the full cold position and all electrical consumers are in the off position, such as headlights, defrosters, climate control fans, and other electrical accessories.

2. Start the engine and hold the engine speed to 3,000 rpm with the transmission in **Park** or **Neutral**, until the radiator cooling fan comes on, then let the engine idle.

3. Connect a tachometer or the Honda PGM Testing Assembly.

4. On 4-cylinder engines, detach the round 2 pin electrical connector from the Idle Air Control (IAC) valve.

5. If the engine stalls, restart pressing the accelerator, hold the engine speed at 1,000 rpm, and slowly release the gas pedal until the engine idles.

6. Check the idle speed making sure all electrical accessories are turned off, with the transmission in **Park** or **Neutral**.

7. The idle speed should be 500–600 rpm

8. If the idle speed must be adjusted, do not turn the adjusting screw located at the top left of the throttle body inlet side more than ¼ of a turn a minute. Make sure no electrical accessories are operating when checking or adjusting the engine idle speed.

9. On the 4-cylinder engines, once the correct test procedure idle speed is attained, perform the following:

a. Turn the ignition switch to the **OFF** position.

b. Reconnect the round 2 pin electrical connector to the Idle Air Control (IAC) valve.

c. Remove the BACK UP (RADIO) 7.5 Amp fuse located in the under-hood fuse/relay box for 10 seconds to reset the Powertrain Control Module (PCM).

Maintenance Service Indicator

The Maintenance Required Indicator used on the Honda Accord and Prelude is one of two types. Early models use a small rectangular window in the lower portion of the instrument cluster that displays

ENGINE TUNE-UP SPECIFICATIONS

Year	Engine Displacement Liters (cc)	Engine ID/VIN	Spark Plugs Gap (in.)	Ignition Timing (deg.) MT	Ignition Timing (deg.) AT	Fuel Pump (psi)	Idle Speed (rpm) MT	Idle Speed (rpm) AT	Valve Clearance In.	Valve Clearance Ex.
1996	2.2 (2156)	F22A1	0.039-0.043	15B	15B	28-35	650-750	650-750	0.009-0.011	0.011-0.013
	2.2 (2156)	F22B1	0.039-0.043	15B	15B	30-37	650-750	650-750	0.009-0.011	0.011-0.013
	2.2 (2156)	F22B2	0.039-0.043	15B	15B	30-37	650-750	650-750	0.009-0.011	0.011-0.013
	2.2 (2157)	H22A1	0.039-0.043	15B	—	24-31	650-750	—	0.006-0.007	0.007-0.008
	2.3 (2259)	H23A1	0.039-0.043	15B	15B	28-35	650-750	650-750	0.003-0.004	0.006-0.007
	2.7 (2675)	C27A4	0.039-0.043	—	15B	30-37	—	650-750	0.009-0.011	0.011-0.013
1997	2.2 (2156)	F22A1	0.039-0.043	15B	15B	28-35	650-750	650-750	0.009-0.011	0.011-0.013
	2.2 (2156)	F22B1	0.039-0.043	15B	15B	30-37	650-750	650-750	0.009-0.011	0.011-0.013
	2.2 (2156)	F22B2	0.039-0.043	15B	15B	30-37	650-750	650-750	0.009-0.011	0.011-0.013
	2.2 (2157)	H22A4	0.039-0.043	15B	15B	47-54	650-750	650-750	0.006-0.007	0.007-0.008
	2.7 (2675)	C27A4	0.039-0.043	—	15B	30-37	—	650-750	0.009-0.011	0.011-0.013
1998	2.3 (2254)	F23A1	0.039-0.043	12B	12B	40-47	650-750	650-750	0.009-0.011	0.011-0.013
	2.3 (2254)	F23A4	0.039-0.043	12B	12B	40-47	650-750	650-750	0.009-0.011	0.011-0.013
	2.3 (2254)	F23A5	0.039-0.043	12B	12B	40-47	650-750	650-750	0.009-0.011	0.011-0.013
	2.2 (2157)	H22A4	0.039-0.043	15B	15B	47-54	650-750	650-750	0.006-0.007	0.007-0.008
	3.0 (2997)	J30A1	0.039-0.043	—	10B	41-48	—	630-730	0.008-0.009	0.011-0.013
1999	2.2 (2157)	H22A4	0.039-0.043	15B	15B	47-54	650-750	650-750	0.006-0.007	0.007-0.008
	2.3 (2254)	F23A1	0.039-0.043	12B	12B	40-47	650-750	650-750	0.009-0.011	0.011-0.013
	2.3 (2254)	F23A4	0.039-0.043	12B	12B	40-47	650-750	650-750	0.009-0.011	0.011-0.013
	2.3 (2254)	F23A5	0.039-0.043	12B	12B	40-47	650-750	650-750	0.009-0.011	0.011-0.013
	3.0 (2997)	J30A1	0.039-0.043	—	10B	41-48	—	630-730	0.008-0.009	0.011-0.013

91181C03

ENGINE TUNE-UP SPECIFICATIONS

Year	Engine Displacement Liters (cc)	Engine ID/VIN	Spark Plugs Gap (in.)	Ignition Timing (deg.)		Fuel Pump (psi)	Idle Speed (rpm)		Valve Clearance	
				MT	AT		MT	AT	In.	Ex.
2000	2.2 (2157)	H22A4	0.039-0.043	15B	15B	47-54	650-750	650-750	0.006-0.007	0.007-0.008
	2.3 (2254)	F23A1	0.039-0.043	12B	12B	40-47	650-750	650-750	0.009-0.011	0.011-0.013
	2.3 (2254)	F23A4	0.039-0.043	12B	12B	40-47	650-750	650-750	0.009-0.011	0.011-0.013
	2.3 (2254)	F23A5	0.039-0.043	12B	12B	40-47	650-750	650-750	0.009-0.011	0.011-0.013
	3.0 (2997)	J30A1	0.039-0.043	—	10B	41-48	—	630-730	0.008-0.009	0.011-0.013

NOTE: The Vehicle Emission Control Information label often reflects specification changes made during production. The label figures must be used if they differ from those in this chart.

B - Before Top Dead Center

91181C04

a colored flag. The flag color remains green until it is time for scheduled maintenance. When the 7,500 mile (12,000 km) maintenance interval approaches, the indicator will turn yellow. If 7,500 miles (12,000 km) is exceeded, the indicator will turn red.

Later models use a Maintenance Required Indicator warning light located in the lower portion of the tachometer. Once reset, the warning light works as follows:

• During the first 6,000 miles (9,600 km), the light operates for two seconds when the ignition is switched **ON**.

• Between 6,000–7,500 miles (9,600–12,000 km), the light operates for two seconds when the ignition is switched **ON**, and then flashes for 10 seconds.

• If 7,500 miles (12,000 km) is exceeded without having the scheduled maintenance performed and the light reset, the light remains on constantly.

RESETTING

Flag Type Maintenance Required Indicators

The indicator can be reset by inserting the ignition key into the slot below the indicator. This will extinguish the indicator for the next 7,500 miles (12,000 km).

Warning Light Type Maintenance Required Indicators

1. Turn the ignition switch to the **OFF** position.
2. Press and hold the Select/Reset button on the instrument panel, then turn the ignition switch to the on position and hold the button for about 10 seconds, until the light stops working.

Air Conditioning System

SYSTEM SERVICE & REPAIR

➡It is recommended that the A/C system be serviced by an EPA Section 609 certified automotive technician utilizing a refrigerant recovery/recycling machine.

The do-it-yourselfer should not service his/her own vehicle's A/C system for many reasons, including legal concerns, personal injury, environmental damage and cost. The following are some of the reasons why you may decide not to service your own vehicle's A/C system.

According to the U.S. Clean Air Act, it is a federal crime to service or repair (involving the refrigerant) a Motor Vehicle Air Conditioning (MVAC) system for money without being EPA certified. It is also illegal to vent R-134a refrigerant into the atmosphere.

State and/or local laws may be more strict than the federal regulations, so be sure to check with your state and/or local authorities for further information. For further federal information on the legality of servicing your A/C system, call the EPA Stratospheric Ozone Hotline.

➡Federal law dictates that a fine of up to $25,000 may be levied on people convicted of venting refrigerant into the atmosphere. Additionally, the EPA may pay up to $10,000 for information or services leading to a criminal conviction of the violation of these laws.

When servicing an A/C system you run the risk of handling or coming in contact with refrigerant, which may result in skin or eye irritation or frostbite. Although low in toxicity (due to chemical stability), inhalation of concentrated refrigerant fumes is dangerous and can result in death; cases of fatal cardiac arrhythmia have been reported in people accidentally subjected to high levels of refrigerant. Some early symptoms include loss of concentration and drowsiness.

Also, refrigerants can decompose at high temperatures (near gas heaters or open flame), which may result in hydrofluoric acid, hydrochloric acid and phosgene (a fatal nerve gas).

R-134a refrigerant is a greenhouse gas which, if allowed to vent into the atmosphere, will contribute to global warming (the Greenhouse Effect).

It is usually more economically feasible to have a certified MVAC automotive technician perform A/C system service to your vehicle. While it is illegal to service an A/C system without the proper equipment, the home mechanic would have to purchase an expensive refrigerant recovery/recycling machine to service his/her own vehicle.

PREVENTIVE MAINTENANCE

◆ See Figures 110 and 111

Although the A/C system should not be serviced by the do-it-yourselfer, preventive maintenance can be practiced and A/C system inspections can be performed to help maintain the efficiency of the vehicle's A/C system. For preventive maintenance, perform the following:

• The easiest and most important preventive maintenance for your A/C system is to be sure that it is used on a regular basis. Running the system for five minutes each month (no matter what the season) will help ensure that the seals and all internal components remain lubricated.

➡Some newer vehicles automatically operate the A/C system compressor whenever the windshield defroster is activated. When running, the compressor lubricates the A/C sys-

TCCS1233

Fig. 110 A coolant tester can be used to determine the freezing and boiling levels of the coolant in your vehicle

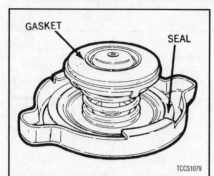

Fig. 111 To ensure efficient cooling system operation, inspect the radiator cap gasket and seal

tem components; therefore, the A/C system would not need to be operated each month.

• In order to prevent heater core freeze-up during A/C operation, it is necessary to maintain a proper antifreeze protection. Use a hand-held coolant tester (hydrometer) to periodically check the condition of the antifreeze in your engine's cooling system.

➡Antifreeze should not be used longer than the manufacturer specifies.

• For efficient operation of an air conditioned vehicle's cooling system, the radiator cap should have a holding pressure which meets manufacturer's specifications. A cap which fails to hold these pressures should be replaced.

• Any obstruction of or damage to the con-

denser configuration will restrict air flow which is essential to its efficient operation. It is, therefore, a good rule to keep this unit clean and in proper physical shape.

➡Bug screens which are mounted in front of the condenser (unless they are original equipment) are regarded as obstructions.

• The condensation drain tube expels any water, which accumulates on the bottom of the evaporator housing, into the engine compartment. If this tube is obstructed, the air conditioning performance can be restricted and condensation buildup can spill over onto the vehicle's floor.

SYSTEM INSPECTION

Although the A/C system should not be serviced by the do-it-yourselfer, preventive maintenance can be practiced and A/C system inspections can be performed to help maintain the efficiency of the vehicle's A/C system. For A/C system inspection, perform the following:

The easiest and often most important check for the air conditioning system consists of a visual inspection of the system components. Visually inspect the air conditioning system for refrigerant leaks, damaged compressor clutch, abnormal compressor drive belt tension and/or condition, plugged evaporator drain tube, blocked condenser fins, disconnected or broken wires, blown fuses, corroded connections and poor insulation.

A refrigerant leak will usually appear as an oily residue at the leakage point in the system. The oily

residue soon picks up dust or dirt particles from the surrounding air and appears greasy. Through time, this will build up and appear to be a heavy dirt impregnated grease.

For a thorough visual and operational inspection, check the following:

• Check the surface of the radiator and condenser for dirt, leaves or other material which might block air flow.

• Check for kinks in hoses and lines. Check the system for leaks.

• Make sure the drive belt is properly tensioned. When the air conditioning is operating, make sure the drive belt is free of noise or slippage.

• Make sure the blower motor operates at all appropriate positions, then check for distribution of the air from all outlets with the blower on HIGH or MAX.

➡Keep in mind that under conditions of high humidity, air discharged from the A/C vents may not feel as cold as expected, even if the system is working properly. This is because vaporized moisture in humid air retains heat more effectively than dry air, thereby making humid air more difficult to cool.

• Make sure the air passage selection lever is operating correctly. Start the engine and warm it to normal operating temperature, then make sure the temperature selection lever is operating correctly.

Windshield Wipers

ELEMENT (REFILL) CARE & REPLACEMENT

▶ See Figures 112 thru 121

For maximum effectiveness and longest element life, the windshield and wiper blades should be kept clean. Dirt, tree sap, road tar and so on will cause streaking, smearing and blade deterioration if left on the glass. It is advisable to wash the windshield carefully with a commercial glass cleaner at least once a month. Wipe off the rubber blades with the wet rag afterwards. Do not attempt to move wipers across the windshield by hand; damage to the motor and drive mechanism will result.

To inspect and/or replace the wiper blade elements, place the wiper switch in the **LOW** speed position and the ignition switch in the **ACC** position. When the wiper blades are approximately vertical on the windshield, turn the ignition switch to **OFF**.

Fig. 112 Bosch® wiper blade and fit kit

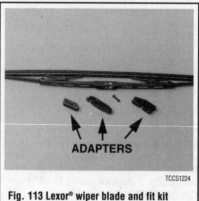

Fig. 113 Lexor® wiper blade and fit kit

Fig. 114 Pylon® wiper blade and adapter

Fig. 115 Trico® wiper blade and fit kit

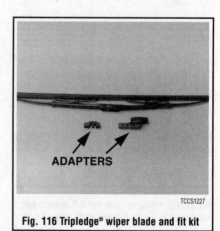

Fig. 116 Tripledge® wiper blade and fit kit

Fig. 117 To remove and install a Lexor® wiper blade refill, slip out the old insert and slide in a new one

Fig. 118 On Pylon® inserts, the clip at the end has to be removed prior to sliding the insert off

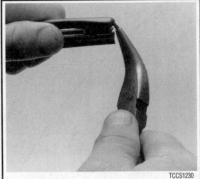

Fig. 119 On Trico® wiper blades, the tab at the end of the blade must be turned up . . .

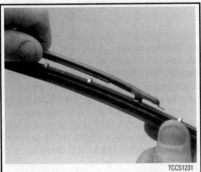

Fig. 120 . . . then the insert can be removed. After installing the replacement insert, bend the tab back

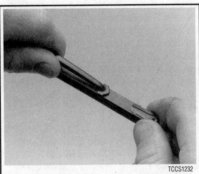

Fig. 121 The Tripledge® wiper blade insert is removed and installed using a securing clip

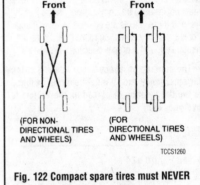

Fig. 122 Compact spare tires must NEVER be used in the rotation pattern

Examine the wiper blade elements. If they are found to be cracked, broken or torn, they should be replaced immediately. Replacement intervals will vary with usage, although ozone deterioration usually limits element life to about one year. If the wiper pattern is smeared or streaked, or if the blade chatters across the glass, the elements should be replaced. It is easiest and most sensible to replace the elements in pairs.

If your vehicle is equipped with aftermarket blades, there are several different types of refills and your vehicle might have any kind. Aftermarket blades and arms rarely use the exact same type blade or refill as the original equipment. Here are some typical aftermarket blades; not all may be available for your vehicle:

The Anco® type uses a release button that is pushed down to allow the refill to slide out of the yoke jaws. The new refill slides back into the frame and locks in place.

Some Trico® refills are removed by locating where the metal backing strip or the refill is wider. Insert a small screwdriver blade between the frame and metal backing strip. Press down to release the refill from the retaining tab.

Other types of Trico® refills have two metal tabs which are unlocked by squeezing them together. The rubber filler can then be withdrawn from the frame jaws. A new refill is installed by inserting the refill into the front frame jaws and sliding it rearward to engage the remaining frame jaws. There are usually four jaws; be certain when installing that the refill is engaged in all of them. At the end of its travel, the tabs will lock into place on the front jaws of the wiper blade frame.

Another type of refill is made from polycarbonate. The refill has a simple locking device at one end which flexes downward out of the groove into which the jaws of the holder fit, allowing easy release. By sliding the new refill through all the jaws and pushing through the slight resistance when it reaches the end of its travel, the refill will lock into position.

To replace the Tridon® refill, it is necessary to remove the wiper blade. This refill has a plastic backing strip with a notch about 1 in. (25mm) from the end. Hold the blade (frame) on a hard surface so that the frame is tightly bowed. Grip the tip of the backing strip and pull up while twisting counterclockwise. The backing strip will snap out of the retaining tab. Do this for the remaining tabs until the refill is free of the blade. The length of these refills is molded into the end and they should be replaced with identical types.

Regardless of the type of refill used, be sure to follow the part manufacturer's instructions closely. Make sure that all of the frame jaws are engaged as the refill is pushed into place and locked. If the metal blade holder and frame are allowed to touch the glass during wiper operation, the glass will be scratched.

Tires and Wheels

Common sense and good driving habits will afford maximum tire life. Fast starts, sudden stops and hard cornering are hard on tires and will shorten their useful life span. Make sure that you don't overload the vehicle or run with incorrect pressure in the tires. Both of these practices will increase tread wear.

➡ For optimum tire life, keep the tires properly inflated, rotate them often and have the wheel alignment checked periodically.

Inspect your tires frequently. Be especially careful to watch for bubbles in the tread or sidewall, deep cuts or underinflation. Replace any tires with bubbles in the sidewall. If cuts are so deep that they penetrate to the cords, discard the tire. Any cut in the sidewall of a radial tire renders it unsafe. Also look for uneven tread wear patterns that may indicate the front end is out of alignment or that the tires are out of balance.

TIRE ROTATION

◆ See Figures 122 and 123

Tires must be rotated periodically to equalize wear patterns that vary with a tire's position on the vehicle. Tires will also wear in an uneven way as the front steering/suspension system wears to the point where the alignment should be reset.

Rotating the tires will ensure maximum life for the tires as a set, so you will not have to discard a tire early due to wear on only part of the tread. Regular rotation is required to equalize wear.

When rotating "unidirectional tires," make sure that they always roll in the same direction. This means that a tire used on the left side of the vehicle must not be switched to the right side and vice-versa. Such tires should only be rotated front-to-rear or rear-to-front, while always remaining on the same side of the vehicle. These tires are marked on the sidewall as to the direction of rotation; observe the marks when reinstalling the tire(s).

Fig. 123 Unidirectional tires are identifiable by sidewall arrows and/or the word "rotation"

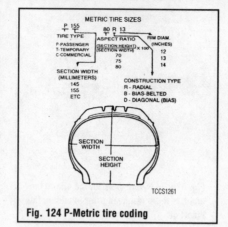

Fig. 124 P-Metric tire coding

Fig. 125 Tires should be checked frequently for any sign of puncture or damage

Some styled or "mag" wheels may have different offsets front to rear. In these cases, the rear wheels must not be used up front and vice-versa. Furthermore, if these wheels are equipped with unidirectional tires, they cannot be rotated unless the tire is remounted for the proper direction of rotation.

➡ **The compact or space-saver spare is strictly for emergency use. It must never be included in the tire rotation or placed on the vehicle for everyday use.**

TIRE DESIGN

▶ **See Figure 124**

For maximum satisfaction, tires should be used in sets of four. Mixing of different types (radial, bias-belted, fiberglass belted) must be avoided. In most cases, the vehicle manufacturer has designated a type of tire on which the vehicle will perform best. Your first choice when replacing tires should be to use the same type of tire that the manufacturer recommends.

When radial tires are used, tire sizes and wheel diameters should be selected to maintain ground clearance and tire load capacity equivalent to the original specified tire. Radial tires should always be used in sets of four.

✳✳ CAUTION

Radial tires should never be used on only the front axle.

When selecting tires, pay attention to the original size as marked on the tire. Most tires are described

using an industry size code sometimes referred to as P-Metric. This allows the exact identification of the tire specifications, regardless of the manufacturer. If selecting a different tire size or brand, remember to check the installed tire for any sign of interference with the body or suspension while the vehicle is stopping, turning sharply or heavily loaded.

Snow Tires

Good radial tires can produce a big advantage in slippery weather, but in snow, a street radial tire does not have sufficient tread to provide traction and control. The small grooves of a street tire quickly pack with snow and the tire behaves like a billiard ball on a marble floor. The more open, chunky tread of a snow tire will self-clean as the tire turns, providing much better grip on snowy surfaces.

To satisfy municipalities requiring snow tires during weather emergencies, most snow tires carry either an M + S designation after the tire size stamped on the sidewall, or the designation "all-season." In general, no change in tire size is necessary when buying snow tires.

Most manufacturers strongly recommend the use of 4 snow tires on their vehicles for reasons of stability. If snow tires are fitted only to the drive wheels, the opposite end of the vehicle may become very unstable when braking or turning on slippery surfaces. This instability can lead to unpleasant endings if the driver can't counteract the slide in time.

Note that snow tires, whether 2 or 4, will affect vehicle handling in all non-snow situations. The stiffer, heavier snow tires will noticeably change the turning and braking characteristics of the vehicle.

Once the snow tires are installed, you must re-learn the behavior of the vehicle and drive accordingly.

➡ **Consider buying extra wheels on which to mount the snow tires. Once done, the "snow wheels" can be installed and removed as needed. This eliminates the potential damage to tires or wheels from seasonal removal and installation. Even if your vehicle has styled wheels, see if inexpensive steel wheels are available. Although the look of the vehicle will change, the expensive wheels will be protected from salt, curb hits and pothole damage.**

TIRE STORAGE

If they are mounted on wheels, store the tires at proper inflation pressure. All tires should be kept in a cool, dry place. If they are stored in the garage or basement, do not let them stand on a concrete floor; set them on strips of wood, a mat or a large stack of newspaper. Keeping them away from direct moisture is of paramount importance. Tires should not be stored upright, but in a flat position.

INFLATION & INSPECTION

▶ **See Figures 125 thru 132**

The importance of proper tire inflation cannot be overemphasized. A tire employs air as part of its structure. It is designed around the supporting strength of the air at a specified pressure. For this reason, improper inflation drastically reduces the tire's ability to perform as intended. A tire will lose

Fig. 126 Tires with deep cuts, or cuts which bulge, should be replaced immediately

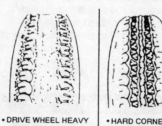

- DRIVE WHEEL HEAVY ACCELERATION
- OVERINFLATION

- HARD CORNERING
- UNDERINFLATION
- LACK OF ROTATION

Fig. 127 Examples of inflation-related tire wear patterns

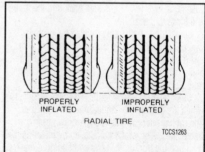

PROPERLY INFLATED   IMPROPERLY INFLATED

RADIAL TIRE

Fig. 128 Radial tires have a characteristic sidewall bulge; don't try to measure pressure by looking at the tire. Use a quality air pressure gauge

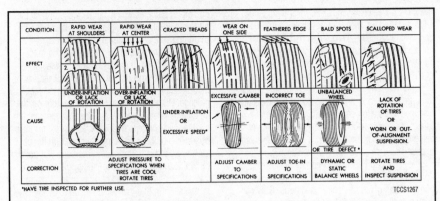

CONDITION	RAPID WEAR AT SHOULDERS	RAPID WEAR AT CENTER	CRACKED TREADS	WEAR ON ONE SIDE	FEATHERED EDGE	BALD SPOTS	SCALLOPED WEAR
EFFECT							
CAUSE	UNDER-INFLATION OR LACK OF ROTATION	OVER-INFLATION OR LACK OF ROTATION	UNDER-INFLATION OR EXCESSIVE SPEED*	EXCESSIVE CAMBER	INCORRECT TOE	UNBALANCED WHEEL OR TIRE DEFECT *	LACK OF ROTATION OF TIRES OR WORN OR OUT-OF-ALIGNMENT SUSPENSION.
CORRECTION		ADJUST PRESSURE TO SPECIFICATIONS WHEN TIRES ARE COOL ROTATE TIRES		ADJUST CAMBER TO SPECIFICATIONS	ADJUST TOE-IN TO SPECIFICATIONS	DYNAMIC OR STATIC BALANCE WHEELS	ROTATE TIRES AND INSPECT SUSPENSION

*HAVE TIRE INSPECTED FOR FURTHER USE.

TCCS1267

Fig. 129 Common tire wear patterns and causes

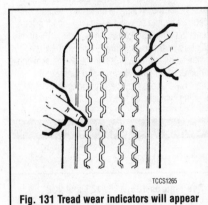

TCCS1265

Fig. 131 Tread wear indicators will appear when the tire is worn

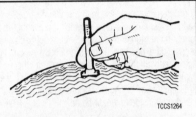

TCCS1264

Fig. 132 Accurate tread depth indicators are inexpensive and handy

✷✷ CAUTION

Never exceed the maximum tire pressure embossed on the tire! This is the pressure to be used when the tire is at maximum loading, but it is rarely the correct pressure for everyday driving. Consult the owner's manual or the tire pressure sticker for the correct tire pressure.

Once you've maintained the correct tire pressures for several weeks, you'll be familiar with the vehicle's braking and handling personality. Slight adjustments in tire pressures can fine-tune these characteristics, but never change the cold pressure specification by more than 2 psi. A slightly softer tire pressure will give a softer ride but also yield lower fuel mileage. A slightly harder tire will give crisper dry road handling but can cause skidding on wet surfaces. Unless you're fully attuned to the vehicle, stick to the recommended inflation pressures.

All tires made since 1968 have built-in tread wear indicator bars that show up as ½ in. (13mm) wide smooth bands across the tire when ¹⁄₁₆ in. (1.5mm) of tread remains. The appearance of tread wear indicators means that the tires should be replaced. In fact, many states have laws prohibiting the use of tires with less than this amount of tread.

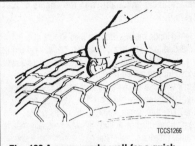

TCCS1266

Fig. 130 A penny works well for a quick check of tread depth

You can check your own tread depth with an inexpensive gauge or by using a Lincoln head penny. Slip the Lincoln penny (with Lincoln's head upside-down) into several tread grooves. If you can see the top of Lincoln's head in 2 adjacent grooves, the tire has less than ¹⁄₁₆ in. (1.5mm) tread left and should be replaced. You can measure snow tires in the same manner by using the "tails" side of the Lincoln penny. If you can see the top of the Lincoln memorial, it's time to replace the snow tire(s).

CARE OF SPECIAL WHEELS

If you have invested money in magnesium, aluminum alloy or sport wheels, special precautions should be taken to make sure your investment is not wasted and that your special wheels look good for the life of the vehicle.

Special wheels are easily damaged and/or scratched. Occasionally check the rims for cracking, impact damage or air leaks. If any of these are found, replace the wheel. But in order to prevent this type of damage and the costly replacement of a special wheel, observe the following precautions:

• Use extra care not to damage the wheels during removal, installation, balancing, etc. After removal of the wheels from the vehicle, place them on a mat or other protective surface. If they are to be stored for any length of time, support them on strips of wood. Never store tires and wheels upright; the tread may develop flat spots.

• When driving, watch for hazards; it doesn't take much to crack a wheel.

• When washing, use a mild soap or non-abrasive dish detergent (keeping in mind that detergent tends to remove wax). Avoid cleansers with abrasives or the use of hard brushes. There are many cleaners and polishes for special wheels.

• If possible, remove the wheels during the winter. Salt and sand used for snow removal can severely damage the finish of a wheel.

• Make certain the recommended lug nut torque is never exceeded or the wheel may crack. Never use snow chains on special wheels; severe scratching will occur.

some air in day-to-day use; having to add a few pounds of air periodically is not necessarily a sign of a leaking tire.

Two items should be a permanent fixture in every glove compartment: an accurate tire pressure gauge and a tread depth gauge. Check the tire pressure (including the spare) regularly with a pocket type gauge. Too often, the gauge on the end of the air hose at your corner garage is not accurate because it suffers too much abuse. Always check tire pressure when the tires are cold, as pressure increases with temperature. If you must move the vehicle to check the tire inflation, do not drive more than a mile before checking. A cold tire is generally one that has not been driven for more than three hours.

A plate or sticker is normally provided somewhere in the vehicle (door post, hood, tailgate or trunk lid) which shows the proper pressure for the tires. Never counteract excessive pressure build-up by bleeding off air pressure (letting some air out). This will cause the tire to run hotter and wear quicker.

FLUIDS AND LUBRICANTS

Fluid Disposal

Used fluids such as engine oil, transmission fluid, antifreeze and brake fluid are hazardous wastes and must be disposed of properly. Before draining any fluids, consult with your local authorities; in many areas, waste oil, antifreeze,

etc. is being accepted as a part of recycling programs. A number of service stations and auto parts stores are also accepting waste fluids for recycling.

Be sure of the recycling center's policies before draining any fluids, as many will not accept different fluids that have been mixed together.

Fuel and Engine Oil Recommendations

➡**Some fuel additives contain chemicals that can damage the catalytic converter and/or oxygen sensor. Read all of the labels carefully**

before using any additive in the engine or fuel system.

All Honda models are designed to run on unleaded fuel. The use of a leaded fuel in a car requiring unleaded fuel will permanently damage a catalytic converter and render it inoperative. A blocked converter will also increase exhaust backpressure to the point where engine output will be severely reduced. The minimum octane rating of the unleaded fuel being used must be at least 87, which usually means regular unleaded, but some high performance engines may require higher ratings. Fuel should be selected for the brand and octane that performs best with the engine. Judge a gasoline by its ability to prevent pinging, its engine starting capabilities (cold and hot) and general all weather performance.

As far as the octane rating is concerned, refer to the General Engine Specifications chart earlier in this section to find the vehicle's engine and its compression ratio. If the compression ratio is 9.0:1 or lower, a regular grade of unleaded gasoline can be used in most cases. If the compression ratio is higher than 9.0:1, use a premium grade of unleaded fuel.

The use of a fuel too low in octane (a measure of anti-knock quality) will result in spark knock or detonation. Since many factors such as altitude, terrain, air temperature and humidity affect operating efficiency, knocking may result although the recommended fuel is being used. If persistent knocking occurs, it may be necessary to switch to a higher grade of fuel. Continuous or heavy knocking may cause internal engine damage.

➡ **The engine's fuel requirement can change with time, mainly due to carbon build-up, which will, in turn, changes the compression ratio. If the engine pings, knocks or diesels (runs with the ignition OFF) switch to a higher grade of fuel. Sometimes, just changing brands will cure the problem. If it becomes necessary to retard the ignition timing from the specifications, don't change it more than a few degrees. Retarded timing will reduce power output and fuel mileage, in addition to making the engine run hotter.**

OIL

▶ **See Figures 133 and 134**

The Society Of Automotive Engineer (SAE) grade number indicates the viscosity of the engine oil and, thus, its ability to lubricate at a given temperature. The lower the SAE grade number, the lighter the oil;

the lower the viscosity, the easier it is to crank the engine in cold weather. Oil viscosities should be chosen from those oils recommended for the lowest anticipated temperatures during the oil change interval. With the proper viscosity, the engine is assured of easy cold starting and sufficient engine protection.

Multi-viscosity oils (5W-30, 10W-30, etc.) offer the important advantage of being adaptable to temperature extremes. They allow easy starting at low temperatures, yet they give good protection at high speeds and engine temperatures. This is a decided advantage in changeable climates or in long distance driving.

The American Petroleum Institute (API) designation indicates the classification of engine oil used under certain given operating conditions. Only oil designated for Service SH, or the latest superseding oil grade, should be used. Oils of the SH type perform a variety of functions inside the engine in addition to their basic function as a lubricant. Through a balanced system of metallic detergents and polymeric dispersants, engine oil prevents the formation of high and low temperature deposits and keeps sludge and particles of dirt in suspension. Acids, particularly sulfuric acid, as well as other byproducts of combustion, are neutralized. Both the SAE grade number and the API designation can be found on the side of the oil bottle.

Synthetic Oils

There are excellent synthetic and fuel-efficient oils available that, under the right circumstances, can help provide better fuel mileage and better engine protection. However, these advantages come at a price, which can be significantly more than the price per quart of conventional motor oils.

Before pouring any synthetic oils into the car's engine, consider the condition of the engine and the type of driving that is done. It is also wise to check the vehicle manufacturer's position on synthetic oils.

Generally, it is best to avoid the use of synthetic oil in both brand new and older, high mileage engines. New engines require a proper break-in, and the synthetics are so slippery that they can impede this; most manufacturers recommend that you wait at least 5,000 miles (8,000 km) before switching to synthetic oil. Conversely, older engines, which have worn parts, tend to lose more oil; synthetics will slip past worn parts more readily than regular oil. If your car already leaks oil, (due to worn parts or bad seals/gaskets), it may leak more with a synthetic inside. Also, because synthetic oils have excellent cleaning abilities, putting a synthetic oil in a high mileage vehicle may flush away built

up carbon particles which can be picked up by the oil pump and trapped in the oil filter, causing a loss of oil pressure and potential engine damage.

Consider the type of driving conditions most often encountered. If mostly on the highway at higher, steadier speeds, synthetic oil will reduce friction and probably help deliver increased fuel mileage. Under such ideal highway conditions, the oil change interval can be extended, as long as the oil filter can continue to operate effectively for the extended life of the oil. If the filter can't do its job for this extended period, dirt and sludge will build up in the engine's crankcase, sump, oil pump and lines, no matter what type of oil is used. If using synthetic oil in this manner, continue to change the oil filter at the recommended intervals.

Cars used under harder, stop-and-go, short hop circumstances should always be serviced more frequently; for these cars, the expense of using synthetic oil should be weighed against the long-term benefits of the oil. Because on average, 80% of an engine's wear occurs during a cold start up, the synthetic oil will help preserve the mechanical condition of the engine. However, the expense of frequent oil changes may offset the long-term benefits of using synthetic oil.

Engine

OIL LEVEL CHECK

▶ **See Figures 135, 136, 137 and 138**

Every time the vehicle is refueled, the engine oil should be checked, making sure the engine has fully warmed and the vehicle is parked on a level surface. Because it takes some time for the oil to drain back to the oil pan, wait a few minutes before checking the oil. When doing this at a fuel stop, first fill the fuel tank, then open the hood and check the oil, but don't get so carried away as to forget to pay for the fuel!

1. Make sure the car is parked on level ground.
2. When checking the oil level, it is best for the engine to be at normal operating temperature, however the engine should be stopped for about 5 minutes before checking. Checking the oil immediately after stopping the engine will lead to a false reading. Waiting a few minutes after turning off the engine allows the oil in the upper engine and cylinder head to drain back into the crankcase.
3. Open the hood and locate the dipstick, which will be in a guide tube located in the front of the

---

API SERVICES SH/CD,SG,SF,CC

API SERVICES SH/CD

SAE 10W-40

ENERGY CONSERVING

DON'T POLLUTE. CONSERVE RESOURCES. RETURN USED OIL TO COLLECTION CENTERS

TCCS1235

Fig. 133 Look for the API oil identification label when choosing your engine oil

---

		10W-30					
	5W-30						
F	−20	0	10	20	32	60	80	100
C	−29	−18	−12	−7	0	16	27	38

ANTICIPATED TEMPERATURE RANGE BEFORE NEXT OIL CHANGE

90901G10

Fig. 134 Recommended SAE engine oil viscosity grades for gasoline engines

---

93131P42

Fig. 135 Locate the engine oil dipstick in the front center of the engine compartment

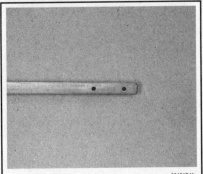

Fig. 136 The engine oil level should measure between the upper and lower dots

Fig. 137 Remove the oil filler cap from the top of the valve cover. Examine the condition of the cap and rubber seal; replace if worn or damaged

Fig. 138 Use a small funnel to avoid spillage, and pour in the proper amount of the correct viscosity engine oil

engine compartment. Pull the dipstick from its tube, wipe it clean (using a clean, lint-free rag), look at the level marks, and then reinsert it.

4. Pull the dipstick out again and, holding it horizontally, read the oil level. The oil should be between the upper and lower dots on the dipstick. If the oil is below the lower dot, add oil of the proper viscosity through the screwed-in capped opening in the top of the valve cover. See the oil and fuel recommendations listed earlier in this section for the proper viscosity and rating of oil to use.

5. Insert the dipstick and check the oil level again after adding any oil. Approximately one quart of oil will raise the level from the lower dot mark to the upper dot mark. Be sure not to overfill the crankcase. Excess oil will generally be consumed at

an accelerated rate and may cause problems. Overfilling the engine oil is much like overfilling a blender. Once running the liquid expands and needs somewhere to go and could force its way past a gasket or oil seal creating a leak or cause sluggish engine operation.

❊❊ WARNING

DO NOT overfill the crankcase. An overfilled crankcase may result in oil fouled spark plugs, oil leaks caused by oil seal failure, or engine damage due to oil foaming.

6. Close the hood.

OIL & FILTER CHANGE

▶ See Figures 139 thru 150

❊❊ CAUTION

The EPA warns that prolonged contact with used engine oil may cause a number of skin disorders, including cancer! Minimize exposure to used engine oil. Protective gloves should be worn when changing the oil. If hands or any other exposed skin is exposed to used engine oil wash them as soon as possible. Soap and water, or a waterless hand cleaner should be used.

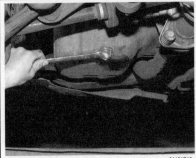

Fig. 139 Most Honda oil drain plugs require the use of a 17mm wrench for removal and installation

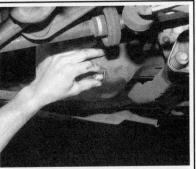

Fig. 140 Once loosened, unthread the oil drain plug by hand

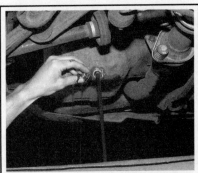

Fig. 141 Pull the oil drain plug away from the pan to allow the oil to drain

Fig. 142 When reinstalling the oil pan drain plug, always use a new crush washer

Fig. 143 Always take the necessary precautions to avoid a spill. Some models may have suspension or steering components in the way which may deflect the oil stream

Fig. 144 A magnetic drain plug will catch any iron shavings that may be suspended in the oil

Fig. 145 A band type filter wrench makes easy work out of oil filter removal

Fig. 146 Once the filter is loosened, finish removing it by hand

Fig. 147 As the filter is removed, promptly position the open end up to prevent spillage. Remember the oil filter holds about 1 quart of hot, dirty oil

Fig. 148 After the oil filter has been removed, wipe the mating surface of the engine block clean with a lint-free cloth

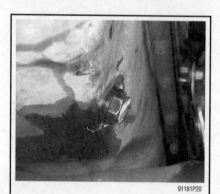

Fig. 149 Install the drain plug, then use a rag to wipe any oil drips off the oil pan

Fig. 150 Honda factory oil filters have numbers stamped on the housing for proper tightening. If other than Honda, follow the instructions provided by the manufacturer of the filter purchased

The manufacturer's recommended oil change interval is 7,500 miles (12,000 km) or at least once a year under normal operating conditions and every 3,750 miles (6,000 km) or twice a year for vehicles driven in severe operating conditions. Because frequent oil changes help to prolong the life of an engine, it's a good idea to adopt an oil change interval of at least twice a year or every 3,000–3,500 miles (4,800–5,600 km) under normal conditions; and more frequently under severe conditions.

The following is a list of what the manufacturer considers severe use. If the vehicle meets any one of these conditions, the severe maintenance schedule should be followed.

• Vehicles operated in Canada or driven in extremely hot (over 90°F or 32°C) conditions

• Vehicles operated in long periods of stop and go driving or conditions requiring extensive idling

• Vehicles driven less than 5 miles (8 km) per trip or, in freezing temperatures driven less than 10 miles (16 km) per trip

• Vehicles driven with car top carriers, used for towing, driven in mountainous areas or on dusty, muddy, or de-iced roadways

Additionally, it is recommended that the oil filter be replaced EVERY time the oil is changed.

➡**Please be considerate of the environment. Dispose of waste oil properly by taking it to a service station, municipal facility or recycling center.**

1. Run the engine until it reaches normal operating temperature. Then turn the engine **OFF**.
2. Remove the oil filler cap.

3. Raise and safely support the front of the vehicle using jackstands.
4. Slide a drain pan of at least 5 quarts 4.7 liters) capacity under the oil pan. Wipe the drain plug and surrounding area clean using an old rag.
5. Loosen the drain plug using 17mm socket on a ratchet, or a suitable box wrench. Turn the plug out by hand, using a rag to shield fingers from the hot oil. Wear disposable latex gloves to protect the skin from exposure to the engine oil. Keep an inward pressure on the plug as it is unscrewed, then the oil won't escape past the threads and it can be removed without being burned by hot oil. Quickly withdraw the plug and move your hands out of the way, but be careful not to drop the plug into the drain pan, as fishing it out can be an unpleasant mess without the use of a magnet. Allow the oil to drain completely.
6. Examine the condition of the drain plug for thread damage or stretching. The manufacturer recommends replacing the aluminum drain plug crush washer with a new one every time the drain plug is removed.
7. Install the drain plug, with a new crush washer, then tighten the plug as follows:
   • Cast aluminum oil pans: 29 ft. lbs. (39 Nm)
   • Steel oil pans: 33 ft. lbs. (44 Nm)
8. Move the drain pan under the oil filter. Use an end cap-type tool to loosen the oil filter. Use disposable gloves to protect the skin from exposure to the used oil and cover the filter with a rag to minimize the risk of slinging engine oil, as the filter is unscrewed from the engine. Keep in mind that the filter holds about a quart of dirty, hot oil.

➡**Be careful when removing the oil filter, because the filter contains about 1 quart of hot, dirty oil.**

9. Empty the old oil filter into the drain pan, then properly dispose of the filter.
10. Using a clean shop towel, wipe off the filter adapter on the engine block. Be sure the towel does not leave any lint, which could clog an oil passage.
11. Coat the rubber gasket and pour some fresh oil into the new filter before installation. This will lubricate the engine more quickly during the initial startup. Spin the filter onto the threaded fitting by hand until it contacts the mounting surface, then tighten it an additional ½–¾ turn. Do NOT overtighten the filter.
12. Carefully lower the vehicle.
13. Refill the crankcase with the correct amount of fresh engine oil. Please refer to the Capacities chart later in this section.
14. Install the oil filler cap.
15. Check the oil level on the dipstick. It is normal for the level to be a bit above the full mark until the engine is run and the new filter is filled with oil. Start the engine and allow it to idle for a few minutes.

✳✳ WARNING

Do not run the engine above idle speed until it has built up oil pressure, as indicated when the oil light goes out.

16. Shut off the engine and allow the oil to flow back to the crankcase for a minute, then recheck the oil level. Check around the filter and drain plug for any leaks, and correct as necessary.

When finished with the job, there are four or five quarts of dirty oil and a used oil filter to be disposed of properly. The best thing to do is to pour the oil into a sealable container, then, locate a service station or automotive parts store that will accept the used oil and oil filter.

➡ **Improperly disposing of used motor oil not only pollutes the environment, it violates federal law. Dispose of waste oil properly.**

Manual Transaxle

FLUID RECOMMENDATIONS

All Honda manual transaxles use the Honda Manual Transmission Fluid (MTF) as the original factory fill. This oil is similar to a 10W-30 or 10W-40 viscosity engine oil, and this oil can be substituted temporarily. However, the manufacturer recommends the use of their MTF when changing the fluid.

LEVEL CHECK

▶ See Figures 151 and 152

The transaxle fluid should be changed every 90,000 miles (144,000 km) or 6 years under normal driving conditions. In severe driving conditions the fluid should be changed every 30,000 miles (48,000 km) or every 2 years, whichever occurs first.

1. Make sure the vehicle is on a level surface. If the vehicle is raised, make sure the vehicle is safely supported and level.

➡ **Do not confuse the drain plug with the fill plug. The fill plug is in the mid section of the transaxle. The drain plug is near the bottom of the transaxle.**

2. The oil level is checked by removing the oil fill plug on the side of the transaxle. The transaxle fluid should just meet the lower threads of the transaxle fill hole.
3. Remove the oil level check bolt from the side of the transaxle. If oil runs out, or if oil can be felt near the threaded fill hole opening, reinstall and retighten the bolt to 33 ft. lbs. (45 Nm).
4. If the level needs to be topped off, pour oil in slowly until it begins to run out then, install and tighten the filler bolt to 33 ft. lbs. (45 Nm).

DRAIN & REFILL

▶ See Figures 152, 153, 154, 155 and 156

1. Raise and safely support the vehicle, making sure it is level.
2. Place a fluid catch pan under the transaxle drain plug.
3. Remove the upper fill and lower drain plugs, and drain the fluid.
4. Using crush new washers, install the bottom plug tightening to 29 ft. lbs. (40 Nm). Refill the transaxle, until the oil is level with the upper filler plug hole, then the filler plug and tighten to 33 ft. lbs. (45 Nm).

➡ **The oil change capacity of the manual transaxle is 1.8 quarts (1.7L).**

Automatic Transaxle

FLUID RECOMMENDATIONS

The manufacturer recommends the use of Honda Premium Automatic Transmission Fluid (ATF) in their vehicles. The Dexron® III automatic transmission fluid can be substituted temporarily.

LEVEL CHECK

▶ See Figures 157 and 158

The first recommended automatic transaxle fluid change, under normal operating conditions, is 45,000 miles (72,000 km) or 3 years whichever occurs first. Thereafter, the interval is every 30,000 miles (48,000 km) or 2 years, whichever occurs first. For severe operating conditions, the interval is every 30,000 miles (48,000 km) or 2 years, whichever occurs first.

The level is checked with the vehicle on level ground and the engine hot, but not running. All models use a standard push in dipstick.

1. Remove the dipstick and wipe it clean, then reinstall it to its fully seated position.
2. Remove the dipstick again, then check the oil level on the stick. The level should be between the upper and lower marks on the dipstick.
3. If the fluid level is low, use a funnel to add the proper type and amount of transaxle fluid to bring it to the correct level.

➡ **It generally takes less than a pint to bring the fluid level from low into the acceptable**

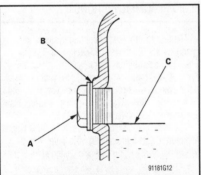

Fig. 151 Unfasten the fluid filler plug (A) and washer (B), then make sure the fluid is at the proper level (C)

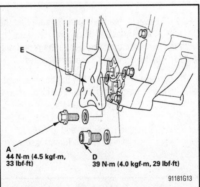

Fig. 152 Location of the manual transaxle fill plug (A) and the drain plug (D)

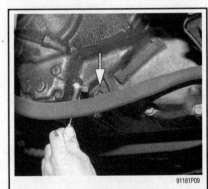

Fig. 153 Using a ⅜ inch ratchet to remove the manual transaxle fluid drain plug

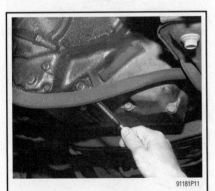

Fig. 154 A ratchet with a button will speed the removal of the fluid drain plug

Fig. 155 Allow fluid to drain completely . . .

Fig. 156 . . . then install the drain plug by hand to prevent cross-threading

Fig. 157 The transmission dipstick is located on the passenger's side of the engine compartment. We removed the air filter housing assembly to fully expose the dipstick's location and oil fill hole

Fig. 158 Just the very top ring of the transmission dipstick is visible with the air filter housing lifted up. Removing the upper air filter housing and the rubber ducting for the intake will allow enough room for a transmission funnel to be used

range. DO NOT overfill the transaxle! If the fluid level is within specifications, simply push the dipstick back into the filler tube completely.

✽✽ WARNING

To avoid getting any dirt or water in the transaxle, always make sure the dipstick is fully seated in the tube.

DRAIN & REFILL

▶ See Figures 159 and 160

1. Drive the vehicle to bring the transaxle fluid up.to operating temperatures.
2. Raise and safely support the front of the vehicle.
3. Place a fluid catch pan under the transaxle.
4. Remove the drain plug, located on the bottom of the transaxle housing, and drain the transaxle.
5. Using a new washer, install the drain plug, and then tighten it to 36 ft. lbs. (49 Nm).
6. Using Honda Premium Automatic Transmission Fluid (ATF) or its temporary substitute, Dexron®III automatic transmission fluid, refill the transaxle using a suitable funnel.

Fig. 159 The transmission drain plug has a square ⅜ inch hole

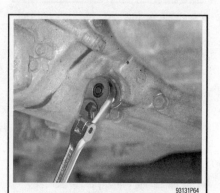

Fig. 160 Use a ⅜ inch drive ratchet to remove the drain plug

➡DO NOT overfill the transaxle. Be sure that the quantity of fluid added is always slightly less than the specified quantity, due to the remaining fluid left in the transaxle housing recesses.

7. Start the engine and allow to idle for at least a minute. With the parking brake set and the brakes depressed, move the gear selector through each position, ending in the Park or Neutral position.
8. Check the fluid level and add just enough fluid to bring the level to ⅛ inch (3mm) below the ADD mark.

9. Allow the engine to fully warm up to normal operating temperature, then check the fluid level. The fluid level should be in the HOT range. If not, add the proper amount of fluid to bring it up to that level. If the fluid level is within specifications, simply push the dipstick back into the filler tube completely.

✽✽ WARNING

To avoid getting any dirt or water in the transaxle, always make sure the dipstick is fully seated in the tube.

Cooling System

▶ See Figures 161, 162 and 163

✽✽ CAUTION

Never remove the radiator cap under any conditions while the engine is hot! Failure to follow these instructions could result in damage to the cooling system, engine and/or personal injury. To avoid having scalding hot coolant or steam blow out of the radiator, use extreme care whenever removing the radiator cap. Wait until the engine has cooled, then wrap a thick cloth around the radiator cap and turn it slowly to the first stop. Step back while the pressure is released from the cooling system. When the pressure has been released, press down on the radiator cap (with the cloth still in position), then turn and remove the cap.

FLUID RECOMMENDATIONS

The first recommended cooling system fluid change is 45,000 miles (72,000 km) or 3 years whichever occurs first. Thereafter, the interval is every 30,000 miles (48,000 km) or 2 years, whichever occurs first. The cooling system should be inspected, flushed and refilled with fresh coolant during these maintenance intervals.

The manufacturer recommends using 50% Honda Antifreeze/Coolant mixed with 50% water. A high quality major-brand, non-silicate designed for use in

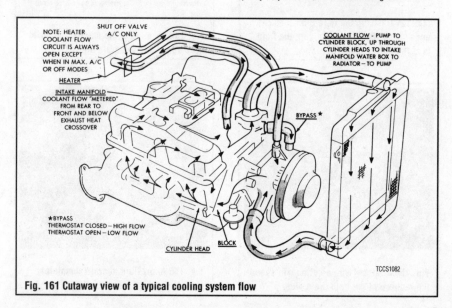

Fig. 161 Cutaway view of a typical cooling system flow

Fig. 162 Cooling systems should be pressure tested for leaks periodically

Fig. 163 The numbers "1.1" on the radiator cap indicate the rated holding pressure of the radiator cap measured in atmospheres. This cap is rated at 1.1 times atmospheric pressure (1.1 x 14.7) or 16 psi

aluminum engines can be substituted temporarily. Using distilled water instead of regular tap water to mix with the antifreeze will also help to keep the cooling system corrosion free, as some of the chemicals found in tap water may corrode aluminum. In addition, if the coolant is left in the system too long, it loses its ability to prevent rust and corrosion.

LEVEL CHECK

▶ See Figures 164 and 165

To check the coolant level, simply verify whether the coolant is up to the MAX line on the expansion tank. Add the proper mixture of coolant to the expansion tank if the level is low. Never add cold water or coolant to a hot engine as damage to both the cooling system and the engine could result.

✳✳ CAUTION

Should it be necessary to remove the radiator cap, make sure the system has had time to cool, reducing the internal pressure.

The radiator cap should be removed only for cleaning or draining the system. The cooling system is under pressure when Hot. Removing the radiator cap when the engine is warm or overheated will cause coolant to spill or be forced out, possibly causing serious burns. The system should be allowed to cool before attempting removal of the radiator cap or other cooling system components.

➡ **If any coolant spills on painted portions of the body, rinse it off immediately.**

DRAIN & REFILL

▶ See Figures 166 thru 171

✳✳ CAUTION

When draining the coolant, keep in mind that small animals and domestic pets are attracted by ethylene glycol antifreeze and may attempt to drink any that is left in an uncovered container or from puddles on the ground. This can be fatal if ingested in sufficient quantity. Always drain the coolant into a sealable container. Coolant should be reused until it becomes contaminated or several years old. To avoid injuries from scalding fluid and steam, DO NOT remove the radiator cap while the engine is running or if the engine or radiator is still hot.

1. Before draining the cooling system, place the heater's temperature selector to the full WARM position while the engine is running.
2. Turn the engine off before it gets hot and the system builds pressure.
3. Make sure the engine is still cool and the vehicle is parked on a level surface.
4. Remove and drain the reservoir recovery tank.
5. Place a fluid catch pan under the radiator. Turn the radiator draincock counterclockwise to open, then allow the coolant to drain.
6. Remove the radiator cap by performing the following:

Fig. 164 If the coolant level is low, remove the coolant reservoir tank cap . . .

Fig. 165 . . . then add coolant to the reservoir

Fig. 166 Using your fingers, loosen the pet cock to drain the radiator

Fig. 167 Allow the coolant to drain into an approved container

Fig. 168 Clean the radiator cap's rubber gasket of any dirt to achieve a proper seal

Fig. 169 Be sure to fill the cooling system to the bottom of the filler neck with a 50/50 mixture of ethylene glycol (or other suitable) antifreeze and water. Always use a funnel to avoid spills

Fig. 170 Also, fill the coolant recovery tank to the proper level

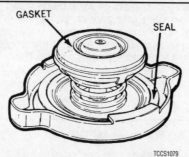

Fig. 171 Always check the condition of the radiator cap gasket and seal. Place a light coating of coolant on the seal and gasket when installing

Fig. 172 Firmly grasp the radiator cap and turn it counterclockwise to remove

a. Slowly rotate the cap counterclockwise to the detent.

b. If any residual pressure is present, WAIT until the hissing stops.

c. After the hissing noise has ceased, press down on the cap and continue rotating it counterclockwise to remove it.

7. Allow the coolant to drain completely from the vehicle.

8. Close the radiator draincock.

➡ When filling the cooling system, be careful not to spill any coolant on the drive belts or alternator.

To refill:

9. Make sure the heater temperature is placed in the full hot position.

10. On 2.2L and 2.3L engines, open the bleed screw on the thermostat housing.

11. Install the reservoir recovery tank and using a 50/50 mixture of the recommended antifreeze and distilled water, fill the cooling system reservoir tank to the FULL mark.

✳✳ WARNING

If any coolant is spilled on a painted surface of the vehicle, wipe it up immediately.

12. Begin filling the radiator with the 50/50 mixture of coolant. On the 2.2L and 2.3L engines, watch for air being released from the open the bleed screw on the thermostat housing. Once coolant mixture begins to steadily flow through the bleeder, close the bleeder.

13. Continue to fill the radiator until the radiator is full.

14. Start the engine and allow the engine to run until the cooling fans operate two times, making sure to top off the system as the fluid level drops.

15. After the cooling fan has run for the second time, top off the system as necessary, then install the radiator cap.

16. Allow the engine to run and inspect the cooling system for leaks.

FLUSHING & CLEANING

▶ **See Figures 172, 173, 174 and 175**

1. Drain the cooling system, as described in the preceding drain and refill procedure.

2. Close the drain valve.

➡ **A flushing solution may be used. Ensure that it is safe for use with aluminum cooling system components, and follow the directions on the container.**

3. If using a flushing solution, remove the thermostat, then reinstall the thermostat housing.

4. Add sufficient water to fill the system.

5. Start the engine and run it for a few minutes. Drain the system.

6. Allow the water to flow out of the radiator until it is clear.

7. Reconnect the heater hose.

8. Drain the cooling system.

9. Reinstall the thermostat.

10. Empty the coolant reservoir or surge tank and flush it.

11. Fill the cooling system, using the correct ratio of antifreeze and water, to the bottom of the filler neck. Fill the reservoir or surge tank to the FULL mark.

12. Install the radiator cap.

Brake Master Cylinder

FLUID RECOMMENDATIONS

Use only Honda® or equivalent brake fluid meeting DOT 3 or DOT 4 specifications from a clean, sealed container. Using any other type of fluid may result in severe brake system damage. Avoid using any brake fluid which has been left open for several hours, or which had been initially opened more than 3 months (90 days) prior to being used.

✳✳ WARNING

Brake fluid damages paint. It is also absorbs moisture from the air. Never leave a container or the master cylinder uncovered longer than necessary. All parts in contact with the brake fluid (master cylinder, hoses, plunger assemblies, etc.) must be kept clean, since any contamination of the brake fluid will adversely affect braking performance.

✳✳ CAUTION

When cleaning a brake component, make sure to use rubbing alcohol, or a suitable

Fig. 173 Twist the cap to the position shown or until the tension is relieved . . .

Fig. 174 . . . then remove the radiator cap

Fig. 175 Always use a funnel while refilling the cooling system to prevent spills

brake cleaner. Use of non-compatible cleaners will cause damage to brake seals and related components.

LEVEL CHECK

▶ See Figures 176, 177 and 178

It should be obvious how important the brake system is to safe operation of your vehicle. The brake fluid is key to the proper operation of your vehicle. Low levels of fluid indicate a need for service (there may be a leak in the system or the brake pads may just be worn and in need of replacement). In any case, the brake fluid level should be inspected at least during every oil change, but more often is desirable. Every time you open the hood is a good time to glance at the master cylinder reservoir.

To check the fluid level, look on the side of the reservoir to see how high the fluid level is against the markings on the side of the reservoir. The level should be at the MAX mark. If not, remove the reservoir cap, then add the proper amount of DOT 3 or DOT 4 brake fluid to bring the level up to MAX.

When making additions of brake fluid, use only fresh, uncontaminated brake fluid which meets or exceeds DOT 3 standards. Be careful not to spill any brake fluid on painted surfaces, as it will quickly eat the paint. Do not allow the brake fluid container or the master cylinder to remain open any longer than necessary; brake fluid absorbs moisture from the air, reducing the fluid's effectiveness and causing corrosion in the lines.

Clutch Master Cylinder

FLUID RECOMMENDATIONS

When adding or changing the fluid in the hydraulic clutch system, use a quality brake fluid conforming to DOT 3 OR DOT 4 specifications such as Honda® Brake Fluid, or equivalent. Never reuse old brake fluid.

LEVEL CHECK

▶ See Figure 179

The fluid in the clutch master cylinder is key to a smooth transition when in the friction zone of the clutch. The fluid condition can effect the clutch engagement while driving. Low levels of fluid indicate a need for service (there may be a leak in the system or the clutch pad lining may just be worn and in need of replacement). The fluid level should be inspected during every oil change, however, more often is desirable. Every time the hood is raised, is a good time to glance at the clutch master cylinder reservoir.

The fluid in the clutch master cylinder reservoir is more likely to become contaminated more quickly than the brake fluid in the brake master cylinder reservoir. When the clutch pedal is pressed, it is pressed completely to the floor during every gear change. Because of this, the seals in the clutch master and slave cylinders travel much further and more often than the brake master cylinder and wheel cylinder or caliper seals, which only travel far enough to achieve proper braking pressure.

To check the clutch master cylinder fluid level, perform the following:

1. Wipe the clutch master cylinder reservoir cap and the surrounding area clean with a shop towel.
2. Inspect the fluid in the reservoir, making sure the fluid level is between the MAX and MIN marks.
3. If required, remove the clutch master cylinder reservoir lid, then add fresh fluid to bring the level up to the MAX mark on the reservoir.

When making additions of fluid, use only fresh, uncontaminated brake fluid which meets DOT 3 or DOT 4 standards. Do not allow the brake fluid container or the master cylinder to remain open any longer than necessary; as brake fluid absorbs moisture from the air, reducing the fluid's effectiveness and causing corrosion in the lines.

✳✳ WARNING

Be careful to avoid spilling any brake fluid on painted surfaces, because the painted surface will become discolored or damaged.

4. Reinstall the lid onto the clutch master cylinder.

Power Steering Pump

FLUID RECOMMENDATIONS

Only genuine Honda power steering fluid should be used when adding fluid. The manufacturer states that ATF or fluids manufactured for use in any other brand of vehicle by their manufacturers or independent suppliers are not compatible with the Honda power steering system.

✳✳ CAUTION

The use of any other fluid may cause the seal failure, increased wear, and poor steering in cold weather.

LEVEL CHECK

▶ See Figures 180, 181, 182 and 183

The fluid in the power steering reservoir should be checked every few weeks for indications of leaks or low fluid level. Check the fluid with the engine cold and the vehicle parked on a level spot. The

Fig. 176 When checking the fluid level, the level should be at the MAX line. Add the proper amount of fluid if necessary

Fig. 177 If the fluid level is low, remove the brake master cylinder reservoir cap . . .

Fig. 178 . . . then pour in enough DOT 3 quality brake fluid until it reaches the MAX level. Be careful not to spill any brake fluid, as it can damage painted surfaces

Fig. 179 The clutch master cylinder reservoir looks very similar to the brake master, but holds much less fluid

Fig. 180 Twist the power steering fluid reservoir cap to remove it

Fig. 181 The power steering reservoir cap is held in place by a series of thin plastic ribs. Use caution not to break these when removing the cap

Fig. 182 The power steering fluid level marks are visible on the side of the reservoir

Fig. 183 Use a funnel to add the proper type and amount of fluid to the power steering pump fluid reservoir

level should be between the upper and lower marks. Fluid need not be added right away unless it has dropped almost to the lower mark. DO NOT overfill the reservoir.

When adding fluid, or making a complete fluid change, use only Honda Power Steering Fluid. NEVER add automatic transmission fluid. Failure to use the proper fluid may cause excessive wear, damage, and fluid leaks.

1. The power steering fluid reservoir has upper and lower level lines cast into the sides of the reservoir. The level is checked while the engine is cold and not running.

2. To top off the system, remove the cap and top off until the fluid level reaches the upper level fluid line, then reinstall the cap.

➡**Be careful not to overfill, as this will cause fluid loss and seal damage. A large loss in fluid volume may indicate a problem, which should be inspected and repaired immediately.**

Chassis Greasing

Inspect the chassis parts every 12 months or 15,000 miles (24,000 km). Look for signs of leak-age, damaged, worn or deteriorating boots and seals.

The Honda vehicles covered in this manual are not equipped with grease fittings, and the suspension components that use grease are sealed units with lifetime lubrication.

Body Lubrication and Maintenance

The body mechanisms and linkages should be inspected, cleaned and lubricated, as necessary, to preserve correct operation and to avoid wear and corrosion. Before lubricating a component, make sure to wipe any dirt or grease from the surface with a suitable rag. If necessary, use a suitable cleaning solvent to clean off the surface. In addition, don't forget to wipe any excess lubricant off the component when finished.

To be sure the hood latch works properly, use white lithium grease to lubricate the latch, safety catch and hood hinges, as necessary. Apply Honda® or equivalent multi-purpose grease sparingly to all pivots and slide contact areas.

Use white lithium grease to lubricate the following components:

- Door hinges—hinge pin and pivot points
- Hood hinges—pivot points
- Trunk lid hinges—pivot points
- Door check mechanism
- Ashtray slides
- Parking brake moving parts
- Front seat tracks

Use multi-purpose grease to lubricate the following components:

- Throttle cable end at the throttle body
- Brake master cylinder pushrod
- Pedal linkage
- Battery terminals
- Fuel fill door latch mechanism
- Clutch master cylinder push rod
- Manual transmission shift lever pivots
- Manual transmission release fork

Wheel Bearings

All Honda vehicles are equipped with sealed hub and bearing assemblies. The hub and bearing assembly is non-serviceable. If the assembly is loose, worn or damaged, the complete unit must be replaced. Refer to Section 8 for the hub and bearing removal and installation procedure.

TOWING THE VEHICLE

◗ See Figure 184

When towing is required, the vehicle should be flat-bedded or towed with the front wheels off of the ground on a wheel lift, to prevent damage to the transaxle. DO NOT allow your vehicle to be towed by a sling type tow truck, if it is at all avoidable. If it is necessary to tow the vehicle from the rear, a wheel dolly should be placed under the front tires. To accommodate a flat-bed tow truck, your vehicle is equipped with a towing hook and tie down hooks. The towing hook can be used with a winch to pull the vehicle onto the truck, and the tie down hooks can be used to secure the vehicle to the truck.

Regardless of whether the vehicle is equipped with a manual transaxle, push starting the vehicle IS NOT RECOMMENDED under any circumstance.

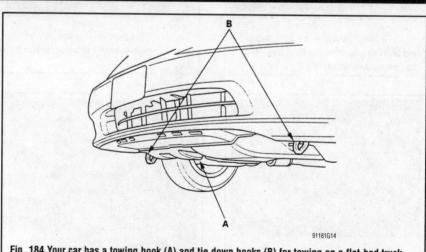

Fig. 184 Your car has a towing hook (A) and tie down hooks (B) for towing on a flat-bed truck

JUMP STARTING A DEAD BATTERY

▶ See Figure 185

Whenever a vehicle is jump started, precautions must be followed in order to prevent the possibility of personal injury. Remember that batteries contain a small amount of explosive hydrogen gas which is a by-product of battery charging. Sparks should always be avoided when working around batteries, especially when attaching jumper cables. To minimize the possibility of accidental sparks, follow the procedure carefully.

✳✳ CAUTION

NEVER hook up the batteries in a series circuit, or the entire electrical system will be severely damaged, including the starter!

Vehicles equipped with a diesel engine may utilize two 12 volt batteries. If so, the batteries are connected in a parallel circuit (positive terminal to positive terminal, negative terminal to negative terminal). Hooking the batteries up in parallel circuit increases battery cranking power without increasing total battery voltage output. Output remains at 12 volts. On the other hand, hooking two 12 volt batteries up in a series circuit (positive terminal to negative terminal, positive terminal to negative terminal) increases total battery output to 24 volts (12 volts plus 12 volts).

Regardless of whether the vehicle is equipped with a manual transaxle, push starting the vehicle IS NOT RECOMMENDED under any circumstance.

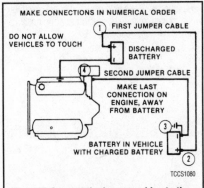

Fig. 185 Connect the jumper cables to the batteries and engine in the order shown

Jump Starting Precautions

- Be sure that both batteries are of the same voltage. Vehicles covered by this manual and most vehicles on the road today utilize a 12 volt charging system.
- Be sure that both batteries are of the same polarity (have the same terminal, in most cases NEGATIVE grounded).
- Be sure that the vehicles are not touching or a short could occur.
- On serviceable batteries, be sure the vent cap holes are not obstructed.
- Do not smoke or allow sparks anywhere near the batteries.
- In cold weather, make sure the battery electrolyte is not frozen. This can occur more readily in a battery that has been in a state of discharge.
- Do not allow the battery electrolyte to contact skin or clothing.

Jump Starting Procedure

1. Make sure that the voltages of the 2 batteries are the same. Most batteries and charging systems are of the 12 volt variety.

2. Pull the jumping vehicle (with the good battery) into a position so the jumper cables can reach the dead battery and that vehicle's engine. Make sure that the vehicles do NOT touch.

3. Place the transmissions/transaxles of both vehicles in **Neutral** (MT) or **P** (AT), as applicable, then firmly set their parking brakes.

➡ **If necessary for safety reasons, the hazard lights on both vehicles may be operated throughout the entire procedure without significantly increasing the difficulty of jumping the dead battery.**

4. Turn all lights and accessories OFF on both vehicles. Make sure the ignition switches on both vehicles are turned to the **OFF** position.

5. Cover the battery cell caps with a rag, but do not cover the terminals.

6. Make sure the terminals on both batteries are clean and free of corrosion or proper electrical connection will be impeded. If necessary, clean the battery terminals before proceeding.

7. Identify the positive (+) and negative (-) terminals on both batteries.

8. Connect the first jumper cable to the positive (+) terminal of the dead battery, then connect the other end of that cable to the positive (+) terminal of the booster (good) battery.

9. Connect one end of the other jumper cable to the negative (-) terminal on the booster battery and the final cable clamp to an engine bolt head, alternator bracket or other solid, metallic point on the engine with the dead battery. Try to pick a ground on the engine that is positioned away from the battery in order to minimize the possibility of the 2 clamps touching should one loosen during the procedure. DO NOT connect this clamp to the negative (-) terminal of the bad battery.

✳✳ CAUTION

Be very careful to keep the jumper cables away from moving parts (cooling fan, belts, etc.) on both engines.

10. Check to make sure that the cables are routed away from any moving parts, then start the donor vehicle's engine. Run the engine at moderate speed for several minutes to allow the dead battery a chance to receive some initial charge.

11. With the donor vehicle's engine still running at idle, try to start the vehicle with the dead battery. Crank the engine for no more than 15 seconds at a time and let the starter cool for at least 15 minutes between tries. If the vehicle does not start in 3 tries, it is likely that something else is also wrong or that the battery needs additional time to charge.

12. Once the vehicle is started, allow it to run at idle for a few seconds to make sure that it is operating properly.

13. Turn ON the headlights, heater blower and, if equipped, the rear defroster of both vehicles in order to reduce the severity of voltage spikes and subsequent risk of damage to the vehicles' electrical systems when the cables are disconnected. This step is especially important to any vehicle equipped with computer control modules.

14. Carefully disconnect the cables in the reverse order of connection. Start with the negative cable that is attached to the engine ground, then negative cable on the donor battery. Disconnect the positive cable from the donor battery and finally, disconnect the positive cable from the formerly dead battery. Be careful when disconnecting the cables from the positive terminals not to allow the alligator clips to touch any metal on either vehicle or a short and sparks will occur.

JACKING

▶ See Figure 186

Your vehicle was supplied with a jack for emergency road repairs. This jack is fine for changing a flat tire or other short term procedures not requiring you to go beneath the vehicle. If it is used in an emergency, carefully follow the instructions provided either with the jack or in the owner's manual. Do not attempt to use the jack on any portions of the vehicle other than those specified by the vehicle manufacturer. Always block the diagonally opposite wheel when using a jack.

Never place the jack under the radiator, engine or transaxle components. Severe and expensive dam-

age will result when the jack is raised. Additionally, never jack under the floorpan or bodywork; the metal will deform.

Whenever working under the vehicle, safely support it on jackstands or ramps. Never use cinder blocks or stacks of wood to support the vehicle, even if only going underneath the vehicle for a few minutes. Never crawl under the vehicle when it is supported only by a jack, whether the jack is the emergency tire changing jack or other floor jack.

➡ **Always position a block of wood or small rubber pad on top of the jack or jackstand to**

protect the lifting point's finish when lifting or supporting the vehicle.

Small hydraulic, screw, or scissors jacks are satisfactory for raising the vehicle. Drive-on trestles or ramps are also a handy and safe way to both raise and support the vehicle. Be careful though, some ramps may be too steep to drive the vehicle onto without scraping the front bottom panels. Never support the vehicle beneath any suspension member (unless specifically instructed to do so by a repair manual) or by an underbody panel.

Jacking Precautions

The following safety points cannot be overemphasized:

• Always block the opposite wheel or wheels to keep the vehicle from rolling off the jack.

• When raising the front of the vehicle, firmly apply the parking brake.

• When the drive wheels are to remain on the ground, leave the vehicle in gear to help prevent it from rolling.

• Always use jackstands to support the vehicle when working underneath. Place the stands beneath the vehicle's jacking brackets. Before climbing underneath, rock the vehicle a bit to make sure it is firmly supported.

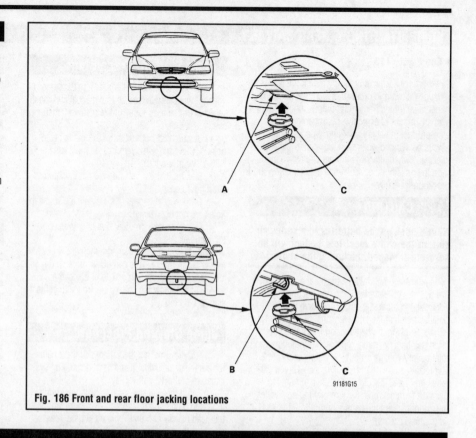

91181G15

Fig. 186 Front and rear floor jacking locations

MAINTENANCE INTERVALS

Both Normal and Severe Maintenance charts are provided in this Total Car Care manual and reflect the recommendations provided by the manufacturer. Maintenance intervals for vehicles operated in severe conditions include any of the following conditions:

• Vehicles operated in Canada or driven in extremely hot (over 90°F or 32°C) conditions

• Vehicles operated in long periods of stop and go driving or conditions requiring extensive idling

• Vehicles driven less than 5 miles (8 km) per trip or, in freezing temperatures, driven less than 10 miles (16 km) per trip

• Vehicles driven with car top carriers, used for towing, driven in mountainous areas or on dusty, muddy, or de-iced roadways

MANUFACTURER RECOMMENDED NORMAL MAINTENANCE INTERVALS ①

Service by time or mileage, whichever occurs first.		VEHICLE MAINTENANCE INTERVALS ①														
miles (x1000)		7.5	15	22.5	30	37.5	45	52.5	60	67.5	75	82.5	90	97.5	105	120
km (x1000)		12	24	36	48	60	72	84	96	108	120	132	144	156	168	180/192
months		12	24		36				48		60		72		84	96
Component	**Procedure**															
Engine oil and filter	Replace	✓	✓	✓	✓	✓	✓	✓	✓	✓	✓	✓	✓	✓	✓	✓
Engine oil level	Inspect ②															
Coolant level	Inspect ②															
Air cleaner	Replace				✓				✓				✓			✓
Valve Adjustment:	Inspect/Adjust		✓				✓				✓				✓	
Spark plugs (except V6)	Replace				✓				✓				✓			✓
Spark plugs (V6)	Replace												✓		✓	✓
Timing belt	Replace														✓	
Balance shaft belt ④	Replace														✓	
Water pump	Inspect														✓	
Drive belts	Inspect/Adjust				✓				✓				✓			✓
Idle speed	Inspect/Adjust								✓							✓
PCV Valve	Inspect								✓							✓
Coolant	Replace						✓						✓			✓
Transmission fluid	Inspect		✓		✓		✓		✓		✓		✓		✓	✓
Front and rear brakes	Inspect	✓	✓		✓		✓		✓				✓		✓	✓
Brake fluid	Replace		✓				✓				✓				✓	
Parking brake	Inspect/Adjust				✓				✓				✓			✓
Air conditioner filter	Replace		✓		✓		✓		✓		✓		✓		✓	✓
Tires	Rotate ⑤	✓	✓	✓	✓	✓	✓	✓	✓	✓	✓	✓	✓	✓	✓	✓
Tire pressure	Adjust ⑤	✓	✓	✓	✓	✓	✓	✓	✓	✓	✓	✓	✓	✓	✓	✓
Steering box	Inspect		✓		✓		✓		✓		✓		✓		✓	✓
Tie rod ends	Inspect		✓		✓		✓		✓		✓		✓		✓	✓
Steering boots	Inspect		✓		✓		✓		✓		✓		✓		✓	✓
Suspension	Inspect		✓		✓		✓		✓		✓		✓		✓	✓
Fluid levels and condition	Inspect		✓		✓		✓		✓		✓		✓		✓	✓
Cooling system connections and hoses	Inspect				✓				✓				✓			✓
Exhaust system	Inspect				✓				✓				✓			✓
CV joint boots	Inspect				✓				✓				✓			✓
Brake lines, fittings and hoses	Inspect				✓				✓				✓			✓
Fuel lines, fittings, and hoses	Inspect				✓				✓				✓			✓
Supplemental restraint	Inspect	Inspect Supplemental Restraint System (SRS) 10 years after date of production														

Perform maintenance at the same intervals for mileage driven beyond that on this chart

① Maintenance chart applies to vehicles driven in the continental United States under normal operating conditions.
Refer to the severe maintenance interval chart if operating conditions include any of the following:
  Vehicles operated in Canada or driven in extremely hot (over 90°F or 32°C) conditions
  Vehicles operated in long periods of stop and go driving or conditions requiring extensive idling
  Vehicles driven less than 5 miles (8 km) per trip or, in freezing temperatures driven less than 10 miles (16 km) per trip
  Vehicles driven with car top carriers, used for towing, driven in mountainous areas or on dusty, muddy, or de-iced roadways
② Check engine oil and coolant levels during each fuel fill up. Top off as necessary. Caution, never open the radiator cap when the engine is hot

91181C05

MANUFACTURER RECOMMENDED SEVERE MAINTENANCE INTERVALS ①

Service by time or mileage, whichever occurs first.		VEHICLE MAINTENANCE INTERVALS ①														
miles (x1000)		7.5	15	22.5	30	37.5	45	52.5	60	67.5	75	82.5	90	97.5	105	120
km (x1000)		12	24	36	48	60	72	84	96	108	120	132	144	156	168	180/192
months		6	12	18	24	30	36	42	48	54	60	66	72	78	84	90/96
Component	**Procedure**															
Engine oil and filter	Replace 6 mo. or 3,750 mi. ②	✓	✓	✓	✓	✓	✓	✓	✓	✓	✓	✓	✓	✓	✓	✓
Engine oil level	Inspect ②															
Coolant level	Inspect ②															
Air cleaner	Replace		✓		✓		✓		✓		✓		✓		✓	✓
Valve Adjustment:																
Spark plugs (except V6)	Replace		✓		✓		✓		✓				✓		✓	✓
Spark plugs (V6)	Replace						✓		✓				✓		✓	✓
Timing belt	Replace															✓
Balance shaft belt ③	Replace								④							✓
Water pump	Inspect								④							✓
Drive belts	Inspect/Adjust				✓				⑤				✓			✓
Idle speed	Inspect/Adjust								⑤							✓
PCV Valve	Inspect								⑤							✓
Coolant	Replace						✓						✓			✓
Transmission fluid	Replace		✓		✓		✓		✓		✓		✓		✓	✓
Front and rear brakes	Inspect	✓	✓	✓	✓	✓	✓	✓	✓	✓	✓	✓	✓	✓	✓	✓
Brake fluid	Replace		✓				✓				✓				✓	
Parking brake	Inspect/Adjust				✓				✓				✓			✓
Air conditioner filter	Replace		⑤				⑤		⑤		⑤				⑤	
Antenna mast	Clean		✓		✓		✓		✓		✓		✓		✓	✓
hinges, locks, and latches	Lubricate		✓		✓		✓		✓		✓		✓		✓	✓
Tires	Inspect/Rotate	✓	✓	✓	✓	✓	✓	✓	✓	✓	✓	✓	✓	✓	✓	✓
Tire pressure	Adjust ⑥	✓	✓	✓	✓	✓	✓	✓	✓	✓	✓	✓	✓	✓	✓	✓
Steering box	Inspect		✓		✓		✓		✓		✓		✓		✓	✓
Tie rod ends	Inspect		✓		✓		✓		✓		✓		✓		✓	✓
Steering boots	Inspect		✓		✓		✓		✓		✓		✓		✓	✓
Suspension	Inspect		✓		✓		✓		✓		✓		✓		✓	✓
Fluid levels and condition	Inspect		✓		✓		✓		✓		✓		✓		✓	✓
Cooling system connections and hoses	Inspect				✓				✓				✓			✓
Exhaust system	Inspect				✓				✓				✓			✓
CV joint boots	Inspect		✓		✓		✓		✓		✓		✓		✓	✓
Brake lines, fittings and hoses	Inspect				✓				✓				✓			✓
ABS	Inspect				✓				✓				✓			✓
Fuel lines, fittings, and hoses	Inspect				✓				✓				✓			✓
Supplemental restraint	Inspect	Inspect supplemental restraint system (SRS) 10 years after date of production														

Perform maintenance at the same intervals for mileage beyond that on this chart

① Maintenance intervals for vehicles operated in severe conditions include any of the following:
  Vehicles operated in Canada or driven in extremely hot (over 90°F or 43°C) conditions
  Vehicles operated in long periods of stop and go driving or conditions requiring extensive idling
  Vehicles driven less than 5 miles (8 km) per trip or, in freezing temperatures driven less than 10 miles (16 km) per trip
  Vehicles driven with car top carriers, used for towing, driven in mountainous areas or on dusty, muddy, or de-iced roadways
② Check engine oil and coolant levels during each fuel fill up. Top off as necessary. Caution, never open the radiator cap when the engine is hot
③ Odyssey 2.2L and 2.3L engines only
④ Replace at 60,000 miles or 100,000 km if driven in high temperatures (above 110°F or 43°C) or very low temperatures (below -20°F or -29°C)
⑤ Replace every 15,000 miles (24,000 km) if driven in congested industrialized urban areas or if climate control air flow is reduced
⑥ Check tire pressure and condition at least once a month

91181C07

CAPACITIES

Year	Model	Engine Displacement Liters (cc)	Engine ID/VIN	Engine Oil with Filter (qts.)	Transmission (pts.) 5-Spd	Transmission (pts.) Auto.	Transfer Case (pts.)	Drive Axle Front (pts.)	Drive Axle Rear (pts.)	Fuel Tank (gal.)	Cooling System (qts.)
1996	Accord DX/LX	2.2 (2156)	F22B2	4.0	4.0	5.0	—	—	—	17.0	①
	Accord EX	2.2 (2156)	F22B1	4.5	4.0	5.0	—	—	—	17.0	①
	Accord V-6	2.7 (2675)	C27A4	4.6	—	6.2	—	—	—	17.0	7.2
	Prelude S	2.2 (2156)	F22A1	4.0	4.0	5.0	—	—	—	15.9	②
	Prelude Si	2.3 (2259)	H23A1	4.5	4.0	5.0	—	—	—	15.9	②
	Prelude Si VTEC	2.2 (2157)	H22A1	5.1	4.0	—	—	—	—	15.9	4.6
1997	Accord Coupe	2.2 (2156)	F22B1	4.5	4.0	5.0	—	—	—	17.0	①
	Accord Coupe	2.2 (2156)	F22B2	4.0	4.0	5.0	—	—	—	17.0	①
	Accord Sedan	2.7 (2675)	C27A4	4.6	—	6.2	—	—	—	17.0	7.2
	Accord Sedan	2.2 (2156)	F22B1	4.5	4.0	5.0	—	—	—	17.0	①
	Accord Sedan	2.2 (2156)	F22B2	4.0	4.0	5.0	—	—	—	17.0	①
	Accord Wagon	2.2 (2156)	F22B1	4.5	4.0	5.0	—	—	—	17.0	①
	Accord Wagon	2.2 (2156)	F22B2	4.0	4.0	5.0	—	—	—	17.0	①
	Prelude	2.2 (2156)	H22A4	5.1	4.0	5.0	—	—	—	15.9	4.6
	Prelude SH	2.2 (2156)	H22A4	5.1	4.0	—	—	—	—	15.9	4.6
1998	Accord Coupe (EX, LX)	2.3 (2254)	F23A1	4.0	4.0	5.0	—	—	—	17.0	③
	Accord Coupe (EX, LX)	2.3 (2254)	F23A4	4.5	4.0	5.0	—	—	—	17.0	③
	Accord Coupe (EX, LX)	3.0 (2997)	J30A1	4.6	—	6.2	—	—	—	17.1	5.9
	Accord Sedan (DX)	2.3 (2254)	F23A5	4.5	4.0	5.2	—	—	—	17.0	③
	Accord Sedan (EX, LX)	2.3 (2254)	F23A1	4.0	4.0	5.0	—	—	—	17.0	③
	Accord Sedan (EX, LX)	2.3 (2254)	F23A4	4.5	4.0	5.2	—	—	—	17.0	③
	Accord Sedan (EX, LX)	3.0 (2997)	J30A1	4.6	—	6.2	—	—	—	17.1	5.9
	Prelude	2.2 (2156)	H22A4	5.1	4.0	—	—	—	—	15.9	4.6
	Prelude SH	2.2 (2156)	H22A4	5.1	4.0	—	—	—	—	15.9	4.6
1999	Accord Coupe (EX, LX)	2.3 (2254)	F23A1	4.0	4.0	5.0	—	—	—	17.0	③
	Accord Coupe (EX, LX)	2.3 (2254)	F23A4	4.5	4.0	5.0	—	—	—	17.0	③
	Accord Coupe (EX, LX)	3.0 (2997)	J30A1	4.6	—	6.2	—	—	—	17.1	5.9
	Accord Sedan (DX)	2.3 (2254)	F23A5	4.5	4.0	5.2	—	—	—	17.0	③
	Accord Sedan (EX, LX)	2.3 (2254)	F23A1	4.0	4.0	5.0	—	—	—	17.0	③
	Accord Sedan (EX, LX)	2.3 (2254)	F23A4	4.5	4.0	5.2	—	—	—	17.0	③
	Accord Sedan (EX, LX)	3.0 (2997)	J30A1	4.6	—	6.2	—	—	—	17.1	5.9
	Prelude	2.2 (2156)	H22A4	5.1	4.0	—	—	—	—	15.9	4.6
	Prelude SH	2.2 (2156)	H22A4	5.1	4.0	—	—	—	—	15.9	4.6
2000	Accord Coupe (EX, LX)	2.3 (2254)	F23A1	4.0	4.0	5.0	—	—	—	17.0	③
	Accord Coupe (EX, LX)	2.3 (2254)	F23A4	4.5	4.0	5.0	—	—	—	17.0	③
	Accord Coupe (EX, LX)	3.0 (2997)	J30A1	4.6	—	6.2	—	—	—	17.1	5.9
	Accord Sedan (DX)	2.3 (2254)	F23A5	4.5	4.0	5.2	—	—	—	17.0	③
	Accord Sedan (EX, LX)	2.3 (2254)	F23A1	4.0	4.0	5.0	—	—	—	17.0	③
	Accord Sedan (EX, LX)	2.3 (2254)	F23A4	4.5	4.0	5.2	—	—	—	17.0	③
	Accord Sedan (EX, LX)	3.0 (2997)	J30A1	4.6	—	6.2	—	—	—	17.1	5.9
	Prelude	2.2 (2156)	H22A4	5.1	4.0	—	—	—	—	15.9	4.6
	Prelude SH	2.2 (2156)	H22A4	5.1	4.0	—	—	—	—	15.9	4.6

NOTE: All capacities are approximate. Add fluid gradually and ensure a proper fluid level is obtained.

① Automatic transaxle: 5.6
Manual transaxle: 5.7

② Automatic transaxle: 4.0
Manual transaxle: 3.8

③ Automatic Transaxle: 5.7
Manual Transaxle: 5.8

91181C06

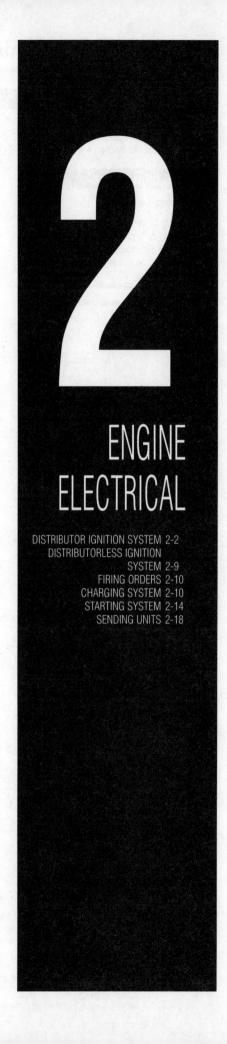

2

ENGINE
ELECTRICAL

DISTRIBUTOR IGNITION SYSTEM

➡For more information about understanding electricity and troubleshooting electrical circuits, please refer to Section 6 of this manual.

General Information

▶ See Figures 1 and 2

The electronic distributor ignition systems used on the Accord and Prelude models is similar to a distributor with the conventional breaker point ignition system found on earlier vehicles. Both systems use a distributor cap and ignition rotor to distribute the ignition spark from the ignition coil to each cylinder's spark plug in the correct order. They both require the cap and rotor to be inspected cleaned and/or replaced during periodic maintenance.

The main difference between the two systems is that the electronic distributor does not have any moving parts that require periodic adjustments, unlike breaker points, which require periodic rubbing block lubrication, adjustment and replacement. To advance the ignition timing relative to engine speed, the breaker point and the initial electronic ignition systems used a mechanical, centrifugal advance unit. The ignition timing would advance based solely on the engine's speed. Those systems worked well for their day, however to meet today's more stringent emission standards, an engine's operating efficiency must be optimized. To meet these standards, and optimize an engine's efficiency requires precise control of the ignition timing.

To achieve this level of efficiency, the ignition timing advance is controlled electronically by the Powertrain Control Module (PCM). This allows the ignition timing to be adjusted electronically based on input from a collection of electronic sensors. This system allows the ignition timing advance to be adjusted and optimized instantly, for changes in engine speed, intake manifold airflow rate and the engine coolant temperature. Some vehicles may have a knock control system, which sets the ideal ignition timing for the octane rating of the gasoline being used.

There are three sensors used to supply information to the PCM. These sensors are the Top Dead Center (TDC), Crankshaft Position (CKP), and Cylinder Position (CYP) sensors. The information these sensors supply to the PCM allows the control module to monitor the mechanical moving components of the engine. The CKP sensor determines the timing for fuel injection and ignition for each cylinder and detects engine speed. The TDC sensor determines ignition timing during start-up and when the crank angle is abnormal. The CYP sensor detects the position of the No. 1 cylinder for sequential fuel injection to each cylinder

Each sensor is each triggered electronically by a reluctor. The reluctors are installed securely onto the distributor shaft, and rotate with the shaft. One reluctor that is pressed onto the distributor shaft looks very similar to a small straight cut gear. As the reluctor rotates with the distributor shaft, the teeth of the reluctor pass very closely to a small sensor, which is simply a small electric coil. As the teeth of the reluctor move toward the sensor, the electric field of the sensor is energized. As the teeth of the reluctor move past the sensor, the electric field of the sensor is collapsed, causing an electric pulse that is sent from the sensor to the control module. As each tooth of the reluctor passes the sensor, it causes an electrical pulse. For each complete revolution of the distributor shaft, the number of pulses generated per revolution, is equal to the number of teeth on the reluctor. The control module uses these electric pulses to gather information about the engine. The faster the engine spins, the faster the distributor spins, the faster the pulses are generated, which allows the control unit to know how fast the engine is spinning.

Reluctors vary is size and shape. Some reluctors look very similar to small gears, however their shape does vary. Another reluctor found in the distributor, has only one tooth, or raised edge. The shape of the reluctor is mostly rounded, with an oblong ramp leading up to a single raised edge. This reluctor operates just like the gear shaped type, however, because it only has one raised edge to pass by the sensor, only one electric pulse is generated for each revolution of the distributor. The control module uses the single pulse of the CYP sensor to recognize the position of No. 1 cylinder for sequential fuel injection to each cylinder.

As the distributor shaft rotates with the attached reluctors, the electrical pulses for each sensor are

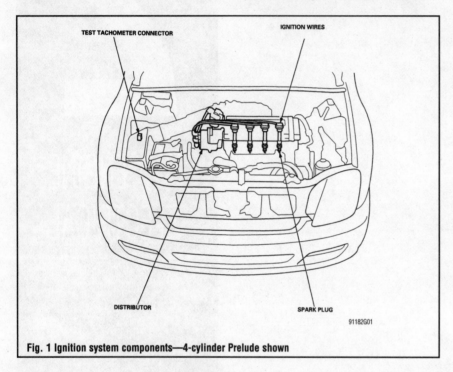

Fig. 1 Ignition system components—4-cylinder Prelude shown

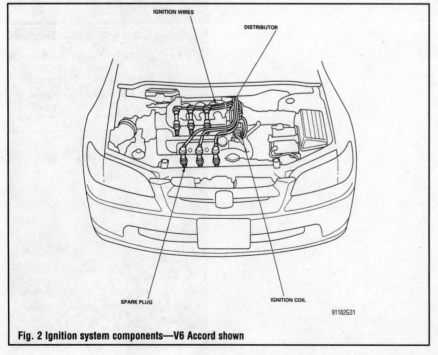

Fig. 2 Ignition system components—V6 Accord shown

used by the control module to track the mechanical moving components of the engine. This allows the control module to keep track of each phase of the four-stroke cycle for each cylinder. The Powertrain Control Module (PCM) can optimize the ignition timing and the amount of ignition advance for the engine's operating conditions (rpm, load and temperature).

The basic ignition timing information for the engine's operating conditions is stored in the memory of the PCM. This is why a jumper must be temporarily installed onto the Service Connector (SCS) when adjusting the idle speed ignition timing as described in the ignition timing adjustment procedure in Section 1 of this manual. Using the jumper allows the base ignition timing to be adjusted manually without the control module over-riding the adjustment. Once the jumper is removed, the control module stores the base timing information into its memory.

As the PCM control module receives input from its sensors, it selects the optimal ignition timing and triggers the ignition coil by sending electric pulses. As with the reluctor collapsing the electrical field of the sensors, the PCM does much the same with the ignition coil. The electrical pulses from the PCM are used to trigger the ignition coil. To do this, the primary ignition current is momentarily cut off by the Powertrain Control Module (PCM). This allows the magnetic field of the ignition coil to collapse, creating a spark that the distributor passes onto the spark plugs via the rotor and spark plug wires.

On 4-cylinder engines, the ignition coil is located within the distributor housing, eliminating the need for a high-tension wire from the ignition coil to the distributor cap. The only high-tension ignition wires used on this ignition system are the spark plug wires, which are connected to the distributor cap and the spark plugs. The V6 engines use a remotely mounted the ignition coil assembly, located near the distributor.

Diagnosis and Testing

Prior to diagnosis or testing procedures, visually inspect the components of the ignition and engine control systems. Check for the following:
- Discharged battery or low alternator output
- Damaged, corroded, or loose electrical connections
- Damaged or worn electrical insulation
- Poor spark plug connections
- Ignition module multi-connector condition
- Blown fuses
- Damaged or corroded ignition wires

- Excessively worn, defective, or damaged spark plugs
- Excessively worn or damaged distributor cap or rotor

Check the spark plug wires and boots for signs of poor insulation that could cause shorting or crossfiring. Make sure the battery is fully charged and that all accessories are off during diagnosis and testing. Make sure the idle speed is properly adjusted and within specification. Check all of the fuel injector electrical connections..

SECONDARY SPARK TEST

✳✳ WARNING

When testing the ignition system for a high-energy spark, make sure the test equipment is sufficiently grounded. Failure to do so may cause severe and expensive internal component damage. When testing for an ignition, spark make sure the area is free of any flammable materials. Do not hold or place hands or fingers near the test equipment when checking for a high voltage spark.

Checking for a high-energy spark is easily performed using a spark tester (available at most automotive parts stores). Three types of spark testers are commonly available.
- The Neon Bulb type: This tool connects to the spark plug wire and flashes with each ignition pulse. This is easy to use as it lights up with each ignition pulse
- The Air Gap type: This tester is adjusted according to the spark plug gap specification for the engine. It is very useful because the gap can be adjusted to check the strength of the electrical spark and the color of the spark can be verified
- The Spark Plug simulator: This looks like a spark plug, and has a grounding alligator style clip on the side. This checker is easy to use, and the spark color can be monitored

The last two types of testers mentioned allow the user to not only detect the presence of spark, but also the intensity (orange/yellow is weak, blue is strong). To use these testers proceed as follows:

1. Disconnect a spark plug wire from the spark plug end.
2. Connect the plug wire to the spark tester and ground the tester to an appropriate location on the engine.

3. Crank the engine and check for spark at the tester.
4. If spark exists at the tester, the ignition system is functioning properly.
5. If all of the spark tests for all of the spark plug wires indicate irregular or weak spark, perform the following:
   a. Refer to the coil test.
   b. Carefully inspect the distributor cap and rotor for damage, corrosion or excessive wear.
   c. Inspect and test the ignition wires. Check the resistance of each spark plug wire. Refer to Section 1 for checking the resistance of the spark plug wires. If the wires are within specification, it will be necessary to diagnose the individual components of the ignition system.
6. If one or more, but not all of the tests indicate irregular, or weak spark, perform the following:
   a. Inspect and test the ignition wire. Check the resistance of each spark plug wire. Refer to Section 1 for checking the resistance of the spark plug wires. If the wire is within specification, it will be necessary to diagnose the individual components of the ignition system.
   b. Carefully inspect the distributor cap and rotor for an internal short, damage, corrosion or excessive wear.
7. If spark does not exist:
   a. Remove the distributor cap, disconnect all of the electrical connectors at the distributor, and ensure that the rotor is turning when the engine is cranked.
   b. Carefully inspect the distributor cap and rotor for damage, corrosion or excessive wear.
   c. Inspect and test the ignition wires. Check the resistance of each spark plug wire. Refer to Section 1 for checking the resistance of the spark plug wires. If the wire is within specification, it will be necessary to diagnose the individual components of the ignition system.

CYLINDER DROP TEST

▶ See Figures 3, 4 and 5

✳✳ WARNING

When performing a cylinder drop make sure the cylinder's high-tension lead for the cylinder being checked is sufficiently grounded. Failure to do so may cause severe and expensive internal component damage.

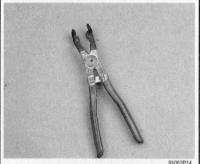

Fig. 3 These pliers are insulated and help protect the user from shock as well as the plug wires from being damaged

91052P14

Fig. 4 To perform the cylinder drop test, remove one wire at a time and . . .

91052P15

Fig. 5 . . . note the idle speed and idle characteristics of the engine. The cylinder(s) with the least drop is the non-contributing cylinder(s)

91052P16

A cylinder drop test can be performed when an engine misfire is present. This test helps determine which cylinder is not contributing to the engine's power. The easiest way to perform this test is to remove and ground the plug wires one at a time for each cylinder with the engine running. A cylinder drop test can be performed when an engine misfire is present

1. Place the transaxle in **P** for automatics or **Neutral** for manuals, and engage the emergency brake. Then start the engine and allow the engine to reach a warm idle.

2. Using a spark plug wire-removing tool, preferably the pliers type, carefully remove and ground the ignition wire from one of the cylinders.

❊❊❊ CAUTION

Make sure not to touch any part of the car that is metal. The secondary voltage from the ignition system is a high-energy spark with enough voltage to significantly cause a painful electrical shock.

3. The engine will sputter, run worse, and possibly nearly stall. If this happens, reinstall the plug wire and move to the next cylinder. If the engine runs no differently, or the difference is minimal, shut the engine off and inspect the spark plug wire, spark plug, and if necessary, perform component diagnostics as covered in this section. Perform this test on all cylinders to verify which cylinders seem low on power.

Adjustments

The only adjustment possible on the ignition system of the Accord and Prelude is the base ignition timing. Please refer to Section 1 for information about setting the base ignition timing.

Ignition Coil

TESTING

2.2L Engines

ACCORD WITH F22B1 ENGINE

▶ See Figures 6 and 7

1. Disconnect the negative battery cable.
2. Remove the distributor cap, as outlined in Section 1 of this manual.

Fig. 6 Squeeze the connector tabs to detach the connector from the ignition coil

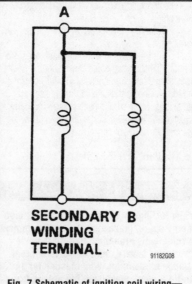

Fig. 7 Schematic of ignition coil wiring— 2.2L (F22B1) engine

3. Remove the black/yellow and white/black wires from the terminals marked A (+) and B (-).

➡**Resistance will vary with coil temperature; therefore all specifications were taken at an ambient temperature of 68°F (20°C)**

4. Measure the resistance between both terminals using an ohmmeter, and compare with the following specifications:

   a. The primary winding resistance should be 0.45–0.55 ohms
   b. The secondary winding resistance should be 16.8–25.2 ohms.

➡**The Powertrain Control Module (PCM) idle memory must be reset after reconnecting the battery. Start the engine and hold it at 3000 rpm until the cooling fan comes on. Then allow the engine to idle for about five minutes with all accessories OFF and with the transmission in Park or Neutral.**

5. Reconnect the negative battery cable.

ACCORD WITH F22B2 ENGINE

▶ See Figures 8 and 9

1. Disconnect the negative battery cable.

➡**Resistance will vary with coil temperature; therefore all specifications were taken at an ambient temperature of 68°F (20°C)**

2. Remove the distributor cap, as outlined in Section 1.
3. Detach the 4-prong connector and igniter wire.
4. Measure the resistance between the terminals and replace the coil if the specifications differ from the following:

   a. The primary winding resistance (measurement between A and B) should be between 0.64–0.78 ohms.
   b. The secondary winding resistance (measurement between A and the secondary winding terminal) should be between 14.4–21.6 kilohms.

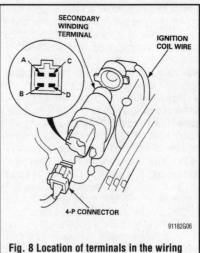

Fig. 8 Location of terminals in the wiring connector—2.2L (F22B2) engine

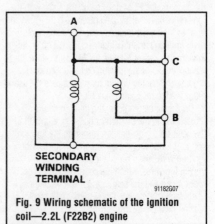

Fig. 9 Wiring schematic of the ignition coil—2.2L (F22B2) engine

PRELUDE

▶ See Figures 10 and 11

1. Turn the ignition switch **OFF**.
2. Detach the 4-prong connector and the ignition coil wire.
3. Using an ohmmeter, measure the primary winding resistance between terminals A and C. The resistance should be 0.64–0.78 ohms. If not, replace the ignition coil.
4. Using an ohmmeter, measure the secondary winding resistance between terminal A and the sec-

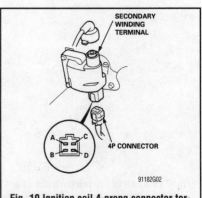

Fig. 10 Ignition coil 4-prong connector terminal identification—Prelude shown

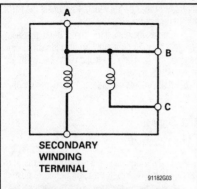

Fig. 11 View of the secondary winding terminal—Prelude shown

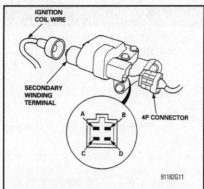

Fig. 13 Terminal identification for the ignition coil 4-prong connector —2.7L engine

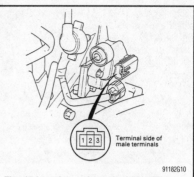

Fig. 15 Location and terminal identification of the 3-prong connector—3.0L engine

ondary winding terminal. The resistance should be 14.4–21.6 kilohms. If not, replace the ignition coil.

5. Check for continuity between the terminals A and B. If there is no continuity, replace the coil.

2.3L Engine

1. Disconnect the negative battery cable.

➡**Resistance will vary with coil temperature; therefore all specifications were taken at an ambient temperature of 68°F (20°C).**

2. Remove the distributor cap, as outlined in Section 1.
3. Detach the wires from the terminals of the coil.
4. Measure the resistance between the coil terminals.
5. Replace the coil if the measurements taken do not fall within the following specifications:
   - Primary winding resistance (F23A1, F23A4 engines): 0.45–0.55 ohms.
   - Primary winding resistance (F23A5 engine): 0.63–0.77 ohms.
   - Secondary winding resistance (F23A1, F23A4 engines): 16.8–25.2 kilohms.
   - Secondary winding resistance (F23A5 engine): 12.8–19.2 kilohms.

2.7L Engine

▶ See Figures 12 and 13

1. Detach the negative battery cable.
2. Remove the distributor cap, as outlined in Section 1.

3. Unplug the 4-prong connector from the ignition coil.
4. Remove the ignition coil wire.
5. Use an ohmmeter to measure the resistance between the terminals on the coil, and compare with the following:
   a. Measure the primary winding resistance, between the A and C terminals, and replace the coil if the resistance is not between 0.3–0.4 ohms.
   b. Measure the secondary winding resistance, between the B and D terminals, and replace the coil if the resistance is not between 14–22 kilohms.

3.0L Engine

▶ See Figures 14 and 15

1. Disconnect the negative battery cable.
2. Remove the distributor cap, as outlined in Section 1.
3. Unplug the 3-prong connector from the ignition coil.
4. Remove the ignition coil wire.
5. Use an ohmmeter to measure the resistance between the terminals on the coil, and compare with the following:
   a. Resistance between the two outer most terminals (#1 and #3) should be between 0.34–0.42 ohms. This is the primary winding side of the coil.
   b. The secondary winding resistance is found by measuring across the middle terminal (#2) of the coil and the secondary winding terminal. The resistance should be between 17.1–20.9 kilohms.

➡**The Powertrain Control Module (PCM) idle memory must be reset after reconnecting the battery. Start the engine and hold it at 3000 rpm until the cooling fan comes on. Then allow the engine to idle for about five minutes with all accessories OFF and with the transmission in Park or Neutral.**

6. Reconnect the negative battery cable.

REMOVAL & INSTALLATION

2.2L and 2.3L Engines

▶ See Figures 16, 17 and 18

1. Disconnect the negative battery cable.
2. Remove the distributor cap, as outlined in Section 1.
3. Mark the position of the rotor to the distributor housing, then remove the ignition rotor.
4. Remove the cap seal.
5. Remove the leak cover.
6. Remove the screws that hold the black/yellow and white/blue wires to the ignition coil.
7. Unfasten the screws that secure the ignition coil, then pull the coil from the housing.
8. Installation is the reverse of the removal procedure.

➡**The Powertrain Control Module (PCM) idle memory must be reset after reconnecting the battery. Start the engine and hold it at 3000 rpm until the cooling fan comes on. Then allow the engine to idle for about five minutes with all accessories OFF and with the transmission in Park or Neutral.**

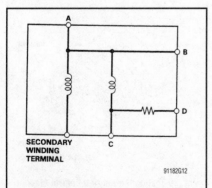

Fig. 12 Schematic of the ignition coil circuit –2.7L engine

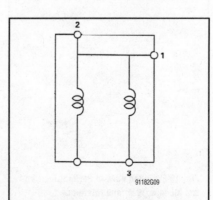

Fig. 14 Schematic of the ignition coil on the 3.0L engine

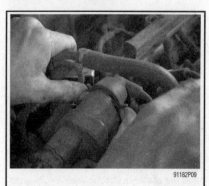

Fig. 16 Using your fingers, push the wire off the coil

Fig. 17 View of the ignition coil wire and ignition coil

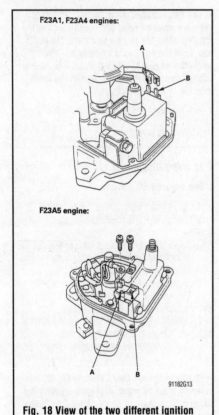

Fig. 18 View of the two different ignition coils used on the 2.3L engines

2.7L and 3.0L Engines

▶ **See Figure 2**

1. Disconnect the negative battery cable.
2. Detach the electrical connector from the coil.
3. Detach the ignition coil wire.
4. Remove the mounting bolts, then remove the ignition coil.
5. Installation is the reverse of the removal procedure.

➡ **The Powertrain Control Module (PCM) idle memory must be reset after reconnecting the battery. Start the engine and hold it at 3000 rpm until the cooling fan comes on. Then allow the engine to idle for about five minutes with all accessories OFF and with the transmission in Park or Neutral.**

Ignition Module

The Ignition Control Module (ICM) on the Accord and Prelude is located in the distributor housing near the ignition coil. To access the module, remove the distributor cap, rotor, and if equipped, the dust cover.

TESTING

Make sure to note the position of the ignition wires on the distributor cap. Use a piece of paper and note the wire locations and connections, or carefully mark the wires before removing them. Failure to reinstall the wires correctly could cause expensive component failure.

2.2L and 2.3L Engines

▶ **See Figure 19**

To test the Ignition Control Module (ICM) on the 2.2L and 2.3L engines, proceed as follows:
1. Remove the distributor cap, as outlined in Section 1.
2. Remove the black/yellow, blue (1), yellow/green, and the blue (2) wires from the ICM
3. Remove the wires from the ICM
4. With the ignition switch **ON**, check for battery voltage between the black/yellow and ground. If voltage is present, proceed with testing. If no voltage is present, check for an open circuit between the wire and the ignition switch.
5. With the ignition switch **ON**, check for battery voltage between the green (white/black on the F22B1 engine) ground. If voltage is present, go to the next step. If no voltage is present, check the ignition coil and the green or white/black wire between the ICM and the coil.
6. Detach the electrical multi-connector from the Powertrain Control Module PCM and check for continuity on the yellow/green wire between the multi-connector and the yellow/green wire at the ICM. There should be continuity. If there is no continuity, check for an open circuit in the yellow/green wire circuit. Check for continuity between the yellow/green wire and ground. There should be no continuity. If there is continuity to ground, locate where the yellow/green wire is

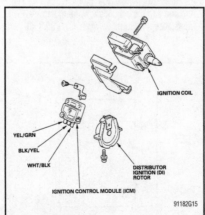

Fig. 19 Exploded view of the Ignition Control Module (ICM) and related system components

shorted to ground, and repair. Reconnect the PCM multi-connector.
7. Detach the connector from the gauge assembly and check for continuity on the blue wire between the ICM and the tachometer. There should be continuity here.
8. If all the test conditions passed, replace the ICM.

2.7L Engine

▶ **See Figure 20**

1. Loosen the fasteners securing the distributor cap to the distributor housing, then remove the cap with the wires attached and place safely aside.
2. Remove the distributor cap seal from the distributor body.
3. Locate the fastener that secures the ignition rotor to the distributor shaft, note the position of the rotor for reinstallation, then remove the fastener and the rotor. If equipped, the protective cover.
4. Locate the Ignition Control Module (ICM), which is near the ignition coil and mounted onto the distributor housing plate. To test the ICM, proceed as follows:
5. Remove the wires from the ICM
6. With the ignition switch **ON**, check for battery voltage between the yellow wire and ground. If voltage is present, proceed with testing. If no voltage is present check for an open circuit between the wire and the ignition switch.
7. With the ignition switch **ON**, check for battery voltage between the green wire and the body ground. If voltage is present, go to the next step. If no voltage is present, check the ignition coil and the green wire between the ICM and the coil.
8. Detach the electrical multi-connector from the Powertrain Control Module PCM and check for continuity on the yellow/green wire between the multi-connector and the yellow/green wire at the ICM. There should be continuity. If there is no continuity, check for an open circuit in the yellow/green wire circuit. Check for continuity between the yellow/green wire and ground. There should be no continuity. If there is continuity to ground, locate where the yellow/green wire is shorted to ground, and repair. Reconnect the PCM multi-connector.
9. If all the test conditions passed, replace the ICM.

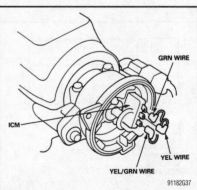

Fig. 20 Testing the Ignition Control Module (ICM)—2.7L engine

3.0L Engine

▶ **See Figure 21**

1. Unplug the 3-prong connector from the distributor.

2. With the ignition switch **ON**, check for voltage between the No. 2 terminal and the body ground. If there is not any battery voltage, check the ignition coil and the BLK/YEL wire between the ICM and the ignition coil.

3. Turn the ignition switch **ON**. Check for voltage between the No. 3 terminal and body ground. If no voltage is detected, check the ignition coil and the BLU wire between the ICM and the ignition coil

4. Detach the weather pack connector from the Powertrain Control Module (PCM). Check continuity at the No. 1 terminal between the ICM connector terminal No. 1 and the PCM connector terminal B13. Continuity should be detected here.

5. Check continuity between the No. 1 terminal and a body ground. No continuity should be detected here. If there is, the ICM is most likely damaged.

6. Attach all detached connectors.

7. If all of the above tests are normal, replace the ICM.

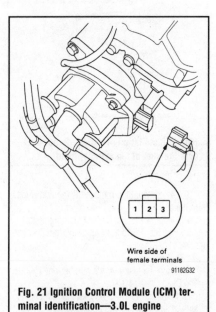

Fig. 21 Ignition Control Module (ICM) terminal identification—3.0L engine

Wire side of female terminals

91182G32

REMOVAL & INSTALLATION

▶ **See Figure 22**

1. Disconnect the negative battery cable.

2. Remove the distributor cap, ignition rotor, and protective leak cover.

3. Detach the wires from the Ignition Control Module (ICM), then remove the ICM.

4. Installation is the reverse of the removal procedure.

➡The Powertrain Control Module (PCM) idle memory must be reset after reconnecting the battery. Start the engine and hold it at 3000 rpm until the cooling fan comes on. Then allow the engine to idle for about five minutes with all accessories OFF and with the transmission in Park or Neutral.

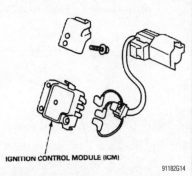

IGNITION CONTROL MODULE (ICM)

91182G14

Fig. 22 Exploded view of a typical Ignition Control Module (ICM)

Distributor

REMOVAL & INSTALLATION

2.2L and 2.3L Engines

▶ **See Figures 23, 24, 25, 26 and 27**

➡The radio may contain a coded theft protection circuit. Always make note of the code before disconnecting the battery.

1. Disconnect the negative battery cable.

2. Access the crankshaft pulley bolt through the left side inner fender liner. Use a socket, long extension and a suitable ratchet to rotate the engine. Rotate the engine counterclockwise until the white Top Dead Center (TDC) mark on the pulley aligns with the pointer on the engine cover.

3. Label the ignition wires to the distributor cap, but do not remove them, unless absolutely necessary.

4. Remove the distributor cap and note the location of the ignition rotor. If the ignition rotor is **not** pointing toward the terminal of the distributor cap for cylinder No. 1, rotate the crankshaft one complete revolution counterclockwise, and align the white (TDC) mark on the pulley with the pointer on the engine cover.

5. If the distributor is going to be reinstalled, make an alignment mark between the distributor housing and the cylinder head using a scribe or a chisel. Then, using a scribe, felt tipped marker or touch up paint, make an alignment mark on the distributor housing for the rotor.

91182P03

Fig. 23 Always matchmark the location of each plug wire before removing it from the distributor cap

91182P62

Fig. 24 Use a wrench to unfasten the distributor hold-down bolts

91182P63

Fig. 25 On some models, you may need to use a ratchet, extension, and shallow socket to reach the rear bolts

91182P61

Fig. 26 After all the mounting bolts have been removed, carefully pull the distributor from the vehicle

91182P60

Fig. 27 Inspect the distributor O-ring for cracks and replace as necessary

6. Uncouple the electrical connectors on the side of the distributor.

7. Remove the three distributor mounting bolts, then carefully remove the distributor from the cylinder head.

To install:

➡If the camshaft or crankshaft has rotated during assembly, rotate the crankshaft counterclockwise until the white Top Dead Center (TDC) mark on the pulley aligns with the pointer on the engine cover. If the valve cover and upper timing cover have been removed, be sure the UP mark on the camshaft is facing up, and that the crankshaft TDC mark aligns with the pointer on the lower timing cover.

8. Coat a new O-ring with clean engine oil and install it onto the distributor shaft.

9. Install the distributor into the cylinder head. The offset lug on the distributor shaft will fit into the groove on the end of the camshaft in only one direction. If the old distributor is being reinstalled, align the marks made during disassembly.

10. Install the three mounting bolts, only hand-tighten them at this time.

11. Couple the electrical connectors on the side of the distributor.

12. If removed, reconnect the ignition wires in the correct order.

13. Reconnect the negative battery cable.

➡The Powertrain Control Module(PCM) idle memory must be reset after reconnecting the battery. Start the engine and hold it at 3000 rpm until the cooling fan comes on. Then allow the engine to idle for about five minutes with all accessories OFF and with the transmission in Park or neutral.

14. Check and adjust the ignition timing. Refer to the ignition timing procedure outlined in Section 1.

15. Enter the radio security code.

2.7L Engine

◆ See Figures 28, 29 and 30

1. Disconnect the negative battery cable.

2. Detach the 3-prong connector from the side of distributor.

3. Matchmark then remove the ignition wires from the distributor cap.

4. Unscrew the distributor mounting bolt(s),

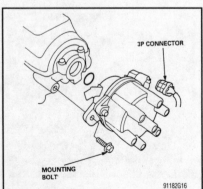

Fig. 28 Exploded view of removing the distributor from the cylinder head

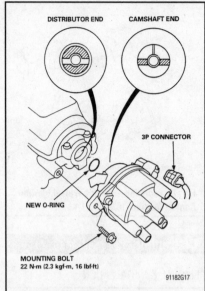

Fig. 29 Proper orientation of the distributor for installation

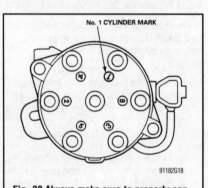

Fig. 30 Always make sure to properly connect the ignition wires to the distributor cap

then carefully pull the distributor unit away from the cylinder head.

To install:

5. Bring the piston in the No. 1 cylinder to Top Dead Center (TDC).

6. Lubricate a new O-ring with light engine oil and install it on the end of the distributor shaft.

7. Slide the distributor into position.

➡The distributor shaft has an offset driveshaft to prevent installing the unit 180° out.

8. Install and hand-tighten the mounting bolt(s).

9. Reconnect the 3-prong connector to the distributor.

10. Install the ignition wires in their correct positions on the cap.

11. Tighten the mounting bolts securely.

12. Attach the negative battery cable and set the base ignition timing, as outlined in Section 1.

3.0L Engines

◆ See Figures 31 and 32

1. Remove the negative battery.

2. Detach the connector from the side of distributor.

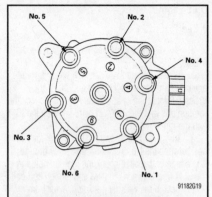

Fig. 31 Always matchmark the installed position of ignition wires to the distributor cap before removal

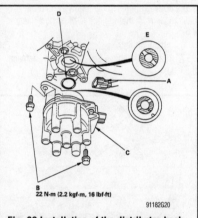

Fig. 32 Installation of the distributor back onto the side of the cylinder head

3. Matchmark then remove the ignition wires from the cap.

4. Unscrew the distributor mounting bolt(s).

5. Pull the distributor unit away from the cylinder head.

To install:

6. Bring the piston in the number one cylinder to Top Dead Center (TDC).

7. Lubricate a new O-ring with a light engine oil and install it on the end of the distributor shaft.

8. Slide the distributor into position.

➡The distributor shaft has an offset driveshaft to prevent installing the unit 180° out.

9. Install and hand-tighten the mounting bolt(s).

10. Reconnect the connector to the distributor.

11. Install the ignition wires in their correct positions on the cap.

Crankshaft Position Sensor

Refer to Electronic Engine Controls in Section 4 for information on servicing the Crankshaft Position (CKP) sensor.

Cylinder Position Sensor

Refer to Electronic Engine Controls in Section 4 for information on servicing the Cylinder Position (CYP) sensor.

DISTRIBUTORLESS IGNITION SYSTEM

General Information

Beginning in 2000, the Accord equipped with the 3.0L V6 engine uses a distributorless ignition system. The ignition timing and the ignition advance are both controlled by the Powertrain Control Module (PCM) to match the driving conditions. The PCM optimizes the ignition timing using input from a collection of sensors. The ignition timing can be checked for diagnostic purposes, although it cannot be adjusted. The distributorless ignition system uses one ignition coil per cylinder, unlike the distributor type system that uses one ignition coil for the entire system and uses the distributor to dispense the high-voltage ignition to the spark plugs.

The distributorless ignition system, which uses individual ignition coils, operates on the same principle as those on the distributor-equipped engines. However, instead of the distributor's rotation being used to trigger the ignition coil, the PCM controls the switching of the current through the primary windings for each of the individual ignition coils. When current to the ignition coil is stopped, a high voltage current flows directly from the ignition coil to the spark plug.

The PCM contains the memory for basic ignition timing for different engine speeds and manifold air-flow rates. The PCM also adjusts the ignition timing according to engine coolant temperature. The Cylinder Position (CYP) Sensor is used by the PCM to monitor the crankshaft speed. A misfire is detected by the PCM if the crankshaft speed fluctuates.

The following sensors are used by the PCM for ignition timing control:

• Top Dead Center (TDC) sensors. These two sensors, TDC1 and TDC2, determine ignition timing during start up and when the crank angle is abnormal

• Cylinder Position (CYP) sensor. This sensor detects engine speed

• Manifold Absolute Pressure (MAP) sensor. This sensor detects the intake manifold air volume

• Engine Coolant Temperature (ECT) sensor. This sensor monitors the engine coolant temperature

• Knock Sensor (KS). Allows the PCM to adjust ignition timing for the octane rating of the gasoline being used

Diagnosis and Testing

The distributorless ignition system can be diagnosed and tested using a logical test sequence. The system can be broken down into three basic components. These components are the inputs (sensors), the processor (Powertrain Control Module (PCM)) and the output components (ignition coils). Basic troubleshooting of the ignition system can be accomplished by testing the input and output components. These simple troubleshooting procedures can be used to help locate and diagnose most problems.

Diagnosing the PCM using basic tools and test equipment requires a process of elimination technique.

1. Check the operation of all input sensors. Please refer to Section 4 for additional information.
2. Check the wiring for all input sensors for continuity or a short to ground.
3. Check the ignition coils. Please refer to the following Ignition Coil Pack section for additional information.
4. Check the ignition coil wiring for continuity or a short to ground.
5. If the sensor inputs and the ignition coils are within specification, and the wiring is connected and functioning properly, the PCM could be faulty.

➡ **The Powertrain Control Module (PCM) has a fault memory to monitor the operation of the system. The PCM has the ability to recognize a problem in the system, and can prioritize the problem. If the problem is severe enough, the Malfunction Indicator Light (MIL) can be turned on by the PCM to indicate the problem is compromising the efficient and optimal operation of the engine. The PCM uses its fault memory to store fault codes that can be accessed using specially designed test equipment which due to its cost and the training required to use this equipment is beyond the scope of this manual. This test equipment is used to read the stored faults, as well as erase the faults from the PCM memory once a repair is completed.**

Adjustments

The programmed ignition system provides an adaptive, optimal ignition timing that is controlled the by the Powertrain Control Module (PCM), based on input sensor information. This system cannot be adjusted.

Ignition Coil

TESTING

3.0L Engine

1. Remove the cover for the ignition coil.
2. Detach the electrical connectors from all 6 ignition coils.
3. Turn the ignition switch to the **ON** position and measure the voltage at the black/yellow wire for each connector. If voltage is present, go to the next step. If voltage is not present, repair the open circuit in the wire between the ignition coil and fuse No. 11 in the left side under dash fuse panel.
4. Turn the ignition switch **OFF** and check for continuity between the black wire and ground. If ground is present, go to the next step. If ground is not present, repair the open circuit in the wire between the ignition coil and the body ground.
5. Detach the 31-pin connector from the Powertrain Control Module (PCM). Hold the 31-pin multiconnector such that the wire connectors are visible, with the locking tab on top. The first row of connectors from left to right are numbered 1 through 10.

On the second row, the number 11 slot is empty and the remaining connectors are numbered 12 through 22. The third row is numbered 23 though 31, with slot number 24 empty. Check the following wires from the provided pin location for continuity to ground. If there is not continuity go to the next step. If there is continuity, repair the short in the wire between the PCM and the ignition coil.

• Blue, pin location No. 3 to ground
• Yellow/green, pin location No. 4 to ground
• Black/red, pin location No. 12
• Yellow, pin location No. 13 to ground
• Red, pin location No. 14
• White/blue, pin location No. 23 to ground

6. Reconnect the PCM multi-plug connector. With the ignition switch in the start position, check for voltage at the multi-plug connector for each ignition coil for the following wires: blue, yellow/green, black/red, yellow, red, and white/blue. If the measured voltage is 0.5 volts, replace the ignition coil. If no voltage is measured, repair the open circuit in the wire between the PCM and the ignition coil.

REMOVAL & INSTALLATION

3.0L Engine

1. Disconnect the negative battery cable.
2. Unfasten the retainers, then remove the ignition coil covers.
3. Remove the multi-plug wiring harness from the ignition coil.
4. Unfasten the ignition coil mounting bolts, then remove the ignition coil.
5. Install in the reverse order of removal.

Ignition Module

➡ **The Ignition Control Module (ICM) on 3.0L Accord models that are equipped with a distributorless ignition, is incorporated into each individual ignition coil, and cannot be replaced separately from the ignition coil. If an ICM failure occurs, the ignition coil assembly must be replaced.**

Top Dead Center Sensors

Refer to Electronic Engine Controls in Section 4 for information on servicing the Top Dead Center (TDC) sensors.

Cylinder Position Sensor

Refer to Electronic Engine Controls in Section 4 for information on servicing the Cylinder Position (CYP) sensor.

Knock Sensor

Refer to Electronic Engine Controls in Section 4 for information on servicing the Knock Sensor (KS).

FIRING ORDERS

▶ **See Figures 33, 34 and 35**

➡**To avoid confusion, remove and tag the spark plug wires one at a time, for replacement.**

If a distributor is not keyed for installation with only one orientation, it could have been removed previously and rewired. The resultant wiring would hold the correct firing order, but could change the relative placement of the plug towers in relation to the engine. For this reason it is imperative that you label all wires before disconnecting any of them. Also, before removal, compare the current wiring with the accompanying illustrations. If the current wiring does not match, make notes in your book to reflect how your engine is wired.

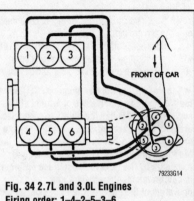

79233G15

Fig. 33 2.2L and 2.3L Engines
Firing order: 1–3–4–2
Distributor rotation: Clockwise

79233G14

Fig. 34 2.7L and 3.0L Engines
Firing order: 1–4–2–5–3–6
Distributor rotation: Counterclockwise

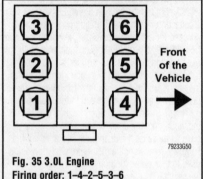

79233G50

Fig. 35 3.0L Engine
Firing order: 1–4–2–5–3–6
Distributorless ignition system (one coil per cylinder)

CHARGING SYSTEM

General Information

▶ **See Figures 36 and 37**

The charging system used on the Honda Accord and Prelude models is a 12 volt DC (Direct Current) negative (-) ground system. The system consists of an alternator with an internal voltage regulator, an alternator belt, a charging system light, an underhood fuse/relay box with a built-in Electrical Load Detector (ELD) Unit, and a battery.

The Powertrain Control Module (PCM) is used as part of the alternator control system by means of sending a signal to the voltage regulator. The signal is used by the regulator to change the voltage generated by the alternator according to the vehicle's operating conditions to improve fuel economy.

The alternator is mounted onto the engine and the alternator rotor is supported by two sealed bearings within the alternator housing. One end of the alternator rotor has two electrical contacts called slip rings, and the other end of the rotor's shaft protrudes through the alternator housing and has a pulley attached to it. The rotor shaft's pulley is belt-driven by another pulley that is attached to the engine's crankshaft.

The slip rings are electrical contacts that allow voltage to be supplied to the rotor's electrical windings while it spins. The voltage is supplied to the two slip rings via a pair of spring loaded brushes. The brushes are soft enough to not damage the slip rings, yet are made of a material that will conduct an electrical current. The rotor has an electrical winding that is surrounded by a series of metal fingers.

The initial voltage is supplied to the rotor from the battery and is called the excitation current. This electrical current is used to energize the field to begin the generation of electricity. When the electrical current is supplied to the rotor field winding via the slip rings, the rotor becomes an electromagnet. The rotor is surrounded by a series of small electrical coils called the stator assembly.

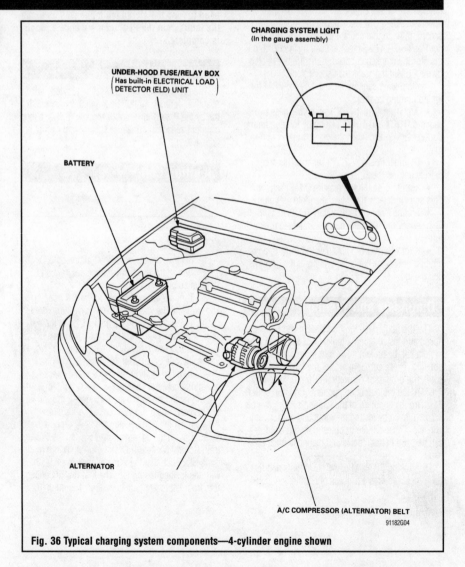

91182G04

Fig. 36 Typical charging system components—4-cylinder engine shown

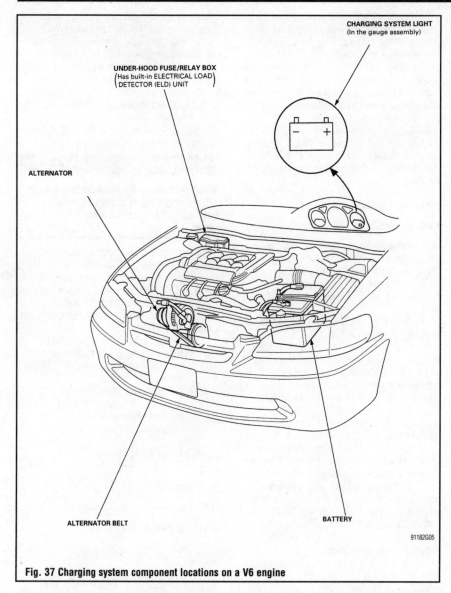

CHARGING SYSTEM LIGHT
(In the gauge assembly)

UNDER-HOOD FUSE/RELAY BOX
(Has built-in ELECTRICAL LOAD
DETECTOR (ELD) UNIT)

ALTERNATOR

ALTERNATOR BELT

BATTERY

91182G05

Fig. 37 Charging system component locations on a V6 engine

When the rotor spins, the magnetic field from the rotor is absorbed by the electrical coils of the stator assembly. This generates a series of positive and negative electrical pulses in the coils of the stator assembly creating an Alternating Current (AC) and AC voltage.

Because the vehicle's battery, electrical system and the electrical accessories are DC voltage, the AC voltage must be converted to DC voltage. The alternating current from the stator assembly is channeled through a series of diodes that are grouped together to form a component known as the rectifier. A diode is essentially a one way valve, and designed to allow current to pass in only one direction. The collection of diodes that form the rectifier assembly allows the current to flow in one direction, changing the electrical pulses from Alternating Current (AC voltage) to Direct Current (DC voltage). Once the alternator rotor begins to rotate and starts to generate electricity, the excitation current comes from its own output, rather than from the battery, although the battery remains as part of the electrical circuit.

Because the electrical needs of the vehicle change depending on operating conditions, the alternator's output needs to be regulated. To

accomplish this, a voltage regulator is used to control the alternator's output. To do this, the regulator controls the voltage to the alternator rotor, which regulates the alternator's output by controlling the strength of the magnetic field. The more voltage the rotor receives, the stronger the magnetic field, and the more electrical current the alternator provides. Conversely, the less voltage the rotor receives, the weaker the magnetic field, and the less electrical current the alternator provides.

The alternator is used to maintain the charge of the battery and to power the components of the electrical system. When the ignition key is turned **ON**, current flows from the battery, through the charging system indicator light on the instrument panel, and to the voltage regulator in the alternator. When the alternator rotor is not moving, the alternator is not producing an electrical current, and the alternator warning light remains on. When the engine is started, the alternator rotor begins to rotate. As the alternator rotor rotates, the alternator generates an electrical current and turns the alternator light off.

When the engine is running, the alternator produces an electrical current that is used to replenish the battery, which is drained slightly during start-up,

and to power the electrical components of the vehicle. The Powertrain Control Module (PCM) fine tunes the alternator output by monitoring the vehicle's electrical demands. The PCM sends a signal to the voltage regulator that allows the regulator to maximize the efficiency of the alternator to improve fuel economy.

Alternator Precautions

Several precautions must be observed with alternator equipped vehicles to avoid damage to the unit.
• ALWAYS observe proper polarity of the battery connections. Use extreme care when jump starting the car. Reversing the battery connections may cause the battery to explode, or result in damage to the one-way rectifiers.
• ALWAYS remove the battery or, at least, disconnect the cables while charging to avoid damaging the alternator.
• ALWAYS match and/or consider the polarity of the battery, alternator and regulator before making any electrical connections within the system.
• ALWAYS disconnect the battery ground terminal while repairing or replacing any electrical components.
• NEVER use a fast battery charger to jump start a vehicle with a dead battery.
• NEVER attempt to polarize an alternator.
• NEVER use test lights of more than 12 volts when checking diode continuity.
• NEVER ground or short out the alternator or regulator terminals.
• NEVER separate the alternator on an open circuit. Make sure all connections within the circuit are clean and tight.
• NEVER use arc welding equipment on the car with the battery cable, PCM or alternator connected.
• NEVER operate the alternator with any of its or the battery's lead wires disconnected.
• NEVER subject the alternator to excessive heat or dampness (for instance, steam cleaning the engine).
• When utilizing a booster battery as a starting aid, always connect the positive to positive terminals and the negative terminal from the booster battery to a good engine ground on the vehicle being started.

Alternator

TESTING

Voltage Drop Test

➡These tests will show the amount of voltage drop across the alternator output wire from the alternator output (B+) terminal to the battery positive post. They will also show the amount of voltage drop from the ground (-) terminal on the alternator.

A voltmeter with a 0–18 volt DC scale should be used for these tests. By repositioning the voltmeter test leads, the point of high resistance (voltage drop) can easily be found. Test points on the alternator can be reached by either removing the air cleaner housing or below by raising the vehicle.

1. Before starting the test, make sure the battery is in good condition and is fully charged. Check the conditions of the battery cables.

2. Start the engine, let it warm up to normal operating temperatures, then turn the engine **OFF**.

3. Connect an engine tachometer, following the manufacturer's directions.

4. Make sure the parking brake is fully engaged.

5. Start the engine, then place the blower on HIGH, and turn on the high beam headlamps and interior lamps.

6. Bring the engine speed up to 2,400 rpm and hold it there.

7. To test the ground (-) circuitry, perform the following:

   a. Touch the negative lead of the voltmeter directly to the positive battery terminal.

   b. Touch the positive lead of the voltmeter to the B+ output terminal stud on the alternator (NOT the terminal mounting nut). The voltage should be no higher than 0.6 volts. If the voltage is higher than 0.6 volts, touch the test lead to the terminal mounting stud nut, and then to the wiring connector. If the voltage is now below 0.6 volts, look for dirty, loose or poor connections at this point. A voltage drop test may be performed at each ground (-) connection in the circuit to locate the excessive resistance.

8. To test the positive (+) circuitry, perform the following:

   a. Touch the positive lead of the voltmeter directly to the negative battery terminal.

   b. Touch the negative lead of the voltmeter to the ground terminal stud on the alternator case

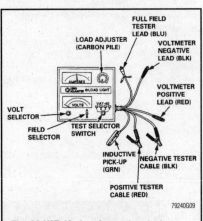

Fig. 38 VAT-40 charging system tester. Similar testers are available that perform as well

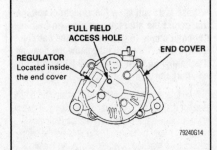

Fig. 39 A rear view of the alternator showing the regulator, end cover and full field access hole locations

(NOT the terminal mounting nut). The voltage should be no higher than 0.3 volts. If the voltage is higher than 0.3 volts, touch the test lead to the terminal mounting stud nut, and then to the wiring connector. If the voltage is now below 0.3 volts, look for dirty, loose or poor connections at this point. A voltage drop test may be performed at each positive (+) connection in the circuit to locate the excessive resistance.

9. This test can also be performed between the alternator case and the engine. If the test voltage is higher than 0.3 volts, check for corrosion at the alternator mounting points or loose alternator mounting.

Output Voltage Test

◀ **See Figures 38 and 39**

1. Before starting the test, make sure the battery is in good condition and is fully charged. Check the conditions of the battery cables.

2. Perform the voltage drop test to ensure clean and tight alternator/battery electrical connections.

3. Be sure the alternator drive belt is properly tensioned, as outlined in Section 1.

4. A volt/amp tester such as the VAT-40 or an equivalent, which is equipped with a battery load control (carbon pile rheostat), full field tester and an inductive-type pickup clamp (ammeter probe) is used for this test. Make sure to follows all directions supplied with the tester.

5. Start the engine and let it run until it reaches normal operating temperature.

6. Connect the VAT-40 or equivalent and turn the selector switch to position 1 (starting). Make sure all electrical accessories and lights are turned OFF.

7. Set the parking brake, place the transmission in Park or Neutral, and start the engine. Operate the throttle and hold the engine at 3,000 rpm with all accessories in the off position, until the radiator cooling fan comes on. Then allow the engine to idle for 15 seconds.

8. Raise the engine speed to 2,000 rpm and check the voltage. If the voltage is less than 15.1 volts, go to the next step. If the voltage is greater than 15.1 volts, replace the alternator.

9. Allow the engine to idle with all electrical accessories turned off. Turn the selector switch on the VAT-40 or equivalent to position 2 (charging).

10. Remove the inductive pick-up and zero the ammeter.

11. Place the inductive pick-up over the B ter-

minal wire from the alternator, making sure the arrow points away from the alternator.

12. Raise the engine speed to 2,000 rpm and read the voltage. If the voltage is 13.5 volts or greater, go to the next step. If the voltage is below 13.5 volts, replace the alternator.

13. Apply a load with the VAT-40 or equivalent until the battery voltage drops to between 12–13.5 volts. If the amperage output is 75 amps or more, the charging system is good. If the amperage output is below 75 amps, go to the next step.

※※ WARNING

When performing the full field test, do not allow the voltage to exceed 18 volts as damage to the electrical system may occur.

14. Perform a full field test by attaching the full field probe from the VAT-40 or equivalent into the full field terminal inside the full field access hole on the back of the alternator. Hold the engine speed to 2,000 rpm, switch the field selector to the A (Ground) position, check the amperage reading and compare with the following:

- Accord models: If the amperage is 65 amps or more, replace the voltage regulator. If the amperage is less than 65 amps, replace the alternator.
- Prelude models: If the amperage is 75 amps or more, replace the voltage regulator. If the amperage is less than 75 amps, replace the alternator.

REMOVAL & INSTALLATION

2.2L Engines

ACCORD

◀ **See Figures 40 thru 49**

1. Note the radio security code and the radio presets.

2. Disconnect the negative battery cable, then the positive.

3. Remove the power steering pump, for details, please refer to Section 8.

4. Detach the wiring from the alternator.

5. Loosen the through bolt, then loosen the adjustment locknut and the adjusting bolt.

6. Remove the alternator belt.

7. Remove all mounting and adjusting bolts

Fig. 40 Location of the alternator on most Honda 4 cylinder engines

Fig. 41 Remove the dust boot for access to wiring connection at the alternator

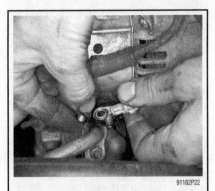

Fig. 42 Unfasten the nut, then remove the closed-ended connector

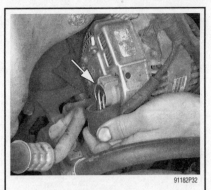

Fig. 43 Unplug the wiring harness from the rear of the alternator

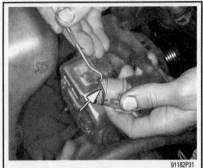

Fig. 44 Check the O-ring on the end of the wiring harness for cracks and or tears in the rubber. Replace as necessary

Fig. 45 After removing the retaining bolts, use a small prytool to remove the alternator from the pivot bracket if it is lodged

Fig. 46 Using both hands, firmly grasp the alternator and remove it from the vehicle

Fig. 47 Front view of a common Honda alternator

Fig. 48 Rear view of a common Honda alternator

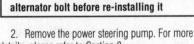

Fig. 49 Always inspect the integrity of the alternator bolt before re-installing it

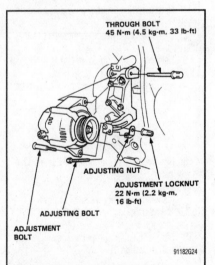

Fig. 50 Alternator mounting bolt locations—Prelude shown

and then remove the alternator unit from the vehicle.

To install:

8. Installation is the reverse of removal. Tighten the adjusting locknut to 16 ft. lbs. (22 Nm) and the through bolt to 33 ft. lbs. (45 Nm).

9. Adjust the alternator belt tension, as outlined in Section 1.

10. Enter the anti-theft code for the radio.

PRELUDE

♦ See Figure 50

1. Disconnect the negative battery cable, then the positive.

2. Remove the power steering pump. For more details, please refer to Section 8.

3. Detach the cruise control actuator, but do not remove the cable.

4. Loosen the through bolt, then loosen adjusting bolt.

5. Remove the alternator belt and the electrical connector.

6. Remove the adjusting bolt.

7. Remove the through bolt, then remove the alternator from the vehicle.

To install:

8. Installation is the reverse of removal. Tighten the alternator locknut to 16 ft. lbs. (22 Nm) and the mounting bolt to 33 ft. lbs. (45 Nm).

9. Adjust the alternator belt tension, as outlined in Section 1.

2.3L Engine

♦ See Figure 51

1. Note the radio security code and the radio presets.

2. Disconnect the negative, then the positive battery cables.

3. Detach the electrical wiring from the alternator.

4. Remove the adjusting bolt, locknut and the mounting bolt.

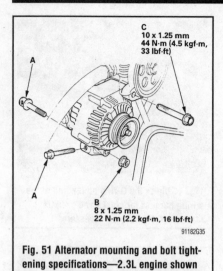

Fig. 51 Alternator mounting and bolt tightening specifications—2.3L engine shown

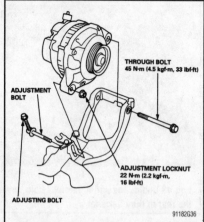

Fig. 52 Alternator mounting and bolt tightening specifications—2.7L engine shown

5. Remove the alternator belt.
6. Pull the alternator from the bracket and remove from the vehicle.

To install:

7. Installation is the reverse of removal. Tighten the adjusting locknut to 16 ft. lbs. (22 Nm) and the through bolt to 33 ft. lbs. (45 Nm).
8. Adjust the alternator belt tension, as outlined in Section 1.
9. Enter the anti-theft code for the radio.

2.7L Engine

▶ **See Figure 52**

1. Note the radio security code and the radio presets.
2. Disconnect the negative, then the positive battery cables.
3. Detach the 4-prong connector from the rear of the alternator.
4. Remove the terminal nut and wire from the alternator.
5. Loosen the bottom through bolt and then the adjusting bolt.
6. Remove the alternator belt.
7. Remove the adjusting bolt and locknut.
8. Remove the through bolt and then remove the alternator.

To install:

9. Installation is the reverse of removal. Tighten the adjusting locknut to 16 ft. lbs. (22 Nm) and the through bolt to 33 ft. lbs. (45 Nm).
10. After installation, properly tension the belt as outlined in Section 1.

3.0L Engine

▶ **See Figures 53, 54 and 55**

1. Note the radio security code and the radio presets.
2. Disconnect the negative, then the positive battery cables.
3. Relieve the alternator belt tension by pulling back on the tensioner, then remove the belt.
4. Detach the condenser fan motor connector from the shroud.
5. Remove the condenser fan assembly.
6. Unplug the 4-prong connector from the rear of the alternator.

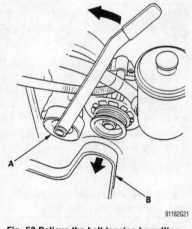

Fig. 53 Relieve the belt tension by pulling back on the tensioner, then remove the belt

7. Remove the alternator mounting bolts.
8. Remove the wiring harness clamp.
9. Remove the alternator assembly.

To install:

10. Alternator installation is the reverse of the removal procedure. Tighten the bolts to the specifications shown in the accompanying figure.
11. Connect the positive battery cable, then the negative battery cable. Enter the radio security code and station presets.

✳✳ WARNING

Be sure to adjust the alternator belt to the proper tension or alternator bearing failure may occur.

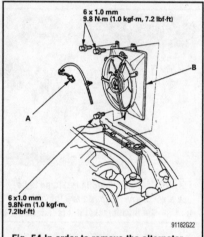

Fig. 54 In order to remove the alternator, you must first remove the condenser fan

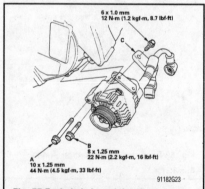

Fig. 55 Exploded view of the alternator mounting and bolt tightening specifications

STARTING SYSTEM

General Information

▶ **See Figures 56 and 57**

The battery and starter motor are linked by very heavy gauge electrical cables designed to minimize resistance to the flow of current. Generally, the major power supply cable that leaves the battery goes directly to the starter, while other electrical system needs are supplied by a smaller gauge cable. During starter operation, the positive (+) bat-

tery power flows from the battery to the starter solenoid, and the starter and is grounded through the engine which is grounded by the battery's negative ground strap.

The starter is a specially designed, direct current electric motor capable of producing a great amount of power for its size. What allows the motor to produce a great deal of power is its tremendous rotating speed. It drives the engine through a tiny pinion gear (attached to the starter's armature), that drives the very large flywheel ring gear at a greatly reduced

speed. Another factor allowing it to produce so much power is that only intermittent operation is required of it. Thus, little allowance for air circulation is necessary, and the windings can be built into a very small space.

The starter solenoid is an electromagnetic device that is triggered by the small current supplied by the start circuit of the ignition switch. This electromagnetic action moves a plunger that mechanically engages the starter gear and closes the high amperage switch connecting the starter to

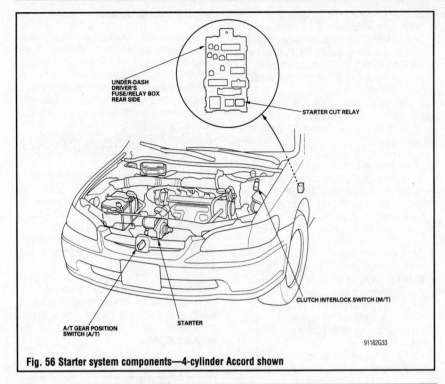

Fig. 56 Starter system components—4-cylinder Accord shown

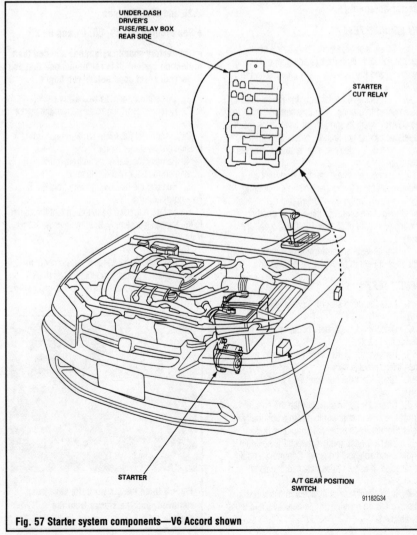

Fig. 57 Starter system components—V6 Accord shown

the battery. The starting switch circuit is part of the ignition switch. The starting circuit wiring includes a safety circuit, such as a neutral safety switch, or clutch pedal switch, that prevents the engine from being started with the transmission engaged. Also included in the starting circuit is the wiring necessary to connect these in series with the starter solenoid.

The pinion, a small gear, is mounted to a one-way drive clutch. This clutch is splined to the starter armature shaft. When the ignition switch is moved to the **START** position, the solenoid plunger slides the pinion toward the flywheel ring gear via a collar and spring. If the teeth on the pinion and flywheel match properly, the pinion will engage the flywheel immediately. If the gear teeth butt one another, the spring will be compressed and will force the gears to mesh as soon as the starter turns far enough to allow them to do so. As the solenoid plunger reaches the end of its travel, it closes the contacts that connect the battery to the starter, and then the engine is cranked.

As soon as the engine starts, the flywheel ring gear begins turning fast enough to drive the pinion at an extremely high rate of speed. At this point, the one-way clutch begins allowing the pinion to spin faster than the starter shaft so that the starter will not operate at excessive speed. When the ignition switch is released from the start position, the solenoid is de-energized, and a spring pulls the gear out of mesh, interrupting the current flow to the starter.

Some starters employ a separate relay, mounted away from the starter, to switch the motor and solenoid current on and off. The relay replaces the solenoid electrical switch, but does not eliminate the need for a solenoid mounted on the starter used to mechanically engage the starter drive gears. The relay is used to reduce the amount of current the start position of the ignition switch must carry.

Starter

TESTING

Testing Preparation

➡**The air temperature should be between 59–100°F before any testing.**

The starting system consists of an ignition switch, starter relay, neutral safety switch, wiring harness, battery, and a starter motor with an integral solenoid. These components form two separate circuits: a high amperage circuit that feeds the starter motor up to 300 or more amps, and a control circuit that operates on less than 20 amps.

Before commencing with the starting system diagnostics, verify:

• The battery top posts and terminals are clean.
• The alternator drive belt tension and condition is correct.
• The battery state-of-charge is correct.
• The battery cable connections at the starter and engine block are clean and free from corrosion.
• The wiring harness connectors and terminals are clean and free from corrosion.
• Proper circuit grounding.

Starter Feed Circuit

> ✻✻ **CAUTION**
>
> **The ignition system must be disabled to prevent engine start while performing the following tests.**

1. Connect a volt-ampere tester (multimeter) to the battery terminals.
2. Disable the ignition system.
3. Verify that all lights and accessories are off, and the transaxle shift selector is in Park (automatic) or Neutral (manual). Set the parking brake.
4. Rotate and hold the ignition switch in the **START** position. Observe the volt-ampere tester:
   - If the voltage reads above 9.6 volts, and the amperage draw reads above 250 amps, go to the starter feed circuit resistance test (following this test).
   - If the voltage reads 12.4 volts or greater and the amperage reads 0–10 amps, refer to the starter solenoid and relay tests.

> ✻✻ **WARNING**
>
> **Do not overheat the starter motor or draw the battery voltage below 9.6 volts during cranking operations.**

5. After the starting system problems have been corrected, verify the battery state of charge and charge the battery if necessary. Disconnect all of the testing equipment and connect the ignition coil cable or ignition coil connector. Start the vehicle several times to assure the problem was corrected.

Starter Feed Circuit Resistance

Before proceeding with this test, refer to the battery tests and starter feed circuit test. The following test will require a voltmeter, which is capable of accuracy to 0.1 volt.

> ✻✻ **CAUTION**
>
> **The ignition system must be disabled to prevent engine start while performing the following tests.**

1. Disable the ignition system.
2. With all wiring harnesses and components (except for the coils) properly connected, perform the following:
   a. Connect the negative (-) lead of the voltmeter to the negative battery post, and the positive (+) lead to the negative (-) battery cable clamp. Rotate and hold the ignition switch in the **START** position. Observe the voltmeter. If the voltage is detected, correct the poor contact between the cable clamp and post.
   b. Connect the positive (+) lead of the voltmeter to the positive battery post, and the negative (-) to the positive battery cable clamp. Rotate and hold the ignition switch key in the **START** position. Observe the voltmeter. If voltage is detected, correct the poor contact between the cable clamp and post.
   c. Connect the negative lead of the voltmeter to the negative (-) battery terminal, and positive lead to the engine block near the battery cable

attaching point. Rotate and hold the ignition switch in the **START** position. If the voltage reads above 0.2 volt, correct the poor contact at ground cable attaching point. If the voltage reading is still above 0.2 volt after correcting the poor contact, replace the negative ground cable with a new one.
3. Remove the heater shield. Refer to removal and installation procedures to gain access to the starter motor and solenoid connections. Perform the following steps:
   a. Connect the positive (+) voltmeter lead to the starter motor housing and the negative (-) lead to the negative battery terminal. Hold the ignition switch key in the **START** position. If the voltage reads above 0.2 volt, correct the poor starter to engine ground.
   b. Connect the positive (+) voltmeter lead to the positive battery terminal, and the negative lead to the battery cable terminal on the starter solenoid. Rotate and hold the ignition key in the **START** position. If the voltage reads above 0.2 volt, correct poor contact at the battery cable to the solenoid connection. If the reading is still above 0.2 volt after correcting the poor contacts, replace the positive battery cable with a new one.
   c. If the resistance tests did not detect feed circuit failures, refer to the starter solenoid test.

Starter Solenoid

ON VEHICLE TEST

1. Before testing, assure the parking brake is set, the transaxle is in Park (automatic) or Neutral (manual), and the battery is fully charged and in good condition.
2. Connect a voltmeter from the (S) terminal on the solenoid to ground. Turn the ignition switch to the **START** position and test for battery voltage. If battery voltage is not found, inspect the ignition switch circuit. If battery voltage is found, proceed to next step.
3. Connect an ohmmeter between the battery negative post and the starter solenoid mounting plate (manual) or the ground terminal (automatic). Turn the ignition switch to the **START** position. The ohmmeter should read zero (0). If not, repair the faulty ground.
4. If both tests are performed and the solenoid still does not energize, replace the solenoid.

BENCH TEST

1. Note the radio security code and the radio presets.
2. Disconnect the battery negative cable then the positive cable.
3. Remove the starter from the vehicle, as outlined later in this section.
4. Disconnect the field coil wire from the field coil terminal.
5. Check for continuity between the solenoid terminal and field coil terminal with a continuity tester. Continuity (resistance) should be present.
6. Check for continuity between the solenoid terminal and solenoid housing. Continuity should be detected. If continuity is detected, the solenoid is good.
7. If continuity is not detected in either test, the solenoid has an open circuit, is defective, and must be replaced.

Starter/Ground Cable Test

When performing these tests, it is important that the voltmeter be connected to the terminals, not the cables themselves.

Before testing, assure that the ignition control module (if equipped) is disconnected, the parking brake is set, the transaxle is in Park (automatic) or Neutral (manual), and the battery is fully charged and in good condition.

1. Check voltage between the positive battery post and the center of the B+ terminal on the starter solenoid stud.
2. Check voltage between the negative battery post and the engine block.
3. Disconnect the ignition coil wire from the distributor cap and connect a suitable jumper wire between the coil cable and a good body ground.
4. Have an assistant crank the engine and measure voltage again. Voltage drop should not exceed 0.5 volts.
5. If voltage drop is greater than 0.5 volts, clean metal surfaces. Apply a thick layer of silicone grease. Install a new cadmium plated bolt and star washer on the battery terminal and a new brass nut on the starter solenoid. Retest and replace cable not within specifications.

REMOVAL & INSTALLATION

2.2L and 2.3L Engines

▶ **See Figures 58, 59, 60, 61 and 62**

➡ **The factory sound system has a coded theft protection system. It is recommended that you know your reset code before you begin.**

1. Disconnect the negative battery cable.
2. Remove the wiring harness from the starter motor.
3. Disconnect the lower radiator hose from the bracket on the starter motor.
4. Remove the starter cable from terminal B located on the back of the solenoid.
5. Remove the black/white wire from the S (solenoid) terminal.
6. Unfasten the two bolts that mount the starter to the transaxle assembly, then remove the starter from the vehicle.

To install:

7. Install the starter in the reverse order of removal. Tighten the starter mounting bolts to 33 ft. lbs. (45 Nm) and the wire terminal nut to 7 ft. lbs. (9 Nm).

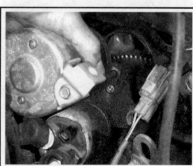

91182P56

Fig. 58 Once the starter bolts have been removed, pull the starter from the vehicle . . .

Fig. 59 . . . and direct the starter between the air conditioning lines and the motor mount to remove it

Fig. 60 View of the starter and solenoid

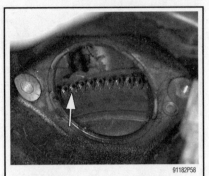

Fig. 61 While the starter is removed, check the engine flywheel teeth for cracks and or chips

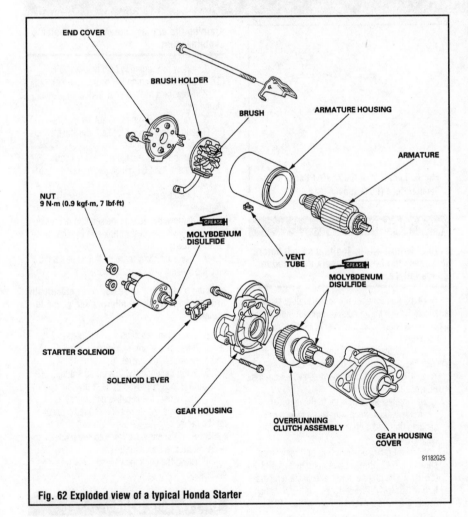

Fig. 62 Exploded view of a typical Honda Starter

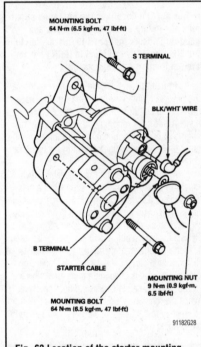

Fig. 63 Location of the starter mounting bolts and wiring

→When installing the heavy gauge starter cable, make sure the crimped side of the terminal end is facing out.

8. Enter the anti-theft code and radio presets.

2.7L Engine

♦ See Figure 63

→The factory sound system has a coded theft protection system. It is recommended that you know your reset code before you begin.

1. Disconnect the negative, then the positive battery cable.
2. Remove the wiring harness from the starter motor.
3. Remove the starter cable from terminal B located on the back of the solenoid.
4. Remove the black/white wire from the S (solenoid) terminal.
5. Unfasten the two bolts that mount the starter the transaxle assembly, then remove the starter.

To install:

6. Install the starter in the reverse order of removal. Torque the starter mounting bolts to 47 ft. lbs. (64 Nm) and the terminal mounting nut to 6.5 ft. lbs. (9 Nm).

→When installing the heavy gauge starter cable, make sure the crimped side of the terminal end is facing out.

7. Enter the anti-theft code and radio presets.

3.0L Engine

♦ See Figure 64

→The factory sound system has a coded theft protection system. It is recommended that you know your reset code before you begin.

1. Disconnect the negative battery cable. Then the positive cable.
2. Remove the Automatic Transmission Fluid (ATF) cooler.
3. Remove the starter cable from terminal B located on the back of the solenoid.

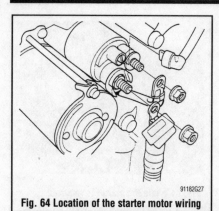

Fig. 64 Location of the starter motor wiring

4. Remove the black/white wire from the S (solenoid) terminal.

5. Unfasten the two bolts that mount the starter to the transaxle assembly, then remove the starter.

To install:

6. Install the starter in the reverse order of removal. Tighten the starter mounting bolts to 33 ft. lbs. (45 Nm) and the wire terminal nut to 7 ft. lbs. (9 Nm).

➡When installing the heavy gauge starter cable, make sure the crimped side of the terminal end is facing out.

7. Enter the anti-theft code and radio presets.

SENDING UNITS

➡This section describes the operating principles of sending units, warning lights and gauges. Sensors that provide information to the Electronic Control Module (ECM) are covered in Section 4 of this manual.

Instrument panels contain a number of indicating devices (gauges and warning lights). These devices are composed of two separate components. One is the sending unit, mounted on the engine or other remote part of the vehicle, and the other is the actual gauge or light in the instrument panel.

Several types of sending units exist, however most can be characterized as being either a pressure type or a resistance type. Pressure type sending units convert liquid pressure into an electrical signal that is sent to the gauge or warning light. Resistance type sending units are most often used to measure temperature and use variable resistance to control the current flow back to the indicating device. Both types of sending units are connected in series to the gauge or warning light by a wire. When the ignition is turned **ON**, current flows from the battery to the gauge or warning light and on to the sending unit.

Engine Coolant Temperature Sending Unit

The coolant temperature information is conveyed to the instrument panel, through the PCM, from the Engine Coolant Temperature (ECT) gauge sending unit. To test the gauge sending unit, first test the gauge operation to make sure the problem is not in the gauge or gauge wiring. To test the gauge operation, perform the following procedures.

TESTING

◆ **See Figure 65**

1. Check the fuses before testing.

2. With the ignition switch **OFF**, disconnect the wire from the ECT gauge sending unit. Then ground it to a place on the engine block (or other known good ground) with a jumper wire.

3. Turn the ignition switch to the **ON** position.

4. Watch the Engine Coolant Temperature (ECT) gauge. It should start moving towards the hot ("H") mark.

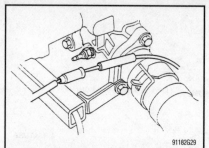

Fig. 65 Location of the Engine Coolant Temperature (ECT) sensor

❊❊ WARNING

Failure to turn off the ignition switch before it reaches the hot ("H") mark may lead to gauge failure.

5. If the pointer does not move at all or moves erratically, check for an open or point of high resistance in the wire. If the wire checks out OK, replace the gauge.

6. If the above steps did not reveal the problem, the test the gauge sending unit as follows:

a. Disconnect the yellow/green wire from the ECT gauge sending unit.

b. Connect an ohmmeter to the terminal where the yellow/green wire was attached to the sending unit and a good known ground on the engine block.

c. The ECT gauge sending unit resistance should be 142 ohms at a temperature of 133°F (56°C). If the engine is hot and has a temperature of 185–212°F (85–100°C) the ECT gauge sending unit resistance should be 32–49 ohms.

REMOVAL & INSTALLATION

◆ **See Figure 65**

❊❊ CAUTION

Engine coolant can spray out causing severe burns if the Engine Coolant Temperature (ECT) gauge sending unit is removed from a hot engine without allowing the engine to cool below 100°F (37°C) and

draining the engine coolant into a sealable container first.

1. Allow the engine to cool below 100°F (37°C) before working on the cooling system.

2. Note the anti-theft code and radio presets for the radio.

3. Locate the Engine Coolant Temperature (ECT) gauge sending unit located near the thermostat housing on the engine.

4. Disconnect the negative battery cable.

5. Detach the ECT gauge sending unit electrical connection.

6. Drain the engine coolant into a sealable container.

7. Remove the ECT gauge sending unit using a pressure switch socket or box-end wrench.

To install:

8. Use a sensor safe liquid thread sealant to coat the threads before installation.

➡Using a tape-type of sealant may electrically insulate the sensor not allowing the gauge to register.

9. Install the new sensor and tighten to 7 ft. lbs. (9 Nm) using a box-end wrench or sending unit pressure switch socket.

10. Refill the engine with a 50/50 solution of water and Honda approved or an equivalent coolant.

11. Reconnect the negative battery cable.

12. Enter the anti-theft code and radio presets for the radio.

13. Start the engine, allow it to reach operating temperature and check for leaks.

14. Bleed the cooling system to remove air as necessary.

Oil Pressure Sender

TESTING

◆ **See Figure 66**

The low oil pressure warning lamp will illuminate anytime the ignition switch is turned to the **ON** position without the engine running. When the engine is running, the light also illuminates if the engine oil pressure drops below a safe oil pressure level. To test the system, perform the following:

If the oil pressure light does not work, perform the following:

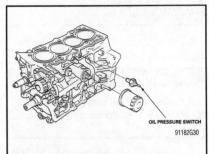

Fig. 66 Location of the oil pressure switch/sender

1. Turn the ignition switch to the **ON** position.
2. If the lamp does not light, check for a broken or disconnected wire around the engine and oil pressure sending unit switch.
3. If the wire at the connector checks out OK, pull the connector loose from the switch and, with a jumper wire, ground the connector to the engine.
4. With the ignition switch turned to the **ON** position, check the warning lamp. If the lamp lights, make sure the oil pressure switch is properly grounded in the cylinder block, and if so replace the oil pressure switch. If the lamp still fails to light, check for a burned out lamp or disconnected socket in the instrument cluster.

To diagnose an oil pressure light that stays on, perform the following:

5. Check the engine oil level and top off as necessary. If the engine was 2 or more quarts low on oil, test start the engine after topping off the oil level and recheck the oil pressure light operation. If the light stays on, stop the engine immediately and go to the next step.
6. Disconnect the wire at the sending unit, then turn the ignition switch to the **ON** position. If the light remains on, check the wire from the sending unit to the gauge for being shorted to ground and repair as necessary. If the light goes out, turn the ignition switch **OFF** and go to the next step.
7. Replace the oil pressure sending switch with a known good switch.
8. Start the engine and check the oil pressure light operation. If the light stays on with the engine running, stop the engine immediately to avoid severe engine damage until the cause of the problem can be determined.

✳✳ WARNING

If the oil pressure light remains on while the engine is started, stop the engine immediately. Do not operate the engine until the cause of the problem can be determined. Operating an engine with low oil pressure will cause severe internal damage.

Possible causes for an oil pressure light to stay on are:
- Pinched or grounded sensor wire
- Defective oil pressure sending unit
- Restricted or severely leaking oil filter
- Excessive internal engine bearing clearance.
- Insufficient or severely contaminated engine oil
- Blocked oil pump pickup screen or severely worn oil pump

REMOVAL & INSTALLATION

♦ See Figure 66

1. Locate the oil pressure sending unit on the engine.
2. Note the anti-theft code and radio presets for the radio.
3. Disconnect the negative battery cable.
4. Disconnect the sending unit electrical harness.
5. Using a pressure switch socket, deep-well socket or wrench, loosen and remove the sending unit from the engine.

To install:

6. Apply a liquid thread sealant to the sending unit and install the sending unit in the engine and tighten securely.
7. Attach the electrical connector to the sending unit.
8. Check the engine oil level and top off as necessary.
9. Connect the negative battery cable.
10. Enter the anti-theft code and radio presets for the radio.
11. Start the engine, allow it to reach operating temperature and check for leaks.
12. Check for proper sending unit operation.

Cooling Fan Switch

The electric cooling fan switch is installed into a coolant passage of the engine near the thermostat housing and operates the radiator electric cooling fans when the coolant temperature reaches a specified temperature.

➡**If the air conditioner is in proper working order, the engine cooling fans will operate when the air conditioner is turned on, regardless of the coolant temperature. When testing the electric cooling fan switch, make sure the air conditioner is OFF.**

Below the specified temperature the switch is off (open), and at or above the specified temperature, the switch is on (closed), and completes a series circuit that triggers the cooling fan relay allowing the cooling fan to operate.

TESTING

✳✳ WARNING

Use care when testing the radiator cooling fans as the fan blades have sharp edges and with the vehicle's battery connected, the cooling fans could begin to operate without notice. Always keep hands, fingers, tools, clothing or other objects away from the cooling fans at all times. Failure to observe this warning could lead to personal and/or equipment damage.

Switch Installed

SINGLE SWITCH MODELS

1. Locate the cooling fan switch near the thermostat housing on the left side of engine behind the distributor assembly. The switch wire colors should be green and black.

2. Disconnect the wire terminal from the cooling fan switch.
3. Allow the engine to reach a coolant temperature of 196–203°F (91–95°C).
4. Using a suitable ohmmeter or continuity tester, check for continuity between the two fan switch terminals. The fan switch should have continuity (switch closed) at the above temperatures. The switch should have no continuity (switch open) when the temperature drops between 5–15°F (3–8°C) from the temperature that the switch first had continuity (switch closed).
5. If the switch does not operate within the range of the supplied information, allow the engine to cool below 100°F (37°C) and replace the switch.

DUAL SWITCH MODELS

Some models have two electric cooling fan switches, switch A and switch B.

1. Locate the cooling fan switch near the thermostat housing as follows:
   a. Switch A: Left side of engine behind the distributor assembly, facing up. The switch wire colors are green and black.
   b. Switch B: Left side of engine behind the distributor assembly, facing the firewall. The switch wire colors are white/green and black.
2. Disconnect the electric wire terminal from the cooling fan switch to be tested.
3. Allow the engine to reach a coolant temperature of:
   a. Switch A: 196–203°F (91–95°C)
   b. Switch B: 217–228°F (103–109°C)
4. Using a suitable ohmmeter or continuity tester, check for continuity between the two fan switch terminals. The fan switch should have continuity (switch closed) at the above temperatures.
5. The switch should have no continuity (switch open) when the temperature drops between:
   a. Switch A: When the temperature drops between 5–15°F (3–8°C) from the temperature that the switch had continuity (switch closed).
   b. Switch B: When the temperature drops between 7–16°F (4–9°C) from the temperature that the switch had continuity (switch closed).
6. If the switch does not operate within the range of the supplied information, allow the engine to cool below 100°F (37°C) and replace the switch.

Switch Removed

♦ See Figure 67

✳✳ WARNING

Submerging the electric cooling fan switch below the threads could damage the component. Coolant must be used for this test as the boiling point of water is below the temperature required for testing some of the sensors. Perform this procedure in a safe and well-ventilated area. Do not breathe any fumes from the heated coolant. Wear eye protection and use care to not come in contact with any of the heated components. Do not use a heating device that produces an open flame.

Testing a radiator fan switch is not difficult, however to do so requires some basic equipment. To properly test the fan switch, the switch's probe must

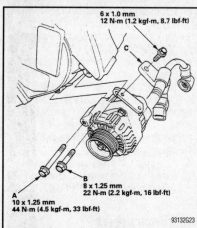

6 x 1.0 mm
12 N·m (1.2 kgf·m, 8.7 lbf·ft)

C

B
8 x 1.25 mm
22 N·m (2.2 kgf·m, 16 lbf·ft)

A
10 x 1.25 mm
44 N·m (4.5 kgf·m, 33 lbf·ft)

93132G23

Fig. 67 Cooling fan switch testing—switch removed from vehicle

be submersed in coolant, only as far as the component's threads. The coolant must be heated and the temperature monitored. When the coolant reaches the specified temperature, the fan switch should be closed. Testing the switch requires the following equipment:

• A safe source of heat, such as a portable electric hot plate

• A container capable of being safely heated by a hot plate and handling heated coolant

• A thermometer safely capable of reading 228°F (109°C)

• A device to safely hold the switch such that only the coolant probe is submerged into the water

• An ohmmeter or continuity tester

1. Refer to the cooling fan switch removal and installation warning and procedures and remove the switch.

Attach a 12 inch wiring sub-harness to the cooling fan switch to avoid having to probe the switch while in the heated coolant. Place the switch into a suitable holding device such that the coolant probe of the switch is submersed in a container of coolant. Make sure the container can be safely heated using a suitable source of heat such as a portable electric hot plate.

2. Using a suitable thermometer to measure the coolant temperature, heat the coolant until the specified temperature is attained.

3. When the specified coolant temperature is attained, using an ohmmeter or a continuity tester, check the continuity between the ends of the two-wire sub-harness attached to the terminals of the switch.

➡**Refer to the information in this section for test temperatures and continuity results.**

REMOVAL & INSTALLATION

The electric cooling fan switches are mounted into the engine cooling system passages.

✳✳ WARNING

When removing a fan switch, make sure the coolant temperature is below 100°F (38°C).

1. Note the radio security code and radio station presets.

2. Disconnect the negative battery cable.

3. Drain the coolant from the radiator drain petcock into a suitable and sealable container.

4. Locate the fan switch, then disconnect the wire terminal from the fan switch

5. Remove the switch using a sensor socket or box-end wrench.

To install:

6. Installation is the reverse of the removal procedure.

7. Reconnect the negative battery cable.

8. Top off coolant level and bleed cooling system as necessary.

9. Enter the radio security code and radio presets.

3

ENGINE AND ENGINE OVERHAUL

ENGINE MECHANICAL

2.2L ENGINE MECHANICAL SPECIFICATIONS

Description	English Specifications	Metric Specifications
Compression		
Pressure check @ 200 rpm wide open throttle		
Nominal	178 psi	1230 kPa
Minimum	135 psi	930 kPa
Maximum variation	28 psi	200 kPa
Cylinder Head		
Warpage	0.02 in.	0.05mm
Height	3.935-3.939 in.	99.95-100.05mm
Camshaft		
Endplay	0.02 in.	0.5mm
Camshaft to holder oil clearance	0.006 in.	0.15mm
Total runout	0.002 in.	0.04mm
Camshaft lobe height		
F22B1 engine		
Intake		
Primary	1.4872 in.	37.775mm
Middle	1.5640 in.	39.725mm
Secondary	1.3575 in.	34.481mm
Exhaust	1.5105 in.	38.366mm
F22B2		
Intake	1.5168 in.	38.526mm
Exhaust	1.5267 in.	38.778mm
Valves		
Clearance (cold)		
Intake	0.009-0.011 in.	0.24-0.28mm
Exhaust	0.011-0.013 in.	0.28-0.32mm
Stem O.D.		
Intake	0.2148 in.	5.455mm
Exhaust	0.2134 in.	5.420mm
Stem to guide clearance		
Intake	0.003 in.	0.08 mm
Exhaust	0.005 in.	0.012mm
Valve Seats		
Width		
Intake	0.079 in.	2.00mm
Exhaust	0.079 in.	2.00mm
Stem installed height		
F22B1 engine		
Intake	1.921 in.	48.80mm
Exhaust	1.879 in.	47.73mm
F22B2 engine		
Intake	1.934 in.	49.13mm
Exhaust	2.016 in.	51.20mm
Valve springs		
Free length		
F22B1 engine		
Intake	2.011 in.	51.08mm
Exhaust	2.188 in.	55.58mm
F22B2 engine		
Intake		
Except associated spring mfg.	2.103 in.	53.42mm
Associated spring mfg.	2.158 in.	54.82mm

9118SC01

2.2L ENGINE MECHANICAL SPECIFICATIONS

Description	English Specifications	Metric Specifications
Valve springs (cont.)		
F22B2 engine		
Exhaust		
Except associated spring mfg.	2.152 in.	54.66mm
Associated spring mfg.	2.216 in.	56.28mm
Valve guides		
I.D.		
Intake	0.219 in.	5.55mm
Exhaust	0.219 in.	5.55mm
Installed height		
F22B1 engine		
Intake	0.835-0.874 in.	21.20-22.20mm
Exhaust	0.812-0.852 in.	20.63-21.63mm
F22B2 engine		
Intake	0.925-0.965 in.	23.50-24.50mm
Exhaust	0.583-0.622 in.	14.80-15.80mm
Rocker arms		
Arm-to-shaft clearance		
Intake	0.003 in.	0.08mm
Exhaust	0.003 in.	0.08mm
Block		
Deck warpage	0.004 in.	0.10mm
Bore diameter		
A or I	3.3492 in.	85.070mm
B or II	3.3492 in.	85.070mm
Bore taper	0.002 in.	0.05mm
Reboring limit	0.02 in.	0.5mm
Piston		
Skirt (O.D. measured 0.8 in (21mm) from bottom of skirt)		
No letter	3.3453 in.	84.970mm
Letter B	3.3449 in.	84.960mm
Clearance in cylinder	0.002 in.	0.05mm
Ring groove width		
Top	0.049 in.	1.25mm
Second	0.049 in.	1.25mm
Oil	0.112 in.	2.85mm
Piston rings		
Ring-to-groove clearance		
Top	0.005 in.	0.13mm
Second	0.005 in.	0.13mm
Ring end gap		
Top	0.024 in.	0.60mm
Second	0.028 in.	0.70mm
Oil	0.031 in.	0.80mm
Piston pin		
O.D.	0.8659-0.8661 in.	21.994-22.00mm
Pin-to-piston clearance	0.0004-0.0009 in.	0.010-0.022mm
Connecting rod		
Pin-to-rod clearance	0.0005-0.0013 in.	0.013-0.032mm
Small end bore diameter	0.8649-0.8654 in.	21.968-21.981mm
Large end bore diameter	2.01 in.	51.0mm
Enplay installed on crankshaft	0.016 in.	0.40mm

9118SC02

2.3L ENGINE MECHANICAL SPECIFICATIONS

Description	English Specifications	Metric Specifications
Compression		
Pressure check @ 200 rpm wide open throttle		
Nominal	178 psi	1230 kPa
Minimum	135 psi	930 kPa
Maximum variation	28 psi	200 kPa
Cylinder Head		
Warpage	0.02 in.	0.05mm
Height	3.935-3.939 in.	99.95-100.05mm
Camshaft		
Endplay	0.02 in.	0.5mm
Camshaft to holder oil clearance	0.006 in.	0.15mm
Total runout	0.002 in.	0.04mm
Camshaft lobe height		
VTEC		
Intake		
Primary	1.4872 in.	37.775mm
Middle	1.5640 in.	39.725mm
Secondary	1.3575 in.	34.481mm
Exhaust		
VTEC exhaust	1.5105 in.	38.366mm
Intake	1.5094 in.	38.339mm
Exhaust	1.4849 in.	37.716mm
Valves		
Clearance (cold)		
Intake	0.009-0.011 in.	0.24-0.28mm
Exhaust	0.011-0.013 in.	0.28-0.32mm
Stem O.D.		
Intake	0.2148 in.	5.455mm
Exhaust	0.2134 in.	5.420mm
Stem to guide clearance		
Intake	0.003 in.	0.08 mm
Exhaust	0.005 in.	0.012mm
Valve Seats		
Width		
Intake	0.079 in.	2.00mm
Exhaust	0.079 in.	2.00mm
Stem installed height		
Intake	1.882 in.	47.80mm
Exhaust	1.879 in.	47.73mm
Valve springs		
Free length		
VTEC		
Intake	2.011 in.	51.08mm
Exhaust	2.188 in.	55.58mm
NON-VTEC		
Intake	2.113 in.	53.66mm
Exhaust	2.188 in.	55.58mm

2.2L ENGINE MECHANICAL SPECIFICATIONS

Description	English Specifications	Metric Specifications
Crankshaft		
Main journal diameter		
No. 1	1.9679-1.9688 in.	49.984-50.008mm
No. 2	1.9676-1.9685 in.	49.976-50.000mm
No. 4	1.9679-1.9688 in.	49.984-50.008mm
No. 3	1.9674-1.9683 in.	49.972-49.996mm
No. 5	1.9680-1.9690 in.	49.988-50.012mm
Rod journal diameter	1.8888-1.8898 in.	47.976-48.000mm
Rod/main journal taper	0.0002 in.	0.006mm
Rod/main journal out or round	0.0002 in.	0.006mm
Endplay	0.018 in.	0.45mm
Runout	0.002 in.	0.04mm
Crankshaft bearing		
Main bearing-to-journal oil clearance		
No. 1	0.0020 in.	0.050mm
No. 2	0.0020 in.	0.050mm
No. 4	0.0020 in.	0.050mm
No. 3	0.022 in.	0.055mm
No. 5	0.0016 in.	0.40mm
Rod bearing clearance	0.0024 in.	0.060mm
Balancer shaft		
Journal diameter		
No. 1 front	1.681 in.	42.71mm
No. 1 rear	0.824 in.	20.92mm
No. 2 front and rear	1.524 in.	38.70mm
No. 3 front and rear	1.367 in.	34.71mm
Balancer shaft		
Journal taper	0.0002 in.	0.005mm
Endplay		
Front	0.004-0.016 in.	0.10-0.40mm
Rear	0.002-0.006 in.	0.04-0.15mm
Total runout	0.001 in.	0.03mm
Shaft to bearing oil clearance		
No. 1, No. 3 front and rear	0.005 in.	0.12mm
No. 1 rear	0.004 in.	0.09mm
No. 2 front and rear	0.005 in.	0.13mm
Balancer shaft bearing		
I.D.		
No. 1 front	1.686 in.	42.83mm
No. 1 rear	0.828 in.	21.02mm
No. 2 front and rear	1.529 in.	38.83mm
No. 3 front and rear	1.371 in.	34.83mm
Oil pump		
Inner-to-outer rotor clearance	0.008 in.	0.20mm
Pump housing-to-outer rotor clearance	0.008 in.	0.21mm
Pump housing-to-outer rotor axial clearance	0.005 in.	0.12mm
Relief valve		
Check with the oil temp. at 176 deg. F or 80 deg. C		
Idle	10 psi min.	70 kPa min.
3000 rpm	50 psi min.	340 kPa min.

91183C03

91183C04

2.3L ENGINE MECHANICAL SPECIFICATIONS

Description	English Specifications	Metric Specifications
Valve guides		
I.D.		
Intake	0.219 in.	5.55mm
Exhaust	0.219 in.	5.55mm
Installed height		
Intake	0.835-0.874 in.	21.20-22.20mm
Exhaust	0.812-0.852 in.	20.63-21.63mm
Rocker arms		
Arm-to-shaft clearance		
Intake	0.003 in.	0.08mm
Exhaust	0.003 in.	0.08mm
Block		
Deck warpage	0.004 in.	0.10mm
Bore diameter		
A or I	3.3886 in.	86.070mm
B or II	3.3886 in.	86.070mm
Bore taper	0.002 in.	0.05mm
Reboring limit	0.01 in.	0.25mm
Piston		
Skirt		
No letter	3.3846 in.	85.970mm
Letter B	3.3842 in.	85.960mm
Clearance in cylinder	0.002 in.	0.05mm
Ring groove width		
Top	0.049 in.	1.25mm
Second	0.049 in.	1.25mm
Oil	0.112 in.	2.85mm
Piston rings		
Ring-to-groove clearance		
Top	0.005 in.	0.13mm
Second	0.005 in.	0.13mm
Ring end gap		
Top	0.024 in.	0.60mm
Second	0.028 in.	0.70mm
Oil	0.031 in.	0.80mm
Piston pin		
O.D.	0.8643 in.	21.954mm
Pin-to-piston clearance	0.0002 in.	0.004mm
Connecting rod		
Pin-to-rod clearance	0.0007 in.	0.019mm
Small end bore diameter	0.8650-0.8652 in.	21.970-21.976mm
Enplay installed on crankshaft	0.006-0.012 in.	0.15-0.30mm

91183C05

2.3L ENGINE MECHANICAL SPECIFICATIONS

Description	English Specifications	Metric Specifications
Crankshaft		
Main journal diameter		
No. 1	2.1655-2.1646 in.	54.980-55.004mm
No. 2	2.1655-2.1646 in.	54.980-55.004mm
No. 4	2.1655-2.1646 in.	54.980-55.004mm
No. 3	2.1644-2.1654 in.	54.976-55.000mm
No. 5	2.1650-2.1660 in.	54.992-55.016mm
Rod journal diameter	1.7707-1.7717 in.	44.976-45.000mm
Rod/main journal taper	0.0002 in.	0.006mm
Rod/main journal out or round	0.0002 in.	0.006mm
Endplay	0.018 in.	0.45mm
Runout	0.002 in.	0.04mm
Crankshaft bearing		
Main bearing-to-journal oil clearance		
No. 1	0.0020 in.	0.050mm
No. 2	0.0020 in.	0.050mm
No. 4	0.0020 in.	0.050mm
No. 3	0.022 in.	0.055mm
No. 5	0.0016 in.	0.40mm
Rod bearing clearance	0.0024 in.	0.060mm
Engine Lubrication		
Engine oil		
Capacity		
Engine overhaul	5.9 US qts.	4.9 Imp qts.
Oil change and filter	4.5 US qts.	3.8 Imp qts.
Oil pump		
Inner-to-outer rotor clearance	0.008 in.	0.20mm
Pump housing-to-outer rotor clearance	0.008 in.	0.21mm
Pump housing-to-outer rotor axial clearance	0.005 in.	0.12mm
Relief valve		
Check with the oil temp. at 176 deg. F or 80 deg. C		
Idle	10 psi min.	70 kPa min.
3000 rpm	50 psi min.	340 kPa min.

91183C06

2.7L ENGINE MECHANICAL SPECIFICATIONS

Description	English Specifications	Metric Specifications
Compression		
Pressure check @ 200 rpm wide open throttle		
Nominal	171 psi	1180 kPa
Minimum	142 psi	980 kPa
Maximum variation	28 psi	200 kPa
Cylinder Head		
Warpage	0.02 in.	0.05mm
Height	5.234-5.239 in.	132.93-133.07mm
Camshaft		
Endplay	0.02 in.	0.5mm
Camshaft to holder oil clearance	0.004 in.	0.10mm
Total runout	0.0012 in.	0.03mm
Camshaft lobe height		
Intake	1.5537 in.	39.463mm
Exhaust	1.5515 in.	39.409mm
Valves		
Clearance (cold)		
Intake	Auto adjusting hydraulic tappets	
Exhaust	Auto adjusting hydraulic tappets	
Stem O.D.		
Intake	0.258 in.	6.55mm
Exhaust	0.257 in.	6.52mm
Stem to guide clearance		
Intake	0.003 in.	0.08 mm
Exhaust	0.004 in.	0.11mm
Valve Seats		
Width		
Intake	0.079 in.	2.00mm
Exhaust	0.079 in.	2.00mm
Stem installed height		
Intake	1.778 in.	45.15mm
Exhaust	1.766 in.	44.85mm
Valve springs		
Free length		
Intake	2.004 in.	50.89mm
Exhaust	1.784 in.	45.31mm
Valve guides		
I.D.		
Intake	0.262 in.	6.65mm
Exhaust	0.262 in.	6.65mm
Installed height		
Intake	0.652-0.671 in.	16.55-17.05mm
Exhaust	0.699-0.719 in.	17.75-18.25mm
Rocker arms		
Arm-to-shaft clearance		
Intake	0.003 in.	0.08mm
Exhaust	0.003 in.	0.08mm
Push rod		
Runout	0.0008 in.	0.02mm
Block		
Deck warpage	0.004 in.	0.10mm

91183C07

2.7L ENGINE MECHANICAL SPECIFICATIONS

Description	English Specifications	Metric Specifications
Block (cont.)		
Bore diameter		
A or I	3.4256-3.4260 in.	87.010-87.020mm
B or II	3.4252-3.4256 in.	87.000-87.010mm
Bore taper	0.002 in.	0.05mm
Reboring limit	0.020 in.	0.50mm
Piston		
Skirt (O.D. measured 0.7 in (18mm) from bottom of skirt)		
No letter	3.4240 in.	86.970mm
Letter B	3.4236 in.	86.960mm
Clearance in cylinder	0.003 in.	0.08mm
Ring groove width		
Top	0.0500 in.	1.270mm
Second	0.0506 in.	1.285mm
Oil	0.1594 in.	4.050mm
Piston rings		
Ring-to-groove clearance		
Top	0.0057 in.	0.145mm
Second	0.0063 in.	0.160mm
Ring end gap		
Top	0.024 in.	0.60mm
Second	0.028 in.	0.70mm
Oil	0.031 in.	0.80mm
Piston pin		
O.D.	0.8659-0.8661 in.	21.994-22.000mm
Pin-to-piston clearance	0.0005-0.0009 in.	0.012-0.024mm
Connecting rod		
Pin-to-rod clearance	0.0005-0.0013 in.	0.013-0.032mm
Small end and bore diameter	0.8649-0.8654 in.	21.968-21.981mm
Large end bore	2.17 in.	55.0mm
Enplay installed on crankshaft	0.016 in.	0.40mm
Crankshaft		
Main journal diameter	2.5187-2.5197 in.	63.976-64.000mm
Rod journal diameter	2.0463-2.0472 in.	51.976-52.000mm
Rod/main journal taper	0.0004 in.	0.01mm
Rod/main journal out or round	0.0004 in.	0.01mm
Endplay	0.018 in.	0.45mm
Runout	0.0012 in.	0.03mm
Crankshaft bearing		
Main bearing-to- journal oil clearance	0.002 in.	0.050mm
Rod bearing clearance	0.002 in.	0.050mm
Engine Lubrication		
Engine oil capacity		
Engine overhaul	5.6 US qts.	5.3 L
Oil change and filter	4.6 US qts.	4.4 L
Oil pump		
Inner-to-outer rotor clearance	0.008 in.	0.2mm
Pump housing-to-outer rotor clearance	0.008 in.	0.2mm
Pump housing-to-outer rotor axial clearance	0.005 in.	0.12mm
Relief valve		
Check with the oil temp. at 176 deg. F or 80 deg. C		
Idle	11 psi min.	78 kPa min.
3000 rpm	63 psi min.	430 kPa min.

91183C08

3.0L ENGINE MECHANICAL SPECIFICATIONS

Description	English Specifications	Metric Specifications
Compression		
Pressure check @ 200 rpm wide open throttle		
Nominal	178 psi	1230 kPa
Minimum	135 psi	930 kPa
Maximum variation	28 psi	200 kPa
Cylinder Head		
Warpage	0.02 in.	0.05mm
Height	4.762-4.766 in.	120.95-121.05mm
Camshaft		
Endplay	0.008 in.	0.20mm
Camshaft to holder oil clearance	0.006 in.	0.15mm
Total runout	0.002 in.	0.04mm
Camshaft lobe height		
Intake		
Primary	1.5537 in.	39.463mm
Mid	1.3628 in.	34.615mm
Secondary	1.4256 in.	36.210mm
Exhaust	1.2279 in.	31.188mm
	1.4203 in.	36.076mm
Valves		
Clearance (cold)		
Intake	0.008-0.009 in.	0.20-0.24mm
Exhaust	0.011-0.013 in.	0.28-0.32mm
Stem O.D.		
Intake	0.2148 in.	5.455mm
Exhaust	0.2134 in.	5.420mm
Stem to guide clearance		
Intake	0.003 in.	0.08 mm
Exhaust	0.005 in.	0.12mm
Valve Seats		
Width		
Intake	0.079 in.	2.00mm
Exhaust	0.079 in.	2.00mm
Stem installed height		
Intake	1.882 in.	47.80mm
Exhaust	1.879 in.	47.43mm
Valve springs		
Free length		
Intake	2.009 in.	51.03mm
Exhaust	2.106 in.	53.48mm
Valve guides		
I.D.		
Intake	0.219 in.	5.55mm
Exhaust	0.219 in.	5.55mm
Installed height		
Intake	0.835-0.874 in.	21.20-22.20mm
Exhaust	0.812-0.852 in.	20.63-21.63mm
Rocker arms		
Arm-to-shaft clearance		
Intake	0.0026 in.	0.067mm
Exhaust	0.0030 in.	0.077mm

91183C09

3.0L ENGINE MECHANICAL SPECIFICATIONS

Description	English Specifications	Metric Specifications
Block		
Deck warpage	0.004 in.	0.10mm
Bore diameter	3.3864 in.	86.065mm
Bore taper	0.002 in.	0.05mm
Reboring limit	0.020 in.	0.50mm
Piston		
Skirt (O.D. measured 0.7 in (18mm) from bottom of skirt)	3.3844 in.	85.995mm
Clearance in cylinder	0.003 in.	0.08mm
Ring groove width		
Top	0.049 in.	1.25mm
Second	0.049 in.	1.25mm
Oil	0.112 in.	2.85mm
Piston rings		
Ring-to-groove clearance		
Top	0.005 in.	0.13mm
Second	0.005 in.	0.13mm
Ring end gap		
Top	0.024 in.	0.60mm
Second	0.028 in.	0.70mm
Oil	0.031 in.	0.80mm
Piston pin		
O.D.	0.8643 in.	21.954mm
Pin-to-piston clearance	0.0002 in.	0.004mm
Connecting rod		
Pin-to-rod clearance	0.0007 in.	0.019mm
Small end and bore diameter	0.8650-0.8652 in.	21.970-21.976mm
Large end bore	2.20 in.	56.0mm
Enplay installed on crankshaft	0.018 in.	0.45mm
Crankshaft		
Main journal diameter	2.8337-2.8346 in.	71.976-72.000mm
Rod journal diameter	2.0857-2.0866 in.	52.976-53.000mm
Rod/main journal taper	0.0004 in.	0.010mm
Rod/main journal out or round	0.0004 in.	0.010mm
Endplay	0.018 in.	0.45mm
Runout	0.0012 in.	0.03mm
Crankshaft bearing		
Main bearing-to-journal oil clearance	0.002 in.	0.050mm
Rod bearing clearance	0.002 in.	0.050mm
Engine Lubrication		
Engine oil capacity		
Engine overhaul	5.3 US qts.	5.0 L
Oil change and filter	4.6 US qts.	4.4 L
Oil pump		
Inner-to-outer rotor clearance	0.008 in.	0.2mm
Pump housing-to-outer rotor clearance	0.008 in.	0.2mm
Pump housing-to-outer rotor axial clearance	0.005 in.	0.12mm
Relief valve		
Check with the oil temp. at 176 deg. F or 80 deg. C		
Idle	10 psi min.	70 kPa min.
3000 rpm	70 psi min.	490 kPa min

91183C10

Engine

REMOVAL & INSTALLATION

In the process of removing the engine, you will come across a number of steps which call for the removal of a separate component or system, such as "disconnect the exhaust system" or "remove the radiator." In most instances, a detailed removal procedure can be found elsewhere in this manual.

It is virtually impossible to list each individual wire and hose which must be disconnected, simply because so many different model and engine combinations have been manufactured. Careful observation and common sense are the best possible approaches to any repair procedure.

Removal and installation of the engine can be made easier if you follow these basic points:

• If you have to drain any of the fluids, use a suitable container.

• Always tag any wires or hoses and, if possible, the components they came from before disconnecting them.

• Because there are so many bolts and fasteners involved, store and label the retainers from components separately in muffin pans, jars or coffee cans. This will prevent confusion during installation.

• After unbolting the transmission or transaxle, always make sure it is properly supported.

• If it is necessary to disconnect the air conditioning system, have this service performed by a qualified technician using a recovery/recycling station. If the system does not have to be disconnected, unbolt the compressor and set it aside.

• When unbolting the engine mounts, always make sure the engine is properly supported. When removing the engine, make sure that any lifting devices are properly attached to the engine. It is recommended that if your engine is supplied with lifting hooks, your lifting apparatus be attached to them.

• Lift the engine from its compartment slowly, checking that no hoses, wires or other components are still connected.

• After the engine is clear of the compartment, place it on an engine stand or workbench.

• After the engine has been removed, you can perform a partial or full teardown of the engine using the procedures outlined in this manual.

1996–97 Accord

2.2L ENGINES

▶ See Figures 1, 2, 3 and 4

1. Secure the hood as far open as possible.
2. Disconnect the negative battery cable, then the positive battery cable.
3. Remove the battery and the battery base. Disconnect the engine ground cable.
4. Remove the throttle cable and the cruise control cable, by loosening the locknuts, then slip the cable ends out of the throttle linkage. Take care not to bend the cables when removing them. Always replace any kinked cable with a new one.
5. Remove the intake air duct and intake air duct/air cleaner housing.
6. Disconnect the Intake Air Resonator (IAR) control solenoid valve connector, then remove the IAR from the vehicle.

7. Remove the battery cables from the under-hood fuse/relay box and under-hood ABS fuse/relay box.
8. Disconnect the engine wiring harness connectors on the right side of the engine compartment.
9. Remove the brake booster vacuum hose, then label and disconnect the other vacuum hoses from the intake manifold.
10. Relieve the pressure from the fuel system, as outlined in Section 5.

✳✳ CAUTION

The fuel injection system remains under pressure after the engine has been turned OFF. Properly relieve fuel pressure before disconnecting any fuel lines. Failure to do so may result in fire or personal injury.

11. Disconnect the fuel feed hose from the fuel rail and disconnect the fuel return line from the fuel pressure regulator.
12. Remove the engine wiring harness connectors, terminal, and clamps on the left side of the engine compartment.
13. Disconnect the injector resistor connector on the left side of the engine compartment.
14. Remove the power steering hose clamp.
15. Remove the power steering pump mounting nuts and adjusting bolt, then remove the power steering pump drive belt and the pump.
16. Loosen the alternator mounting bolt, nut, and adjusting bolt, then remove the alternator belt.
17. If equipped with a manual transaxle perform the following:

91183P19

Fig. 1 Using a closed end wrench to remove the motor mount through bolt

91183P20

Fig. 2 Top view of a common Honda motor mount and retaining bolts

a. Disconnect the shift cable and the select cable from the transaxle. Do not bend the cables when removing them. Replace any kinked cable with a new one.

b. Disconnect the back-up light switch connectors and starter motor cable.

c. Remove the clutch slave cylinder and the pipe/hose assembly. Do not depress the clutch pedal once the slave cylinder has been removed.

18. Disconnect the VSS.
19. Remove the radiator cap.
20. Raise and safely support the vehicle. Remove the front wheels and the engine splash shield.
21. Drain the engine coolant into a sealable container.
22. Drain the transaxle fluid into a sealable container. Install the drain plug with a new gasket.
23. Drain the engine oil into a sealable container.
24. Lower the vehicle to a working level.
25. Remove the upper and lower radiator hoses, then disconnect the heater hoses from the engine.
26. If equipped with an automatic transaxle, disconnect the ATF cooler hoses.
27. Remove the radiator assembly from the vehicle.
28. Loosen the air conditioning mounting bolts, then remove the compressor. Do not disconnect the air conditioning hoses. Detach the compressor electrical connector and support the compressor with a strong wire.
29. Remove the center beam from under the engine.
30. Remove the nuts attaching the exhaust pipe to the exhaust manifold and the catalytic converter. Remove the nuts from the exhaust pipe hanger, then remove the exhaust pipe and discard the gaskets.
31. If equipped with an automatic transaxle, remove the shift cable cover, then disconnect the shift cable. Do not bend the cable and replace the cable if it becomes kinked.
32. Remove the left and the right side damper forks.
33. Disconnect the lower ball joints from the lower control arms.
34. Pry the halfshafts from the transaxle. Cover the inner CV-joints with plastic bags to protect them.
35. Swing the halfshaft under the fender out of the way.
36. Attach an engine hoist to the engine lifting points and raise the hoist to remove all slack from the chain.
37. Remove the rear engine mount bracket.
38. Remove the front engine mount bracket.
39. Remove the side engine mount.
40. Remove the transaxle mount and the mount bracket.
41. Check that the engine is completely free of vacuum hoses, fuel and coolant hoses, and electrical wiring.
42. Slowly raise the engine approximately 6 in. (150mm). Check once again that all hoses and wires have been disconnected from the engine.
43. Raise the engine all the way and remove it from the vehicle.
44. Remove the transaxle from the engine.
45. If equipped with a manual transaxle, remove the clutch cover (pressure plate) and clutch disc.
46. Mount the engine on an engine stand, mak-

ing sure the mounting bolts are tight. If an engine stand is not available, support the engine in an upright position with blocks. Never leave an engine hanging from a lift or hoist.

To install:

47. Assemble the clutch disc and pressure plate to the flywheel, if equipped with a manual transaxle.

48. Install the transaxle to the engine.

49. Lift the engine into position and lower it into the car, aligning the mounts and bushings.

➡When installing the engine mounts and vibration dampers in the following steps, they must be tightened to the correct tension in the correct order if they are to damp vibration properly.

50. Install the side engine mount. Install a 6 x 100mm bolt to the mount to properly position the mount. Do not tighten the nut and bolt attaching the mount to the engine. Tighten the through-bolt to 47 ft. lbs. (64 Nm), then remove the 6 x 100mm bolt from the mount.

51. Install the transaxle mount. Install a 6 x 100mm bolt to the mount to properly position the mount. Do not tighten the nuts attaching the mount to the transaxle at this time. Tighten the through-bolt to 47 ft. lbs. (64 Nm), then remove the 6x100mm bolt from the mount.

52. Install the rear engine mount bracket using new bolts. Tighten the new bolts attaching the

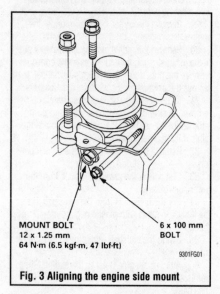

MOUNT BOLT
12 x 1.25 mm
64 N·m (6.5 kgf·m, 47 lbf·ft)

6 x 100 mm BOLT

9301FG01

Fig. 3 Aligning the engine side mount

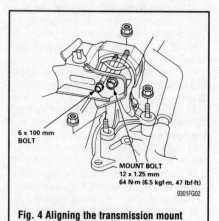

6 x 100 mm BOLT

MOUNT BOLT
12 x 1.25 mm
64 N·m (6.5 kgf·m, 47 lbf·ft)

9301FG02

Fig. 4 Aligning the transmission mount

mount to the engine assembly to 40 ft. lbs. (54 Nm). Install a new rear engine mount through-bolt. Tighten the new through-bolt to 47 ft. lbs. (64 Nm).

➡Tighten the bolts attaching the mount to the engine assembly first, then the through-bolt. If this order is not followed, excessive engine vibration may be felt and mount damage may occur.

53. Install the front mount bracket. Do not tighten the nuts attaching the mount to the engine assembly, only snug the nuts in place. Install a new through-bolt to the front mount. Tighten the new through-bolt to 47 ft. lbs. (64 Nm).

54. Tighten the side engine mount nut and bolt to 47 ft. lbs. (64 Nm).

55. Tighten the nuts attaching the transaxle mount to the transaxle to 28 ft. lbs. (38 Nm).

56. Tighten the 3 bolts attaching the front mount bracket to the engine to 28 ft. lbs. (38 Nm).

57. Remove the hoist equipment from the engine.

58. Install new spring clips to the inner CV-joints. Install the halfshafts into the transaxle, be sure that the spring clips on the inner joints click into place.

59. Connect the lower ball joints to the lower control arms and tighten the nuts to 36–43 ft. lbs. (49–59 Nm). Install a new cotter pin to the ball joint stud.

60. Using new self-locking bolts, attach the damper forks to the struts and tighten to 32 ft. lbs. (43 Nm). Tighten the new nut and bolt attaching the damper fork to the lower control arm to 47 ft. lbs. (64 Nm).

61. If equipped with an automatic transaxle, connect the shift cable to the transaxle. Install a new lockwasher and tighten the attaching bolt to 10 ft. lbs. (14 Nm). Install the shift cable cover and tighten the shift cable cover attaching bolts to 13 ft. lbs. (18 Nm).

62. Install the exhaust pipe with new gaskets. Tighten new nuts attaching the exhaust pipe to the exhaust manifold to 40 ft. lbs. (54 Nm). Tighten new nuts attaching exhaust pipe to the catalytic converter to 16 ft. lbs. (22 Nm). Install new attaching nuts on the exhaust pipe hanger, and tighten the nuts to 13 ft. lbs. (18 Nm).

63. Install the center beam and tighten the bolts attaching the center beam to 37 ft. lbs. (50 Nm).

64. Install the air conditioning compressor, attach the electrical connector and tighten the mounting bolts to 16 ft. lbs. (22 Nm).

65. Install the radiator assembly.

66. If equipped with an automatic transaxle, connect the ATF cooler hoses.

67. Install the upper and lower radiator hoses and connect the heater hoses to the engine.

68. Install the engine splash shield and the front wheels.

69. Attach the VSS electrical connector.

70. If equipped with a manual transaxle, perform the following:

a. Install the clutch slave cylinder and the pipe/hose assembly. Tighten the slave cylinder mounting bolts to 16 ft. lbs. (22 Nm).

b. Connect the starter motor cable and the back-up light switch connectors.

c. Connect the shift cable and the select cable to the transaxle. Adjust the shift cable and select cable.

71. Install and adjust the alternator drive belt.

72. Install the power steering pump and drive belt. Adjust the drive belt and tighten the attaching nuts and bolts to 16 ft. lbs. (22 Nm).

73. Install the power steering hose clamp.

74. Attach the injector resistor connector on the left of the engine compartment.

75. Attach the engine wiring harness connectors, terminal and clamps on the left side of the engine compartment.

76. Connect the fuel return hose to the regulator. Connect the fuel feed hose to the fuel rail with new washers and tighten the banjo nut to 16 ft. lbs. (22 Nm).

77. Connect the vacuum hoses to the intake manifold.

78. Attach the engine wiring harness connectors on the right side of the engine compartment.

79. Connect the battery cables to the under-hood fuse/relay box and under-hood ABS fuse/relay box.

80. Install the vacuum hose and IAR, then connect the IAR control solenoid valve connector.

81. Install the intake air duct/air cleaner housing, then the intake air duct.

82. Install and adjust the throttle cable.

83. Connect the engine ground cable and install the battery base. Tighten the base mounting bolts to 16 ft. lbs. (22 Nm).

84. Install the battery and connect the positive, then the negative battery cables. Enter the radio security code.

85. Fill the engine with oil and the transaxle with fluid.

86. Fill and bleed the air from the cooling system.

87. Switch the ignition **ON** but do not engage the starter. The fuel pump should run for approximately 2 seconds, building pressure within the lines. Switch the ignition **OFF**, then **ON** 2 or 3 more times to build full system pressure. Check for fuel leaks.

88. Start the engine, allowing it to idle. Check the hoses and lines carefully for any sign of leakage.

89. Check the timing and idle speed, as outlined in Section 1.

90. After the engine has warmed up fully and the fan(s) have come on at least once, recheck the engine for fluid leaks. Switch the engine **OFF**.

91. Adjust the belts, clutch and throttle cable as necessary.

2.7L ENGINES

▶ **See Figures 5 and 6**

1. Disconnect the support struts from the engine hood, then fix the hood in a vertical position.

2. Disconnect the negative, then the positive battery cables.

3. Remove the battery, battery base, and bracket. Disconnect the engine ground cable, located next to the battery.

4. Remove the intake air duct.

5. Remove intake manifold cover, then disconnect the throttle cable and cruise control cables from the throttle linkage. Loosen the cable locknuts, then slip the cables ends out of the accelerator linkage. Take care to not bend the cables. Always replaced a kinked cable.

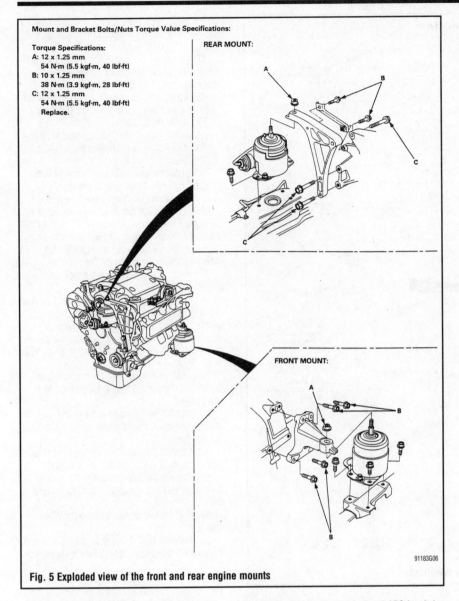

Mount and Bracket Bolts/Nuts Torque Value Specifications:

Torque Specifications:
A: 12 x 1.25 mm
   54 N·m (5.5 kgf·m, 40 lbf·ft)
B: 10 x 1.25 mm
   38 N·m (3.9 kgf·m, 28 lbf·ft)
C: 12 x 1.25 mm
   54 N·m (5.5 kgf·m, 40 lbf·ft)
   Replace.

REAR MOUNT:

FRONT MOUNT:

91183G06

Fig. 5 Exploded view of the front and rear engine mounts

6. Remove the starter cable from the strut brace, then remove the strut brace.

7. Disconnect the engine wiring harness connectors on the left side of the engine compartment.

8. Disconnect the injector resistor connector on the left side of the engine compartment.

9. Relieve the pressure from the fuel system, as outlined in Section 5.

✳✳ CAUTION

The fuel injection system remains under pressure after the engine has been turned OFF. Properly relieve fuel pressure before disconnecting any fuel lines. Failure to do so may result in fire or personal injury.

10. Disconnect the fuel feed hose from the fuel filter. Disconnect the fuel return hose from the regulator.

11. Disconnect the brake booster vacuum hose and the EVAP control canister hose.

12. Label, then disconnect the vacuum hoses from the engine.

13. Remove the battery cables from the under-hood fuse/relay box and under-hood ABS fuse/relay box.

14. Disconnect the engine wiring harness connectors on the right side of the engine compartment.

15. Remove the side engine mount and discard the bolts attaching the mount to the engine.

16. Loosen the air conditioning idler pulley center nut and adjusting bolt, then remove the drive belt.

17. Disconnect the ground cable from the body, located toward the front of the vehicle by the drive belts.

18. Loosen the alternator mounting nut, bolt, and adjusting bolt, then remove the drive belt.

19. Loosen the power steering pump mounting and adjusting nuts, then remove the drive belt.

20. Disconnect the power steering inlet hose from the pump. Plug or cap the connections.

21. Remove the power steering pump mounting nuts and adjusting bolt, then remove the pump.

22. Remove the radiator cap.

23. Raise and safely support the vehicle.

24. Remove the front wheels and the splash shield.

25. Drain the engine coolant into a sealable container.

26. Drain the transaxle fluid into a sealable container. Install the drain plug with a new gasket.

27. Drain the engine oil into a sealable container. Install the drain plug with a new gasket.

28. Remove the center beam from under the engine.

29. Detach the O_2S electrical connector. Remove the nuts attaching the exhaust pipe to the exhaust manifolds. Remove the nuts attaching the exhaust pipe to the catalytic converter and remove the exhaust pipe. Discard the locknuts and gaskets.

30. Remove the crankshaft pulley bolt and remove the crankshaft pulley. Use a crank pulley holder (part # 07MAB-PY3010A) and holder handle (part # 07JAB-001020A) to hold the crankshaft pulley in place while removing the bolt.

31. Remove the oil filter.

32. Disconnect the oil pressure switch terminal, then remove the oil filter base attaching bolts.

33. Remove the oil filter base and discard the O-rings.

34. Remove the shift cable cover, then remove the shift cable attaching bolts. Discard the lockwasher.

35. Remove the left and right damper forks.

36. Disconnect the lower ball joints from the lower control arms.

37. Remove the halfshafts from the vehicle.

38. Remove the upper and lower radiator hoses, then disconnect the heater hoses from the engine.

39. Disconnect the transaxle cooler hoses, then plug the pipes and hoses.

40. Remove the radiator from the vehicle.

41. Unplug the air conditioning compressor electrical connector. Remove the air conditioning compressor mounting bolts, position the compressor out of the way and support it with a strong wire. Do not disconnect the air conditioning hoses from the compressor.

42. Attach an engine hoist to the engine lifting points and raise the hoist to remove all slack from the chain.

43. Remove the transaxle mount.

44. Remove the bolts attaching the front mount to the beam.

45. Disconnect the vacuum hose from the rear engine mount control solenoid valve.

46. Remove the bolts attaching the rear mount to the beam.

47. Check that the engine is completely free of vacuum hoses, fuel lines, coolant hoses, and electrical wiring.

48. Slowly raise the engine approximately 6 in. (150mm). Check once again that all hoses and wires have been disconnected from the engine.

49. Raise the engine all the way and remove it from the vehicle.

50. Remove the transaxle from the engine.

51. Mount the engine on an engine stand, making sure the mounting bolts are tight. If an engine stand is not available, support the engine in an upright position with blocks. Never leave an engine hanging from a lift or hoist.

To install:

52. Install the transaxle.

53. Install the front and rear engine mounts to their mounting brackets and tighten the attaching nuts to 40 ft. lbs. (54 Nm).

54. Lift the engine into position and lower it into the car, aligning the mounts and bushings.

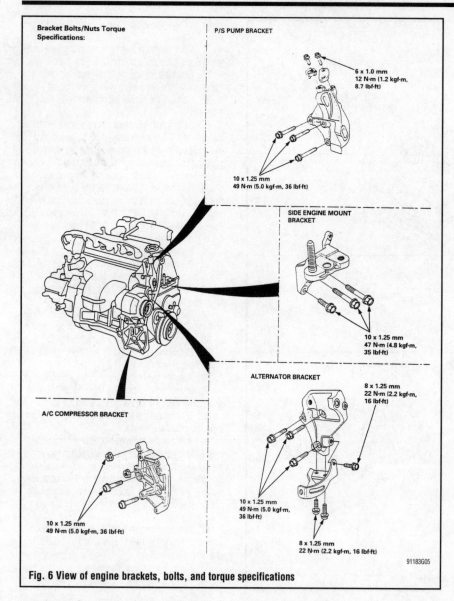

Fig. 6 View of engine brackets, bolts, and torque specifications

Bracket Bolts/Nuts Torque Specifications:

P/S PUMP BRACKET

6 x 1.0 mm
12 N·m (1.2 kgf-m, 8.7 lbf-ft)

10 x 1.25 mm
49 N·m (5.0 kgf-m, 36 lbf-ft)

SIDE ENGINE MOUNT BRACKET

10 x 1.25 mm
47 N·m (4.8 kgf-m, 35 lbf-ft)

A/C COMPRESSOR BRACKET

10 x 1.25 mm
49 N·m (5.0 kgf-m, 36 lbf-ft)

ALTERNATOR BRACKET

8 x 1.25 mm
22 N·m (2.2 kgf-m, 16 lbf-ft)

10 x 1.25 mm
49 N·m (5.0 kgf-m, 36 lbf-ft)

8 x 1.25 mm
22 N·m (2.2 kgf-m, 16 lbf-ft)

91183G05

55. Place the power steering pump drive belt over the bracket the side engine mount attaches to.

➡When installing the engine mounts and vibration dampers in the following steps, they must be tightened to the correct tension in the correct order if they are to damp vibration properly.

56. Install the rear mount and tighten the bolts attaching the mount to the beam to 43 ft. lbs. (59 Nm).

57. Install the front mount and tighten the bolts attaching the mount to the beam to 43 ft. lbs. (59 Nm).

58. Install the side engine mount. Use 3 new bolts to attach the mount to the engine and tighten the bolts to 40 ft. lbs. (54 Nm). Do not tighten the through-bolt at this time.

59. Install the transaxle mount and tighten the 3 nuts attaching the mount to the transaxle to 28 ft. lbs. (38 Nm). Do not tighten the through-bolt at this time.

60. Tighten the side engine mount through-bolt to 47 ft. lbs. (64 Nm).

61. Tighten the transaxle mount through-bolt to 47 ft. lbs. (64 Nm).

62. Remove the engine hoist.

63. Position the air conditioning compressor on the engine and install the mounting bolts. Tighten the mounting bolts to 16 ft. lbs. (22 Nm), then attach the air conditioning compressor electrical connector.

64. Install the radiator assembly.

65. Connect the transaxle cooler hoses to the transaxle cooler lines.

66. Install the upper and lower radiator hoses and connect the heater hoses to the engine.

67. Install the halfshafts with new snaprings, be sure the snaprings click into place.

68. Connect the lower ball joints to the lower control arms. Tighten the ball joint nuts to 36–43 ft. lbs. (49–59 Nm), then install a new cotter pin.

69. Install the damper forks and tighten the flange bolt to 32 ft. lbs. (43 Nm). Install the lower bolt and a new locknut and tighten the nut to 47 ft. lbs. (64 Nm).

70. Connect the shift cable to the transaxle and install a new lockwasher to the attaching bolt. Tighten the bolt attaching the shift cable end to the transaxle to 10 ft. lbs. (14 Nm). Install the shift cable cover and tighten the cover attaching bolts to

20 ft. lbs. (26 Nm). Tighten the 2 bolts attaching the cable housing to the transaxle to 108 inch lbs. (12 Nm).

71. Install new O-rings to the oil filter base and install the oil filter base to the engine. Tighten the mounting bolts to 16 ft. lbs. (22 Nm).

72. Connect the oil pressure switch terminal and tighten the attaching bolt to 1.8 ft. lbs. (2.5 Nm).

73. Install the oil filter.

74. Install the crankshaft pulley. Use the pulley holder when installing and tighten the pulley bolt. Tighten the bolt to 181 ft. lbs. (245 Nm).

75. Install the exhaust pipe with new gaskets and new locknuts. Tighten the nuts attaching the exhaust pipe to the catalytic converter to 25 ft. lbs. (33 Nm). Tighten the nuts attaching the exhaust pipe to the exhaust manifolds to 40 ft. lbs. (54 Nm). Attach the oxygen sensor electrical connector.

76. Install the center beam and tighten the attaching bolts to 37 ft. lbs. (50 Nm).

77. Install the splash shield and the front wheels.

78. Install the power steering pump and connect the inlet hose. Do not tighten the power steering pump mounting bolts and nuts at this time.

79. Install and adjust the power steering pump belt and tighten the mounting nuts to 16 ft. lbs. (22 Nm).

80. Install and adjust the alternator belt, then tighten the alternator mounting nut and bolt to 16 ft. lbs. (22 Nm).

81. Install the air conditioning belt and adjust the belt tension. Tighten the idler center nut to 33 ft. lbs. (44 Nm).

82. Connect the engine wiring harness connectors on the right side of the engine compartment.

83. Connect the battery cables to the under-hood fuse/relay box and under-hood ABS fuse/relay box.

84. Connect the vacuum hoses to the intake manifold.

85. Connect the EVAP control canister hose and the power brake booster hose to the engine assembly.

86. Connect the fuel return hose to the regulator. Connect the fuel feed hose to the fuel filter with new washers. Tighten the banjo nut to 16 ft. lbs. (22 Nm) and tighten the service bolt to 108 inch lbs. (12 Nm).

87. Connect the injector resistor connector on the left of the engine compartment.

88. Connect the engine wiring harness connectors on the left side of the engine compartment.

89. Install the strut brace and tighten the strut brace bolts to 16 ft. lbs. (22 Nm). Install the starter cable to the strut brace.

90. Connect the throttle cable and cruise control cables to the throttle linkage, adjust the cable as necessary. Install the intake manifold cover and tighten the attaching bolt to 108 inch lbs. (12 Nm).

91. Install the intake air duct.

92. Connect the engine ground cable and install the battery base and bracket. Tighten the base mounting bolts to 16 ft. lbs. (22 Nm).

93. Install the battery and connect the positive, then the negative battery cables. Enter the radio security code.

94. Fill the engine with oil and the transaxle with fluid.

95. Fill and bleed the air from the cooling system.

96. Switch the ignition **ON** but do not engage the starter. The fuel pump should run for approximately 2 seconds, building pressure within the lines. Switch the ignition **OFF**, then **ON** 2 or 3 more times to build full system pressure. Check for fuel leaks.

97. Start the engine, allowing it to idle. Check the hoses and lines carefully for any sign of leakage.

98. Check the timing and idle speed, as outlined in Section 1.

99. After the engine has warmed up fully and the fan(s) have come on at least once, recheck the engine for fluid leaks. Switch the engine **OFF**.

1998–00 Accord

2.3L AND 3.0L ENGINES

▶ See Figures 7 thru 13

1. Obtain the anti-theft code for the radio, then disconnect the battery cables. Be sure to disconnect the negative cable first.

2. Remove the air intake duct.

3. Secure the hood in the open position with a long prop rod such as P/N 74145-S84-A00.

4. Detach the negative, then the positive battery cables and the connector from the underhood relay box. On the 3.0L engine, remove the battery and tray.

5. Remove the bolt securing the relay box to the body.

6. Remove the accelerator and cruise control cables from the throttle body and bracket.

7. Properly relieve the fuel system pressure, as outlined in Section 5.

8. Detach the fuel hoses from the fuel rail.

9. Remove the following hoses:
  • Brake booster vacuum
  • EVAP canister
  • Vacuum hose from the canister

10. Remove the hose securing the power steering hose on the engine.

11. Remove the power steering pump belt, then remove the pump and position it out of the way. Use wire if necessary. Do not disconnect the fluid lines.

12. Detach the PCM connectors from the control module. Remove the grommet and pull the connectors through.

13. Detach the wiring harness connectors from the right side of the engine compartment for 2.3L engines and from the left side of the engine compartment for the 3.0L engine.

14. On the 2.3L engine, remove the starter cable and clamp. Remove the ground cable and back-up light switch connectors. On the 3.0L engine, remove

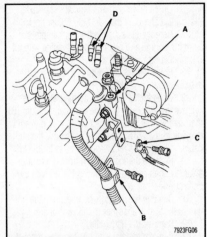

Fig. 8 Starter cable (A), clamp (B), ground cable (C) and back-up light switch connector (D) locations—1998–00 2.3L engine

the starter wiring from the engine compartment attaching points.

15. On vehicles with a manual transaxle, disconnect the shift and select cables from the transaxle. Remove the slave cylinder mounting bolts and position the cylinder out of the way. Be sure not to bend the line.

16. Remove the rear engine mount through-bolt and stiffener.

17. Remove the front engine mount bracket mounting bolts and loosen the through-bolt.

18. Remove the radiator cap.

19. Raise and safely support the vehicle.

20. Remove the front tires.

21. Remove the engine under cover.

22. Loosen the radiator drain plug and drain the coolant into a suitable container.

23. Drain the transaxle oil or fluid into a suitable container, then reinstall the plug using a new washer.

24. Drain the engine oil into a suitable container, then reinstall the plug using a new washer.

25. Lower the vehicle and remove the upper and lower radiator hoses and heater hoses from the engine.

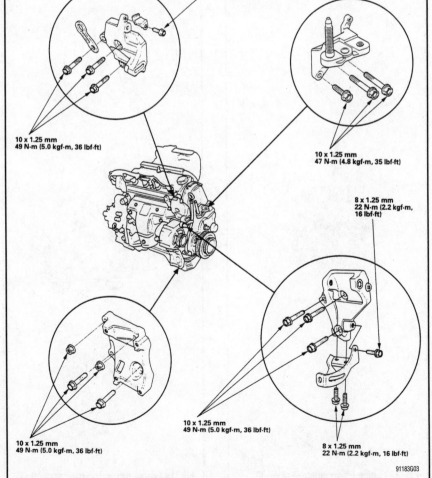

Fig. 7 View of the engine mounts and torque specifications—2.3L engine shown

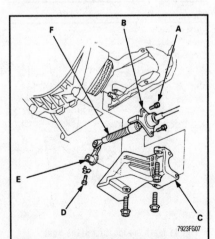

Fig. 9 Automatic transaxle linkage components (letters referenced in Steps 29 and 30)—1998–00 2.3L engine

26. On vehicles with an automatic transaxle, disconnect and plug the ATF fluid cooler lines.

27. Remove the air conditioning compressor from the engine and position it to the side without disconnecting the hoses.

28. Raise the vehicle and remove the front exhaust pipe.

29. On vehicles with an automatic transaxle, remove the 2 bolts (A) for the shift cable holder (B), then remove the shift cable cover (C). To prevent damage to the linkage, be sure to remove the shift cable holder before removing the bolts for the cover.

30. Remove the lockbolt (D) from the control lever (E), then remove the shift cable (F) with the control lever.

31. Remove the through-bolt securing the bottom of the shock absorber to the control arm.

32. Remove the halfshafts.

33. Remove the rear engine mounting bracket.

34. Remove the 2 flange bolts from each of the radius rods.

35. Mark the location of the front beams (A) on the rear beams (B). Remove the 4 bolts and the subframe.

36. Lower the vehicle about halfway and attach a chain hoist to the engine lifting points as shown. Apply slight upward pressure to the engine/transaxle assembly.

37. Remove the remaining engine and transaxle mounting brackets.

38. Lower the engine about 6 in. (150mm) and check that the engine/transaxle is free of any hoses, cables or wiring.

39. Lower the assembly completely and remove it from under the vehicle.

To install:

40. Lift the engine into position and install the engine mounting brackets. Tighten the retainers as follows:
- On the 2.3L engine, tighten the engine mounting bolts and nuts to 40 ft. lbs. (54 Nm).
- On the 3.0L engine, tighten the bolts to 28 ft. lbs. (38 Nm).

41. On the 3.0L engine, install the air conditioning compressor. Tighten the bolts to 16 ft. lbs. (22 Nm).

42. Install the transaxle mounting bracket and tighten the retainers as follows:
- On the 2.3L engine, tighten the nuts to 28 ft. lbs. (38 Nm) and the through-bolt to 40 ft. lbs. (54 Nm).
- On the 3.0L engine, tighten the bolts to 28 ft. lbs. (38 Nm).

43. Install the sub-frame in its original position. Tighten the bolts as follows:
- On the 2.3L engine, tighten the rear bolts to 47 ft. lbs. (64 Nm) and the front bolts to 76 ft. lbs. (103 Nm).

- On the 3.0L engine, tighten the rear bolts to 40 ft. lbs. (54 Nm), front bolts to 76 ft. lbs. (103 Nm) and the nuts to 28 ft. lbs. (38 Nm).

44. On the 2.3L engine, perform the following:
- Install the radius rod bolts. Tighten them to 119 ft. lbs. (162 Nm).
- Install the rear mount bracket. Tighten the bolts to 40 ft. lbs. (54 Nm).
- On vehicles with manual transaxles, install the stiffener and tighten the through-bolt to 47 ft. lbs. (64 Nm). On vehicles with automatic transaxles, install the stiffener and tighten the nut and bolt to 28 ft. lbs. (38 Nm).
- Tighten the 3 front mounting bracket bolts to 28 ft. lbs. (38 Nm). Then, tighten the through-bolt to 47 ft. lbs. (64 Nm).
- Install the air conditioning compressor. Tighten the bolts to 16 ft. lbs. (22 Nm).

45. On the 3.0L engine, perform the following:
- Install the radius rod bolts. Tighten them to 119 ft. lbs. (162 Nm).
- Install the front mounting bracket support nut. Tighten it to 40 ft. lbs. (54 Nm).
- Install the rear mounting bracket nut and bolt. Tighten the nut to 40 ft. lbs. (54 Nm) and the bolt to 28 ft. lbs. (38 Nm).
- Install the side mounting bracket. Tighten the bolts to 40 ft. lbs. (54 Nm) and the through-bolt to 40 ft. lbs. (54 Nm).

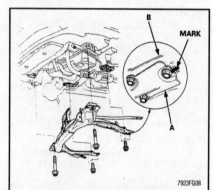

Fig. 10 Be sure to mark the location of the front beams (A) on the rear beams (B) before removing the subframe—1998–00 2.3L engine

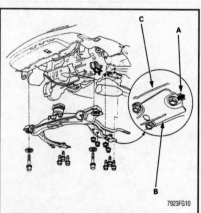

Fig. 11 Mark the location of the front beams (A) on the rear beams (B) before removing the subframe—1998–00 3.0L engine

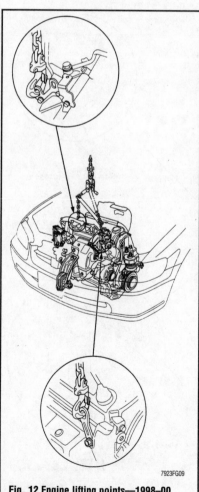

Fig. 12 Engine lifting points—1998–00 2.3L engine

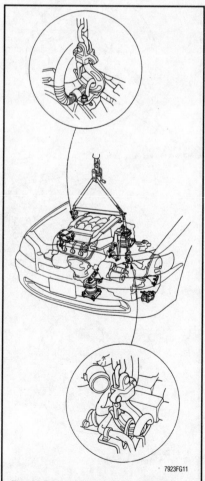

Fig. 13 Engine lifting points—1998–00 3.0L engine

46. Assemble the exhaust system.

47. If equipped with an automatic transaxle, connect the shift linkage.

48. The remainder of the installation is the reverse of the removal.

49. Refill and bleed the cooling system.

※ WARNING

Operating the engine without the proper amount and type of engine oil will result in severe engine damage.

50. Fill the engine and transaxle with the correct types and amount of oil.

51. Install the battery if removed. Start the engine and check for leaks.

Prelude

♦ See Figure 14

1. Secure the hood as far open as possible.

2. Disconnect the negative battery cable, then the positive battery cable.

3. Remove the radiator cap.

4. Raise and safely support the vehicle. Remove the front wheels and the engine splash shield.

5. Drain the engine coolant into a sealable container.

6. Drain the transaxle fluid into a sealable container. Install the drain plug with a new gasket.

7. Lower the vehicle to a suitable working level.

8. Remove the air intake duct and the air cleaner case.

9. Remove the vacuum tank and bracket.

10. Remove the battery and the battery base. Disconnect the battery cable and starter cable harnesses from the body.

11. Relieve the pressure from the fuel system, as outlined in Section 5.

※ CAUTION

The fuel injection system remains under pressure after the engine has been turned OFF. Properly relieve fuel pressure before disconnecting any fuel lines. Failure to do so may result in fire or personal injury.

12. Disconnect the fuel feed hose from the fuel rail and disconnect the fuel return line from the fuel pressure regulator.

13. Detach the injector resistor connector from the left side of the engine compartment.

14. Remove the throttle cable by loosening the

locknut, then slip the cable end out of the throttle linkage. Take care not to bend the cable when removing it. Always replace any kinked cable with a new one.

15. Disconnect the engine wiring harness connectors, terminal, and clamps on the right side of the engine.

16. Remove the power cable from the under-hood fuse/relay box.

17. Disconnect the brake booster vacuum hose and emissions control vacuum tubes from the intake manifold.

18. Detach the cruise control actuator electrical connector and vacuum tube, then remove the actuator.

19. Remove the engine ground cable from the body side.

20. Remove the power steering pump drive belt, then remove the pump.

21. Remove the air conditioning condenser fan, then install a protector plate on the radiator.

22. Loosen the alternator mounting bolt, nut, and adjusting nut, then remove the alternator drive belt.

23. Detach the air conditioning compressor electrical connector and loosen the compressor mounting bolts. Remove the compressor without disconnecting the air conditioning hoses. Support the compressor with a strong wire out of the way.

24. Remove the upper and lower radiator hoses, then disconnect the heater hoses from the engine.

25. Remove the transaxle ground cable.

26. If equipped with an automatic transaxle, disconnect the cooler hoses.

27. If equipped with a manual transaxle perform the following:

a. Disconnect the shift cable and the select cable from the transaxle. Do not bend the cables when removing them. Replace any kinked cable with a new one.

b. Remove the clutch slave cylinder and the pipe/hose assembly. Do not depress the clutch pedal once the slave cylinder has been removed.

c. Remove the clutch damper assembly.

28. Remove the VSS/Power Steering speed sensor assembly. Do not disconnect the hoses.

29. Remove the nuts attaching the exhaust pipe to the exhaust manifold and the catalytic converter. Remove the bolts from the exhaust pipe hanger, then remove the exhaust pipe and discard the gaskets.

30. If equipped with an automatic transaxle, remove the shift cable cover, then disconnect the shift cable. Do not bend the cable and replace the cable if it becomes kinked.

31. Remove the left and the right side damper forks.

32. Disconnect the lower ball joints from the lower control arms.

33. Pry the halfshafts from the transaxle. Cover the inner CV-joints with plastic bags to protect them.

34. Swing the halfshafts under the fender out of the way.

35. Attach an engine hoist to the engine lifting points and raise the hoist to remove all slack from the chain.

36. Remove the rear engine mount bracket.

37. Remove the front engine mount bracket.

38. Remove the left side engine mount.

39. Remove the transaxle mount and the mount bracket.

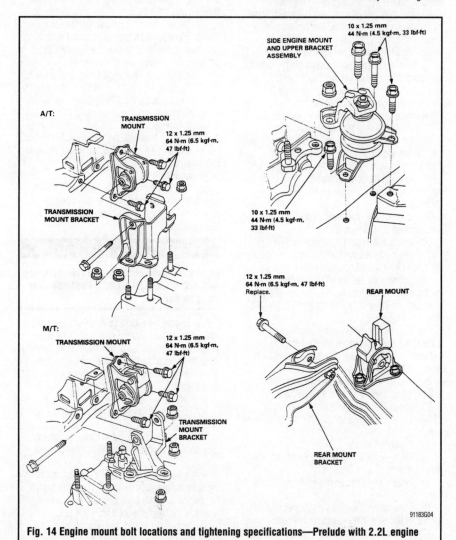

91183G04

Fig. 14 Engine mount bolt locations and tightening specifications—Prelude with 2.2L engine

40. Check that the engine is completely free of vacuum hoses, fuel and coolant hoses, and electrical wiring.

41. Slowly raise the engine approximately 6 in. (150mm). Check once again that all hoses and wires have been disconnected from the engine.

42. Raise the engine all the way and remove it from the vehicle.

43. Remove the transaxle.

44. If equipped with a manual transaxle, remove the clutch cover (pressure plate) and clutch disc.

45. Mount the engine on an engine stand, making sure the mounting bolts are tight. If an engine stand is not available, support the engine in an upright position with blocks. Never leave an engine hanging from a lift or hoist.

To install:

46. If equipped with a manual transaxle, assemble the clutch disc and pressure plate to the flywheel.

47. Install the transaxle.

48. Lift the engine into position and lower it into the car, aligning the mounts and bushings.

➡**When installing the engine mounts and vibration dampers in the following steps, they must be tightened to the correct tension in the correct order if they are to damp vibration properly.**

49. Install the side engine mount and the through-bolt. Do not tighten the through-bolt at this time. Install the nut and bolt attaching the mount to the engine. Tighten the nut and bolt attaching the side mount to the engine to 40 ft. lbs. (55 Nm).

50. Install the transaxle mount and through-bolt. Do not tighten the through-bolt at this time.

51. Install the rear engine mount and new bolts attaching the mount to the engine. Tighten the 3 new bolts attaching the mount to the engine assembly to 40 ft. lbs. (55 Nm). Install a new rear engine mount through-bolt and tighten the new through-bolt to 47 ft. lbs. (65 Nm).

52. Install the front mount and the 3 bolts attaching the mount to the engine assembly, only snug the bolts in place. Install a new through-bolt to the front mount and tighten the new through-bolt to 47 ft. lbs. (65 Nm).

53. Install the nuts to the transaxle mount. Tighten the nuts to 28 ft. lbs. (39 Nm).

54. Tighten the side engine mount through-bolt to 47 ft. lbs. (65 Nm).

55. Tighten the transaxle mount through-bolt to 47 ft. lbs. (65 Nm).

56. Tighten the 3 bolts attaching the front mount to the engine to 28 ft. lbs. (39 Nm).

57. Remove the hoist equipment from the engine.

58. Install new spring clips to the inner CV-joints. Install the halfshafts into the transaxle. Be sure that the inner joint spring clips click into place.

59. Connect the lower ball joints to the lower control arms. Tighten the nuts to 36–43 ft. lbs. (50–60 Nm). Install a new cotter pin to the ball joint stud.

60. Install the damper forks. Using new self-locking bolts, attach the damper forks to the struts and tighten to 32 ft. lbs. (44 Nm). Tighten the new nut and bolt attaching the damper fork to the lower control arm to 47 ft. lbs. (65 Nm).

61. If equipped with an automatic transaxle, connect the shift cable to the transaxle. Install a new

lockwasher and tighten the attaching bolt to 84 inch lbs. (10 Nm). Install the shift cable cover. Tighten the shift cable cover attaching bolts to 13 ft. lbs. (18 Nm).

62. Install the exhaust pipe with new gaskets. Tighten the new nuts attaching the exhaust pipe to the exhaust manifold to 40 ft. lbs. (55 Nm). Tighten the new nuts attaching the exhaust pipe to the catalytic converter to 25 ft. lbs. (34 Nm). Install new attaching bolts to the exhaust pipe hanger and tighten the bolts to 13 ft. lbs. (18 Nm).

63. Install the VSS, attach the electrical connector, and tighten the mounting bolt to 13 ft. lbs. (18 Nm).

64. If equipped with a manual transaxle perform the following:

a. Install the clutch damper assembly and tighten the attaching bolts to 16 ft. lbs. (22 Nm).

b. Install the clutch slave cylinder and the pipe/hose assembly and tighten the slave cylinder mounting bolts to 16 ft. lbs. (22 Nm).

c. Connect the shift cable and the select cable to the transaxle. Adjust the shift cable and select cable.

65. If equipped with an automatic transaxle, connect the cooler hoses.

66. Install the transaxle ground cable.

67. Install the upper and lower radiator hoses and connect the heater hoses to the engine.

68. Install the air conditioning compressor and attach the electrical connector. Tighten the mounting bolts to 16 ft. lbs. (22 Nm).

69. Install and adjust the alternator drive belt.

70. Remove the protector plate from the radiator and install the air conditioning condenser fan.

71. Install and the power steering pump and drive belt. Adjust the drive belt tension, then tighten the attaching nuts and bolts to 16 ft. lbs. (22 Nm).

72. Attach the engine ground cable to the body.

73. Install the cruise control actuator, then connect the electrical connector and vacuum tube. Tighten the mounting bolts to 84 inch lbs. (10 Nm).

74. Connect the brake booster vacuum hose and the emissions control vacuum tubes to the intake manifold.

75. Connect the engine wiring harness connectors, terminal, and clamps.

76. Install and adjust the throttle cable.

77. Attach the injector resistor connector on the left side of the engine compartment.

78. Connect the fuel return hose to the regulator. Connect the fuel feed hose to the fuel rail with new washers. Tighten the cap nut to 16 ft. lbs. (22 Nm).

79. Connect the battery cable and the starter cable to the body. Install the battery base and the battery. Tighten the battery base attaching bolts to 16 ft. lbs. (22 Nm).

80. Install the PAIR vacuum tank and bracket. Tighten the mounting bolts to 96 inch lbs. (10 Nm).

81. Install the air cleaner duct and housing.

82. Install the engine splash shield and the front wheels.

83. Lower the vehicle.

84. Fill the engine with oil and the transaxle with fluid.

85. Fill and bleed the air from the cooling system.

86. Connect the positive, then the negative battery cable and enter the radio security code.

87. Switch the ignition **ON** but do not engage

the starter. The fuel pump should run for approximately 2 seconds, building pressure within the lines. Switch the ignition **OFF**, then **ON** 2 or 3 more times to build full system pressure. Check for fuel leaks.

88. Start the engine, allowing it to idle. Check the hoses and lines carefully for any sign of leakage.

89. Check the timing and idle speed, as outlined in Section 1.

90. After the engine has warmed up fully and the fan(s) have come on at least once, recheck the engine for fluid leaks. Switch the engine **OFF**.

91. Adjust the belts and throttle cable as necessary.

92. Road test the vehicle, then loosen and retighten the 3 bolts attaching the front engine mount to the engine. Tighten the bolts to 28 ft. lbs. (39 Nm).

Rocker Arm (Valve) Cover

REMOVAL & INSTALLATION

◆ **See Figures 15 thru 20**

1. Remove the spark plug wires by twisting side to side and gently pulling. Note or label their location and place aside.

2. Starting from the outside and working inward, using a 10mm wrench or socket with an extension and ratchet, remove the fasteners securing the valve cover to the cylinder head.

3. If equipped, remove all hoses and brackets.

4. Carefully lift the cover off the cylinder head. Use care to not loose the sealing grommets when lifting the cover. Place the cover upright in a clean, protected area. If the cover is stuck onto the cylinder head, using a suitable prytool carefully pry the cover upward at the corners. Move each corner no more than a 1/16 inch at a time.

To install:

5. Thoroughly clean and inspect the gasket surface of the cover and cylinder head. Rubbing alcohol or a suitable brake cleaner works well for this application.

✳✳ WARNING

Protect the eyes and exposed skin from contact with cleaning agents. Do not use near an open flame.

6. Inspect the rubber valve cover gasket, the sealing grommets, and the seal around the spark plug holes. If the gasket or seals are brittle, cracked or damaged, replace them. If the old gasket and seals are not worn or damaged they can be reused once cleaned.

To clean the valve cover gasket:

• Place the gasket in a suitable, clear plastic bag.

• Spray a small amount of brake cleaner, or pour about 2 ounces of rubbing alcohol into the bag.

• Close the end of the bag and swish the cleaning fluid around, making certain the entire gasket has been thoroughly saturated. Do not leave the gasket in the bag for more than 5 minutes.

• Remove the gasket, and wipe clean with a paper towel or clean soft cloth.

Fig. 15 Use a pick tool to carefully remove the valve cover-to-spark plug tube grommets

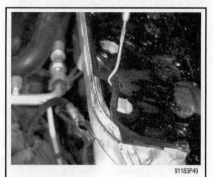

Fig. 16 Carefully remove and inspect the valve cover gasket and replace it if it is damaged

Fig. 17 Install the valve cover properly in the cylinder head groove—1996 Accord shown

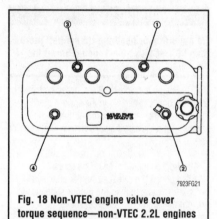

Fig. 18 Non-VTEC engine valve cover torque sequence—non-VTEC 2.2L engines

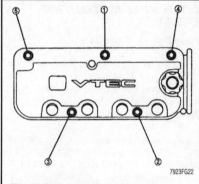

Fig. 19 Rocker arm (valve) cover torque sequence—VTEC 2.2L engines

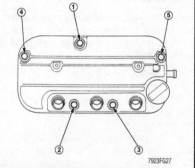

Fig. 20 Tighten the rocker arm (valve) cover bolts in the sequence shown—3.0L engine

7. Apply a liquid, non-hardening gasket sealant, such as Honda sealant part No. 08718–0001 or 08718–0003 to the valve cover side of the spark plug opening seals and press them into the valve cover.

8. Install the valve cover gasket securely into the groove in the valve cover.

9. Apply a ½ inch bead of sealant to the corners of the gasket, where the gasket meets the cylinder head and the camshaft journal cap.

10. Install the grommets if removed, and tighten the valve cover fasteners from the inside out evenly in three steps. For the 2.2L and 3.0L engines, tighten the retainers in the sequence shown in the accompanying figures. Tighten the valve cover fastener, as follows:

    a. 4-cylinder engines: to 86 inch lbs. (9.8 Nm).

    b. 2.7L engine: 11 ft. lbs. (15 Nm)

    c. 3.0L engine: 108 inch lbs. (12 Nm)

11. The remainder of the assembly procedure is the reverse of the removal sequence.

Rocker Arm/Shafts

REMOVAL & INSTALLATION

2.2L (H22A1) Engine

▶ See Figures 21 thru 26

1. Disconnect the negative battery cable.
2. Remove the cylinder head from the engine assembly, as outlined later in this section.

3. Remove the VTEC solenoid valve and filter from the cylinder head. Discard the filter.

4. Install rubber bands to each of the rocker arm assemblies, this will hold the rocker arms together and prevent them from separating.

5. Remove the intake and exhaust rocker shaft orifices. The intake and exhaust shaft orifices are different, note their locations for installation.

6. Remove the rocker arm shaft sealing bolts from the cylinder head. Discard the washers.

7. Install 12mm bolts into the rocker arm shafts. Remove each rocker arm while slowly pulling out the intake and exhaust rocker arm shafts.

8. Remove the lost motion assemblies from the cylinder head and inspect it. Pushing it gently with a finger will cause it to sink slightly. Increasing the force on it will cause it to sink deeper.

Fig. 21 The major carbon build-up on these rocker arms is due to a lack of oil changes at the proper intervals

Fig. 22 View of the rocker arm assembly, removed from the vehicle

Fig. 23 Location of the valve clearance adjusting screw

Fig. 24 There may be grooves worn into the bottoms of the rocker arms where they ride on the camshaft if there is a loss of oil pressure

Fig. 25 View of the rocker arms as they sit on the shaft

Fig. 26 Clean all bolt threads thoroughly before installing the rocker assembly

To install:

➡Clean the rocker shaft orifices and install new O-rings. Clean the rocker arms and the shafts in solvent, dry them, and apply clean oil to any contact surfaces.

9. Install the lost motion assemblies to the cylinder head.

10. Install the rocker arms to their original locations while passing the rocker arm shaft through the cylinder head.

11. Install the rocker arm shaft orifices. If the holes in the rocker arm shaft and cylinder head are not in line with each other, thread a 12mm bolt into the rocker arm shaft and rotate the shaft. Be sure that the orifices are installed in the correct locations, the intake and exhaust orifices are different. The rocker shafts should not turn if the orifices are installed correctly.

12. Install the rocker arm sealing bolts with new washers and tighten the bolts to 43 ft. lbs. (60 Nm). Remove the rubber bands from the rocker arm assemblies.

13. Install the VTEC solenoid valve with a new filter. Tighten the mounting bolts to 108 inch lbs. (12 Nm).

14. Install the cylinder head onto the engine block.

15. Adjust the valves.

16. Connect the negative battery cable and enter the radio security code.

17. Check and adjust the ignition timing.

18. Run the engine and check for leaks, then road test the vehicle.

2.2L (F22A1, F22A6, F22B1, F22B2) ENGINES

▶ See Figures 27 thru 34

1. Disconnect the negative battery cable.
2. Remove the air intake duct.
3. Remove the PCV hose, then remove the rocker arm (valve) cover. Replace the rubber seals if damaged or deteriorated.
4. Remove the timing belt upper cover.
5. Bring the No. 1 cylinder to TDC. The white mark on the crankshaft pulley should align with the pointer on the timing belt cover. The words **UP** embossed on the camshaft pulley should be aligned in the upward position. The marks on the edge of the pulley should be aligned with the cylinder head or the back cover upper edge. Once in this position, the engine must NOT be turned or disturbed.
6. Label, then detach the electrical connectors from the distributor and the spark plug wires from the spark plugs. Mark the position of the distributor and remove it from the cylinder head.
7. Loosen the power steering mounting bolts and remove drive belt from the pump.
8. Mark the rotation of the timing belt if it is to be used again. Loosen the timing belt adjusting bolt ¾–1 turn, then release the tension on the timing belt. Push the tensioner to release tension from the belt, then tighten the adjusting bolt.
9. Remove the timing belt from the camshaft sprocket, as outlined later in this section.

✳✳ WARNING

Do not crimp or bend the timing belt more than 90°, or less than 1 inch (25mm) in diameter

10. Ensure the words **UP** embossed on the camshaft pulley is aligned in the upward position, then remove the camshaft sprocket bolt. Pull the sprocket from the camshaft and remove the sprocket key.

11. Remove the timing belt back cover.

12. Loosen the valve adjusting screws.

13. Loosen the camshaft holder attaching bolts 2 turns at a time in the proper sequence to prevent damaging the valves or rocker arm assemblies.

➡When removing the rocker arm assembly, do not remove the camshaft holder bolts. The bolts will keep the camshaft holders, springs, and the rocker arms on the shafts.

14. Carefully remove the camshaft holders and rocker arm assembly. If the rocker arm and shaft assembly needs to be disassembled for service, note the location of the components as they are removed. Install a rubber band around the VTEC rocker arm assemblies to keep them from coming apart during disassembly of the rocker arm assembly. The rocker arms must be installed in the same position if reused.

15. Remove the camshaft from the cylinder head and discard the seal.

16. Remove the oil control orifice.

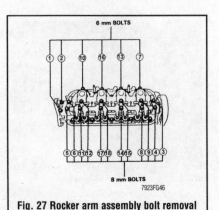

Fig. 27 Rocker arm assembly bolt removal sequence—2.2L (F22A1, F22A6) engines

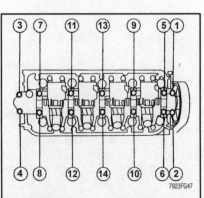

Fig. 28 Rocker arm assembly bolt loosening sequence—2.2L (F22B1) engine

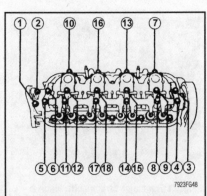

Fig. 29 Rocker arm assembly bolt loosening sequence—2.2L (F22B2) engine

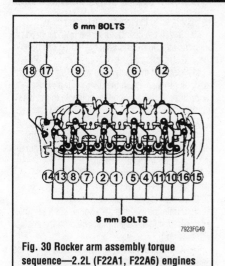

Fig. 30 Rocker arm assembly torque sequence—2.2L (F22A1, F22A6) engines

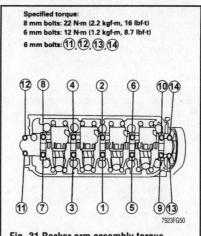

Fig. 31 Rocker arm assembly torque sequence—2.2L (F22B1) engine

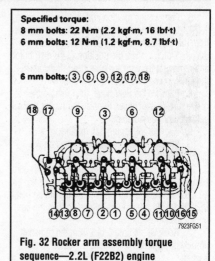

Fig. 32 Rocker arm assembly torque sequence—2.2L (F22B2) engine

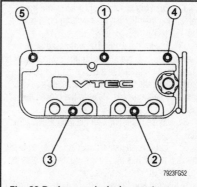

Fig. 33 Rocker arm (valve) cover torque sequence—2.2L (F22B1) engine

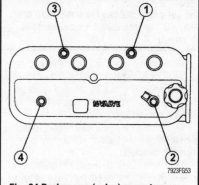

Fig. 34 Rocker arm (valve) cover torque sequence—2.2L (F22B2) engine

To install:

17. Wipe the camshaft and the camshaft journals clean, then lubricate both surfaces, and install the camshaft.

18. Turn the camshaft so that its keyway is facing up (No. 1 cylinder will be at TDC).

19. Clean the oil control orifice and install a new O-ring, then install the oil control orifice.

20. Reassemble the rocker arm and shaft assembly, if it was disassembled. Lubricate the rocker arm and shaft assembly with clean oil, then apply liquid gasket to the head mating surfaces of the No. 1 and No. 6 camshaft holders.

21. Set the camshaft holders and rocker arm assembly in place, then loosely install the attaching bolts.

22. Apply clean oil to the camshaft oil seal lip and the seal guide (part # 07NAG-PT0010A), then install the seal to the seal guide. Install the seal guide to the camshaft, then the installer cup (part # 07NAF-PT0010A), and the installer shaft (part # 07NAF-PT0020A). Tighten the nut on the installer shaft to press the seal into the cylinder head.

23. Tighten the camshaft holder bolts 2 turns at a time in the proper sequence, as shown in the accompanying figures. The final torque for the 8mm bolts is 16 ft. lbs. (22 Nm) and the final torque for the 6mm bolts is 108 inch lbs. (12 Nm).

24. Install the timing belt back cover and a new gasket, if necessary. Tighten the bolt toward the exhaust manifold to 84 inch lbs. (10 Nm) and tighten the bolt toward the intake manifold to 108 inch lbs. (12 Nm).

25. Install the camshaft sprocket key to the camshaft, then install the camshaft sprocket. Install the bolt and tighten it to 27 ft. lbs. (37 Nm).

26. Ensure the words **UP** embossed on the camshaft pulley is aligned in the upward position, then install the timing belt onto the camshaft sprocket. Loosen, then tighten the timing belt adjusting nut. Refer to the procedure located in this section.

27. Rotate the crankshaft pulley 5 or 6 turns to position the timing belt on the pulleys.

28. Set the No. 1 cylinder to TDC and loosen the timing belt adjusting nut 1 turn. Turn the crankshaft counterclockwise until the cam pulley has moved 3 teeth; this creates tension on the timing belt. Loosen, then tighten the adjusting nut, and tighten it to 33 ft. lbs. (45 Nm).

29. Adjust the valves.

30. Tighten the crankshaft pulley bolt to 181 ft. lbs. (245 Nm) on (F22B1) engines and 159 ft. lbs. (220 Nm) on all other engines.

31. Install the upper timing belt cover. Tighten the bolt toward the exhaust manifold to 84 inch lbs. (10 Nm) and tighten the bolt toward the intake manifold to 108 inch lbs. (12 Nm).

32. Install the rocker arm (valve) cover gasket cover to the groove of the rocker arm (valve) cover. Before installing the gasket, thoroughly clean the seal and the groove. Seat the recesses for the camshaft first, then work it into the groove around the outside edges. Be sure the gasket is seated securely in the corners of the recesses.

33. Apply liquid gasket to the 4 corners of the recesses of the rocker arm (valve) cover gasket. Do not install the parts if 5 minutes or more have elapsed since applying liquid gasket. After assembly, wait at least 20 minutes before filling the engine with oil.

34. Install the cylinder head (valve) cover. Tighten the bolts attaching the rocker arm (valve) cover in the proper sequence to 84 inch lbs. (10 Nm).

35. Install the PCV hose to the rocker arm (valve) cover.

36. Install and adjust the power steering belt.

37. Install the distributor to the cylinder head. Snug the attaching bolts until the timing has been checked and adjusted.

38. Connect the spark plug wires to the correct spark plugs, then connect the distributor electrical connectors.

39. Install the air intake duct.

40. Drain the oil from the engine into a sealable container. Install the drain plug and refill the engine with clean oil.

41. Connect the negative battery cable and enter the radio security code.

42. Start the engine and check carefully for any leaks.

43. Check and adjust the ignition timing as necessary, then tighten the distributor bolts to 13 ft. lbs. (18 Nm).

2.3L ENGINE

▶ See Figure 35

1. Disconnect the negative battery cable.

2. Turn the crankshaft so the No. 1 piston is at Top Dead Center (TDC).

➡**The No. 1 piston is at TDC when the pointer on the block aligns with the white painted mark on the flywheel (manual transaxle) or driveplate (automatic transaxle).**

3. Remove the air intake duct.

4. Remove the engine ground cable from the rocker arm (valve) cover.

5. Remove the connector and the terminal from the alternator, then remove the engine wiring harness from the valve cover.

6. Remove the ignition coil.

7. Label, then detach the electrical connectors from the distributor and the spark plug wires from the spark plugs. Mark the position of the distributor and remove it from the cylinder head. Disconnect the ignition coil wire from the distributor.

8. Remove the PCV hose, then remove the rocker arm (valve) cover. Replace the rubber seals if damaged or deteriorated.

9. Remove the timing belt middle cover.

10. Ensure the words **UP** embossed on the camshaft pulleys are aligned in the upward position.

11. Mark the rotation of the timing belt if it is to be used again. Loosen the timing belt adjusting nut ½ turn, then release the tension on the timing belt. Push the tensioner to release tension from the belt, then tighten the adjusting nut.

12. Remove the timing belt from the camshaft sprockets. Refer to the procedure located in this section.

✳✳ WARNING

Do not crimp or bend the timing belt more than 90˚, or less than 1 inch (25mm) in diameter

13. Insert a 5.0mm pin punch in each of the camshaft caps, nearest to the sprockets, through the holes provided. Remove the camshaft sprocket attaching bolts, then remove the sprockets. Do not lose the sprocket keys.

14. Remove the side engine mount bracket B, then the timing belt back cover from behind the camshaft sprockets.

15. Loosen all of the rocker arm adjusting screws, then remove the pin punches from the camshaft caps.

16. Remove the camshaft holders. Note the holders locations for ease of installation. Loosen the bolts in the reverse order of the holder bolts torque sequence.

17. Remove the camshafts from the cylinder head, then discard the camshaft seals.

18. Remove the rubber cap from the head, located at the end of the intake camshaft.

19. Remove the rocker arms from the cylinder head. Note the locations of the rocker arms.

➡The rocker arms have to be installed to their original locations if being reused.

To install:

20. Lubricate the rocker arms with clean oil, then install the rocker arms on the pivot bolts and the valve stems. If the rocker arms are being reused, install them to their original locations. The locknuts and adjustment screws should be loosened before installing the rocker arms.

21. Lubricate the camshafts with clean oil.

22. Install the camshaft seals to the end of the camshafts that the timing belt sprockets attach to. The open side (spring) should be facing into the cylinder head when installed.

23. Be sure the keyways on the camshafts are facing up and install the camshafts to the cylinder head.

24. Install the rubber plug to the cylinder head at the end of the intake camshaft.

25. Apply liquid gasket to the head mating surfaces of the No. 1 and No. 6 camshaft holders, then install them along with No. 2, 3, 4 and 5. **I** or **E** marks are stamped on the camshaft holders to iden-

tify them as Intake or Exhaust side holders. The arrows stamped on the holders should point toward the timing belt.

26. Snug the camshaft holders in place.

27. Press the camshaft seals securely into place.

28. Tighten the camshaft holder bolts in 2 steps, following the proper sequence, to ensure that the rockers do not bind on the valves. Tighten all the bolts, except the 4 studs, to 84 inch lbs. (10 Nm). Tighten the studs (number 5 and 7 bolts in the correct sequence) to 108 inch lbs. (12 Nm).

29. Install the timing belt back cover.

30. Install the side engine mount bracket B. Tighten the bolt attaching the bracket to the cylinder head to 33 ft. lbs. (45 Nm). Tighten the bolts attaching the bracket to the side engine mount to 16 ft. lbs. (22 Nm).

31. Insert a 5.0mm pin punch in each of the camshaft caps, nearest to the pulleys, through the holes provided. Install the keys into the camshaft grooves.

32. Push the camshaft sprockets onto the camshafts, then tighten the retaining bolts to 27 ft. lbs. (38 Nm).

33. Ensure the words **UP** embossed on the camshaft pulleys are aligned in the upward position. Install the timing belt to the camshaft sprockets, then remove the 2, 5.0mm pin punches from the camshaft bearing caps. Refer to the procedure located in this section.

34. Loosen, then tighten the timing belt adjuster nut.

35. Turn the crankshaft counterclockwise until the cam pulley has moved 3 teeth; this creates tension on the timing belt. Loosen, then tighten the adjusting nut and tighten it to 33 ft. lbs. (45 Nm).

36. Adjust the valves.

37. Tighten the crankshaft pulley bolt to 181 ft. lbs. (250 Nm).

38. Install the middle timing belt cover and tighten the attaching bolts to 108 inch lbs. (12 Nm).

39. Install the rocker arm (valve) cover and tighten the cap nuts to 84 inch lbs. (10 Nm). Install

the PCV hose to the rocker arm (valve) cover.

40. Install the distributor to the cylinder head. Snug the attaching bolts until the timing has been checked and adjusted.

41. Connect the spark plug wires to the correct spark plugs, then attach the distributor electrical connectors. Install the ignition coil wire to the distributor.

42. Install the ignition coil.

43. Install the alternator wiring harness to the rocker arm (valve) cover, then connect the terminal and connector to the alternator.

44. Connect the engine ground cable to the rocker arm (valve) cover.

45. Install the air intake duct.

46. Drain the oil from the engine into a sealable container. Install the drain plug and refill the engine with clean oil.

47. Connect the negative battery cable and enter the radio security code.

48. Start the engine and check carefully for any leaks.

49. Check and adjust the ignition timing. Tighten the distributor bolts to 13 ft. lbs. (18 Nm).

2.7L ENGINE

▶ **See Figures 36, 37 and 38**

1. Disconnect the negative battery cable.

2. Remove the timing belt covers and the timing belt. Refer to the procedure located in this section.

3. Remove the camshafts from the cylinder heads.

4. Remove the intake rocker arms, exhaust inside rocker arms and the pushrods. Identify the location of the parts as they are removed, to ensure reinstallation to the original locations.

5. Remove the valve lifters (hydraulic tappets) from the cylinder heads.

6. Remove the intake manifold, then the cylinder heads from the vehicle.

7. Remove the rocker arm shaft sealing bolt from the cylinder head and discard the washer.

8. Install a 12 x 1.25mm bolt into the rocker arm shaft. Slowly remove the shaft from the cylinder head and remove the exhaust rocker arms and

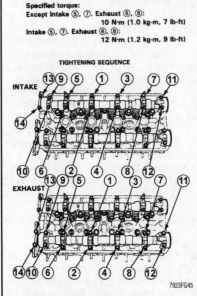

Fig. 35 Camshaft holders torque sequence—2.3L engine

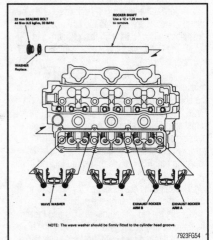

Fig. 36 Exhaust rocker arms and rocker arm shaft component locations—2.7L engine

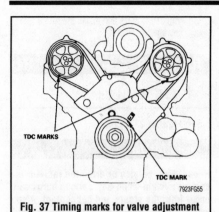

Fig. 37 Timing marks for valve adjustment for cylinders 3, 5 and 6—2.7L engine

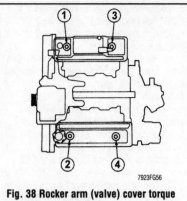

Fig. 38 Rocker arm (valve) cover torque sequence—2.7L engine

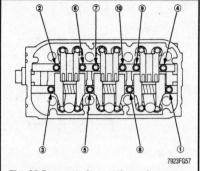

Fig. 39 Be sure to loosen the rocker arm shaft bolts in the correct order as shown—3.0L engine

washers. Identify the location of the parts as they are removed, to ensure reinstallation to the original locations.

To install:

9. Clean the rocker arms and rocker arm shafts in solvent and dry them, then oil the contact surfaces of the parts.

10. Install a 12 x 1.25mm bolt into the rocker arm shaft. Install the rocker arms to their original locations while passing the rocker arm shaft through the cylinder head.

11. Remove the bolt from the rocker arm shaft and install the sealing bolt with a new washer. Tighten the sealing bolt to 33 ft. lbs. (44 Nm).

12. Install the cylinder heads and the intake manifold.

13. Fill the valve lifter (hydraulic tappets) mounting hole and the oil fillers with clean engine oil.

14. Install the valve lifters.

✵✵ WARNING

Do not rotate the valve lifters while installing them.

15. Apply clean engine oil to the rocker arms, pushrods, and the camshafts.

16. Loosen the exhaust rocker arm adjusting screws and locknuts, then install the pushrods, exhaust inside rocker arms, and the intake rocker arms. Install the parts to their original locations.

17. Be sure the rocker arms are properly positioned on the valve stems. Advance the crankshaft 30° from Top Dead Center (TDC) to prevent interference between the pistons and valves when the camshafts are installed.

18. Install the camshafts and camshaft holders.

19. Install the timing belt and set No. 1 cylinder to TDC.

20. Tighten the adjusting screws for No. 1, No. 2 and No. 4 cylinders. Tighten the screw until it contacts the valve, then tighten the screw 1 turn. Hold the screw in place and tighten the locknut to 14 ft. lbs. (20 Nm).

21. Rotate the crankshaft pulley 1 turn clockwise, then tighten the adjusting screws for No. 3, No. 5 and No. 6 cylinders. Tighten the screw until it contacts the valve, then tighten the screw 1⅛ turns. Hold the screw in place and tighten the locknut to 14 ft. lbs. (20 Nm).

22. Install the cylinder head gasket into the groove of the rocker arm (valve) cover. Seat the recesses for the camshaft first, then work it into the groove around the outside edges.

➡**Before installing the rocker arm (valve) cover gasket, thoroughly clean the seal groove.**

23. Apply liquid gasket to the rocker arm (valve) cover gasket at the 4 corners of the recesses. Use a shop towel and wipe the cylinder heads where the rocker arm (valve) covers will come in contact.

24. Install the rocker arm (valve) covers, hold the gasket in the groove by placing your fingers on the camshaft contacting surfaces. With the rocker arm (valve) cover on the cylinder heads, slide the covers slightly back and forth to seat the rocker arm (valve) cover gaskets. Replace the washers if damaged or deteriorated

25. Install the cylinder head side covers with new O-rings and tighten the bolts to 108 inch lbs. (12 Nm).

26. Tighten the rocker arm (valve) cover bolts in 2 or 3 steps. In the final step, tighten all the bolts, in sequence, to 11 ft. lbs. (15 Nm).

27. Install the distributor to the cylinder head and tighten the mounting bolt to 16 ft. lbs. (22 Nm).

28. Connect the spark plug wires to the correct spark plugs, then attach the distributor electrical connectors.

29. Drain the engine oil into a sealable container, then refill the engine with clean oil.

30. Connect the negative battery cable and enter the radio security code.

31. Start the engine, allowing it to idle, and check for any signs of leakage.

3.0L ENGINE

◆ **See Figures 39, 40 and 41**

1. Remove the valve (cylinder head) cover, as outlined earlier in this section.

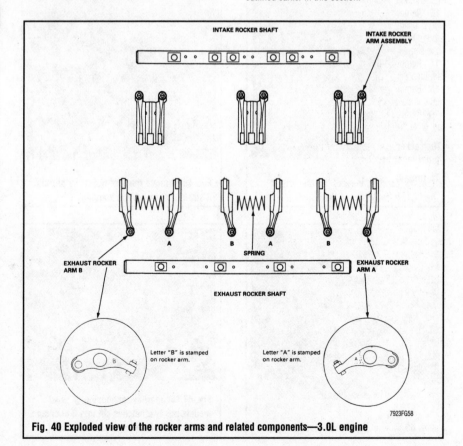

Fig. 40 Exploded view of the rocker arms and related components—3.0L engine

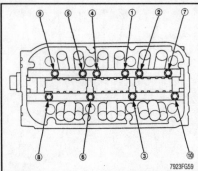

Fig. 41 Tighten the rocker arm bolts 2 turns at a time in the sequence shown—3.0L engine

2. Loosen the jam nuts on the adjusters, then back out the screws.

3. Loosen the rocker arm shaft bolts 2 turns at a time in the sequence shown.

4. Lift the rocker arm assembly from the cylinder head. Leave the bolts in the shafts to retain the rocker arms and springs.

To install:

5. Clean all parts in solvent, dry with compressed air and lubricate with clean engine oil.

6. Place the rocker arm assemblies on the cylinder head and install the bolts loosely. Be sure that all rocker arms are in alignment with their valves.

7. Tighten each bolt 2 turns at a time in the correct sequence. Tighten the bolts to 17 ft. lbs. (24 Nm).

8. Adjust the valves and install the rocker arm (valve) covers.

Thermostat

REMOVAL & INSTALLATION

▶ See Figures 42 thru 50

✳✳ CAUTION

Never open, service or drain the radiator or cooling system when hot; serious burns can occur from the steam and hot coolant. Also, when draining engine coolant, keep in mind that cats and dogs are attracted to ethylene

Fig. 42 After loosening the hose clamp, disconnect the hose from the thermostat housing

Fig. 43 Unthread the bolts from the thermostat housing

Fig. 44 Once all the bolts have been removed, pull the thermostat housing away from the engine

Fig. 45 Installed view of the thermostat and gasket as it sits in the housing

Fig. 46 Remove the thermostat by pulling it straight out from the housing

Fig. 47 Remove the gasket from the thermostat and replace, if necessary

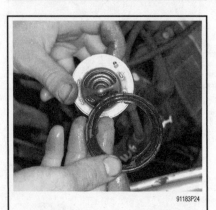

Fig. 48 View of the thermostat and gasket

Fig. 49 The thermostat housing on most models has two notches cut into it to ensure the correct installation of the thermostat

Fig. 50 During installation, always position the air bleed at the top of the thermostat

glycol antifreeze and could drink any that is left in an uncovered container or in puddles on the ground. This will prove fatal in sufficient quantities. Always drain coolant into a sealable container. Coolant should be reused unless it is contaminated or is several years old.

1. Note the radio security code and station presets.
2. Disconnect the negative battery cable.
3. Drain the engine coolant into a sealable container, to a level below the thermostat.
4. Use a pair of pliers to release the tension from the hose clamp, then disconnect the hose from the thermostat housing.
5. Remove the fasteners from the thermostat housing, remove the housing, then remove the thermostat.

To install:

6. Install the thermostat using a new seal. If the thermostat has a small bleed hole, make sure the bleed hole is on the top.
7. Apply an anti-seize compound to the threads of the fasteners.
8. Position the thermostat housing and secure with the retaining bolts.
9. Attach the hose to the housing and secure with the hose clamp
10. Set the heater to the "full hot" position.
11. On the 2.2L and 2.3L engines, locate the coolant bleed valve near the thermostat housing and open the valve ½ turn.

➡When mixing a 50/50 solution of antifreeze and water, using distilled water may help to keep the cooling system from building up mineral deposits and internal blockage.

12. Top off the cooling system and overflow reservoir with a 50/50 mixture of a recommended antifreeze and water solution and bleed the system to remove any air pockets as necessary. Simultaneously squeeze the upper and lower radiator hoses to help push any captured air pockets out of the system.

❄❄ WARNING

The manufacturer does not recommend using a coolant concentration of greater than 60% antifreeze.

13. Inspect all coolant hoses and fittings to make sure they are properly installed and if previously opened, close the bleed valve.
14. Connect the negative battery cable.
15. Install the radiator cap loosely and start the engine. Allow the engine to run until the cooling fan has cycled two times, then turn the engine off and top off the cooling system as necessary.
16. Install the radiator cap and inspect for leaks.
17. Enter the radio security code.

Intake Manifold

REMOVAL & INSTALLATION

➡The radio may contain a coded theft protection circuit. Always obtain the code number before disconnecting the battery.

2.2L and 2.3L Engines

▸ **See Figures 51 and 52**

1. Disconnect the negative battery cable.
2. Drain the engine coolant into a sealable container.
3. Disconnect the cooling hoses from the intake manifold.
4. Label and unplug the vacuum hoses and electrical connectors on the manifold and throttle body. Unplug the connector from the EGR valve. Position the wiring harnesses out of the way.
5. Disconnect the throttle cable from the throttle body.
6. Relieve the fuel pressure, as outlined in Section 5.
7. Remove the fuel rail and fuel injectors.
8. Remove the thermostat housing mounting bolts. Remove the thermostat housing from the intake manifold and the connecting pipe by pulling and twisting the housing. Discard the O-rings.
9. It may be necessary to remove the upper intake manifold plenum and throttle body assembly in order to access the nuts securing the manifold to the head.
10. Remove the intake manifold support bracket bolts and the bracket. If it is necessary to access it from under the vehicle; raise and support the vehicle safely.
11. While supporting the intake manifold, remove the nuts attaching the intake manifold to the

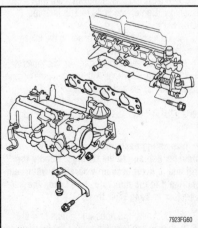

Fig. 51 It is recommended to use a closed-end wrench to remove the intake manifold-to-cylinder head bolts

Fig. 52 Intake manifold and related components—2.3L engine shown

cylinder head, then remove the manifold. Remove the old gasket from the cylinder head.
12. Clean any old gasket material from the cylinder head and the intake manifold. Check and clean the FIA chamber on the cylinder head.

To install:

13. Using a new gasket, place the manifold into position and support.
14. Install the support bracket to the manifold. Tighten the bolt holding the bracket to the manifold to 16 ft. lbs. (22 Nm).
15. Starting with the inner or center nuts, tighten the nuts, in a crisscross pattern, to the correct torque. The tension must be even across the entire face of the manifold if leaks are to be prevented. Correct torque is 16 ft. lbs. (22 Nm).
16. Using a new gasket, install the upper intake manifold and throttle body assembly, if removed as a separate unit. Tighten the nuts and bolts holding the chamber to 16 ft. lbs. (22 Nm).
17. Install a new O-ring to the coolant connecting pipe, and to the thermostat housing. Install the housing to the coolant pipe and the intake manifold. Tighten the mounting bolts to 16 ft. lbs. (22 Nm).
18. Connect and adjust the throttle cable.
19. Install the fuel rail/injector assembly. Connect the fuel lines.
20. Properly position the wiring harnesses and attach the electrical connectors, as tagged during removal.
21. Connect the vacuum hoses, as tagged during removal.
22. Fill and bleed the air from the cooling system.
23. Connect the negative battery cable and enter the radio security code.
24. Start the engine and check carefully for any leaks of fuel, coolant or vacuum. Check the manifold gasket areas carefully for any leakage of vacuum.

2.7L Engines

▸ **See Figure 53**

1. Disconnect the negative battery cable.
2. Drain the engine coolant into a sealable container.
3. Relieve the fuel pressure, as outlined in Section 5.
4. Disconnect the feed hose from the fuel filter.
5. Remove the PCV valve from the rocker arm (valve) cover.
6. Remove the air intake duct.
7. Remove the intake manifold covers.
8. Remove the throttle cable and cruise control cable by loosening the locknut, then slip the cable end out of the accelerator linkage.
9. Label and unplug all electrical connections on the manifold and throttle body.
10. Disconnect the hoses from the brake booster and the evaporative canister.
11. Remove the wiring harness holders and position them out of the way.
12. Disconnect the vacuum hose from the fuel pressure regulator.
13. Remove the fuel rail attaching nuts.
14. Remove the fuel rail from the injectors, leaving the injectors in the manifold.
15. Remove each injector, noting its position, and remove the seal ring from each manifold port.
16. Remove the cushion ring and O-ring from each injector.

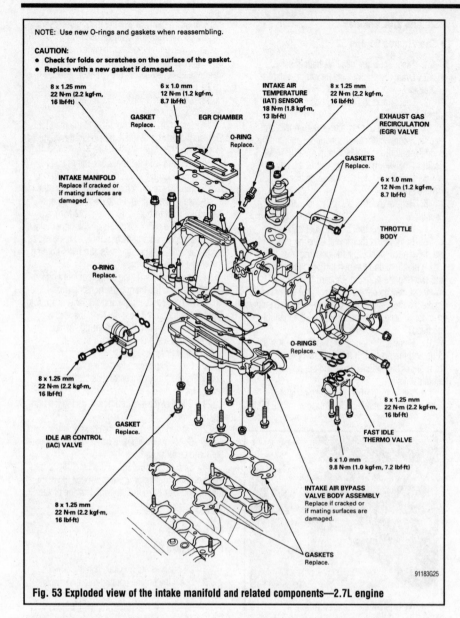

NOTE: Use new O-rings and gaskets when reassembling.

CAUTION:
- Check for folds or scratches on the surface of the gasket.
- Replace with a new gasket if damaged.

8 x 1.25 mm
22 N·m (2.2 kgf·m,
16 lbf·ft)

6 x 1.0 mm
12 N·m (1.2 kgf·m,
8.7 lbf·ft)

INTAKE AIR
TEMPERATURE
(IAT) SENSOR
18 N·m (1.8 kgf·m,
13 lbf·ft)

8 x 1.25 mm
22 N·m (2.2 kgf·m,
16 lbf·ft)

GASKET
Replace.

EGR CHAMBER

O-RING
Replace.

EXHAUST GAS
RECIRCULATION
(EGR) VALVE

INTAKE MANIFOLD
Replace if cracked or
if mating surfaces are
damaged.

GASKETS
Replace.

6 x 1.0 mm
12 N·m (1.2 kgf·m,
8.7 lbf·ft)

THROTTLE
BODY

O-RING
Replace.

O-RINGS
Replace.

8 x 1.25 mm
22 N·m (2.2 kgf·m,
16 lbf·ft)

8 x 1.25 mm
22 N·m (2.2 kgf·m,
16 lbf·ft)

IDLE AIR CONTROL
(IAC) VALVE

GASKET
Replace.

FAST IDLE
THERMO VALVE

6 x 1.0 mm
9.8 N·m (1.0 kgf·m, 7.2 lbf·ft)

INTAKE AIR BYPASS
VALVE BODY ASSEMBLY
Replace if cracked or
if mating surfaces are
damaged.

8 x 1.25 mm
22 N·m (2.2 kgf·m,
16 lbf·ft)

GASKETS
Replace.

91183G25

Fig. 53 Exploded view of the intake manifold and related components—2.7L engine

17. Label and disconnect all vacuum and coolant hoses from the intake manifold and throttle body. If necessary, remove the vacuum pipe assembly.

18. Remove the EGR crossover pipe. Discard the gasket.

19. Remove the bolts and nuts securing the intake manifold to the engine. Be sure all vacuum and electrical connections are unplugged. Carefully lift the manifold from the engine. Discard the gaskets.

To install:

20. Using new gaskets, place the manifold into position. Install the nuts/bolts until just snug.

21. Starting with the inner/center bolts, tighten the nuts and bolts in a crisscross pattern to the correct torque. The tension must be even across the entire face of the manifold if leaks are to be prevented. Correct torque is 16 ft. lbs. (22 Nm).

22. Install the EGR crossover pipe using a new gasket. Tighten the nuts (to the intake manifold) to

108 inch lbs. (12 Nm) and the pipe (to the exhaust manifold) to 43 ft. lbs. (59 Nm).

23. If removed, install the vacuum pipe assembly. Tighten the bolts to 108 inch lbs. (12 Nm).

24. Connect the coolant hoses to the intake manifold and the throttle body.

25. Install new cushion rings on each injector.

26. Coat new O-rings with clean engine oil and install them on the fuel injectors.

27. Install the injectors into the fuel rail. Make certain the O-rings seat properly and are not distorted.

➡ Assembling each injector into the fuel rail prevents damage to the O-rings. Handle the rail and injector assembly carefully when reinstalling it to the manifold. Don't drop the injectors or bang their tips.

28. Coat new seal rings with a light coat of clean, thin oil and install them into the manifold.

29. Install the fuel rail and injectors to the intake manifold.

30. With all injectors seated in the manifold, be sure each injector is positioned properly.

31. Install the fuel rail retaining nuts and tighten them evenly to 108 inch lbs. (12 Nm).

32. Connect the vacuum hose to the regulator.

33. Install the wiring harness to the fuel rail and tighten the mounting bolts to 108 inch lbs. (12 Nm).

34. Connect the electrical harness to the injectors.

35. Attach all electrical and vacuum connections to the throttle body and manifold.

36. Connect the brake booster, evaporative canister, and fuel return hoses.

37. Connect the feed hose to the fuel filter with new gaskets. Tighten the union bolt to 16 ft. lbs. (22 Nm) and the service bolt to 108 inch lbs. (12 Nm).

38. Install and adjust the throttle and cruise control cables.

39. Install the air intake duct.

40. Install the PCV valve to the rocker arm (valve) cover.

41. Refill and bleed the air from the cooling system.

42. Connect the negative battery cable and enter the radio security code.

43. Switch the ignition **ON** but do not engage the starter. The fuel pump should run for approximately 2 seconds, building pressure within the lines. Switch the ignition **OFF**, then **ON** 2 or 3 more times to build full system pressure. Check for fuel leaks.

44. Start the engine and check carefully for any leaks of fuel, coolant, or vacuum. Check the manifold gasket areas carefully for any leakage of vacuum.

45. Install the intake manifold covers and tighten the attaching bolts to 108 inch lbs. (12 Nm).

3.0L ENGINE

▶ See Figure 54

1. Obtain the security code for the radio.

2. Disconnect the negative battery cable.

3. Drain the coolant into a suitable container.

4. Disconnect the EVAP canister hose from the throttle body.

5. Remove the air intake duct.

6. Remove the upper engine covers.

7. Disconnect the accelerator and cruise control cables from the throttle body.

8. Ensure that all components have been removed from the intake manifold.

9. Unfasten the retaining bolts, then remove the intake manifold.

To install:

10. Clean the mounting surfaces.

11. Install a new gasket on the engine and install the manifold.

12. Starting with the inner/center bolts, tighten the nuts and bolts in a crisscross pattern to the correct torque. The tension must be even across the entire face of the manifold if leaks are to be prevented. Correct torque is 16 ft. lbs. (22 Nm).

13. Install all removed hoses and wiring on the intake manifold and throttle body.

14. Install the engine covers.

15. Install the intake air duct.

16. Refill the cooling system.

17. Connect the negative battery cable, start the engine, and check for leaks.

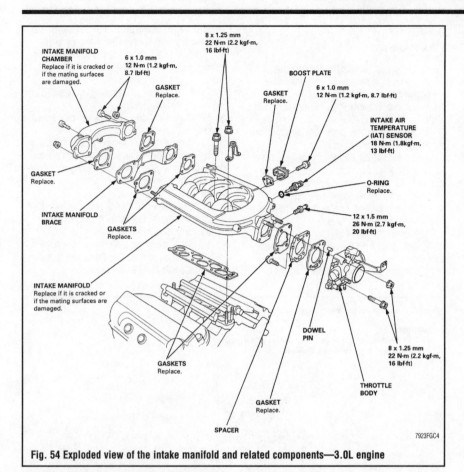

INTAKE MANIFOLD CHAMBER
Replace if it is cracked or if the mating surfaces are damaged.

6 x 1.0 mm
12 N·m (1.2 kgf·m, 8.7 lbf·ft)

8 x 1.25 mm
22 N·m (2.2 kgf·m, 16 lbf·ft)

GASKET
Replace.

BOOST PLATE

GASKET
Replace.

6 x 1.0 mm
12 N·m (1.2 kgf·m, 8.7 lbf·ft)

INTAKE AIR TEMPERATURE (IAT) SENSOR
18 N·m (1.8kgf·m, 13 lbf·ft)

GASKET
Replace.

INTAKE MANIFOLD BRACE

O-RING
Replace.

GASKETS
Replace.

12 x 1.5 mm
26 N·m (2.7 kgf·m, 20 lbf·ft)

INTAKE MANIFOLD
Replace if it is cracked or if the mating surfaces are damaged.

GASKETS
Replace.

DOWEL PIN

8 x 1.25 mm
22 N·m (2.2 kgf·m, 16 lbf·ft)

THROTTLE BODY

GASKET
Replace.

SPACER

7923FGC4

Fig. 54 Exploded view of the intake manifold and related components—3.0L engine

Exhaust Manifold

REMOVAL & INSTALLATION

➡The radio may contain a coded theft protection circuit. Always obtain the code number before disconnecting the battery.

✳✳ CAUTION

The exhaust system should be serviced with the engine cold.

2.2L and 2.3L Engines

▶ **See Figures 55 thru 62**

1. Disconnect the negative battery cable.
2. Safely raise and support the vehicle.
3. If the Oxygen Sensor (O2S) is located in the exhaust manifold, detach the O2S connector.
4. Remove the exhaust manifold upper cover/heat shield.
5. If equipped with air conditioning, remove the heat insulator from the manifold.
6. Remove the nuts attaching the exhaust manifold to the front exhaust pipe. Separate the pipe from the manifold and discard the gasket. Support the pipe with wire; do not allow it to hang by itself.
7. Remove the exhaust manifold bracket(s) bolts and remove the bracket(s).
8. Using a crisscross pattern (starting from the center), remove the exhaust manifold attaching nuts.

91183P17

Fig. 55 Unfasten the retainers, then remove the exhaust manifold heat shield

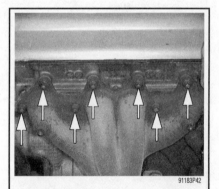

91183P42

Fig. 56 Location of the exhaust manifold mounting bolts

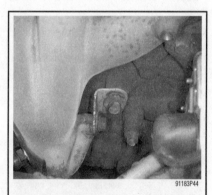

91183P44

Fig. 57 Remove the manifold-to-block support bracket

91183P45

Fig. 58 There are three manifold-to-down pipe bolts that must be removed

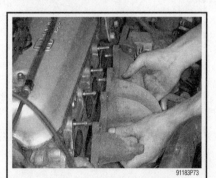

91183P73

Fig. 59 After all of the retainers are removed, you can remove the exhaust manifold

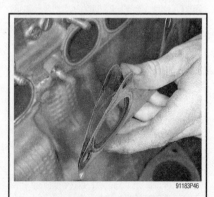

91183P46

Fig. 60 View of the exhaust manifold gasket

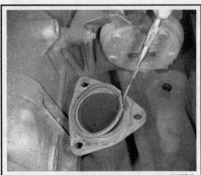

Fig. 61 Use a pick tool to remove the exhaust manifold to down pipe gasket

Fig. 62 Once the exhaust manifold has been installed, use a torque wrench to tighten the mounting nuts

9. Remove the manifold and discard the gasket. Clean the manifold and cylinder head mating surfaces.

10. If equipped, remove the lower manifold cover from the manifold.

To install:

11. If equipped, install the lower manifold cover and tighten the attaching bolts to 16 ft. lbs. (22 Nm).

12. Using a new gasket and nuts, place the manifold into position and support it. Install the nuts snug on the studs.

13. Install the support bracket(s) below the manifold. Tighten the bracket(s) mounting bolts to 33 ft. lbs. (44 Nm).

14. Starting with the manifold inner or center nuts, tighten the nuts in a crisscross pattern to the correct torque. The tension must be even across the entire face of the manifold if leaks are to be prevented. Tighten the nuts to 23 ft. lbs. (31 Nm).

15. If equipped with air conditioning, install the heat insulator to the manifold. Tighten the attaching bolts to 84 inch lbs. (10 Nm) on Prelude models and 108 inch lbs. (12 Nm) on Accord models.

16. Install the upper manifold cover and tighten the bolts to 16 ft. lbs. (22 Nm).

17. If disconnected, attach the Oxygen Sensor (O_2S) connector.

18. Connect the front exhaust pipe using new gaskets and nuts. Tighten the exhaust pipe attaching nuts to 40 ft. lbs. (55 Nm).

19. Connect the negative battery cable and enter the radio security code.

20. Start the engine and check for exhaust leaks.

2.7L Engines

▶ **See Figure 63**

1. Disconnect the negative battery cable.
2. Remove the radiator cap and drain the cooling system into a sealable container.
3. Remove the radiator, as outlined later in this section.
4. Detach the starter cable from the strut tower brace. Remove the strut tower brace.
5. If necessary for additional clearance, remove the vacuum control box on the bulkhead. Position it aside with the vacuum hoses attached.
6. Raise and safely support the vehicle.
7. Remove the front wheels, then remove the splash shield from under the engine.
8. Remove the center beam.
9. Detach the front Oxygen sensor (O_2S) electrical connector.
10. Disconnect the exhaust pipe from the exhaust manifolds and the catalytic converter. Discard the locknuts attaching the downpipe to the manifolds and the catalytic converter. Remove the exhaust pipe from the vehicle and discard the gaskets.
11. Remove the bolts securing the heat shields on the exhaust manifolds.
12. Disconnect the EGR crossover pipe from the engine.
13. Remove the nuts securing the manifolds to the cylinder heads. Remove the manifolds and gaskets from the engine. Remove any old gasket material from the cylinder heads.

To install:

14. Using new gaskets and nuts, place the manifolds into position. Lightly oil the threads, then install the nuts snug on the studs.
15. Starting with the center nuts, tighten the nuts in a crisscross pattern to the correct torque. Tighten the nuts to 22 ft. lbs. (30 Nm).

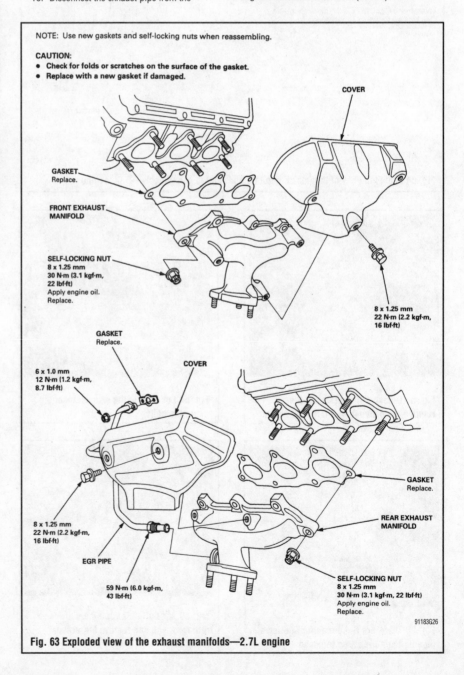

NOTE: Use new gaskets and self-locking nuts when reassembling.

CAUTION:
● Check for folds or scratches on the surface of the gasket.
● Replace with a new gasket if damaged.

COVER

GASKET
Replace.

FRONT EXHAUST MANIFOLD

SELF-LOCKING NUT
8 x 1.25 mm
30 N·m (3.1 kgf·m,
22 lbf·ft)
Apply engine oil.
Replace.

8 x 1.25 mm
22 N·m (2.2 kgf·m,
16 lbf·ft)

GASKET
Replace.

COVER

6 x 1.0 mm
12 N·m (1.2 kgf·m,
8.7 lbf·ft)

GASKET
Replace.

REAR EXHAUST MANIFOLD

8 x 1.25 mm
22 N·m (2.2 kgf·m,
16 lbf·ft)

EGR PIPE

59 N·m (6.0 kgf·m,
43 lbf·ft)

SELF-LOCKING NUT
8 x 1.25 mm
30 N·m (3.1 kgf·m, 22 lbf·ft)
Apply engine oil.
Replace.

Fig. 63 Exploded view of the exhaust manifolds—2.7L engine

16. Install the EGR crossover pipe with a new gasket. Tighten the nuts to 108 inch lbs. (12 Nm) and the exhaust manifold connection to 43 ft. lbs. (59 Nm).

17. Install the heat shields to the manifolds. Tighten the bolts to 16 ft. lbs. (22 Nm).

18. Install the exhaust pipe with new nuts and gaskets. Tighten the exhaust manifold connections to 40 ft. lbs. (54 Nm) and the catalytic converter to 25 ft. lbs. (33 Nm).

19. Attach the front O₂S electrical connector.

20. Install the center beam. Tighten the bolts to 37 ft. lbs. (50 Nm).

21. Install the splash shield and front wheels.

22. Install the vacuum control box and the radiator.

23. Install the strut tower brace and secure the starter cable. Tighten the strut tower bolts to 16 ft. lbs. (22 Nm).

24. Fill and bleed the air from the cooling system.

25. Connect the negative battery cable and enter the radio security code.

26. Start the engine and allow it to reach normal operating temperature. Check for leaks.

3.0L Engine

♦ **See Figure 64**

1. Raise and safely support the vehicle.

2. Remove the engine undercover.

3. Disconnect the exhaust pipe from the manifold to be removed.

4. Lower the vehicle.

5. Remove the exhaust manifold heat shield.

6. Remove the mounting nuts and the exhaust manifold.

To install:

7. Clean the mounting surfaces.

8. Position a new gasket on the cylinder head.

9. Install the exhaust manifold. Tighten the nuts to 23 ft. lbs. (31 Nm).

10. Install the heat shield. Tighten the bolts to 16 ft. lbs. (22 Nm).

11. Raise the vehicle and connect the exhaust pipe to the manifold using a new gasket. Tighten the nuts to 40 ft. lbs. (54 Nm).

Radiator

REMOVAL & INSTALLATION

♦ **See Figure 65**

❊ CAUTION

Never open a radiator cap or cooling system when the coolant temperature is above 100°F (38°C). Avoid physical contact at all times, wear protective clothing and eye protection. Always drain coolant into a sealable container. If spillage occurs take care to clean the spill as quickly as possible.

1. Drain the coolant into a sealable container by loosening the radiator drain plug.

2. Remove the upper and lower radiator hoses.

3. If equipped with an automatic transaxle, place a separate sealable drain container under the transaxle Automatic Transmission Fluid (ATF) cool-

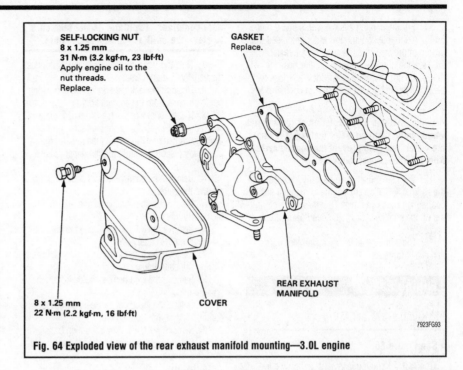

Fig. 64 Exploded view of the rear exhaust manifold mounting—3.0L engine

SELF-LOCKING NUT
8 x 1.25 mm
31 N·m (3.2 kgf·m, 23 lbf·ft)
Apply engine oil to the nut threads.
Replace.

GASKET
Replace.

REAR EXHAUST MANIFOLD

COVER

8 x 1.25 mm
22 N·m (2.2 kgf·m, 16 lbf·ft)

7923FG93

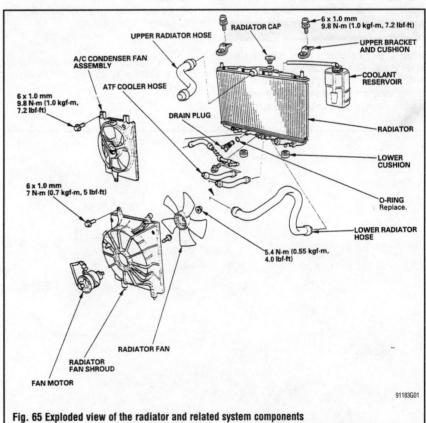

Fig. 65 Exploded view of the radiator and related system components

UPPER RADIATOR HOSE

RADIATOR CAP

6 x 1.0 mm
9.8 N·m (1.0 kgf·m, 7.2 lbf·ft)

A/C CONDENSER FAN ASSEMBLY

UPPER BRACKET AND CUSHION

ATF COOLER HOSE

COOLANT RESERVOIR

6 x 1.0 mm
9.8 N·m (1.0 kgf·m, 7.2 lbf·ft)

DRAIN PLUG

RADIATOR

LOWER CUSHION

6 x 1.0 mm
7 N·m (0.7 kgf·m, 5 lbf·ft)

O-RING
Replace.

LOWER RADIATOR HOSE

5.4 N·m (0.55 kgf·m, 4.0 lbf·ft)

RADIATOR FAN

FAN MOTOR

RADIATOR FAN SHROUD

91183G01

ing lines and disconnect, drain and plug the lines and radiator fittings.

4. Detach the electrical connectors from the radiator cooling fans.

5. Remove the upper radiator support brackets and cushion assemblies.

6. Carefully lift the radiator upward and away from the vehicle.

7. Remove the fasteners that secure the cooling fans to the radiator.

To install:

8. Install the radiator in the reverse order of disassembly.

9. Once installed open the bleed valve on the thermostat housing ½ a turn.

10. Set the heater to the "full hot" position.

11. Fill the cooling system with a 50/50 mixture of a suitable coolant and water and bleed the air out of the system as necessary. Alternately squeeze the upper and lower radiator hoses to help force out any trapped air pockets. Close the bleed valve once a steady stream of coolant is visible.

→When mixing a 50/50 solution of coolant and water, using distilled water instead of regular tap water may help prevent the cooling system from internal deposit build-up.

12. With the radiator cap partially installed, start the engine, and allow the engine to run until the cooling fan runs two times. Turn the engine off and top up the cooling system and overflow reservoir as necessary.

13. Close the radiator cap, restart the engine and check for leaks.

Engine Fan

REMOVAL & INSTALLATION

♦ See Figure 66

The radiator cooling fans are electrically operated and mount directly to the radiator.

✳✳ CAUTION

Never open a radiator cap or cooling system when the coolant temperature is above 100°F (38°C). Avoid physical contact at all times, wear protective clothing and eye protection. Always drain coolant into a sealable container. If spillage occurs take care to clean the spill as quickly as possible.

1. Note the radio security code and disconnect the negative battery cable.
2. Detach the electrical connectors and wiring guide brackets from the cooling fans
3. If additional work space is needed, drain about 3 quarts of coolant from the radiator into a sealable container by loosening the radiator drain plug, then disconnect and plug the upper radiator hose.
4. Remove the positive battery cable and remove the battery.
5. Disconnect the wire harness guides from the battery tray.
6. Remove the ground strap and the relay box bracket from the battery tray.
7. Remove the battery tray mounting bolts and remove the battery tray.
8. Remove the wire harness holders from the upper radiator support.
9. Detach the electrical connectors from the air conditioning compressor clutch.
10. Remove the fan shroud mounting bolts.
11. Carefully remove the cooling fan assembly from the vehicle.

To install:

12. The installation is in the reverse order of removal except for the following.
13. Top off and bleed the cooling system as necessary.
14. When connecting the battery cables, connect the positive battery cable first, then the negative cable.
15. Enter the radio security code.

16. Start the engine and check for coolant leaks and normal operation of the cooling fans.

TESTING

✳✳ WARNING

The electrically operated cooling fans can begin to operate without notice, should an electrical component fail or if a circuit interference occurs. Always keep fingers, hands and objects clear of the cooling fans as unexpected operation of the cooling fans could cause physical injury. Always use care when testing or working with the cooling fans or related equipment.

The electric cooling fans are electrically operated and controlled by two basic electrical circuits.

One of the electrical circuits has a temperature sensor which triggers a relay to power the fans. The cooling fan will begin to operate once the coolant temperature reaches the designated temperature of the temperature sensor, which completes the circuit for the fan relay causing the fan to operate.

Possible failures in this circuit include the following:
- A failed relay
- A failed fan motor
- A blown or missing fuse
- A defective ignition switch
- A defective temperature sensor
- Damaged, shorted or disconnected wiring or electrical connector

Possible cooling system problems that could affect the cooling fan operation include:
- Coolant leaks
- Low coolant level
- A restricted radiator
- A failed head gasket
- A defective water pump
- A defective radiator cap
- Excessively contaminated coolant

The second electrical circuit that controls the cooling fans is the air conditioner circuit. When the air conditioning is used, the cooling fans automatically operate, regardless of the engine coolant temperature.

This can be a handy tidbit of information to know should the temperature sensor fail. If the air conditioner is turned on, the cooling fans should function if the A/C system is in proper working order.

Possible failures in this circuit include a faulty A/C switch as well as those items from the previous list.

Electric cooling fan circuit failures can be one of several types:
- The fans fail to operate, either completely or not within the designed temperature range
- The fans run continuously regardless of the coolant temperature with the A/C and ignition switch off
- The fans run continuously regardless of the coolant temperature only when the ignition switch is on but with the A/C switch off

The danger of a cooling fan that fails to operate is an overheated engine. A cooling fan that runs all the time only when the ignition is **ON** never allows the engine to fully warm up and driveability and fuel economy may suffer. A cooling fan that runs all the time even when the ignition is switched **OFF**, never

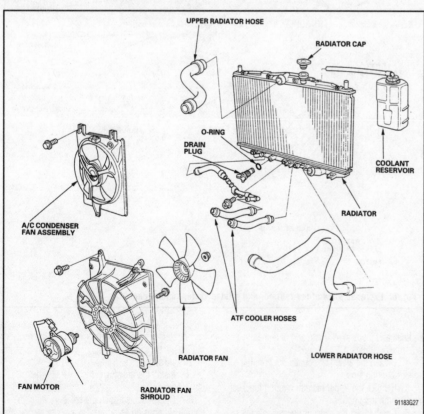

Fig. 66 Exploded view of common radiator cooling fans and related components

UPPER RADIATOR HOSE

RADIATOR CAP

O-RING

DRAIN PLUG

COOLANT RESERVOIR

RADIATOR

A/C CONDENSER FAN ASSEMBLY

ATF COOLER HOSES

RADIATOR FAN

LOWER RADIATOR HOSE

FAN MOTOR

RADIATOR FAN SHROUD

91183G27

allows the engine to fully warm up, the driveability and fuel economy may suffer, and the battery will eventually discharge.

To test the cooling fans, proceed as follows:

1. Detach the electrical connector for the cooling fan. Consult the wiring schematic in Section 6 for the exact wire color for each fan. The black wire is ground and the colored, striped wire is positive.

2. Carefully connect a 30 amp fused jumper wire between the fan positive wire and the battery positive terminal.

3. Connect a jumper wire between the fan ground terminal and a known good chassis ground and the fan should operate. If the fan fails to operate, check the test circuit with a known good 12 Volt test light to make sure the jumper leads are functioning properly. If the circuit tests ok and the fan fails to function when connected to the jumper circuit, replace the fan. If the jumper circuit fuse blows, check for a shorted fan wire and test again. If the jumper circuit continues to blow the fuse the fan motor is internally shorted and must be replaced.

Water Pump

REMOVAL & INSTALLATION

2.2L and 2.3L Engines

♦ See Figures 67 and 68

➡The original radio contains a coded anti-theft circuit. Obtain the security code number before disconnecting the battery cables.

1. Disconnect the negative battery cable.
2. Drain the cooling system into a suitable container.
3. Remove the accessory drive belts, the valve cover, and the upper timing belt cover.
4. Set the timing at TDC/compression for the No. 1 piston.
5. Remove the crankshaft pulley and lower timing belt cover.
6. Remove the timing belt. Replace the timing belt if it is contaminated with oil or coolant or shows any signs of wear and damage. Refer to the procedure located in this section.
7. If equipped with a Crankshaft Speed Fluctuation (CKF) sensor at the crankshaft sprocket, unbolt the sensor bracket and move the sensor out of the way. Cover the sensor with a shop towel to keep coolant off of it.

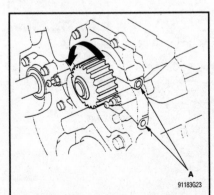

Fig. 67 Direction of rotation of the water pump pulley

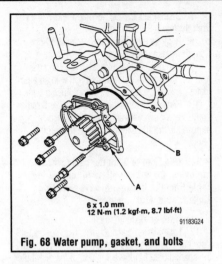

6 x 1.0 mm
12 N·m (1.2 kgf·m, 8.7 lbf·ft)

91183G24

Fig. 68 Water pump, gasket, and bolts

8. Unbolt the water pump and remove it from the engine block.

To install:

9. Clean the water pump and O-ring mating surfaces before installation.
10. Install the water pump with a new O-ring. Coat only the bolt threads with liquid gasket and tighten them to 108 inch lbs. (12 Nm).
11. Install the timing belt. Be sure it is fitted and adjusted properly. Refer to the procedure located in this section.
12. If equipped, install the CKF sensor and tighten the bracket bolts to 108 inch lbs. (12 Nm).
13. Install the lower belt cover and crankshaft pulley.
14. Install the upper timing belt cover, the valve cover, and the accessory drive belts.
15. Be sure the cooling system drain plug is closed. Refill and bleed the cooling system.
16. Connect the negative battery cable and enter the radio security code.
17. Start the engine, allow it to reach normal operating temperature, and check for coolant leaks.

2.7L Engine

♦ See Figure 69

1. Disconnect the negative battery cable.
2. Drain the coolant into a sealable container.
3. Remove the timing belt covers and the timing belt. Refer to the procedure located in this section.
4. Remove the timing belt tensioner.
5. Remove the 9 water pump bolts, take note of their locations for reinstallation.
6. Remove the water pump from the engine and discard the O-ring. Remove the dowel pins.

To install:

7. Clean the water pump mounting surface and O-ring groove, then install the dowel pins to the engine.
8. Install a new O-ring to the engine, then install the water pump. Be careful not to pinch the O-ring. Install the mounting bolts to their original locations. When tightening the bolts, be sure that the O-ring does not bulge out of the groove. Tighten the 6mm bolts to 108 inch lbs. (12 Nm), and tighten the 8mm bolts to 16 ft. lbs. (22 Nm).

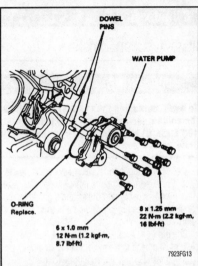

DOWEL PINS

WATER PUMP

O-RING Replace.

6 x 1.0 mm
12 N·m (1.2 kgf·m, 8.7 lbf·ft)

8 x 1.25 mm
22 N·m (2.2 kgf·m, 16 lbf·ft)

7923FG13

Fig. 69 Exploded view of the water pump—2.7L engine

9. Inspect the water pump, making sure that the pump turns freely.
10. Install the timing belt tensioner.
11. Install the timing belt and timing belt covers. Refer to the procedure located in this section.
12. Refill and bleed the air from the cooling system.
13. Connect the negative battery cable and enter the radio security code.

3.0L Engine

♦ See Figure 70

1. Remove the timing belt. Refer to the procedure located in this section.
2. Remove the timing belt tensioner.
3. Remove the 5 water pump mounting bolts, then remove the pump and seal.

To install:

4. Clean the seal groove and mating surfaces.
5. Using a new seal, install the water pump. Tighten the bolts to 104 inch lbs. (12 Nm).
6. Install the timing belt tensioner.
7. Install the timing belt. Refer to the procedure located in this section.
8. Refill the cooling system.
9. Start the engine and check for leaks.
10. Top off the cooling system if necessary after the engine has cooled.

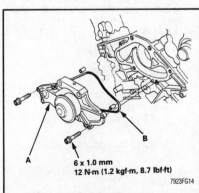

6 x 1.0 mm
12 N·m (1.2 kgf·m, 8.7 lbf·ft)

7923FG14

Fig. 70 Exploded view of the water pump mounting—3.0L engine

Cylinder Head

REMOVAL & INSTALLATION

✳✳ WARNING

To avoid damaging the cylinder head, allow the coolant temperature to drop below 100°F (38°C) before removing the head bolts.

Carefully thought and a clean work environment should be a priority when removing a cylinder head. Have plenty of cardboard boxes and a good marker handy to label and organize the parts as they are removed.

Be sure to have an ample supply of sealable clear plastic bags that can be labeled for the removed fasteners. Make sure to investigate whether or not certain fasteners can be reused or must be replaced.

Have sealable containers available for the used coolant and engine oil which must be drained during the procedure. Have a pencil and note pad handy to make drawings and make notes of cable routing , wire and bracket locations.

Follow the installation procedures carefully to know whether certain fasteners should be lubricated or not when being installed.

Read the procedures before starting to get a thorough understanding of the tools and equipment needed. Many of the components of the cylinder head are precision machined pieces that need to be thoroughly cleaned and inspected before reinstalling. For specific details on the basics of the cylinder head, refer to the ENGINE RECONDITIONING information located further along in this section.

When machined components are removed **NEVER:**
• Allow two machined pieces to rest or contact one another
• Lay the component directly on the ground or garage floor
• Mix up the location from which they were removed

Use wood or cardboard to protect a machined component, especially items such as a cylinder head.

➡**The radio may contain a coded theft protection circuit. Always obtain the code number before disconnecting the battery. After connecting the battery, turn the steering wheel lock-to-lock to reset the steering control unit.**

2.2L Engines

F22B1 AND F22B2 ENGINES

▶ **See Figures 71 thru 83**

1. Disconnect the negative battery cable.
2. Bring the No. 1 cylinder to TDC.
3. Drain the engine coolant into a sealable container.
4. Relieve the fuel pressure, as outlined in Section 5.
5. Remove the vacuum hose, breather hose and air intake duct.
6. Remove the water bypass hose from the cylinder head.

7. Disconnect the fuel feed and return hose from the fuel rail.
8. Remove the EVAP control canister hose from the intake manifold.
9. Remove the brake booster vacuum hose from the intake manifold. If equipped with an automatic transaxle, remove the vacuum hose mount.
10. Remove the throttle cable from the throttle body. If equipped with an automatic transaxle, remove the throttle control cable at the throttle body.

➡**Be careful not to bend the cable when removing. Do not use pliers to remove the cable from the linkage. Always replace a kinked cable with a new one.**

11. Remove the ignition coil.
12. Label, then detach the electrical connectors from the distributor and the spark plug wires from the spark plugs. Mark the position of the distributor and remove it from the cylinder head. Disconnect the ignition coil wire from the distributor.
13. Remove the connector and the terminal from the alternator, then remove the engine wiring harness from the valve cover.
14. Label and detach the following engine wiring harness connectors:
   a. Fuel injector connectors
   b. IAT sensor connector, if equipped
   c. IAC valve connector

   d. TP sensor connector
   e. EGR valve lift sensor
   f. Ground cable terminals
   g. ECT switch B connector, if equipped
   h. HO2S connector
   i. ECT sensor
   j. ECT gauge sending unit connector
   k. CKP/CYP sensor connector, if equipped
   l. VSS connector
   m. ECT switch **A** connector

15. Remove the upper radiator hose and the heater inlet hose from the cylinder head.
16. Remove the lower radiator hose and heater outlet hose from the intake manifold.
17. Remove the bypass hose from the thermostat housing and intake manifold.
18. Remove the thermostat housing mounting bolts. Remove the thermostat housing from the intake manifold and the connecting pipe by pulling and twisting the housing. Discard the O-rings.
19. Tag, then disconnect the emissions vacuum hoses from the intake manifold assembly.
20. Disconnect the cruise control actuator electrical connector and the vacuum tube, then remove the cruise control actuator.
21. Remove the engine ground cable from the body.
22. Remove the mounting bolts and drive belt from the power steering pump. Pull the pump away

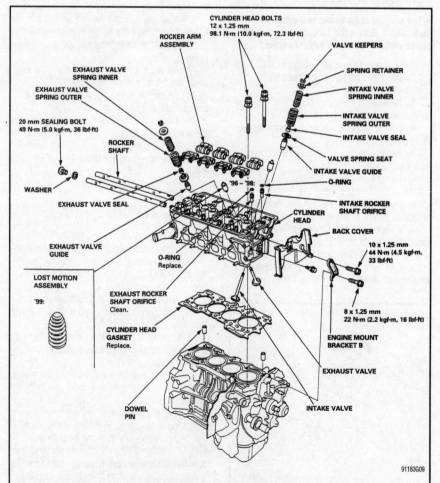

Fig. 71 Exploded view of the cylinder head and related components—2.2L engines (except F22B1 & F22B2)

Fig. 72 The cylinder head and valve train components can easily be seen with the valve cover removed

Fig. 73 Use a breaker bar to break the cylinder head bolts loose

Fig. 74 Once the head bolts have been broken loose with a breaker bar, you may use a ratchet to speed up the removal process

Fig. 75 Noting their installed location, remove the bolts from the cylinder head . . .

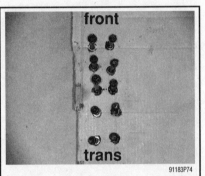

Fig. 76 . . . and use a piece of cardboard as a holder to keep them in the proper order

Fig. 77 Marking the position of each head bolt is extremely important because they are of unequal length

Fig. 78 Firmly grasp the cylinder head and slowly and carefully lift it off the block

Fig. 79 You may want to leave the intake manifold attached to the head until it has been removed from the block. This will speed up the removal process

Fig. 80 Once the head has been removed, the cylinders can easily be inspected for wear

Fig. 81 Always replace the head gasket with a new one that meets or exceeds the factory specifications

Fig. 82 View of the head gasket alignment dowel

Fig. 83 It is easier to remove the intake manifold from the cylinder head once the head has been removed from the block

from the mounting bracket without disconnecting the hoses. Support the pump out of the way.

23. Raise and safely support the vehicle.
24. Remove the front wheel and tire assemblies.
25. Remove the splash shield.

➡You can also leave the intake manifold attached to the cylinder head, then separate the two components once they are removed from the engine.

26. Remove the intake manifold bracket bolts.
27. Remove the intake manifold.
28. Disconnect the exhaust pipe from the exhaust manifold.
29. Remove the exhaust manifold and the exhaust manifold heat insulator.
30. Remove the power steering pump mounting bracket.
31. Remove the PCV hose, then remove the rocker arm (valve) cover. Replace the rubber seals if damages or deteriorated.
32. Remove the timing belt. Refer to the procedure located in this section.
33. Remove the cylinder head bolts in the reverse order of installation.

➡To prevent warpage, unscrew the bolts in sequence ⅓ turn at a time. Repeat the sequence until all bolts are loosened.

34. Separate the cylinder head from the engine block with a suitable flat-bladed prytool.

To install:

35. Be sure all cylinder head and block gasket surfaces are clean. Check the cylinder head for warpage. If warpage is less than 0.002 in. (0.05mm), cylinder head resurfacing is not required. Maximum resurface limit is 0.008 in. (0.2mm) based on a cylinder head height of 3.94 in. (100mm). Refer to engine rebuilding at the end of this section for more information.
36. Always use a new head gasket.
37. The **UP** mark on the camshaft pulley should be at the top.
38. Be sure the No. 1 cylinder is at TDC.
39. Clean the oil control orifice and install a new O-ring. Install and align the cylinder head dowel pins and oil control jet.
40. Install the bolts that secure the intake manifold to its bracket but do not tighten them.
41. Install the cylinder head, then tighten the cylinder head bolts sequentially in 3 steps:
- Step 1: 29 ft. lbs. (40 Nm).
- Step 2: 51 ft. lbs. (70 Nm).
- Step 3: 72 ft. lbs. (100 Nm).
42. Install the intake manifold and tighten the nuts in a crisscross pattern, in 2 or 3 steps, beginning with the inner nuts. Final torque should be 16 ft. lbs. (22 Nm). Always use a new intake manifold gasket.
43. Connect the intake manifold bracket to the intake manifold. Tighten the bolt to 16 ft. lbs. (22 Nm).
44. Install the heat insulator to the cylinder head and the block.
45. Install the power steering pump mounting bracket to the cylinder head. Tighten the 2 10mm bolts to 36 ft. lbs. (50 Nm). Torque the 8mm bolt to 16 ft. lbs. (22 Nm).
46. Install the exhaust manifold and tighten the nuts in a crisscross pattern in 2 or 3 steps, beginning with the inner nut. Final torque should be 23

ft. lbs. (32 Nm). Always use a new exhaust manifold gasket.

47. Install the exhaust manifold bracket, then install the exhaust pipe, bracket and upper shroud.
48. Be sure the camshaft sprocket and the crankshaft pulleys are aligned to TDC. Install the timing belt. Refer to the procedure located in this section.
49. Install the splash shield and the front wheels.
50. Lower the vehicle.
51. Check and adjust the valves, as necessary.
52. Tighten the crankshaft pulley bolt to 181 ft. lbs. (250 Nm).
53. Installation of the remaining components is the reverse of the removal procedure.
54. Fill the cooling system.
55. Connect the negative battery cable and enter the radio security code.
56. Start the engine and check carefully for any leaks.
57. Check the ignition timing and tighten the distributor bolts to 13 ft. lbs. (18 Nm).

F22B1 AND F22B2 ENGINES

♦ **See Figures 84, 85, 86, 87 and 88**

1. Disconnect the negative battery cable, then the positive battery cable.

2. Turn the engine to align the timing marks and set cylinder No.1 to TDC. The white mark on the crankshaft pulley should align with the pointer on the timing belt cover.
3. Raise and safely support the vehicle.
4. Drain the engine coolant into a sealable container.
5. Remove the front wheel and tire assemblies.
6. Remove the splash shield.
7. Disconnect the exhaust pipe from the exhaust manifold.
8. Remove the intake manifold bracket bolts.
9. Lower the vehicle to a working level without placing it on the floor.
10. Remove the throttle cable from the throttle body. On automatic transaxle equipped vehicles, remove the throttle control cable. If equipped with cruise control, remove the cruise control cable.

➡Be careful not to bend the cable when removing it. Always replace a kinked cable with a new one. Do not use pliers to remove the cable from the linkage.

11. Remove the intake air duct.
12. Remove the breather hose, PCV hose, and EVAP control canister hose.
13. Relieve the fuel pressure, as outlined in Section 5.

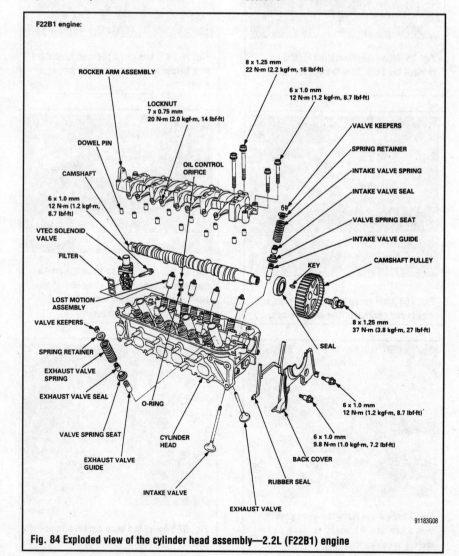

F22B1 engine:

ROCKER ARM ASSEMBLY
8 x 1.25 mm
22 N·m (2.2 kgf·m, 16 lbf·ft)
6 x 1.0 mm
12 N·m (1.2 kgf·m, 8.7 lbf·ft)
LOCKNUT
7 x 0.75 mm
20 N·m (2.0 kgf·m, 14 lbf·ft)
VALVE KEEPERS
SPRING RETAINER
DOWEL PIN
OIL CONTROL ORIFICE
INTAKE VALVE SPRING
CAMSHAFT
INTAKE VALVE SEAL
6 x 1.0 mm
12 N·m (1.2 kgf·m, 8.7 lbf·ft)
VALVE SPRING SEAT
VTEC SOLENOID VALVE
INTAKE VALVE GUIDE
FILTER
KEY
CAMSHAFT PULLEY
LOST MOTION ASSEMBLY
8 x 1.25 mm
37 N·m (3.8 kgf·m, 27 lbf·ft)
VALVE KEEPERS
SEAL
SPRING RETAINER
EXHAUST VALVE SPRING
6 x 1.0 mm
12 N·m (1.2 kgf·m, 8.7 lbf·ft)
EXHAUST VALVE SEAL
O-RING
6 x 1.0 mm
9.8 N·m (1.0 kgf·m, 7.2 lbf·ft)
VALVE SPRING SEAT
CYLINDER HEAD
BACK COVER
EXHAUST VALVE GUIDE
RUBBER SEAL
INTAKE VALVE
EXHAUST VALVE

91183G08

Fig. 84 Exploded view of the cylinder head assembly—2.2L (F22B1) engine

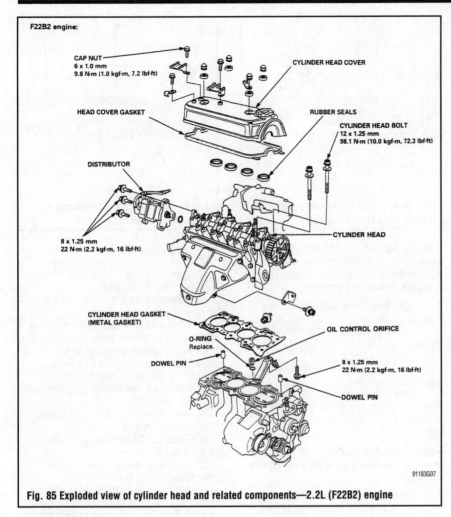

Fig. 85 Exploded view of cylinder head and related components—2.2L (F22B2) engine

14. Remove the fuel feed and return hose from the fuel rail.

15. Disconnect the vacuum hoses attached to the engine located near the fuel feed and return hoses.

16. Remove the brake booster vacuum hose from the intake manifold. Label and remove the other vacuum hoses from the intake manifold.

17. Remove the clamp holding the power steering hose to the strut tower.

18. Remove the wiring harness clamp and the ground cable from the intake manifold.

19. Remove the connector and the terminal from the alternator, then remove the engine wiring harness from the valve cover.

20. Remove the mounting bolts and drive belt from the power steering pump. Pull the pump away from the mounting bracket without disconnecting the hoses. Support the pump out of the way.

21. Loosen the adjusting and mounting bolts for the alternator and remove the drive belt.

22. Remove the engine wiring harness and bypass hose from the lower side of the intake manifold.

23. Label and detach the following engine wiring harness connectors:
- Fuel injector connectors
- IAT sensor connector
- IAC valve connector
- TP sensor connector
- MAP sensor connector

- HO$_2$S connector
- ECT sensor connector
- ECT switch connector
- ECT gauge sending unit connector
- VTEC solenoid valve connector
- VTEC pressure switch connector
- EGR valve lift sensor
- CKP/CYP sensor connector
- Ignition coil connector (Non VTEC engine)
- Fuel Injection Air (FIA) control solenoid valve connector (VTEC engine)

24. Label, then detach the electrical connectors from the distributor and the spark plug wires from the spark plugs. Mark the position of the distributor and remove it from the cylinder head. Disconnect the ignition coil wire from the distributor.

25. Remove the upper radiator hose and the heater inlet hose from the cylinder head.

26. Remove the lower radiator hose from the thermostat housing.

27. Remove the coolant bypass hoses.

28. Use a jack to support the engine. Be sure to place a cushion between the oil pan and the jack. Remove the through-bolt from the side engine mount and remove the mount.

29. Remove the rocker arm (valve) cover. Replace the rubber seals if damaged or deteriorated.

30. Remove the timing belt covers and the timing belt. Refer to the procedure located in this section.

31. Remove the camshaft sprocket and the back cover. Do not lose the sprocket key.

32. Remove the exhaust manifold heat insulator and the exhaust manifold.

33. Remove the thermostat housing mounting bolts. Remove the thermostat housing from the intake manifold and the connecting pipe, by pulling and twisting the housing. Discard the O-rings.

34. Remove the fuel rail and fuel injectors.

35. Remove the intake manifold.

36. Remove the cylinder head bolts in the reverse order proper sequence, then remove the cylinder head.

➡ **To prevent warpage, unscrew the bolts in sequence ⅓ turn at a time. Repeat the sequence until all bolts are loosened.**

To install:

37. Be sure all cylinder head and block gasket surfaces are clean. Check the cylinder head for warpage. If warpage is less than 0.002 in. (0.05mm), cylinder head resurfacing is not required. Maximum resurface limit is 0.008 in. (0.2mm) based on a cylinder head height of 3.94 in. (100mm). Refer to engine rebuilding, at the end of this section for more information.

38. Always use a new head gasket.

39. Be sure the No. 1 cylinder is at TDC.

40. Clean the oil control orifice and install a new O-ring (VTEC engine only).

41. Install the dowel pins to the engine block.

42. Install the bolts that secure the intake manifold to its bracket but do not tighten them.

43. Position the camshaft correctly.

44. Install the cylinder head, then tighten the cylinder head bolts sequentially in 3 steps:
- Step 1: 29 ft. lbs. (39 Nm).
- Step 2: 51 ft. lbs. (69 Nm).
- Step 3: 72 ft. lbs. (98 Nm).

45. Install the intake manifold with a new gasket.

46. Connect the intake manifold bracket to the intake manifold and tighten the bolt to 16 ft. lbs. (22 Nm).

47. Install the fuel rail with the fuel injectors.

48. Install the exhaust manifold with a new gasket.

49. Install the exhaust manifold bracket.

50. Install the timing belt back cover to the cylinder head. Tighten the cover bolt on the non VTEC engine to 108 inch lbs. (12 Nm). On the VTEC engine tighten the bolt on the intake side of the head to 108 inch lbs. (12 Nm) and tighten the bolt on the exhaust side of the head to 84 inch lbs. (10 Nm).

51. Install the key to the camshaft, then install the camshaft sprocket. Tighten the sprocket bolt to 27 ft. lbs. (37 Nm).

52. Be sure the camshaft sprocket and the crankshaft pulleys are aligned to TDC and install the timing belt. Refer to the procedure located in this section.

53. Install the lower timing belt cover and tighten the bolts to 108 inch lbs. (12 Nm).

54. Install a new seal around the adjusting nut. Do not loosen the adjusting nut.

55. Install the crankshaft pulley. Coat the threads and seating face of the pulley bolt with engine oil. Install and tighten the bolt to 181 ft. lbs. (250 Nm).

56. Install the side engine mount. Tighten the bolt and nut attaching the mount to the engine to 40 ft. lbs. (55 Nm). Tighten the through nut and bolt to

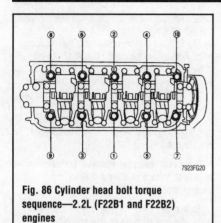

Fig. 86 Cylinder head bolt torque sequence—2.2L (F22B1 and F22B2) engines

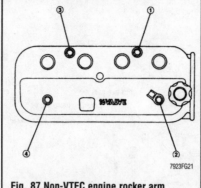

Fig. 87 Non-VTEC engine rocker arm (valve) cover torque sequence

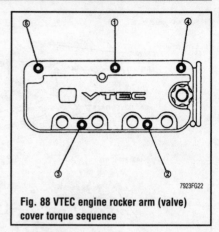

Fig. 88 VTEC engine rocker arm (valve) cover torque sequence

47 ft. lbs. (65 Nm), remove the jack from under the center beam.

57. Adjust the valves.

58. Install the upper timing belt cover. Tighten the bolt on the intake side of the head to 108 inch lbs. (12 Nm) and tighten the bolt on the exhaust side of the head to 84 inch lbs. (10 Nm).

59. Raise and safely support the vehicle.

60. Connect the exhaust pipe to the exhaust manifold with new gaskets. Tighten the nuts 40 ft. lbs. (54 Nm).

61. Install the splash shield and the front wheels.

62. Lower the vehicle.

63. Install the rocker arm (valve) cover gasket cover to the groove of the rocker arm (valve) cover. Before installing the gasket thoroughly clean the seal and the groove. Seat the recesses for the camshaft first, then work it into the groove around the outside edges. Be sure the gasket is seated securely in the corners of the recesses.

64. Apply liquid gasket to the 4 corners of the recesses of the rocker arm (valve) cover gasket. Do not install the parts if 5 minutes or more have elapsed since applying liquid gasket. After assembly, wait at least 20 minutes before filling the engine with oil.

65. If equipped with a VTEC engine, install the spark plug seals on the spark plug pipes. Take care not to damage the spark plug seals when installing the rocker arm (valve) cover.

66. Clean the rocker arm (valve) cover contacting surface with a shop towel. Install the rocker arm (valve) cover and tighten the rocker arm (valve) cover bolts in 2 or 3 steps. Tighten the cap nuts in the proper sequence to 84 inch lbs. (10 Nm).

67. Install the remaining components in the reverse order of removal.

68. Fill the crankcase to the proper level with clean oil.

69. Fill and bleed the air from the cooling system.

70. Connect the positive, then the negative battery cable. Enter the radio security code.

71. Start the engine and check carefully for any leaks.

72. Check the ignition timing, as outlined in Section 1.

2.3L Engines

▶ See Figures 89 and 90

1. Disconnect the negative battery cable.

2. Turn the crankshaft so the No. 1 piston is at TDC.

➡The No. 1 piston is at TDC when the pointer on the block aligns with the white painted mark on the flywheel (manual transaxle) or driveplate (automatic transaxle).

3. Drain the engine coolant into a sealable container.

4. Relieve the fuel pressure, as outlined in Section 5.

5. Remove the air intake duct.

6. Remove the EVAP control canister hose from the intake manifold.

7. Remove the throttle cable from the throttle body. If equipped with an automatic transaxle, remove the throttle control cable from the throttle body.

➡Be careful not to bend the cable when removing. Always replace a kinked cable with a new one.

8. Disconnect the fuel feed and return hose.

9. Remove the brake booster vacuum hose from the intake manifold.

10. Tag and detach the following engine wiring harness connectors:
   - Fuel injector connectors
   - IAT sensor connector
   - IAC valve connector
   - TP sensor connector
   - EGR valve lift sensor
   - Ground cable terminals
   - ECT switch **B** connector
   - Heated Oxygen sensor (HO$_2$S) connector
   - ECT sensor
   - ECT gauge sending unit connector
   - ICM connector
   - CKP/CYP sensor connector
   - VSS connector
   - Ignition coil connector
   - Intake air bypass solenoid valve connector
   - ECT switch **A** connector
   - Knock sensor connector

11. Remove the engine ground cable from the rocker arm (valve) cover.

12. Remove the connector and the terminal from the alternator, then remove the engine wiring harness from the valve cover.

13. Remove the mounting bolts and drive belt from the power steering pump. Pull the pump away from the mounting bracket, without disconnecting the hoses. Support the pump out of the way.

14. Remove the ignition coil.

15. Tag, then disconnect the emissions vacuum hoses from the intake manifold assembly.

16. Remove the bypass hose from the intake manifold.

17. Remove the upper radiator hose and the heater hose from the cylinder head.

18. Remove the lower radiator hose and bypass hose from the thermostat housing.

19. Remove the thermostat housing mounting bolts. Remove the thermostat housing from the intake manifold and the connecting pipe, by pulling and twisting the housing. Discard the O-rings.

20. Raise and safely support the vehicle.

21. Remove the front wheel and tire assemblies.

22. Remove the splash shield.

23. Remove the intake manifold bracket bolts.

24. Remove the intake manifold.

25. Disconnect the exhaust pipe from the exhaust manifold.

26. Remove the exhaust manifold and the exhaust manifold heat insulator.

27. Label, then detach the electrical connectors from the distributor and the spark plug wires from the spark plugs. Mark the position of the distributor and remove it from the cylinder head. Disconnect the ignition coil wire from the distributor.

28. Remove the PCV hose, then remove the rocker arm (valve) cover. Replace the rubber seals if damaged or deteriorated.

29. Remove the timing belt. Refer to the procedure located in this section.

30. Insert a 5.0mm pin punch in each of the camshaft caps, nearest to the sprockets, through the holes provided. Remove the camshaft sprocket attaching bolts, then remove the sprockets. Do not lose the sprocket keys.

31. Loosen all of the rocker arm adjusting screws, then remove the pin punches from the camshaft caps.

32. Remove the camshaft holders, note the holders locations for ease of installation.

33. Remove the rubber cap from the head, located at the end of the intake camshaft.

34. Remove the rocker arms from the cylinder head. Note the locations of the rocker arms.

➡The rocker arms have to be installed to their original locations if being reused.

35. Remove the side engine mount bracket B, then the back cover from behind the camshaft sprockets.

36. Remove the cylinder head bolts in the proper sequence.

➡To prevent warpage, unscrew the bolts in sequence ⅓ turn at a time. Repeat the sequence until all bolts are loosened.

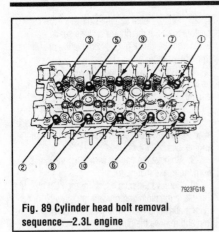

Fig. 89 Cylinder head bolt removal sequence—2.3L engine

37. Separate the cylinder head from the engine block with a suitable flat-bladed prytool.

To install:

38. Be sure all cylinder head and block gasket surfaces are clean. Check the cylinder head for warpage. If warpage is less than 0.002 in. (0.05mm), cylinder head resurfacing is not required. Maximum resurface limit is 0.008 in. (0.2mm) based on a cylinder head height of 5.20 in. (132.0mm). Refer to engine rebuilding, at the end of this section for more information.

39. Always use a new head gasket.

40. Be sure the No. 1 cylinder is at TDC.

41. Clean the oil control orifice and install a new O-ring. The cylinder head dowel pins and oil control jet must be aligned.

42. Install the bolts that secure the intake manifold to its bracket but do not tighten them.

43. Install the cylinder head, then tighten the cylinder head bolts sequentially in 3 steps:
- Step 1: 29 ft. lbs. (40 Nm).
- Step 2: 51 ft. lbs. (70 Nm).
- Step 3: 72 ft. lbs. (100 Nm).

➡**A beam type torque wrench is recommended. If a bolt makes any noise while being tightened, loosen the bolt and retighten it.**

44. Install the intake manifold with a new gasket.

45. Install the exhaust manifold with a new gasket.

46. Install the exhaust manifold bracket, then install the exhaust pipe, bracket, and upper shroud.

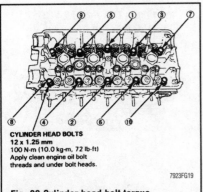

CYLINDER HEAD BOLTS
12 x 1.25 mm
100 N·m (10.0 kg-m, 72 lb-ft)
Apply clean engine oil bolt
threads and under bolt heads.

7923FG19

Fig. 90 Cylinder head bolt torque sequence—2.3L engine

47. Install the camshafts and rocker arms.

48. Install the timing belt back cover.

49. Install the side engine mount bracket B. Tighten the bolt attaching the bracket to the cylinder head to 33 ft. lbs. (45 Nm). Tighten the bolts attaching the bracket to the side engine mount to 16 ft. lbs. (22 Nm).

50. Install the camshaft sprockets onto the camshafts.

51. Install the timing belt. Refer to the procedure located in this section.

52. Adjust the valves, as outlined in Section 1.

53. Tighten the crankshaft pulley bolt to 181 ft. lbs. (250 Nm).

54. Install the splash shield and the front wheels.

55. Lower the vehicle.

56. Install the remaining components in the reverse order of removal.

57. Drain the oil from the engine into a sealable container. Install the drain plug and refill the engine with clean oil.

58. Fill and bleed the air from the cooling system.

59. Connect the negative battery cable and enter the radio security code.

60. Start the engine and check carefully for any leaks.

61. Check and adjust the ignition timing. Tighten the distributor bolts to 13 ft. lbs. (18 Nm).

2.7L Engines

▶ **See Figures 91, 92, 93 and 94**

1. Disconnect the negative battery cable.

2. Turn the engine to align the timing marks and set cylinder No.1 to Top Dead Center (TDC). Remove the inspection caps on the upper timing belt covers to check the alignment of the timing marks. The white mark on the crankshaft pulley should align with the pointer on the timing belt cover. The pointers for the camshafts should align with the green marks on the camshaft pulleys.

3. Drain the engine coolant into a sealable container.

4. Remove the intake air duct.

5. Remove intake manifold cover **B**, then disconnect the throttle cable and cruise control cables from the throttle linkage. Take care to not bend the cables. Always replaced a kinked cable.

6. Remove the starter cable from the strut brace, then remove the strut brace.

7. Relieve the pressure from the fuel system, as outlined in Section 5.

❋❋ CAUTION

The fuel injection system remains under pressure after the engine has been turned OFF. Properly relieve fuel pressure before disconnecting any fuel lines. Failure to do so may result in fire or personal injury.

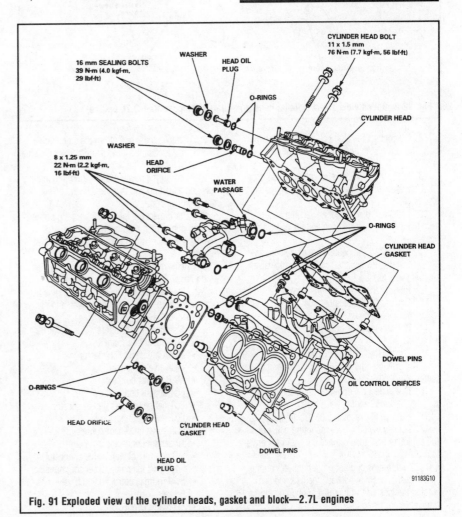

Fig. 91 Exploded view of the cylinder heads, gasket and block—2.7L engines

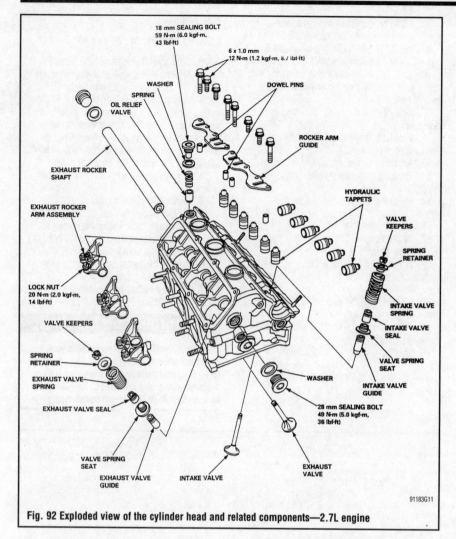

Fig. 92 Exploded view of the cylinder head and related components—2.7L engine

18 mm SEALING BOLT
59 N·m (6.0 kgf·m, 43 lbf·ft)

6 x 1.0 mm
12 N·m (1.2 kgf·m, 8.7 lbf·ft)

WASHER
SPRING
OIL RELIEF VALVE

DOWEL PINS

ROCKER ARM GUIDE

EXHAUST ROCKER SHAFT

HYDRAULIC TAPPETS

EXHAUST ROCKER ARM ASSEMBLY

VALVE KEEPERS

SPRING RETAINER

LOCK NUT
20 N·m (2.0 kgf·m, 14 lbf·ft)

INTAKE VALVE SPRING

INTAKE VALVE SEAL

VALVE KEEPERS

VALVE SPRING SEAT

SPRING RETAINER

EXHAUST VALVE SPRING

WASHER

INTAKE VALVE GUIDE

EXHAUST VALVE SEAL

28 mm SEALING BOLT
49 N·m (5.0 kgf·m, 36 lbf·ft)

VALVE SPRING SEAT

EXHAUST VALVE GUIDE

INTAKE VALVE

EXHAUST VALVE

91183G11

25. Label, then disconnect the electrical connectors from the distributor and the spark plug wires from the spark plugs. Remove the distributor from the cylinder head.

26. Remove the upper and lower radiator hoses, then disconnect the heater hoses from the engine.

27. Remove the intake air bypass vacuum tank.

28. Remove the bolts attaching the water passage to the cylinder heads, then remove it from the engine. Discard the O-rings.

29. Remove the engine wiring harness covers from the intake manifold.

30. Remove the nuts attaching the EGR pipe to the intake manifold and discard the gasket. Loosen the nut attaching the EGR pipe to the exhaust manifold and remove the pipe from the vehicle.

31. Remove the intake manifold.

32. Remove the exhaust manifolds from the engine.

33. Remove the rocker arm (valve) covers and the side covers.

34. Remove the timing belt covers and the timing belt. Refer to the procedure located in this section.

35. Remove the camshaft sprockets and the timing belt back covers.

36. Remove the bolts attaching the camshaft holder plates and camshaft holders in the reverse order of installation.

37. Remove the camshaft holder plates, camshaft holders, and the dowel pins from the cylinder head.

38. Remove the camshafts from the cylinder heads and the rubber cap from the rear cylinder head. Discard the camshaft seals.

39. Remove the intake rocker arms, exhaust inside rocker arms and the pushrods. Identify the location of the parts as they are removed to ensure reinstallation to the original locations.

40. Remove the cylinder head bolts in the proper sequence.

➡ **To prevent warpage, loosen the bolts in sequence ⅓ turn at a time. Repeat the sequence until all bolts are removed.**

41. Remove the cylinder heads from the engine block.

42. Remove and clean the oil control orifices, then install new O-rings to the orifices.

To install:

43. Be sure all cylinder head and block gasket surfaces are clean. Check the cylinder head for

8. Disconnect the fuel feed hose from the fuel filter. Disconnect the fuel return hose from the regulator.

9. Disconnect the brake booster vacuum hose and the evaporative emissions (EVAP) control canister hose.

10. Label and disconnect all vacuum hoses from the throttle body, intake manifold, and cylinder head.

11. Disconnect the coolant hoses from the Idle Air Control (IAC) valve, the fast idle thermo valve, and the water passage.

12. Remove the intake manifold cover.

13. Disconnect the breather hose from the rocker arm (valve) cover.

14. Remove the PCV hose from the rocker arm (valve) cover.

15. Loosen the idler pulley center nut and adjusting bolt, then remove the air conditioning compressor belt.

16. Disconnect the engine ground cable from the body, located near the drive belts.

17. Remove the vacuum pipe assembly.

18. Loosen the alternator mounting bolt, nut, and adjusting bolt, then remove the alternator drive belt.

19. Support the engine with a floor jack on the oil pan (use a cushion between the jack and pan). Tension the jack so that it is just supporting the engine but not lifting it.

20. Remove the 3 bolts from the side engine mount, then loosen the through-bolt. Pivot the side engine mount out of the way.

21. Loosen the power steering pump mounting nuts and adjusting nut, then remove the power steering drive belt.

22. Disconnect the inlet hose from the power steering pump, then plug the hose and pump. Remove the power steering pump and place it out of the way.

23. Remove the wiring harness cover and the ground cable from the water passage inlet.

24. Label and detach the following engine harness connectors from the cylinder head and the intake manifold:

- Six injector connectors
- IAT sensor connector
- TDC/CYP sensor connector
- IAC valve connector
- MAP sensor connector
- ECT sensor connector
- ECT gauge sending unit connector
- ECT switch connector
- EGR valve lift sensor connector
- TP sensor connector
- IAB control solenoid valve connector
- Engine oil temperature sensor connector
- EVAP purge control solenoid valve connector
- Alternator connector

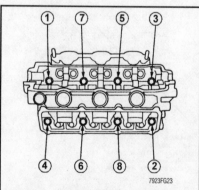

7923FG23

Fig. 93 Cylinder head bolt removal sequence—2.7L engine

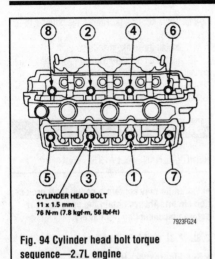

Fig. 94 Cylinder head bolt torque sequence—2.7L engine

warpage. If warpage is less than 0.002 in. (0.05mm), cylinder head resurfacing is not required. Maximum resurface limit is 0.008 in. (0.2mm) based on a cylinder head height of 5.24 in. (133mm). Refer to engine rebuilding, at the end of this section for more information.

44. Install new head gaskets.

45. Be sure the No. 1 cylinder is at TDC.

46. Install and align the cylinder head dowel pins and oil control orifices.

47. Install the cylinder heads. Apply clean oil to the threads of the cylinder head bolts and washers, then install and tighten the cylinder head bolts sequentially in 2 steps:
- Step 1: 29 ft. lbs. (39 Nm).
- Step 2: 56 ft. lbs. (76 Nm).

48. Fill the hydraulic tappet mounting hole and the oil fillers with clean engine oil.

49. Install the hydraulic tappets.

✳✳ WARNING

Do not rotate the hydraulic tappets while installing them.

50. Apply clean engine oil to the rocker arms, pushrods, and the camshafts.

51. Loosen the exhaust rocker arm adjusting screws and locknuts, then install the pushrods, exhaust inside rocker arms, and the intake rocker arms. Install the parts to their original locations.

52. Be sure the rocker arms are properly positioned on the valve stems. Advance the crankshaft 30° from TDC to prevent interference between the pistons and valves, then install the camshafts. Position the rear camshaft on the cylinder head so the cam is not pushing on any valves.

53. Install the timing belt back covers and tighten the attaching bolts to 108 inch lbs. (12 Nm).

54. Install the camshaft sprockets and tighten the attaching bolts to 23 ft. lbs. (31 Nm).

55. Set the camshaft sprockets so that the No. 1 piston is at TDC. Align the TDC marks (green mark) on the camshaft pulleys to the pointers on the back covers.

56. Turn the crankshaft counterclockwise to set it at TDC. Align the TDC mark on the tooth of the timing belt drive pulley with the pointer on the oil pump.

57. Install the timing belt and timing belt covers. Refer to the procedure located in this section.

58. Set No. 1 cylinder to TDC.

59. Tighten the adjusting screws for No. 1, No. 2, and No. 4 cylinders. Tighten the screw until it contacts the valve, then tighten the screw 1⅛ turns. Hold the screw in place and tighten the locknut to 14 ft. lbs. (20 Nm).

60. Rotate the crankshaft pulley 1 turn clockwise, then tighten the adjusting screws for No. 3, No. 5 and No. 6 cylinders. Tighten the screw until it contacts the valve, then tighten the screw 1⅛ turns. Hold the screw in place and tighten the locknut to 14 ft. lbs. (20 Nm).

61. Install the rocker arm (valve) cover gasket into the groove of the rocker arm (valve) cover. Seat the recesses for the camshaft first, then work it into the groove around the outside edges.

➡**Before installing the rocker arm (valve) cover gasket, thoroughly clean the seal groove.**

62. Apply liquid gasket to the rocker arm (valve) cover gasket at the 4 corners of the recesses. Use a shop towel and wipe the cylinder heads where the rocker arm (valve) covers will come in contact.

63. Install the rocker arm (valve) covers, hold the gasket in the groove by placing your fingers on the camshaft contacting surfaces. With the rocker arm (valve) cover on the cylinder heads, slide the covers slightly back and forth to seat the rocker arm (valve) cover gaskets. Replace the washers if damaged or deteriorated.

64. Tighten the rocker arm (valve) cover bolts in 2 or 3 steps. In the final step, tighten all the bolts, in sequence, to 11 ft. lbs. (15 Nm).

65. Install the cylinder head side covers with new O-rings and tighten the bolts to 108 inch lbs. (12 Nm).

66. Install the intake manifold.

67. Install the exhaust manifolds.

68. Install new O-rings to the water passage and install the water passage to the engine and tighten the mounting bolts to 16 ft. lbs. (22 Nm).

69. Install the EGR pipe with a new gasket at the intake manifold. Tighten the nuts attaching the pipe to the intake manifold to 108 inch lbs. (12 Nm) and tighten the exhaust manifold fitting to 43 ft. lbs. (59 Nm).

70. Install the side engine mount. Use 3 new bolts to attach the mount to the engine and tighten the bolts to 40 ft. lbs. (54 Nm).

71. Tighten the side engine mount through-bolt to 47 ft. lbs. (64 Nm).

72. Install the remaining components in the reverse of removal.

73. Drain the engine oil into a sealable container, then refill the engine with clean oil.

74. Connect the negative battery cable and enter the radio security code.

75. Fill and bleed the air from the cooling system.

76. Switch the ignition **ON** but do not engage the starter. The fuel pump should run for approximately 2 seconds, building pressure within the lines. Switch the ignition **OFF**, then **ON** 2 or 3 more times to build full system pressure. Check for fuel leaks.

77. Start the engine, allow it to idle and check for any signs of leakage.

3.0L Engine

◆ **See Figures 95, 96, 97 and 98**

1. Obtain the security code for the radio.

2. Disconnect the negative battery cable.

3. Drain the coolant into a suitable container.

4. Remove the EVAP canister hose from the throttle body.

5. Remove the air intake duct.

6. Remove the upper engine covers.

7. Disconnect the accelerator and cruise control cables from the throttle body.

8. Remove the spark plug wire holder, cover, and intake manifold covers.

9. Properly relieve the fuel system pressure, as outlined in Section 5.

10. Disconnect the fuel hoses from the supply rail.

11. Tag and disconnect the following hoses and lines:
- Brake booster vacuum hose
- PCV hose
- Breather hose
- Water bypass hose
- Vacuum hose from the throttle body

12. Remove the ground cable from the engine.

13. Remove the alternator belt.

14. Support the engine with a jack and a block of wood and remove the side engine mounting bracket.

15. Remove the power steering pump without disconnecting the hoses.

16. Remove the alternator.

17. Detach the wiring harness connectors from the components on the engine that may interfere with removing the cylinder head.

18. Remove the distributor and spark plug wires.

19. Remove the intake manifold.

20. Detach the connectors from the fuel injectors.

21. Remove the fuel supply rails.

22. Remove the vacuum hoses from the fuel control valve.

23. Set the engine to TDC by aligning the marks on the crankshaft and camshaft pulleys.

24. Remove the timing belt. Refer to the procedure located in this section.

25. Remove the upper and lower radiator hoses.

26. Disconnect the heater hoses.

27. Remove both exhaust manifolds.

28. Remove the water passage assembly.

29. Remove the camshaft pulleys and rear timing belt covers.

30. Loosen each cylinder head bolt ⅓ turn at a time in the correct sequence. This will take several passes.

31. Remove the cylinder heads.

To install:

32. Clean the cylinder head and the surface of the cylinder block.

33. Install the oil control orifices and install them using new o-rings.

34. If removed, install the dowel pins.

35. Position new cylinder head gaskets on the cylinder block.

36. If moved, set the crankshaft and camshaft pulleys to TDC by aligning the marks on the pulley and oil pump.

37. Carefully position the cylinder heads on the engine.

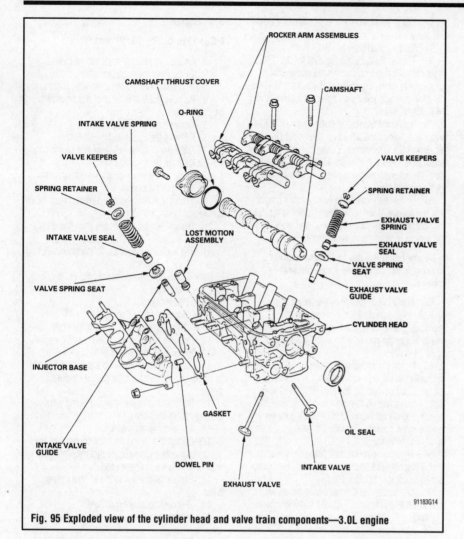

Fig. 95 Exploded view of the cylinder head and valve train components—3.0L engine

new gaskets and o-rings. Tighten the bolts to 16 ft. lbs. (22 Nm).

47. Install the intake manifold.

48. Install all of the remaining hoses, tubes, and connectors are installed correctly.

49. Connect the negative battery cable.

50. Enter the security code for the radio.

Oil Pan

REMOVAL & INSTALLATION

➡**The radio may contain a coded theft protection circuit. Always obtain the code number before disconnecting the battery.**

2.2L, 2.3L and 2.7L Engines

▶**See Figures 99, 100 and 101**

1. Disconnect the negative battery cable.

2. Raise and safely support the vehicle.

3. Drain the engine oil into a sealable container.

4. Install the drain bolt with a new gasket. Tighten the bolt to 33 ft. lbs. (44 Nm).

5. Remove the front wheels and the splash shield.

6. Remove the center beam.

7. Detach the Oxygen sensor (O2S) electrical connector.

8. Remove the bolts from the support bracket on the exhaust pipe.

9. Remove the nuts attaching the exhaust pipe to the exhaust manifold and the catalytic converter.

10. Remove the exhaust pipe and discard the gaskets.

11. If equipped with an automatic transaxle, remove the converter cover.

12. If equipped with a manual transaxle, remove the clutch cover.

13. Remove the oil pan nuts and bolts (in a criss-cross pattern) and the oil pan; if necessary, use a mallet to tap the corners of the oil pan. DO NOT pry on the pan to get it loose.

14. Clean the oil pan mounting surface of old gasket material and engine oil.

To install:

15. Install a new oil pan gasket to the oil pan. Apply liquid gasket to the corners of the curved section of the gasket.

16. Install the oil pan to the engine.

17. Install the oil pan nuts and bolts and tighten

---

38. Lubricate the cylinder head bolts with clean engine oil.

➡**If any cylinder head bolt makes noise while being tightened, loosen the bolts and begin the tightening sequence again.**

39. Tighten the cylinder head bolts in sequence, in 3 separate steps. First tighten each bolt in sequence to 29 ft. lbs. (39 Nm).

40. Tighten each bolt in sequence to 51 ft. lbs. (69 Nm).

41. Tighten each bolt a third time in sequence to a final torque of 72 ft. lbs. (98 Nm).

42. Install the exhaust manifolds.

43. Install the timing belt. Refer to the procedure located in this section.

44. Check and adjust the valve clearance if necessary.

45. Install the rocker arm (valve) cover. Tighten the bolts in sequence to 108 inch lbs. (12 Nm).

46. Install the water passage. Be sure to use

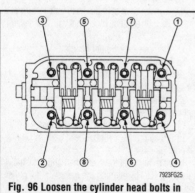

Fig. 96 Loosen the cylinder head bolts in the sequence shown to prevent damage to the head—3.0L engine

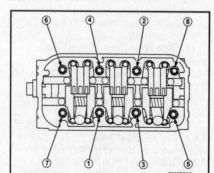

Fig. 97 Tighten the cylinder head bolts in the sequence shown to prevent damage to the head—3.0L engine

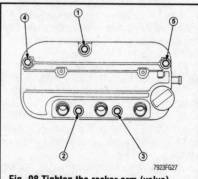

Fig. 98 Tighten the rocker arm (valve) cover bolts in the sequence shown—3.0L engine

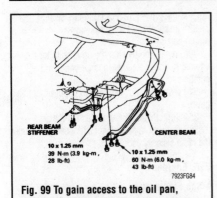

Fig. 99 To gain access to the oil pan, remove the center beam—2.2L and 2.3L engines

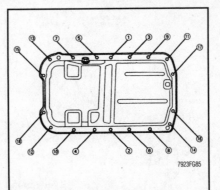

Fig. 100 Oil pan mounting bolt tightening sequence—2.2L and 2.3L engines

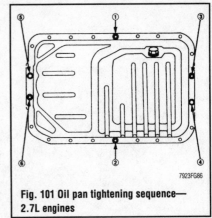

Fig. 101 Oil pan tightening sequence— 2.7L engines

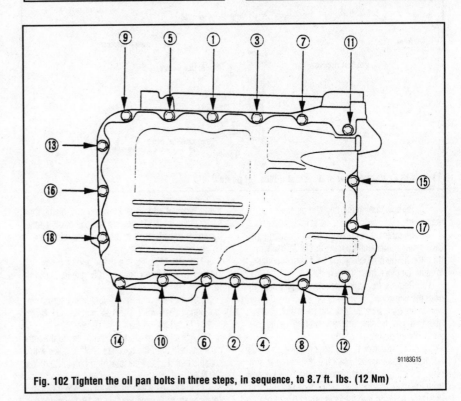

Fig. 102 Tighten the oil pan bolts in three steps, in sequence, to 8.7 ft. lbs. (12 Nm)

the nuts and bolts in sequence. Tighten the nuts and bolts in 2 steps to 10 ft. lbs. (14 Nm).

18. If equipped with an automatic transaxle, install the torque converter cover. Tighten the bolts to 108 inch lbs. (12 Nm).

19. If equipped with a manual transaxle, install the clutch cover. Tighten the bolts to 108 inch lbs. (12 Nm).

20. Install the exhaust pipe with new gaskets and new locknuts. Tighten the nuts attaching the exhaust pipe to the manifold to 40 ft. lbs. (54 Nm)and tighten the nuts attaching the exhaust pipe to the catalytic converter to 25 ft. lbs. (33 Nm). Install the bolts to the exhaust pipe support bracket and tighten the bolts to 13 ft. lbs. (18 Nm).

21. Attach the Oxygen sensor (O$_2$S) electrical connector.

22. Install the center beam and tighten the mounting bolts as follows:
   • Prelude: 43 ft. lbs. (60 Nm)
   • Accord: 37 ft. lbs. (50 Nm)

23. Install the splash shield and tighten the mounting bolts to 84 inch lbs. (10 Nm).

24. Install the front wheels.

25. Lower the vehicle and fill the engine with oil.

26. Connect the negative battery cable and enter the radio security code.

27. Start the engine and check for leaks.

3.0L Engine

♦ **See Figure 102**

1. Disconnect the negative battery cable.
2. Raise and safely support the vehicle.
3. Remove the engine undercover.
4. Drain the engine oil and replace the drain plug.
5. Remove the front exhaust pipe.
6. Remove the oil pan mounting bolts.
7. Hammer a seal cutter between the engine block and oil pan to break the seal.
8. Remove the oil pan.

To install:

9. Clean the oil pan flange and engine block mounting surface.
10. Apply sealant to the oil pan flange. Be sure to apply sealant toward the inside of the bolt holes.
11. Install the oil pan on the engine. Tighten the bolts in sequence to 8.7 ft. lbs. (12 Nm).
12. Install the exhaust pipe.
13. Install the undercover.
14. Lower the vehicle.

> ⁕⁕⁕ WARNING
>
> **Operating the engine without the proper amount and type of engine oil will result in severe engine damage.**

15. Refill the engine with the correct amount of oil.
16. Connect the negative battery cable.
17. Start the engine and check for leaks.

Oil Pump

REMOVAL & INSTALLATION

➡The original radio may contain a coded anti-theft circuit. Always obtain the security code number before disconnecting the battery cables.

2.2L and 2.3L Engines

♦ **See Figure 103**

1. Disconnect the negative battery cable.
2. Drain the engine oil into a sealable container.
3. Turn the engine to align the timing marks and set cylinder No.1 to TDC. The white mark on the crankshaft pulley should align with the pointer on the timing belt cover.
4. Remove the valve cover and upper timing belt cover.
5. Remove the power steering pump belt and the alternator belt, also the air conditioning belt if so equipped.
6. Remove the crankshaft pulley and the lower timing belt cover.
7. Remove the balancer belt and the timing belt. Be sure to mark the rotation of the timing belt if it is going to be reused. Refer to the procedure located in this section.

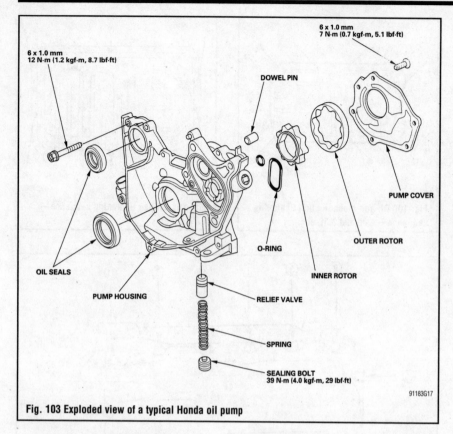

6 x 1.0 mm
12 N·m (1.2 kgf·m, 8.7 lbf·ft)

6 x 1.0 mm
7 N·m (0.7 kgf·m, 5.1 lbf·ft)

DOWEL PIN

PUMP COVER

OUTER ROTOR

O-RING

INNER ROTOR

OIL SEALS

RELIEF VALVE

PUMP HOUSING

SPRING

SEALING BOLT
39 N·m (4.0 kgf·m, 29 lbf·ft)

91183G17

Fig. 103 Exploded view of a typical Honda oil pump

8. Remove the timing belt and balancer belt tensioners.

9. If equipped, remove the bolts mounting the CKP sensor and carefully remove the CKP sensor from the oil pump. Detach the CKP sensor connector and remove it from the vehicle.

10. Remove the timing belt drive pulley and key from the crankshaft.

11. Insert a suitable tool into the maintenance hole in the front balancer shaft and remove the balancer driven pulley.

12. Align the rear timing balancer pulley using a 6 x 100mm bolt or rod. Mark the bolt or rod at a point 2.9 in. (74mm) from the end. Remove the bolt from the maintenance hole on the side of the block; insert the bolt/rod into the hole. Align the 74mm mark with the face of the hole. This pin will hold the shaft in place.

13. Remove the balancer gear case and the dowel pins. Discard the O-ring.

14. Remove the balancer driven gear attaching bolt and the balancer driven gear.

15. Remove the oil pan and the oil screen. Discard the screen gasket.

16. Remove the oil pump mounting bolts and remove the oil pump assembly. Remove the dowel pins from the engine and clean the oil pump mating surfaces of old gasket material and oil. Discard the O-rings.

To install:

17. Install the 2 dowel pins and new O-rings to the cylinder block.

18. Be sure that the mating surfaces are clean and dry. Apply a liquid gasket evenly in a narrow bead, centered on the mating surface. Once the sealant is applied, do not wait longer than 20 minutes to install the parts; the sealant will become ineffective. After final assembly, wait at least 30

minutes before adding oil to the engine, giving the sealant time to set. To prevent leakage of oil, apply a suitable thread sealer to the inner threads of the bolt holes.

19. Install the oil pump to the engine block. Tighten the mounting bolts to 108 inch lbs. (12 Nm).

20. Install the oil screen. Tighten the screen mounting bolts and nuts to 108 inch lbs. (12 Nm).

21. Install the oil pan.

22. Install the balancer driven pulley to the front balancer belt, hold the balancer shaft in place with a suitable tool. Tighten the attaching bolt to 22 ft. lbs. (29 Nm).

23. Install the balancer driven gear to the rear balancer shaft. Tighten the bolt to 18 ft. lbs. (25 Nm).

24. Before installing the balancer driven gear and the gear case, apply molybdenum disulfide (lithium grease) to the thrust surfaces of the balancer gears.

25. Align the groove on the pulley edge to the pointer on the balancer gear case.

26. Install the balancer gear case to the engine and install the mounting bolts and nut. The rear balancer shaft is being held in place with a 6 x 100mm bolt. Tighten the mounting bolts and nut to 18 ft. lbs. (25 Nm).

27. Check the alignment of the pointer on the balancer pulley to the pointer on the oil pump.

28. Install the drive pulley to the crankshaft.

29. If equipped, connect the CKP sensor connector to the wiring harness on the engine. Install the CKP sensor to the oil pump and install the mounting bolts. Tighten the mounting bolts to 108 inch lbs. (12 Nm).

30. Install the timing belt tensioners.

31. Install the timing belt and the balancer belt.

Refer to the procedure located in this section.

32. Install the crankshaft pulley and the lower timing belt cover.

33. Install and tension the drive belts for the alternator, power steering, and air conditioning compressor.

34. Install the valve cover and upper timing belt cover.

35. Refill the engine with clean, fresh oil.

36. Connect the negative battery cable and enter the radio security code.

2.7L Engines

▶ See Figure 104

➡**The radio may contain a coded theft protection circuit. Always obtain the code before disconnecting the battery.**

1. Disconnect the negative battery cable.

2. Turn the engine to align the timing marks and set cylinder No.1 to TDC. The white mark on the crankshaft pulley should align with the pointer on the timing belt cover. Remove the inspection caps on the upper timing belt covers to check the alignment of the timing marks. The pointers for the camshafts should align with the green marks on the camshaft pulleys.

3. Raise and safely support the vehicle.

4. Drain the engine oil into a sealable container.

5. Remove the front wheels and the engine splash shield.

6. Remove the timing belt covers and the timing belt. Refer to the procedure located in this section.

7. Detach the CKP sensor electrical connector, then remove the CKP sensor from the oil pump.

8. Remove the timing belt tensioner.

9. Remove the stopper plate from the oil pump, then remove the timing belt drive pulley.

10. Remove the oil filter.

11. Disconnect the oil pressure switch terminal, then remove the oil filter base attaching bolts.

12. Remove the oil filter base and discard the O-rings.

13. Remove the oil pan.

14. Remove the oil screen and baffle plate.

15. Remove the oil pass pipe attaching bolts, then remove the pipe from the oil pump. Discard the O-rings.

16. Remove the bolts from the oil pump. Note the location of the bolts.

17. Remove the oil pump and dowel pins from the engine.

To install:

18. Install the 2 dowel pins to the cylinder block.

19. Be sure that the mating surfaces are clean and dry. Apply a liquid gasket evenly in a narrow bead centered on the mating surface. Once the sealant is applied, do not wait longer than 20 minutes to install the parts; the sealant will become ineffective. After final assembly, wait at least 30 minutes before adding oil to the engine, giving the sealant time to set. To prevent leakage of oil, apply a suitable thread sealer to the inner threads of the bolt holes.

20. Apply grease to the lips of the crankshaft oil seal. Install the oil pump to the engine block. Tighten the 6mm mounting bolts to 108 inch lbs. (12 Nm) and tighten the 8mm mounting bolts to 16

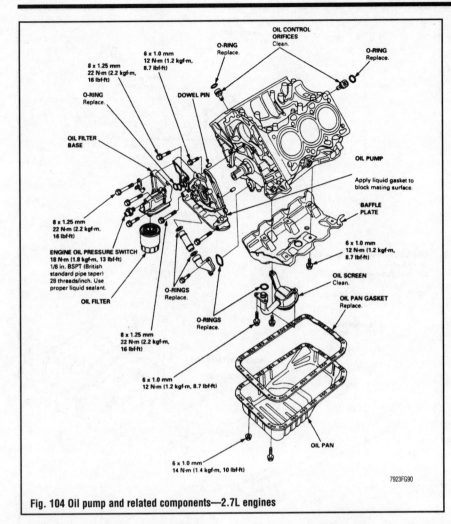

Fig. 104 Oil pump and related components—2.7L engines

7923FG90

33. Lower the vehicle and fill the engine with oil.

34. Connect the negative battery cable and enter the radio security code.

35. Run the engine and check for leaks.

3.0L Engine

◆ See Figures 105 and 106

1. Raise and safely support the vehicle.

2. Drain the engine oil into a suitable container.

3. Turn the crankshaft to position the No. 1 piston at TDC on the compression stroke.

4. Remove the timing belt. Refer to the procedure located in this section.

5. Remove the idler pulley.

6. Remove the CKP sensor.

7. Remove the VTEC solenoid valve and the oil filter.

8. Remove the oil pan and pick-up.

9. Remove the oil pump assembly.

To install:

10. Install a new crankshaft seal in the oil pump.

11. Apply sealant to the oil pump mounting surface and bolt holes on the engine block.

12. Grease the lip of the new seal and apply engine oil to the o-ring.

13. Install the dowel pin and oil pump while aligning the inner rotor with the crankshaft. Tighten the bolts to 108 inch lbs. (12 Nm).

14. Install the oil pump pick-up. Tighten the mounting bolts to 108 inch lbs. (12 Nm).

15. Install the oil pan, VTEC solenoid, oil filter, CKP, and idler pulley.

16. Install the timing belt. Refer to the procedure located in this section.

ft. lbs. (22 Nm). Clean any excess grease from the crankshaft and check that the seal lips are not distorted.

21. Install new O-rings to the oil pass pipe, then install the pass pipe to the oil pump and the crankshaft bridge. Tighten the attaching bolts to 108 inch lbs. (12 Nm).

22. Install the baffle plate. Tighten the baffle plate mounting bolts to 108 inch lbs. (12 Nm).

23. Install the oil screen with a new O-ring. Tighten the screen mounting bolts to 108 inch lbs. (12 Nm).

24. Install the oil pan.

25. Install new O-rings to the oil filter base and install the oil filter base to the engine. Tighten the mounting bolts to 16 ft. lbs. (22 Nm).

26. Connect the oil pressure switch terminal. Tighten the attaching bolt to 22 inch lbs. (2.5 Nm).

27. Install the oil filter.

28. Install the timing belt drive pulley and the stopper plate. Tighten the stopper plate mounting bolts to 108 inch lbs. (12 Nm).

29. Install the timing belt tensioner.

30. Install the CKP sensor to the oil pump and connect the electrical connector. Tighten the mounting bolts to 108 inch lbs. (12 Nm).

31. Install the timing belt and the timing belt covers. Refer to the procedure located in this section.

32. Install the engine splash shield and the front wheels.

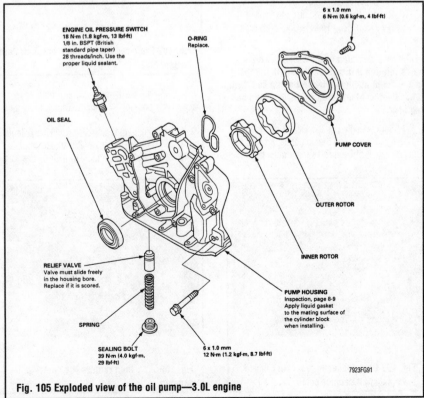

Fig. 105 Exploded view of the oil pump—3.0L engine

7923FG91

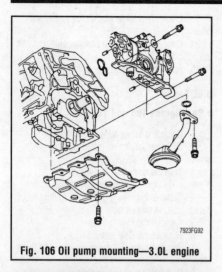

Fig. 106 Oil pump mounting—3.0L engine

❊❊ WARNING

Operating the engine without the proper amount and type of engine oil will result in severe engine damage.

17. Fill the crankcase with the proper amount of new engine oil.

Crankshaft Damper

REMOVAL & INSTALLATION

▶ **See Figures 107, 108, 109 and 110**

1. Note the radio security code and station presets.
2. Disconnect the negative battery cable.
3. Raise and safely support the vehicle.
4. Remove the lower engine splash shield.
5. Remove the engine accessory drive belts. For specific details, refer to Section 1.

➡ **Mark the direction of the accessory drive belt's rotation if it is to be reinstalled. If there is any doubt about the condition of a belt, or if it has been contaminated by oil, it should be replaced.**

6. Set the engine at Top Dead Center (TDC) for the No. 1 piston on the compression stroke. The crankshaft pulley **white** mark must be

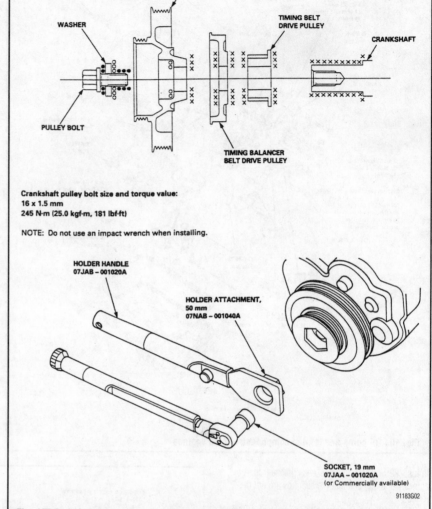

Crankshaft pulley bolt size and torque value:
16 x 1.5 mm
245 N·m (25.0 kgf·m, 181 lbf·ft)

NOTE: Do not use an impact wrench when installing.

Fig. 107 Exploded view of the crankshaft damper and the special tool needed to loosen the damper bolt

aligned with the mark on the lower timing cover. Once in this position, the engine must not be disturbed.

7. Hold the crankshaft pulley with Honda Tool Nos. 07MAB–PY3010A Holder Attachment and 07JAB–001020A Holder Handle or their equivalents and remove the crankshaft pulley bolt by turning it in a counterclockwise direction.

8. Remove the crankshaft pulley.

To install:

9. Install the crankshaft pulley. Tighten the crankshaft pulley bolt to 181 ft. lbs. (245 Nm)

Fig. 108 Once loosened, you can remove the crankshaft damper bolt . . .

Fig. 109 . . . then remove the crankshaft damper

Fig. 110 The crankshaft is keyed for proper position during installation

10. Install and adjust the accessory drive belts.
11. Verify that all engine components that may have been removed have been reinstalled correctly.
12. Install the splash shield and lower the vehicle.
13. Connect the negative battery cable.
14. Enter the security code for the radio.

Timing Belt Cover and Seal

REMOVAL & INSTALLATION

Upper Timing Belt Cover & Seal

▶ See Figures 111 and 112

1. Note the radio security code and disconnect the negative battery cable.
2. Remove the valve cover.
3. Remove the upper timing belt cover fasteners, then remove the cover.
4. Remove the seal from the groove in the cover.

To install:

5. Secure the seal in the cover. It may be helpful to use a semi drying gasket sealant to hold the seal in place.
6. The remainder of the installation procedure is the reverse of disassembly.
7. Enter the radio security code.

Lower Timing Belt Cover & Seal

▶ See Figures 111, 112, 113 and 114

1. Note the radio security code and disconnect the negative battery cable.

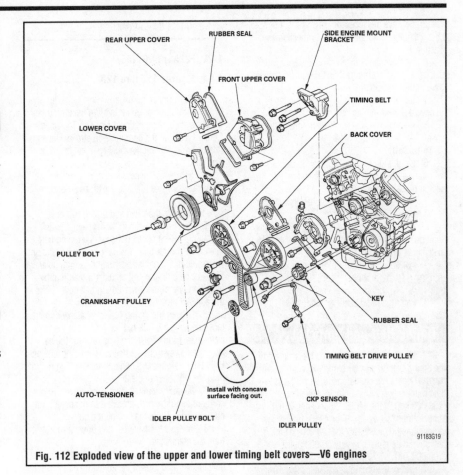

Fig. 112 Exploded view of the upper and lower timing belt covers—V6 engines

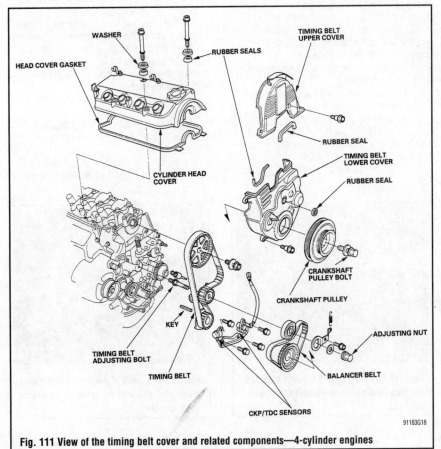

Fig. 111 View of the timing belt cover and related components—4-cylinder engines

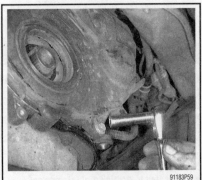

Fig. 113 Unfasten the bolt located at the bottom of the lower timing belt cover

Fig. 114 Once all of the fasteners are loose, pull out the lower timing belt cover

2. Remove the accessory drive belts. For specific details, refer to the drive belt procedures in Section 1.

3. Remove the crankshaft pulley. For specific details, refer to the removal and installation procedure in this section.

4. Remove any necessary fasteners, then remove the lower timing belt cover.

5. Remove the seal from the groove in the cover.

To install:

6. Secure the seal in the cover. It may be helpful to use a semi drying gasket sealant to hold the seal in place.

7. The remainder of the installation procedure is the reverse of disassembly.

8. For specific details pertaining to the crankshaft pulley installation, refer to the removal and installation procedure in this section.

9. For specific detail on drive belt installation, refer to the drive belt procedures in Section 1.

10. Enter the radio security code.

Timing Belt and Sprockets

The manufacturer recommends replacement of the timing belt (and water pump inspection) under **normal** operating conditions for Accord and Prelude models every 84 months (7 years) or 105,000 (168,000 km). If the vehicle is operated in high temperatures (above 110°F or 43°C) or very low temperatures (below -20°F or -29°C) the timing belt should be replaced every 60,000 miles (100,000 km).

If, however, the timing belt is inspected earlier or more frequently than suggested, and shows signs of wear or defects, the belt should be replaced at that time.

❊❊ WARNING

On interference engines, it is very important to replace the timing belt at the recommended intervals, otherwise expensive engine damage will likely result if the belt fails.

➡ **For manufacturer's recommended service intervals, refer to the maintenance interval chart located in Section 1 of this manual.**

REMOVAL & INSTALLATION

2.2L (F22A1) ENGINES

♦ **See Figures 115 thru 120**

1. Disconnect the negative battery cable.

2. Turn the crankshaft to align the timing belt matchmarks and set cylinder No. 1 to Top Dead Center (TDC) on the compression stroke. Once in this position, the engine must NOT be turned or disturbed.

3. Remove all necessary components to gain access to the valve (cylinder head) cover and timing belt covers.

4. Remove the valve and timing belt covers.

5. There are 2 belts in this system; the belt running to the camshaft pulley is the timing belt. The other, shorter belt drives the balance shafts and is referred to as the balancer belt or timing balancer belt. Lock the timing belt adjuster in position by installing one of the lower timing belt cover bolts to the adjuster arm.

6. Loosen the timing belt and balancer shafts tensioner adjuster nut, but do not loosen the nut more than 1 turn. Push the tensioner for the balancer belt away from the belt to relieve the tension. Hold the tensioner and tighten the adjusting nut to hold the tensioner in place.

7. Carefully remove the balancer belt. Do not crimp or bend the belt; protect it from contact with oil or coolant. Slide the belt off the pulleys.

8. Remove the balancer belt drive sprocket from the crankshaft.

9. Loosen the lockbolt installed to the timing belt adjuster and loosen the adjusting nut. Push the timing belt adjuster to remove the tension on the timing belt, then tighten the adjuster nut.

10. Remove the timing belt. Do not crimp or bend the belt; protect it from contact with oil or coolant. Slide the belt off the pulleys.

11. If defective, remove the belt tensioners by performing the following:

a. Remove the springs from the balancer belt and the timing belt tensioners.

b. Remove the adjusting nut.

c. Remove the bolt from the balancer belt adjuster lever, then remove the lever and the tensioner pulley.

d. Remove the lockbolt from the timing belt

tensioner lever, then remove the tensioner pulley and lever from the engine.

➡ **This is an excellent time to check or replace the water pump. Even if the timing belt is only being replaced as part of a good maintenance schedule, consider replacing the pump at the same time.**

To install:

12. If the water pump was replaced, install a new O-ring and make certain it is properly seated. Install the water pump and retaining bolts. Tighten the mounting bolts to 106 inch lbs. (12 Nm).

13. If the tensioners were removed, perform the following to install them:

a. Install the timing belt tensioner lever and tensioner pulley.

➡ **The tensioner lever must be properly positioned on its pivot pin located on the oil pump. Be sure that the timing belt lever and tensioner moves freely and does not bind.**

b. Install the lockbolt to the timing belt tensioner, do not tighten the lockbolt at this time.

c. Install the balancer belt pulley and adjuster lever.

d. Install the adjusting nut and the bolt to the balancer belt adjuster lever. Do not tighten the adjuster nut or bolt at this time.

➡ **Be sure that the balancer lever and tensioner moves freely and does not bind.**

e. Install the springs to the tensioners.

f. Move the timing belt tensioner its full deflection and tighten the lockbolt.

g. Move the balancer its full deflection and tighten the adjusting nut.

14. The crankshaft timing pointer must be perfectly aligned with the white mark on the flywheel or flex-plate; the camshaft pulley must be aligned so that the word **UP** is at the top of the pulley and the marks on the edge of the pulley are aligned with the surfaces of the head.

15. Install the timing belt over the pulleys and tensioners.

16. Loosen the bolt used to lock the timing belt tensioner. Loosen, then tighten the timing belt adjusting nut.

17. Turn the crankshaft counterclockwise until the cam pulley has moved 3 teeth; this creates ten-

Fig. 115 Installed view of the balance shafts and belts

Fig. 116 You can remove the belt from the balance shafts once the tension has been relieved

Fig. 117 The teeth of the timing belt must mesh perfectly with the teeth on the crankshaft sprocket

sion on the timing belt. Loosen, then tighten the

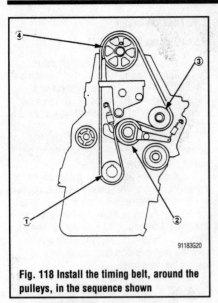

Fig. 118 Install the timing belt, around the pulleys, in the sequence shown

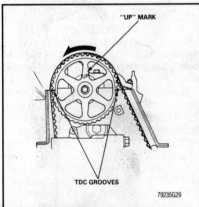

Fig. 119 Camshaft timing belt sprocket alignment mark positioning for timing belt installation—2.2L (F22A1) engines

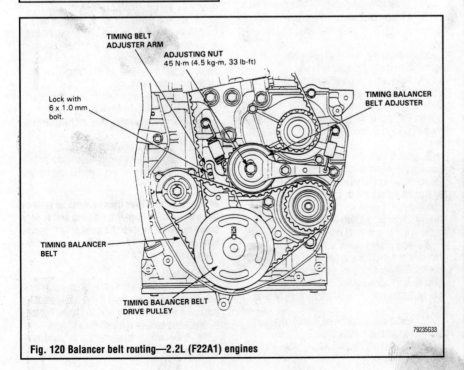

Fig. 120 Balancer belt routing—2.2L (F22A1) engines

adjusting nut and tighten it to 33 ft. lbs. (45 Nm). Tighten the bolt used to lock the timing belt tensioner.

18. Realign the timing belt marks, then install the balancer belt drive sprocket on the crankshaft.

19. Align the front balancer pulley; the face of the front timing balancer pulley has a mark, which must be aligned with the notch on the oil pump body. This pulley is the one at 10 o'clock to the crank pulley when viewed from the pulley end.

20. Align the rear timing balancer pulley (2 o'clock from the crank pulley) using a 6 x 100mm bolt or rod. Mark the bolt or rod at a point 2.9 in. (74mm) from the end. Remove the bolt from the maintenance hole on the side of the block; insert the bolt or rod into the hole. Align the 2.9 in. (74mm) mark with the face of the hole. This pin will hold the shaft in place during installation.

21. Install the balancer belt. Once the belts are in place, be sure that all the engine alignment marks are still correct. If not, remove the belts, realign the engine and reinstall the belts. Once the belts are properly installed, slowly loosen the adjusting nut, allowing the tensioner to move against the belt. Remove the pin from the maintenance hole and reinstall the bolt and washer.

22. Turn the crankshaft 1 full turn, then tighten the adjuster nut to 33 ft. lbs. (45 Nm). Remove the bolt used to lock the timing belt tensioner.

23. Install the lower cover, ensuring the rubber seals are in place. Install a new seal around the adjusting nut, DO NOT loosen the adjusting nut.

24. Install the key on the crankshaft and install the crankshaft pulley. Apply oil to the bolt threads and tighten it to 181 ft. lbs. (250 Nm).

25. Install the upper timing belt cover and all applicable components. When installing the side engine mount, tighten the bolt and nut attaching the mount to the engine to 40 ft. lbs. (55 Nm) and the through-bolt and nut to 47 ft. lbs. (65 Nm).

26. Installation of the remaining components is the reverse of the removal procedure.

27. Connect the negative battery cable.

2.2L (F22B1 and F22B2) Engines

▶ **See Figures 118, 121 and 122**

1. Disconnect the negative battery cable.

2. Remove the cylinder head (valve) and upper timing belt covers.

3. Turn the engine to align the timing marks and set cylinder No. 1 to Top Dead Center (TDC) on the compression stroke. The white mark on the crankshaft sprocket should align with the pointer on the timing belt cover. The words **UP** embossed on the camshaft sprocket should be aligned in the upward position. The marks on the edge of the sprocket should be aligned with the cylinder head or the back cover upper edge. Once in this position, the engine must NOT be turned or disturbed.

4. Remove all necessary components for access to the lower timing belt cover, then remove the cover.

5. There are 2 belts in this system; the one running to the camshaft sprocket is the timing belt. The other, shorter one drives the balance shaft and is referred to as the balancer shaft belt or timing balancer belt. Lock the timing belt adjuster in position, by installing one of the lower timing belt cover bolts to the adjuster arm.

6. Loosen the timing belt and balancer shafts tensioner adjuster nut, do not loosen the nut more than 1 turn. Push the tensioner for the balancer belt away from the belt to relieve the tension. Hold the tensioner and tighten the adjusting nut to hold the tensioner in place.

7. Carefully remove the balancer belt. Do not crimp or bend the belt; protect it from contact with oil or coolant.

8. Remove the balancer belt sprocket from the crankshaft.

9. Loosen the lockbolt installed to the timing belt adjuster and loosen the adjusting nut. Push the timing belt adjuster to remove the tension on the timing belt, then tighten the adjuster nut.

10. Remove the timing belt by sliding it off the sprockets. Do not crimp or bend the belt; protect it from contact with oil or coolant.

11. If defective, remove the belt tensioners by performing the following:

   a. Remove the springs from the balancer belt and the timing belt tensioners.

   b. Remove the adjusting nut from the belt tensioners.

   c. Remove the bolt from the balancer belt adjuster lever, then remove the lever and the tensioner pulley.

   d. Remove the lockbolt from the timing belt tensioner lever, then remove the tensioner pulley and lever from the engine.

➡ **This is an excellent time to check or replace the water pump. Even if the timing belt is only being replaced as part of a good maintenance schedule, consider replacing the pump at the same time.**

To install:

12. If the water pump was replaced, install a new O-ring and make certain it is properly seated. Install the water pump and tighten the mounting bolts to 106 inch lbs. (12 Nm).

13. If the tensioners were removed, perform the following procedures:

   a. Install the timing belt tensioner lever and the tensioner pulley.

b. Install the balancer belt pulley and adjuster lever.

c. Install the adjusting nut and the bolt to the balancer belt adjuster lever.

d. Install the springs to the tensioners.

e. Install the lockbolt to the timing belt tensioner, then move it its full deflection and tighten the lockbolt.

f. Move the balancer it's full deflection and tighten the adjusting nut to hold its position.

14. The pointer on the crankshaft sprocket should be aligned with the pointer on the oil pump. The camshaft sprocket must be aligned so that the word **UP** is at the top of the sprocket and the marks on the edge of the sprocket are aligned with the surfaces of the head or the back cover upper edge.

15. Install the timing belt on the sprockets in the following sequence: crankshaft sprocket, tensioner sprocket, water pump sprocket and camshaft sprocket.

16. Check the timing marks to be sure that they did not move.

17. Loosen, then retighten the timing belt

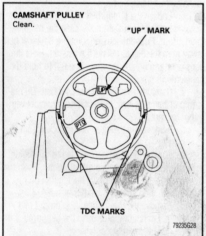

Fig. 121 Position the camshaft sprocket as indicated for timing belt installation— 2.2L (F22B1 and F22B2) engines

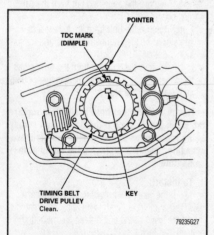

Fig. 122 Before installing the timing belt, ensure the crankshaft sprocket marks are properly aligned—2.2L (F22B1 and F22B2) engines

adjusting nut; this will apply the proper amount of tension to the timing belt.

18. Install the timing balancer belt drive sprocket and the lower timing belt cover.

19. Install the crankshaft pulley and bolt, tighten the bolt to 181 ft. lbs. (245 Nm). Rotate the crankshaft sprocket 5–6 turns to position the timing belt on the sprockets.

20. Set the No. 1 cylinder to TDC and loosen the timing belt adjusting nut 1 turn. Turn the crankshaft counterclockwise until the cam sprocket has moved 3 teeth; this creates tension on the timing belt.

21. Tighten the timing belt adjusting nut.

22. Set the crankshaft sprocket and the camshaft sprocket to TDC. If the sprockets do not align, remove the belt to realign the marks, then install the belt.

23. Remove the crankshaft pulley and the lower cover.

24. With the timing marks aligned, lock the timing belt adjuster in place with one of the lower cover mounting bolts.

25. Loosen the adjusting nut and ensure the timing balancer belt adjuster moves freely.

26. Align the rear timing balancer sprocket using a 6 x 100mm bolt or rod. Mark the bolt or rod at a point 2.9 in. (74mm) from the end. Remove the bolt from the maintenance hole on the side of the block; insert the bolt/rod into the hole and align the 2.9 in. (74mm) mark with the face of the hole. This will hold the shaft in place during installation.

27. Align the groove on the front balancer shaft sprocket with the pointer on the oil pump.

28. Install the balancer belt. Once the belts are in place, be sure that all the engine alignment marks are still correct. If not, remove the belts, realign the engine and reinstall the belts. Once the belts are properly installed, slowly loosen the adjusting nut, allowing the tensioner to move against the belt. Remove the bolt from the maintenance hole and reinstall the bolt and washer.

29. Install the crankshaft pulley, then turn the crankshaft sprocket 1 turn counterclockwise and tighten the timing belt adjusting nut to 33 ft. lbs. (45 Nm).

30. Remove the crankshaft pulley and the bolt locking the timing belt adjuster in place.

31. Install the lower and upper timing belt covers, and all applicable components. When installing the crankshaft pulley, coat the threads and seating face of the pulley bolt with engine oil, then install and tighten the bolt to 181 ft. lbs. (250 Nm).

32. Install the rocker arm (valve) cover gasket cover to the groove of the rocker arm (valve) cover. Before installing the gasket thoroughly clean the seal and the groove. Seat the recesses for the camshaft first, then work it into the groove around the outside edges. Be sure the gasket is seated securely in the corners of the recesses.

33. Apply liquid gasket to the 4 corners of the recesses of the rocker arm (valve) cover gasket. Do not install the parts if 5 minutes or more have elapsed since applying liquid gasket. After assembly, wait at least 20 minutes before filling the engine with oil.

34. Install the cylinder head (valve) cover and all other applicable components.

35. Connect the negative battery cable.

2.2L (H22A1) Engine

◆ See Figures 123 and 124

1. Disconnect the negative battery cable.

2. Turn the crankshaft so the No. 1 piston is at Top Dead Center (TDC) on the compression stroke. The No. 1 piston is TDC when the pointer on the block aligns with the white painted mark on the driveplate.

3. Remove all necessary components for access to the cylinder head and upper timing belt covers. Then, remove the covers.

4. Ensure the words **UP** embossed on the camshaft pulleys are aligned in the upward position.

5. Support the engine with a floor jack below the center of the center beam. Tension the jack so that it is just supporting the beam but not lifting it. Remove the 2 rear bolts from the center beam to allow the engine to drop down for clearance to remove the lower cover.

6. Remove and discard the rubber seal from the timing belt adjuster. Do not loosen the adjusting nut.

7. Remove the lock pin from the maintenance bolt.

8. Remove the lower timing belt cover.

9. There are 2 belts in this system; the belt running to the camshaft pulley is the timing belt. The other, shorter belt drives the balance shafts and is referred to as the balancer belt or timing balancer belt.

10. Loosen the balancer shafts tensioner adjusting nut, do not loosen the nut more than 1 turn. Push the tensioner for the balancer belt away from the belt to relieve the tension. Hold the tensioner and tighten the adjusting nut to hold the tensioner in place.

11. Carefully remove the balancer belt by sliding it off of the pulleys. Do not crimp or bend the belt; protect it from contact with oil or coolant.

12. Remove the balancer belt drive sprocket from the crankshaft.

13. Remove the bolts attaching the Crankshaft Position/Top Dead Center (CKP/TDC) sensor and remove the sensor.

14. Remove the timing belt by sliding it off of the pulleys. Do not crimp or bend the belt; protect it from contact with oil or coolant.

15. If defective, remove the 2 bolts mounting the timing belt auto-tensioner and remove the tensioner from the vehicle.

16. If defective, remove the balancer belt tensioner by performing the following:

a. Remove the spring from the balancer belt tensioner.

b. Remove the adjusting nut.

c. Remove the bolt from the balancer belt adjuster lever, then remove the lever and the tensioner pulley.

➡This is an excellent time to check or replace the water pump. Even if the timing belt is only being replaced as part of a good maintenance schedule, consider replacing the pump at the same time.

To install:

17. If the water pump was replaced, install a new O-ring and make certain it is properly seated. Install the water pump and retaining bolts. Tighten the mounting bolts to 106 inch lbs. (12 Nm).

18. If the balancer tensioner was removed, perform the following to install it:

a. Install the balancer belt pulley and adjuster lever.

b. Install the adjusting nut and the bolt to the balancer belt adjuster lever. Do not tighten the adjuster nut or bolt at this time.

➡**Be sure that the balancer lever and tensioner moves freely and does not bind.**

c. Install the spring to the tensioner.

d. Move the balancer its full deflection and tighten the adjusting nut.

19. Hold the auto-tensioner with the maintenance bolt pointing up. Remove the maintenance bolt and discard the gasket.

➡**Handle the tensioner carefully so the oil inside does not spill or leak. Replenish the auto-tensioner with oil if any spills or leaks out. The auto-tensioner total capacity is ¼ oz. (8 ml).**

20. Clamp the mounting boss of the auto-tensioner in a vise. Use pieces of wood or a cloth to protect the mounting boss.

✳✳✳ WARNING

Do not clamp the housing of the auto-tensioner, component damage may occur.

21. Insert a flat-bladed prytool into the maintenance hole. Place the stopper (part No. 14540-P13-003) on the auto-tensioner while turning the prytool clockwise to compress the tensioner. Take care not to damage the threads or the gasket contact surface with the prytool.

22. Remove the prytool and install the maintenance bolt with a new gasket. Tighten the maintenance bolt to 71 inch lbs. (8 Nm).

23. Be sure no oil is leaking from the maintenance bolt and install the auto-tensioner to the engine. Tighten the auto-tensioner mounting bolts to 16 ft. lbs. (22 Nm).

24. The pointer on the crankshaft pulley should be aligned with the pointer on the oil pump. The camshaft pulley must be aligned so that the word **UP** is at the top of the pulley and the marks on the edge of the pulley are aligned with the surfaces of the head.

25. Install the timing belt.

26. Remove the stopper from the timing belt adjuster.

27. Install the CKP/TDC sensors and tighten the bolts to 106 inch lbs. (12 Nm). Connect the CKP/TDC sensor connectors.

28. Install the balancer belt drive sprocket to the crankshaft.

29. Align the groove on the front balancer shaft pulley with the pointer on the oil pump.

30. Align the rear timing balancer pulley using a 6 x 100mm bolt or rod. Mark the bolt or rod at a point 2.9 in. (74mm) from the end. Remove the bolt from the maintenance hole on the side of the block; insert the bolt/rod into the hole and align the 2.9 in. (74mm) mark with the face of the hole. This pin will hold the shaft in place during installation.

31. Ensure the timing balancer belt adjuster moves freely.

32. Install the balancer belt. Once the belts are in place, be sure that all the engine alignment marks are still correct. If not, remove the belts, realign the engine and reinstall the belts. Once the belts are properly installed, slowly loosen the adjusting nut, allowing the tensioner to move against the belt. Remove the pin from the maintenance hole and reinstall the bolt and washer.

33. Turn the crankshaft pulley 1 full turn, then tighten the adjusting nut to 33 ft. lbs. (45 Nm).

✳✳✳ WARNING

Do not apply extra pressure to the pulleys or tensioners while performing the adjustment.

34. Install the timing belt and rocker arm (valve) covers, and any other applicable components. When installing the side engine mount, tighten the bolt and nut attaching the mount to the engine to 40

ft. lbs. (55 Nm), and the through-bolt and nut to 47 ft. lbs. (65 Nm).

35. Connect the negative battery cable.

2.3L (H23A1) Engine

♦ See Figures 123 and 124

1. Disconnect the negative battery cable.

2. Turn the crankshaft so the No. 1 piston is at Top Dead Center (TDC) on the compression stroke.

➡**The No. 1 piston is at TDC when the pointer on the block aligns with the white painted mark on the flywheel for manual transmission or driveplate for automatic transmission.**

3. Remove all necessary components for access to the rocker arm (valve) cover, then remove the rocker arm (valve) cover.

4. Ensure the words **UP** embossed on the camshaft pulleys are aligned in the upward position.

5. Insert a 5.0mm pin punch in each of the camshaft caps, nearest to the pulleys, through the holes provided.

6. Remove the upper and middle timing belt covers.

7. Support the engine with a floor jack below the center of the center beam. Tension the jack so that it is just supporting the beam but not lifting it. Remove the 2 rear bolts from the center beam to allow the engine to drop down for clearance to remove the lower cover.

8. Remove and discard the rubber seal from the timing belt adjuster. Do not loosen the adjusting nut.

9. Remove the lower timing belt cover.

10. There are 2 belts in this system; the one running to the camshaft pulley is the timing belt. The other, shorter belt drives the balance shaft and is referred to as the balancer belt or timing balancer belt. Lock the timing belt adjuster in position, by installing one of the lower timing belt cover bolts to the adjuster arm.

11. Loosen the timing belt and balancer shaft tensioner adjuster nut(s), do not loosen the nut(s) more than 1 turn. Push the tensioner for the bal-

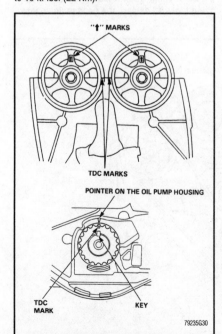

Fig. 123 Camshaft and crankshaft alignment mark positioning for TDC—2.2L (H22A1) and 2.3L engines

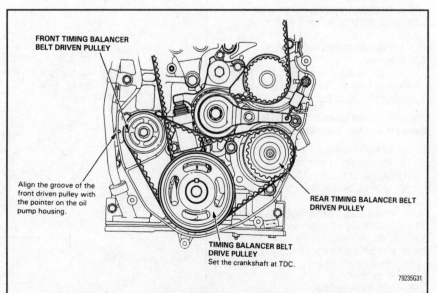

Fig. 124 View of the balancer belt and the related timing marks— 2.2L (H22A1) and 2.3L engines

ancer belt away from the belt to relieve the tension. Hold the tensioner and tighten the adjusting nut to hold the tensioner in place.

12. Carefully remove the balancer belt by sliding it off of the pulleys. Do not crimp or bend the belt; protect it from contact with oil or coolant.

13. Remove the balancer belt drive sprocket from the crankshaft.

14. Loosen the lockbolt installed in the timing belt adjuster and loosen the adjusting nut. Push the timing belt adjuster to remove the tension on the timing belt, then tighten the adjuster nut.

15. Remove the timing belt by sliding it off of the pulleys. Do not crimp or bend the belt; protect it from contact with oil or coolant.

16. If defective, remove the belt tensioners by performing the following:

   a. Remove the springs from the balancer belt and the timing belt tensioners.

   b. Remove the adjusting nut.

   c. Remove the bolt from the balancer belt adjuster lever, then remove the lever and the tensioner pulley.

   d. Remove the lockbolt from the timing belt tensioner lever, then remove the tensioner pulley and lever from the engine.

➡ **This is an excellent time to check or replace the water pump. Even if the timing belt is only being replaced as part of a good maintenance schedule, consider replacing the pump at the same time.**

To install:

17. If the water pump was replaced, install a new O-ring and make certain it is properly seated. Install the water pump and retaining bolts. Tighten the mounting bolts to 106 inch lbs. (12 Nm).

18. If the tensioners were removed perform the following to install them:

   a. Install the timing belt tensioner lever and tensioner pulley.

➡ **The tensioner lever must be properly positioned on its pivot pin located on the oil pump. Be sure that the timing belt lever and tensioner moves freely and does not bind.**

   b. Install the lockbolt to the timing belt tensioner, do not tighten the lockbolt at this time.

   c. Install the balancer belt pulley and adjuster lever.

   d. Install the adjusting nut and the bolt to the balancer belt adjuster lever. Do not tighten the adjuster nut or bolt at this time.

➡ **Be sure that the balancer lever and tensioner moves freely and does not bind.**

   e. Install the springs to the tensioners.

   f. Move the timing belt tensioner its full deflection and tighten the lockbolt.

   g. Move the balancer its full deflection and tighten the adjusting nut.

19. The crankshaft timing pointer must be perfectly aligned with the white mark on the flywheel or flex-plate. The camshaft pulley must be aligned so that the word **UP** is at the top of the pulley and the marks on the edge of the pulley are aligned with the surfaces of the head.

20. Install the timing belt.

21. Install the balancer belt drive sprocket to the crankshaft.

22. Remove the 2, 5.0mm pin punches from the camshaft bearing caps.

23. Loosen the bolt used to lock the timing belt tensioner. Loosen, then tighten the timing belt adjuster nut.

24. Turn the crankshaft counterclockwise until the cam pulley has moved 3 teeth; this creates tension on the timing belt. Loosen, then tighten the adjusting nut and tighten it to 33 ft. lbs. (45 Nm). Tighten the bolt used to lock the timing belt tensioner.

25. Realign the timing belt timing marks.

26. Align the groove on the front balancer shaft pulley with the pointer on the oil pump.

27. Align the rear timing balancer pulley using a 6 x 100mm bolt or rod. Mark the bolt or rod at a point 2.913 in. (74mm) from the end. Remove the bolt from the maintenance hole on the side of the block; insert the bolt/rod into the hole and align the 74mm mark with the face of the hole. This pin will hold the shaft in place during installation.

28. Loosen the adjusting nut and ensure the timing balancer belt adjuster moves freely.

29. Install the balancer belt. Once the belts are in place, be sure that all the engine alignment marks are still correct. If not, remove the belts, realign the engine and reinstall the belts. Once the belts are properly installed, slowly loosen the adjusting nut, allowing the tensioner to move against the belt. Remove the pin from the maintenance hole and reinstall the bolt and washer.

30. Turn the crankshaft pulley 1 full turn and tighten the adjusting nut to 33 ft. lbs. (45 Nm).

➡ **Both belt adjusters are spring loaded to properly tension the belts. Do not apply extra pressure to the pulleys or tensioners while performing the adjustment.**

31. Remove the 6 x 100mm bolt from the timing belt adjuster arm.

32. Install the timing belt and rocker arm (valve) covers. Reinstall all applicable components. When installing the crankshaft pulley, coat the threads and seating face of the pulley bolt with engine oil, then

install and tighten the bolt to 181 ft. lbs. (250 Nm). When installing the side engine mount, tighten the bolt and nut attaching the mount to the engine to 40 ft. lbs. (55 Nm), and the through-bolt and nut to 47 ft. lbs. (65 Nm). Remove the jack from under the center beam.

33. Connect the negative battery cable.

2.7L and 3.0L Engines

▶ **See Figures 125, 126, 127, 128 and 129**

1. Disconnect the negative battery cable.

2. Turn the engine to align the timing marks and set cylinder No. 1 to Top Dead Center (TDC) on the compression stroke. The white mark on the crankshaft pulley should align with the pointer on the timing belt cover. Remove the inspection caps on the upper timing belt covers to check the alignment of the timing marks. The pointers for the camshafts should align with the green marks on the camshaft sprockets.

3. Remove all necessary components for access to the timing belt covers, then remove the covers.

➡ **Do not use the covers to store removed items.**

4. Loosen the timing belt adjuster bolt 180 degrees (½ turn). Push the tensioner to remove the tension from the timing belt, then retighten the adjusting bolt.

5. Remove the timing belt. Do not crimp or bend the belt; protect it from contact with oil or coolant. Slide the belt off the sprockets.

6. Remove the bolts attaching the camshaft sprockets to the camshafts, then remove the sprockets.

7. If the timing belt tensioner is defective, remove the spring from the timing belt tensioner. Remove the tensioner pulley adjusting bolt and the adjuster assembly from the engine.

➡ **This is an excellent time to check or replace the water pump. Even if the timing belt is only being replaced as part of a good maintenance**

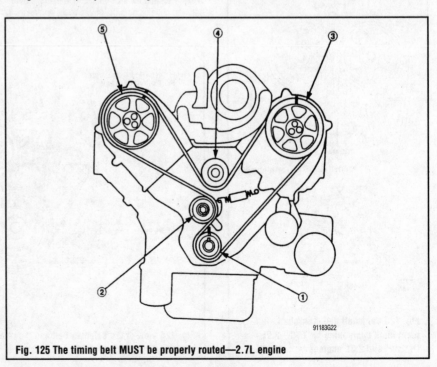

Fig. 125 The timing belt MUST be properly routed—2.7L engine

91183G22

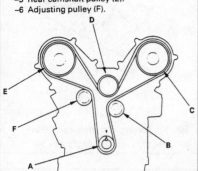

-1 Drive pulley (A).
-2 Idler pulley (B).
-3 Front camshaft pulley (C).
-4 Water pump pulley (D).
-5 Rear camshaft pulley (E).
-6 Adjusting pulley (F).

91183G21

Fig. 126 Following this routing diagram when installing the timing belt—3.0L engine

schedule, consider replacing the pump at the same time.

To install:

8. If the water pump was replaced, install a new O-ring and make certain it is properly seated.

Install the water pump and retaining bolts. Tighten the mounting bolts to 16 ft. lbs. (22 Nm).

9. If removed, install the tensioner pulley and the adjusting bolt, be sure the tensioner is properly positioned on its pivot pin. Install the spring to the tensioner, then push the tensioner to its full deflection and tighten the adjusting bolt.

10. Set the timing belt drive sprocket so that the No. 1 piston is at TDC. Align the TDC mark on the tooth of the timing belt drive sprocket with the pointer on the oil pump.

11. Set the camshaft sprockets so that the No. 1 piston is at TDC. Align the TDC marks (green mark) on the camshaft sprockets to the pointers on the back covers.

12. Install the timing belt onto the sprockets in the following sequence: crankshaft sprocket, tensioner pulley, front camshaft sprocket, water pump pulley and rear camshaft sprocket.

13. Loosen, then retighten the timing belt adjuster bolt to tension the timing belt.

14. Install the lower timing belt cover.

15. Install the crankshaft sprocket and the crankshaft pulley bolt. Tighten the bolt to 181 ft. lbs. (245 Nm) with the aid of the crank pulley holder.

16. Rotate the crankshaft 5–6 turns clockwise so that the timing belt positions on the sprockets.

17. Set cylinder No. 1 to TDC by aligning the timing marks. If the timing marks do not align,

remove the timing belt, then adjust the components and reinstall the timing belt.

18. Loosen the timing belt adjusting bolt 180 degrees (½ turn) and retighten the adjusting bolt. Tighten the adjusting bolt to 31 ft. lbs. (42 Nm).

19. Install the upper timing belt cover and all other applicable components. When installing the side engine mount to the engine, use 3 new attaching bolts. Tighten the new bolts to 40 ft. lbs. (54 Nm).

20. Install any remaining components in the reverse of the removal procedure.

21. Connect the negative battery cable.

INSPECTION

▶ **See Figures 130 thru 138**

Inspect both sides of the timing belt. Replace the belt with a new one if any of the following conditions exist:

- Hardening of the rubber—back side is glossy without resilience and leaves no indentation when pressed with a fingernail
- Cracks on the rubber backing
- Cracks or peeling of the canvas backing
- Cracks on rib root
- Cracks on belt sides
- Missing teeth or chunks of teeth

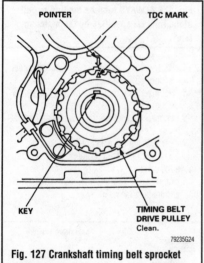

79235G24

Fig. 127 Crankshaft timing belt sprocket alignment mark locations—2.7L and 3.0L engines

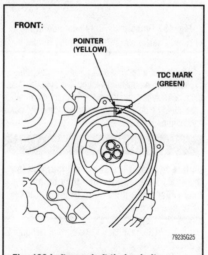

79235G25

Fig. 128 Left camshaft timing belt sprocket alignment mark location—2.7L and 3.0L engines

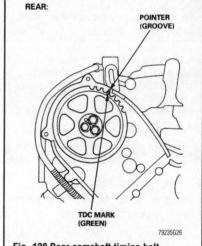

79235G26

Fig. 129 Rear camshaft timing belt sprocket alignment mark location—2.7L and 3.0L engines

TCCS1242

Fig. 130 Never bend or twist a timing belt excessively, and do not allow solvents, antifreeze, gasoline, acid or oil to come into contact with the belt

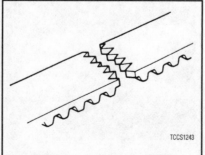

TCCS1243

Fig. 131 Check for premature parting of the belt

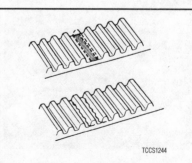

TCCS1244

Fig. 132 Check if the teeth are cracked or damaged

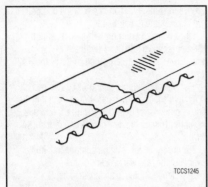

Fig. 133 Look for noticeable cracks or wear on the belt face

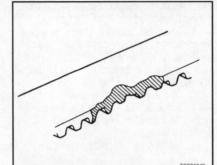

Fig. 134 You may only have damage on one side of the belt; if so, the guide could be the culprit

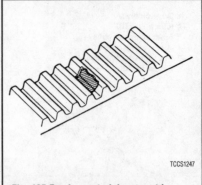

Fig. 135 Foreign materials can get in between the teeth and cause damage

Fig. 136 Inspect the timing belt for cracks, fraying, glazing or damage of any kind

Fig. 137 Damage on only one side of the timing belt may indicate a faulty guide

Fig. 138 ALWAYS replace the timing belt at the interval specified by the manufacturer

• Abnormal wear of belt sides—the sides are normal if they are sharp, as if cut by a knife.

If none of these conditions exist, the belt does not need replacement unless it is at the recommended interval. The belt MUST be replaced at the recommended interval.

REMOVAL & INSTALLATION

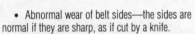

▶ See Figures 139, 140 and 141

The camshaft(s) rotate in journals with journal caps that have been machined into the cylinder head. No bearings are used between the camshaft

and the cylinder head. If a camshaft journal in the cylinder head has been damaged, the cylinder head must be replaced and the cause of the journal failure should be determined before replacing the damaged components.

✳✳ WARNING

Failure to install the camshaft journals in the exact location in which they belong, may cause severe damage to the cylinder head and camshaft.

1. Note the radio security code and station presets.
2. Disconnect the negative battery cable.
3. Label and disconnect the spark plug wires.

4. Remove the valve cover, as outlined earlier in this section.
5. Remove the timing belt, as outlined earlier in this section.
6. Loosen the rocker arm locknuts and adjusting screws.
7. Remove the camshaft bearing caps or camshaft holder plates and holders, then carefully remove the camshafts.
8. Remove the rocker arms, noting their positions, and inspect for wear.

Fig. 139 Lack of sufficient oil will cause damage to the camshaft journals, as shown here

Fig. 140 To ensure sufficient lubrication, the oil galleries must be free of carbon deposits

Fig. 141 Exploded view of the camshafts—V6 engine shown; 4-cylinder similar

To install:

➡**Use new O-rings, seals, and gaskets when installing the camshaft.**

9. Clean and inspect the camshaft bearing caps in the cylinder head.

10. Lubricate the lobes and journals of the camshaft prior to installation. Install the camshaft and the bearing caps.

11. Tighten the camshaft bearing caps to 86 inch lbs. (9.8 Nm), in sequence.

12. Set the camshafts at Top Dead Center (TDC) for No. 1 piston, align the holes in the camshafts with the holes in the No. 1 camshaft holder and insert a 5mm pin punch into the holes.

13. Install the keys into the keyways on the camshafts and install the pulleys, then tighten the retaining bolts to 27 ft. lbs. (37 Nm).

14. Install the timing belt, as outlined in this section.

15. Adjust the valve clearance, as outlined in Section 1.

16. Install the valve cover and tighten the nuts to 86 inch lbs. (9.8 Nm).

17. Connect the spark plug wires, as tagged during removal.

18. Connect the negative battery cable.

19. Enter the security code for the radio.

INSPECTION

♦ **See Figures 142, 143 and 144**

Using solvent, degrease the camshaft and clean out all of the oil holes. Visually inspect the cam lobes and bearing journals for excessive wear. If a lobe is questionable, check all of the lobes as indicated. If a journal or lobe is worn, the camshaft MUST BE or replaced.

➡**If a journal is worn, there is a good chance that the bearings or journals are worn and need replacement.**

If the lobes and journals appear intact, place the front and rear journals in V-blocks and rest a dial indicator on the center journal. Rotate the camshaft to check the straightness. If deviation exceeds 0.001 in. (0.0254mm), replace the camshaft.

Check the camshaft lobes with a micrometer, by measuring the lobes from the nose to the base and again at 90° (see illustration). The lobe lift is determined by subtracting the second measurement from the first. If all of the exhaust and intake lobes are not identical, the camshaft must be reground or replace.

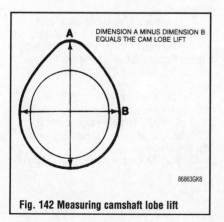

DIMENSION A MINUS DIMENSION B
EQUALS THE CAM LOBE LIFT

86863GK8

Fig. 142 Measuring camshaft lobe lift

Balance Shaft

REMOVAL & INSTALLATION

2.2L and 2.3L Engines

♦ **See Figure 145**

1. Note the radio security code and station presets.

2. Disconnect the negative and positive battery cables.

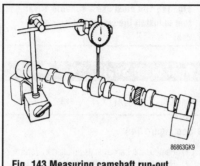

86863GK9

Fig. 143 Measuring camshaft run-out

3. Remove the engine assembly. For specific details refer to the engine removal procedures in this section.

4. Remove the rocker arm (valve) cover.

5. Remove the upper timing belt cover.

6. Turn the crankshaft to align the timing marks and set cylinder No.1 to Top Dead Center (TDC) for the compression stroke.

7. Remove the crankshaft pulley bolt and

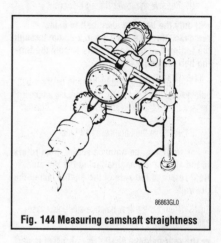

86863GL0

Fig. 144 Measuring camshaft straightness

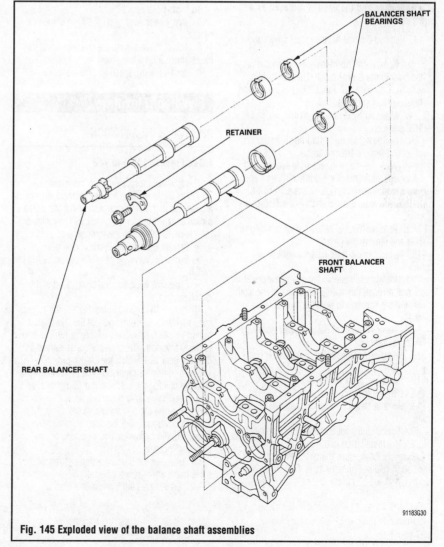

BALANCER SHAFT BEARINGS

RETAINER

FRONT BALANCER SHAFT

REAR BALANCER SHAFT

91183G30

Fig. 145 Exploded view of the balance shaft assemblies

remove the crankshaft pulley. Use a Crank Pulley Holder tool No. 07MAB-PY3010A and Holder Handle tool No. 07JAB-001020A or their equivalents, to hold the crankshaft pulley while removing the bolt.

8. Remove the dipstick and the dipstick tube.

9. Remove the through-bolt for the side engine mount and remove the mount.

10. Remove the lower timing belt cover.

➡If only the balance shaft belt is being removed, thread a 6 x 1.0mm x 25mm through the timing belt tensioner plate to hold the timing belt tensioner in place.

11. Loosen the timing belt/timing balancer belt adjuster nut ⅔–1 turn. Move the tension adjuster to release the belt tension and retighten the adjuster nut.

12. Remove the balancer shaft belt.

➡For servicing the balance shafts, front refers to the side of the engine facing the radiator. Rear refers to the side of the engine facing the firewall.

13. Remove the rear balance shaft/gear case assembly.

➡The rear balance shaft drive sprocket is part of a gear case and the case is removed as a unit.

14. Remove the rear balance shaft driven gear as follows:

   a. Remove the maintenance bolt located on the back of the engine block. The bolt is inline with the balance shaft about 3 inches behind the balance shaft sprocket.

   b. Make sure the balance shaft is still in the TDC position.

   c. Scribe a 3 inch (74mm) line from the end of a 6 x 1.0mm x 100mm bolt.

   d. With the maintenance hole sealing bolt removed, insert the 6 x 1.0mm x 100mm bolt into the maintenance hole to the scribed line to lock the rear balance shaft in the TDC position.

   e. Remove the rear balance shaft driven gear bolt and remove the gear.

15. To remove the front balance shaft drive sprocket:

   a. Install a suitable and sturdy screw driver or drift through the maintenance hole in the shaft behind the sprocket to hold the front balance shaft.

   b. Remove the front balance shaft mounting nut and sprocket.

16. Remove the front balance shaft outer bearing cap.

17. Remove the oil pan.

18. Remove the oil pump assembly.

19. Remove the front balance shaft retainer plate bolts.

20. Remove the front and rear balance shafts.

21. The installation is the reverse order of disassembly. Make sure to tighten the front balance shaft retainer plate bolts to 14 ft. lbs. (20 Nm).

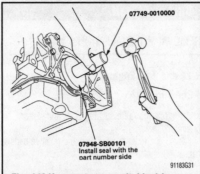

Fig. 146 You must use a suitable driver tool to install the crankshaft rear main seal

Rear Main Seal

REMOVAL & INSTALLATION

▶ **See Figure 146**

1. Remove the transaxle, as outlined in Section 7.
2. Remove the driveplate from the crankshaft.
3. Carefully pry the crankshaft rear main seal out of the retainer.

To install:

4. Apply clean engine oil to the lip of the new seal.

5. Install the seal onto the crankshaft and into the retainer using the appropriate seal driver.

6. Install the driveplate and the transaxle.

Flywheel/Flexplate

REMOVAL & INSTALLATION

▶ **See Figures 147 and 148**

The flywheel on cars with manual transaxles serves as the forward clutch engagement surface. It also serves as the ring gear with which the starter pinion engages to crank the engine. The most common reasons to replace the flywheel are:

- Broken teeth on the flywheel ring gear
- Excessive driveline chatter when engaging the clutch
- Excessive wear, scoring or cracking of the clutch surface

On cars with automatic transaxles, the torque converter actually forms part of the flywheel. It is bolted to a thin driveplate which, in turn, is bolted to the crankshaft. The driveplate also serves as the ring gear with which the starter pinion engages in engine cranking. The driveplate occasionally cracks; the teeth on the ring gear may also break, especially if the starter is often engaged while the pinion is still spinning. The torque converter and driveplate must be separated, and the converter and transaxle are be removed together.

1. Remove the transaxle from the vehicle. For more information, refer to Section 7.

2. On vehicles equipped with a manual

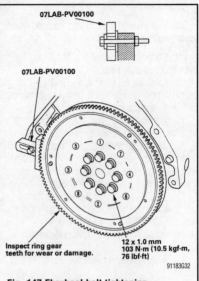

Fig. 147 Flywheel bolt tightening sequence—with manual transaxles

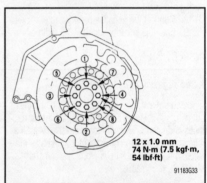

Fig. 148 Driveplate/flexplate bolt tightening sequence—with automatic transaxles

transaxle, remove the clutch assembly from the flywheel, as described in Section 7.

3. Support the flywheel in a secure manner (the flywheel on manual transaxle-equipped vehicles can be heavy).

4. Matchmark the flywheel/flexplate to the rear flange of the crankshaft.

5. Remove the attaching bolts and remove the flywheel/flexplate from the crankshaft.

To install:

6. Clean the flywheel/flexplate attaching bolts, the flywheel/flexplate and the rear crankshaft mounting flange.

7. Position the flywheel/flexplate onto the crankshaft flange so that the matchmarks align.

8. Torque the mounting bolts in a three step crisscross pattern, to the following specifications:

   a. Flywheel bolts (MT vehicles): 76 ft. lbs. (103 Nm)

   b. Driveplate/flexplate bolts (AT vehicles): 54 ft. lbs. (74 Nm)

9. On manual transaxle-equipped vehicles, install the clutch assembly. For more information, refer to Section 7.

10. Install the transaxle, as described in Section 7.

EXHAUST SYSTEM

Inspection

▶ See Figures 149 thru 155

→Safety glasses should be worn at all times when working on or near the exhaust system. Older exhaust systems will almost always be covered with loose rust particles which will shower you when disturbed. These particles are more than a nuisance and could injure your eye.

❋❋ CAUTION

DO NOT perform exhaust repairs or inspection with the engine or exhaust hot. Allow the system to cool completely before attempting any work. Exhaust systems are noted for sharp edges, flaking metal and rusted bolts. Gloves and eye protection are required. A healthy supply of penetrating oil and rags is highly recommended.

Your vehicle must be raised and supported safely to inspect the exhaust system properly. By placing 4 safety stands under the vehicle for support should provide enough room for you to slide under the vehicle and inspect the system completely. Start the inspection at the exhaust manifold or turbocharger pipe where the header pipe is attached and work your way to the back of the vehicle. On dual exhaust systems, remember to inspect both sides of the vehicle. Check the complete exhaust system for open seams, holes loose connections, or other deterioration which could permit exhaust fumes to seep into the passenger compartment. Inspect all mounting brackets and hangers for deterioration, some models may have rubber O-rings that can be overstretched and non-supportive. These components will need to be replaced if found. It has always been a practice to use a pointed tool to poke up into the exhaust system where the deterioration spots are to see whether or not they crumble. Some models may have heat shield covering certain parts of the exhaust system , it will be necessary to remove these shields to have the exhaust visible for inspection also.

REPLACEMENT

▶ See Figures 156, 157 and 158

There are basically two types of exhaust systems. One is the flange type where the component ends are attached with bolts and a gasket in-between. The other exhaust system is the slip joint type. These components slip into one another using clamps to retain them together.

❋❋ CAUTION

Allow the exhaust system to cool sufficiently before spraying a solvent exhaust fasteners. Some solvents are highly flammable and

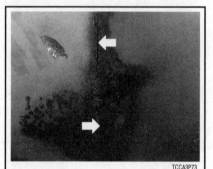

TCCA3P73

Fig. 149 Cracks in the muffler are a guaranteed leak

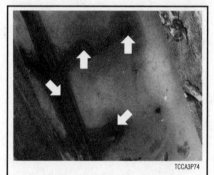

TCCA3P74

Fig. 150 Check the muffler for rotted spot welds and seams

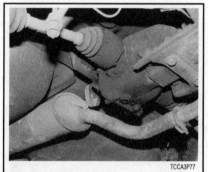

TCCA3P77

Fig. 151 Make sure the exhaust components are not contacting the body or suspension

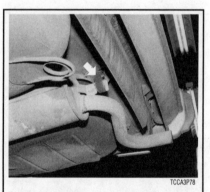

TCCA3P78

Fig. 152 Check for overstretched or torn exhaust hangers

TCCA3P75

Fig. 153 Example of a badly deteriorated exhaust pipe

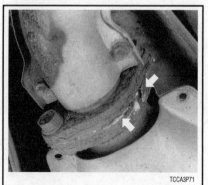

TCCA3P71

Fig. 154 Inspect flanges for gaskets that have deteriorated and need replacement

TCCA3P76

Fig. 155 Some systems, like this one, use large O-rings (doughnuts) in between the flanges

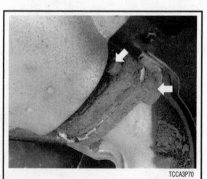

TCCA3P70

Fig. 156 Nuts and bolts will be extremely difficult to remove when deteriorated with rust

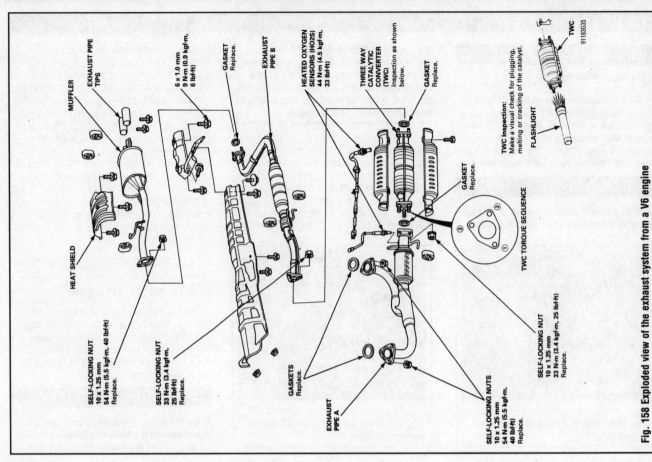

Fig. 158 Exploded view of the exhaust system from a V6 engine

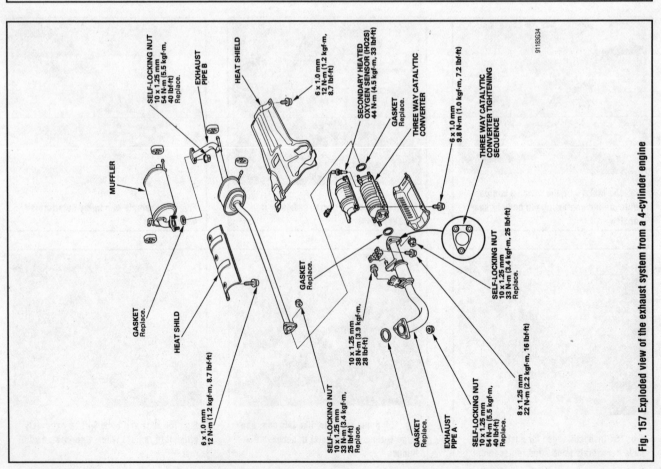

Fig. 157 Exploded view of the exhaust system from a 4-cylinder engine

could ignite when sprayed on hot exhaust components.

Before removing any component of the exhaust system, ALWAYS squirt a liquid rust dissolving agent onto the fasteners for ease of removal. A lot of knuckle skin will be saved by following this rule. It may even be wise to spray the fasteners and allow them to sit overnight.

Flange Type

▶ See Figure 159

✳✳ CAUTION

Do NOT perform exhaust repairs or inspection with the engine or exhaust hot. Allow

Fig. 159 Example of a flange type exhaust system joint

the system to cool completely before attempting any work. Exhaust systems are noted for sharp edges, flaking metal and rusted bolts. Gloves and eye protection are required. A healthy supply of penetrating oil and rags is highly recommended. Never spray liquid rust dissolving agent onto a hot exhaust component.

Before removing any component on a flange type system, ALWAYS squirt a liquid rust dissolving agent onto the fasteners for ease of removal. Start by unbolting the exhaust piece at both ends (if required). When unbolting the headpipe from the manifold, make sure that the bolts are free before trying to remove them. if you snap a stud in the exhaust manifold, the stud will have to be removed with a bolt extractor, which often means removal of the manifold itself. Next, disconnect the component from the mounting; slight twisting and turning may be required to remove the component completely from the vehicle. You may need to tap on the component with a rubber mallet to loosen the component. If all else fails, use a hacksaw to separate the parts. An oxy-acetylene cutting torch may be faster but the sparks are DANGEROUS near the fuel tank, and at the very least, accidents could happen, resulting in damage to the under-car parts, not to mention yourself.

Slip Joint Type

▶ See Figure 160

Before removing any component on the slip joint type exhaust system, ALWAYS squirt a liquid

rust dissolving agent onto the fasteners for ease of removal. Start by unbolting the exhaust piece at both ends (if required). When unbolting the headpipe from the manifold, make sure that the bolts are free before trying to remove them. if you snap a stud in the exhaust manifold, the stud will have to be removed with a bolt extractor, which often means removal of the manifold itself. Next, remove the mounting U-bolts from around the exhaust pipe you are extracting from the vehicle. Don't be surprised if the U-bolts break while removing the nuts. Loosen the exhaust pipe from any mounting brackets retaining it to the floor pan and separate the components.

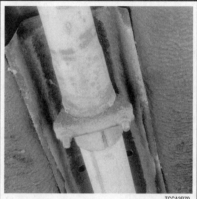

Fig. 160 Example of a common slip joint type system

ENGINE RECONDITIONING

Determining Engine Condition

Anything that generates heat and/or friction will eventually burn or wear out (for example, a light bulb generates heat, therefore its life span is limited). With this in mind, a running engine generates tremendous amounts of both; friction is encountered by the moving and rotating parts inside the engine and heat is created by friction and combustion of the fuel. However, the engine has systems designed to help reduce the effects of heat and friction and provide added longevity. The oiling system reduces the amount of friction encountered by the moving parts inside the engine, while the cooling system reduces heat created by friction and combustion. If either system is not maintained, a break-down will be inevitable. Therefore, you can see how regular maintenance can affect the service life of your vehicle. If you do not drain, flush and refill your cooling system at the proper intervals, deposits will begin to accumulate in the radiator, thereby reducing the amount of heat it can extract from the coolant. The same applies to your oil and filter; if it is not changed often enough it becomes laden with contaminates and is unable to properly lubricate the engine. This increases friction and wear.

There are a number of methods for evaluating the condition of your engine. A compression test can reveal the condition of your pistons, piston rings, cylinder bores, head gasket(s), valves and valve seats. An oil pressure test can warn you of

possible engine bearing, or oil pump failures. Excessive oil consumption, evidence of oil in the engine air intake area and/or bluish smoke from the tailpipe may indicate worn piston rings, worn valve guides and/or valve seals. As a general rule, an engine that uses no more than one quart of oil every 1000 miles is in good condition. Engines that use one quart of oil or more in less than 1000 miles should first be checked for oil leaks. If any oil leaks are present, have them fixed before determining how much oil is consumed by the engine, especially if blue smoke is not visible at the tailpipe.

COMPRESSION TEST

A noticeable lack of engine power, excessive oil consumption and/or poor fuel mileage measured over an extended period are all indicators of internal engine wear. Worn piston rings, scored or worn cylinder bores, blown head gaskets, sticking or burnt valves, and worn valve seats are all possible culprits. A check of each cylinder's compression will help locate the problem.

▶ See Figure 161

➡A screw-in type compression gauge is more accurate than the type you simply hold against the spark plug hole. Although it takes slightly longer to use, it's worth the effort to obtain a more accurate reading.

1. Make sure that the proper amount and viscosity of engine oil is in the crankcase, then ensure the battery is fully charged.
2. Warm-up the engine to normal operating temperature, then shut the engine **OFF**.
3. Disable the ignition system.
4. Label and disconnect all of the spark plug wires from the plugs.
5. Thoroughly clean the cylinder head area around the spark plug ports, then remove the spark plugs.
6. Set the throttle plate to the fully open (wide-open throttle) position. You can block the accelera-

Fig. 161 A screw-in type compression gauge is more accurate and easier to use without an assistant

tor linkage open for this, or you can have an assistant fully depress the accelerator pedal.

7. Install a screw-in type compression gauge into the No. 1 spark plug hole until the fitting is snug.

✷✷ WARNING

Be careful not to crossthread the spark plug hole.

8. According to the tool manufacturer's instructions, connect a remote starting switch to the starting circuit.

9. With the ignition switch in the **OFF** position, use the remote starting switch to crank the engine through at least five compression strokes (approximately 5 seconds of cranking) and record the highest reading on the gauge.

10. Repeat the test on each cylinder, cranking the engine approximately the same number of compression strokes and/or time as the first.

11. Compare the highest readings from each cylinder to that of the others. The indicated compression pressures are considered within specifications if the lowest reading cylinder is within 75 percent of the pressure recorded for the highest reading cylinder. For example, if your highest reading cylinder pressure was 150 psi (1034 kPa), then 75 percent of that would be 113 psi (779 kPa). So the lowest reading cylinder should be no less than 113 psi (779 kPa).

12. If a cylinder exhibits an unusually low compression reading, pour a tablespoon of clean engine oil into the cylinder through the spark plug hole and repeat the compression test. If the compression rises after adding oil, it means that the cylinder's piston rings and/or cylinder bore are damaged or worn. If the pressure remains low, the valves may not be seating properly (a valve job is needed), or the head gasket may be blown near that cylinder. If compression in any two adjacent cylinders is low, and if the addition of oil doesn't help raise compression, there is leakage past the head gasket. Oil and coolant in the combustion chamber, combined with blue or constant white smoke from the tailpipe, are symptoms of this problem. However, don't be alarmed by the normal white smoke emitted from the tailpipe during engine warm-up or from cold weather driving. There may be evidence of water droplets on the engine dipstick and/or oil droplets in the cooling system if a head gasket is blown.

OIL PRESSURE TEST

Check for proper oil pressure at the sending unit passage with an externally mounted mechanical oil pressure gauge (as opposed to relying on a factory installed dash-mounted gauge). A tachometer may also be needed, as some specifications may require running the engine at a specific rpm.

1. With the engine cold, locate and remove the oil pressure sending unit.

2. Following the manufacturer's instructions, connect a mechanical oil pressure gauge and, if necessary, a tachometer to the engine.

3. Start the engine and allow it to idle.

4. Check the oil pressure reading when cold and record the number. You may need to run the engine at a specified rpm, so check the specifications.

5. Run the engine until normal operating temperature is reached (upper radiator hose will feel warm).

6. Check the oil pressure reading again with the engine hot and record the number. Turn the engine **OFF**.

7. Compare your hot oil pressure reading to that given in the chart. If the reading is low, check the cold pressure reading against the chart. If the cold pressure is well above the specification, and the hot reading was lower than the specification, you may have the wrong viscosity oil in the engine. Change the oil, making sure to use the proper grade and quantity, then repeat the test.

Low oil pressure readings could be attributed to internal component wear, pump related problems, a low oil level, or oil viscosity that is too low. High oil pressure readings could be caused by an overfilled crankcase, too high of an oil viscosity or a faulty pressure relief valve.

Buy or Rebuild?

Now that you have determined that your engine is worn out, you must make some decisions. The question of whether or not an engine is worth rebuilding is largely a subjective matter and one of personal worth. Is the engine a popular one, or is it an obsolete model? Are parts available? Will it get acceptable gas mileage once it is rebuilt? Is the car it's being put into worth keeping? Would it be less expensive to buy a new engine, have your engine rebuilt by a pro, rebuild it yourself or buy a used engine from a salvage yard? Or would it be simpler and less expensive to buy another car? If you have considered all these matters and more, and have still decided to rebuild the engine, then it is time to decide how you will rebuild it.

➡**The editors at Chilton feel that most engine machining should be performed by a professional machine shop. Don't think of it as wasting money, rather, as an assurance that the job has been done right the first time. There are many expensive and specialized tools required to perform such tasks as boring and honing an engine block or having a valve job done on a cylinder head. Even inspecting the parts requires expensive micrometers and gauges to properly measure wear and clearances. Also, a machine shop can deliver to you clean, and ready to assemble parts, saving you time and aggravation. Your maximum savings will come from performing the removal, disassembly, assembly and installation of the engine and purchasing or renting only the tools required to perform the above tasks. Depending on the particular circumstances, you may save 40 to 60 percent of the cost doing these yourself.**

A complete rebuild or overhaul of an engine involves replacing all of the moving parts (pistons, rods, crankshaft, camshaft, etc.) with new ones and machining the non-moving wearing surfaces of the block and heads. Unfortunately, this may not be cost effective. For instance, your crankshaft may have been damaged or worn, but it can be machined undersize for a minimal fee.

So, as you can see, you can replace everything inside the engine, but, it is wiser to replace only those parts which are really needed, and, if possible, repair the more expensive ones. Later in this section,

we will break the engine down into its two main components: the cylinder head and the engine block. We will discuss each component, and the recommended parts to replace during a rebuild on each.

Engine Overhaul Tips

Most engine overhaul procedures are fairly standard. In addition to specific parts replacement procedures and specifications for your individual engine, this section is also a guide to acceptable rebuilding procedures. Examples of standard rebuilding practice are given and should be used along with specific details concerning your particular engine.

Competent and accurate machine shop services will ensure maximum performance, reliability and engine life. In most instances it is more profitable for the do-it-yourself mechanic to remove, clean and inspect the component, buy the necessary parts and deliver these to a shop for actual machine work.

Much of the assembly work (crankshaft, bearings, piston rods, and other components) is well within the scope of the do-it-yourself mechanic's tools and abilities. You will have to decide for yourself the depth of involvement you desire in an engine repair or rebuild.

TOOLS

The tools required for an engine overhaul or parts replacement will depend on the depth of your involvement. With a few exceptions, they will be the tools found in a mechanic's tool kit (see Section 1 of this manual). More in-depth work will require some or all of the following:

• A dial indicator (reading in thousandths) mounted on a universal base
• Micrometers and telescope gauges
• Jaw and screw-type pullers
• Scraper
• Valve spring compressor
• Ring groove cleaner
• Piston ring expander and compressor
• Ridge reamer
• Cylinder hone or glaze breaker
• Plastigage®
• Engine stand

The use of most of these tools is illustrated in this section. Many can be rented for a one-time use from a local parts jobber or tool supply house specializing in automotive work.

Occasionally, the use of special tools is called for. See the information on Special Tools and the Safety Notice in the front of this book before substituting another tool.

OVERHAUL TIPS

Aluminum has become extremely popular for use in engines, due to its low weight. Observe the following precautions when handling aluminum parts:

• Never hot tank aluminum parts (the caustic hot tank solution will eat the aluminum.
• Remove all aluminum parts (identification tag, etc.) from engine parts prior to the tanking.
• Always coat threads lightly with engine oil or anti-seize compounds before installation, to prevent seizure.
• Never overtighten bolts or spark plugs especially in aluminum threads.

When assembling the engine, any parts that will be exposed to frictional contact must be prelubed to provide lubrication at initial start-up. Any product specifically formulated for this purpose can be used, but engine oil is not recommended as a pre-lube in most cases.

When semi-permanent (locked, but removable) installation of bolts or nuts is desired, threads should be cleaned and coated with Loctite• or another similar, commercial non-hardening sealant.

CLEANING

♦ **See Figures 162, 163, 164 and 165**

Before the engine and its components are inspected, they must be thoroughly cleaned. You

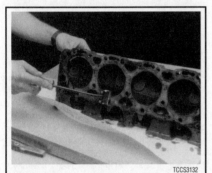

TCCS3132

Fig. 162 Use a gasket scraper to remove the old gasket material from the mating surfaces

will need to remove any engine varnish, oil sludge and/or carbon deposits from all of the components to insure an accurate inspection. A crack in the engine block or cylinder head can easily become overlooked if hidden by a layer of sludge or carbon.

Most of the cleaning process can be carried out with common hand tools and readily available solvents or solutions. Carbon deposits can be chipped away using a hammer and a hard wooden chisel. Old gasket material and varnish or sludge can usually be removed using a scraper and/or cleaning solvent. Extremely stubborn deposits may require the use of a power drill with a wire brush. If using a wire brush, use extreme care around any critical machined surfaces (such as the gasket surfaces, bearing saddles, cylinder bores, etc.). Use of a wire brush is NOT RECOMMENDED on any aluminum components. Always follow any safety recommendations given by the manufacturer of the tool and/or solvent. You should always wear eye protection during any cleaning process involving scraping, chipping or spraying of solvents.

An alternative to the mess and hassle of cleaning the parts yourself is to drop them off at a local garage or machine shop. They will, more than likely, have the necessary equipment to properly clean all of the parts for a nominal fee.

✳✳ CAUTION

Always wear eye protection during any cleaning process involving scraping, chipping or spraying of solvents.

Remove any oil galley plugs, freeze plugs and/or pressed-in bearings and carefully wash and degrease all of the engine components including the fasteners and bolts. Small parts such as the valves, springs, etc., should be placed in a metal basket and allowed to soak. Use pipe cleaner type brushes, and clean all passageways in the components. Use a ring expander and remove the rings from the pistons. Clean the piston ring grooves with a special tool or a piece of broken ring. Scrape the carbon off of the top of the piston. You should never use a wire brush on the pistons. After preparing all of the piston assemblies in this manner, wash and degrease them again.

✳✳ WARNING

Use extreme care when cleaning around the cylinder head valve seats. A mistake or slip may cost you a new seat.

When cleaning the cylinder head, remove carbon from the combustion chamber with the valves installed. This will avoid damaging the valve seats.

REPAIRING DAMAGED THREADS

♦ **See Figures 166, 167, 168, 169 and 170**

Several methods of repairing damaged threads are available. Heli-Coil® (shown here), Keenserts® and Microdot® are among the most widely used. All involve basically the same principle—drilling out stripped threads, tapping the hole and installing a prewound insert—making welding, plugging and oversize fasteners unnecessary.

TCCS3211

Fig. 163 Use a ring expander tool to remove the piston rings

TCCS3208

Fig. 164 Clean the piston ring grooves using a ring groove cleaner tool, or . . .

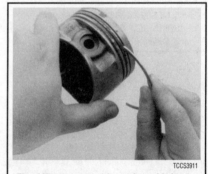

TCCS3911

Fig. 165 . . . use a piece of an old ring to clean the grooves. Be careful, the ring can be quite sharp

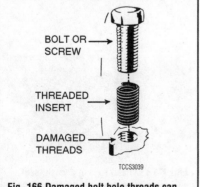

TCCS3039

Fig. 166 Damaged bolt hole threads can be replaced with thread repair inserts

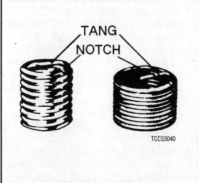

TCCS3040

Fig. 167 Standard thread repair insert (left), and spark plug thread insert

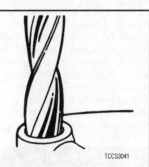

TCCS3041

Fig. 168 Drill out the damaged threads with the specified size bit. Be sure to drill completely through the hole or to the bottom of a blind hole

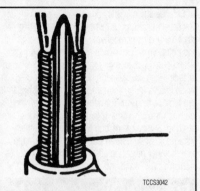

Fig. 169 Using the kit, tap the hole in order to receive the thread insert. Keep the tap well oiled and back it out frequently to avoid clogging the threads

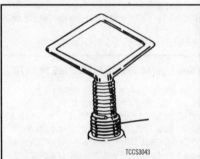

Fig. 170 Screw the insert onto the installer tool until the tang engages the slot. Thread the insert into the hole until it is ¼–½ turn below the top surface, then remove the tool and break off the tang using a punch

Two types of thread repair inserts are usually supplied: a standard type for most inch coarse, inch fine, metric course and metric fine thread sizes and a spark lug type to fit most spark plug port sizes. Consult the individual tool manufacturer's catalog to determine exact applications. Typical thread repair kits will contain a selection of prewound threaded inserts, a tap (corresponding to the outside diameter threads of the insert) and an installation tool. Spark plug inserts usually differ because they require a tap equipped with pilot threads and a combined reamer/tap section. Most manufacturers also supply blister-packed thread repair inserts separately in addition to a master kit containing a variety of taps and inserts plus installation tools.

Before attempting to repair a threaded hole, remove any snapped, broken or damaged bolts or studs. Penetrating oil can be used to free frozen threads. The offending item can usually be removed with locking pliers or using a screw/stud extractor. After the hole is clear, the thread can be repaired, as shown in the series of accompanying illustrations and in the kit manufacturer's instructions.

Engine Preparation

To properly rebuild an engine, you must first remove it from the vehicle, then disassemble and diagnose it. Ideally you should place your engine on an engine stand. This affords you the best

access to the engine components. Follow the manufacturer's directions for using the stand with your particular engine. Remove the flywheel or flexplate before installing the engine to the stand.

Now that you have the engine on a stand, and assuming that you have drained the oil and coolant from the engine, it's time to strip it of all but the necessary components. Before you start disassembling the engine, you may want to take a moment to draw some pictures, or fabricate some labels or containers to mark the locations of various components and the bolts and/or studs which fasten them. Modern day engines use a lot of little brackets and clips which hold wiring harnesses and such, and these holders are often mounted on studs and/or bolts that can be easily mixed up. The manufacturer spent a lot of time and money designing your vehicle, and they wouldn't have wasted any of it by haphazardly placing brackets, clips or fasteners on the vehicle. If it's present when you disassemble it, put it back when you assemble, you will regret not remembering that little bracket which holds a wire harness out of the path of a rotating part.

You should begin by unbolting any accessories still attached to the engine, such as the water pump, power steering pump, alternator, etc. Then, unfasten any manifolds (intake or exhaust) which were not removed during the engine removal procedure. Finally, remove any covers remaining on the engine such as the rocker arm, front or timing cover and oil pan. Some front covers may require the vibration damper and/or crank pulley to be removed beforehand. The idea is to reduce the engine to the bare necessities (cylinder head(s), valve train, engine block, crankshaft, pistons and connecting rods), plus any other 'in block' components such as oil pumps, balance shafts and auxiliary shafts.

Finally, remove the cylinder head(s) from the engine block and carefully place on a bench. Disassembly instructions for each component follow later in this section.

Cylinder Head

There are two basic types of cylinder heads used on today's automobiles: the Overhead Valve (OHV) and the Overhead Camshaft (OHC). The latter can also be broken down into two subgroups: the Single Overhead Camshaft (SOHC) and the Dual Overhead Camshaft (DOHC). Generally, if there is only a single camshaft on a head, it is just referred to as an OHC head. Also, an engine with an OHV cylinder head is also known as a pushrod engine.

Most cylinder heads these days are made of an aluminum alloy due to its light weight, durability and heat transfer qualities. However, cast iron was the material of choice in the past, and is still used on many vehicles today. Whether made from aluminum or iron, all cylinder heads have valves and seats. Some use two valves per cylinder, while the more hi-tech engines will utilize a multi-valve configuration using 3, 4 and even 5 valves per cylinder. When the valve contacts the seat, it does so on precision machined surfaces, which seals the combustion chamber. All cylinder heads have a valve guide for each valve. The guide centers the valve to the seat and allows it to move up and down within it. The clearance between the valve and guide can be critical. Too much clearance and the engine may consume oil, lose vacuum and/or damage the seat. Too little, and the valve can stick in the guide caus-

ing the engine to run poorly if at all, and possibly causing severe damage. The last component all cylinder heads have are valve springs. The spring holds the valve against its seat. It also returns the valve to this position when the valve has been opened by the valve train or camshaft. The spring is fastened to the valve by a retainer and valve locks (sometimes called keepers). Aluminum heads will also have a valve spring shim to keep the spring from wearing away the aluminum.

An ideal method of rebuilding the cylinder head would involve replacing all of the valves, guides, seats, springs, etc. with new ones. However, depending on how the engine was maintained, often this is not necessary. A major cause of valve, guide and seat wear is an improperly tuned engine. An engine that is running too rich, will often wash the lubricating oil out of the guide with gasoline, causing it to wear rapidly. Conversely, an engine which is running too lean will place higher combustion temperatures on the valves and seats allowing them to wear or even burn. Springs fall victim to the driving habits of the individual. A driver who often runs the engine rpm to the redline will wear out or break the springs faster then one that stays well below it. Unfortunately, mileage takes it toll on all of the parts. Generally, the valves, guides, springs and seats in a cylinder head can be machined and re-used, saving you money. However, if a valve is burnt, it may be wise to replace all of the valves, since they were all operating in the same environment. The same goes for any other component on the cylinder head. Think of it as an insurance policy against future problems related to that component.

Unfortunately, the only way to find out which components need replacing, is to disassemble and carefully check each piece. After the cylinder head(s) are disassembled, thoroughly clean all of the components.

DISASSEMBLY

OHC Heads

▶ **See Figures 171 and 172**

Whether it is a single or dual overhead camshaft cylinder head, the disassembly procedure is rela-

Fig. 171 Exploded view of a valve, seal, spring, retainer and locks from an OHC cylinder head

Fig. 172 Example of a multi-valve cylinder head. Note how it has 2 intake and 2 exhaust valve ports

tively unchanged. One aspect to pay attention to is careful labeling of the parts on the dual camshaft cylinder head. There will be an intake camshaft and followers as well as an exhaust camshaft and followers and they must be labeled as such. In some cases, the components are identical and could easily be installed incorrectly. DO NOT MIX THEM UP! Determining which is which is very simple; the intake camshaft and components are on the same side of the head as was the intake manifold. Conversely, the exhaust camshaft and components are on the same side of the head as was the exhaust manifold.

CUP TYPE CAMSHAFT FOLLOWERS

♦ See Figures 173, 174 and 175

Most cylinder heads with cup type camshaft followers will have the valve spring, retainer and locks recessed within the follower's bore. You will need a C-clamp style valve spring compressor tool, an OHC spring removal tool (or equivalent) and a small magnet to disassemble the head.

Fig. 173 C-clamp type spring compressor and an OHC spring removal tool (center) for cup type followers

1. If not already removed, remove the camshaft(s) and/or followers. Mark their positions for assembly.
2. Position the cylinder head to allow use of a C-clamp style valve spring compressor tool.

➥It is preferred to position the cylinder head gasket surface facing you with the valve springs facing the opposite direction and the head laying horizontal.

3. With the OHC spring removal adapter tool positioned inside of the follower bore, compress the valve spring using the C-clamp style valve spring compressor.
4. Remove the valve locks. A small magnetic tool or screwdriver will aid in removal.
5. Release the compressor tool and remove the spring assembly.
6. Withdraw the valve from the cylinder head.
7. If equipped, remove the valve seal.

➥Special valve seal removal tools are available. Regular or needlenose type pliers, if used with care, will work just as well. If using

Fig. 174 Most cup type follower cylinder heads retain the camshaft using bolt-on bearing caps

Fig. 175 Position the OHC spring tool in the follower bore, then compress the spring with a C-clamp type tool

ordinary pliers, be sure not to damage the follower bore. The follower and its bore are machined to close tolerances and any damage to the bore will effect this relationship.

8. If equipped, remove the valve spring shim. A small magnetic tool or screwdriver will aid in removal.
9. Repeat Steps 3 through 8 until all of the valves have been removed.

ROCKER ARM TYPE CAMSHAFT FOLLOWERS

♦ See Figures 176 thru 184

Most cylinder heads with rocker arm-type camshaft followers are easily disassembled using a standard valve spring compressor. However, certain models may not have enough open space around the spring for the standard tool and may require you to use a C-clamp style compressor tool instead.

1. If not already removed, remove the rocker arms and/or shafts and the camshaft. If applicable, also remove the hydraulic lash adjusters. Mark their positions for assembly.
2. Position the cylinder head to allow access to the valve spring.
3. Use a valve spring compressor tool to relieve the spring tension from the retainer.

➥Due to engine varnish, the retainer may stick to the valve locks. A gentle tap with a hammer may help to break it loose.

4. Remove the valve locks from the valve tip and/or retainer. A small magnet may help in removing the small locks.

Fig. 176 Example of the shaft mounted rocker arms on some OHC heads

Fig. 177 Another example of the rocker arm type OHC head. This model uses a follower under the camshaft

Fig. 178 Before the camshaft can be removed, all of the followers must first be removed . . .

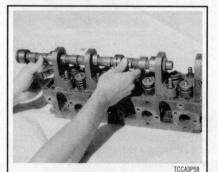

Fig. 179 . . . then the camshaft can be removed by sliding it out (shown), or unbolting a bearing cap (not shown)

Fig. 180 Compress the valve spring . . .

Fig. 181 . . . then remove the valve locks from the valve stem and spring retainer

Fig. 182 Remove the valve spring and retainer from the cylinder head

Fig. 183 Remove the valve seal from the guide. Some gentle prying or pliers may help to remove stubborn ones

5. Lift the valve spring, tool and all, off of the valve stem.

6. If equipped, remove the valve seal. If the seal is difficult to remove with the valve in place, try removing the valve first, then the seal. Follow the steps below for valve removal.

7. Position the head to allow access for withdrawing the valve.

➥Cylinder heads that have seen a lot of miles and/or abuse may have mushroomed the valve lock grove and/or tip, causing difficulty in removal of the valve. If this has happened, use a metal file to carefully remove the high spots around the lock grooves and/or tip. Only file it enough to allow removal.

8. Remove the valve from the cylinder head.

9. If equipped, remove the valve spring shim. A small magnetic tool or screwdriver will aid in removal.

10. Repeat Steps 3 though 9 until all of the valves have been removed.

INSPECTION

Now that all of the cylinder head components are clean, it's time to inspect them for wear and/or damage. To accurately inspect them, you will need some specialized tools:

• A 0–1 in. micrometer for the valves
• A dial indicator or inside diameter gauge for the valve guides
• A spring pressure test gauge

If you do not have access to the proper tools, you may want to bring the components to a shop that does.

Valves

▶ See Figures 185, 186 and 187

The first thing to inspect are the valve heads. Look closely at the head, margin and face for any cracks, excessive wear or burning. The margin is the best place to look for burning. It should have a squared edge with an even width all around the diameter. When a valve burns, the margin will look melted and the edges rounded. Also inspect the valve head for any signs of tulipping. This will show as a lifting of the edges or dishing in the center of the head and will usually not occur to all of the

Fig. 184 All aluminum and some cast iron heads will have these valve spring shims. Remove all of them as well

Fig. 185 Honda valve springs have been known to even go several hundred thousand miles and still meet the manufacturer's rigid specifications

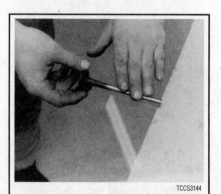

Fig. 186 Valve stems may be rolled on a flat surface to check for bends

Fig. 187 Use a micrometer to check the valve stem diameter

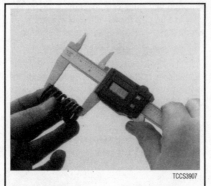

Fig. 188 Use a caliper to check the valve spring free-length

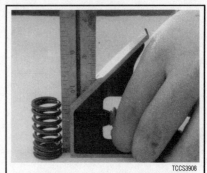

Fig. 189 Check the valve spring for squareness on a flat surface; a carpenter's square can be used

valves. All of the heads should look the same, any that seem dished more than others are probably bad. Next, inspect the valve lock grooves and valve tips. Check for any burrs around the lock grooves, especially if you had to file them to remove the valve. Valve tips should appear flat, although slight rounding with high mileage engines is normal. Slightly worn valve tips will need to be machined flat. Last, measure the valve stem diameter with the micrometer. Measure the area that rides within the guide, especially towards the tip where most of the wear occurs. Take several measurements along its length and compare them to each other. Wear should be even along the length with little to no taper. If no minimum diameter is given in the specifications, then the stem should not read more than 0.001 in. (0.025mm) below the unworn area of the valve stem. Any valves that fail these inspections should be replaced.

Springs, Retainers and Valve Locks

♦ See Figures 188 and 189

The first thing to check is the most obvious, broken springs. Next check the free length and squareness of each spring. If applicable, insure to distinguish between intake and exhaust springs. Use a ruler and/or carpenter's square to measure the length. A carpenter's square should be used to check the springs for squareness. If a spring pressure test gauge is available, check each springs rating and compare to the specifications chart. Check the readings against the specifications given. Any springs that fail these inspections should be replaced.

The spring retainers rarely need replacing, however they should still be checked as a precaution. Inspect the spring mating surface and the valve lock retention area for any signs of excessive wear. Also check for any signs of cracking. Replace any retainers that are questionable.

Valve locks should be inspected for excessive wear on the outside contact area as well as on the inner notched surface. Any locks which appear worn or broken and its respective valve should be replaced.

Cylinder Head

There are several things to check on the cylinder head: valve guides, seats, cylinder head surface flatness, cracks and physical damage.

VALVE GUIDES

♦ See Figure 190

Now that you know the valves are good, you can use them to check the guides, although a new valve, if available, is preferred. Before you measure anything, look at the guides carefully and inspect them for any cracks, chips or breakage. Also if the guide is a removable style (as in most aluminum heads), check them for any looseness or evidence of movement. All of the guides should appear to be at the same height from the spring seat. If any seem lower (or higher) from another, the guide has moved. Mount a dial indicator onto the spring side of the cylinder head. Lightly oil the valve stem and insert it into the cylinder head. Position the dial indicator against the valve stem near the tip and zero the

gauge. Grasp the valve stem and wiggle towards and away from the dial indicator and observe the readings. Mount the dial indicator 90 degrees from the initial point and zero the gauge and again take a reading. Compare the two readings for a out of round condition. Check the readings against the specifications given. An Inside Diameter (I.D.) gauge designed for valve guides will give you an accurate valve guide bore measurement. If the I.D. gauge is used, compare the readings with the specifications given. Any guides that fail these inspections should be replaced or machined.

VALVE SEATS

A visual inspection of the valve seats should show a slightly worn and pitted surface where the valve face contacts the seat. Inspect the seat carefully for severe pitting or cracks. Also, a seat that is badly worn will be recessed into the cylinder head. A severely worn or recessed seat may need to be replaced. All cracked seats must be replaced. A seat concentricity gauge, if available, should be used to check the seat run-out. If run-out exceeds specifications the seat must be machined (if no specification is given use 0.002 in. or 0.051mm).

CYLINDER HEAD SURFACE FLATNESS

♦ See Figures 191 and 192

After you have cleaned the gasket surface of the cylinder head of any old gasket material, check the head for flatness.

Place a straightedge across the gasket surface. Using feeler gauges, determine the clearance at the center of the straightedge and across the cylinder

Fig. 190 A dial gauge may be used to check valve stem-to-guide clearance; read the gauge while moving the valve stem

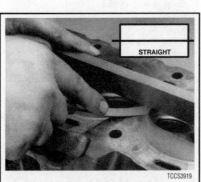

Fig. 191 Check the head for flatness across the center of the head surface using a straightedge and feeler gauge

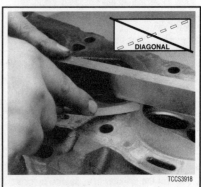

Fig. 192 Checks should also be made along both diagonals of the head surface

head at several points. Check along the centerline and diagonally on the head surface. If the warpage exceeds 0.003 in. (0.076mm) within a 6.0 in. (15.2cm) span, or 0.006 in. (0.152mm) over the total length of the head, the cylinder head must be resurfaced. After resurfacing the heads of a V-type engine, the intake manifold flange surface should be checked, and if necessary, milled proportionally to allow for the change in its mounting position.

CRACKS AND PHYSICAL DAMAGE

Generally, cracks are limited to the combustion chamber, however, it is not uncommon for the head to crack in a spark plug hole, port, outside of the head or in the valve spring/rocker arm area. The first area to inspect is always the hottest: the exhaust seat/port area.

A visual inspection should be performed, but just because you don't see a crack does not mean it is not there. Some more reliable methods for inspecting for cracks include Magnaflux®, a magnetic process or Zyglo®, a dye penetrant. Magnaflux® is used only on ferrous metal (cast iron) heads. Zyglo® uses a spray on fluorescent mixture along with a black light to reveal the cracks. It is strongly recommended to have your cylinder head checked professionally for cracks, especially if the engine was known to have overheated and/or leaked or consumed coolant. Contact a local shop for availability and pricing of these services.

Physical damage is usually very evident. For example, a broken mounting ear from dropping the head or a bent or broken stud and/or bolt. All of these defects should be fixed or, if unrepairable, the head should be replaced.

Camshaft and Followers

Inspect the camshaft(s) and followers as described earlier in this section.

REFINISHING & REPAIRING

Many of the procedures given for refinishing and repairing the cylinder head components must be performed by a machine shop. Certain steps, if the inspected part is not worn, can be performed yourself inexpensively. However, you spent a lot of time and effort so far, why risk trying to save a couple bucks if you might have to do it all over again?

Valves

Any valves that were not replaced should be refaced and the tips ground flat. Unless you have access to a valve grinding machine, this should be done by a machine shop. If the valves are in extremely good condition, as well as the valve seats and guides, they may be lapped in without performing machine work.

It is a recommended practice to lap the valves even after machine work has been performed and/or new valves have been purchased. This insures a positive seal between the valve and seat.

LAPPING THE VALVES

➡**Before lapping the valves to the seats, read the rest of the cylinder head section to insure that any related parts are in acceptable enough condition to continue.**

➡**Before any valve seat machining and/or lapping can be performed, the guides must be within factory recommended specifications.**

1. Invert the cylinder head.
2. Lightly lubricate the valve stems and insert them into the cylinder head in their numbered order.
3. Raise the valve from the seat and apply a small amount of fine lapping compound to the seat.
4. Moisten the suction head of a hand-lapping tool and attach it to the head of the valve.
5. Rotate the tool between the palms of both hands, changing the position of the valve on the valve seat and lifting the tool often to prevent grooving.
6. Lap the valve until a smooth, polished circle is evident on the valve and seat.
7. Remove the tool and the valve. Wipe away all traces of the grinding compound and store the valve to maintain its lapped location.

✳✳ WARNING

Do not get the valves out of order after they have been lapped. They must be put back with the same valve seat with which they were lapped.

Springs, Retainers and Valve Locks

There is no repair or refinishing possible with the springs, retainers and valve locks. If they are found to be worn or defective, they must be replaced with new (or known good) parts.

Cylinder Head

Most refinishing procedures dealing with the cylinder head must be performed by a machine shop. Read the sections below and review your inspection data to determine whether or not machining is necessary.

VALVE GUIDE

➡**If any machining or replacements are made to the valve guides, the seats must be machined.**

Unless the valve guides need machining or replacing, the only service to perform is to thoroughly clean them of any dirt or oil residue.

There are only two types of valve guides used on automobile engines: the replaceable-type (all aluminum heads) and the cast-in integral-type (most cast iron heads). There are four recommended methods for repairing worn guides.
- Knurling
- Inserts
- Reaming oversize
- Replacing

Knurling is a process in which metal is displaced and raised, thereby reducing clearance, giving a true center, and providing oil control. It is the least expensive way of repairing the valve guides. However, it is not necessarily the best, and in some cases, a knurled valve guide will not stand up for more than a short time. It requires a special knurlizer and precision reaming tools to obtain proper clearances. It would not be cost effective to purchase these tools, unless you plan on rebuilding several of the same cylinder head.

Installing a guide insert involves machining the guide to accept a bronze insert. One style is the coil-type which is installed into a threaded guide. Another is the thin-walled insert where the guide is reamed oversize to accept a split-sleeve insert. After the insert is installed, a special tool is then run through the guide to expand the insert, locking it to the guide. The insert is then reamed to the standard size for proper valve clearance.

Reaming for oversize valves restores normal clearances and provides a true valve seat. Most cast-in type guides can be reamed to accept an valve with an oversize stem. The cost factor for this can become quite high as you will need to purchase the reamer and new, oversize stem valves for all guides which were reamed. Oversizes are generally 0.003 to 0.030 in. (0.076 to 0.762mm), with 0.015 in. (0.381mm) being the most common.

To replace cast-in type valve guides, they must be drilled out, then reamed to accept replacement guides. This must be done on a fixture which will allow centering and leveling off of the original valve seat or guide, otherwise a serious guide-to-seat misalignment may occur making it impossible to properly machine the seat.

Replaceable-type guides are pressed into the cylinder head. A hammer and a stepped drift or punch may be used to install and remove the guides. Before removing the guides, measure the protrusion on the spring side of the head and record it for installation. Use the stepped drift to hammer out the old guide from the combustion chamber side of the head. When installing, determine whether or not the guide also seals a water jacket in the head, and if it does, use the recommended sealing agent. If there is no water jacket, grease the valve guide and its bore. Use the stepped drift, and hammer the new guide into the cylinder head from the spring side of the cylinder head. A stack of washers the same thickness as the measured protrusion may help the installation process.

VALVE SEATS

➡**Before any valve seat machining can be performed, the guides must be within factory recommended specifications.**

➡**If any machining or replacements were made to the valve guides, the seats must be machined.**

If the seats are in good condition, the valves can be lapped to the seats, and the cylinder head assembled. See the valves section for instructions on lapping.

If the valve seats are worn, cracked or damaged, they must be serviced by a machine shop. The valve seat must be perfectly centered to the valve guide, which requires very accurate machining.

CYLINDER HEAD SURFACE

If the cylinder head is warped, it must be machined flat. If the warpage is extremely severe, the head may need to be replaced. In some instances, it may be possible to straighten a warped head enough to allow machining. In either case, contact a professional machine shop for service.

➡**Any OHC cylinder head that shows excessive warpage should have the camshaft bearing journals align bored after the cylinder head has been resurfaced.**

Failure to align bore the camshaft bearing journals could result in severe engine damage including but not limited to: valve and piston damage, connecting rod damage, camshaft and/or crankshaft breakage.

CRACKS AND PHYSICAL DAMAGE

Certain cracks can be repaired in both cast iron and aluminum heads. For cast iron, a tapered threaded insert is installed along the length of the crack. Aluminum can also use the tapered inserts, however welding is the preferred method. Some physical damage can be repaired through brazing or welding. Contact a machine shop to get expert advice for your particular dilemma.

ASSEMBLY

The first step for any assembly job is to have a clean area in which to work. Next, thoroughly clean all of the parts and components that are to be assembled. Finally, place all of the components onto a suitable work space and, if necessary, arrange the parts to their respective positions.

OHV Engines

1. Lightly lubricate the valve stems and insert all of the valves into the cylinder head. If possible, maintain their original locations.
2. If equipped, install any valve spring shims which were removed.
3. If equipped, install the new valve seals, keeping the following in mind:
   - If the valve seal presses over the guide, lightly lubricate the outer guide surfaces.
   - If the seal is an O-ring type, it is installed just after compressing the spring but before the valve locks.
4. Place the valve spring and retainer over the stem.
5. Position the spring compressor tool and compress the spring.
6. Assemble the valve locks to the stem.
7. Relieve the spring pressure slowly and insure that neither valve lock becomes dislodged by the retainer.
8. Remove the spring compressor tool.
9. Repeat Steps 2 through 8 until all of the springs have been installed.

OHC Engines

▶ See Figure 193

CUP TYPE CAMSHAFT FOLLOWERS

To install the springs, retainers and valve locks on heads which have these components recessed into the camshaft follower's bore, you will need a small screwdriver-type tool, some clean white grease and a lot of patience. You will also need the C-clamp style spring compressor and the OHC tool used to disassemble the head.

1. Lightly lubricate the valve stems and insert all of the valves into the cylinder head. If possible, maintain their original locations.
2. If equipped, install any valve spring shims which were removed.

Fig. 193 Once assembled, check the valve clearance and correct as needed

3. If equipped, install the new valve seals, keeping the following in mind:
   - If the valve seal presses over the guide, lightly lubricate the outer guide surfaces.
   - If the seal is an O-ring type, it is installed just after compressing the spring but before the valve locks.
4. Place the valve spring and retainer over the stem.
5. Position the spring compressor and the OHC tool, then compress the spring.
6. Using a small screwdriver as a spatula, fill the valve stem side of the lock with white grease. Use the excess grease on the screwdriver to fasten the lock to the driver.
7. Carefully install the valve lock, which is stuck to the end of the screwdriver, to the valve stem then press on it with the screwdriver until the grease squeezes out. The valve lock should now be stuck to the stem.
8. Repeat Steps 6 and 7 for the remaining valve lock.
9. Relieve the spring pressure slowly and insure that neither valve lock becomes dislodged by the retainer.
10. Remove the spring compressor tool.
11. Repeat Steps 2 through 10 until all of the springs have been installed.
12. Install the followers, camshaft(s) and any other components that were removed for disassembly.

ROCKER ARM TYPE CAMSHAFT FOLLOWERS

1. Lightly lubricate the valve stems and insert all of the valves into the cylinder head. If possible, maintain their original locations.
2. If equipped, install any valve spring shims which were removed.
3. If equipped, install the new valve seals, keeping the following in mind:
   - If the valve seal presses over the guide, lightly lubricate the outer guide surfaces.
   - If the seal is an O-ring type, it is installed just after compressing the spring but before the valve locks.
4. Place the valve spring and retainer over the stem.
5. Position the spring compressor tool and compress the spring.
6. Assemble the valve locks to the stem.
7. Relieve the spring pressure slowly and insure that neither valve lock becomes dislodged by the retainer.

8. Remove the spring compressor tool.
9. Repeat Steps 2 through 8 until all of the springs have been installed.
10. Install the camshaft(s), rockers, shafts and any other components that were removed for disassembly.

Engine Block

GENERAL INFORMATION

A thorough overhaul or rebuild of an engine block would include replacing the pistons, rings, bearings, timing belt/chain assembly and oil pump. For OHV engines also include a new camshaft and lifters. The block would then have the cylinders bored and honed oversize (or if using removable cylinder sleeves, new sleeves installed) and the crankshaft would be cut undersize to provide new wearing surfaces and perfect clearances. However, your particular engine may not have everything worn out. What if only the piston rings have worn out and the clearances on everything else are still within factory specifications? Well, you could just replace the rings and put it back together, but this would be a very rare example. Chances are, if one component in your engine is worn, other components are sure to follow, and soon. At the very least, you should always replace the rings, bearings and oil pump. This is what is commonly called a "freshen up".

Cylinder Ridge Removal

Because the top piston ring does not travel to the very top of the cylinder, a ridge is built up between the end of the travel and the top of the cylinder bore.

Pushing the piston and connecting rod assembly past the ridge can be difficult, and damage to the piston ring lands could occur. If the ridge is not removed before installing a new piston or not removed at all, piston ring breakage and piston damage may occur.

➡It is always recommended that you remove any cylinder ridges before removing the piston and connecting rod assemblies. If you know that new pistons are going to be installed and the engine block will be bored oversize, you may be able to forego this step. However, some ridges may actually prevent the assemblies from being removed, necessitating its removal.

There are several different types of ridge reamers on the market, none of which are inexpensive. Unless a great deal of engine rebuilding is anticipated, borrow or rent a reamer.

1. Turn the crankshaft until the piston is at the bottom of its travel.
2. Cover the head of the piston with a rag.
3. Follow the tool manufacturers instructions and cut away the ridge, exercising extreme care to avoid cutting too deeply.
4. Remove the ridge reamer, the rag and as many of the cuttings as possible. Continue until all of the cylinder ridges have been removed.

DISASSEMBLY

▶ See Figures 194 and 195

The engine disassembly instructions following assume that you have the engine mounted on an engine stand. If not, it is easiest to disassemble the engine on a bench or the floor with it resting on the bell housing or transmission mounting surface. You must be able to access the connecting rod fasteners and turn the crankshaft during disassembly. Also, all engine covers (timing, front, side, oil pan, whatever) should have already been removed. Engines which are seized or locked up may not be able to be completely disassembled, and a core (salvage yard) engine should be purchased.

If not done during the cylinder head removal, remove the timing chain/belt and/or gear/sprocket assembly. Remove the oil pick-up and pump assembly and, if necessary, the pump drive. If equipped, remove any balance or auxiliary shafts. If necessary, remove the cylinder ridge from the top of the bore. See the cylinder ridge removal procedure earlier in this section.

Rotate the engine over so that the crankshaft is exposed. Use a number punch or scribe and mark each connecting rod with its respective cylinder number. The cylinder closest to the front of the engine is always number 1. However, depending on the engine placement, the front of the engine could either be the flywheel or damper/pulley end. Generally the front of the engine faces the front of the vehicle. Use a number punch or scribe and also mark the main bearing caps from front to rear with the front most cap being number 1 (if there are five caps, mark them 1 through 5, front to rear).

❊❊ WARNING

Take special care when pushing the connecting rod up from the crankshaft because the sharp threads of the rod bolts/studs will score the crankshaft journal. Insure that special plastic caps are installed over them, or cut two pieces of rubber hose to do the same.

Again, rotate the engine, this time to position the number one cylinder bore (head surface) up. Turn the crankshaft until the number one piston is at the bottom of its travel, this should allow the maximum access to its connecting rod. Remove the number one connecting rods fasteners and cap and place two lengths of rubber hose over the rod bolts/studs to protect the crankshaft from damage. Using a sturdy wooden dowel and a hammer, push the connecting rod up about 1 in. (25mm) from the crankshaft and remove the upper bearing insert. Continue pushing or tapping the connecting rod up until the

Fig. 194 Place rubber hose over the connecting rod studs to protect the crankshaft and cylinder bores from damage

Fig. 195 Carefully tap the piston out of the bore using a wooden dowel

piston rings are out of the cylinder bore. Remove the piston and rod by hand, put the upper half of the bearing insert back into the rod, install the cap with its bearing insert installed, and hand-tighten the cap fasteners. If the parts are kept in order in this manner, they will not get lost and you will be able to tell which bearings came form what cylinder if any problems are discovered and diagnosis is necessary. Remove all the other piston assemblies in the same manner. On V-style engines, remove all of the pistons from one bank, then reposition the engine with the other cylinder bank head surface up, and remove that banks piston assemblies.

The only remaining component in the engine block should now be the crankshaft. Loosen the main bearing caps evenly until the fasteners can be turned by hand, then remove them and the caps. Remove the crankshaft from the engine block. Thoroughly clean all of the components.

INSPECTION

Now that the engine block and all of its components are clean, it's time to inspect them for wear and/or damage. To accurately inspect them, you will need some specialized tools:

- Two or three separate micrometers to measure the pistons and crankshaft journals
- A dial indicator
- Telescoping gauges for the cylinder bores
- A rod alignment fixture to check for bent connecting rods

If you do not have access to the proper tools, you may want to bring the components to a shop that does.

Generally, you shouldn't expect cracks in the engine block or its components unless it was known to leak, consume or mix engine fluids, it was severely overheated, or there was evidence of bad bearings and/or crankshaft damage. A visual inspection should be performed on all of the components, but just because you don't see a crack does not mean it is not there. Some more reliable methods for inspecting for cracks include Mag-

naflux®, a magnetic process or Zyglo®, a dye penetrant. Magnaflux® is used only on ferrous metal (cast iron). Zyglo® uses a spray on fluorescent mixture along with a black light to reveal the cracks. It is strongly recommended to have your engine block checked professionally for cracks, especially if the engine was known to have overheated and/or leaked or consumed coolant. Contact a local shop for availability and pricing of these services.

Engine Block

ENGINE BLOCK BEARING ALIGNMENT

Remove the main bearing caps and, if still installed, the main bearing inserts. Inspect all of the main bearing saddles and caps for damage, burrs or high spots. If damage is found, and it is caused from a spun main bearing, the block will need to be align-bored or, if severe enough, replacement. Any burrs or high spots should be carefully removed with a metal file.

Place a straightedge on the bearing saddles, in the engine block, along the centerline of the crankshaft. If any clearance exists between the straightedge and the saddles, the block must be align-bored.

Align-boring consists of machining the main bearing saddles and caps by means of a flycutter that runs through the bearing saddles.

DECK FLATNESS

The top of the engine block where the cylinder head mounts is called the deck. Insure that the deck surface is clean of dirt, carbon deposits and old gasket material. Place a straightedge across the surface of the deck along its centerline and, using feeler gauges, check the clearance along several points. Repeat the checking procedure with the straightedge placed along both diagonals of the deck surface. If the reading exceeds 0.003 in. (0.076mm) within a 6.0 in. (15.2cm) span, or 0.006 in. (0.152mm) over the total length of the deck, it must be machined.

CYLINDER BORES

▶ See Figure 196

The cylinder bores house the pistons and are slightly larger than the pistons themselves. A common piston-to-bore clearance is 0.0015–0.0025 in. (0.0381mm–0.0635mm). Inspect and measure the cylinder bores. The bore should be checked for out-of-roundness, taper and size. The results of this

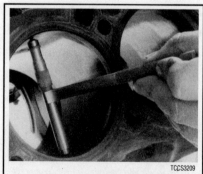

Fig. 196 Use a telescoping gauge to measure the cylinder bore diameter—take several readings within the same bore

inspection will determine whether the cylinder can be used in its existing size and condition, or a rebore to the next oversize is required (or in the case of removable sleeves, have replacements installed).

The amount of cylinder wall wear is always greater at the top of the cylinder than at the bottom. This wear is known as taper. Any cylinder that has a taper of 0.0012 in. (0.305mm) or more, must be rebored. Measurements are taken at a number of positions in each cylinder: at the top, middle and bottom and at two points at each position; that is, at a point 90 degrees from the crankshaft centerline, as well as a point parallel to the crankshaft centerline. The measurements are made with either a special dial indicator or a telescopic gauge and micrometer. If the necessary precision tools to check the bore are not available, take the block to a machine shop and have them mike it. Also if you don't have the tools to check the cylinder bores, chances are you will not have the necessary devices to check the pistons, connecting rods and crankshaft. Take these components with you and save yourself an extra trip.

For our procedures, we will use a telescopic gauge and a micrometer. You will need one of each, with a measuring range which covers your cylinder bore size.

1. Position the telescopic gauge in the cylinder bore, loosen the gauges lock and allow it to expand.

➡️**Your first two readings will be at the top of the cylinder bore, then proceed to the middle and finally the bottom, making a total of six measurements.**

2. Hold the gauge square in the bore, 90 degrees from the crankshaft centerline, and gently tighten the lock. Tilt the gauge back to remove it from the bore.

3. Measure the gauge with the micrometer and record the reading.

4. Again, hold the gauge square in the bore, this time parallel to the crankshaft centerline, and gently tighten the lock. Again, you will tilt the gauge back to remove it from the bore.

5. Measure the gauge with the micrometer and record this reading. The difference between these two readings is the out-of-round measurement of the cylinder.

6. Repeat steps 1 through 5, each time going to the next lower position, until you reach the bottom of the cylinder. Then go to the next cylinder, and continue until all of the cylinders have been measured.

The difference between these measurements will tell you all about the wear in your cylinders. The measurements which were taken 90 degrees from the crankshaft centerline will always reflect the most wear. That is because at this position is where the engine power presses the piston against the cylinder bore the hardest. This is known as thrust wear. Take your top, 90 degree measurement and compare it to your bottom, 90 degree measurement. The difference between them is the taper. When you measure your pistons, you will compare these readings to your piston sizes and determine piston-to-wall clearance.

Crankshaft

Inspect the crankshaft for visible signs of wear or damage. All of the journals should be perfectly round and smooth. Slight scores are normal for a used crankshaft, but you should hardly feel them with your fingernail. When measuring the crankshaft with a micrometer, you will take readings at the front and rear of each journal, then turn the micrometer 90 degrees and take two more readings, front and rear. The difference between the front-to-rear readings is the journal taper and the first-to-90 degree reading is the out-of-round measurement. Generally, there should be no taper or out-of-roundness found, however, up to 0.0005 in. (0.0127mm) for either can be overlooked. Also, the readings should fall within the factory specifications for journal diameters.

If the crankshaft journals fall within specifications, it is recommended that it be polished before being returned to service. Polishing the crankshaft insures that any minor burrs or high spots are smoothed, thereby reducing the chance of scoring the new bearings.

Pistons and Connecting Rods

PISTONS

▶ See Figure 197

The piston should be visually inspected for any signs of cracking or burning (caused by hot spots or detonation), and scuffing or excessive wear on the skirts. The wrist pin attaches the piston to the connecting rod. The piston should move freely on the wrist pin, both sliding and pivoting. Grasp the connecting rod securely, or mount it in a vise, and try to rock the piston back and forth along the centerline of the wrist pin. There should not be any excessive play evident between the piston and the pin. If there are C-clips retaining the pin in the piston then you have wrist pin bushings in the rods. There should not be any excessive play between the wrist pin and the rod bushing. Normal clearance for the wrist pin is approx. 0.001–0.002 in. (0.025mm–0.051mm).

Use a micrometer and measure the diameter of the piston, perpendicular to the wrist pin, on the skirt. Compare the reading to its original cylinder measurement obtained earlier. The difference between the two readings is the piston-to-wall clearance. If the clearance is within specifications, the piston may be used as is. If the piston is out of specification, but the bore is not, you will need a new piston. If both are out of specification, you will need the cylinder rebored and oversize pistons installed. Generally if two or more pistons/bores are

Fig. 197 Measure the piston's outer diameter, perpendicular to the wrist pin, with a micrometer

out of specification, it is best to rebore the entire block and purchase a complete set of oversize pistons.

CONNECTING ROD

You should have the connecting rod checked for straightness at a machine shop. If the connecting rod is bent, it will unevenly wear the bearing and piston, as well as place greater stress on these components. Any bent or twisted connecting rods must be replaced. If the rods are straight and the wrist pin clearance is within specifications, then only the bearing end of the rod need be checked. Place the connecting rod into a vice, with the bearing inserts in place, install the cap to the rod and torque the fasteners to specifications. Use a telescoping gauge and carefully measure the inside diameter of the bearings. Compare this reading to the rods original crankshaft journal diameter measurement. The difference is the oil clearance. If the oil clearance is not within specifications, install new bearings in the rod and take another measurement. If the clearance is still out of specifications, and the crankshaft is not, the rod will need to be reconditioned by a machine shop.

➡️**You can also use Plastigage® to check the bearing clearances. The assembling section has complete instructions on its use.**

Camshaft

Inspect the camshaft and lifters/followers as described earlier in this section.

Bearings

All of the engine bearings should be visually inspected for wear and/or damage. The bearing should look evenly worn all around with no deep scores or pits. If the bearing is severely worn, scored, pitted or heat blued, then the bearing, and the components that use it, should be brought to a machine shop for inspection. Full-circle bearings (used on most camshafts, auxiliary shafts, balance shafts, etc.) require specialized tools for removal and installation, and should be brought to a machine shop for service.

Oil Pump

➡️**The oil pump is responsible for providing constant lubrication to the whole engine and so it is recommended that a new oil pump be installed when rebuilding the engine.**

Completely disassemble the oil pump and thoroughly clean all of the components. Inspect the oil pump gears and housing for wear and/or damage. Insure that the pressure relief valve operates properly and there is no binding or sticking due to varnish or debris. If all of the parts are in proper working condition, lubricate the gears and relief valve, and assemble the pump.

REFINISHING

▶ See Figure 198

Almost all engine block refinishing must be performed by a machine shop. If the cylinders are not to be rebored, then the cylinder glaze can be removed with a ball hone. When removing cylinder glaze with a ball hone, use a light or penetrating

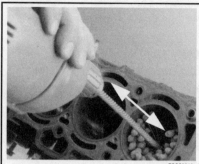

Fig. 198 Use a ball type cylinder hone to remove any glaze and provide a new surface for seating the piston rings

type oil to lubricate the hone. Do not allow the hone to run dry as this may cause excessive scoring of the cylinder bores and wear on the hone. If new pistons are required, they will need to be installed to the connecting rods. This should be performed by a machine shop as the pistons must be installed in the correct relationship to the rod or engine damage can occur.

Pistons and Connecting Rods

▶ See Figure 199

Only pistons with the wrist pin retained by C-clips are serviceable by the home-mechanic. Press fit pistons require special presses and/or heaters to remove/install the connecting rod and should only be performed by a machine shop.

All pistons will have a mark indicating the direction to the front of the engine and the must be installed into the engine in that manner. Usually it is a notch or arrow on the top of the piston, or it may be the letter F cast or stamped into the piston.

Fig. 199 Most pistons are marked to indicate positioning in the engine (usually a mark means the side facing the front)

C-CLIP TYPE PISTONS

1. Note the location of the forward mark on the piston and mark the connecting rod in relation.
2. Remove the C-clips from the piston and withdraw the wrist pin.

➡Varnish build-up or C-clip groove burrs may increase the difficulty of removing the wrist pin. If necessary, use a punch or drift to carefully tap the wrist pin out.

3. Insure that the wrist pin bushing in the connecting rod is usable, and lubricate it with assembly lube.
4. Remove the wrist pin from the new piston and lubricate the pin bores on the piston.
5. Align the forward marks on the piston and the connecting rod and install the wrist pin.
6. The new C-clips will have a flat and a rounded side to them. Install both C-clips with the flat side facing out.
7. Repeat all of the steps for each piston being replaced.

ASSEMBLY

Before you begin assembling the engine, first give yourself a clean, dirt free work area. Next, clean every engine component again. The key to a good assembly is cleanliness.

Mount the engine block into the engine stand and wash it one last time using water and detergent (dishwashing detergent works well). While washing it, scrub the cylinder bores with a soft bristle brush and thoroughly clean all of the oil passages. Completely dry the engine and spray the entire assembly down with an anti-rust solution such as WD-40® or similar product. Take a clean lint-free rag and wipe up any excess anti-rust solution from the bores, bearing saddles, etc. Repeat the final cleaning process on the crankshaft. Replace any freeze or oil galley plugs which were removed during disassembly.

Crankshaft

▶ See Figures 200, 201, 202 and 203

1. Remove the main bearing inserts from the block and bearing caps.

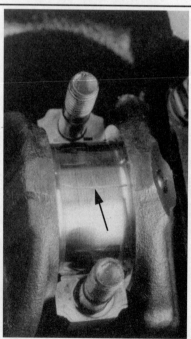

Fig. 200 Apply a strip of gauging material to the bearing journal, then install and torque the cap

2. If the crankshaft main bearing journals have been refinished to a definite undersize, install the correct undersize bearing. Be sure that the bearing inserts and bearing bores are clean. Foreign material under inserts will distort bearing and cause failure.
3. Place the upper main bearing inserts in bores with tang in slot.

➡The oil holes in the bearing inserts must be aligned with the oil holes in the cylinder block.

4. Install the lower main bearing inserts in bearing caps.
5. Clean the mating surfaces of block and rear main bearing cap.
6. Carefully lower the crankshaft into place. Be careful not to damage bearing surfaces.
7. Check the clearance of each main bearing by using the following procedure:
   a. Place a piece of Plastigage® or its equivalent, on bearing surface across full width of bearing cap and about ¼ in. off center.
   b. Install cap and tighten bolts to specifications. Do not turn crankshaft while Plastigage® is in place.
   c. Remove the cap. Using the supplied Plastigage® scale, check width of Plastigage® at widest point to get maximum clearance. Difference between readings is taper of journal.
   d. If clearance exceeds specified limits, try a 0.001 in. or 0.002 in. undersize bearing in combination with the standard bearing. Bearing clearance must be within specified limits. If standard and 0.002 in. undersize bearing does not bring clearance within desired limits, refinish crankshaft journal, then install undersize bearings.
8. Install the rear main seal.
9. After the bearings have been fitted, apply a light coat of engine oil to the journals and bearings. Install the rear main bearing cap. Install all bearing caps except the thrust bearing cap. Be sure that main bearing caps are installed in original locations. Tighten the bearing cap bolts to specifications.
10. Install the thrust bearing cap with bolts finger-tight.
11. Pry the crankshaft forward against the thrust surface of upper half of bearing.
12. Hold the crankshaft forward and pry the thrust bearing cap to the rear. This aligns the thrust surfaces of both halves of the bearing.
13. Retain the forward pressure on the crankshaft. Tighten the cap bolts to specifications.
14. Measure the crankshaft end-play as follows:
    a. Mount a dial gauge to the engine block and position the tip of the gauge to read from the crankshaft end.
    b. Carefully pry the crankshaft toward the rear of the engine and hold it there while you zero the gauge.
    c. Carefully pry the crankshaft toward the front of the engine and read the gauge.
    d. Confirm that the reading is within specifications. If not, install a new thrust bearing and repeat the procedure. If the reading is still out of specifications with a new bearing, have a machine shop inspect the thrust surfaces of the crankshaft, and if possible, repair it.
15. Rotate the crankshaft so as to position the first rod journal to the bottom of its stroke.

Fig. 201 After the cap is removed again, use the scale supplied with the gauging material to check the clearance

Fig. 202 A dial gauge may be used to check crankshaft end-play

Fig. 203 Carefully pry the crankshaft back and forth while reading the dial gauge for end-play

Pistons and Connecting Rods

▶ **See Figures 204, 205, 206 and 207**

1. Before installing the piston/connecting rod assembly, oil the pistons, piston rings and the cylinder walls with light engine oil. Install connecting rod bolt protectors or rubber hose onto the connecting rod bolts/studs. Also perform the following:

   a. Select the proper ring set for the size cylinder bore.

   b. Position the ring in the bore in which it is going to be used.

   c. Push the ring down into the bore area where normal ring wear is not encountered.

   d. Use the head of the piston to position the ring in the bore so that the ring is square with

Fig. 204 Checking the piston ring-to-ring groove side clearance using the ring and a feeler gauge

the cylinder wall. Use caution to avoid damage to the ring or cylinder bore.

   e. Measure the gap between the ends of the ring with a feeler gauge. Ring gap in a worn cylinder is normally greater than specification. If the ring gap is greater than the specified limits, try an oversize ring set.

   f. Check the ring side clearance of the compression rings with a feeler gauge inserted between the ring and its lower land according to specification. The gauge should slide freely around the entire ring circumference without binding. Any wear that occurs will form a step at the inner portion of the lower land. If the lower lands have high steps, the piston should be replaced.

2. Unless new pistons are installed, be sure to install the pistons in the cylinders from which they were removed. The numbers on the connecting rod and bearing cap must be on the same side when installed in the cylinder bore. If a connecting rod is ever transposed from one engine or cylinder to another, new bearings should be fitted and the connecting rod should be numbered to correspond with the new cylinder number. The notch on the piston head goes toward the front of the engine.

3. Install all of the rod bearing inserts into the rods and caps.

4. Install the rings to the pistons. Install the oil control ring first, then the second compression ring and finally the top compression ring. Use a piston ring expander tool to aid in installation and to help reduce the chance of breakage.

5. Make sure the ring gaps are properly spaced around the circumference of the piston. Fit a

piston ring compressor around the piston and slide the piston and connecting rod assembly down into the cylinder bore, pushing it in with the wooden hammer handle. Push the piston down until it is only slightly below the top of the cylinder bore. Guide the connecting rod onto the crankshaft bearing journal carefully, to avoid damaging the crankshaft.

6. Check the bearing clearance of all the rod bearings, fitting them to the crankshaft bearing journals. Follow the procedure in the crankshaft installation above.

7. After the bearings have been fitted, apply a light coating of assembly oil to the journals and bearings.

8. Turn the crankshaft until the appropriate bearing journal is at the bottom of its stroke, then push the piston assembly all the way down until the connecting rod bearing seats on the crankshaft journal. Be careful not to allow the bearing cap screws to strike the crankshaft bearing journals and damage them.

9. After the piston and connecting rod assemblies have been installed, check the connecting rod side clearance on each crankshaft journal.

10. Prime and install the oil pump and the oil pump intake tube.

OHV Engines

CAMSHAFT, LIFTERS AND TIMING ASSEMBLY

1. Install the camshaft.
2. Install the lifters/followers into their bores.
3. Install the timing gears/chain assembly.

Fig. 205 The notch on the side of the bearing cap matches the tang on the bearing insert

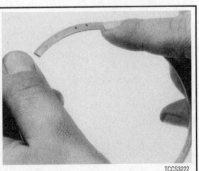

Fig. 206 Most rings are marked to show which side of the ring should face up when installed to the piston

Fig. 207 Install the piston and rod assembly into the block using a ring compressor and the handle of a hammer

CYLINDER HEAD(S)

1. Install the cylinder head(s) using new gaskets.
2. Assemble the rest of the valve train (pushrods and rocker arms and/or shafts).

OHC Engines

CYLINDER HEAD(S)

1. Install the cylinder head(s) using new gaskets.
2. Install the timing sprockets/gears and the belt/chain assemblies.

Engine Covers and Components

Install the timing cover(s) and oil pan. Refer to your notes and drawings made prior to disassembly and install all of the components that were removed. Install the engine into the vehicle.

Engine Start-up and Break-in

STARTING THE ENGINE

Now that the engine is installed and every wire and hose is properly connected, go back and double check that all coolant and vacuum hoses are connected. Check that your oil drain plug is installed and properly tightened. If not already done, install a new oil filter onto the engine. Fill the crankcase with the proper amount and grade of engine oil. Fill the cooling system with a 50/50 mixture of coolant/water.

1. Connect the vehicle battery.
2. Start the engine. Keep your eye on your oil pressure indicator; if it does not indicate oil pressure within 10 seconds of starting, turn the vehicle off.

✴✴ WARNING

Damage to the engine can result if it is allowed to run with no oil pressure. Check the engine oil level to make sure that it is full. Check for any leaks and if found, repair the leaks before continuing. If there is still no indication of oil pressure, you may need to prime the system.

3. Confirm that there are no fluid leaks (oil or other).
4. Allow the engine to reach normal operating temperature (the upper radiator hose will be hot to the touch).
5. At this point you can perform any necessary checks or adjustments, such as checking the ignition timing.
6. Install any remaining components or body panels which were removed.

BREAKING IT IN

Make the first miles on the new engine, easy ones. Vary the speed but do not accelerate hard. Most importantly, do not lug the engine, and avoid sustained high speeds until at least 100 miles. Check the engine oil and coolant levels frequently. Expect the engine to use a little oil until the rings seat. Change the oil and filter at 500 miles, 1500 miles, then every 3000 miles past that.

KEEP IT MAINTAINED

Now that you have just gone through all of that hard work, keep yourself from doing it all over again by thoroughly maintaining it. Not that you may not have maintained it before, you could have had one to two hundred thousand miles on it before doing this. However, you may have bought the vehicle used, and the previous owner did not keep up on maintenance. Which is why you just went through all of that hard work. See?

2.2L/2.3L ENGINE TORQUE SPECIFICATIONS

Component	English	Metric
Balance shaft		
Balance shaft gear case bolt	18 ft. lbs.	25 Nm
Rear balance shaft sealing bolt	22 ft. lbs.	29 Nm
Rear balance shaft driven gear	18 ft. lbs.	25 Nm
Front balance shaft belt driven pulley	22 ft. lbs.	29 Nm
Rear balance shaft retainer plate bolts	14 ft. lbs.	20 Nm
Camshaft		
Camshaft sprocket bolt		
2.2L engine	27 ft. lbs.	37 Nm
2.3L engine	43 ft. lbs.	59 Nm
Bearing journal-to-cylinder head (follow tightening sequence)		
6 x 1.0 mm bolts	104 inch lbs.	12 Nm
8 x 1.25 mm bolts	16 ft. lbs.	22 Nm
Connecting Rod Bearings		
Rod journal cap bolts (apply engine oil to bolt threads)		
2.2L engine	34 ft. lbs.	46 Nm
2.3L engine		
Step 1	14 ft. lbs.	20 Nm
Step 2	90°	90°
Crankshaft		
Pulley bolt	181 ft. lbs.	245 Nm
Flywheel oil seal housing-to-block bolts	86 inch lbs.	9.8 Nm
Flywheel-to-crankshaft (manual transmission)	76 ft. lbs.	103 Nm
Drive plate-to-crankshaft (automatic transmission)	54 ft. lbs.	74 Nm
Cylinder Head		
Valve cover fasteners	86 inch lbs.	9.8 Nm
Cylinder head bolts (Oil bolt threads and follow torque sequence)		
2.2L engines		
Step 1	29 ft. lbs.	39 Nm
Step 2	51 ft. lbs.	69 Nm
Step 3	72.3 ft. lbs.	98.1 Nm
2.3L engine		
Step 1	22 ft. lbs.	29 Nm
Step 2	90°	90°
Step 3	90°	90°
Step 4 (Only if using new bolts)	90°	90°
Distributor		
Mounting bolts		
2.2L engine	16 ft. lbs.	22 Nm
2.3L engine	13 ft. lbs.	18 Nm

9183C11

2.2L/2.3L ENGINE TORQUE SPECIFICATIONS

Component	English	Metric
Exhaust Manifold		
Exhaust manifold-to-cylinder head	23 ft. lbs.	31 Nm
Front pipe-to-exhaust manifold nuts	40 ft. lbs.	54 Nm
Intake Manifold		
Intake manifold-to-cylinder head	16 ft. lbs.	22 Nm
Main Bearings		
Cap bolts (apply engine oil to bolt threads)		
2.2L engine		
Step 1	22 ft. lbs.	29 Nm
Step 2	54 ft. lbs.	74 Nm
2.3L engine		
Step 1 (11 x 1.5 mm bolts)	22 ft. lbs.	29 Nm
Step 2 (11 x 1.5 mm bolts)	58 ft. lbs.	78 Nm
Step 3 (6 x 1.0 mm bolts)	104 inch lbs.	12 Nm
Oil Pan		
Oil pan fasteners		
2.2L engine	120 inch lbs.	14 Nm
2.3L engine	104 inch lbs.	12 Nm
Drain plug (always use a new crush washer)		
2.2L and 2.3L engines	33 ft. lbs.	44 Nm
Oil Pump		
Relief valve sealing bolt	29 ft. lbs.	39 Nm
Pump cover-to-housing bolts		
2.2L and 2.3L engine	61 inch lbs.	7 Nm
Housing-to-block 6 x 1.0 mm bolts (apply liquid sealant to threads)	104 inch lbs.	12 Nm
Balancer gear case-to-housing 8 x 1.25 mm bolts (2.2L and 2.3L engine only)	18 ft. lbs.	25 Nm
Rocker Arms		
Valve adjustment locknut	14 ft. lbs.	20 Nm
Thermostat		
Thermostat housing-to-cover	104 inch lbs.	12 Nm
Thermostat housing-to-cylinder head	16 ft. lbs.	22 Nm
Timing Belt and Cover		
Cover bolts	104 inch lbs.	12 Nm
Tensioner nut	33 ft. lbs.	44 Nm
Water Pump		
Water pump-to-block bolts	104 inch lbs.	12 Nm

9183C12

2.7L/3.0L ENGINE TORQUE SPECIFICATIONS

Component	English	Metric
Camshaft		
Camshaft sprocket bolt		
2.7L engine	23 ft. lbs.	31 Nm
3.0L engine	67 ft. lbs.	90 Nm
Camshaft (Valve/Cylinder Head) Cover		
2.7L engine		
8mm bolts	20 ft. lbs.	27 Nm
6mm bolts	104 inch lbs.	12 Nm
3.0L engine (in 3 steps)	104 inch lbs.	12 Nm
Crankshaft		
Pulley bolt	181 ft. lbs.	245 Nm
Flywheel oil seal housing-to-block bolts	86 inch lbs.	9.8 Nm
Flywheel-to-crankshaft (manual transmission)	76 ft. lbs.	103 Nm
Drive plate-to-crankshaft (automatic transmission)	54 ft. lbs.	74 Nm
Cylinder Head		
Cylinder head bolts (Oil bolt threads and follow torque sequence)		
2.7L engines		
Step 1	29 ft. lbs.	39 Nm
Step 2	56 ft. lbs.	76 Nm
3.0L engine		
Step 1	29 ft. lbs.	39 Nm
Step 2	51 ft. lbs.	69 Nm
Step 3	72 ft. lbs.	98 Nm
Drive Plate (Flex Plate)		
Mounting bolts		
2.7L & 3.0L engines	54 ft. lbs.	74 Nm
Exhaust Manifold		
Exhaust manifold-to-cylinder head	23 ft. lbs.	31 Nm
Front pipe-to-exhaust manifold nuts	40 ft. lbs.	54 Nm
Intake Manifold		
Intake manifold-to-cylinder head	16 ft. lbs.	22 Nm
Main Bearings		
Cap bolts (apply engine oil to bolt threads)		
2.7L engine	33 ft. lbs.	44 Nm
3.0L engine		
Step 1 (11 x 1.5 mm bolts)	22 ft. lbs.	29 Nm
Step 2 (11 x 1.5 mm bolts)	58 ft. lbs.	78 Nm
Step 3 (6 x 1.0 mm bolts)	104 inch lbs.	12 Nm
Oil Pan		
Oil pan fasteners		
2.7L engine	120 inch lbs.	14 Nm
3.0L engine	104 inch lbs.	12 Nm
Drain plug (always use a new crush washer)	33 ft. lbs.	44 Nm
Oil Pump		
Screen bolts		
2.7L & 3.0L engines	104 inch lbs.	12 Nm
Pump bolts		
2.7L engine	16 ft. lbs.	22 Nm
3.0L engine	104 inch lbs.	12 Nm
Thermostat		
Thermostat housing-to-cylinder head	104 inch lbs.	12 Nm
Timing Belt and Cover		
Cover bolts	104 inch lbs.	12 Nm
Tensioner nut	33 ft. lbs.	44 Nm
Water Pump		
2.7L engine		
6 x 1.0mm bolts	104 inch lbs.	12 Nm
8 x 1.25mm bolts	16 ft. lbs.	22 Nm
3.0L engine	104 inch lbs.	12 Nm

91183C13

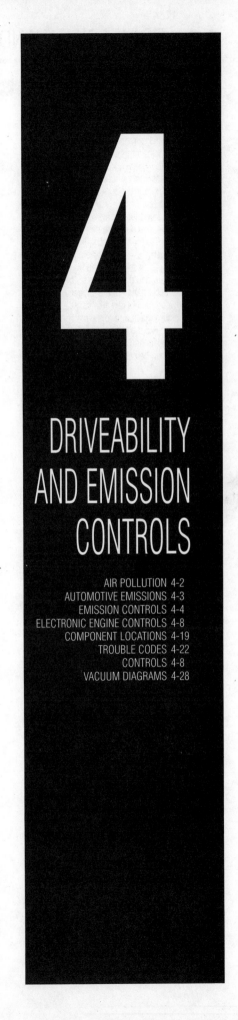

4

DRIVEABILITY AND EMISSION CONTROLS

AIR POLLUTION

The earth's atmosphere, at or near sea level, consists approximately of 78 percent nitrogen, 21 percent oxygen and 1 percent other gases. If it were possible to remain in this state, 100 percent clean air would result. However, many varied sources allow other gases and particulates to mix with the clean air, causing our atmosphere to become unclean or polluted.

Some of these pollutants are visible while others are invisible, with each having the capability of causing distress to the eyes, ears, throat, skin and respiratory system. Should these pollutants become concentrated in a specific area and under certain conditions, death could result due to the displacement or chemical change of the oxygen content in the air. These pollutants can also cause great damage to the environment and to the many man made objects that are exposed to the elements.

To better understand the causes of air pollution, the pollutants can be categorized into 3 separate types, natural, industrial and automotive.

Natural Pollutants

Natural pollution has been present on earth since before man appeared and continues to be a factor when discussing air pollution, although it causes only a small percentage of the overall pollution problem. It is the direct result of decaying organic matter, wind born smoke and particulates from such natural events as plain and forest fires (ignited by heat or lightning), volcanic ash, sand and dust which can spread over a large area of the countryside.

Such a phenomenon of natural pollution has been seen in the form of volcanic eruptions, with the resulting plume of smoke, steam and volcanic ash blotting out the sun's rays as it spreads and rises higher into the atmosphere. As it travels into the atmosphere the upper air currents catch and carry the smoke and ash, while condensing the steam back into water vapor. As the water vapor, smoke and ash travel on their journey, the smoke dissipates into the atmosphere while the ash and moisture settle back to earth in a trail hundreds of miles long. In some cases, lives are lost and millions of dollars of property damage result.

Industrial Pollutants

Industrial pollution is caused primarily by industrial processes, the burning of coal, oil and natural gas, which in turn produce smoke and fumes. Because the burning fuels contain large amounts of sulfur, the principal ingredients of smoke and fumes are sulfur dioxide and particulate matter. This type of pollutant occurs most severely during still, damp and cool weather, such as at night. Even in its less severe form, this pollutant is not confined to just cities. Because of air movements, the pollutants move for miles over the surrounding countryside, leaving in its path a barren and unhealthy environment for all living things.

Working with Federal, State and Local mandated regulations and by carefully monitoring emissions, big business has greatly reduced the amount of pollutant introduced from its industrial sources, striving to obtain an acceptable level. Because of the mandated industrial emission clean up, many land areas and streams in and around the cities that were formerly barren of vegetation and life, have now begun to move back in the direction of nature's intended balance.

Automotive Pollutants

The third major source of air pollution is automotive emissions. The emissions from the internal combustion engines were not an appreciable problem years ago because of the small number of registered vehicles and the nation's small highway system. However, during the early 1950's, the trend of the American people was to move from the cities to the surrounding suburbs. This caused an immediate problem in transportation because the majority of suburbs were not afforded mass transit conveniences. This lack of transportation created an attractive market for the automobile manufacturers, which resulted in a dramatic increase in the number of vehicles produced and sold, along with a marked increase in highway construction between cities and the suburbs. Multi-vehicle families emerged with a growing emphasis placed on an individual vehicle per family member. As the increase in vehicle ownership and usage occurred, so did pollutant levels in and around the cities, as suburbanites drove daily to their businesses and employment, returning at the end of the day to their homes in the suburbs.

It was noted that a smoke and fog type haze was being formed and at times, remained in suspension over the cities, taking time to dissipate. At first this "smog," derived from the words "smoke" and "fog," was thought to result from industrial pollution but it was determined that automobile emissions shared the blame. It was discovered that when normal automobile emissions were exposed to sunlight for a period of time, complex chemical reactions would take place.

It is now known that smog is a photo chemical layer, which develops when certain oxides of nitrogen (NOx) and unburned hydrocarbons (HC) from automobile emissions are exposed to sunlight. Pollution was more severe when smog would become stagnant over an area in which a warm layer of air settled over the top of the cooler air mass, trapping and holding the cooler mass at ground level. The trapped cooler air would keep the emissions from being dispersed and diluted through normal air flows. This type of air stagnation was given the name "Temperature Inversion."

TEMPERATURE INVERSION

In normal weather situations, surface air is warmed by heat radiating from the earth's surface and the sun's rays. This causes it to rise upward, into the atmosphere. Upon rising, it will cool through a convection type heat exchange with the cooler upper air. As warm air rises, the surface pollutants are carried upward and dissipated into the atmosphere.

When a temperature inversion occurs, we find the higher air is no longer cooler, but is warmer than the surface air, causing the cooler surface air to become trapped. This warm air blanket can extend from above ground level to a few hundred or even a few thousand feet into the air. As the surface air is trapped, so are the pollutants, causing a severe smog condition. Should this stagnant air mass extend to a few thousand feet high, enough air movement with the inversion takes place to allow the smog layer to rise above ground level but the pollutants still cannot dissipate. This inversion can remain for days over an area, with the smog level only rising or lowering from ground level to a few hundred feet high. Meanwhile, the pollutant levels increase, causing eye irritation, respiratory problems, reduced visibility, plant damage and in some cases, even disease.

This inversion phenomenon was first noted in the Los Angeles, California area. The city lies in terrain resembling a basin and with certain weather conditions, a cold air mass is held in the basin while a warmer air mass covers it like a lid.

Because this type of condition was first documented as prevalent in the Los Angeles area, this type of trapped pollution was named Los Angeles Smog, although it occurs in other areas where a large concentration of automobiles are used and the air remains stagnant for any length of time.

HEAT TRANSFER

Consider the internal combustion engine as a machine in which raw materials must be placed so a finished product comes out. As in any machine operation, a certain amount of wasted material is formed. When we relate this to the internal combustion engine, we find that through the input of air and fuel, we obtain power during the combustion process to drive the vehicle. The by-product or waste of this power is, in part, heat and exhaust gases with which we must dispose.

The heat from the combustion process can rise to over 4000°F (2204°C). The dissipation of this heat is controlled by a ram air effect, the use of cooling fans to cause air flow and a liquid coolant solution surrounding the combustion area to transfer the heat of combustion through the cylinder walls and into the coolant. The coolant is then directed to a thin-finned, multi-tube radiator, from which the excess heat is transferred to the atmosphere by 1 of the 3 heat transfer methods, conduction, convection or radiation.

The cooling of the combustion area is an important part in the control of exhaust emissions. To understand the behavior of the combustion and transfer of its heat, consider the air/fuel charge. It is ignited and the flame front burns progressively across the combustion chamber until the burning charge reaches the cylinder walls. Some of the fuel in contact with the walls is not hot enough to burn, thereby snuffing out or quenching the combustion process. This leaves unburned fuel in the combustion chamber. This unburned fuel is then forced out of the cylinder and into the exhaust system, along with the exhaust gases.

Many attempts have been made to minimize the amount of unburned fuel in the combustion chambers due to quenching, by increasing the coolant temperature and lessening the contact area of the coolant around the combustion area. However, design limitations within the combustion chambers prevent the complete burning of the air/fuel charge, so a certain amount of the unburned fuel is still expelled into the exhaust system, regardless of modifications to the engine.

AUTOMOTIVE EMISSIONS

Before emission controls were mandated on internal combustion engines, other sources of engine pollutants were discovered along with the exhaust emissions. It was determined that engine combustion exhaust produced approximately 60 percent of the total emission pollutants, fuel evaporation from the fuel tank and carburetor vents produced 20 percent, with the final 20 percent being produced through the crankcase as a by-product of the combustion process.

Exhaust Gases

The exhaust gases emitted into the atmosphere are a combination of burned and unburned fuel. To understand the exhaust emission and its composition, we must review some basic chemistry.

When the air/fuel mixture is introduced into the engine, we are mixing air, composed of nitrogen (78 percent), oxygen (21 percent) and other gases (1 percent) with the fuel, which is 100 percent hydrocarbons (HC), in a semi-controlled ratio. As the combustion process is accomplished, power is produced to move the vehicle while the heat of combustion is transferred to the cooling system. The exhaust gases are then composed of nitrogen, a diatomic gas (N_2), the same as was introduced in the engine, carbon dioxide (CO_2), the same gas that is used in beverage carbonation, and water vapor (H_2O). The nitrogen (N_2), for the most part, passes through the engine unchanged, while the oxygen (O_2) reacts (burns) with the hydrocarbons (HC) and produces the carbon dioxide (CO_2) and the water vapors (H_2O). If this chemical process would be the only process to take place, the exhaust emissions would be harmless. However, during the combustion process, other compounds are formed which are considered dangerous. These pollutants are hydrocarbons (HC), carbon monoxide (CO), oxides of nitrogen (NOx) oxides of sulfur (SOx) and engine particulates.

HYDROCARBONS

Hydrocarbons (HC) are essentially fuel which was not burned during the combustion process or which has escaped into the atmosphere through fuel evaporation. The main sources of incomplete combustion are rich air/fuel mixtures, low engine temperatures and improper spark timing. The main sources of hydrocarbon emission through fuel evaporation on most vehicles used to be the vehicle's fuel tank and carburetor float bowl.

To reduce combustion hydrocarbon emission, engine modifications were made to minimize dead space and surface area in the combustion chamber. In addition, the air/fuel mixture was made leaner through the improved control which feedback carburetion and fuel injection offers and by the addition of external controls to aid in further combustion of the hydrocarbons outside the engine. Two such methods were the addition of air injection systems, to inject fresh air into the exhaust manifolds and the installation of catalytic converters, units that are able to burn traces of hydrocarbons without affecting the internal combustion process or fuel economy.

To control hydrocarbon emissions through fuel evaporation, modifications were made to the fuel tank to allow storage of the fuel vapors during periods of engine shutdown. Modifications were also made to the air intake system so that at specific times during engine operation, these vapors may be purged and burned by blending them with the air/fuel mixture.

CARBON MONOXIDE

Carbon monoxide is formed when not enough oxygen is present during the combustion process to convert carbon (C) to carbon dioxide (CO_2). An increase in the carbon monoxide (CO) emission is normally accompanied by an increase in the hydrocarbon (HC) emission because of the lack of oxygen to completely burn all of the fuel mixture.

Carbon monoxide (CO) also increases the rate at which the photo chemical smog is formed by speeding up the conversion of nitric oxide (NO) to nitrogen dioxide (NO_2). To accomplish this, carbon monoxide (CO) combines with oxygen (O_2) and nitric oxide (NO) to produce carbon dioxide (CO_2) and nitrogen dioxide (NO_2). ($CO + O_2 + NO = CO_2 + NO_2$).

The dangers of carbon monoxide, which is an odorless and colorless toxic gas, are many. When carbon monoxide is inhaled into the lungs and passed into the blood stream, oxygen is replaced by the carbon monoxide in the red blood cells, causing a reduction in the amount of oxygen supplied to the many parts of the body. This lack of oxygen causes headaches, lack of coordination, reduced mental alertness and, should the carbon monoxide concentration be high enough, death could result.

NITROGEN

Normally, nitrogen is an inert gas. When heated to approximately 2500°F (1371°C) through the combustion process, this gas becomes active and causes an increase in the nitric oxide (NO) emission.

Oxides of nitrogen (NOx) are composed of approximately 97–98 percent nitric oxide (NO). Nitric oxide is a colorless gas but when it is passed into the atmosphere, it combines with oxygen and forms nitrogen dioxide (NO_2). The nitrogen dioxide then combines with chemically active hydrocarbons (HC) and when in the presence of sunlight, causes the formation of photochemical smog.

Ozone

To further complicate matters, some of the nitrogen dioxide (NO_2) is broken apart by the sunlight to form nitric oxide and oxygen. ($NO_2 + $ sunlight $= NO + O$). This single atom of oxygen then combines with diatomic (meaning 2 atoms) oxygen (O_2) to form ozone (O_3). Ozone is one of the smells associated with smog. It has a pungent and offensive odor, irritates the eyes and lung tissues, affects the growth of plant life and causes rapid deterioration of rubber products. Ozone can be formed by sunlight as well as electrical discharge into the air.

The most common discharge area on the automobile engine is the secondary ignition electrical system, especially when inferior quality spark plug cables are used. As the surge of high voltage is routed through the secondary cable, the circuit builds up an electrical field around the wire, which acts upon the oxygen in the surrounding air to form the ozone. The faint glow along the cable with the engine running that may be visible on a dark night, is called the "corona discharge." It is the result of the electrical field passing from a high along the cable, to a low in the surrounding air, which forms the ozone gas. The combination of corona and ozone has been a major cause of cable deterioration. Recently, different and better quality insulating materials have lengthened the life of the electrical cables.

Although ozone at ground level can be harmful, ozone is beneficial to the earth's inhabitants. By having a concentrated ozone layer called the "ozonosphere," between 10 and 20 miles (16–32 km) up in the atmosphere, much of the ultra violet radiation from the sun's rays are absorbed and screened. If this ozone layer were not present, much of the earth's surface would be burned, dried and unfit for human life.

OXIDES OF SULFUR

Oxides of sulfur (SOx) were initially ignored in the exhaust system emissions, since the sulfur content of gasoline as a fuel is less than 1/10TH of 1 percent. Because of this small amount, it was felt that it contributed very little to the overall pollution problem. However, because of the difficulty in solving the sulfur emissions in industrial pollution and the introduction of catalytic converters to automobile exhaust systems, a change was mandated. The automobile exhaust system, when equipped with a catalytic converter, changes the sulfur dioxide (SO_2) into sulfur trioxide (SO_3).

When this combines with water vapors (H_2O), a sulfuric acid mist (H_2SO_4) is formed and is a very difficult pollutant to handle since it is extremely corrosive. The sulfuric acid mist that is formed, is the same mist that rises from the vents of an automobile battery when an active chemical reaction takes place within the battery cells.

When a large concentration of vehicles equipped with catalytic converters are operating in an area, this acid mist may rise and be distributed over a large ground area causing land, plant, crop, paint and building damage.

PARTICULATE MATTER

A certain amount of particulate matter is present in the burning of any fuel, with carbon constituting the largest percentage of the particulates. In gasoline, the remaining particulates are the burned remains of the various other compounds used in its manufacture. When a gasoline engine is in good internal condition, the particulate emissions are low but as the engine wears internally, the particulate emissions increase. By visually inspecting the tail pipe emissions, a determination can be made as to where an engine defect may exist. An engine with light gray or blue smoke emitting from the tail pipe normally indicates an increase in the oil consumption through burning due to internal engine wear. Black smoke would indicate a defective fuel delivery system, causing the engine to operate in a rich mode. Regardless of the color of the smoke, the internal part of the engine or the fuel delivery system should be repaired to prevent excess particulate emissions.

Diesel and turbine engines emit a darkened plume of smoke from the exhaust system because of the type of fuel used. Emission control regulations are mandated for this type of emission and measures that are more stringent are being used to prevent excess emission of the particulate matter. Electronic components are being introduced to control the injection of the fuel at precisely the proper time of piston travel, to achieve the optimum in fuel ignition and fuel usage. Other particulate after-burning components are being tested to achieve a cleaner emission.

Good grades of engine lubricating oils should be used, which meet the manufacturer's specification. Cut-rate oils can contribute to the particulate emission problem because of their low flash or ignition temperature point. Such oils burn prematurely during the combustion process causing emission of particulate matter.

The cooling system is an important factor in the reduction of particulate matter. The optimum combustion will occur, with the cooling system operating at a temperature specified by the manufacturer. The cooling system must be maintained in the same manner as the engine oiling system, as each system is required to perform properly in order for the engine to operate efficiently for a long time.

Crankcase Emissions

Crankcase emissions are made up of water, acids, unburned fuel, oil fumes and particulates. These emissions are classified as hydrocarbons (HC) and are formed by the small amount of unburned, compressed air/fuel mixture entering the crankcase from the combustion area (between the cylinder walls and piston rings) during the compression and power strokes. The head of the compression and combustion help to form the remaining crankcase emissions.

Since the first engines, crankcase emissions were allowed into the atmosphere through a road draft tube, mounted on the lower side of the engine block. Fresh air came in through an open oil filler cap or

breather. The air passed through the crankcase mixing with blow-by gases. The motion of the vehicle and the air blowing past the open end of the road draft tube caused a low pressure area (vacuum) at the end of the tube. Crankcase emissions were simply drawn out of the road draft tube into the air.

To control the crankcase emission, the crankcase breather road draft tube was deleted. A hose and/or tubing was routed from the crankcase to the intake manifold so the blow-by emission could be burned with the air/fuel mixture. However, it was found that intake manifold vacuum, used to draw the crankcase emissions into the manifold, would vary in strength at the wrong time and not allow the proper emission flow. A regulating valve was needed to control the flow of air through the crankcase.

Testing, showed the removal of the blow-by gases from the crankcase as quickly as possible, was most important to the longevity of the engine. Should large accumulations of blow-by gases remain and condense, dilution of the engine oil would occur to form water, soot, resins, acids and lead salts, resulting in the formation of sludge and varnishes. This condensation of the blow-by gases occurs during cold engine start up and most frequently to vehicles used in stop and go driving. These severe operating conditions include numerous engine starting and stopping conditions, excessive idling and not allowing the engine to attain normal operating temperature through short runs. Vehicles that accumulate mostly continuous speed highway miles tend to purge the condensation blow-by gases from the engine oil that occur during start up.

Because the engine oil can accumulate these blow-by gasses, dirty engine oil can contribute to increased emissions as well as increased engine wear. For this reason, oil change intervals for vehicles driven in severe conditions are more frequent than for vehicles driven primarily on the open highway.

Evaporative Emissions

Gasoline fuel is a major source of pollution, before and after it is burned in the automobile engine. From the time the fuel is refined, stored,

pumped and transported, again stored until it is pumped into the fuel tank of the vehicle, the gasoline gives off unburned hydrocarbons (HC) into the atmosphere. Through the redesign of storage areas and venting systems, the pollution factor was diminished, but not eliminated, from the refinery standpoint. However, the automobile remained the primary source of vaporized, unburned hydrocarbon (HC) emissions.

Fuel pumped from an underground storage tank is cool but when exposed to a warmer ambient temperature, will expand. Before controls were mandated, an owner might fill the fuel tank with fuel from an underground storage tank and park the vehicle for some time in warm area, such as a parking lot. As the fuel would warm, it would expand and should no provisions or area be provided for the expansion, the fuel would spill out of the filler neck and onto the ground, causing hydrocarbon (HC) pollution and creating a severe fire hazard. To correct this condition, the vehicle manufacturers added overflow plumbing and/or gasoline tanks with built in expansion areas or domes.

However, this did not control the fuel vapor emission from the fuel tank. It was determined that most of the fuel evaporation occurred when the vehicle was stationary and the engine not operating. Most vehicles carry 5–25 gallons (19–95 liters) of gasoline. Should a large concentration of vehicles be parked in one area, such as a large parking lot, excessive fuel vapor emissions would take place, increasing as the temperature increases.

To prevent the vapor emission from escaping into the atmosphere, the fuel systems were designed to trap the vapors while the vehicle is stationary, by sealing the system from the atmosphere. A storage system is used to collect and hold the fuel vapors from the carburetor (if equipped) and the fuel tank when the engine is not operating. When the engine is started, the storage system is then purged of the fuel vapors, which are drawn into the engine and burned with the air/fuel mixture.

EMISSION CONTROLS

Positive Crankcase Ventilation (PCV) System

OPERATION

♦ See Figures 1 and 2

The Positive Crankcase Ventilation (PCV) system is used to control and purge the crankcase blow-by vapors. The gases are recycled in the following way:

As the engine is running, clean, filtered air is drawn through the air filter and into the crankcase. As the air passes through the crankcase, it picks up the combustion gases and carries them out of the crankcase, through the PCV valve, and into the induction system. As they enter the intake manifold, they are drawn into the combustion chamber where they are burned.

The most critical component in the system is the PCV valve. This valve controls the amount of gases that are recycled into the combustion cham-

ber. At low engine speeds, the valve is partially closed, limiting the flow of gases into the intake manifold. As engine speed increases, the valve opens to admit greater quantities of gases into the intake manifold. If the PCV valve becomes

clogged, the system is designed to allow excessive amounts of blow-by gases to back flow through the crankcase tube into the air cleaner to be consumed by normal combustion.

The Positive Crankcase Ventilation (PCV) sys-

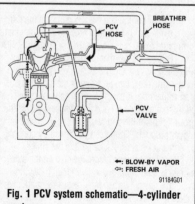

Fig. 1 PCV system schematic—4-cylinder engines

←: BLOW-BY VAPOR
⇐: FRESH AIR

91184G01

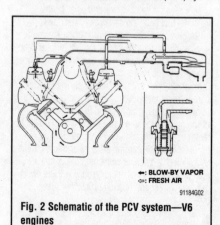

Fig. 2 Schematic of the PCV system—V6 engines

←: BLOW-BY VAPOR
⇐: FRESH AIR

91184G02

tem must be operating correctly to provide complete removal of the crankcase vapors. Fresh air is supplied to the crankcase from the air filter, mixed with the internal exhaust gases, passed through the PCV valve and into the intake manifold.

The PCV valve meters the flow at a rate depending upon the manifold vacuum. If the manifold vacuum is high, the PCV restricts the flow to the intake manifold. If abnormal operating conditions occur, excessive amounts of internal exhaust gases back flow through the crankcase vent tube into the air filter to be burned by normal combustion.

Because the PCV valve vents the crankcase, a defective valve allows the build up of harmful blow-by gases that dilute and damage the lubricating properties of the engine oil. Additionally, the crankcase operating pressure increases and may cause a gasket or seal failure, resulting in an engine oil leak. In extreme cases, a seal or gasket could be completely forced away from the sealing surfaces, causing a severe oil leak.

TESTING

➡️**Never operate an engine without a PCV valve or a crankcase ventilation system, except as directed by testing procedures, for it can become damaged.**

Incorrect operation of the PCV system can cause multiple driveability symptoms.
A plugged valve or hose may cause:
- Rough idle
- Stalling or slow idle speed
- Oil leaks
- Sludge in engine
A leaking valve or hose would cause:
- Rough idle
- Stalling
- High idle speed

PCV Valve

▶ **See Figures 3 and 4**

1. Check the PCV lines and connections for restrictions and leaks.
2. Start the engine and allow the engine to reach a warm idle.
3. With the engine running at idle, using a suitable pliers or fingers, squeeze the hose between the

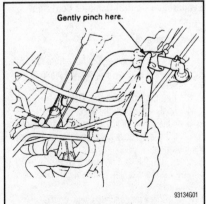

Gently pinch here.

93134G01

Fig. 3 When the engine is at a warm idle, a clicking sound should be heard from the PCV valve when the PCV hose is pinched

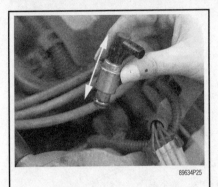

89634P25

Fig. 4 Remove and shake the PCV valve; if a rattling noise is heard, the valve is OK

PCV valve and the intake manifold. The PCV valve should make a clicking noise when the hose is squeezed closed.
4. If the PCV does not make a clicking noise:
a. Shut off the engine, refer to PCV valve removal as outlined in Section 1 and remove the valve.
b. Shake the valve and listen for a rattling noise:
c. If the PCV valve doesn't rattle or doesn't

move freely when shaken, replace it and recheck the system.
d. If the PCV valve does rattle freely when shaken, check the valve's grommet and hoses for leaks and replace any parts that are cracked or damaged. Recheck the PCV valve operation.

REMOVAL & INSTALLATION

Refer to Section 1 for removal and installation of the PCV valve. The PCV valve should be inspected every 2 years or 60,000 miles (96,000 km) and replaced as necessary.

Evaporative Emission Controls

OPERATION

▶ **See Figures 5, 6 and 7**

Changes in atmospheric temperature cause fuel tanks to breathe, that is, the air within the tank expands and contracts with outside temperature changes. If an unsealed system was used, when the temperature rises, air would escape through the tank vent tube or the vent in the tank cap. The air which escapes contains gasoline vapors.

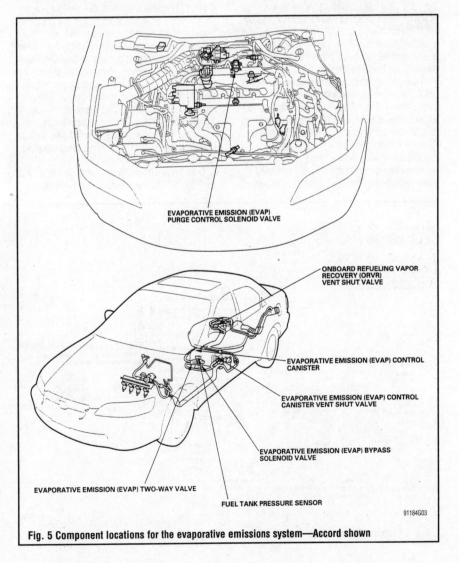

EVAPORATIVE EMISSION (EVAP) PURGE CONTROL SOLENOID VALVE

ONBOARD REFUELING VAPOR RECOVERY (ORVR) VENT SHUT VALVE

EVAPORATIVE EMISSION (EVAP) CONTROL CANISTER

EVAPORATIVE EMISSION (EVAP) CONTROL CANISTER VENT SHUT VALVE

EVAPORATIVE EMISSION (EVAP) BYPASS SOLENOID VALVE

EVAPORATIVE EMISSION (EVAP) TWO-WAY VALVE

FUEL TANK PRESSURE SENSOR

91184G03

Fig. 5 Component locations for the evaporative emissions system—Accord shown

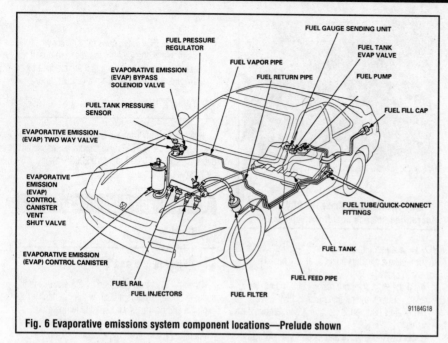

Fig. 6 Evaporative emissions system component locations—Prelude shown

The Evaporative Emission Control System provides a sealed fuel system with the capability to store and condense fuel vapors. When the fuel evaporates in the fuel tank, the vapor passes through the EVAP emission valve, through vent hoses or tubes to a carbon filled evaporative canister. When the engine is operating the vapors are drawn into the intake manifold and burned during combustion.

A sealed, maintenance free evaporative canister is used. The canister is filled with granules of an activated carbon mixture. Fuel vapors entering the canister are absorbed by the charcoal granules. A vent cap is located on the top of the canister to provide fresh air to the canister when it is being purged. The vent cap opens to provide fresh air into the canister, which circulates through the charcoal, releasing trapped vapors and carrying them to the engine to be burned.

Fuel tank pressure vents fuel vapors into the canister. They are held in the canister until they can be drawn into the intake manifold. The canister purge valve allows the canister to be purged at a pre-determined time and engine operating conditions.

Vacuum to the canister is controlled by the canister purge valve. The valve is operated by the PCM. The PCM regulates the valve by switching the ground circuit on and off based on engine operating conditions. When energized, the valve prevents vacuum from reaching the canister. When not energized, the valve allows vacuum to purge the vapors from the canister.

During warm up and for a specified time during hot starts, the PCM energizes the valve, preventing vacuum from reaching the canister

Once the proper coolant temperature is achieved, the PCM controls the ground circuit to the valve.

When the PCM opens the ground, this allows vacuum to flow through the canister and vapors are purged from the canister into the throttle body. During certain idle conditions, the PCM may energize the purge valve to control fuel mixture calibrations.

The fuel tank is sealed with a pressure-vacuum relief filler cap. The relief valve in the cap is a safety feature, preventing excessive pressure or vacuum in the fuel tank. If the cap is malfunctioning, and needs to be replaced, ensure that the replacement is the identical cap to ensure correct system operation.

The following components are part of and affect the operation of the EVAP (Evaporative Emission) Control system

- Fuel Tank
- Fuel Fill Cap
- Evap Two Way Valve
- Evap Control Canister
- Evap Three Way Valve
- Fuel Tank Pressure Sensor
- Powertrain Control Module (PCM)
- Evap Purge Control Solenoid Valve
- Evap Control Canister Vent Shut Valve

COMPONENT TESTING

The Evaporative Emission (EVAP) Controls are monitored by the Powertrain Control Module (PCM) and, if found to be malfunctioning, the PCM records the problem in the fault memory as a Diagnostic Trouble Code (DTC). If the problem persists or compromises the vehicle's emissions, the Malfunction Indicator Light (MIL) could be activated.

Evaporative Emissions (EVAP) Control Canister

This canister is used as a storage facility for fuel vapors that have escaped from components such as the fuel tank. This canister prevents these vapors from entering the atmosphere.

Generally, the only testing done to the canister is a visual inspection. Look the canister over and replace it with a new one if there is any evidence of cracks or other damage.

Evaporative Hoses and Tubes

Inspect all system hoses and tubes for signs of damage or cracks. Any damage or leakage must be repaired.

Evaporative Control Canister Vent Shut Valve

▶ See Figure 8

1. Disconnect the vacuum hose from the valve.
2. Connect a hand-held vacuum pump to the vacuum hose.
3. Turn the ignition switch **ON**.
4. Apply vacuum to the hose.
5. If the valve holds vacuum, the valve is ok.
6. If the valve does not hold vacuum, perform the following:
   a. Turn the ignition switch **OFF**.
   b. Disconnect the electrical connector from the valve.
   c. Check for continuity between the orange/green or light green/white wire and ground. If continuity is present, replace the valve. If no continuity is present, check for an open circuit in the wire between the valve and the PCM.

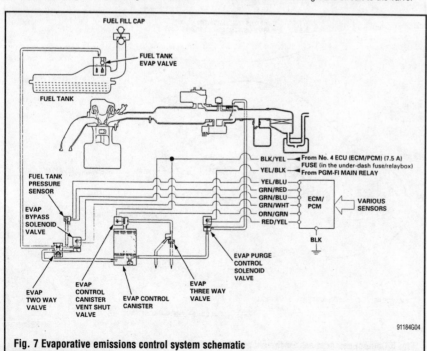

Fig. 7 Evaporative emissions control system schematic

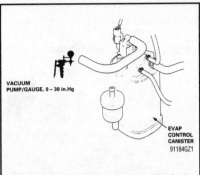

Fig. 8 You can use a vacuum pump to test the evaporative control vent shut valve—Prelude shown, others similar

Fig. 9 View of the evaporative emissions canister

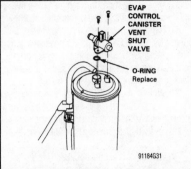

Fig. 10 Some vehicles have an EVAP control shut valve that just has a vacuum hose and 2 retaining screws . . .

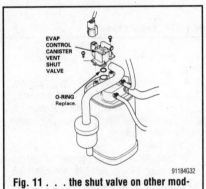

Fig. 11 . . . the shut valve on other models also has an electrical connector that must be detached

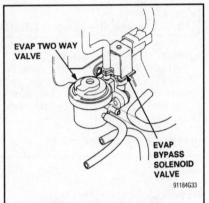

Fig. 12 EVAP 2-way valve mounting

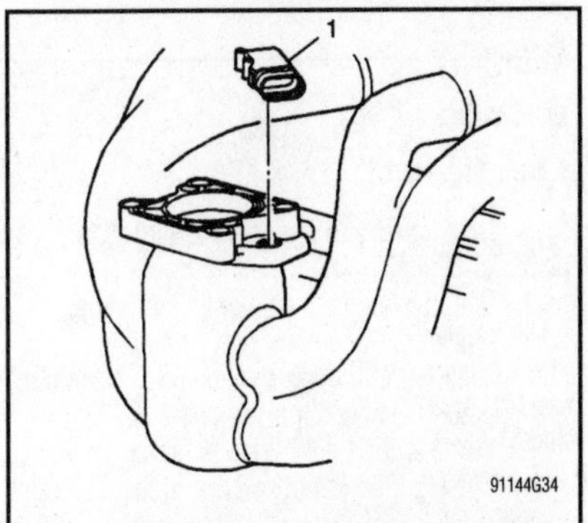

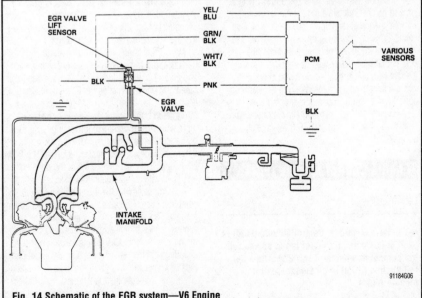

Fig. 13 Exhaust Gas Recirculation (EGR) system schematic—4-cylinder engines

7. When finished testing, attach all disconnected hoses, connectors, and wires.

REMOVAL & INSTALLATION

Evaporative Emissions Canister

▶ See Figure 9

➡Depending upon the model, you may have to raise and support the vehicle for access to the canister.

1. If necessary, raise and safely support the vehicle.
2. Remove the bolts retaining the Evaporative Emissions (EVAP) canister and bracket assembly.
3. Label and disconnect the vapor hoses from the canister.
4. Remove the canister from the bracket.
5. Installation is the reverse of removal.

Evaporative Emissions Control Shut Valve

▶ See Figures 10 and 11

1. Disconnect the vacuum hose and electrical connector (if equipped) from the EVAP shut valve.
2. Remove the fasteners that hold the EVAP shut valve to the canister.
3. Remove the EVAP control shut valve from the canister.
To install:
4. Install the EVAP control shunt valve and fasteners.
5. Connect all vacuum hoses and electrical connectors as necessary.

Canister Purge Valve (Two-way Valve)

▶ See Figure 12

1. Raise and support the vehicle.
2. Unplug the electrical harness from the valve.
3. Disconnect the fuel vapor hoses, then remove the valve.
4. Installation is the reverse of removal.

Exhaust Gas Recirculation System

OPERATION

▶ See Figures 13 and 14

The Exhaust Gas Recirculation (EGR) system is designed to reduce Oxides of Nitrogen (NO_x) by

Fig. 14 Schematic of the EGR system—V6 Engine

recirculating exhaust gas through the EGR valve and into the intake manifold and combustion chambers.

The EGR valve is controlled by the Powertrain Control Module (PCM) that relies on feedback from various sensors. The PCM contains a memory for ideal EGR valve operation and lift suited to various operating conditions.

The amount of exhaust gas that is reintroduced into the combustion cycle is determined by several factors, such as: engine speed, engine vacuum, exhaust system backpressure, coolant temperature, and throttle position.

The EGR valve is vacuum operated via an inline solenoid. The EGR vacuum diagram for your particular year and model of vehicle is displayed on the Vehicle Emission Control Information (VECI) label found on the underside of the hood.

COMPONENT TESTING

EGR Valve

▶ See Figure 15

1. Disconnect and plug the vacuum supply hose from the EGR valve.
2. Start the engine, then apply the parking brake, block the rear wheels and position the transaxle in Neutral. Allow the engine to reach normal operating temperature.
3. Using a hand-held vacuum pump, slowly apply 8 in. Hg (26 kPa) of vacuum to the EGR valve nipple.

    a. If the idle speed drops more than 100 rpm with the vacuum applied and returns to normal after the vacuum is removed, the EGR valve is OK.

    b. If the idle speed does not drop more than

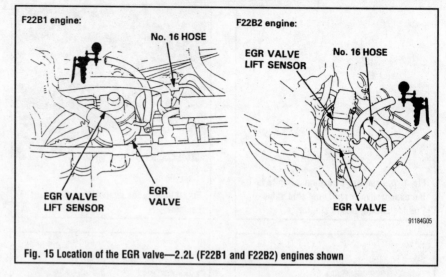

Fig. 15 Location of the EGR valve—2.2L (F22B1 and F22B2) engines shown

100 rpm with the vacuum applied and return to normal after the vacuum is removed, inspect the EGR valve for a blockage; clean it if a blockage is found. Replace the EGR valve if no blockage is found, or if cleaning the valve does not remedy the malfunction.

REMOVAL & INSTALLATION

EGR Valve

▶ See Figure 15

1. Disconnect the negative battery cable.
2. On models equipped with the EGR lift sensor, remove the EGR lift sensor electrical connector.

3. Detach the vacuum hose from the EGR valve.
4. Remove the EGR valve mounting fasteners, then separate the valve from the intake manifold.
5. Remove and discard the old EGR valve gasket. Clean the gasket mating surfaces on the valve and the intake manifold.

To install:
6. Install the EGR valve, along with a new gasket, on the upper intake manifold, then install and tighten the mounting bolts securely.
7. Attach the vacuum hose to the EGR valve.
8. If equipped, attach the EGR lift sensor electrical connector.
9. Connect the negative battery cable.

ELECTRONIC ENGINE CONTROLS

The following systems can be checked individually, and most of them can be checked using suitable diagnostic equipment. Beginning with model year 1996 Honda passenger vehicles are On Board Diagnostic version II (OBD-II) compliant. Using a suitable OBD-II Data Scan Tool (DST) can save precious diagnostic time and allows the systems to be checked while the engine is running without chance of damaging the component, wire connections or the insulation.

Another advantage of using a suitable OBD-II DST is that the systems can be checked how they interact with one another, and can be checked during initial start-up, monitored during the warm up period and at normal operating temperatures.

A suitable OBD-II DST also allows for any stored Diagnostic Trouble Codes (DTCs) faults to be accessed and cleared.

Engine Control Module (ECM)

OPERATION

➡The term Electronic Control Module (ECM) is used in this manual to refer to the engine control computer, whether it is a Powertrain Control Module (PCM) or an Engine Control Module (ECM).

The heart of the electronic engine management system, which is found on the vehicles covered by this manual, is the computer control module. On vehicles equipped with a manual transaxle, there is no need for a control unit to control shift points as the transaxle is shifted manually. On these models, the engine management system uses an ECM. Some models used a separate Transmission Control Module (TCM) that is linked with the ECM to control the automatic transaxle shift points.

Many models equipped with an automatic transaxle, the Transmission Control Module (TCM) and Engine Control Module (ECM) have been combined into one unit, called the Powertrain Control Module (PCM). The ECM/PCM processes input information from various sensors, compares the input with pre-programmed information and sends output signals to control the fuel supply, ignition timing, and the engine emission system. The PCM also controls the shift functions of the on vehicles equipped with an automatic transaxle.

Regardless of who the manufacturer may be, all computer control modules are serviced in a similar manner. Care must be taken when handling these expensive electronic components in order to protect them from damage. Carefully follow all instructions included with the replacement part. Avoid touching pins or connectors to prevent damage from static electricity or contaminating the electrical connection. Some input voltages and resistance values are

quite small and the readings very sensitive. A poor electrical connection could drastically affect the values recognized by the PCM and cause a poor running condition.

Since the PCM is a sensitive electronic component and must be kept away from areas of heat, debris and fluids, it is located in the interior.

All of the computer control modules contain a Programmable Read Only Memory (PROM) chip that contains calibration information specific to the vehicle application.

✱✱ WARNING

To prevent the possibility of permanent control module damage, the ignition switch MUST always be OFF when disconnecting power from or reconnecting power to the module. This includes unplugging the module connector, disconnecting the negative battery cable, removing the module fuse or even attempting to jump start your dead battery using jumper cables.

In case of an ECM failure, the system will default to a pre-programmed set of values. These are compromise values which allow the engine to operate, although at a reduced efficiency. This is variously known as the default, limp or back-up mode. Driveability is usually affected when the ECM enters this mode and should trigger the Malfunction Indicator Lamp (MIL) indicator.

REMOVAL & INSTALLATION

▶ See Figures 16 and 17

Sometimes substituting a known good ECM/PCM can be helpful when attempting to diagnose a problem in the engine management system. When substituting a control unit, make sure that both control units are identical. Installing the wrong control unit could damage the substituted unit, and/or possibly damage other related sensors or components in the vehicle being tested.

The control units are very sensitive to changes in the charging system operating voltage and voltage spikes. Make sure the alternator and battery are functioning properly. An alternator that is over charging will not only damages the battery, the voltage output may be enough to cause damage to other electrical components and control units.

Operating a vehicle with a discharged or defective battery can cause the vehicle's charging system to be overworked. Never operate a vehicle with a battery cable disconnected. If the vehicle requires a jump start, be careful to connect the battery cables properly, and wait at least one minute after the cables have been installed the start the vehicle.

1. Make sure the ignition switch is turned **OFF**, then disconnect the negative battery cable.

✳✳ WARNING

To prevent the possibility of permanent control module damage, the ignition switch

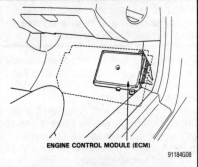

ENGINE CONTROL MODULE (ECM)

91184G08

Fig. 16 The ECM is located under the carpeting of the passenger's side floor pan, on earlier models

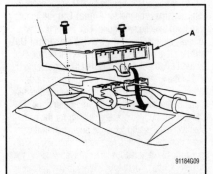

91184G09

Fig. 17 On later models of the Accord and Prelude, the ECM is located closer to the front console

MUST always be OFF when disconnecting power from or reconnecting power to the module. This includes unplugging the module connector, disconnecting the negative battery cable, removing the module fuse or even attempting to jump your dead battery using jumper cables.

2. Locate the computer control module.

➡**Always ground yourself when handling an ECM. This can easily be done by connecting a small jumper lead to you and then to the metal chassis of the vehicle.**

3. Pull back the carpeting from the passenger's side floor and front console. This will expose the ECM.
4. If necessary, remove the ECM cover retaining bolts and cover.
5. Remove the retaining bolts from the control module. On models with 4-cylinder engines, there are usually 2 bolts. On V6 equipped models, there are usually 3 mounting bolts.
6. Remove the wiring harnesses from the ECM.
7. Carefully lift the ECM from the vehicle.

➡**Remember to properly ground yourself when handling the ECM. It only takes a small spark of static electricity to destroy the fragile electronics within the ECM.**

8. Installation is the reverse of removal.

Oxygen Sensor

OPERATION

▶ See Figure 18

An Oxygen (O$_2$) sensor is an input device used by the ECM to monitor the amount of oxygen in the exhaust gas stream. The information is used by the computer, along with other inputs, to fine-tune the air/fuel mixture so that the engine can run with the greatest efficiency in all conditions. The O$_2$ sensor sends this information to the computer control module in the form of a 100–900 millivolt (mV) reference signal. The signal is actually created by the O$_2$ sensor itself through chemical interactions between the sensor tip material (zirconium dioxide in almost all cases) and the oxygen levels in the exhaust gas stream and ambient atmosphere gas. At operating temperatures, approximately 1100°F

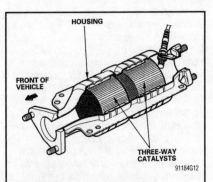

HOUSING

FRONT OF VEHICLE

THREE-WAY CATALYSTS

91184G12

Fig. 18 Many Honda vehicles have the oxygen sensor mounted in the catalytic converter

(600°C), the element becomes a semiconductor. Essentially, through the differing levels of oxygen in the exhaust gas stream and in the surrounding atmosphere, the sensor creates a voltage signal that is directly and consistently related to the concentration of oxygen in the exhaust stream. Typically, a higher than normal amount of oxygen in the exhaust stream indicates that not all of the available oxygen was used in the combustion process, because there was not enough fuel (lean condition) present. Inversely, a lower than normal concentration of oxygen in the exhaust stream indicates that a large amount was used in the combustion process, because a larger than necessary amount of fuel was present (rich condition). Thus, the engine ECM/PCM can correct the amount of fuel introduced into the combustion chambers by controlling the fuel injector opening time.

To improve O$_2$ sensor efficiency, newer O$_2$ sensors were designed with a built-in heating element, and were called Heated Oxygen (HO$_2$) Sensors. The heating element was incorporated into the sensor so that the sensor would reach optimal operating temperature quicker, meaning that the O$_2$ sensor output signal could be used by the engine control computer sooner and also stabilizes the sensor's output. Because the sensor reaches optimal temperature quicker, vehicles can enjoy improved driveability and fuel economy even before the engine reaches normal operating temperature.

Beginning with model year 1996, the On-Board Diagnostics second generation (OBD-II), an updated system based on the former OBD-I became mandatory for passenger vehicles produced for sale in the United States. The OBD-II system used on the Accord and Prelude models is also installed on vehicles sold in Canada. This system requires the use of two HO$_2$ sensors, the Primary Heated Oxygen (PHO$_2$) sensor and the Secondary Heated Oxygen (SHO$_2$) sensor. The PHO$_2$ sensor is located before the catalytic converter and performs the same functions as the HO$_2$ sensor found on vehicles equipped with a single sensor. The Secondary Heated Oxygen (SHO$_2$) sensor is located after the catalytic converter and enables the ECM/PCM to monitor the PHO$_2$ sensor and catalytic converter efficiency. The SHO$_2$ sensor mounted in the exhaust system after the catalytic converter is not used to affect air/fuel mixture, it is used solely to monitor the catalytic converter and PHO$_2$ sensor efficiency.

The ECM/PCM uses the HO$_2$ sensor output voltage as an indication of the oxygen content of the burnt exhaust gases. Because the oxygen content directly affects the HO$_2$ sensor output, the signal voltage from the sensor to the ECM/PCM fluctuates constantly. This fluctuation is caused by interaction between the ECM/PCM and the HO$_2$ sensor, which follows a general pattern: detect, compare, compensate, detect, compare, compensate, etc. This means that when the ECM/PCM detects a lean signal from the HO$_2$ sensor, it compares the reading with known parameters stored within its memory. It calculates that there is too much oxygen present in the exhaust gases, so it compensates by adding more fuel to the air/fuel mixture. This, in turn, causes the HO$_2$ sensor to send a rich signal to the computer, which, then compares this new signal, and adjusts the air/fuel mixture again. This pattern constantly repeats itself: detect rich, compare, compensate lean, detect lean, compare, compensate rich, etc. Since the HO$_2$ sensor fluctuates between rich and lean, and because the lean limit for sensor output is 100 mV and the rich limit is 900 mV, the proper voltage signal from a normally functioning O_2 sensor consistently fluctuates between 100–300 and 700–900 mV.

➡ **The sensor voltage may never quite reach 100 or 900 mV, but it should fluctuate from at least below 300 mV to above 700 mV, and the mid-point of the fluctuations should be centered around 500 mV.**

TESTING

The best, and most accurate method to test the operation of an O_2 sensor is with the use of either an oscilloscope or a Diagnostic Scan Tool (DST), following their specific instructions for testing. It is possible, however, to test whether the O_2 sensor is functioning properly within general parameters using a Digital Volt-Ohmmeter (DVOM), also referred to as a Digital Multi-Meter (DMM). Newer DMM's are often designed to perform many advanced diagnostic functions. Some are constructed to be used as an oscilloscope. Two in-vehicle-testing procedures, and 1 bench test procedure, will be provided for the common zirconium dioxide oxygen sensor. The first in-vehicle test makes use of a standard DVOM with a 10 megohms impedance, whereas the second in-vehicle test presented necessitates the usage of an advanced DMM with MIN/MAX/Average functions. Both of these in-vehicle test procedures are likely to set Diagnostic Trouble Codes (DTC's) in the engine control computer. Therefore, after testing, be sure to clear all DTC's before retesting the sensor, if necessary.

✲✲ WARNING

When testing or servicing a Heated Oxygen (O_2) Sensor, the vehicle will need to be started and the engine warmed up to operating temperature in order to perform the necessary testing procedures or to easily remove the sensor from its threaded fitting. This will create a situation that requires working around a HOT exhaust system. The following is a list of precautions to consider during this service:

• Do not pierce any wires when testing a HO_2 sensor, as this can lead to wiring harness damage. Backprobe the connector, when necessary.
• While testing the sensor, be sure to keep out of the way of moving engine components, such as the cooling fan. Refrain from wearing loose clothing that may become tangled in moving engine components.
• Safety glasses must be worn at all times when working on or near the exhaust system. Older exhaust systems may be covered with loose rust particles that can fall off when disturbed. These particles are not only a nuisance, they can cause eye injuries.
• Be cautious when working on and around the hot exhaust system. Painful burns will result if skin is exposed to the exhaust system pipes or manifolds.
• The HO_2 sensor may be difficult to remove when the engine temperature is below 120°F (48°C). Excessive force may damage the threads in

the exhaust pipe, therefore always start the engine and allow it to reach normal operating temperature prior to removal.
• Since HO_2 sensors are usually designed with a permanently attached wiring pigtail (this allows the wiring harness and sensor connectors to be positioned away from the hot exhaust system), it may be necessary to use a socket or wrench that is designed specifically for this purpose.

Four Wire Heated Oxygen Sensor

✲✲ WARNING

The four wire Heated Oxygen (HO_2) Sensor have two separate circuits, the signal circuit and the heater circuit which must not be confused. Never apply voltage to the signal wiring of a HO_2 sensor, otherwise it may be damaged. Also, never connect an ohmmeter (or a DVOM set on the ohm function) to both of the signal wires of a HO_2 sensor at the same time, otherwise the sensor may be damaged.

The color of the wires for the HO_2 sensor vary from model to model, however the positioning of the wires is consistent. With HO_2 sensor disconnected, hold the electrical multi-connector such that the locking tab is at the top, while facing the electrical connectors. The two top electrical connectors are the sensor terminals. The two bottom electrical connectors are the heater terminals. The two electrical connectors on the left side are the (+) positive part of the circuit and the two electrical connectors on the right side are the (-) negative part of the circuit.

Test 1 makes use of a standard DVOM with a 10 megohms impedance, where as Test 2 necessitates the usage of an advanced Digital Multi-Meter (DMM) with MIN/MAX/Average functions or a sliding bar graph function. Both of these in-vehicle test procedures are likely to set Diagnostic Trouble Codes (DTC's) in the Engine Control Module/Powertrain Control Module (ECM/PCM). Therefore, after testing, be sure to clear all DTC's before retesting the sensor, if necessary. The Test 3 in-vehicle test is designed for the use of a scan tool or oscilloscope. The Test 4 Heating Circuit Test is designed to check the function of the heating circuit of the HO_2 sensor.

The Honda models covered in this book produced prior to 1996 use one Heated Oxygen (HO_2). Beginning with model year 1996, passenger vehicles sold in the United States were mandated to be On Board Diagnostic version II (OBD-II) compliant. The OBD-II equipped vehicles use two HO_2 sensors. The Primary Heated Oxygen (PHO_2) Sensor is located before the catalytic converter and is also referred to as Sensor 1 (S1). This is the sensor the ECM/PCM uses to monitor the oxygen content of the exhaust. The sensor located down stream from the catalytic converter is the Secondary Heated Oxygen (SHO_2). This sensor is also referred to as Sensor 2 (S2), and is used only to monitor the efficiency of the PHO_2 and the catalytic converter.

The in-vehicle tests may be performed for the SHO_2 sensor, however under normal conditions, the SHO_2 sensor should not fluctuate like the PHO_2). Because the SHO_2 sensor is used only to monitor the efficiency of the PHO_2 sensor and the catalytic

converter, if the HO_2 sensor exhibits a fluctuating signal, the catalytic converter is most likely defective.

TEST 1—DIGITAL VOLT-OHMMETER

This test will not only verify proper sensor functioning, but is also designed to ensure the engine control computer and associated wiring is functioning properly as well.

1. Start the engine and allow it to warm up to normal operating temperature.

➡ **If you are using the opening of the thermostat to gauge normal operating temperature, be forewarned: a defective thermostat can open too early and prevent the engine from reaching normal operating temperature. This can cause a slightly rich condition in the exhaust, which can throw the HO_2 sensor readings off slightly.**

2. Turn the ignition switch **OFF**, then locate the two signal wires of the HO_2 sensor pigtail connector.
3. Perform a visual inspection of the connector to ensure it is properly engaged and all terminals are straight, tight and free from corrosion or damage.
4. Disengage the sensor pigtail connector from the vehicle harness connector.
5. Using a DVOM set to read DC voltage, attach the positive lead to the **Signal Output** terminal of the sensor pigtail connector, and the DVOM negative lead to a good engine ground.

✲✲ CAUTION

While the engine is running, keep clear of all moving and hot components. Do not wear loose clothing. Otherwise severe personal injury or death may occur.

6. Have an assistant start the engine and hold it at approximately 2000 rpm. Wait at least 1 minute before commencing with the test to allow the HO_2 sensor to sufficiently warm up.
7. Using a jumper wire, connect the **Signal Output** terminal of the **vehicle harness connector** to a good engine ground. This will fool the engine control computer into thinking it is receiving a lean signal from the HO_2 sensor, therefore, the computer will richen the air/fuel ratio. With the **Signal Output** terminal so grounded, the DVOM should register at least 800 mV, as the control computer adds additional fuel to the air/fuel ratio.
8. While observing the DVOM, disconnect the vehicle harness connector **Signal Output** jumper wire from the engine ground. Use the jumper wire to apply slightly less than 1 volt to the **signal Output** terminal of the vehicle harness connector. One method to do this is by grasping and squeezing the end of the jumper between your forefinger and thumb of one hand while touching the positive terminal of the battery post with your other hand. This allows your body to act as a resistor for the battery positive voltage, and fools the engine control computer into thinking it is receiving a rich signal. Or, use a mostly-drained AA battery by connecting the positive terminal of the AA battery to the jumper wire and the negative terminal of the battery to a good engine ground. (Another jumper wire may be necessary to do this.) The computer should lean the

air/fuel mixture out. This lean mixture should register as 150 mV or less on the DVOM while connected to the **Signal Output** terminals of the HO2 sensor.

9. If the DVOM did not register millivoltages as indicated, the problem may be either the sensor, the engine control computer or the associated wiring. Perform the following to determine which is the defective component:

a. Remove the vehicle harness connector **Signal Output** jumper wire.

b. While observing the DVOM, artificially enrich the air/fuel charge using propane. The DVOM reading should register higher than normal millivoltages. (Normal voltage for an ideal air/fuel mixture is approximately 450–550 mV DC). Then, lean the air/fuel intake charger by either disconnecting one of the fuel injector wiring harness connectors (to prevent the injector from delivering fuel) or by detaching 1 or 2 vacuum lines (to add additional non-metered air into the engine). The DVOM should now register lower than normal millivoltages. If the DVOM functioned as indicated, the problem lies elsewhere in the fuel delivery and control system. If the DVOM readings were still unresponsive, the O2 sensor is defective; replace the sensor and retest.

➡ **Poor wire connections and/or ground circuits may shift a normal O2 sensor's millivoltage readings up into the rich range or down into the lean range. It is a good idea to check the wire condition and continuity before replacing a component that will not fix the problem.**

10. Turn the engine **OFF**, remove the DVOM and all associated jumper wires. Reattach the vehicle harness connector to the sensor pigtail connector. If applicable, reattach the fuel injector wiring connector and/or the vacuum line(s).

11. Clear any DTCs present in the ECM/PCM memory, as necessary.

TEST 2—DIGITAL MULTI-METER

This test method is a more straightforward Heated Oxygen (HO2) Sensor test, and does not test the engine control computer's response to the HO2 sensor signal. The use of a DMM with the MIN/MAX/Average function or sliding bar graph/wave function is necessary for this test. Don't forget that the Secondary Heated Oxygen (SHO2) Sensor mounted after the catalytic converter (if equipped) will not fluctuate like the other Primary Heated Oxygen (PHO2) Sensor will.

1. Start the engine and allow it to warm up to normal operating temperature.

➡ **If using the opening of the thermostat to gauge normal operating temperature, be forewarned: a defective thermostat can open too early and prevent the engine from reaching normal operating temperature. This can cause a slightly rich condition in the exhaust, which can throw the HO2 sensor readings off slightly.**

2. Turn the ignition switch **OFF**, then locate the HO2 sensor pigtail connector.

3. Perform a visual inspection of the connector to ensure it is properly engaged and all terminals are straight, tight and free from corrosion or damage.

4. Backprobe the HO2 sensor connector termi-

nals. Attach the DMM positive test lead to the **Signal Output** terminal of the sensor pigtail connector. Attach the negative lead to either the **Signal Ground** terminal of the sensor pigtail or to a good, clean engine ground.

5. Activate the MIN/MAX/Average or sliding bar graph/wave function on the DMM.

❋❋ CAUTION

While the engine is running, keep clear of all moving and hot components. Do not wear loose clothing. Otherwise severe personal injury or death may occur.

6. Have an assistant start the engine and wait a few minutes before commencing with the test to allow the HO2 sensor to sufficiently warm up.

7. Read the minimum, maximum and average readings exhibited by the HO2 sensor or observe the bar graph/wave form. The average reading for a properly functioning HO2 sensor is be approximately 450–550 mV DC. The minimum and maximum readings should vary more than 300–600 mV. A typical HO2 sensor can fluctuate from as low as 100 mV to as high as 900 mV; if the sensor range of fluctuation is not large enough, the sensor is defective. Also, if the fluctuation range is biased up or down in the scale. For example, if the fluctuation range is 400 mV to 900 mV the sensor is defective, because the readings are pushed up into the rich range (as long as the fuel delivery system is functioning properly). The same goes for a fluctuation range pushed down into the lean range. The midpoint of the fluctuation range should be around 400–500 mV. Finally, if the HO2 sensor voltage fluctuates too slowly (usually the voltage wave should oscillate past the mid-way point of 500 mV several times per second) the sensor is defective. (When an O2 sensor fluctuates too slowly, it is referred to as being "lazy.")

➡ **Poor wire connections and/or ground circuits may shift a normal HO2 sensor's millivoltage readings up into the rich range or down into the lean range. It is a good idea to check the wire condition and continuity before replacing a component that will not fix the problem.**

8. Using the propane method, richen the air/fuel mixture and observe the DMM readings. The average HO2 sensor output signal voltage should rise into the rich range.

9. Lean the air/fuel mixture by either disconnecting a fuel injector wiring harness connector or by disconnecting a vacuum line. The HO2 sensor average output signal voltage should drop into the lean range.

10. If the HO2 sensor did not react as indicated, the sensor is defective and should be replaced.

11. Turn the engine **OFF**, remove the DMM and all associated jumper wires. Reattach the vehicle harness connector to the sensor pigtail connector. If applicable, reattach the fuel injector wiring connector and/or the vacuum line(s).

12. Clear any DTC's present in the ECM/PCM memory, as necessary.

TEST 3—OSCILLOSCOPE

▶ See Figure 19

This test is designed for the use of an oscilloscope to test the functioning of a Heated Oxygen (HO2) Sensor.

➡ **This test is only applicable for HO2 and Primary Heated Oxygen (PHO2) Sensors mounted in the exhaust system before the catalytic converter.**

1. Start the engine and allow it to reach normal operating temperature.

2. Turn the engine **OFF**, and locate the HO2 sensor connector. Backprobe the scope lead to the O2

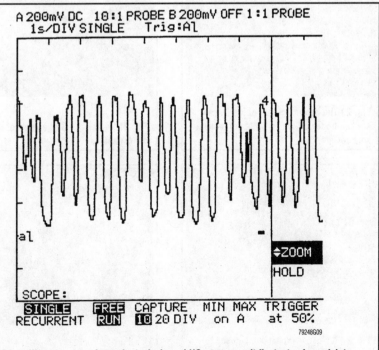

Fig. 19 An oscilloscope wave form of a typical good HO2 sensor as it fluctuates from rich to lean

sensor connector **Signal Output** terminal. Refer to the scope manufacturer's instructions for more information on attaching the scope to the vehicle.

3. Turn the scope ON.

4. Set the oscilloscope amplitude to 200 mV per division, and the time to 1 second per division. Use the 1:1 setting of the probe, and be sure to connect the scope's ground lead to a good, clean engine ground. Set the signal function to automatic or internal triggering.

5. Start the engine and run it at 2000 rpm.

6. The oscilloscope should display a waveform, representative of the HO$_2$ sensor switching between lean (100–300 mV) and rich (700–900 mV). The sensor should switch between rich and lean, or lean and rich (crossing the mid-point of 500 mV) several times per second. In addition, the range of each wave should reach at least above 700 mV and below 300 mV. However, an occasional low peak is acceptable.

7. Force the air/fuel mixture rich by introducing propane into the engine, then observe the oscilloscope readings. The fluctuating range of the HO$_2$ sensor should climb into the rich range.

8. Lean the air/fuel mixture out by either detaching a vacuum line or by disengaging one of the fuel injector's wiring connectors. Watch the scope readings; the HO$_2$ sensor waveform should drop toward the lean range.

9. If the HO$_2$ sensor's wave form does not fluctuate adequately, is not centered around 500 mV during normal engine operation, does not climb toward the rich range when propane is added to the engine, or does not drop toward the lean range when a vacuum hose or fuel injector connector is detached, the sensor is defective.

10. Reattach the fuel injector connector or vacuum hose.

11. Disconnect the oscilloscope from the vehicle.

TEST 4—HEATING CIRCUIT TEST

▶ See Figure 20

The heating circuit in a Heated Oxygen (HO$_2$) Sensor is designed heat and stabilize the sensor quicker than a non-heated sensor. This provides an advantage of increased engine driveability and fuel economy while the engine temperature is still below normal operating temperature, because the fuel management system can enter closed loop operation (more efficient than open loop operation) sooner.

Therefore, if the heating element goes bad, the HO$_2$ sensor may still function properly once the sensor warms up to its normal temperature. This will take longer than normal and may cause mild driveability-related problems while the engine has not reached normal operating temperature.

If the heating element is found to be defective, replace the HO$_2$ sensor.

1. Locate the O$_2$ sensor pigtail connector.

2. Perform a visual inspection of the connector to ensure it is properly engaged and all terminals are straight, tight and free from corrosion or damage.

3. Disengage the sensor pigtail connector from the vehicle harness connector.

4. Using a DVOM set to read resistance (ohms), attach 1 DVOM test lead to the **Heater Element Power** terminal, and the other lead to the **Heater Element Ground** terminal, of the sensor pigtail connector, then observe the resistance readings.

a. If there is no continuity between the **Heater Element Power** and **Heater Element Ground** terminals, the sensor is defective. Replace it with a new one and retest.

b. If there is continuity between the 2 terminals, but the resistance is less than 10 ohms or greater than 40 ohms, the sensor is defective. Replace it with a new one and retest.

5. Turn the engine **OFF**, remove the DVOM and all associated jumper wires. Reattach the vehicle harness connector to the sensor pigtail connector.

6. Clear any DTC's present in the ECM/PCM memory, as necessary.

REMOVAL & INSTALLATION

▶ See Figures 21, 22, 23, 24 and 25

✳✳ WARNING

The sensors use a pigtail and connector. This pigtail should not be removed from the sensor. Damage or removal of the pigtail or connector could affect proper operation of the oxygen sensor. Keep the electrical connector and louvered end of the sensor clean and free of grease. NEVER use cleaning solvents of any type on the sensor! The sensor may be difficult to remove when the engine temperature is below 120°F (48°C). Excessive removal force may damage the threads in the exhaust manifold or pipe; follow the removal procedure carefully.

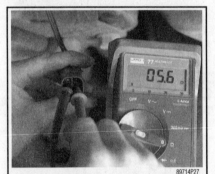

Fig. 20 The heating circuit of the O$_2$ sensor can be tested with a DMM set to measure resistance

Fig. 21 Detach the Oxygen sensor electrical connector

Fig. 22 There is a special socket available that is specifically for removing the Oxygen sensor

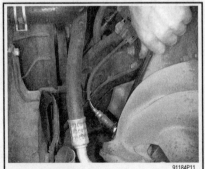

Fig. 23 A closed wrench can be used to remove the Oxygen sensor if there is sufficient space

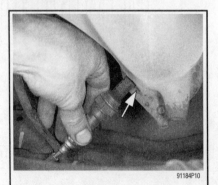

Fig. 24 Unthread, then carefully remove the Oxygen sensor

Fig. 25 Apply an suitable anti-seize lubricant to the threads of the Oxygen sensor before installation

1. Make sure the ignition is **OFF**, then disconnect the negative battery cable.

2. Raise and safely support the vehicle.

3. Locate the oxygen sensor. It protrudes from the exhaust pipe (it looks somewhat like a spark plug).

4. Unplug the sensor electrical connector.

➡ **There are special wrenches, either socket or open-end available from reputable retail outlets for removing the oxygen sensor. These tools make the job much easier and often prevent unnecessary sensor damage.**

5. Carefully unscrew the sensor counterclockwise, then remove the oxygen sensor from the manifold or pipe.

To install:

6. During and after the removal, be very careful to protect the tip of the sensor if it is to be reused. Do not let it to come in contact with fluids or dirt. Do not clean it or wash it.

7. Apply a light coat of anti-seize compound to the sensor threads but DO NOT allow any to get on the tip of the sensor.

8. Install the sensor into the exhaust pipe.

9. Attach the electrical connector and ensure a clean, tight connection.

10. Carefully lower the vehicle.

11. Connect the negative battery cable and enter the radio security code.

Idle Air Control Valve

OPERATION

▶ **See Figure 26**

The engine idle speed is monitored and controlled by the Engine Control Module/Powertrain Control Module (ECM/PCM) which uses the Idle Air Control (IAC) valve to regulate the idle speed. The valve controls the amount of air that is allowed

to bypass the intake throttle plate, which enables the engine idle speed to remain constant even though the engine loads change during idle. This is especially true when electrical consumers such as the air conditioner are used.

The minimum idle air speed is set at the factory with a stop screw. This setting allows a certain amount of air to bypass the throttle valves regardless of IAC valve positioning. A combination of this airflow and IAC positioning allows the ECM/PCM to control engine idle speed. During normal engine idle operation, the IAC valve is controlled by the ECM/PCM and properly positioned. No adjustment should be required during routine maintenance. Tampering with the minimum idle speed adjustment may result in premature failure of the IAC valve or improperly controlled engine idle operation.

TESTING

▶ **See Figure 27**

Prior to testing the Idle Air Control (IAC) valve, inspect the IAC valve mounting, hoses, connections and O-rings for damage, looseness or leakage.

1. Start the vehicle's engine.

2. Allow to run until it reaches normal operating temperature that is indicated by one complete fan cycle.

3. Detach the electrical connector from the IAC valve.

➡ **With the IAC valve disconnected, there should be a noticeable drop in engine speed. If a drop in idle speed was noted but an intermittent idle still persists, check the wiring harness for high resistance connections or exposed wires.**

4. A vacuum leak in the throttle body could also cause a poor idle. Check for this by placing your finger over the hole in the inner throttle body. The idle should drop. If it does not, a vacuum leak may be present.

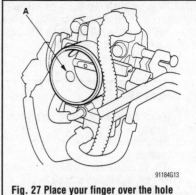

Fig. 27 Place your finger over the hole marked "A" to test the IAC system

REMOVAL & INSTALLATION

1. Disconnect the negative battery cable.

2. Detach the wiring harness from the IAC valve.

3. Remove the two retaining bolts.

4. Remove the IAC valve and discard the old seals or gaskets.

To install:

5. Clean the gasket mating surfaces thoroughly.

6. Using new seals or gaskets, position the IAC valve on the throttle body.

7. Install and tighten the retaining bolts.

8. Connect the wiring harness to the IAC valve:

9. If raised, lower the vehicle.

10. Connect the negative battery cable.

Engine Coolant Temperature Sensor

OPERATION

▶ **See Figure 28**

The Engine Coolant Temperature (ECT) sensor is a thermistor, which means it's resistance changes in response to engine coolant temperature. The sensor resistance decreases as the coolant temperature increases, and increases as the coolant temperature decreases. This input signal is used by the ECM/PCM help determine the correct air-to-fuel ratio for the engine's operating temperature. The ECM/PCM controls the fuel mixture by controlling how long the electrically triggered fuel injectors stay open. If the ECT sensor is unplugged, the

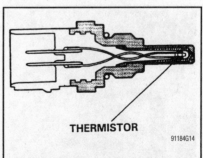

Fig. 28 The Engine Coolant Temperature (ECT) sensor is a thermistor; a sensor whose resistance changes is response to coolant temperature

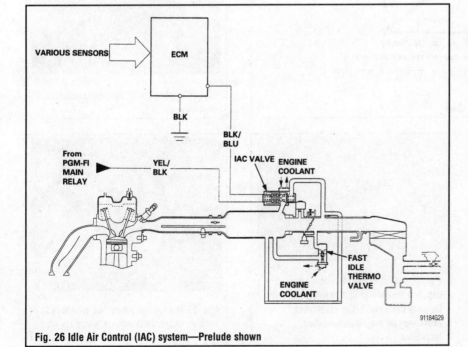

Fig. 26 Idle Air Control (IAC) system—Prelude shown

ECM/PCM senses a very high resistance, and the engine may start when cold, however as the engine's temperature increases, a rich running condition will cause the engine to loose power and stall.

TESTING

▶ **See Figure 29**

1. Disconnect the engine wiring harness from the ECT sensor.
2. Connect an ohmmeter between the two ECT sensor terminals.
3. With the engine cold and the ignition switch in the **OFF** position, measure and note the ECT sensor resistance.
4. Connect the engine wiring harness to the sensor.
5. Start the engine and allow the engine to reach normal operating temperature.
6. Once the engine has reached normal operating temperature, turn the engine **OFF**.
7. Again, disconnect the engine wiring harness from the ECT sensor.
8. Measure and note the ECT sensor resistance with the engine hot.
9. The ECT sensor should have 5,000 ohms resistance when the engine coolant temperature is cold. The ECT sensor resistance should decrease as the engine temperature increases. At operating temperature the ECT sensor resistance should be 100–400 ohms.

10. If readings are not close, the sensor may be faulty.

REMOVAL & INSTALLATION

▶ **See Figures 30 and 31**

1. Disconnect the negative battery cable.
2. Drain and recycle the engine coolant, to a level below the sensor.

✳✳ CAUTION

Never open, service or drain the radiator or cooling system when hot; serious burns can occur from the steam and hot coolant. In addition, when draining engine coolant, keep in mind that cats and dogs are attracted to ethylene glycol antifreeze and could drink any that is left in an uncovered container or in puddles on the ground. This will prove fatal in sufficient quantities. Always drain coolant into a sealable container. Coolant should be reused unless it is contaminated or is several years old.

3. Detach the ECT sensor electrical connector.
4. Unthread and remove the ECT sensor from the thermostat housing.
   To install:
5. Coat the sensor threads with a suitable Teflon® sealant.

6. Thread the sensor into position and tighten securely.
7. Attach the ECT sensor connector.
8. Connect the negative battery cable.
9. Refill the engine cooling system.
10. Start the engine and check for coolant leaks.
11. Bleed the cooling system as necessary.

Intake Air Temperature Sensor

OPERATION

▶ **See Figure 32**

The Intake Air Temperature (IAT) Sensor is used by the ECM/PCM to monitor the air temperature inside the intake manifold. The resistance decreases as the air temperature increases. This provides a signal to the ECM/PCM indicating the temperature of the incoming air charge. This sensor helps the ECM/PCM to determine spark timing and the air-to-fuel ratio. Information from this sensor is added to the pressure sensor information to calculate the density of the air mass being sent to the cylinders.

TESTING

▶ **See Figures 33 and 34**

1. Turn the ignition switch **OFF**.
2. Disconnect the wiring harness from the IAT sensor.
3. Measure the resistance between the sensor terminals.

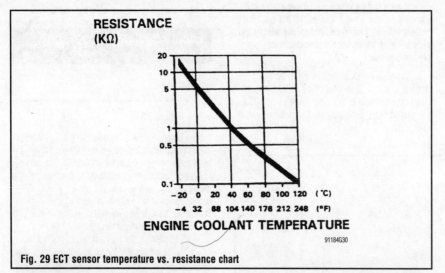

RESISTANCE (KΩ)

ENGINE COOLANT TEMPERATURE

91184G30

Fig. 29 ECT sensor temperature vs. resistance chart

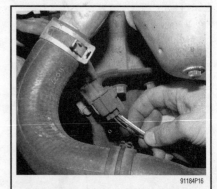

91184P16

Fig. 30 Unplug the ECT sensor electrical connector . . .

91184P17

Fig. 31 . . . then remove the ECT sensor from the thermostat housing

91054P41

Fig. 32 The tip of the IAT sensor has an exposed thermistor that changes the resistance of the sensor. The resistance decreases as the air temperature increases

91054P09

Fig. 33 The IAT sensor can be monitored with an appropriate and Data-stream scan tool

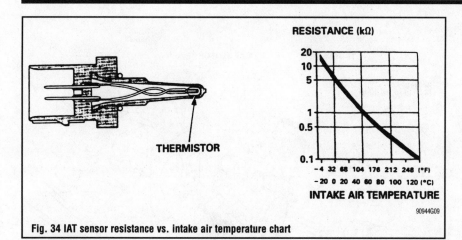

Fig. 34 IAT sensor resistance vs. intake air temperature chart

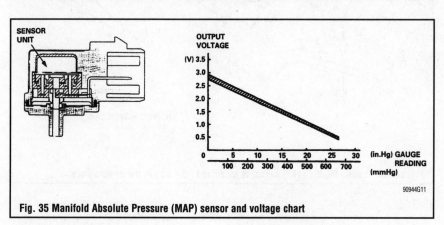

Fig. 35 Manifold Absolute Pressure (MAP) sensor and voltage chart

4. Compare the resistance reading with the accompanying chart.

5. If the resistance is not within specification, the IAT may be faulty.

6. Connect the wiring harness to the sensor.

REMOVAL & INSTALLATION

1. Disconnect the negative battery cable.
2. Detach the IAT sensor electrical connector.
3. Remove the retaining screws from the sensor (some models may unscrew from the manifold).
4. Remove the IAT sensor from the intake manifold.

To install:

5. Coat the sensor threads with a suitable Teflon® sealant.
6. Install the sensor into the intake manifold.
7. Attach the connectors to the IAT sensor.
8. Connect the negative battery cable.

Manifold Absolute Pressure Sensor

OPERATION

▶ See Figure 35

The Manifold Absolute Pressure (MAP) sensor measures and converts intake manifold vacuum into a voltage signal. The higher the vacuum, the lower the voltage signal that is sent to the ECM/PCM. The range of operation of the MAP sensor varies from approximately 0.5–3.0 volts. The ECM/PCM com-

pares the Throttle Position (TP) sensor with the MAP sensor readings to verify proper operation. Any discrepancy between the MAP sensor and the TP sensor is likely to trigger the Malfunction Indicator Lamp (MIL). The MAP sensor provides the ECM/PCM information on engine load.

TESTING

▶ See Figure 35

1. Check the connection at the MAP sensor connector.
2. Check the terminals within the connector for corrosion or poor contacts causing high resistance.
3. Repair or replace electrical connections as necessary.
4. If code three is detected, an electrical problem in the system may be present.
5. Remove the electrical connector from the MAP sensor.
6. Turn the ignition key to the **ON** position.
7. Connect the positive lead of a voltmeter to the terminal No. 1, the leftmost electrical terminal.
8. Connect the negative probe to the terminal No. 2, the middle electrical terminal harness. Do not probe the MAP sensor side.
9. With the voltmeter connected properly there should be a 5 volts reference signal.

REMOVAL & INSTALLATION

▶ See Figure 36

1. Disconnect the negative battery cable.
2. Disconnect the MAP sensor vacuum lines.
3. Remove the mounting screws from the MAP sensor.
4. Remove the MAP sensor.
5. Installation is the reverse of removal.

Throttle Position Sensor

OPERATION

▶ See Figures 37 and 38

The Throttle Position (TP) sensor is a potentiometer that provides a signal to the ECM/PCM

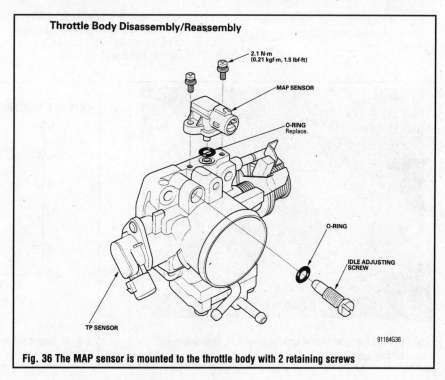

Fig. 36 The MAP sensor is mounted to the throttle body with 2 retaining screws

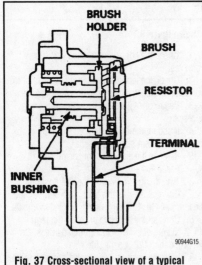

Fig. 37 Cross-sectional view of a typical Honda Throttle Position (TP) sensor

BRUSH HOLDER

BRUSH

RESISTOR

TERMINAL

INNER BUSHING

90944G15

that is directly proportional to the throttle plate position. The TP sensor is mounted on the side of the throttle body and is connected to the throttle plate shaft. The TP sensor monitors throttle plate movement and position, and transmits an appropriate electrical signal to the ECM/PCM. These signals are used by the ECM/PCM to adjust the air/fuel mixture, spark timing and if installed, EGR operation according to engine load at idle, part throttle, or full throttle. The TP sensor is not adjustable.

The TP sensor receives a 5 volt reference signal and a ground circuit from the PCM. A return signal circuit is connected to wiper that runs on a resistor internally on the sensor. The further the throttle is opened, the further the wiper moves along the resistor. At full throttle, the wiper essentially creates a loop between the reference signal and the signal return returning the full or nearly full 5 volt signal back to the PCM. At idle the signal return should be approximately 0.9 volts.

The ECM/PCM compares the TP sensor with the MAP sensor to determine if the system is functioning properly.

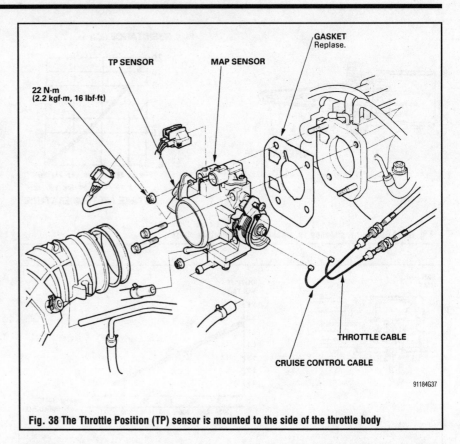

Fig. 38 The Throttle Position (TP) sensor is mounted to the side of the throttle body

22 N·m (2.2 kgf·m, 16 lbf·ft)

TP SENSOR

MAP SENSOR

GASKET Replase.

THROTTLE CABLE

CRUISE CONTROL CABLE

91184G37

TESTING

♦ See Figures 39 and 40

1. With the engine **OFF** and the ignition **ON**, check the voltage at the signal return circuit of the TP sensor by carefully backprobing the connector using a DVOM.

2. Voltage should be between 0.2 and 1.4 volts at idle.

3. Slowly move the throttle pulley to the Wide Open Throttle (WOT) position and watch the voltage on the DVOM. The voltage should slowly rise to slightly less than 4.8v at WOT.

4. If no voltage is present, check the wiring harness for supply voltage (5.0v) and ground (0.3v or less), by referring to your corresponding wiring guide. If supply voltage and ground are present, but no output voltage from TP, replace the TP sensor. If supply voltage and ground do not meet specifications, make necessary repairs to the harness or PCM.

REMOVAL & INSTALLATION

♦ See Figure 41

➡On some models, the TP sensor is not removable from the throttle body. If the TP

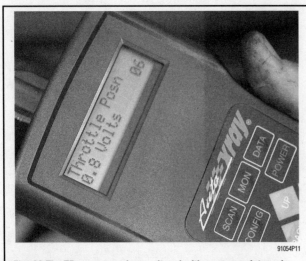

Fig. 39 The TP sensor can be monitored with an appropriate and Data-stream capable scan tool

91054P11

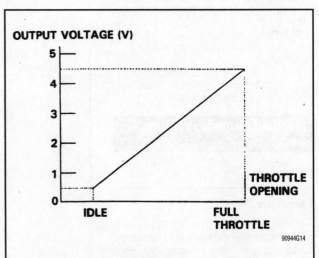

OUTPUT VOLTAGE (V)

THROTTLE OPENING

IDLE

FULL THROTTLE

90944G14

Fig. 40 Output voltage vs. throttle opening of a Throttle Position (TP) sensor

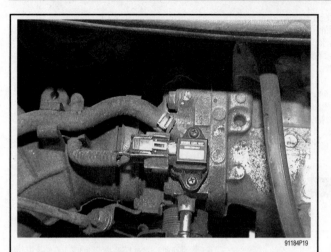

Fig. 41 On models such as this 1996 Accord, the TP sensor can be removed from the throttle body by detaching the wiring, then unfastening the mounting screws

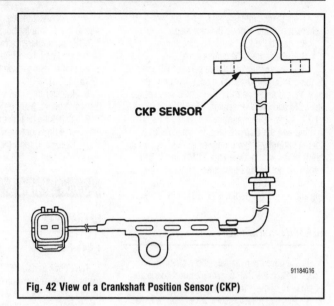

Fig. 42 View of a Crankshaft Position Sensor (CKP)

sensor goes bad, the entire throttle body must be replaced.

1. Disconnect the negative battery cable.
2. Unplug the wiring harness from the TP sensor.
3. Remove the two sensor mounting screws.
4. Pull the TP sensor off the throttle shaft.

To install:

5. Install the TP sensor onto the shaft.
6. Install and tighten the sensor mounting screws.
7. Attach the wiring harness to the sensor.
8. Connect the negative battery cable.

Crankshaft Position Sensor

OPERATION

♦ See Figures 42 and 43

The Crankshaft Position (CKP) sensor is used to monitor engine speed and determines the timing for the for the fuel injectors for each cylinder.

On some vehicles, the CKP sensor is integral with a Top Dead Center (TDC) sensor. The TDC sensor determines ignition timing at startup and also detects when crank angle is abnormal.

The CKP sensor is located behind the crankshaft pulley.

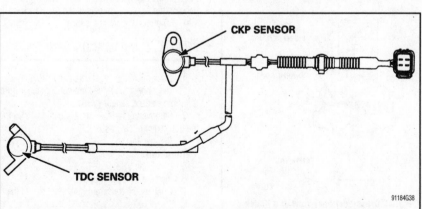

Fig. 43 On some models, the CKP sensor is integral with the TDC sensor as a single assembly

TESTING

4-Cylinder Engines

If the Diagnostic Trouble Code (DTC) PO335 and or PO336 is thrown, perform the following test.

1. Reset the Electronic Control Module (ECM).
2. Start the engine. Does the code reoccur? If so proceed on to the next step. If not, the problem is intermittent and you should check for loose connections and poor grounds.
3. Position the ignition switch in the **OFF** position.
4. Detach the Crankshaft Position (CKP)/Top Dead Center (TDC) sensor electrical connector.
5. Measure the resistance between the terminals.
6. The resistance should measure, as follows:
   a. 1996 Accord: 0.5–1.0 kohms.
   b. 1979–00 Accord: 1,850–2,450 ohms.
   c. Prelude: 1.2–3.2 kohms.
7. If the resistance is not in the above specified range, replace the sensor.

V6 Engines

2.7L ENGINE

If the Diagnostic Trouble Code (DTC) PO335 and or PO336 is thrown, perform the following test.

1. Reset the Electronic Control Module (ECM), as outlined under clearing codes later in this section.
2. Start the engine. Does the code reoccur? If so proceed on to the next step. If not, the problem is intermittent and you should check for loose connections and poor grounds.
3. Turn the ignition switch **OFF**.
4. Detach the Crankshaft Position Sensor (CKP) 2-prong connector.
5. Check the resistance between terminals No. 1 and No. 2. Is there 1850–2450 ohms? If not, replace the sensor. If so, go on to the next step.
6. Check for ground between both terminals and the body of the vehicle.
7. Is there continuity? If so, replace the CKP sensor. If not, move on to the next step.
8. Attach the CKP sensor connector.
9. Detach the ECM connector "C".
10. Measure the resistance between B8 and B16. Is there 1850–2450 ohms? If so, move on to the next step. If not, repair the open in the wire between the ECM and the CKP sensor.
11. Check the continuity between the body ground and the ECM connector terminal B8. Is there continuity? If your answer is YES, repair the short in the wire between the ECM and the CKP sensor. If not, Honda recommends substituting a known good ECM. If the vehicle stops throwing the above code(s), replace the ECM with a new unit.

3.0L ENGINE

If the Diagnostic Trouble Code (DTC) PO335 and or PO336 is thrown, perform the following test.

1. Reset the Electronic Control Module (ECM), as outlined under clearing codes later in this section.
2. Start the engine. Does the code reoccur? If so proceed on to the next step. If not, the problem is intermittent and you should check for loose connections and poor grounds.
3. Turn the ignition switch **OFF**.
4. Detach the Crankshaft Position (CKP) sensor 2-prong connector.
5. Check the resistance between terminals No. 1 and No. 2. Is there 1850–2450 ohms? If not, replace the sensor. If so, go on to the next step.
6. Check for ground between both terminals and the body of the vehicle.

7. Is there continuity? If so, replace the CKP sensor. If not, move on to the next step.

8. Attach the CKP sensor connector.

9. Detach the ECM connector "C".

10. Measure the resistance between C8 and C9. Is there 1850–2450 ohms? If so, move on to the next step. If not, repair the open in the wire between the ECM and the CKP sensor.

11. Check the continuity between the body ground and the ECM connector terminal C8. Is there continuity? If your answer is YES, repair the short in the wire between the ECM and the CKP sensor. If not, Honda recommends substituting a known good ECM. If the vehicle stops throwing the above code(s), replace the ECM with a new unit.

REMOVAL & INSTALLATION

1. Remove the negative battery cable.

2. Detach the CKP sensor electrical connector at the front of the lower timing belt cover.

3. Remove the accessory drive belts. Refer to Section 1 for specific details on belt removal.

4. Remove the crankshaft pulley. Refer to

5. Remove the lower timing belt cover.

6. Remove the CKP sensor.

➡The CKP sensor is part of the Top Dead Center (TDC) Sensor on some models and must be replaced as an unit.

7. Install the CKP sensor in the reverse order of removal.

Cylinder Position Sensor

OPERATION

♦ See Figure 44

The Cylinder Position (CYP) sensor detects the position of the No. 1 cylinder as a reference for fuel injection to each cylinder. The CYP sensor is located in the lower distributor housing. If the CYP sensor in the distributor housing fails, the distributor ignition housing must be replaced.

REMOVAL & INSTALLATION

1. Remove the negative battery cable.

2. Remove the distributor cap leaving the wires attached and place aside.

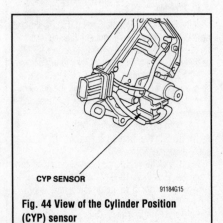

CYP SENSOR

91184G15

Fig. 44 View of the Cylinder Position (CYP) sensor

3. Disconnect the electrical connectors at the side of the distributor housing.

4. Make a reference mark between the distributor housing and the cylinder head and remove the distributor housing assembly.

To install:

5. Transfer the components not supplied with the replacement distributor housing assembly.

6. Install the distributor housing assembly in the reverse order of removal.

7. Check and reset the ignition timing as outlined in Section 1.

Knock Sensor

OPERATION

♦ See Figure 45

The Knock Sensor (KS) is used to monitor detonation in the combustion chamber. Detonation occurs when the fuel does not burn evenly and completely in the combustion chamber. Detonation is also referred to as pre-ignition, "engine knocks" or "engine pinging." Detonation can be caused by a variety of conditions including excessive ignition timing advance, excessive carbon build up in the combustion chamber, incorrect spark plug heat range and/or gap or using gasoline with too low of an octane rating.

To maximize the efficiency of the engine, a knock sensor is used to send a signal to the PCM. If a knock is detected, the PCM responds by adjusting the ignition timing until the "knock" stops. The sensor works by generating a signal produced by the frequency of the knock as recorded by the piezo-electric ceramic disc inside the KS. The disc absorbs the shock waves from the knocks and exerts a pressure on the metal diaphragm inside the KS. This compresses the crystals inside the disc and the disc generates a voltage signal proportional to the frequency of the knocks ranging from zero to 1 volt.

TESTING

Although the sensor is designed to detect internal engine knocks, a loose bracket or fastener near the sensor location could cause the sensor to mistake a loose bracket or fastener for an internal knock. A sensor that has come loose or has been replaced but over-tightened during installation,

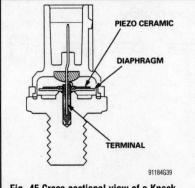

PIEZO CERAMIC

DIAPHRAGM

TERMINAL

91184G39

Fig. 45 Cross-sectional view of a Knock Sensor (KS)

could also cause an incorrect signal to be sent to the ECM/PCM.

There is real no test for this sensor, the sensor produces it's own signal based on information gathered while the engine is running. The sensors also are mounted on the side of the engine block near the cylinder head. The sensor can be monitored with an appropriate scan tool using a data display or other data stream information. Follow the instructions included with the scan tool for information on accessing the data. The only test available is to test the continuity of the harness from the PCM to the sensor and make sure all of the electrical connectors are clean and secure.

REMOVAL & INSTALLATION

1. Disconnect the negative battery cable.

2. Locate the sensor installed in the side of the engine block. If the vehicle needs to be raised, raise and securely support the vehicle in a safe manner.

3. Unplug the sensor connector.

4. Using the proper size socket, loosen and remove the knock sensor.

To install:

5. Carefully thread the sensor into the engine block.

6. Tighten the sensor to 23 ft. lbs. (31 Nm).

7. Attach the sensor connector.

8. Lower the vehicle if raised for accessibility.

9. Connect the negative battery cable.

Vehicle Speed Sensor

OPERATION

The Vehicle Speed Sensor (VSS) is a magnetic pick-up sensor that sends a signal to the Powertrain Control Module (PCM) and the speedometer. The sensor measures the rotation of the output shaft on the transaxle and sends an AC voltage signal to the PCM that determines the corresponding vehicle speed.

TESTING

1. Disconnect the negative battery cable.

2. Disengage the wiring harness connector from the VSS.

3. Using a Digital Volt-Ohmmeter (DVOM), measure the resistance (ohmmeter function) between the sensor terminals. If the resistance is 190–250 ohms, the sensor is okay.

REMOVAL & INSTALLATION

1. Disconnect the negative battery cable.

2. Disconnect the three terminal connector from the vehicle speed sensor (VSS).

3. Remove the fasteners that secure the VSS to the transaxle housing assembly.

4. Remove the VSS.

To install:

5. Install the VSS.

6. Install the mounting bolts.

7. Connect the three terminal connector to the sensor.

8. Connect the negative battery cable.

COMPONENT LOCATIONS

UNDERHOOD EMISSIONS AND ELECTRONIC ENGINE CONTROL COMPONENT LOCATIONS—2.2L ENGINE

1. Electrical load detector
2. Throttle Position (TP) sensor
3. Manifold Absolute Pressure (MAP) sensor
4. Exhaust Gas Recirculation (EGR) valve
5. Vacuum port
6. PCV valve
7. Crankshaft Position (CKP) sensor
8. Primary oxygen sensor (located in the exhaust, before the catalytic converter)
9. Secondary oxygen sensor (located in the exhaust, after the catalytic converter)

UNDERHOOD EMISSIONS AND ELECTRONIC ENGINE CONTROL COMPONENT LOCATIONS—2.7L ENGINE

1. Electrical load detector
2. Control box
3. Crankshaft Position (CKP) sensor (located behind the timing cover)
4. Top Dead Center (TDC) position sensor
5. Intake Air Temperature (IAT) sensor
6. Secondary heated oxygen sensor
7. Manifold vacuum ports
8. Idle Air Control (IAC) valve
9. PCV valve
10. Evaporative emissions purge control solenoid valve
11. Exhaust Gas Recirculation (EGR) valve and lift solenoid
12. Manifold Absolute Pressure (MAP) sensor
13. Charcoal canister
14. Engine Coolant Temperature (ECT) sensor
15. Throttle Position (TP) sensor
16. Ignition control module (located inside the distributor housing)
17. Intake air bypass solenoid

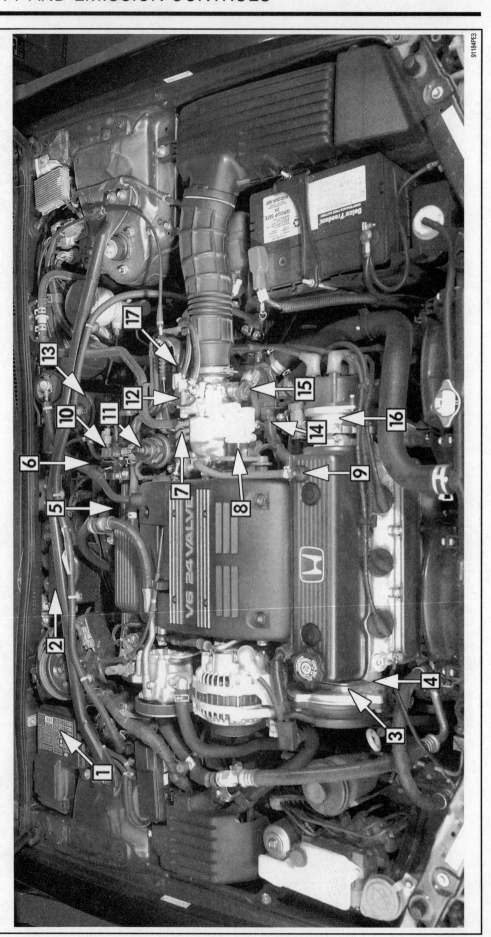

UNDERHOOD EMISSIONS AND ELECTRONIC ENGINE CONTROL COMPONENT LOCATIONS—3.0L ENGINE

1. Crankshaft Position (CKP) sensor
2. Top Dead Center (TDC) sensor #1
3. Top Dead Center (TDC) sensor #2
4. Secondary oxygen sensor (located in the exhaust, after the catalytic converter)
5. Primary oxygen sensor (located in the exhaust, before the catalytic converter)
6. Engine Coolant Temperature (ECT) sensor
7. PCV valve
8. Intake Air Temperature (IAT) sensor
9. Manifold Absolute Pressure (MAP) sensor
10. Throttle Position (TP) sensor
11. Idle Air Control (IAC) valve

9118RPE1

TROUBLE CODES

General Information

▶ See Figure 46

All Accord and Prelude models use an Engine Control Module/Powertrain Control Module (ECM/PCM) to control the fuel, ignition and emission systems of the engine. The ECM/PCM relies on a variety of sensors to evaluate the engine's operating condition. The ECM/PCM also has the ability to recognize when a sensor's value or input is beyond the normal operating range for that component.

If a sensor's wire is damaged, disconnected, or the sensor fails, the ECM/PCM receives an invalid signal for that sensor. The ECM/PCM has no idea what the cause of the problem is, however it does recognize that the signal is not within the acceptable operating range for that particular component. In order for the engine to run, the ECM/PCM will substitute a default value for the sensor that allows the engine to continue running, however the engine's performance and efficiency may be compromised. When this condition occurs, the ECM/PCM stores Diagnostic Trouble Codes (DTCs) into its fault memory.

If the condition is severe enough to cause potential damage to another component, the MALFUNCTION INDICATOR LAMP or the CHECK ENGINE LIGHT is turned on and the warning light remains on after the vehicle is started.

Diagnostic testing is done by checking the inputs and the outputs for the ECM/PCM control unit, and by accessing the fault memory of the ECM/PCM. The ECM used has on board diagnostic capabilities that are decoded by using the blink code method. All models covered are OBD-II compliant and the PCM fault memory is accessed by using a suitable OBD-II capable Data Scan Tool (DST), and the fault codes are displayed on the DST screen.

SCAN TOOLS

On all 1996–00 models, an OBD-II compliant scan tool must be used. To retrieve the Diagnostic Trouble Codes (DTCs). There are many manufacturers of these tools; a purchaser must be certain that the tool is proper for the intended use. A suitable good quality Data Scan Tool (DST) should come

with comprehensive instructions on its proper use. Be sure to follow the instructions that came with the unit if they differ from what is provided in this manual.

The scan tool allows any stored codes to be read from the ECM/PCM memory. The tool also allows the operator to view the data being sent to the computer control module while the engine is running. This ability has obvious diagnostic advantages; as the use of the scan tool is frequently required for component testing. The scan tool makes collecting information easier; however, an operator familiar with the system must correctly interpret the data.

An example of the usefulness of the scan tool may be seen in the case of a temperature sensor, which has changed its electrical characteristics. The ECM/PCM is reacting to an apparently warmer engine (causing a driveability problem), but the sensor's voltage has not changed enough to set a fault code. Connecting the scan tool, the voltage signal being sent to the ECM/PCM may be viewed; and comparison to normal values or a known good vehicle reveals the problem quickly.

ELECTRICAL TOOLS

The most commonly required electrical diagnostic tool is the digital multimeter, allowing voltage, ohms (resistance) and amperage to be read by one instrument. The multimeter must be a high-impedance unit, with 10 megohms of impedance in the voltmeter. This type of meter will not place an additional load on the circuit it is testing; which is extremely important in low voltage circuits. The multimeter must be of high quality in all respects. It should be handled carefully and protected from impact or damage. Replace batteries frequently in the unit.

Other necessary tools include an unpowered test light, and electrical leads capable of back-probing electrical terminals without damaging them. A vacuum pump/gauge is also needed for checking some sensors, solenoids and valves.

Diagnosis and Testing

Diagnosis of a driveability and/or emissions problems requires attention to detail and following the diagnostic procedures in the correct order. Resist the temptation to perform any repairs before performing the preliminary diagnostic steps. In many cases this will shorten diagnostic time and often cure the problem without electronic testing.

The proper troubleshooting procedure for these vehicles is as follows:

VISUAL/PHYSICAL INSPECTION

This is possibly the most critical step of diagnosis and should be performed immediately after retrieving any codes. A detailed examination of connectors, wiring and vacuum hoses can often lead to a repair without further diagnosis. Performance of this step relies on the skill of the technician performing it; a careful inspector will check the undersides of hoses as well as the integrity of hard-to-reach hoses blocked by the air cleaner or other component. Wiring should be checked carefully for any sign of strain, burning, crimping, or terminal pullout from a connector. Checking connectors at components or in harnesses is required; usually, pushing them together will reveal a loose fit.

INTERMITTENTS

If a fault occurs intermittently, such as a loose connector pin breaking contact as the vehicle hits a bump, the PCM will note the fault as it occurs and may energize the dash-warning lamp. If the problem self-corrects, as with the terminal pin again making contact, the dash lamp will extinguish after 10 seconds but a code will remain stored in the computer control module's memory.

When an unexpected code appears during diagnostics, it may have been set during an intermittent failure that self-corrected itself. These codes are still useful in diagnosis and should not be discounted.

CIRCUIT/COMPONENT REPAIR

The fault codes and the scan tool data will lead to diagnosis and checking of a particular circuit. It is important to note that the fault code indicates a fault or loss of signal in an ECM/PCM controlled system, not necessarily in the specific component. A sensor's wire may be shorted, corroded or disconnected, and though the actual sensor is operating properly, the signal received by the ECM/PCM is beyond specification.

Refer to the appropriate Diagnostic Code chart to determine the code's meaning. The component may then be tested following the appropriate component test procedures found in this section. If the component is OK, check the wiring for shorts or an open circuit. Sometimes a second opinion is valuable from an experienced driveability technician.

If a code indicates the ECM/PCM to be faulty and the ECM/PCM is replaced, but does not correct the problem, one of the following may be the reason:

• There is a problem with the ECM/PCM terminal connections: The terminals may have to be removed from the connector in order to check them properly.

• The ECM/PCM or PROM is not correct for the application: The incorrect ECM/PCM or PROM may cause a malfunction and may or may not set a code.

• The problem is intermittent: This means that the problem is not present at the time the system is being checked. In this case, make a careful physical inspection of all portions of the system involved.

• Shorted solenoid, relay coils or harness: Solenoids and relays are turned on and off by the ECM/PCM using internal electronic switches called drivers. Each driver is part of a group of four called Quad-Drivers. A shorted solenoid, relay coil or harness could cause an PCM to fail, and a replacement PCM to fail when it is installed.

• The Programmable Read Only Memory (PROM) may be faulty: Although the PROM rarely fails, it operates as part of the ECM/PCM. Therefore, it could be the cause of the problem. Substitute a known good PROM.

• The replacement ECM/PCM may be faulty: After the ECM/PCM is replaced, the system should

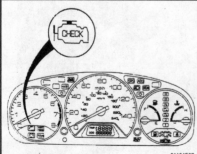

91184G07

Fig. 46 If a DTC is stored in the PCM, the Check Engine Light, or Malfunction Indicator Lamp (MIL) will illuminate

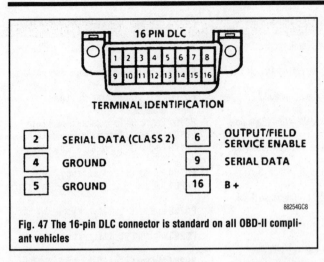

16 PIN DLC

TERMINAL IDENTIFICATION

2	SERIAL DATA (CLASS 2)	6	OUTPUT/FIELD SERVICE ENABLE
4	GROUND	9	SERIAL DATA
5	GROUND	16	B +

Fig. 47 The 16-pin DLC connector is standard on all OBD-II compliant vehicles

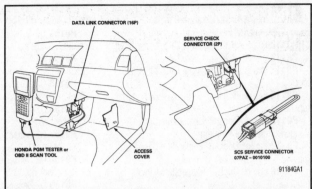

Fig. 48 On some models such as this Prelude, the Data Link Connector is located under the dash, on the passenger side of the vehicle near the center console

be rechecked for proper operation. If the diagnostic code again indicates the ECM/PCM is the problem, substitute a known good PCM. Although this is a very rare condition, it could happen.

Diagnostic Connector

▶ See Figures 47, 48 and 49

The 16-pin On Board Diagnostic version II (OBD-II) compliant Data Link Connector (DLC) is used to access the Diagnostic Trouble Codes (DTCs) using an OBD-II compliant Data Scan Tool (DST). It is an electrical connector with a gray housing located under the dash, either near the center console, on the passenger side of the vehicle or to the left of the driver side of the vehicle.

The two wire electrical connector with a blue housing next to the DLC is the Service Check Connector (SCS).

Reading Codes

▶ See Figures 48 and 49

On all 1996–00 models, an On Board Diagnostic version II (OBD-II) compliant Data Scan Tool (DST) must be used to retrieve the Diagnostic Trouble Codes (DTCs). Follow the DST manufacturer's

instructions on how to connect the scan tool to the vehicle and how to retrieve the DTCs.

Clearing Codes

▶ See Figure 50

The Diagnostic Trouble Codes (DTCs) can be cleared using one of two methods. A suitable On Board Diagnostic version II (OBD-II) Data Scan Tool (DST) can be used to clear the DTCs or the Back-Up Radio (clock) fuse can be removed to clear the codes.

The advantage of using a DST is that all of the stored fault codes can be read before clearing them. This may be handy for future diagnostic purposes. When clearing the stored DTCs by removing the fuse, all of the codes are cleared at one time. Once the codes are cleared, the stored information is lost.

To clear the DTCs using a Data Scan Tool (DST), connect the tool and proceed, following the tool manufacturer's directions.

✷✷ WARNING

The ignition switch must be OFF any time power is disconnected or restored to the ECM/PCM. Severe damage may result if this precaution is not observed.

To clear the stored DTCs by removing the clock fuse, perform the following:
1. Locate the 7.5 amp **BACK-UP** (Radio) fuse.
2. Turn the ignition switch to the **OFF** position
3. Remove the fuse for 10 seconds, then reinstall the fuse.

Diagnostic Trouble Codes

The following is a list of On Board Diagnostic version II (OBD-II) Diagnostic Trouble Codes (DTCs).

P0000 No Failures
P0100 Mass or Volume Air Flow Circuit Malfunction
P0101 Mass or Volume Air Flow Circuit Range/Performance Problem
P0102 Mass or Volume Air Flow Circuit Low Input
P0103 Mass or Volume Air Flow Circuit High Input
P0104 Mass or Volume Air Flow Circuit Intermittent
P0105 Manifold Absolute Pressure/Barometric Pressure Circuit Malfunction
P0106 Manifold Absolute Pressure/Barometric Pressure Circuit Range/Performance Problem
P0107 Manifold Absolute Pressure/Barometric Pressure Circuit Low Input
P0108 Manifold Absolute Pressure/Barometric Pressure Circuit High Input
P0109 Manifold Absolute Pressure/Barometric Pressure Circuit Intermittent

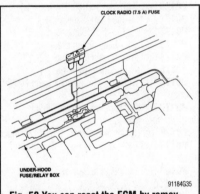

Fig. 50 You can reset the ECM by removing the clock radio fuse for 10 seconds

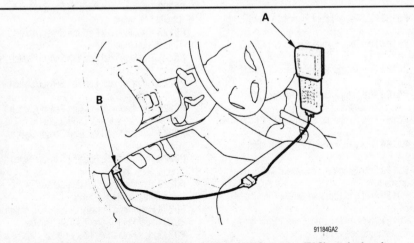

Fig. 49 On other models such as this Accord, the Data Link Connector (DLC) can be found under the dash, toward the left of the driver's side footwell

P0110 Intake Air Temperature Circuit Malfunction
P0111 Intake Air Temperature Circuit Range/Performance Problem
P0112 Intake Air Temperature Circuit Low Input
P0113 Intake Air Temperature Circuit High Input
P0114 Intake Air Temperature Circuit Intermittent
P0115 Engine Coolant Temperature Circuit Malfunction
P0116 Engine Coolant Temperature Circuit Range/Performance Problem
P0117 Engine Coolant Temperature Circuit Low Input
P0118 Engine Coolant Temperature Circuit High Input
P0119 Engine Coolant Temperature Circuit Intermittent
P0120 Throttle/Pedal Position Sensor/Switch "A" Circuit Malfunction
P0121 Throttle/Pedal Position Sensor/Switch "A" Circuit Range/Performance Problem
P0122 Throttle/Pedal Position Sensor/Switch "A" Circuit Low Input
P0123 Throttle/Pedal Position Sensor/Switch "A" Circuit High Input
P0124 Throttle/Pedal Position Sensor/Switch "A" Circuit Intermittent
P0125 Insufficient Coolant Temperature For Closed Loop Fuel Control
P0126 Insufficient Coolant Temperature For Stable Operation
P0130 O2 Circuit Malfunction (Bank no. 1 Sensor no. 1)
P0131 O2 Sensor Circuit Low Voltage (Bank no. 1 Sensor no. 1)
P0132 O2 Sensor Circuit High Voltage (Bank no. 1 Sensor no. 1)
P0133 O2 Sensor Circuit Slow Response (Bank no. 1 Sensor no. 1)
P0134 O2 Sensor Circuit No Activity Detected (Bank no. 1 Sensor no. 1)
P0135 O2 Sensor Heater Circuit Malfunction (Bank no. 1 Sensor no. 1)
P0136 O2 Sensor Circuit Malfunction (Bank no. 1 Sensor no. 2)
P0137 O2 Sensor Circuit Low Voltage (Bank no. 1 Sensor no. 2)
P0138 O2 Sensor Circuit High Voltage (Bank no. 1 Sensor no. 2)
P0139 O2 Sensor Circuit Slow Response (Bank no. 1 Sensor no. 2)
P0140 O2 Sensor Circuit No Activity Detected (Bank no. 1 Sensor no. 2)
P0141 O2 Sensor Heater Circuit Malfunction (Bank no. 1 Sensor no. 2)
P0142 O2 Sensor Circuit Malfunction (Bank no. 1 Sensor no. 3)
P0143 O2 Sensor Circuit Low Voltage (Bank no. 1 Sensor no. 3)
P0144 O2 Sensor Circuit High Voltage (Bank no. 1 Sensor no. 3)
P0145 O2 Sensor Circuit Slow Response (Bank no. 1 Sensor no. 3)
P0146 O2 Sensor Circuit No Activity Detected (Bank no. 1 Sensor no. 3)
P0147 O2 Sensor Heater Circuit Malfunction (Bank no. 1 Sensor no. 3)
P0150 O2 Sensor Circuit Malfunction (Bank no. 2 Sensor no. 1)
P0151 O2 Sensor Circuit Low Voltage (Bank no. 2 Sensor no. 1)

P0152 O2 Sensor Circuit High Voltage (Bank no. 2 Sensor no. 1)
P0153 O2 Sensor Circuit Slow Response (Bank no. 2 Sensor no. 1)
P0154 O2 Sensor Circuit No Activity Detected (Bank no. 2 Sensor no. 1)
P0155 O2 Sensor Heater Circuit Malfunction (Bank no. 2 Sensor no. 1)
P0156 O2 Sensor Circuit Malfunction (Bank no. 2 Sensor no. 2)
P0157 O2 Sensor Circuit Low Voltage (Bank no. 2 Sensor no. 2)
P0158 O2 Sensor Circuit High Voltage (Bank no. 2 Sensor no. 2)
P0159 O2 Sensor Circuit Slow Response (Bank no. 2 Sensor no. 2)
P0160 O2 Sensor Circuit No Activity Detected (Bank no. 2 Sensor no. 2)
P0161 O2 Sensor Heater Circuit Malfunction (Bank no. 2 Sensor no. 2)
P0162 O2 Sensor Circuit Malfunction (Bank no. 2 Sensor no. 3)
P0163 O2 Sensor Circuit Low Voltage (Bank no. 2 Sensor no. 3)
P0164 O2 Sensor Circuit High Voltage (Bank no. 2 Sensor no. 3)
P0165 O2 Sensor Circuit Slow Response (Bank no. 2 Sensor no. 3)
P0166 O2 Sensor Circuit No Activity Detected (Bank no. 2 Sensor no. 3)
P0167 O2 Sensor Heater Circuit Malfunction (Bank no. 2 Sensor no. 3)
P0170 Fuel Trim Malfunction (Bank no. 1)
P0171 System Too Lean (Bank no. 1)
P0172 System Too Rich (Bank no. 1)
P0173 Fuel Trim Malfunction (Bank no. 2)
P0174 System Too Lean (Bank no. 2)
P0175 System Too Rich (Bank no. 2)
P0176 Fuel Composition Sensor Circuit Malfunction
P0177 Fuel Composition Sensor Circuit Range/Performance
P0178 Fuel Composition Sensor Circuit Low Input
P0179 Fuel Composition Sensor Circuit High Input
P0180 Fuel Temperature Sensor "A" Circuit Malfunction
P0181 Fuel Temperature Sensor "A" Circuit Range/Performance
P0182 Fuel Temperature Sensor "A" Circuit Low Input
P0183 Fuel Temperature Sensor "A" Circuit High Input
P0184 Fuel Temperature Sensor "A" Circuit Intermittent
P0185 Fuel Temperature Sensor "B" Circuit Malfunction
P0186 Fuel Temperature Sensor "B" Circuit Range/Performance
P0187 Fuel Temperature Sensor "B" Circuit Low Input
P0188 Fuel Temperature Sensor "B" Circuit High Input
P0189 Fuel Temperature Sensor "B" Circuit Intermittent
P0190 Fuel Rail Pressure Sensor Circuit Malfunction
P0191 Fuel Rail Pressure Sensor Circuit Range/Performance
P0192 Fuel Rail Pressure Sensor Circuit Low Input

P0193 Fuel Rail Pressure Sensor Circuit High Input
P0194 Fuel Rail Pressure Sensor Circuit Intermittent
P0195 Engine Oil Temperature Sensor Malfunction
P0196 Engine Oil Temperature Sensor Range/Performance
P0197 Engine Oil Temperature Sensor Low
P0198 Engine Oil Temperature Sensor High
P0199 Engine Oil Temperature Sensor Intermittent
P0200 Injector Circuit Malfunction
P0201 Injector Circuit Malfunction—Cylinder no. 1
P0202 Injector Circuit Malfunction—Cylinder no. 2
P0203 Injector Circuit Malfunction—Cylinder no. 3
P0204 Injector Circuit Malfunction—Cylinder no. 4
P0205 Injector Circuit Malfunction—Cylinder no. 5
P0206 Injector Circuit Malfunction—Cylinder no. 6
P0207 Injector Circuit Malfunction—Cylinder no. 7
P0208 Injector Circuit Malfunction—Cylinder no. 8
P0209 Injector Circuit Malfunction—Cylinder no. 9
P0210 Injector Circuit Malfunction—Cylinder no. 10
P0211 Injector Circuit Malfunction—Cylinder no. 11
P0212 Injector Circuit Malfunction—Cylinder no. 12
P0213 Cold Start Injector no. 1 Malfunction
P0214 Cold Start Injector no. 2 Malfunction
P0215 Engine Shutoff Solenoid Malfunction
P0216 Injection Timing Control Circuit Malfunction
P0217 Engine Over Temperature Condition
P0218 Transmission Over Temperature Condition
P0219 Engine Over Speed Condition
P0220 Throttle/Pedal Position Sensor/Switch "B" Circuit Malfunction
P0221 Throttle/Pedal Position Sensor/Switch "B" Circuit Range/Performance Problem
P0222 Throttle/Pedal Position Sensor/Switch "B" Circuit Low Input
P0223 Throttle/Pedal Position Sensor/Switch "B" Circuit High Input
P0224 Throttle/Pedal Position Sensor/Switch "B" Circuit Intermittent
P0225 Throttle/Pedal Position Sensor/Switch "C" Circuit Malfunction
P0226 Throttle/Pedal Position Sensor/Switch "C" Circuit Range/Performance Problem
P0227 Throttle/Pedal Position Sensor/Switch "C" Circuit Low Input
P0228 Throttle/Pedal Position Sensor/Switch "C" Circuit High Input
P0229 Throttle/Pedal Position Sensor/Switch "C" Circuit Intermittent
P0230 Fuel Pump Primary Circuit Malfunction
P0231 Fuel Pump Secondary Circuit Low
P0232 Fuel Pump Secondary Circuit High
P0233 Fuel Pump Secondary Circuit Intermittent

P0234 Engine Over Boost Condition
P0261 Cylinder no. 1 Injector Circuit Low
P0262 Cylinder no. 1 Injector Circuit High
P0263 Cylinder no. 1 Contribution/Balance Fault
P0264 Cylinder no. 2 Injector Circuit Low
P0265 Cylinder no. 2 Injector Circuit High
P0266 Cylinder no. 2 Contribution/Balance Fault
P0267 Cylinder no. 3 Injector Circuit Low
P0268 Cylinder no. 3 Injector Circuit High
P0269 Cylinder no. 3 Contribution/Balance Fault
P0270 Cylinder no. 4 Injector Circuit Low
P0271 Cylinder no. 4 Injector Circuit High
P0272 Cylinder no. 4 Contribution/Balance Fault
P0273 Cylinder no. 5 Injector Circuit Low
P0274 Cylinder no. 5 Injector Circuit High
P0275 Cylinder no. 5 Contribution/Balance Fault
P0276 Cylinder no. 6 Injector Circuit Low
P0277 Cylinder no. 6 Injector Circuit High
P0278 Cylinder no. 6 Contribution/Balance Fault
P0279 Cylinder no. 7 Injector Circuit Low
P0280 Cylinder no. 7 Injector Circuit High
P0281 Cylinder no. 7 Contribution/Balance Fault
P0282 Cylinder no. 8 Injector Circuit Low
P0283 Cylinder no. 8 Injector Circuit High
P0284 Cylinder no. 8 Contribution/Balance Fault
P0285 Cylinder no. 9 Injector Circuit Low
P0286 Cylinder no. 9 Injector Circuit High
P0287 Cylinder no. 9 Contribution/Balance Fault
P0288 Cylinder no. 10 Injector Circuit Low
P0289 Cylinder no. 10 Injector Circuit High
P0290 Cylinder no. 10 Contribution/Balance Fault
P0291 Cylinder no. 11 Injector Circuit Low
P0292 Cylinder no. 11 Injector Circuit High
P0293 Cylinder no. 11 Contribution/Balance Fault
P0294 Cylinder no. 12 Injector Circuit Low
P0295 Cylinder no. 12 Injector Circuit High
P0296 Cylinder no. 12 Contribution/Balance Fault
P0300 Random/Multiple Cylinder Misfire Detected
P0301 Cylinder no. 1—Misfire Detected
P0302 Cylinder no. 2—Misfire Detected
P0303 Cylinder no. 3—Misfire Detected
P0304 Cylinder no. 4—Misfire Detected
P0305 Cylinder no. 5—Misfire Detected
P0306 Cylinder no. 6—Misfire Detected
P0307 Cylinder no. 7—Misfire Detected
P0308 Cylinder no. 8—Misfire Detected
P0309 Cylinder no. 9—Misfire Detected
P0310 Cylinder no. 10—Misfire Detected
P0311 Cylinder no. 11—Misfire Detected
P0312 Cylinder no. 12—Misfire Detected
P0320 Ignition/Distributor Engine Speed Input Circuit Malfunction
P0321 Ignition/Distributor Engine Speed Input Circuit Range/Performance
P0322 Ignition/Distributor Engine Speed Input Circuit No Signal
P0323 Ignition/Distributor Engine Speed Input Circuit Intermittent

P0325 Knock Sensor no. 1—Circuit Malfunction (Bank no. 1 or Single Sensor)
P0326 Knock Sensor no. 1—Circuit Range/Performance (Bank no. 1 or Single Sensor)
P0327 Knock Sensor no. 1—Circuit Low Input (Bank no. 1 or Single Sensor)
P0328 Knock Sensor no. 1—Circuit High Input (Bank no. 1 or Single Sensor)
P0329 Knock Sensor no. 1—Circuit Input Intermittent (Bank No. 1 or Single Sensor)
P0330 Knock Sensor no. 2—Circuit Malfunction (Bank no. 2)
P0331 Knock Sensor no. 2—Circuit Range/Performance (Bank no. 2)
P0332 Knock Sensor no. 2—Circuit Low Input (Bank no. 2)
P0333 Knock Sensor no. 2—Circuit High Input (Bank no. 2)
P0334 Knock Sensor no. 2—Circuit Input Intermittent (Bank no. 2)
P0335 Crankshaft Position Sensor "A" Circuit Malfunction
P0336 Crankshaft Position Sensor "A" Circuit Range/Performance
P0337 Crankshaft Position Sensor "A" Circuit Low Input
P0338 Crankshaft Position Sensor "A" Circuit High Input
P0339 Crankshaft Position Sensor "A" Circuit Intermittent
P0340 Camshaft Position Sensor Circuit Malfunction
P0341 Camshaft Position Sensor Circuit Range/Performance
P0342 Camshaft Position Sensor Circuit Low Input
P0343 Camshaft Position Sensor Circuit High Input
P0344 Camshaft Position Sensor Circuit Intermittent
P0350 Ignition Coil Primary/Secondary Circuit Malfunction
P0351 Ignition Coil "A" Primary/Secondary Circuit Malfunction
P0352 Ignition Coil "B" Primary/Secondary Circuit Malfunction
P0353 Ignition Coil "C" Primary/Secondary Circuit Malfunction
P0354 Ignition Coil "D" Primary/Secondary Circuit Malfunction
P0355 Ignition Coil "E" Primary/Secondary Circuit Malfunction
P0356 Ignition Coil "F" Primary/Secondary Circuit Malfunction
P0357 Ignition Coil "G" Primary/Secondary Circuit Malfunction
P0358 Ignition Coil "H" Primary/Secondary Circuit Malfunction
P0359 Ignition Coil "I" Primary/Secondary Circuit Malfunction
P0360 Ignition Coil "J" Primary/Secondary Circuit Malfunction
P0361 Ignition Coil "K" Primary/Secondary Circuit Malfunction
P0362 Ignition Coil "L" Primary/Secondary Circuit Malfunction
P0370 Timing Reference High Resolution Signal "A" Malfunction
P0371 Timing Reference High Resolution Signal "A" Too Many Pulses
P0372 Timing Reference High Resolution Signal "A" Too Few Pulses

P0373 Timing Reference High Resolution Signal "A" Intermittent/Erratic Pulses
P0374 Timing Reference High Resolution Signal "A" No Pulses
P0375 Timing Reference High Resolution Signal "B" Malfunction
P0376 Timing Reference High Resolution Signal "B" Too Many Pulses
P0377 Timing Reference High Resolution Signal "B" Too Few Pulses
P0378 Timing Reference High Resolution Signal "B" Intermittent/Erratic Pulses
P0379 Timing Reference High Resolution Signal "B" No Pulses
P0380 Glow Plug/Heater Circuit "A" Malfunction
P0381 Glow Plug/Heater Indicator Circuit Malfunction
P0382 Glow Plug/Heater Circuit "B" Malfunction
P0385 Crankshaft Position Sensor "B" Circuit Malfunction
P0386 Crankshaft Position Sensor "B" Circuit Range/Performance
P0387 Crankshaft Position Sensor "B" Circuit Low Input
P0388 Crankshaft Position Sensor "B" Circuit High Input
P0389 Crankshaft Position Sensor "B" Circuit Intermittent
P0400 Exhaust Gas Recirculation Flow Malfunction
P0401 Exhaust Gas Recirculation Flow Insufficient Detected
P0402 Exhaust Gas Recirculation Flow Excessive Detected
P0403 Exhaust Gas Recirculation Circuit Malfunction
P0404 Exhaust Gas Recirculation Circuit Range/Performance
P0405 Exhaust Gas Recirculation Sensor "A" Circuit Low
P0406 Exhaust Gas Recirculation Sensor "A" Circuit High
P0407 Exhaust Gas Recirculation Sensor "B" Circuit Low
P0408 Exhaust Gas Recirculation Sensor "B" Circuit High
P0410 Secondary Air Injection System Malfunction
P0411 Secondary Air Injection System Incorrect Flow Detected
P0412 Secondary Air Injection System Switching Valve "A" Circuit Malfunction
P0413 Secondary Air Injection System Switching Valve "A" Circuit Open
P0414 Secondary Air Injection System Switching Valve "A" Circuit Shorted
P0415 Secondary Air Injection System Switching Valve "B" Circuit Malfunction
P0416 Secondary Air Injection System Switching Valve "B" Circuit Open
P0417 Secondary Air Injection System Switching Valve "B" Circuit Shorted
P0418 Secondary Air Injection System Relay "A" Circuit Malfunction
P0419 Secondary Air Injection System Relay "B" Circuit Malfunction
P0420 Catalyst System Efficiency Below Threshold (Bank no. 1)
P0421 Warm Up Catalyst Efficiency Below Threshold (Bank no. 1)

P0422 Main Catalyst Efficiency Below Threshold (Bank no. 1)

P0423 Heated Catalyst Efficiency Below Threshold (Bank no. 1)

P0424 Heated Catalyst Temperature Below Threshold (Bank no. 1)

P0430 Catalyst System Efficiency Below Threshold (Bank no. 2)

P0431 Warm Up Catalyst Efficiency Below Threshold (Bank no. 2)

P0432 Main Catalyst Efficiency Below Threshold (Bank no. 2)

P0433 Heated Catalyst Efficiency Below Threshold (Bank no. 2)

P0434 Heated Catalyst Temperature Below Threshold (Bank no. 2)

P0440 Evaporative Emission Control System Malfunction

P0441 Evaporative Emission Control System Incorrect Purge Flow

P0442 Evaporative Emission Control System Leak Detected (Small Leak)

P0443 Evaporative Emission Control System Purge Control Valve Circuit Malfunction

P0444 Evaporative Emission Control System Purge Control Valve Circuit Open

P0445 Evaporative Emission Control System Purge Control Valve Circuit Shorted

P0446 Evaporative Emission Control System Vent Control Circuit   Malfunction

P0447 Evaporative Emission Control System Vent Control Circuit Open

P0448 Evaporative Emission Control System Vent Control Circuit Shorted

P0449 Evaporative Emission Control System Vent Valve/Solenoid Circuit Malfunction

P0450 Evaporative Emission Control System Pressure Sensor Malfunction

P0451 Evaporative Emission Control System Fuel Tank Pressure Sensor Range/Performance

P0452 Evaporative Emission Control System Fuel Tank Pressure Sensor Low Input

P0453 Evaporative Emission Control System Fuel Tank Pressure Sensor High Input

P0454 Evaporative Emission Control System Pressure Sensor Intermittent

P0455 Evaporative Emission Control System Leak Detected (Gross Leak)

P0460 Fuel Level Sensor Circuit Malfunction

P0461 Fuel Level Sensor Circuit Range/Performance

P0462 Fuel Level Sensor Circuit Low Input

P0463 Fuel Level Sensor Circuit High Input

P0464 Fuel Level Sensor Circuit Intermittent

P0465 Purge Flow Sensor Circuit Malfunction

P0466 Purge Flow Sensor Circuit Range/Performance

P0467 Purge Flow Sensor Circuit Low Input

P0468 Purge Flow Sensor Circuit High Input

P0469 Purge Flow Sensor Circuit Intermittent

P0470 Exhaust Pressure Sensor Malfunction

P0471 Exhaust Pressure Sensor Range/Performance

P0472 Exhaust Pressure Sensor Low

P0473 Exhaust Pressure Sensor High

P0474 Exhaust Pressure Sensor Intermittent

P0475 Exhaust Pressure Control Valve Malfunction

P0476 Exhaust Pressure Control Valve Range/Performance

P0477 Exhaust Pressure Control Valve Low

P0478 Exhaust Pressure Control Valve High

P0479 Exhaust Pressure Control Valve Intermittent

P0480 Cooling Fan no. 1 Control Circuit Malfunction

P0481 Cooling Fan no. 2 Control Circuit Malfunction

P0482 Cooling Fan no. 3 Control Circuit Malfunction

P0483 Cooling Fan Rationality Check Malfunction

P0484 Cooling Fan Circuit Over Current

P0485 Cooling Fan Power/Ground Circuit Malfunction

P0500 Vehicle Speed Sensor Malfunction

P0501 Vehicle Speed Sensor Range/Performance

P0502 Vehicle Speed Sensor Circuit Low Input

P0503 Vehicle Speed Sensor Intermittent/Erratic/High

P0505 Idle Control System Malfunction

P0506 Idle Control System RPM Lower Than Expected

P0507 Idle Control System RPM Higher Than Expected

P0510 Closed Throttle Position Switch Malfunction

P0520 Engine Oil Pressure Sensor/Switch Circuit Malfunction

P0521 Engine Oil Pressure Sensor/Switch Range/Performance

P0522 Engine Oil Pressure Sensor/Switch Low Voltage

P0523 Engine Oil Pressure Sensor/Switch High Voltage

P0530 A/C Refrigerant Pressure Sensor Circuit Malfunction

P0531 A/C Refrigerant Pressure Sensor Circuit Range/Performance

P0532 A/C Refrigerant Pressure Sensor Circuit Low Input

P0533 A/C Refrigerant Pressure Sensor Circuit High Input

P0534 A/C Refrigerant Charge Loss

P0550 Power Steering Pressure Sensor Circuit Malfunction

P0551 Power Steering Pressure Sensor Circuit Range/Performance

P0552 Power Steering Pressure Sensor Circuit Low Input

P0553 Power Steering Pressure Sensor Circuit High Input

P0554 Power Steering Pressure Sensor Circuit Intermittent

P0560 System Voltage Malfunction

P0561 System Voltage Unstable

P0562 System Voltage Low

P0563 System Voltage High

P0565 Cruise Control On Signal Malfunction

P0566 Cruise Control Off Signal Malfunction

P0567 Cruise Control Resume Signal Malfunction

P0568 Cruise Control Set Signal Malfunction

P0569 Cruise Control Coast Signal Malfunction

P0570 Cruise Control Accel Signal Malfunction

P0571 Cruise Control/Brake Switch "A" Circuit Malfunction

P0572 Cruise Control/Brake Switch "A" Circuit Low

P0573 Cruise Control/Brake Switch "A" Circuit High

P0574 Through P0580 Reserved for Cruise Codes

P0600 Serial Communication Link Malfunction

P0601 Internal Control Module Memory Check Sum Error

P0602 Control Module Programming Error

P0603 Internal Control Module Keep Alive Memory (KAM) Error

P0604 Internal Control Module Random Access Memory (RAM) Error

P0605 Internal Control Module Read Only Memory (ROM) Error

P0606 PCM Processor Fault

P0608 Control Module VSS Output "A" Malfunction

P0609 Control Module VSS Output "B" Malfunction

P0620 Generator Control Circuit Malfunction

P0621 Generator Lamp "L" Control Circuit Malfunction

P0622 Generator Field "F" Control Circuit Malfunction

P0650 Malfunction Indicator Lamp (MIL) Control Circuit Malfunction

P0654 Engine RPM Output Circuit Malfunction

P0655 Engine Hot Lamp Output Control Circuit Malfunction

P0656 Fuel Level Output Circuit Malfunction

P0700 Transmission Control System Malfunction

P0701 Transmission Control System Range/Performance

P0702 Transmission Control System Electrical

P0703 Torque Converter/Brake Switch "B" Circuit Malfunction

P0704 Clutch Switch Input Circuit Malfunction

P0705 Transmission Range Sensor Circuit Malfunction (PRNDL Input)

P0706 Transmission Range Sensor Circuit Range/Performance

P0707 Transmission Range Sensor Circuit Low Input

P0708 Transmission Range Sensor Circuit High Input

P0709 Transmission Range Sensor Circuit Intermittent

P0710 Transmission Fluid Temperature Sensor Circuit Malfunction

P0711 Transmission Fluid Temperature Sensor Circuit Range/Performance

P0712 Transmission Fluid Temperature Sensor Circuit Low Input

P0713 Transmission Fluid Temperature Sensor Circuit High Input

P0714 Transmission Fluid Temperature Sensor Circuit Intermittent

P0715 Input/Turbine Speed Sensor Circuit Malfunction

P0716 Input/Turbine Speed Sensor Circuit Range/Performance

P0717 Input/Turbine Speed Sensor Circuit No Signal

P0718 Input/Turbine Speed Sensor Circuit Intermittent

P0719 Torque Converter/Brake Switch "B" Circuit Low

P0720 Output Speed Sensor Circuit Malfunction

P0721 Output Speed Sensor Circuit Range/Performance

P0722 Output Speed Sensor Circuit No Signal

P0723 Output Speed Sensor Circuit Intermittent

P0724 Torque Converter/Brake Switch "B" Circuit High

P0725 Engine Speed Input Circuit Malfunction

P0726 Engine Speed Input Circuit Range/Performance

P0727 Engine Speed Input Circuit No Signal

P0728 Engine Speed Input Circuit Intermittent

P0730 Incorrect Gear Ratio

P0731 Gear no. 1 Incorrect Ratio

P0732 Gear no. 2 Incorrect Ratio

P0733 Gear no. 3 Incorrect Ratio

P0734 Gear no. 4 Incorrect Ratio

P0735 Gear no. 5 Incorrect Ratio

P0736 Reverse Incorrect Ratio

P0740 Torque Converter Clutch Circuit Malfunction

P0741 Torque Converter Clutch Circuit Performance or Stuck Off

P0742 Torque Converter Clutch Circuit Stuck On

P0743 Torque Converter Clutch Circuit Electrical

P0744 Torque Converter Clutch Circuit Intermittent

P0745 Pressure Control Solenoid Malfunction

P0746 Pressure Control Solenoid Performance or Stuck Off

P0747 Pressure Control Solenoid Stuck On

P0748 Pressure Control Solenoid Electrical

P0749 Pressure Control Solenoid Intermittent

P0750 Shift Solenoid "A" Malfunction

P0751 Shift Solenoid "A" Performance or Stuck Off

P0752 Shift Solenoid "A" Stuck On

P0753 Shift Solenoid "A" Electrical

P0754 Shift Solenoid "A" Intermittent

P0755 Shift Solenoid "B" Malfunction

P0756 Shift Solenoid "B" Performance or Stuck Oft

P0757 Shift Solenoid "B" Stuck On

P0758 Shift Solenoid "B" Electrical

P0759 Shift Solenoid "B" Intermittent

P0760 Shift Solenoid "C" Malfunction

P0761 Shift Solenoid "C" Performance Or Stuck Oft

P0762 Shift Solenoid "C" Stuck On

P0763 Shift Solenoid "C" Electrical

P0764 Shift Solenoid "C" Intermittent

P0765 Shift Solenoid "D" Malfunction

P0766 Shift Solenoid "D" Performance Or Stuck Oft

P0767 Shift Solenoid "D" Stuck On

P0768 Shift Solenoid "D" Electrical

P0769 Shift Solenoid "D" Intermittent

P0770 Shift Solenoid "E" Malfunction

P0771 Shift Solenoid "E" Performance Or Stuck Oft

P0772 Shift Solenoid "E" Stuck On

P0773 Shift Solenoid "E" Electrical

P0774 Shift Solenoid "E" Intermittent

P0780 Shift Malfunction

P0781 1–2 Shift Malfunction

P0782 2–3 Shift Malfunction

P0783 3–4 Shift Malfunction

P0784 4–5 Shift Malfunction

P0785 Shift/Timing Solenoid Malfunction

P0786 Shift/Timing Solenoid Range/Performance

P0787 Shift/Timing Solenoid Low

P0788 Shift/Timing Solenoid High

P0789 Shift/Timing Solenoid Intermittent

P0790 Normal/Performance Switch Circuit Malfunction

P0801 Reverse Inhibit Control Circuit Malfunction

P0803 1–4 Upshift (Skip Shift) Solenoid Control Circuit Malfunction

P0804 1–4 Upshift (Skip Shift) Lamp Control Circuit Malfunction

P1106 Barometric Pressure Circuit Range Performance Problem

P1107 Barometric Pressure Circuit Low Input

P1108 Barometric Pressure Circuit High Input

P1111 IAT Sensor Circuit Intermittent High Voltage

P1112 IAT Sensor Circuit Intermittent Low Voltage

P1114 ECT Sensor Circuit Intermittent Low Voltage

P1115 ECT Sensor Circuit Intermittent High Voltage

P1121 Throttle Position Lower Than Expected

P1122 Throttle Position Higher Than Expected

P1128 Manifold Absolute Pressure Lower Than Expected

P1129 Manifold Absolute Pressure Higher Than Expected

P1133 HO2S-11 Insufficient Switching (Bank 1 Sensor 1)

P1134 HO2S-11 Transition Time Ratio (Bank 1 Sensor 1)

P1153 HO2S-21 Insufficient Switching (Bank 2 Sensor I)

P1154 HO2S-21 Transition Time Ratio (Bank 2 Sensor 1)

P1171 Fuel System Lean During Acceleration

P1259 VTEC System Malfunction

P1297 Electrical Load Detector Circuit Low Input

P1298 Electrical Load Detector Circuit High Input

P1300 Random Misfire

P1336 Crankshaft Speed Fluctuation Sensor Intermittent Interruption

P1337 Crankshaft Speed Fluctuation Sensor No Signal

P1359 Crankshaft Position/Top Dead Center Sensor/Cylinder Position Connector Disconnected

P1361 Top Dead Center Sensor Intermittent Interruption

P1362 Top Dead Center Sensor No Signal

P1366 Top Dead Center Sensor2 Intermittent Interruption

P1367 Top Dead Center Sensor2 No Signal

P1381 Cylinder Position Sensor Intermittent Interruption

P1382 Cylinder Position Sensor No Signal

P1391 G-Acceleration Sensor Intermittent Low Voltage

P1390 G-Acceleration (Low G) Sensor Performance

P1392 Rough Road G-Sensor Circuit Low Voltage

P1393 Rough Road G-Sensor Circuit High Voltage

P1394 G-Acceleration Sensor Intermittent High Voltage

P1406 EGR Valve Pintle Position Sensor Circuit Fault

P1441 EVAP System Flow During Non-Purge

P1442 EVAP System Flow During Non-Purge

P1456 EVAP System Leak Detected (Fuel Tank)

P1457 EVAP System Leak Detected (Control Canister)

P1491 EGR Valve Lift Insufficient Detected

P1498 EGR Valve Lift Sensor High Voltage

P1508 Idle Speed Control System-Low

P1509 Idle Speed Control System-High

P1607 Powertrain Control Module Internal Circuit Failure A

P1618 Serial Peripheral Interface Communication Error

P1640 Output Driver Module 'A' Fault

P1676 FPTDR Signal Line Failure

P1678 FPTDR Signal Line Failure

P1705 Automatic Transaxle

P1706 Automatic Transaxle

P1709 Automatic Transaxle

P1738 Automatic Transaxle

P1739 Automatic Transaxle

P1753 Automatic Transaxle

P1768 Automatic Transaxle

P1773 Automatic Transaxle

P1790 PCM ROM (Transmission Side) Check Sum Error

P1792 PCM EPROM (Transmission Side) Check Sum Error

P1835 Kick Down Switch Always On

P1850 Brake Band Apply Solenoid Electrical Fault

P1860 TCC PWM Solenoid Electrical Fault

P1870 Transmission Component Slipping

VACUUM DIAGRAMS

▶ **See Figures 51 thru 60**

Following are vacuum diagrams for most of the engine and emissions package combinations covered by this manual. Because vacuum circuits will vary based on various engine and vehicle options,

always refer first to the vehicle emission control information label, if present. Should the label be missing, or should vehicle be equipped with a different engine from the vehicle's original equipment, refer to the diagrams below for the same or similar configuration.

If you wish to obtain a replacement emissions label, most manufacturers make the labels available for purchase. The labels can usually be ordered from a local dealer.

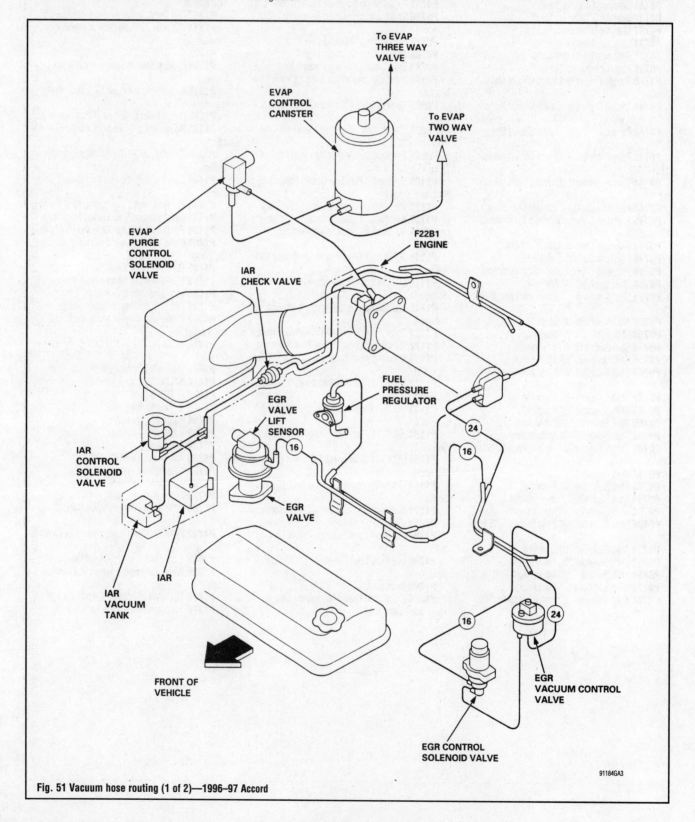

Fig. 51 Vacuum hose routing (1 of 2)—1996–97 Accord

91184GA3

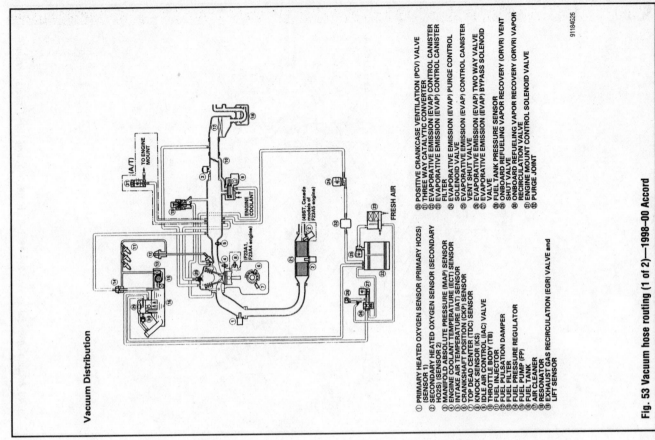

Vacuum Distribution

91184G26

① PRIMARY HEATED OXYGEN SENSOR (PRIMARY HO2S) (SENSOR 1)
② SECONDARY HEATED OXYGEN SENSOR (SECONDARY HO2S) (SENSOR 2)
③ MANIFOLD ABSOLUTE PRESSURE (MAP) SENSOR
④ ENGINE COOLANT TEMPERATURE (ECT) SENSOR
⑤ INTAKE AIR TEMPERATURE (IAT) SENSOR
⑥ CRANKSHAFT POSITION (CKP) SENSOR
⑦ TOP DEAD CENTER (TDC) SENSOR
⑧ IDLE AIR CONTROL (IAC) VALVE
⑨ KNOCK SENSOR (KS)
⑩ THROTTLE BODY (TB)
⑪ FUEL INJECTOR
⑫ FUEL PULSATION DAMPER
⑬ FUEL FILTER
⑭ FUEL PRESSURE REGULATOR
⑮ FUEL PUMP (FP)
⑯ FUEL TANK
⑰ AIR CLEANER
⑱ RESONATOR
⑲ EXHAUST GAS RECIRCULATION (EGR) VALVE and LIFT SENSOR

⑳ POSITIVE CRANKCASE VENTILATION (PCV) VALVE
㉑ THREE WAY CATALYTIC CONVERTER
㉒ EVAPORATIVE EMISSION (EVAP) CONTROL CANISTER
㉓ EVAPORATIVE EMISSION (EVAP) CONTROL CANISTER FILTER
㉔ EVAPORATIVE EMISSION (EVAP) PURGE CONTROL SOLENOID VALVE
㉕ EVAPORATIVE EMISSION (EVAP) CONTROL CANISTER VENT SHUT VALVE
㉖ EVAPORATIVE EMISSION (EVAP) TWO WAY VALVE
㉗ EVAPORATIVE EMISSION (EVAP) BYPASS SOLENOID VALVE
㉘ FUEL TANK PRESSURE SENSOR
㉙ ONBOARD REFUELING VAPOR RECOVERY (ORVR) VENT SHUT VALVE
㉚ ONBOARD REFUELING VAPOR RECOVERY (ORVR) VAPOR RECIRCULATION VALVE
㉛ ENGINE MOUNT CONTROL SOLENOID VALVE
㉜ PURGE JOINT

Fig. 53 Vacuum hose routing (1 of 2)—1998–00 Accord

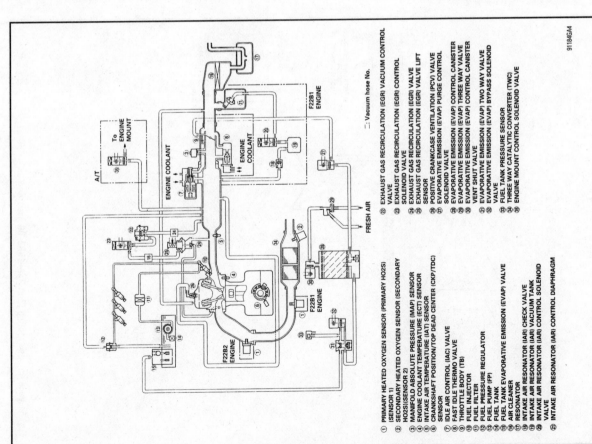

91184GA4

▭ : Vacuum hose No.

① PRIMARY HEATED OXYGEN SENSOR (PRIMARY HO2S) (SENSOR 1)
② SECONDARY HEATED OXYGEN SENSOR (SECONDARY HO2S) (SENSOR 2)
③ MANIFOLD ABSOLUTE PRESSURE (MAP) SENSOR
④ ENGINE COOLANT TEMPERATURE (ECT) SENSOR
⑤ INTAKE AIR TEMPERATURE (IAT) SENSOR
⑥ CRANKSHAFT POSITION/TOP DEAD CENTER (CKP/TDC) SENSOR
⑦ IDLE AIR CONTROL (IAC) VALVE
⑧ FAST IDLE THERMO VALVE
⑨ THROTTLE BODY (TB)
⑩ FUEL INJECTOR
⑪ FUEL FILTER
⑫ FUEL PRESSURE REGULATOR
⑬ FUEL PUMP (FP)
⑭ FUEL TANK
⑮ FUEL TANK EVAPORATIVE EMISSION (EVAP) VALVE
⑯ AIR CLEANER
⑰ RESONATOR
⑱ INTAKE AIR RESONATOR (IAR) CHECK VALVE
⑲ INTAKE AIR RESONATOR (IAR) VACUUM TANK
⑳ INTAKE AIR RESONATOR (IAR) CONTROL SOLENOID VALVE
㉑ INTAKE AIR RESONATOR (IAR) CONTROL DIAPHRAGM

㉒ EXHAUST GAS RECIRCULATION (EGR) VACUUM CONTROL VALVE
㉓ EXHAUST GAS RECIRCULATION (EGR) CONTROL SOLENOID VALVE
㉔ EXHAUST GAS RECIRCULATION (EGR) VALVE
㉕ EXHAUST GAS RECIRCULATION (EGR) VALVE LIFT SENSOR
㉖ POSITIVE CRANKCASE VENTILATION (PCV) VALVE
㉗ EVAPORATIVE EMISSION (EVAP) CONTROL CANISTER SOLENOID VALVE
㉘ EVAPORATIVE EMISSION (EVAP) THREE WAY VALVE
㉙ EVAPORATIVE EMISSION (EVAP) CONTROL CANISTER VENT SHUT VALVE
㉚ EVAPORATIVE EMISSION (EVAP) TWO WAY VALVE
㉛ EVAPORATIVE EMISSION (EVAP) BYPASS SOLENOID VALVE
㉜ FUEL TANK PRESSURE SENSOR
㉝ THREE WAY CATALYTIC CONVERTER (TWC)
㉞ ENGINE MOUNT CONTROL SOLENOID VALVE

Fig. 52 Vacuum hose routing (2 of 2) —1996–97 Accord

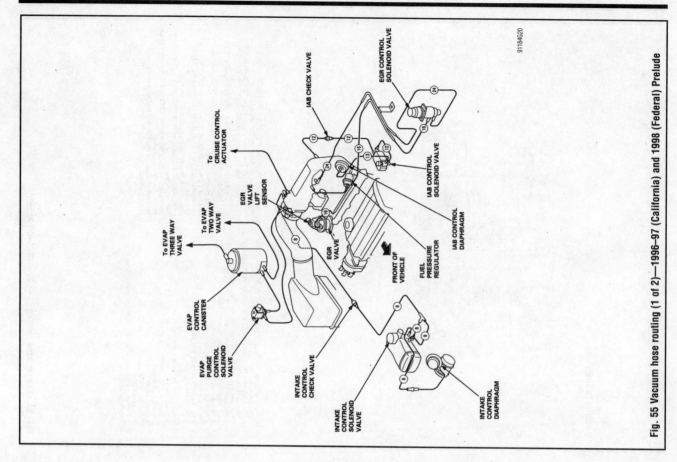

Fig. 55 Vacuum hose routing (1 of 2)—1996–97 (California) and 1998 (Federal) Prelude

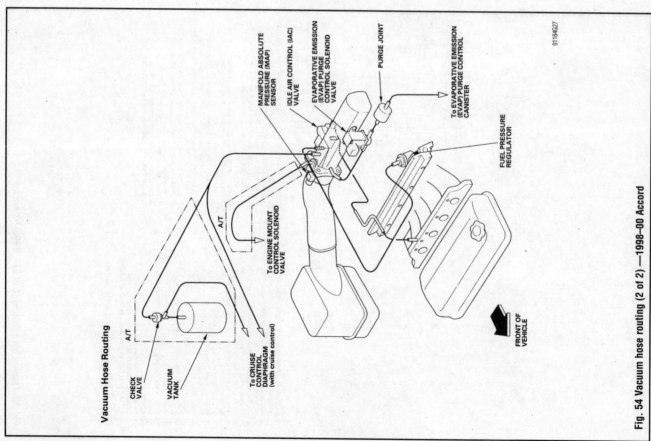

Fig. 54 Vacuum hose routing (2 of 2)—1998–00 Accord

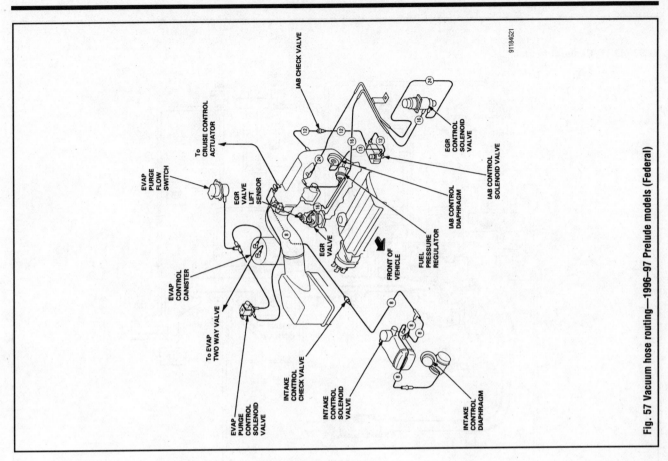

Fig. 57 Vacuum hose routing—1996-97 Prelude models (Federal)

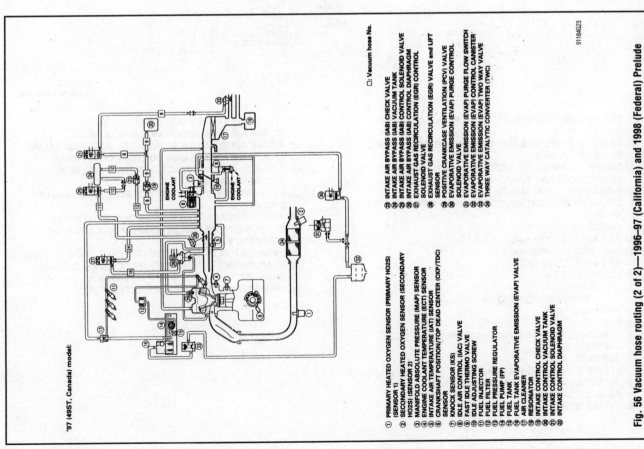

'97 (49ST, Canada) model:

① PRIMARY HEATED OXYGEN SENSOR (PRIMARY HO2S) (SENSOR 1)
② SECONDARY HEATED OXYGEN SENSOR (SECONDARY HO2S) (SENSOR 2)
③ MANIFOLD ABSOLUTE PRESSURE (MAP) SENSOR
④ ENGINE COOLANT TEMPERATURE (ECT) SENSOR
⑤ INTAKE AIR TEMPERATURE (IAT) SENSOR
⑥ CRANKSHAFT POSITION/TOP DEAD CENTER (CKP/TDC) SENSOR
⑦ KNOCK SENSOR (KS)
⑧ IDLE AIR CONTROL (IAC) VALVE
⑨ FAST IDLE THERMO VALVE
⑩ IDLE ADJUSTING SCREW
⑪ FUEL INJECTOR
⑫ FUEL FILTER
⑬ FUEL PRESSURE REGULATOR
⑭ FUEL PUMP (FP)
⑮ FUEL TANK
⑯ FUEL TANK EVAPORATIVE EMISSION (EVAP) VALVE
⑰ AIR CLEANER
⑱ RESONATOR
⑲ INTAKE CONTROL CHECK VALVE
⑳ INTAKE CONTROL VACUUM TANK
㉑ INTAKE CONTROL SOLENOID VALVE
㉒ INTAKE CONTROL DIAPHRAGM

☐: Vacuum hose No.

㉒ INTAKE AIR BYPASS (IAB) CHECK VALVE
㉓ INTAKE AIR BYPASS (IAB) VACUUM TANK
㉔ INTAKE AIR BYPASS (IAB) CONTROL SOLENOID VALVE
㉕ INTAKE AIR BYPASS (IAB) CONTROL DIAPHRAGM
㉗ EXHAUST GAS RECIRCULATION (EGR) CONTROL SOLENOID VALVE
㉘ EXHAUST GAS RECIRCULATION (EGR) VALVE and LIFT SENSOR
㉙ POSITIVE CRANKCASE VENTILATION (PCV) VALVE
㉚ EVAPORATIVE EMISSION (EVAP) PURGE CONTROL SOLENOID VALVE
㉛ EVAPORATIVE EMISSION (EVAP) PURGE FLOW SWITCH
㉜ EVAPORATIVE EMISSION (EVAP) CONTROL CANISTER
㉝ EVAPORATIVE EMISSION (EVAP) TWO WAY VALVE
㉞ THREE WAY CATALYTIC CONVERTER (TWC)

Fig. 56 Vacuum hose routing (2 of 2)—1996-97 (California) and 1998 (Federal) Prelude

'97 (49ST, Canada) model:

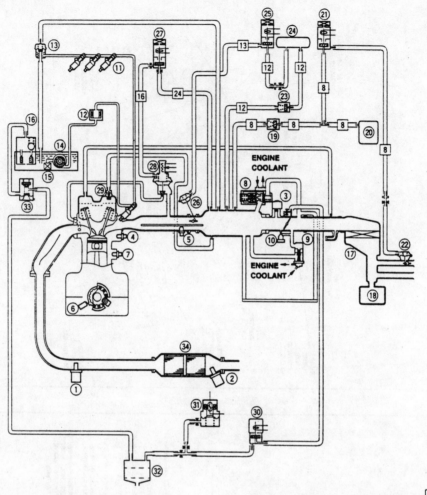

□: Vacuum hose No.

① PRIMARY HEATED OXYGEN SENSOR (PRIMARY HO2S) (SENSOR 1)
② SECONDARY HEATED OXYGEN SENSOR (SECONDARY HO2S) (SENSOR 2)
③ MANIFOLD ABSOLUTE PRESSURE (MAP) SENSOR
④ ENGINE COOLANT TEMPERATURE (ECT) SENSOR
⑤ INTAKE AIR TEMPERATURE (IAT) SENSOR
⑥ CRANKSHAFT POSITION/TOP DEAD CENTER (CKP/TDC) SENSOR
⑦ KNOCK SENSOR (KS)
⑧ IDLE AIR CONTROL (IAC) VALVE
⑨ FAST IDLE THERMO VALVE
⑩ IDLE ADJUSTING SCREW
⑪ FUEL INJECTOR
⑫ FUEL FILTER
⑬ FUEL PRESSURE REGULATOR
⑭ FUEL PUMP (FP)
⑮ FUEL TANK
⑯ FUEL TANK EVAPORATIVE EMISSION (EVAP) VALVE
⑰ AIR CLEANER
⑱ RESONATOR
⑲ INTAKE CONTROL CHECK VALVE
⑳ INTAKE CONTROL VACUUM TANK
㉑ INTAKE CONTROL SOLENOID VALVE
㉒ INTAKE CONTROL DIAPHRAGM

㉓ INTAKE AIR BYPASS (IAB) CHECK VALVE
㉔ INTAKE AIR BYPASS (IAB) VACUUM TANK
㉕ INTAKE AIR BYPASS (IAB) CONTROL SOLENOID VALVE
㉖ INTAKE AIR BYPASS (IAB) CONTROL DIAPHRAGM
㉗ EXHAUST GAS RECIRCULATION (EGR) CONTROL SOLENOID VALVE
㉘ EXHAUST GAS RECIRCULATION (EGR) VALVE and LIFT SENSOR
㉙ POSITIVE CRANKCASE VENTILATION (PCV) VALVE
㉚ EVAPORATIVE EMISSION (EVAP) PURGE CONTROL SOLENOID VALVE
㉛ EVAPORATIVE EMISSION (EVAP) PURGE FLOW SWITCH
㉜ EVAPORATIVE EMISSION (EVAP) CONTROL CANISTER
㉝ EVAPORATIVE EMISSION (EVAP) TWO WAY VALVE
㉞ THREE WAY CATALYTIC CONVERTER (TWC)

91184G24

Fig. 58 Vacuum hose routing—1997 Prelude models (Canadian)

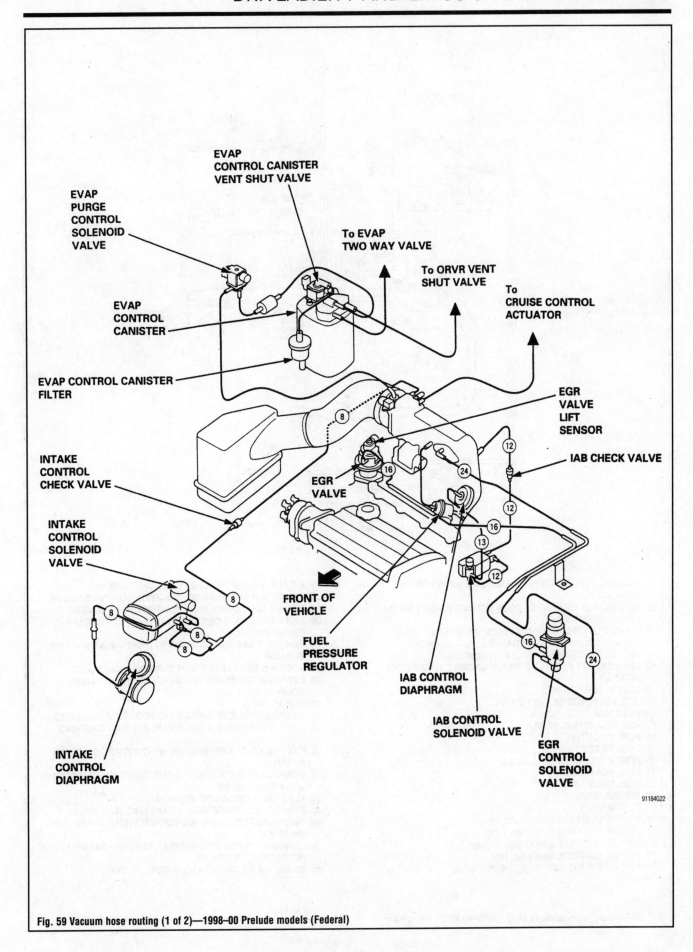

Fig. 59 Vacuum hose routing (1 of 2)—1998–00 Prelude models (Federal)

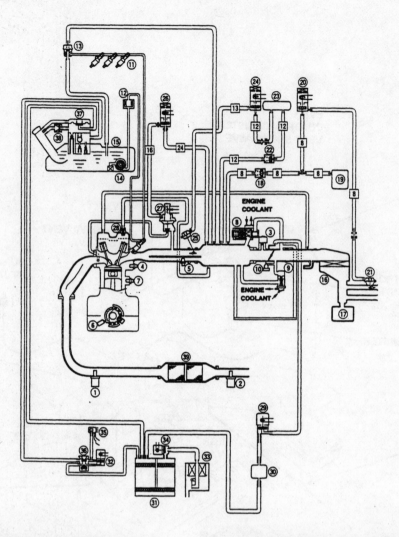

□: Vacuum hose No.

① PRIMARY HEATED OXYGEN SENSOR (PRIMARY HO2S) (SENSOR 1)
② SECONDARY HEATED OXYGEN SENSOR (SECONDARY HO2S) (SENSOR 2)
③ MANIFOLD ABSOLUTE PRESSURE (MAP) SENSOR
④ ENGINE COOLANT TEMPERATURE (ECT) SENSOR
⑤ INTAKE AIR TEMPERATURE (IAT) SENSOR
⑥ CRANKSHAFT POSITION/TOP DEAD CENTER (CKP/TDC) SENSOR
⑦ KNOCK SENSOR (KS)
⑧ IDLE AIR CONTROL (IAC) VALVE
⑨ FAST IDLE THERMO VALVE
⑩ IDLE ADJUSTING SCREW
⑪ FUEL INJECTOR
⑫ FUEL FILTER
⑬ FUEL PRESSURE REGULATOR
⑭ FUEL PUMP (FP)
⑮ FUEL TANK
⑯ AIR CLEANER
⑰ RESONATOR
⑱ INTAKE CONTROL CHECK VALVE
⑲ INTAKE CONTROL VACUUM TANK
⑳ INTAKE CONTROL SOLENOID VALVE
㉑ INTAKE CONTROL DIAPHRAGM
㉒ INTAKE AIR BYPASS (IAB) CHECK VALVE

㉓ INTAKE AIR BYPASS (IAB) VACUUM TANK
㉔ INTAKE AIR BYPASS (IAB) CONTROL SOLENOID VALVE
㉕ INTAKE AIR BYPASS (IAB) CONTROL DIAPHRAGM
㉖ EXHAUST GAS RECIRCULATION (EGR) CONTROL SOLENOID VALVE
㉗ EXHAUST GAS RECIRCULATION (EGR) VALVE and LIFT SENSOR
㉘ POSITIVE CRANKCASE VENTILATION (PCV) VALVE
㉙ EVAPORATIVE EMISSION (EVAP) PURGE CONTROL SOLENOID VALVE
㉚ PURGE JOINT
㉛ EVAPORATIVE EMISSION (EVAP) CONTROL CANISTER
㉜ EVAPORATIVE EMISSION (EVAP) BYPASS SOLENOID VALVE
㉝ EVAPORATIVE EMISSION (EVAP) CONTROL CANISTER FILTER
㉞ EVAPORATIVE EMISSION (EVAP) CONTROL CANISTER VENT SHUT VALVE
㉟ FUEL TANK PRESSURE SENSOR
㊱ EVAPORATIVE EMISSION (EVAP) TWO WAY VALVE
㊲ ONBOARD REFUELING VAPOR RECOVERY (ORVR) VENT SHUT VALVE
㊳ ONBOARD REFUELING VAPOR RECOVERY (ORVR) VAPOR RECIRCULATION VALVE
㊴ THREE WAY CATALYTIC CONVERTER (TWC)

91184G25

Fig. 60 Vacuum hose routing (2 of 2)—1998–00 Prelude (Federal)

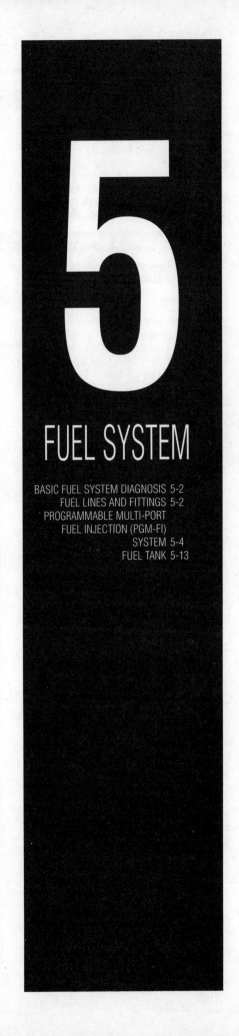

5

FUEL SYSTEM

BASIC FUEL SYSTEM DIAGNOSIS

When there is a problem starting or driving a vehicle, two of the most important checks involve the ignition and the fuel systems. The questions most mechanics attempt to answer first, "is there spark?" and "is there fuel?" will often lead to solving most basic problems. For ignition system diagnosis and testing, please refer to the information on engine electrical components and ignition systems found earlier in this manual. If the ignition system checks out (there is spark), then you must determine if the fuel system is operating properly (is there fuel?).

Of course when diagnosing a running or no-start condition, knowing the engine's mechanical condition is helpful. If the engine's mechanical condition is in good working order, the engine can be expected to run well if the fuel and ignition systems are up to par.

Some of the Honda vehicles covered in this manual do have mechanically adjusted valves; therefore, it is possible to have a "tight" valve contribute to a running problem. Establishing an engine's mechanical condition should be the first step in a logical diagnosis procedure.

FUEL LINES AND FITTINGS

✱✱ CAUTION

Do not smoke while working on the fuel system!

The fuel system is inter-connected using a network of lines and connectors. At times these connectors must be disconnected in order to properly repair the system. Pay careful attention to the following.

The fuel lines and fittings found on the Accord and Prelude models are one of four basic types.

• The conventional clamped fitting: A flexible fuel hose is installed over a fitting with a clamp to secure the hose to the fitting. The clamp is either spring loaded and released using a flat-nosed pliers, or mechanically tightened, requiring a screwdriver or related tool to loosen or tighten.

• The compression fitting: This type of fitting has a flared metal line that is installed through an externally threaded flare nut, or compressed collar called a ferrule installed over a metal or plastic line and held in place by an internally threaded flare nut. Because the line is flared or has a compressed ferrule installed on it, the threaded nut cannot be removed and is considered part of the pressure line assembly.

• The banjo bolt fitting: This fitting uses a hollow bolt that threads through a round hollowed out chamber with a hose fitting incorporated onto the chamber. The hollowed out chamber and hose fitting resemble the shape of a banjo, hence the name banjo bolt. The banjo bolt uses sealing washers on each side of the hollowed chamber that should be replaced during reassembly.

• The quick-connect fitting: These fittings allow the pipe and connector to be removed from one another by releasing a retainer tab and disconnect the fitting. They can be disconnected and reconnected quickly, and the fittings are an integral part of the fuel line.

Due to the construction of the fuel lines, acid may damage the integrity of the line. Replace the fuel tubing if there is any suspect of an acid or electrolyte contamination. When disconnecting the lines, be cautious not to twist the connectors. As always, replace any component if damaged.

Clamped Fittings

REMOVAL & INSTALLATION

▸ See Figures 1 and 2

The conventional clamped fitting is used when a flexible hose is installed over a fitting and clamped in place. This type of fuel fitting is found in a variety of locations and sizes throughout the vehicle, such as the fuel filler neck and Evaporative Canister hoses. The flexible fuel hose is installed over a fitting with a clamp to secure the hose to the fitting. The clamp is either spring loaded and released using a pliers, or mechanically tightened, requiring a screwdriver or related tool to loosen or tighten.

To remove a clamped type fitting, perform the following:

1. Release the clamp's tension and slide the clamp off the section of hose that is attached to the fitting.

2. Carefully slide the hose off the fitting.

To install:

3. Carefully slide the hose over the fitting.

4. Center the clamp over the middle of the section of hose covering the fitting.

5. Release the clamp or tighten as necessary.

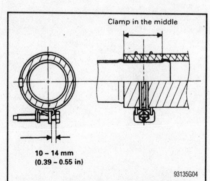

Fig. 1 The mechanically tightened clamp should be centered on the fitting and properly secured. Use care to not overtighten

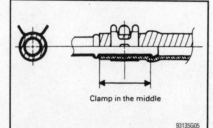

Fig. 2 The spring-loaded clamp is released by using flat-nosed pliers to squeeze the tabs together and slide the clamp off the clamped portion of the fitting

Compression Fittings

REMOVAL & INSTALLATION

▸ See Figures 3, 4, 5, 6 and 7

The compression fitting has a flared metal tube or a compression fitting that is surrounded by a threaded flare nut. Because the tube is flared or has a compression fitting installed, the threaded flare nut cannot be removed from the line and is considered part of the assembly.

Compression fittings are most often used when a pressure line attaches to an assembly, much like the fluid lines found at the brake master cylinder or on the inlet fuel line for the firewall-mounted fuel filter found on some Accord and Prelude models.

The compression fitting does not have a gasket or seal, rather it uses the threaded flare nut to seal the flared end of the line or a compression fitting on the line to the assembly. The flared end of the fuel line or the compression fitting is sealed between the component and the flare nut.

A compression fitting is most often found where the fluid in the line is under considerable pressure.

The flare nut is one of two types:

• The externally threaded flare nut: An example of this type of fitting is most easily seen on models where the flare nut is threaded into the brake master cylinder.

• An internally threaded flare nut: This type of fitting uses a compression fitting on the line and the nut threads onto a threaded fitting.

Fig. 3 An example of an internally threaded flare nut on this fuel line. Note the use of a flare nut wrench to loosen the nut while the component is held with another wrench

Fig. 4 The open-end wrench on the left compared to a flare nut wrench on the right. The slot allows the flare nut wrench to clear the line, yet will grip the flare nut on all 6 sides

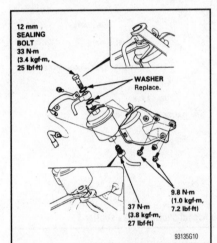

Fig. 7 An exploded view of the Honda firewall mounted fuel filter and mounting bracket. The filter outlet (Top) uses a banjo bolt fitting, the inlet (Bottom) is a compression fitting

To disconnect a fuel line using a compression fitting:

1. Hold the component that the flare nut is threaded onto securely, and using a flare nut type wrench, loosen the flare nut.

2. Installation is the reverse of the removal procedure.

Banjo Bolt Fittings

REMOVAL & INSTALLATION

▶ **See Figures 8 and 9**

The banjo bolt fitting has a hollow bolt that is installed through a round hollowed out chamber with a hose fitting incorporated onto the chamber. The hollowed out chamber and hose fitting resemble the shape of a banjo, hence the name banjo bolt. The banjo bolt uses a sealing washer on each side of the hollowed chamber that should be replaced during reassembly.

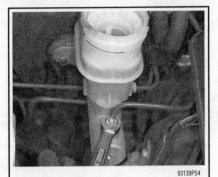

Fig. 5 An externally threaded flare nut is used on both fuel lines and hydraulic brake lines. A flare nut wrench is shown loosening the flare nut on a hydraulic brake line fitting

Banjo bolt fittings are used where the fluid in the fluid lines is under pressure.

To remove a banjo bolt type of fitting, perform the following:

1. Secure the component the banjo bolt is threaded into and loosen the banjo bolt using a boxed end wrench if room permits.

To install:

2. Using new sealing washer on either side of the banjo fitting, install the banjo bolt and carefully tighten to specification. The sealing washers should be slightly "crushed" between the banjo bolt the banjo fitting and the component.

Fig. 8 Use a box-end wrench to remove the banjo bolt fitting from the fuel rail–1996 Accord shown

Fig. 9 The outlet line of on a Honda firewall-mounted fuel filter uses a banjo bolt type fitting. Always use new sealing washers when reinstalling the banjo bolt

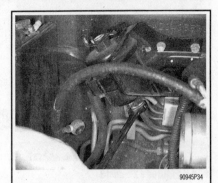

Fig. 6 The fuel inlet line on a Honda firewall mounted fuel filter is a compression fitting. The flare nut has external threads and is threaded into the bottom of the fuel filter

Quick-Connect Fittings

REMOVAL & INSTALLATION

▶ **See Figures 10 and 11**

A disconnected quick-connect fitting can be re-attached. The retainer on the mating pipe should not be reused once disconnected. It should be replaced when:
- Replacing the fuel pump.
- Replacing the fuel feed pipe.
- It has been removed from the pipe.
- It is damaged.

To disconnect a quick-connect fitting, perform the following:

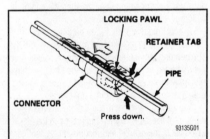

Fig. 10 Press both retainer tabs in to release the fuel line from the connector on quick-connect fittings

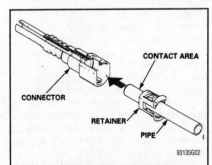

Fig. 11 Once separated, inspect the fuel line connector and replace the retainer. Coat the contact area of the pipe with a light coating of fresh engine oil

1. Properly relieve the fuel system pressure, as outlined later in this section.

2. Clean all dirt off the fuel system connectors before removal of the fitting.

3. Hold the connector with one hand, then pull the connector off with your other hand by pressing down on the retainer tabs.

4. Inspect the contact area of the connector for dirt and grime. If the surface is dirty, clean it. If the surface area is rusty or damaged, replace it.

5. To keep foreign material out of the fitting, cover the end of the line/fitting assembly with a plastic bag such as a sandwich style or locking freezer bag.

To install:

6. Insert a new retainer into the connector.

7. Apply a light coating of fresh engine oil to the fuel pipe.

8. Carefully press the fuel pipe into the connector making sure the retainer snaps in place completely.

9. Inspect for leakage and repair as necessary.

PROGRAMMABLE MULTI-PORT FUEL INJECTION (PGM-FI) SYSTEM

General Information

▶ See Figures 12 and 13

The fuel system includes components such as the fuel tank, fuel filler cap, fuel lines, a high-pressure fuel pump, PGM-FI main relay, filter, pressure regulator, injectors, and fuel pulsation damper. The fuel injection system delivers pressurized fuel to the injectors with the engine **ON** and cuts that fuel delivery when the engine is turned **OFF**.

The fuel is circulated in a pressurized loop from the fuel tank to the injectors and back to the fuel tank. That is why some of the components are labeled in and out, or feed and return, as the component must be installed properly. This is also useful when doing system diagnosis, because the fuel pressure characteristics could differ depending on where it is being checked.

The fuel is circulated in a loop so each fuel injector has a continuous supply of fuel. The fuel injectors are electrically operated and their operation is controlled by the Powertrain Control Module (PCM). Each injector has a small electromagnet, that when triggered by electricity, causes the injector to open and spray fuel. Sometimes an audible clicking noise can be heard from an electrically operated injector when the engine is running.

The fuel requirements for an engine differ depending on the temperature of the engine and the surrounding atmospheric conditions. A cold engine being started in freezing temperatures requires significantly more fuel to be delivered to the cylinders than a warm engine idling in a hot climate.

Any atmospheric condition that affects the amount of available oxygen molecules in the air also affects the needed fuel mixture for a gasoline engine. The amount of available oxygen molecules in the air is affected by both temperature and altitude, and the fuel injection system must be able to adapt to ensure the correct fuel delivery for the engine to run properly.

During a cold engine startup more fuel is needed to get the engine started. The fuel does not atomize efficiently on a cold engine, as the fuel tends to enter the combustion chamber in the form of small droplets, which are more difficult to ignite than an atomized vapor. Once the engine has reached operating temperature, the fuel is atomized into a highly combustible vapor by the engine's increased operating temperature. This fuel vapor is much more combustible than raw fuel droplets, therefore the engine needs less fuel to operate.

To accommodate the ever-changing fuel requirements for an engine to run and perform properly, the PCM must be capable of monitoring the atmospheric conditions and the engine's operating parameters.

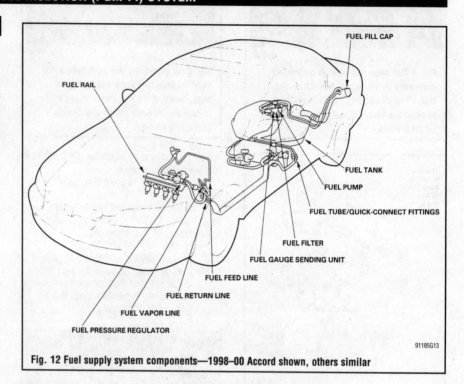

Fig. 12 Fuel supply system components—1998–00 Accord shown, others similar

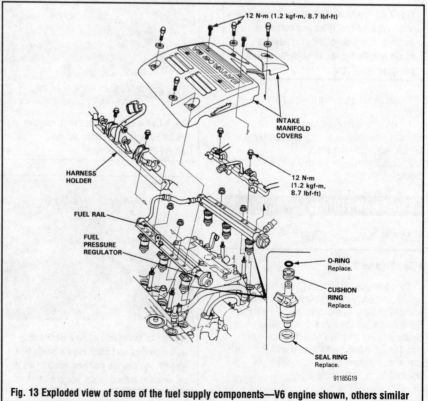

Fig. 13 Exploded view of some of the fuel supply components—V6 engine shown, others similar

The following engine related conditions affect fuel requirements:

- Engine operating temperature
- Engine speed (RPM)
- Throttle position
- Engine load

The following atmospheric conditions affect the engine's fuel requirements:

- Altitude
- Outside air (ambient air) temperature

Based on the information provided to the PCM via the input sensors, the PCM manages the fuel delivery by controlling the amount of time that it allows each injector to stay open. Because the fuel injectors are in a fuel loop where the pressure is relatively constant, the fuel mixture can be controlled by the amount of time a fuel injector stays open.

The added benefits of a precisely controlled fuel delivery system include:

- Reduced emissions
- Improved driveability
- Increased performance
- Improved fuel economy

The fuel injection system rarely requires maintenance and there are no routine adjustments to the fuel metering system that can be performed. Preventative maintenance tips that will help prolong the life of a fuel injection system include:

- Frequently inspect the air filter, and replace as needed
- Never operate the vehicle with a missing fuel filler cap
- Keeping the fuel system free of contaminants and debris
- Follow the recommended fuel filter replacement intervals
- Keep the fuel injector and engine management sensor wiring and connectors clean and dry

FUEL SYSTEM SERVICE PRECAUTIONS

Safety is an important factor when servicing the fuel system. Failure to conduct maintenance and repairs in a safe manner may result in serious personal injury. Maintenance and testing of the vehicle's fuel system components can be accomplished safely and effectively by adhering to the following rules and guidelines.

- To avoid the possibility of fire and personal injury, always disconnect the negative battery cable unless the repair or test procedure requires that battery voltage be applied.
- Always relieve the fuel system pressure prior to disconnecting any fuel system component (injector, fuel rail, pressure regulator, etc.), fitting or fuel line connection. Exercise extreme caution whenever relieving fuel system pressure to avoid exposing skin, face and eyes to fuel spray. Please be advised that fuel under pressure may penetrate the skin or any part of the body that it contacts.
- Always place a shop towel or cloth around the fitting or connection prior to loosening to absorb any excess fuel due to spillage. Ensure that all fuel spillage is quickly removed from engine surfaces. Ensure that all fuel soaked cloths or towels are deposited into a suitable waste container.
- Always keep a dry chemical (Class B) fire extinguisher near the work area.

- Do not allow fuel spray or fuel vapors to come into contact with a spark or open flame.
- Always use a backup wrench when loosening and tightening fuel line connection fittings. This will prevent unnecessary stress and torsion to fuel line piping. Always follow the proper torque specifications.
- Always replace worn fuel fitting O-rings. Do not substitute fuel hose where fuel pipe is installed.

Relieving Fuel System Pressure

❈❈ CAUTION

Be sure that the ignition switch is OFF before relieving the fuel system. Never work near an open flame, a source of sparks or smoke while working on the fuel system!

PROCEDURE

Accord

1996 4-CYLINDER ENGINES

▶ See Figure 14

1. Disconnect the negative battery cable.
2. Remove the fuel filler cap.

➡**Place a shop towel over the service bolt to absorb any fuel that may spray out as the bolt is loosened.**

3. Place a 6mm box-end wrench, over the service bolt on the fuel rail, while holding the banjo bolt with a back-up wrench.
4. Slowly loosen the service bolt one complete turn.
5. Always replace the service or banjo bolt sealing washers whenever the bolt is loosened.
6. After the fuel system pressure is relieved, tighten the bolt, install the fuel filler cap, then connect the negative battery cable.

1997 4-CYLINDER ENGINES

To relieve the fuel system pressure on these vehicles, please refer to the procedure for Prelude models.

Fig. 14 Using a back-up wrench, loosen the service bolt to relieve the fuel system pressure—1996 4-cylinder Accord shown

1996—97 V6 ENGINES

▶ See Figure 15

1. Disconnect the negative battery cable.
2. Remove the fuel filler cap.

➡**Place a shop towel over the service bolt to absorb any fuel that may spray out as the bolt is loosened.**

3. If equipped with a service bolt, place a 6mm box-end wrench, over the service bolt on the fuel filter, while holding the banjo bolt with a back-up wrench.
4. If not equipped with a service bolt, place a box-end wrench over the banjo bolt on the fuel filter.
5. Slowly loosen the service or banjo bolt one complete turn.
6. Always replace the service or banjo bolt sealing washers whenever the bolt is loosened.
7. After the fuel system pressure is relieved, tighten the service bolt to 9 ft. lbs. (12 Nm) or the banjo bolt to 25 ft. lbs. (34 Nm),
8. Install the fuel filler cap, then connect the negative battery cable.

1998—00 MODELS

▶ See Figure 16

1. Disconnect the negative battery cable.
2. Remove the fuel filler cap.
3. Use a wrench to loosen the fuel pulsation damper on the fuel rail near the throttle linkage.

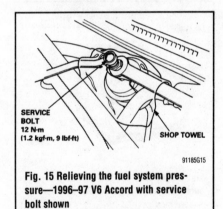

Fig. 15 Relieving the fuel system pressure—1996—97 V6 Accord with service bolt shown

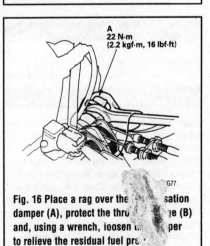

Fig. 16 Place a rag over the ___ sation damper (A), protect the thro___ ___e (B) and, using a wrench, loosen ___ ___per to relieve the residual fuel pr___

4. Place a shop towel over the fuel pulsation damper to absorb any fuel that may leak out as the damper is loosened.

5. Slowly unscrew the fuel pulsation damper one turn.

6. Always replace the sealing washer whenever the fuel pulsation damper loosened.

7. After the fuel system pressure is relieved, tighten the fuel pulsation damper, install the fuel filler cap, then connect the negative battery cable.

Prelude

▶ See Figure 17

➡This procedure also covers 1997 4-cylinder Accord models.

1. Disconnect the negative battery cable.
2. Remove the fuel filler cap.

➡Place a shop towel over the service bolt to absorb any fuel that may spray out as the bolt is loosened.

3. Using a 12mm box-end wrench, loosen the service bolt (sealing bolt) from the fuel rail.

4. Slowly unscrew the banjo bolt one turn.

5. Always replace the banjo bolt sealing washers whenever the bolt is loosened.

6. After the fuel system pressure is relieved, tighten the bolt to 16 ft. lbs. (22 Nm), install the fuel filler cap, then connect the negative battery cable.

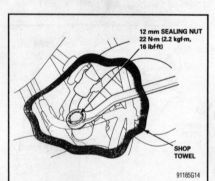

Fig. 17 Relieving the fuel system pressure—Prelude shown, 1997 4-cylinder Accord similar

Fuel Pump

REMOVAL & INSTALLATION

❊❊ CAUTION

Observe all applicable safety precautions when working around fuel. Whenever servicing the fuel system, always work in a well-ventilated area. Do not allow fuel spray or vapors to come in contact with a spark or open flame. Keep a dry chemical fire extinguisher near the work area. Always keep fuel in a container specifically designed for fuel storage; also, always properly seal fuel containers to avoid the possibility of fire or explosion.

Prelude

1996 MODELS

❊❊ CAUTION

The fuel injection system remains under pressure, even after the engine has been turned OFF. The fuel system pressure MUST BE relieved before disconnecting any fuel lines. Failure to do so may result in fire and/or personal injury.

1. Disconnect the negative battery cable.
2. Open the fuel tank filler cap to vent off pressure in the tank.
3. Relieve the fuel pressure, as outlined earlier in this section.
4. Remove the access panel in the trunk.
5. Detach the electrical connector from the fuel pump.
6. Remove the fuel pump mounting nuts.
7. Remove the fuel pump assembly from the tank.
8. Installation is the reverse of removal.
9. Torque the fuel pump mounting nuts to 4 ft. lbs. (6 Nm).

1997—00 MODELS

▶ See Figures 18 and 19

❊❊ CAUTION

The fuel injection system remains under pressure, even after the engine has been turned OFF. The fuel system pressure MUST BE relieved before disconnecting any fuel lines. Failure to do so may result in fire and/or personal injury.

1. Disconnect the negative battery cable.
2. Open the fuel tank filler cap to vent off pressure in the tank.
3. Relieve the fuel pressure, as outlined earlier in this section.
4. Remove the rear seat cushion.
5. Pull the carpet up.
6. Remove the rear floor beam.
7. Pull the access panel from the floor.
8. Remove the fuel pump wiring harness from the pump.
9. Using square-nosed pliers, squeeze the spring loaded fuel clamp tabs together to release

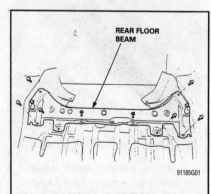

Fig. 18 You must remove the rear floor beam to get to the fuel pump access panel

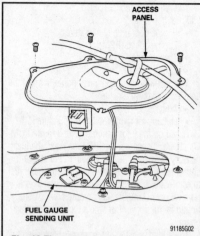

Fig. 19 The access panel is secured with retaining screws

the clamp's tension and slide the clamp down the fuel line.

10. Press the two tabs on the quick-connect fuel line in, and slide the fuel hose away from the fuel line.

11. Remove the 8mm nuts securing the fuel pump mounting plate to the fuel tank, and carefully extract the fuel pump assembly from the fuel tank.

❊❊ WARNING

Ensure that the battery is disconnected before any wires are removed.

12. Installation is the reverse of the removal procedure, making sure to replace the fuel pump mounting plate seal.

Accord

1996–97 MODELS

▶ See Figure 20

1. Remove the negative battery cable.
2. Remove the fuel tank as outlined later in this section.

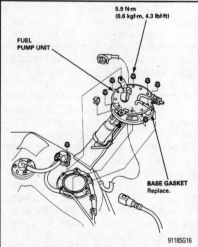

Fig. 20 Once the fuel tank is removed, unfasten the retainers, then remove the fuel pump from the tank

3. Detach the fuel pump electrical connector.
4. Remove the fuel pump mounting nuts.
5. Pull the pump from the tank.
6. Install the fuel pump in the reverse order of removal.
7. Torque the fuel pump mounting nuts to 4.3 ft. lbs. (5.8 Nm).

1998—00 MODELS

▶ See Figures 21 and 22

✳✳ CAUTION

The fuel injection system remains under pressure, even after the engine has been turned OFF. The fuel system pressure MUST BE relieved before disconnecting any fuel lines. Failure to do so may result in fire and/or personal injury.

1. Disconnect the negative battery cable.
2. Open the fuel tank filler cap to vent off pressure in the tank.
3. Relieve the fuel pressure, as outlined earlier in this section.
4. Open the trunk and remove the spare tire lid.
5. Remove the access panel from the floor.
6. Detach the fuel pump electrical connector.

✳✳ WARNING

Ensure that the battery is disconnected before any wires are removed.

7. Detach the fuel lines from the pump.
8. Unscrew the bolts and remove the fuel pump assembly.
9. If necessary, remove the bracket, the fuel filter, the fuel gauge sending unit, the hose, and the wire harness.
10. Installation is the reverse of the removal procedure, making sure to replace the fuel pump mounting plate seal.

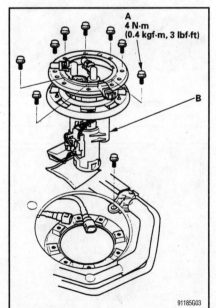

Fig. 21 Unfasten the fuel pump retaining bolts (A), then remove the fuel pump assembly (B) from the tank

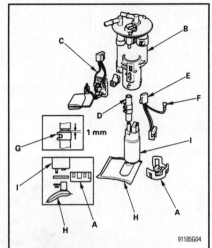

Fig. 22 Remove the bracket (A), the fuel filter (B), the fuel gauge sending unit (C), the hose (D), and the wire harness (E)

TESTING

Fuel Pump Circuit

If you suspect a problem with the fuel pump, listen for the pump to operate by removing the fuel fill cap and checking to see if the pump can be heard running during the first two seconds after the ignition key is turned to the **ON** position. You should hear the fuel pump motor run.

➡**If the fuel pump can be heard running, the fuel pump's electrical circuit is likely to be OK and the fuel pump operating pressure should be checked as outlined later in this section.**

Once the engine has started, the fuel pump operation is controlled by the Powertrain Control Module (PCM) via the PGM-FI Main Relay. The fuel pump receives its electrical power from the PGM-FI Main Relay, which is triggered for two seconds when the ignition switch is initially turned to the on position.

After the initial two-second startup signal is received, the PGM-FI Main Relay is controlled by the PCM. Because the fuel pump receives its power from the PGM-FI Main Relay, a problem with the ignition switch, PCM, or electrical wiring may not allow battery voltage to reach the pump.

To check the fuel pump wiring proceed as follows:
1. Make sure the ignition switch is in the **OFF** position.
2. Locate and detach the fuel pump electrical connector at the fuel tank.
3. You may have to remove the floor access panel. For specific details, see the fuel pump removal procedure in this section.
4. Fuel pump access is limited on some 1996–97 models of the Accord and may require you to work under the vehicle. Perform the following steps if that is the situation:
   a. Raise the vehicle and safely support it on suitable jackstands.
   b. Remove the protective cover from the fuel tank fuel hoses.
5. Detach the fuel pump electrical connector.
6. Connect a suitable Voltmeter between the fuel pump positive terminal of the electrical connector and a known good chassis ground.

7. Hold the electrical connector of the PGM–FI Main Relay so the wire side of the female terminals is visible and install a jumper wire between terminal Nos. 4 and 5.
8. When the ignition switch is turned **ON**, battery voltage should be present at the fuel pump electrical connector.
9. If the battery voltage is present, check the fuel pump's ground.
10. If the ground is "OK", check the fuel pump.
11. If battery voltage is not present, trace the wiring harness and check the cause for an open or shorted circuit.
12. If all wiring checks out, test the fuel pressure, as outlined later in this section.

Fuel Pump Pressure

The fuel pressure should be checked at the fuel rail or at the fuel feed line for the fuel rail. The fuel pressure is checked with the engine started, thus the fuel pressure gauge must not interrupt the flow of fuel to the fuel rail and the fuel injectors.

To attach a fuel pressure gauge to the pressurized fuel loop requires the use of an adapter that is capable of safely withstanding the fuel system fuel pressure.

✳✳ WARNING

Checking the fuel system fuel pressure requires the use of an in-line fuel pressure gauge with the engine running. Do not perform this check if suitable test equipment and fuel fittings are not available. The fuel system operates under pressure, if any fuel leakage is noticed while performing this check STOP immediately and do not continue until the source of the leak is resolved. Do not perform this test near sources of heat, spark, or flames. This test must be performed in a well-ventilated area.

✳✳ CAUTION

The fuel injection system remains under pressure, even after the engine has been turned OFF. The fuel system pressure MUST BE relieved before disconnecting any fuel lines. Failure to do so may result in fire and/or personal injury.

To check the fuel system pressure proceed as follows:
1. Remove the fuel filler cap and relieve the residual fuel pressure. For specific details, refer to the relieving fuel pressure coverage in this section.
2. Attach a suitable fuel pressure gauge to the fuel injection fuel loop as follows:

➡**Models such as the 1998—00 Accord have a fuel pulsation dampener which must be removed in place of the banjo bolt for testing.**

- 1996–97 Accord with 4-cylinder engines and 1996–00 Prelude: Remove the service/banjo bolt from the end of the fuel rail. Install the fuel pressure gauge using a suitable fitting to temporarily substitute for the banjo bolt or in place of the service bolt that will allow fuel to be supplied to the gauge and the fuel rail.

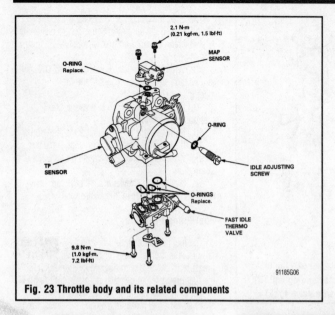

Fig. 23 Throttle body and its related components

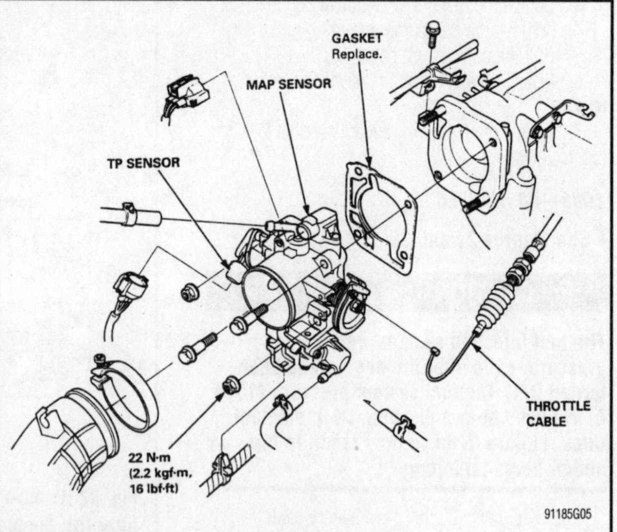

Fig. 24 Exploded view of a Honda throttle body

- 1996–97 Accord with V6 engines: Remove the banjo bolt from the fuel filter outlet and install the pressure gauge using a suitable fitting to temporarily substitute for the banjo bolt and supply fuel to the gauge and the fuel rail.
- 1998–00 Accord: Remove the fuel pulsation damper from the end of the fuel rail and install a suitable fuel pressure gauge in its place.

3. Remove and plug the vacuum line for the fuel pressure regulator located near the end of the fuel rail.

4. Start the engine and note the fuel pressure. With the pressure regulator vacuum hose disconnected and plugged, the fuel pressure should register as follows:
- 2.2L engines: 38–46 psi (260–310 kPa)
- 2.3L engines: 47–54 psi (320–370 kPa)
- 2.7L engines: 40–47 psi (270–320 kPa)
- 3.0L engines: 41–48 psi (280–330 kPa)

➡**If the engine wont start, turn on the ignition switch ON, wait two seconds, then turn off the ignition switch OFF. Turn the ignition switch back ON again and read the fuel pressure.**

5. If the fuel pressure is higher than specification check for a pinched or restricted fuel return hose or line.

6. If the fuel pressure is lower than the specification check for a damaged fuel pressure regulator, clogged fuel filter, fuel feed line or a leak in the fuel feed line. If the fuel pressure regulator, fuel feed lines, and fuel pump are OK, replace the fuel pump and fuel filter.

➡**The fuel pressure regulator testing procedures are located later in this section.**

Once the test is complete, perform the following:

7. Carefully remove the fuel pressure gauge and test fittings.

8. Install the removed fasteners using new sealing washers.

9. Install the fuel filler cap.

10. Start the engine and check for any fuel leaks, and repair as necessary.

Throttle Body

▶ **See Figures 23 and 24**

The throttle body used on both Accord and Prelude models is a single-barrel side draft design. The lower portion of the throttle body has a coolant passage that is heated by the coolant flowing from the cylinder head. The throttle body is heated to prevent throttle icing and to help stabilize the fuel mixture.

The Throttle Position (TP) sensor and the Manifold Absolute Pressure (MAP) sensor are attached to the throttle body. The TP sensor and the MAP sensor are important input sensors used by the PCM, and based on the information received will affect the ignition timing and fuel mixture.

The idle speed adjusting screw is located toward the top of the throttle body, in a vertical position facing the air inlet of the throttle body. The idle speed screw is used to increase/decrease the bypass air required to achieve the recommended idle speed.

The throttle cable is attached to the throttle body, and should have enough free play such that the cable has 0.39–0.47 inches (10–12mm) of deflection.

The throttle stop screw is located on the side of the throttle body, near the throttle linkage. The throttle stop screw is non-adjustable and **MUST NOT** be disturbed. The throttle stop screw is set at the factory and usually has a light coat of paint on it to permanently lock it in place. With the throttle in the closed or idle position, if there is clearance between the throttle stop screw and the throttle stop, the throttle body must be replaced.

➡**Replace the throttle body if there is excessive play in the throttle shaft, if the shaft is sticking or binding, or if clearance exists between the throttle stop screw and the throttle stop.**

REMOVAL & INSTALLATION

▶ **See Figures 25, 26, 27, 28 and 29**

1. Disconnect the negative battery cable.
2. Remove the air duct from the throttle body.

3. Remove the wiring harness connector from the throttle body.

4. Label and detach all vacuum hoses from the throttle body.

5. Detach the accelerator cable.

6. Detach and plug the coolant hoses from the throttle body.

7. Unfasten the throttle body mounting fasteners, then remove the throttle body. Remove and discard the throttle body gasket.

8. Using a suitable plastic scraper, remove any

Fig. 25 Installed view of the throttle body assembly

Fig. 26 Remove the bolts that fasten the throttle body to the intake manifold

Fig. 27 Separate the throttle body from the intake manifold

Fig. 28 Remove and discard the throttle body gasket

Fig. 29 Clean the surface of the intake manifold before a new gasket is installed

Fig. 30 You must replace the fuel injector sealing O-ring anytime the injector is removed

Fig. 31 The fuel injector O-ring may be stuck in the intake manifold

Fig. 32 You may need to thoroughly clean the injector tips if there is excessive carbon around the needle and seat

gasket material from the throttle body and air intake plenum.

9. Installation is the reverse of the removal procedure making sure of the following:

- The throttle cable is properly routed, installed, and has 0.39–0.47 inches (10–12mm) of deflection.
- If equipped, make sure the transaxle and cruise control cables are properly routed and installed correctly. With the engine at a warm idle the cruise control cable should have 0.18–0.22 inches (4.5–5.5mm) of free play.
- The cooling system is topped off and bled as necessary.

Fuel Injector(s)

REMOVAL & INSTALLATION

▶ See Figures 30, 31, 32, 33 and 34

❊❊ CAUTION

Observe all applicable safety precautions when working around fuel. Whenever servicing the fuel system, always work in a well-ventilated area. Do not allow fuel spray or vapors to come in contact with a spark or open flame. Keep a dry chemical fire extinguisher near the work area. Always keep fuel in a container specifically designed for fuel storage; also, always properly seal fuel containers to avoid the possibility of fire or explosion.

1. Disconnect the negative battery cable.
2. Relieve the fuel system pressure.

❊❊ CAUTION

Fuel injection systems remain under pressure, even after the engine has been turned OFF. The fuel system pressure must be relieved before disconnecting any fuel lines. Failure to do so may result in fire and/or personal injury.

3. Detach the electrical connectors from the fuel rail.

4. Disconnect the vacuum hose and fuel return from the fuel pressure regulator.

5. Loosen and remove the fasteners on the fuel rail, then remove the fuel rail. For more information on fuel rail removal, refer to the procedure in this section.

6. Grasp the fuel injector body and pull up while gently rocking the fuel injector from side to side.

7. Once removed, inspect the fuel injector cap

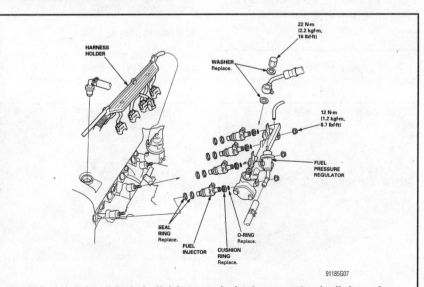

Fig. 33 Exploded view of the fuel rail, injectors and related components—4-cylinder engine shown

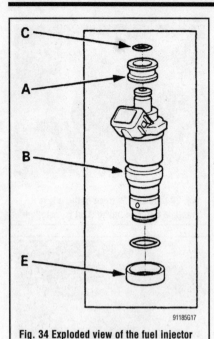

Fig. 34 Exploded view of the fuel injector (B), O-rings (C), and seal rings (E)

and body for signs of deterioration. Replace as required.

8. Remove and discard the injector O-rings. If an O-ring or end cap is missing, look in the intake manifold for the missing part.

To install:

9. Replace the O-rings and apply a small amount of clean engine oil to them. Install the lubricated O-rings onto each injector.

10. Install the injectors using a slight twisting downward motion.

11. Install the injector retaining clips.

12. Install the fuel injection supply manifold (fuel rail).

13. Connect the negative battery cable.

14. Turn the ignition switch **ON** for 5 seconds, then turn it **OFF** and check for fuel leaks.

15. If no fuel leaks are noticed, run the engine at idle for 2 minutes, then turn the engine **OFF** and recheck for fuel leaks and proper operation.

TESTING

The easiest way to test the operation of the fuel injectors is to listen for a clicking sound coming from the injectors while the engine is running. This is accomplished using a mechanic's stethoscope, or a long screwdriver.

Place the end of the stethoscope or the screwdriver (tip end, not handle) onto the body of the injector. Place the two earpieces of the stethoscope in your ears, or if using a screwdriver, place your ear on top of the handle. An audible clicking noise should be heard; as the solenoid in the injector is operating. If the injector makes this noise, the injector driver circuit and computer are operating as designed. Continue testing all the injectors this way.

❋❋ CAUTION

Be extremely careful while working on an operating engine, make sure you have no dangling jewelry, extremely loose clothes, power tool cords or other items that might get caught in a moving part of the engine.

The Honda fuel injectors are triggered by electrical pulses. The injector is either on (open) or off (closed). The amount of fuel the injector provides is determined by the fuel pressure and how long the injector is opened.

When diagnosing a fuel related running problem, it's a good idea to remove the spark plugs and check their color. A rich mixture (too much fuel) is characterized by a black sooty appearing spark plug electrode. A lean mixture (too little fuel) is characterized by a dry, very whitish colored spark plug.

A fuel injector could cause a rich mixture if:
- The pressure regulator is defective
- The system fuel pressure is too high
- The injector leaks when not being triggered
- The pressure regulator vacuum line is restricted

A fuel injector could cause a lean mixture if:
- The pressure regulator is defective
- The system fuel pressure is too low
- The injector has fuel flow related blockage
- The injector sticks or binds when being triggered
- The internal electrical windings of the injector have failed
- The injector does not receive an electrical pulse or has a bad ground

All Injectors Clicking

If all the injectors are clicking, but you have determined that the fuel system is the cause of your driveability problem, continue diagnostics. Make sure that you have checked fuel pump pressure as outlined earlier in this section. An easy way to determine a weak or unproductive cylinder is a cylinder drop test. This is accomplished by grounding one spark plug wire at a time, or interrupting the voltage signal to an individual ignition coil pack, one unit at a time and seeing which cylinder causes the least difference in the idle. The one that causes the least change is the weak cylinder.

If the injectors were all clicking and the ignition system is functioning properly, remove the injector of the suspect cylinder and bench test it. This is accomplished by checking for a spray pattern from the injector itself. Install a fuel supply line to the injector (or rail if the injector is left attached to the rail) and momentarily apply 12 volts DC and a ground to the injector itself; a visible fuel spray should appear. If no spray is achieved, replace the injector and check the running condition of the engine. If the injector leaks fuel without being triggered, replace the leaking injector.

One or More Injectors Are Not Clicking

▶ See Figures 35, 36, 37 and 38

If one or more injectors are found to be not operating, testing the injector driver circuit and computer can be accomplished using a "noid" light. First, with the engine not running and the ignition key in the **OFF** position, remove the connector from the injector to be tested, then plug the "noid" light tool into the injector connector. Start the engine and the "noid" light should flash, signaling that the injector driver circuit is working. If the "noid" light flashes, but the injector does not click when plugged in, test the injector's resistance. The resistance should be between 1.5–2.5 ohms.

If the "noid" light does not flash, the injector driver circuit is faulty. Check the PGM-FI Main Relay operation and the wiring between the PCM. Disconnect the negative battery cable. Unplug the "noid" light from the injector connector and also unplug the PCM. Check the harness between the appropriate pins on the harness side of the PCM connector and the injector connector. Resistance should be less than 5.0 ohms; if not, repair the circuit. If resistance is within specifications, the injector driver inside the PCM is faulty. If available, substitute a known good PCM for diagnostic purposes. If defective, replacement of the PCM will be necessary.

Fig. 35 Unplug the fuel injector connector

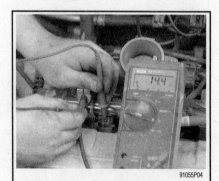

Fig. 36 Probe the two terminals of a fuel injector to check its resistance

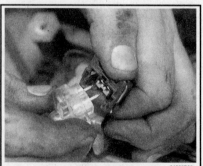

Fig. 37 Plug the correct "noid" light directly into the injector harness connector

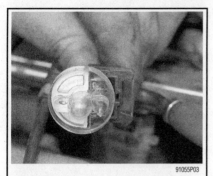

Fig. 38 If the correct "noid" light flashes while the engine is running, the injector driver circuit of the PCM is working

Fig. 39 Detach the electrical connectors from the fuel injectors

Fig. 40 Pull the injector wiring up and place it out of your way

Fig. 41 Place a rag under the connection, then disconnect the fuel line from the rail

Fig. 42 Removing the bolts from the fuel rail

Fig. 43 Using both hands, gently rock the fuel rail until the injectors are freed

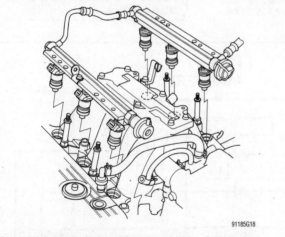

Fig. 44 Exploded view of the fuel rail assembly—2.7L engine shown, 3.0L similar

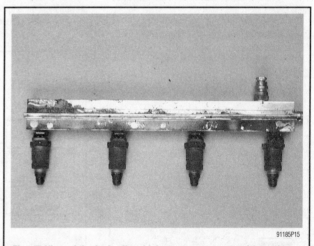

Fig. 45 View of the fuel rail and injectors, once removed from the vehicle

Fuel Rail Assembly

REMOVAL & INSTALLATION

▶ See Figures 33, 39 thru 45

1. Disconnect the negative battery cable.

❊❊ CAUTION

Fuel injection systems remain under pressure, even after the engine has been turned OFF. The fuel system pressure must be relieved before disconnecting any fuel lines. Failure to do so may result in fire and/or personal injury.

2. Relieve the fuel system pressure, as outlined earlier in this section.

3. Detach the fuel rail electrical harness connectors. Move the harness out of the way.

4. Remove the vacuum hose and fuel return hose from the fuel pressure regulator.

5. Place a rag under the fuel line connection to absorb any leaking fuel, then disconnect the fuel line from the fuel rail.

6. Unfasten the fuel rail retaining nuts then, use a gently rocking motion to free the fuel injectors and remove the fuel rail.

To install:

➡ When installing the fuel rail, be sure to lubricate all rubber O-rings with fresh engine oil and to replace any sealing washer that was removed.

7. Coat the fuel injector O-rings with a light coating of fresh engine oil and install the fuel rail and secure with the retaining fasteners.

8. Connect the fuel line to the fuel rail.

9. Install the vacuum hose and fuel return hose to the fuel pressure regulator.

10. Attach the electrical harness connectors.

11. Connect the negative battery cable.

12. Pressurize the fuel system by turning the ignition switch to the **ON** position.

13. Check for leaks, if none are found, start the engine and recheck for any leaks. If any leakage is found, repair as necessary.

Fuel Pressure Regulator

REMOVAL & INSTALLATION

▶ See Figure 46

※※ CAUTION

Observe all applicable safety precautions when working around fuel. Whenever servicing the fuel system, always work in a well ventilated area. Do not allow fuel spray or vapors to come in contact with a spark or open flame. Keep a dry chemical fire extinguisher near the work area. Always keep fuel in a container specifically designed for fuel storage; also, always properly seal fuel containers to avoid the possibility of fire or explosion.

1. Properly relieve the fuel system pressure, as outlined earlier in this section.

2. Disconnect the negative battery cable.

3. Detach the vacuum hose from the fuel pressure regulator.

4. Unfasten the two fuel pressure regulator retaining bolts.

5. Remove the fuel pressure regulator and the O-rings. Discard the O-rings.

To install:

6. Lubricate the new O-rings with light engine oil.

7. Position a new O-ring onto the fuel pressure regulator.

8. Place the fuel pressure regulator into position and install the retainers. Tighten to 9 ft. lbs. (12 Nm).

9. Attach the vacuum line to the fuel pressure regulator.

10. Connect the negative battery cable.

11. Run the engine at idle for 2 minutes, then turn the engine **OFF** and check for fuel leaks and proper operation.

PGM-FI Main Relay

▶ See Figure 47

The PGM-FI Main Relay is actually comprised of two individual internal relays. When the ignition switch is initially turned **ON**, the Powertrain Control Module (PCM) supplies ground to the PGM-FI Main Relay. This ground triggers one of the PGM-FI internal relays that sends battery voltage to the fuel pump for two seconds to pressurize the fuel system.

When the engine is running the PCM supplies a continuous ground to the PGM-FI Main Relay. The supplied ground keeps the relay in the "closed" position providing electrical current to the fuel pump, keeping the fuel loop pressurized while the engine runs.

If the engine is not running with the ignition **ON**, the PCM cuts the ground to the PGM-FI Main Relay, causing the relay to "open" and stop the electric current flow to the fuel pump. As mentioned previously, if the engine is not running, the PCM will only supply ground to the PGM-FI Main Relay

for two seconds when the ignition switch is initially switched to the **ON** position.

The PGM-FI Main Relay also supplies electrical power to the Idle Air Control (IAC) valve and to the fuel injectors.

TESTING

▶ See Figure 48

➡ **If the engine starts and continues to run, the PGM-FI Main Relay is working and does not need to be replaced.**

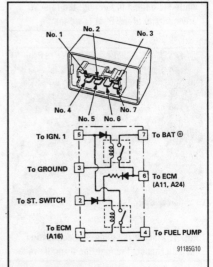

Fig. 48 View of the PGM-FI relay and terminal identification

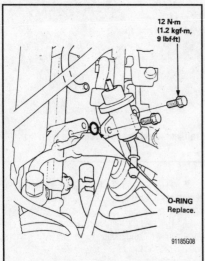

Fig. 46 Exploded view of the fuel pressure regulator-to-rail mounting

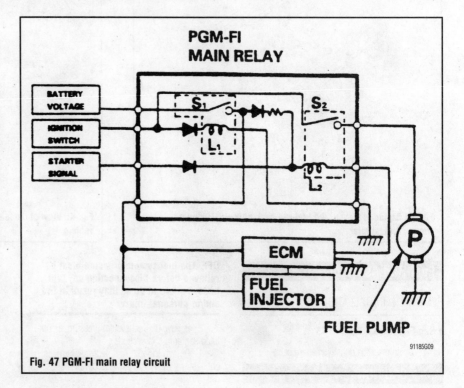

Fig. 47 PGM-FI main relay circuit

1. Locate and remove the relay.
2. Apply battery voltage to the No. 3 terminal.
3. Ground the No. 2 terminal.
4. Check for continuity between terminal Nos. 5 and 2.
5. If continuity is detected, proceed to the step 7.

6. If there is no continuity, replace the relay.
7. Connect the No. 4 terminal to the positive side of the battery.
8. Ground the No. 2 terminal of the relay.
9. Check for continuity between the No. 5 terminal and the No. 2 terminal of the relay.

10. If there is continuity, the relay checks out OK. If the fuel pump still does not function, check the wiring harness and electrical connectors.
11. If there is no continuity, replace the relay and retest.

FUEL TANK

Tank Assembly

REMOVAL & INSTALLATION

♦ See Figures 49 thru 54

✳✳ CAUTION

Observe all applicable safety precautions when working around fuel. Whenever servicing the fuel system, always work in a well ventilated area. Do not allow fuel spray or vapors to come in contact with a spark or open flame. Keep a dry chemical fire extinguisher near the work area. Always keep fuel in a container specifically designed for fuel storage; also, always properly seal fuel containers to avoid the possibility of fire or explosion.

The vehicle must be raised and safely supported to allow the fuel tank to be removed from underneath the vehicle.

1. Note the radio security code and disconnect the negative battery cable.
2. Relieve the residual fuel system pressure as outlined in this section.
3. On some models, fold the left rear seat cushion forward and remove the plastic seat base, then remove the floor pan access panel.

91185P07

Fig. 49 Most Honda fuel tanks are equipped with a drain plug

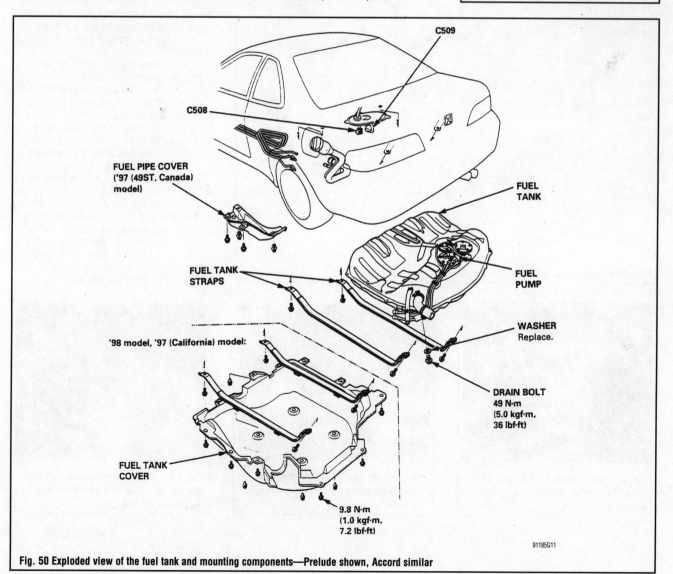

C509

C508

FUEL PIPE COVER ('97 (49ST, Canada) model)

FUEL TANK STRAPS

'98 model, '97 (California) model:

FUEL TANK COVER

9.8 N·m (1.0 kgf·m, 7.2 lbf·ft)

FUEL TANK

FUEL PUMP

WASHER Replace.

DRAIN BOLT 49 N·m (5.0 kgf·m, 36 lbf·ft)

91185G11

Fig. 50 Exploded view of the fuel tank and mounting components—Prelude shown, Accord similar

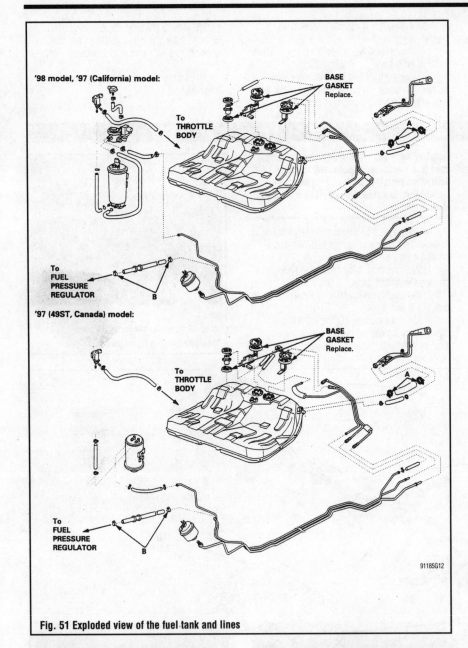

'98 model, '97 (California) model:

BASE GASKET
Replace.

To THROTTLE BODY

To FUEL PRESSURE REGULATOR

B

A

'97 (49ST, Canada) model:

BASE GASKET
Replace.

To THROTTLE BODY

To FUEL PRESSURE REGULATOR

B

A

91185G12

Fig. 51 Exploded view of the fuel tank and lines

a. Detach the fuel pump electrical connector, then disconnect the fuel feed and return lines.

4. On V6 models, perform the following:

a. Disconnect the fuel feed and return lines, and detach the fuel pump electrical connector.

b. Remove the fuel pump. For specific details, see the fuel pump removal procedures in this section.

c. Using an approved hand pump and storage container, remove the fuel from the fuel tank through the fuel pump access hole.

5. Carefully jack up and safely support the vehicle.

6. On some Prelude models, perform the following:

a. Remove the middle floor beam.

b. Remove the fuel tank drain bolt and drain the fuel into an approved container.

c. Install the fuel tank drain bolt using a new sealing washer, tighten the bolt to 36 ft. lbs. (49 Nm) and apply a coating of a rust preventative to the bolt.

7. On early (Canadian) 4-cylinder Accord models:

a. Remove the fuel tank drain bolt and drain the fuel into an approved container.

b. Remove the fuel hose joint protection cover.

c. Install the fuel tank drain bolt using a new sealing washer, tighten the bolt to 36 ft. lbs. (49 Nm) and apply a coating of a rust preventative to the bolt.

d. Disconnect the fuel return hose, vapor hose and quick-connect fittings.

e. Detach the fuel pump electrical connector.

8. On clamped fuel lines, release the clamp tension and slide the hose clamps away from the fitting. Carefully twist the hoses while pulling to remove them. Make sure all fuel hoses and electrical connectors have been properly disconnected.

9. Support the fuel tank with a jack.

10. Remove the fuel tank strap fasteners and allow the straps to fall freely.

11. Carefully remove the fuel tank. The tank may stick in place due to being undercoated. Carefully using a suitable prytool, remove it from its mount.

The installation is in the reverse order of disassembly. If the tank is to be replaced, transfer the needed components as necessary using new seals, O-rings, and quick-connect connectors.

91185P12

Fig. 52 Always ground the fuel tank, as shown here, when you are working on or around it

91185P09

Fig. 53 Make sure to have the fuel tank properly supported before removing any of the mounting fasteners

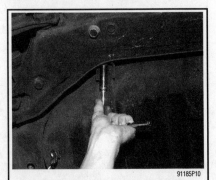

91185P10

Fig. 54 With the tank supported, unfasten the fuel tank strap fasteners, then carefully lower the fuel tank

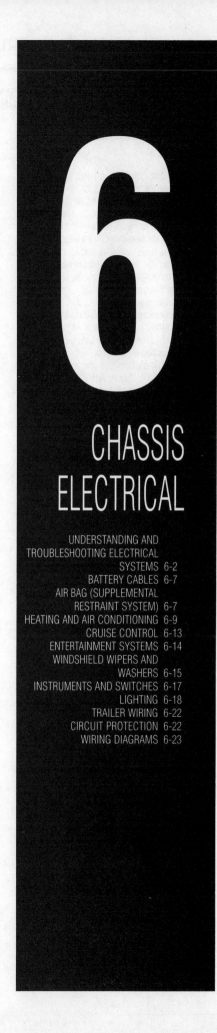

6

CHASSIS

ELECTRICAL

UNDERSTANDING AND TROUBLESHOOTING ELECTRICAL SYSTEMS

Basic Electrical Theory

♦ See Figure 1

For any 12 volt, negative ground, electrical system to operate, the electricity must travel in a complete circuit. This simply means that current (power) from the positive (+) terminal of the battery must eventually return to the negative (-) terminal of the battery. Along the way, this current will travel through wires, fuses, switches and components. If, for any reason, the flow of current through the circuit is interrupted, the component fed by that circuit will cease to function properly.

Perhaps the easiest way to visualize a circuit is to think of connecting a light bulb (with two wires attached to it) to the battery—one wire attached to the negative (-) terminal of the battery and the other wire to the positive (+) terminal. With the two wires touching the battery terminals, the circuit would be complete and the light bulb would illuminate. Electricity would follow a path from the battery to the bulb and back to the battery. It's easy to see that with longer wires on our light bulb, it could be mounted anywhere. Further, one wire could be fitted with a switch so that the light could be turned on and off.

The normal automotive circuit differs from this simple example in two ways. First, instead of having a return wire from the bulb to the battery, the current travels through the frame of the vehicle. Since the negative (-) battery cable is attached to the frame (made of electrically conductive metal), the frame of the vehicle can serve as a ground wire to complete the circuit. Secondly, most automotive circuits contain multiple components which receive power from a single circuit. This lessens the amount of wire needed to power components on the vehicle.

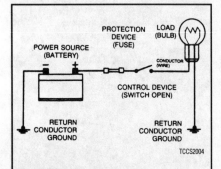

TCCS2004

Fig. 1 This example illustrates a simple circuit. When the switch is closed, power from the positive (+) battery terminal flows through the fuse and the switch, and then to the light bulb. The light illuminates and the circuit is completed through the ground wire back to the negative (-) battery terminal. In reality, the two ground points shown in the illustration are attached to the metal frame of the vehicle, which completes the circuit back to the battery

HOW DOES ELECTRICITY WORK: THE WATER ANALOGY

Electricity is the flow of electrons—the sub-atomic particles that constitute the outer shell of an atom. Electrons spin in an orbit around the center core of an atom. The center core is comprised of protons (positive charge) and neutrons (neutral charge). Electrons have a negative charge and balance out the positive charge of the protons. When an outside force causes the number of electrons to unbalance the charge of the protons, the electrons will split off the atom and look for another atom to balance out. If this imbalance is kept up, electrons will continue to move and an electrical flow will exist.

Many people have been taught electrical theory using an analogy with water. In a comparison with water flowing through a pipe, the electrons would be the water and the wire is the pipe.

The flow of electricity can be measured much like the flow of water through a pipe. The unit of measurement used is amperes, frequently abbreviated as amps (a). You can compare amperage to the volume of water flowing through a pipe. When connected to a circuit, an ammeter will measure the actual amount of current flowing through the circuit. When relatively few electrons flow through a circuit, the amperage is low. When many electrons flow, the amperage is high.

Water pressure is measured in units such as pounds per square inch (psi); the electrical pressure is measured in units called volts (v). When a voltmeter is connected to a circuit, it is measuring the electrical pressure.

The actual flow of electricity depends not only on voltage and amperage, but also on the resistance of the circuit. The higher the resistance, the higher the force necessary to push the current through the circuit. The standard unit for measuring resistance is an ohm. Resistance in a circuit varies depending on the amount and type of components used in the circuit. The main factors which determine resistance are:

• Material—some materials have more resistance than others. Those with high resistance are said to be insulators. Rubber materials (or rubber-like plastics) are some of the most common insulators used in vehicles as they have a very high resistance to electricity. Very low resistance materials are said to be conductors. Copper wire is among the best conductors. Silver is actually a superior conductor to copper and is used in some relay contacts, but its high cost prohibits its use as common wiring. Most automotive wiring is made of copper.

• Size—the larger the wire size being used, the less resistance the wire will have. This is why components which use large amounts of electricity usually have large wires supplying current to them.

• Length—for a given thickness of wire, the longer the wire, the greater the resistance. The shorter the wire, the less the resistance. When determining the proper wire for a circuit, both size and length must be considered to design a circuit that can handle the current needs of the component.

• Temperature—with many materials, the higher the temperature, the greater the resistance

(positive temperature coefficient). Some materials exhibit the opposite trait of lower resistance with higher temperatures (negative temperature coefficient). These principles are used in many of the sensors on the engine.

OHM'S LAW

There is a direct relationship between current, voltage and resistance. The relationship between current, voltage and resistance can be summed up by a statement known as Ohm's law.

Voltage (E) is equal to amperage (I) times resistance (R): $E = I \times R$

Other forms of the formula are $R = E/I$ and $I = E/R$

In each of these formulas, E is the voltage in volts, I is the current in amps and R is the resistance in ohms. The basic point to remember is that as the resistance of a circuit goes up, the amount of current that flows in the circuit will go down, if voltage remains the same.

The amount of work that the electricity can perform is expressed as power. The unit of power is the watt (w). The relationship between power, voltage and current is expressed as:

Power (w) is equal to amperage (I) times voltage (E): $W = I \times E$

This is only true for direct current (DC) circuits; The alternating current formula is a tad different, but since the electrical circuits in most vehicles are DC type, we need not get into AC circuit theory.

Electrical Components

POWER SOURCE

Power is supplied to the vehicle by two devices: The battery and the alternator. The battery supplies electrical power during starting or during periods when the current demand of the vehicle's electrical system exceeds the output capacity of the alternator. The alternator supplies electrical current when the engine is running. Just not does the alternator supply the current needs of the vehicle, but it recharges the battery.

The Battery

In most modern vehicles, the battery is a lead/acid electrochemical device consisting of six 2 volt subsections (cells) connected in series, so that the unit is capable of producing approximately 12 volts of electrical pressure. Each subsection consists of a series of positive and negative plates held a short distance apart in a solution of sulfuric acid and water.

The two types of plates are of dissimilar metals. This sets up a chemical reaction, and it is this reaction which produces current flow from the battery when its positive and negative terminals are connected to an electrical load. The power removed from the battery is replaced by the alternator, restoring the battery to its original chemical state.

The Alternator

On some vehicles there isn't an alternator, but a generator. The difference is that an alternator supplies alternating current which is then changed to direct current for use on the vehicle, while a generator produces direct current. Alternators tend to be more efficient and that is why they are used.

Alternators and generators are devices that consist of coils of wires wound together making big electromagnets. One group of coils spins within another set and the interaction of the magnetic fields causes a current to flow. This current is then drawn off the coils and fed into the vehicles electrical system.

GROUND

Two types of grounds are used in automotive electric circuits. Direct ground components are grounded to the frame through their mounting points. All other components use some sort of ground wire which is attached to the frame or chassis of the vehicle. The electrical current runs through the chassis of the vehicle and returns to the battery through the ground (-) cable; if you look, you'll see that the battery ground cable connects between the battery and the frame or chassis of the vehicle.

➡**It should be noted that a good percentage of electrical problems can be traced to bad grounds.**

PROTECTIVE DEVICES

It is possible for large surges of current to pass through the electrical system of your vehicle. If this surge of current were to reach the load in the circuit, the surge could burn it out or severely damage it. It can also overload the wiring, causing the harness to get hot and melt the insulation. To prevent this, fuses, circuit breakers and/or fusible links are connected into the supply wires of the electrical system. These items are nothing more than a built-in weak spot in the system. When an abnormal amount of current flows through the system, these protective devices work as follows to protect the circuit:

• Fuse—when an excessive electrical current passes through a fuse, the fuse "blows" (the conductor melts) and opens the circuit, preventing the passage of current.

• Circuit Breaker—a circuit breaker is basically a self-repairing fuse. It will open the circuit in the same fashion as a fuse, but when the surge subsides, the circuit breaker can be reset and does not need replacement.

• Fusible Link—a fusible link (fuse link or main link) is a short length of special, high temperature insulated wire that acts as a fuse. When an excessive electrical current passes through a fusible link, the thin gauge wire inside the link melts, creating an intentional open to protect the circuit. To repair the circuit, the link must be replaced. Some newer type fusible links are housed in plug-in modules, which are simply replaced like a fuse, while older type fusible links must be cut and spliced if they melt. Since this link is very early in the electrical path, it's the first place to look if nothing on the vehicle works, yet the battery seems to be charged and is properly connected.

Always replace fuses, circuit breakers and fusible links with identically rated components. Under no circumstances should a component of higher or lower amperage rating be substituted.

SWITCHES & RELAYS

▶ **See Figure 2**

Switches are used in electrical circuits to control the passage of current. The most common use is to open and close circuits between the battery and the various electric devices in the system. Switches are rated according to the amount of amperage they can handle. If a sufficient amperage rated switch is not used in a circuit, the switch could overload and cause damage.

Some electrical components which require a large amount of current to operate use a special switch called a relay. Since these circuits carry a large amount of current, the thickness of the wire in the circuit is also greater. If this large wire were connected from the load to the control switch, the switch would have to carry the high amperage load and the fairing or dash would be twice as large to accommodate the increased size of the wiring harness. To prevent these problems, a relay is used.

Relays are composed of a coil and a set of contacts. When the coil has a current passed though it, a magnetic field is formed and this field causes the contacts to move together, completing the circuit. Most relays are normally open, preventing current from passing through the circuit, but they can take any electrical form depending on the job they are intended to do. Relays can be considered "remote control switches." They allow a smaller current to operate devices that require higher amperages. When a small current operates the coil, a larger current is allowed to pass by the contacts. Some common circuits which may use relays are the horn, headlights, starter, electric fuel pump and other high draw circuits.

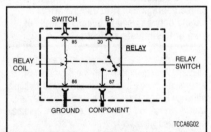

TCCA6G02

Fig. 2 Relays are composed of a coil and a switch. These two components are linked together so that when one operates, the other operates at the same time. The large wires in the circuit are connected from the battery to one side of the relay switch (B+) and from the opposite side of the relay switch to the load (component). Smaller wires are connected from the relay coil to the control switch for the circuit and from the opposite side of the relay coil to ground

LOAD

Every electrical circuit must include a "load" (something to use the electricity coming from the source). Without this load, the battery would attempt to deliver its entire power supply from one pole to another. This is called a "short circuit." All this electricity would take a short cut to ground and cause a great amount of damage to other components in the circuit by developing a tremendous amount of heat. This condition could develop sufficient heat to melt the insulation on all the surrounding wires and reduce a multiple wire cable to a lump of plastic and copper.

WIRING & HARNESSES

The average vehicle contains meters and meters of wiring, with hundreds of individual connections. To protect the many wires from damage and to keep them from becoming a confusing tangle, they are organized into bundles, enclosed in plastic or taped together and called wiring harnesses. Different harnesses serve different parts of the vehicle. Individual wires are color coded to help trace them through a harness where sections are hidden from view.

Automotive wiring or circuit conductors can be either single strand wire, multi-strand wire or printed circuitry. Single strand wire has a solid metal core and is usually used inside such components as alternators, motors, relays and other devices. Multi-strand wire has a core made of many small strands of wire twisted together into a single conductor. Most of the wiring in an automotive electrical system is made up of multi-strand wire, either as a single conductor or grouped together in a harness. All wiring is color coded on the insulator, either as a solid color or as a colored wire with an identification stripe. A printed circuit is a thin film of copper or other conductor that is printed on an insulator backing. Occasionally, a printed circuit is sandwiched between two sheets of plastic for more protection and flexibility. A complete printed circuit, consisting of conductors, insulating material and connectors for lamps or other components is called a printed circuit board. Printed circuitry is used in place of individual wires or harnesses in places where space is limited, such as behind instrument panels.

Since automotive electrical systems are very sensitive to changes in resistance, the selection of properly sized wires is critical when systems are repaired. A loose or corroded connection or a replacement wire that is too small for the circuit will add extra resistance and an additional voltage drop to the circuit.

The wire gauge number is an expression of the cross-section area of the conductor. Vehicles from countries that use the metric system will typically describe the wire size as its cross-sectional area in square millimeters. In this method, the larger the wire, the greater the number. Another common system for expressing wire size is the American Wire Gauge (AWG) system. As gauge number increases, area decreases and the wire becomes smaller. An 18 gauge wire is smaller than a 4 gauge wire. A wire with a higher gauge number will carry less current than a wire with a lower gauge number. Gauge wire size refers to the size of the strands of the conductor, not the size of the complete wire with insulator. It is possible, therefore, to have two wires of the same gauge with different diameters because one may have thicker insulation than the other.

It is essential to understand how a circuit works before trying to figure out why it doesn't. An electrical schematic shows the electrical current paths when a circuit is operating properly. Schematics break the entire electrical system down into individual circuits. In a schematic, usually no attempt is made to represent wiring and components as they physically appear on the vehicle; switches and other components are shown as simply as possible. Face views of harness connectors show the cavity or terminal locations in all multi-pin connectors to help locate test points.

CONNECTORS

▶ **See Figures 3 and 4**

Three types of connectors are commonly used in automotive applications—weatherproof, molded and hard shell.

• Weatherproof—these connectors are most commonly used where the connector is exposed to the elements. Terminals are protected against moisture and dirt by sealing rings which provide a weather-tight seal. All repairs require the use of a special terminal and the tool required to service it. Unlike standard blade type terminals, these weatherproof terminals cannot be straightened once they are bent. Make certain that the connectors are properly seated and all of the sealing rings are in place when connecting leads.

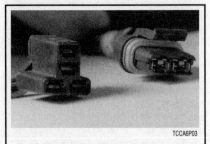

Fig. 3 Hard shell (left) and weatherproof (right) connectors have replaceable terminals

Fig. 4 Weatherproof connectors are most commonly used in the engine compartment or where the connector is exposed to the elements

• Molded—these connectors require complete replacement of the connector if found to be defective. This means splicing a new connector assembly into the harness. All splices should be soldered to insure proper contact. Use care when probing the connections or replacing terminals in them, as it is possible to create a short circuit between opposite terminals. If this happens to the wrong terminal pair, it is possible to damage certain components. Always use jumper wires between connectors for circuit checking and NEVER probe through weatherproof seals.

• Hard Shell—unlike molded connectors, the terminal contacts in hard-shell connectors can be replaced. Replacement usually involves the use of a special terminal removal tool that depresses the locking tangs (barbs) on the connector terminal and allows the connector to be removed from the rear of the shell. The connector shell should be replaced if it shows any evidence of burning, melting, cracks, or breaks. Replace individual terminals that are burnt, corroded, distorted or loose.

Test Equipment

Pinpointing the exact cause of trouble in an electrical circuit is most times accomplished by the use of special test equipment. The following describes different types of commonly used test equipment and briefly explains how to use them in diagnosis. In addition to the information covered below, the tool manufacturer's instructions booklet (provided with the tester) should be read and clearly understood before attempting any test procedures.

JUMPER WIRES

> ✳✳ **CAUTION**
>
> Never use jumper wires made from a thinner gauge wire than the circuit being tested. If the jumper wire is of too small a gauge, it may overheat and possibly melt. Never use jumpers to bypass high resistance loads in a circuit. Bypassing resistances, in effect, creates a short circuit. This may, in turn, cause damage and fire. Jumper wires should only be used to bypass lengths of wire or to simulate switches.

Jumper wires are simple, yet extremely valuable, pieces of test equipment. They are basically test wires which are used to bypass sections of a circuit. Although jumper wires can be purchased, they are usually fabricated from lengths of standard automotive wire and whatever type of connector (alligator clip, spade connector or pin connector) that is required for the particular application being tested. In cramped, hard-to-reach areas, it is advisable to have insulated boots over the jumper wire terminals in order to prevent accidental grounding. It is also advisable to include a standard automotive fuse in any jumper wire. This is commonly referred to as a "fused jumper". By inserting an in-line fuse holder between a set of test leads, a fused jumper wire can be used for bypassing open circuits. Use a 5 amp fuse to provide protection against voltage spikes.

Jumper wires are used primarily to locate open electrical circuits, on either the ground (-) side of the circuit or on the power (+) side. If an electrical

component fails to operate, connect the jumper wire between the component and a good ground. If the component operates only with the jumper installed, the ground circuit is open. If the ground circuit is good, but the component does not operate, the circuit between the power feed and component may be open. By moving the jumper wire successively back from the component toward the power source, you can isolate the area of the circuit where the open is located. When the component stops functioning, or the power is cut off, the open is in the segment of wire between the jumper and the point previously tested.

You can sometimes connect the jumper wire directly from the battery to the "hot" terminal of the component, but first make sure the component uses 12 volts in operation. Some electrical components, such as fuel injectors or sensors, are designed to operate on about 4 to 5 volts, and running 12 volts directly to these components will cause damage.

TEST LIGHTS

▶ **See Figure 5**

The test light is used to check circuits and components while electrical current is flowing through them. It is used for voltage and ground tests. To use a 12 volt test light, connect the ground clip to a good ground and probe wherever necessary with the pick. The test light will illuminate when voltage is detected. This does not necessarily mean that 12 volts (or any particular amount of voltage) is present; it only means that some voltage is present. It is advisable before using the test light to touch its ground clip and probe across the battery posts or terminals to make sure the light is operating properly.

> ✳✳ **WARNING**
>
> Do not use a test light to probe electronic ignition, spark plug or coil wires. Never use a pick-type test light to probe wiring on computer controlled systems unless specifically instructed to do so. Any wire insulation that is pierced by the test light probe should be taped and sealed with silicone after testing.

Like the jumper wire, the 12 volt test light is used to isolate opens in circuits. But, whereas the jumper wire is used to bypass the open to operate the load, the 12 volt test light is used to locate the

Fig. 5 A 12 volt test light is used to detect the presence of voltage in a circuit

presence of voltage in a circuit. If the test light illuminates, there is power up to that point in the circuit; if the test light does not illuminate, there is an open circuit (no power). Move the test light in successive steps back toward the power source until the light in the handle illuminates. The open is between the probe and a point which was previously probed.

The self-powered test light is similar in design to the 12 volt test light, but contains a 1.5 volt penlight battery in the handle. It is most often used in place of a multimeter to check for open or short circuits when power is isolated from the circuit (continuity test).

The battery in a self-powered test light does not provide much current. A weak battery may not provide enough power to illuminate the test light even when a complete circuit is made (especially if there is high resistance in the circuit). Always make sure that the test battery is strong. To check the battery, briefly touch the ground clip to the probe; if the light glows brightly, the battery is strong enough for testing.

➥**A self-powered test light should not be used on any computer controlled system or component. The small amount of electricity transmitted by the test light is enough to damage many electronic automotive components.**

MULTIMETERS

Multimeters are an extremely useful tool for troubleshooting electrical problems. They can be purchased in either analog or digital form and have a price range to suit any budget. A multimeter is a voltmeter, ammeter and ohmmeter (along with other features) combined into one instrument. It is often used when testing solid state circuits because of its high input impedance (usually 10 megaohms or more). A brief description of the multimeter main test functions follows:

• Voltmeter—the voltmeter is used to measure voltage at any point in a circuit, or to measure the voltage drop across any part of a circuit. Voltmeters usually have various scales and a selector switch to allow the reading of different voltage ranges. The voltmeter has a positive and a negative lead. To avoid damage to the meter, always connect the negative lead to the negative (-) side of the circuit (to ground or nearest the ground side of the circuit) and connect the positive lead to the positive (+) side of the circuit (to the power source or the nearest power source). Note that the negative voltmeter lead will always be black and that the positive voltmeter will always be some color other than black (usually red).

• Ohmmeter—the ohmmeter is designed to read resistance (measured in ohms) in a circuit or component. Most ohmmeters will have a selector switch which permits the measurement of different ranges of resistance (usually the selector switch allows the multiplication of the meter reading by 10, 100, 1,000 and 10,000). Some ohmmeters are "auto-ranging" which means the meter itself will determine which scale to use. Since the meters are powered by an internal battery, the ohmmeter can be used like a self-powered test light. When the ohmmeter is connected, current from the ohmmeter flows through the circuit or component being tested. Since the ohmmeter's internal resistance and

voltage are known values, the amount of current flow through the meter depends on the resistance of the circuit or component being tested. The ohmmeter can also be used to perform a continuity test for suspected open circuits. In using the meter for making continuity checks, do not be concerned with the actual resistance readings. Zero resistance, or any ohm reading, indicates continuity in the circuit. Infinite resistance indicates an opening in the circuit. A high resistance reading where there should be none indicates a problem in the circuit. Checks for short circuits are made in the same manner as checks for open circuits, except that the circuit must be isolated from both power and normal ground. Infinite resistance indicates no continuity, while zero resistance indicates a dead short.

✶✶ WARNING

Never use an ohmmeter to check the resistance of a component or wire while there is voltage applied to the circuit.

• Ammeter—an ammeter measures the amount of current flowing through a circuit in units called amperes or amps. At normal operating voltage, most circuits have a characteristic amount of amperes, called "current draw" which can be measured using an ammeter. By referring to a specified current draw rating, then measuring the amperes and comparing the two values, one can determine what is happening within the circuit to aid in diagnosis. An open circuit, for example, will not allow any current to flow, so the ammeter reading will be zero. A damaged component or circuit will have an increased current draw, so the reading will be high. The ammeter is always connected in series with the circuit being tested. All of the current that normally flows through the circuit must also flow through the ammeter; if there is any other path for the current to follow, the ammeter reading will not be accurate. The ammeter itself has very little resistance to current flow and, therefore, will not affect the circuit, but it will measure current draw only when the circuit is closed and electricity is flowing. Excessive current draw can blow fuses and drain the battery, while a reduced current draw can cause motors to run slowly, lights to dim and other components to not operate properly.

Troubleshooting Electrical Systems

When diagnosing a specific problem, organized troubleshooting is a must. The complexity of a modern automotive vehicle demands that you approach any problem in a logical, organized manner. There are certain troubleshooting techniques, however, which are standard:

• Establish when the problem occurs. Does the problem appear only under certain conditions? Were there any noises, odors or other unusual symptoms? Isolate the problem area. To do this, make some simple tests and observations, then eliminate the systems that are working properly. Check for obvious problems, such as broken wires and loose or dirty connections. Always check the obvious before assuming something complicated is the cause.

• Test for problems systematically to determine the cause once the problem area is isolated. Are all

the components functioning properly? Is there power going to electrical switches and motors. Performing careful, systematic checks will often turn up most causes on the first inspection, without wasting time checking components that have little or no relationship to the problem.

• Test all repairs after the work is done to make sure that the problem is fixed. Some causes can be traced to more than one component, so a careful verification of repair work is important in order to pick up additional malfunctions that may cause a problem to reappear or a different problem to arise. A blown fuse, for example, is a simple problem that may require more than another fuse to repair. If you don't look for a problem that caused a fuse to blow, a shorted wire (for example) may go undetected.

Experience has shown that most problems tend to be the result of a fairly simple and obvious cause, such as loose or corroded connectors, bad grounds or damaged wire insulation which causes a short. This makes careful visual inspection of components during testing essential to quick and accurate troubleshooting.

Testing

OPEN CIRCUITS

▶ See Figure 6

This test already assumes the existence of an open in the circuit and it is used to help locate the open portion.

1. Isolate the circuit from power and ground.
2. Connect the self-powered test light or ohmmeter ground clip to the ground side of the circuit and probe sections of the circuit sequentially.
3. If the light is out or there is infinite resistance, the open is between the probe and the circuit ground.
4. If the light is on or the meter shows continuity, the open is between the probe and the end of the circuit toward the power source.

SHORT CIRCUITS

➥**Never use a self-powered test light to perform checks for opens or shorts when power is applied to the circuit under test. The test light can be damaged by outside power.**

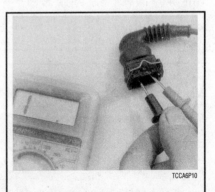

TCCA6P10

Fig. 6 The infinite reading on this multimeter indicates that the circuit is open

1. Isolate the circuit from power and ground.
2. Connect the self-powered test light or ohmmeter ground clip to a good ground and probe any easy-to-reach point in the circuit.
3. If the light comes on or there is continuity, there is a short somewhere in the circuit.
4. To isolate the short, probe a test point at either end of the isolated circuit (the light should be on or the meter should indicate continuity).
5. Leave the test light probe engaged and sequentially open connectors or switches, remove parts, etc. until the light goes out or continuity is broken.
6. When the light goes out, the short is between the last two circuit components which were opened.

If a short circuit has caused a blown fuse, a suitable automotive test light can be used to help locate the cause. A test light is connected in series to the fuse terminals to diagnose the source of the short circuit. Using a suitable automotive test light proceed as follows:

7. Carefully remove the blown fuse.

✳✳ WARNING

Make sure the test light leads and jumper wires, if used, are properly insulated and DO NOT contact any other electrical terminals, wiring or chassis grounds. Failure to properly attach or insulate the test light and/or jumper wires could cause physical injury or component damage.

8. Attach one lead of the automotive test light to one of the fuse terminals, and the second lead of the test light to the other fuse terminal.

➡**It may be necessary to use a suitable jumper wire to properly connect the test light leads to the fuse terminals.**

9. If the circuit is a switched circuit, turn on the ignition switch and/or the switch for the component that is causing the fuse to blow. When the appropriate switch is turned on, the test light should begin working.
10. Once the test light is operating, begin to inspect the wiring and components of the circuit. Systematically disconnect and reconnect the electrical connectors in the circuit being tested. When the test light goes out, the shorted portion of the circuit has been located. The short could be either a failed component or a shorted portion of the electrical circuit for the component.
11. Repair the short, or replace the shorted component and reinstall the correct amperage fuse and retest.

VOLTAGE

This test determines voltage available from the battery and should be the first step in any electrical troubleshooting procedure after visual inspection. Many electrical problems, especially on computer controlled systems, can be caused by a low state of charge in the battery. Excessive corrosion at the battery cable terminals can cause poor contact that will prevent proper charging and full battery current flow.

1. Set the voltmeter selector switch to the 20V position.
2. Connect the multimeter negative lead to the battery's negative (-) post or terminal and the positive lead to the battery's positive (+) post or terminal.
3. Turn the ignition switch **ON** to provide a load.
4. A well charged battery should register over 12 volts. If the meter reads below 11.5 volts, the battery power may be insufficient to operate the electrical system properly.

VOLTAGE DROP

▶ **See Figure 7**

When current flows through a load, the voltage beyond the load drops. This voltage drop is due to the resistance created by the load and also by small resistances created by corrosion at the connectors and damaged insulation on the wires. The maximum allowable voltage drop under load is critical, especially if there is more than one load in the circuit, since all voltage drops are cumulative.

1. Set the voltmeter selector switch to the 20 volt position.
2. Connect the multimeter negative lead to a good ground.
3. Operate the circuit and check the voltage prior to the first component (load).
4. There should be little or no voltage drop in the circuit prior to the first component. If a voltage drop exists, the wire or connectors in the circuit are suspect.
5. While operating the first component in the circuit, probe the ground side of the component with the positive meter lead and observe the voltage readings. A small voltage drop should be noticed. This voltage drop is caused by the resistance of the component.
6. Repeat the test for each component (load) down the circuit.
7. If a large voltage drop is noticed, the preceding component, wire or connector is suspect.

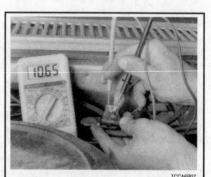

Fig. 7 This voltage drop test revealed high resistance (low voltage) in the circuit

RESISTANCE

▶ **See Figures 8 and 9**

✳✳ WARNING

Never use an ohmmeter with power applied to the circuit. The ohmmeter is designed to operate on its own power supply. The normal 12 volt electrical system voltage could damage the meter!

Fig. 8 Checking the resistance of a coolant temperature sensor with an ohmmeter. Reading is 1.04 kilohms

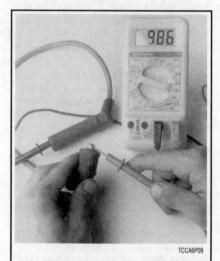

Fig. 9 Spark plug wires can be checked for excessive resistance using an ohmmeter

1. Isolate the circuit from the vehicle's power source.
2. Ensure that the ignition key is **OFF** when disconnecting any components or the battery.
3. Where necessary, also isolate at least one side of the circuit to be checked, in order to avoid reading parallel resistances. Parallel circuit resistances will always give a lower reading than the actual resistance of either of the branches.
4. Connect the meter leads to both sides of the circuit (wire or component) and read the actual measured ohms on the meter scale. Make sure the selector switch is set to the proper ohm scale for the circuit being tested, to avoid misreading the ohmmeter test value.

Wire and Connector Repair

Almost anyone can replace damaged wires, as long as the proper tools and parts are available. Wire and terminals are available to fit almost any need. Even the specialized weatherproof, molded and hard shell connectors are now available from aftermarket suppliers.

Be sure the ends of all the wires are fitted with the proper terminal hardware and connectors. Wrapping a wire around a stud is never a permanent solution and will only cause trouble later. Replace wires one at a time to avoid confusion.

Always route wires exactly the same as the factory.

➡ If connector repair is necessary, only attempt it if you have the proper tools. Weatherproof and hard shell connectors require special tools to release the pins inside the connector. Attempting to repair these connectors with conventional hand tools will damage them.

If reliability is a concern, solder wires with rosin core solder whenever possible and insulate them using shrink wrap, or a good quality electrical tape. Exercise care when soldering wires, as proper heat sinks may be needed to prevent component damage from excessive heat. Do not solder a wire or component if there is a potential for heat related damage to occur.

BATTERY CABLES

Disconnecting the Battery Cables

When working on any electrical component on the vehicle, it is always a good idea to disconnect the negative (-) battery cable. This will prevent potential damage to many sensitive electrical components such as the Powertrain Control Module (PCM), radio, alternator, etc.

※ WARNING

Never disconnect a battery cable when the engine is running. Disconnecting a battery cable with the engine running is likely to cause expensive and permanent damage to the alternator, voltage regulator, and control modules, such as the PCM.

➡ Any time you disconnect or remove the battery cables, it is recommended that you disconnect the negative (-) battery cable first. This will prevent your accidentally grounding the positive (+) terminal to the body of the vehicle when disconnecting it, thereby preventing damage to the above mentioned components.

Before you disconnect the cable(s), first turn the ignition to the OFF position. This will prevent a draw on the battery which could cause arcing (electricity trying to ground itself to the body of a vehicle, just like a spark plug jumping the gap) and, of course, damaging some components such as the alternator diodes.

When reconnecting or installing a battery, always attach the negative cable last. This is done as a safety measure, should a tool or component slip while installing the positive battery cable. If the tool touches the battery positive terminal and a chassis ground simultaneously, as long as the negative battery cable is not connected, no damage will occur. Make sure when installing a battery that the positive battery cable is fully installed and tightened before installing the negative battery cable.

When the battery cable(s) are reconnected (negative cable last), be sure to check that your lights, windshield wipers and other electrically operated safety components are all working correctly. If your vehicle contains an Electronically Tuned Radio (ETR), don't forget to reset your radio security code, the radio station presets, and reset the clock.

AIR BAG (SUPPLEMENTAL RESTRAINT SYSTEM)

General Information

The Air Bag is referred to as a Supplemental Restraint System (SRS) component because it is designed to work with, or as a supplement to, the seat belts supplied with the vehicle.

※ CAUTION

Air bags should never be assumed to take the place of seat belts. The air bag is designed to work in conjunction with the seat belts. Most states have instituted laws requiring the use of seat belts. Consult your local and state laws regarding seat belt usage.

※ WARNING

If the air bags have deployed, the air bags, SRS control unit, and if installed, the seat belt tensioner assemblies must be replaced.

A basic SRS is comprised of the following components:
• SRS Airbag
• SRS Sensors
• SRS Control Unit
• SRS Indicator Light (SRS Warning Light)
The SRS Sensors are used by the SRS Control Unit to detect a moderate to severe frontal collision. If such is the case, the SRS Sensors send a signal to the SRS Control Unit, which in turn activates the SRS Airbag. The SRS Control Unit also has it's own emergency backup power in case the vehicle's electrical system is disconnected in a crash.

The SRS Control Unit also monitors the integrity of the SRS System once the ignition key is switched ON. Under normal operating conditions, when the ignition key is initially turned to the ON position, the SRS Indicator Light should come on for 6 seconds, and then go out. This serves as a bulb check for the SRS Indicator Light. If the SRS Control Unit detects a problem in the SRS system, the SRS Indicator Light will remain ON until the problem is resolved and the SRS Diagnostic Trouble Codes (DTCs) erased.

※ CAUTION

If the SRS Indicator Light fails to light, or is on continuously, the cause should be determined immediately. The system may have a problem that could compromise the safe operation and/or deployment of the SRS system.

SERVICE PRECAUTIONS

◆ See Figures 10 and 11

※ WARNING

The Supplemental Restraint System (SRS) must be disabled before performing service on or around system components, steering column, instrument panel components, wiring and sensors. Failure to follow safety and disabling procedures could result in accidental air bag deployment, possible personal injury and unnecessary system repairs.

Please take note of the following precautions whenever working on or near SRS air bag system components:
• When carrying a live air bag module, point the bag and trim cushion away from your body. When placing a live air bag on a bench or other surface, always face the bag and trim cushion up, away from the surface. Following these precautions will reduce the chance of injury if the air bag is accidentally deployed.
• Use only a digital multimeter when checking any part of the air bag system. The multimeter's output must be 0.01Amps (10mA) or less when it is switched to its smallest ohmmeter range value.
• Do not bump, strike, or drop any SRS component. Store SRS components away from any source of electricity, including static electricity, moisture, oil, grease, and extreme heat and humidity.
• Do not cut, damage, or attempt to alter the SRS wiring harness or its yellow insulation.
• Do not install SRS components that have been recovered from wrecked or dismantled vehicles.
• Always disconnect both battery cables when working around SRS components or wiring.

93138P10
Fig. 10 If removed, always place the inflator module facing up to avoid injury should accidental deployment occur

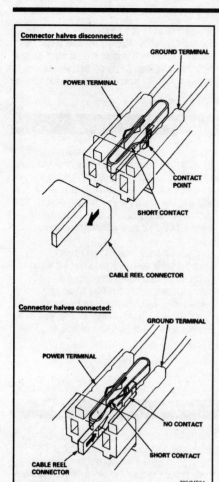

Connector halves disconnected:

GROUND TERMINAL

POWER TERMINAL

CONTACT POINT

SHORT CONTACT

CABLE REEL CONNECTOR

Connector halves connected:

GROUND TERMINAL

POWER TERMINAL

NO CONTACT

SHORT CONTACT

CABLE REEL CONNECTOR

7924MG34

Fig. 11 Cut away view of a spring-loaded SRS electrical connector. Never modify an SRS electrical connector

- Always disable the air bag when working under the dashboard.
- Always check the alignment of the air bag cable reel during steering-related service procedures.
- Take extra care when working in the area of the dashboard. Avoid direct exposure of the SRS unit or wiring to heat guns, welding, or spraying equipment.
- Disconnect the driver's/front passenger's air bag and if equipped, the seat belt tensioner connections before working below the dashboard close to the SRS control unit.
- If the vehicle is involved in a frontal impact or after a collision without airbag deployment, inspect the SRS unit for physical damage. If the SRS control unit is dented, cracked, or deformed, replace it.
- If removed or replaced, make sure the SRS control unit is installed securely.
- Never disassemble the SRS control unit.
- When installing or replacing the SRS control unit, be careful not to bump or strike the area around the SRS control unit. Avoid using impact wrenches, hammers, etc. in the area surrounding the SRS control unit
- Never reach through the steering wheel to start an air bag equipped vehicle.
- If the air bag has deployed, the air bags, control unit, and if equipped, the seat belt tensioners must be replaced.

DISARMING THE SRS

✳✳ CAUTION

The Supplemental Restraint System (SRS) must be disarmed before any of its components are disconnected or the air bag is removed. Failing to disarm the SRS before servicing its components may cause accidental deployment of the air bag, resulting in unnecessary SRS repairs and possible personal injury.

➡**To fully disarm the SRS, both the driver's and passenger's air bag be disconnected.**

The battery must be disconnected at least 3 minutes prior to proceeding with disarming the SRS components, otherwise DTCs will be stored and the SRS Indicator Light will remain on once the system is activated. If DTCs are stored in the process of disarming the SRS, consult the SRS Indicator Light resetting procedures in this section.

Driver's Side Air Bag

➡**Write down the sound system security code before disconnecting the battery.**

1. Disconnect the negative, then the positive battery cables.

✳✳ WARNING

Wait at least three minutes after disconnecting the battery before working on or around the air bag.

2. On all models, except the 1996 Prelude with the 2.2L engine, remove the steering wheel lower access cover and detach the driver's side 2-pin air bag electrical connector.
3. On the 1996 Prelude with the 2.2L engine, remove the steering wheel lower access panel and locate the red shorting connector. Detach the driver's side air bag 3-pin electrical connector, then install the red shorting connector onto the 3-pin air bag connector.

Passenger's Side Air Bag

1. If not already disconnected, disconnect negative battery cable first and then the positive battery cable.

✳✳ WARNING

Wait at least three minutes after disconnecting the battery before working on or around the air bag.

2. Remove the glove box or dashboard compartment. The air bag electrical connector is located in the dash just above the glove or storage box.
3. Depending on the vehicle, the air bag connector may be a 2 or 3-pin connection. Locate the passenger's side air bag connector, and proceed as follows:
   a. If the air bag connector is a 2-pin electrical connector, detach the connector.
   b. If the air bag connector is a 3-pin electrical connector, locate the red shorting connector. Disconnect the 3-pin passenger's side air bag

connector, and then install the air bag 3-pin electrical connector onto the red shorting connector.

ARMING THE SRS

➡**To properly arm the Supplemental Restraint (SRS) System, all SRS components must be completely and properly installed. This includes the driver's and passenger's air bag.**

Driver's Side Air Bag

1. On all models, except the 1996 2.2L Prelude, attach the driver's side 2-pin air bag electrical connector.
2. On 1996 2.2L Prelude models, perform the following:
   a. Remove the red shorting connector from the air bag module connector.
   b. Immediately couple the air bag and cable reel connectors.
   c. Place the red shorting connector back into its holder.
3. Install the steering wheel lower access panel.
4. Make sure the passenger's air bag and, if equipped, the driver's and passenger's seat belt tensioners are properly installed before connecting the battery.
5. Connect the positive battery cable first and then the negative battery cable.
6. Enter the sound system security code.
7. Turn the ignition switch to the **ON** position, but don't start the engine. The SRS indicator light should turn on for 6 seconds and then turn off. If the SRS indicator light doesn't come on, or stays on longer than six seconds, the system fault must be diagnosed, repaired and the SRS DTC fault memory cleared.

Passenger's Side Air Bag

1. On all models except the 1996 2.2L Prelude, attach the 2-pin passenger's side air bag connector.
2. On 2.2L Prelude models, locate the front passenger's air bag connector and proceed as follows:
   a. If the air bag connector is a 2-pin electrical connector, attach the electrical connector.
   b. If the air bag connector is a 3-pin electrical connector, remove the red shorting connector and immediately connect the 3-pin passenger's side air bag electrical connector. Then place the red shorting connector back into its holder.
3. Install the glove box or dashboard compartment.
4. Make sure the driver's air bag and, if equipped, the driver's and passenger's seat belt tensioners are properly installed before connecting the battery.
5. Connect the positive battery cable first and then the negative battery cable.
6. Enter the sound system security code.
7. Turn the ignition switch to the **ON** position, but don't start the engine. The SRS indicator light should turn on for 6 seconds and then turn off. If the SRS indicator light doesn't come on, or stays on longer than six seconds, the system fault must be diagnosed, repaired and the SRS DTC fault memory cleared.

RESETTING THE SRS INDICATOR

The Supplemental Restraint System (SRS) Indicator Light should extinguish 6 seconds after the ignition is switched **ON** if the system is in proper working order. If the light fails to illuminate, or the light stays on, the cause of the problem should be determined immediately.

If the SRS Warning Light stays on after the 6 second bulb check function, the control unit is sending a signal indicating there are stored faults in the system. These stored faults are referred to as Diagnostic Trouble Codes (DTCs). The DTCs can be read by using a suitable Data Scan Tool (DST) or by activating the blink codes using the yellow Memory Erase Signal (MES) Connector and the Service Connector (SCS) tool No. 07PAZ-0010100.

To read the stored DTCs, switch the ignition **OFF** for at least 10 seconds and install the Service Connector SCS tool to the Service Check Connector as outlined in Section 4. Turn the ignition switch to the **ON** position and the SRS indicator light should come on for 6 seconds and then go off momentarily. If DTCs are stored the SRS will then begin to flash the codes, the main code is flashed first, fol-

lowed by the sub-code. A main code flash lasts 1.2 seconds, the sub-code flash lasts 0.3 seconds. The blink code system is capable of displaying a maximum of three codes. If no codes are stored, the SRS indicator light will come on for 6 seconds, go off momentarily, and then come back on.

To erase the DTC memory and reset the SRS Indicator Light, first locate the yellow plastic Memory Erase Signal (MES) connector:

• The SRS connector is plugged into the upper right corner of the driver's side under dash fuse panel or behind the driver's side left kick panel.

The two wire color combinations found housed in the MES yellow connector should be as follows:

• 2.2L engines: Gray, gray or black, white
• 2.3L engines: Green, green or black, white
• V6 engines: Green, green or black, light green/black

Once the MES connector has been properly located and identified, proceed as follows:

1. Verify and make sure the ignition is switched **OFF**.
2. Connect the SCS service connector Tool No. 07PAZ-0010100 to the MES connector.
3. Turn the ignition switch **ON**.
4. The SRS Indicator Light should come on for 6 seconds and then go off. Remove the SCS connec-

tor within 4 seconds of when the SRS light goes off.

5. The SRS Indicator Light should come back on again. Reconnect the SCS service connector to the MES connector within 4 seconds of the time when the SRS Indicator Light comes back on.

6. The SRS Indicator Light should go off. Remove the SCS service connector from the MES connector within 4 seconds of the light going off.

7. If the process was successful, the SRS Indicator Light will blink two times.

8. Turn the ignition switch **OFF** and wait 10 seconds.

9. Turn the ignition switch **ON** and the SRS Indicator Light should come on for 6 seconds and then go off if all of the codes have been successfully cleared.

10. If the SRS Indicator Light does not go off, repeat the erasing the DTCs procedure. If after several attempts to erase the DTCs the SRS Indicator Light stays on, use the blink codes to help locate the problem in the SRS system. Inspect and make sure that all the components and electrical connectors are properly installed and connected.

11. Once the DTCs have been successfully erased, reinstall the yellow MES connector to its holder in the fuse panel.

HEATING AND AIR CONDITIONING

> ※※ **WARNING**
>
> **When working on components located near or under the dash be aware of the location of the Supplemental Restraint (SRS) System components and wiring and take care not to damage them.**

> ※※ **CAUTION**
>
> **The SRS system should always be disarmed before performing dash related repairs, otherwise physical injury or component damage could occur.**

Blower Motor

REMOVAL & INSTALLATION

➡**On some models of the Accord and Prelude you may have to remove the air conditioning evaporator to allow access to the blower motor. Removal of the air conditioner evaporator requires the A/C system to be discharged. The legal ramifications of discharging A/C systems without the proper EPA certification, experience, and equipment dictate that the A/C components on your vehicle should be serviced only by a Motor Vehicle Air Conditioning (MVAC) trained, and EPA certified automotive technician using approved equipment.**

If you insist upon servicing the heater core and you are not a Motor Vehicle Air Conditioning (MVAC) trained, and EPA certified automotive technician and/or you do have the approved equipment for discharging and recovery of the A/C refrigerant,

before disabling your vehicle, take your vehicle to an approved repair facility and have the A/C system discharged prior to beginning the heater core repair procedure.

Accord

1996–97 MODELS

▶ **See Figures 12, 13, 14 and 15**

The front blower motor is located in the front passenger's right side foot well area.

1. If additional access is needed, remove the front passenger's right side lower kick panel.
2. Detach the negative battery cable.
3. Remove the glove box door and frame.

4. On models without A/C, remove the self-tapping screws from the heater duct.
5. On models equipped with A/C, remove the evaporator.
6. Detach the electrical connectors from the blower motor.
7. Remove the fasteners on the blower motor mounting flange.
8. Remove the blower motor downward from the blower unit.
9. Installation is the reverse of the removal procedure.
10. Check for air leaks.

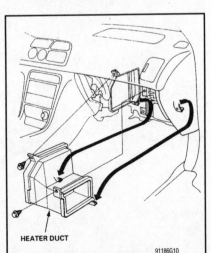

HEATER DUCT

91186G10

Fig. 12 If your vehicle is not equipped with A/C, unfasten the 2 self-tapping screws, then remove the heater duct

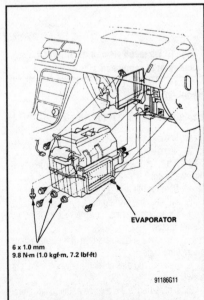

EVAPORATOR

6 x 1.0 mm
9.8 N·m (1.0 kgf·m, 7.2 lbf·ft)

91186G11

Fig. 13 If your vehicle has A/C, you must remove the evaporator

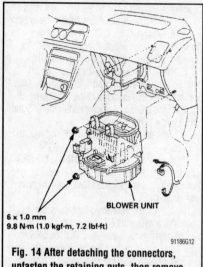

6 x 1.0 mm
9.8 N·m (1.0 kgf·m, 7.2 lbf·ft)

BLOWER UNIT

91186G12

Fig. 14 After detaching the connectors, unfasten the retaining nuts, then remove the blower unit

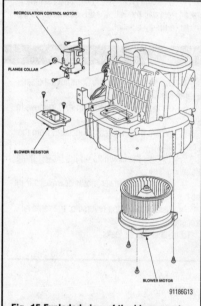

RECIRCULATION CONTROL MOTOR

FLANGE COLLAR

BLOWER RESISTOR

BLOWER MOTOR

91186G13

Fig. 15 Exploded view of the blower motor and related components

1998–00 MODELS

▶ See Figures 16, 17 and 18

1. Remove the negative battery cable.
2. Remove the dashboard.
3. If the vehicle is equipped with A/C, remove the evaporator.
4. Remove the self-tapping screws, nut and bolts, and then the heating duct.
5. Detach the electrical connectors from the blower motor.
6. Remove the fasteners from the blower motor mounting flange.
7. Remove the blower motor downward from the blower unit.
8. Installation is the reverse of the removal procedure.
9. Check for air leaks.

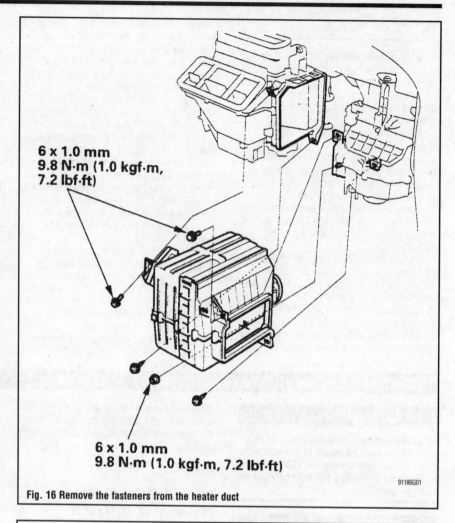

6 x 1.0 mm
9.8 N·m (1.0 kgf·m, 7.2 lbf·ft)

6 x 1.0 mm
9.8 N·m (1.0 kgf·m, 7.2 lbf·ft)

91186G01

Fig. 16 Remove the fasteners from the heater duct

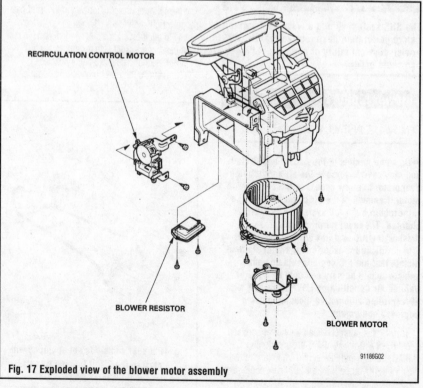

RECIRCULATION CONTROL MOTOR

BLOWER RESISTOR

BLOWER MOTOR

91186G02

Fig. 17 Exploded view of the blower motor assembly

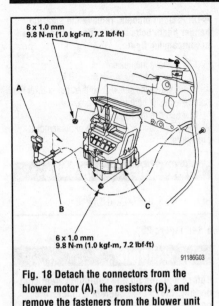

6 x 1.0 mm
9.8 N·m (1.0 kgf·m, 7.2 lbf·ft)

A

B   C

6 x 1.0 mm
9.8 N·m (1.0 kgf·m, 7.2 lbf·ft)

91186G03

Fig. 18 Detach the connectors from the blower motor (A), the resistors (B), and remove the fasteners from the blower unit (C)

Prelude

1996 MODELS

▶ See Figures 12, 13 and 14

1. Detach the negative battery cable.
2. Remove the glove box and frame.
3. Remove the self-tapping screws and the heater duct on models without A/C.
4. On models with A/C, remove the evaporator.
5. Detach all electrical connections from the blower motor.
6. Remove the blower resistor.
7. Remove the recirculation motor.
8. Remove the two nuts from the bolts, then pull the blower unit from the vehicle.
9. Installation is the reverse of removal.
10. Check for air leaks.

1997–00 MODELS

▶ See Figures 12, 13 and 14

1. Detach the negative battery cable.
2. Remove the evaporator.
3. Detach the wiring connectors from the recirculation motor.
4. Remove the blower motor connector.
5. Detach the wiring from the blower motor resistors.
6. Remove the blower motor mounting bolts.
7. Pull the blower housing from the vehicle.

Heater Core

REMOVAL & INSTALLATION

1996–97 Models

▶ See Figure 19

➡**Removing the heater core may require removal of the dashboard and the air conditioner evaporator. Removal of the air conditioner evaporator requires the A/C system to be discharged. The legal ramifications of dis-**

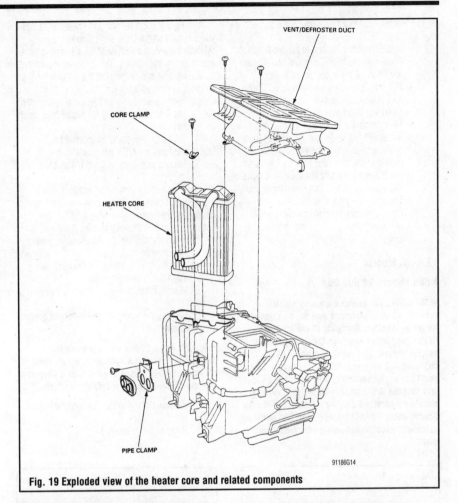

VENT/DEFROSTER DUCT

CORE CLAMP

HEATER CORE

PIPE CLAMP

91186G14

Fig. 19 Exploded view of the heater core and related components

charging A/C systems without the proper EPA certification, experience, and equipment dictate that the A/C components on your vehicle should be serviced only by a Motor Vehicle Air Conditioning (MVAC) trained, and EPA certified automotive technician using approved equipment.

If you insist upon servicing the heater core and you are not a Motor Vehicle Air Conditioning (MVAC) trained, and EPA certified automotive technician and/or you do have the approved equipment for discharging and recovery of the A/C refrigerant, before disabling your vehicle, take your vehicle to an approved repair facility and have the A/C system discharged prior to beginning the heater core repair procedure.

1. Take your vehicle to an approved repair facility and have the A/C system discharged.
2. Record your vehicle's radio anti-theft code.
3. Disconnect the negative battery cable.

➡**Allow the engine to cool if the coolant temperature is above 100°F (37°C).**

4. From under the hood, locate the heater control valve on the lower passenger's side firewall area just below the fuel filter. Manually turn the heater control valve to the opened position.
5. Make sure the heater valve is in the full hot position by pressing the arm toward the firewall.
6. Drain the engine coolant from the radiator into a suitable and sealable container.
7. Remove the heater control valve.

8. Place a drain pan below the two heater hoses at the firewall, release the tension on both heater hose clamps and slide the clamps up the heater hose away from the firewall and remove the two hoses.
9. Drain the coolant from the hoses into the drain pan and then into a suitable and sealable container.
10. Remove the nut attached to the stud protruding through the firewall, just above and to the right of the heater hoses.
11. Remove the dashboard assembly. Refer to Section 10 for specific details.
12. Remove the heater duct.
13. Detach the heater unit from the fire wall.
14. Remove the self-tapping screws and the bracket.
15. Pull the heater core out of the housing.

To install:

The installation procedure is in reverse order of disassembly making note of the following points.

16. For the air conditioning system, perform the following:

- Replace any removed A/C O-rings and coat them with a light coating of refrigerant oil before installing them.
- Make sure any replaced O-rings are compatible with R-134a refrigerant.
- Once the repair procedure is completed, have a certified repair facility add the proper type and amount of refrigerant oil if necessary, charge the A/C system, and test for normal operation and refrigerant leaks.

17. For the heater system, perform the following:

- Apply a suitable sealant to the grommets.
- Make sure the heater inlet and outlet hoses are installed in the correct location.
- Refill the engine coolant with a 50/50 mixture of approved coolant and water, and bleed as necessary.
- Once the heater core repair is completed, make sure the heater control valve is properly adjusted by placing the temperature setting to the max cool position. Unclamp the heater valve cable sheathing and move the heater valve arm away from the firewall. The apply a light pull to the cable and cable sheathing to make sure all slack is removed from the cable, and reinstall the cable.

1998–00 Models

▶ **See Figures 20 thru 25**

➡Removing the heater core may require removal of the dashboard and the air conditioner evaporator. Removal of the air conditioner evaporator requires the A/C system to be discharged. The legal ramifications of discharging A/C systems without the proper EPA certification, experience, and equipment dictate that the A/C components on your vehicle should be serviced only by a Motor Vehicle Air Conditioning (MVAC) trained, and EPA certified automotive technician using approved equipment.

If you insist upon servicing the heater core and you are not a Motor Vehicle Air Conditioning (MVAC) trained, and EPA certified automotive technician and/or you do have the approved equipment for discharging and recovery of the A/C refrigerant, before disabling your vehicle, take your vehicle to an approved repair facility and have the A/C system discharged prior to beginning the heater core repair procedure.

1. Take your vehicle to an approved repair facility and have the A/C system discharged.
2. Record your vehicle's radio anti-theft code.
3. Disconnect the negative battery cable.
4. From under the hood, open the cable clamp, disconnect the heater valve cable, and turn the heater valve arm to the fully opened position.
5. Drain the coolant into a suitable container. The engine must be cool.
6. Remove the mounting nut from the heater.
7. Push the hose clamps back.
8. Place a small drip pan under the heater hoses.
9. Remove the inlet and then the outlet hoses from the heater unit.

➡Always keep engine coolant away from painted surfaces. If a spill does occur, rinse it off immediately. Never wipe it with a shop rag, this may further smear it into the surface.

10. Remove the mounting nut from the heater unit.
11. Remove the dashboard.

➡On Prelude models, remove the steering hanger beam bolts in the order shown in the accompanying figure.

12. Remove the heater duct.
13. Remove the heater unit.
14. Remove the screws and then the bracket that holds the heater core in the air box.
15. Remove the heater core.
16. Installation is the reverse of the removal procedure.

Heater Water Control Valve

REMOVAL & INSTALLATION

▶ **See Figure 26**

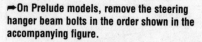

✳✳ **WARNING**

Before working on any cooling system component, the engine coolant temperature must be below 100°F (37°C).

1. Turn the ignition switch to the **ON** position, then turn the heater temperature control to full hot, then turn the ignition switch **OFF**.
2. Drain the coolant from the radiator into a suitable sealable container, or using two pair of suitable hose crimping pliers, carefully clamp shut the two heater hoses attached to the heater control valve.
3. Squeeze the hose clamp ends together using

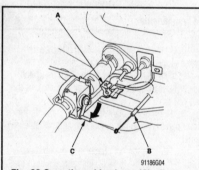

Fig. 20 Open the cable clamp (A), disconnect the heater valve cable (B), and turn the heater valve arm (C) to the fully opened position

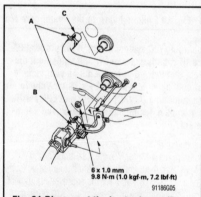

6 x 1.0 mm
9.8 N·m (1.0 kgf·m, 7.2 lbf·ft)
91186G05

Fig. 21 Disconnect the heater hoses (B and C) from the heater unit

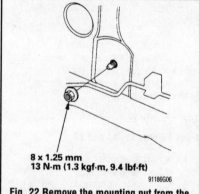

8 x 1.25 mm
13 N·m (1.3 kgf·m, 9.4 lbf·ft)
91186G06

Fig. 22 Remove the mounting nut from the heater unit

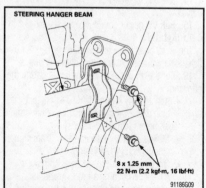

STEERING HANGER BEAM

8 x 1.25 mm
22 N·m (2.2 kgf·m, 16 lbf·ft)
91186G09

Fig. 23 On Prelude models, remove the steering hanger beam bolts

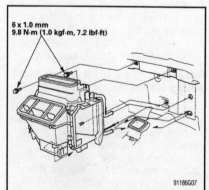

6 x 1.0 mm
9.8 N·m (1.0 kgf·m, 7.2 lbf·ft)
91186G07

Fig. 24 Remove the heater unit assembly from the vehicle

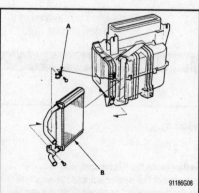

91186G08

Fig. 25 Pull the heater core (B) from the air distribution box

Fig. 26 A pair of hose crimping pliers is useful when doing cooling system related repairs

a flat-nosed pliers to release the tension of the hose clamps, and slide the clamps off of the heater valve spigots.

4. Place a suitable coolant drain pan below the heater control valve, then remove the control valve cable clamp and control valve cable.

5. Carefully remove the heater hoses from the control valve and remove the control valve from the vehicle.

To install:

The installation is the reverse of the removal procedure making sure of the following points:
- Make sure the cooling system is topped off with the proper mixture of coolant and bled if necessary.
- Once the repair is completed, check the operation of the heater control valve.

Air Conditioning Components

REMOVAL & INSTALLATION

Repair or service of air conditioning components is not covered by this manual, because of the risk of personal injury or death, and because of the legal ramifications of servicing these components without the proper EPA certification and experience. Cost, personal injury or death, environmental damage, and legal considerations (such as the fact that it is a federal crime to vent refrigerant into the atmo-

sphere), dictate that the A/C components on your vehicle should be serviced only by a Motor Vehicle Air Conditioning (MVAC) trained, and EPA certified automotive technician.

→ **If your vehicle's A/C system uses R-12 refrigerant and is in need of recharging, the A/C system can be converted over to R-134a refrigerant (less environmentally harmful and expensive). Refer to Section 1 for additional information on R-12 to R-134a conversions, and for additional considerations dealing with your vehicle's A/C system.**

Control Cables

REMOVAL & INSTALLATION

Temperature Control Cable

1. Locate the heater control valve under the hood and disconnect the temperature control cable from the heater control valve and arm.

2. Locate the air mix control arm and heater control cable under the dash and disconnect the cable.

To install:

3. Set the climate control temperature to MAX COOL with the ignition switched **ON**.

4. Reconnect the heater control cable to the air mix control arm assembly under the dash. Make sure the cable sheathing is flush against the stop.

5. Access the heater control valve under the hood and move the heater valve arm away from the firewall to the fully closed position.

6. Attach the cable end to the heater valve arm.

7. Hold the heater valve arm in the fully closed position while applying a light load toward the firewall on the cable sheathing to remove any slack in the cable.

8. Clamp the cable into the heater control valve.

9. Test the operation of the unit to make sure no binding occurs and repair as necessary.

CONTROL CABLE ADJUSTMENT

1. Under the hood, open the clamp and disconnect the heater control valve cable from the arm.

2. Under the dash, detach the air mix control

cable from the clamp. Pull the cable from the control arm.

3. Position the temperature control at MAX COOL.

4. Turn the air mix control arm counterclockwise until it stops.

5. Attach the air mix control cable to the arm.

6. Snap the air mix cable hook into the cable clamp.

7. Under the hood, turn the control valve to the fully closed position.

8. Install the heater valve cable to the arm.

9. Gently pull on the cable housing to remove any slack.

10. Insert the cable into the clamp.

Control Panel

REMOVAL & INSTALLATION

▶ **See Figure 27**

1. Remove the center trim panel, by unfastening any necessary retainers, then carefully prying it off.

2. Detach the air mix control cable from the heater unit.

3. Remove the panel retaining screws then pull the heater control panel from the dash.

4. Detach the wiring connectors from the back of the control panel, then remove the heater control panel.

5. Installation is the reverse of removal.

Fig. 27 You must remove the center trim panel for access to the control panel retainers

CRUISE CONTROL

The cruise control system is a vacuum-based system and is designed to work at speeds above 25 mph. To activate the system, the cruise control dash mounted main switch must be in the on position. The main switch toggles between on and off by simply pressing it. When in the on position, an indicator light in the switch will light.

The cruise control system works a mechanical linkage to the throttle by way of a vacuum motor which is inside a server. This is a diaphragm moved by vacuum applied to one side. A solenoid driven valve connects the vacuum motor to a vacuum tank. Another solenoid vents the vacuum. The cruise control module controls the servo and the

throttle by pulsing these solenoid valves on and off.

One input to the cruise control module is the vehicle speed, which is sent to the Powertrain Control Module (PCM) by the Vehicle Speed Sensor (VSS)

To diagnose the system, first note the symptom.

If the system does not engage at all:
- Check the main switch, make sure it is in the on position.
- Check the brake and clutch (if installed) pedal adjustments.
- Check the wiring for the cruise vacuum unit and control unit.

- Check the vacuum hose connections for the vacuum unit.
- Check the vacuum unit throttle cable and verify that it is connected.
- Check the speedometer operation. If the speedometer does not work, the VSS may be faulty.

If the system loses speed:
- Check the vacuum hoses for the vacuum unit for leaks.
- Check the vacuum storage tank for leaks.

If the vehicle loses speed before the system engages:
- Check the cable adjustment from the vacuum unit to the throttle for excessive free play.

ENTERTAINMENT SYSTEMS

Radio Receiver/Amplifier/Tape Player/CD Player

REMOVAL & INSTALLATION

♦ **See Figures 28, 29, 30 and 31**

1. Note the radio security code, then disconnect the negative battery cable..
2. Remove the center console. For specific details, refer to Section 10.
3. Detach the cup holder (if applicable). For specific details, refer to Section 10.
4. Remove the mounting bolts/screws from the console.
5. Remove the mounting screws from the radio and then pull the unit out slightly for access to the connectors on the rear of the radio.
6. Detach the electrical connectors and antenna lead, then remove the radio from the vehicle.

7. Installation is the reverse of the removal procedure. Once installed, enter the security code.

Fig. 28 Remove all switches that may inhibit removal of the radio

Speakers

REMOVAL & INSTALLATION

♦ **See Figures 32 thru 37**

1. If necessary, remove the door panel, as outlined in Section 10.
2. Locate the small rectangular opening at the bottom of the speaker grilles.
3. Using a suitable, small flat blade prytool, carefully pry the speaker grille up.
4. Remove the Phillips screws that mount the speaker.
5. Carefully remove the speaker from the door panel, instrument panel or rear deck to gain access to the electrical connector.
6. Remove the wire connector from the speaker, then remove the speaker from the vehicle.
7. Installation is the reverse of the removal procedure.

Fig. 29 Pull the radio partially out from the dashboard for access to the connectors

Fig. 30 Unplug the antenna cable. Never allow the radio to hang from the antenna cable, as this may damage the cable

Fig. 31 Detach the wiring harness from the rear of the radio

Fig. 32 Remove the speaker cover by carefully prying it off

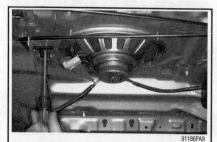

Fig. 33 Detach all speaker wire looms by unfastening the retaining screws

Fig. 34 Use a ratchet and socket to remove the speaker mounting screws

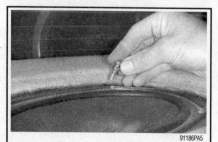

Fig. 35 Note the spacer on the end of the speaker mounting screw

Fig. 36 Carefully lift the speaker up . . .

Fig. 37 . . . then detach the wiring harness and remove the speaker

WINDSHIELD WIPERS AND WASHERS

Windshield Wiper Blade and Arm

REMOVAL & INSTALLATION

Front

▶ See Figures 38, 39, 40 and 41

1. Remove the mounting nut from the wiper pivot.

2. Mark the wiper arm and pivot bolt alignment using touch up paint or a suitable maker.

3. Carefully press down on the wiper arm about 4 inches (100mm) from the wiper pivot bolt. Press down and release several times until the wiper arm releases from the pivot. If you have trouble removing the arm, you can try using a suitable puller to release the arm from the pivot.

4. While holding the wiper arm on the pivot, fold the arm upward until it locks in position.

5. Lift the wiper arm off of the pivot.

To install:

➡Be sure to properly align the wiper arm with the pivot bolt.

6. Installation is the reverse of removal.

➡Once the arms are installed, operate the wipers in the fast position with the windshield wet. Use the washers to wet the windshield. If the wipers strike the windshield trim, reposition the arms to so they do not touch the surrounding trim.

Rear

The rear wiper arm removal is the same as the front wiper arm procedure, with exception of the wrench size needed. Most of the rear wiper assemblies typically require a 12mm wrench for removal.

Windshield Wiper Motor

REMOVAL & INSTALLATION

Front

▶ See Figures 42, 43, 44, 45 and 46

1. Make sure the wipers are in the park position. If not, turn the ignition key to the **ON** position and operate the wipers one time. Turn the wiper switch to the off position and then turn the ignition switch **OFF**.

2. Remove the wiper arms from the wiper pivots.

3. Using a suitable trim panel removal tool, remove the upper clips from the plastic windshield wiper linkage cover.

4. Using two small suitable prytools, carefully remove the lower panel clips from the wiper linkage cover.

5. Remove the 2 wiper pivot trim covers, and then remove the plastic wiper linkage cover.

6. Using a 10mm socket, extension and ratchet, remove the four wiper assembly mounting bolts.

7. Remove the wiper motor electrical connector from the wiper motor.

8. Carefully remove the wiper motor and linkage assembly from the center cowling.

9. Make a reference mark with touch up paint or a suitable marker between the motor pivot shaft and the pivot arm.

10. Using a 12mm wrench, remove the pivot arm mounting nut, and then tap the arm with a suitable plastic handle of a screwdriver. It may take several taps to loosen the link arm. Once the arm is loose, lift it off of the pivot shaft.

11. Using a 10mm socket, extension and ratchet, remove the three bolts that mount the motor to the bracket assembly, then remove the motor assembly.

To install:

12. Installation is the reverse of the removal. If the wiper motor is being replaced, cycle the motor one time to make sure it is in the park position. To do this proceed as follows:

a. Before installing the wiper motor onto the linkage assembly, plug the wiper electrical connector onto the wiper motor.

b. Secure and place the wiper motor such that it can be operated safely and will not contact a painted surface.

Fig. 38 After removing the wiper arm mounting nut, matchmark the installed position of the wiper arm to the pivot bolt

Fig. 39 Carefully press down on the arm about 4 inches from the pivot bolt a few times. This should release the blade and arm from the pivot

Fig. 40 If you encounter difficulty removing the wiper arm from the pivot, you can try using a puller to separate the arm . . .

Fig. 41 . . . then lift the wiper arm from the pivot

Fig. 42 Remove the wiper arm from the wiper pivots

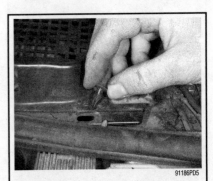

Fig. 43 Remove the retaining clips from the windshield wiper linkage cover (cowl) . . .

Fig. 44 . . . then remove the cover for access to the wiper motor and linkage

Fig. 45 Installed view of the windshield wiper motor and linkage

Fig. 46 Unfasten the retaining bolts, then remove the wiper motor assembly

c. Turn the ignition switch to the **ON** position, but do not start the engine.

d. While the ignition switch is in the **ON** position, turn the wiper switch to the low speed on position. Make sure the wiper motor spins, then turn the wiper switch **OFF**. The wiper motor should stop moving once it reaches the park position.

e. Turn the ignition switch to the **OFF** position, and install the wiper motor in the reverse order as removal.

Rear

♦ See Figure 47

1. Make sure the wipers are in the park position. If not, turn the ignition key to the **ON** position and operate the wipers one time. Turn the wiper switch to the off position and then turn the ignition switch **OFF**.

2. Lift up the rear wiper pivot cover, and using a 10mm wrench, remove the rear wiper mounting nut.

3. Matchmark the wiper arm and the wiper pivot, then remove the wiper arm from the wiper pivot.

4. Remove the outer wiper pivot trim from the wiper pivot.

5. Using a suitable 23mm wrench, loosen and remove the wiper pivot mounting nut.

6. Open the rear hatch glass and press in on

the two wiper motor cover tabs, and remove the cover.

7. Detach the electrical connector from the wiper motor.

8. Using a 10mm socket, extension and ratchet, remove the fastener that secures the motor assembly to the window lift handle and carefully remove the wiper motor and bracket assembly from the rear hatch glass.

9. Using a 10mm socket, extension and ratchet, remove the fasteners that secure the motor to the wiper motor bracket assembly.

To install:

10. Installation is the reverse of the removal procedure. If the wiper motor is being replaced, cycle the motor one time to make sure it is in the park position. To do this proceed as follows:

a. Before installing the wiper motor onto the linkage assembly, plug the wiper electrical connector onto the wiper motor.

b. Carefully hold the wiper motor such that it can be operated safely and will not contact a painted surface or the rear hatch glass.

c. Turn the ignition switch to the **ON** position, but do not start the engine.

d. While the ignition switch is in the **ON** position, turn the wiper switch to the low speed on position. Make sure the wiper motor spins, then turn the wiper switch off. The wiper motor should stop moving once it reaches the park position.

e. Turn the ignition switch to the **OFF** position and install the wiper motor in the reverse order of removal.

➡Use extreme care to not overtighten the fasteners.

Windshield Washer Pump

REMOVAL & INSTALLATION

♦ See Figures 48 and 49

The front and rear windshield washer pumps are attached to the washer bottle.

➡Some later models of the Accord and Prelude may require the removal of the front bumper to gain access to the washer solvent container. All others will require the removal of the front inner fender well.

1. Remove the front bumper or inner fender well as necessary for access to the windshield washer pump.

2. Disconnect the washer motor electrical connector and fluid hose.

3. Release the washer pump from the washer bottle and grommet.

Installation is the reverse of the removal procedure.

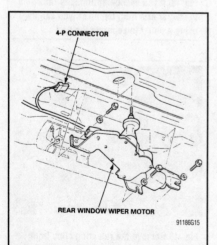

Fig. 47 View of the rear window wiper motor

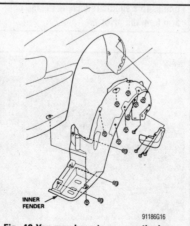

Fig. 48 You may have to remove the inner fender well to get the windshield washer pump

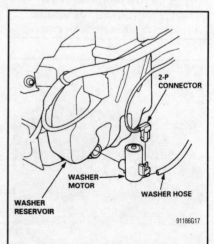

Fig. 49 The windshield washer pump is mounted to the washer fluid reservoir

INSTRUMENTS AND SWITCHES

Instrument Cluster

REMOVAL & INSTALLATION

♦ See Figures 50 thru 55

1. Remove the fasteners from the trim around the instrument cluster.
2. Use a small prytool to pop out one side of the trim cover.
3. With your fingers, gently pull the instrument cluster cover out.

➡ **This component is fragile. Use caution and good judgement when ever you are removing dashboard components to avoid any damage.**

4. Remove the instrument cluster mounting screws.
5. Pull the instrument cluster forward.
6. Detach all electrical connections from the rear of the cluster.
7. If applicable, remove the speedometer cable.
8. Remove the instrument cluster from the dash and place it on a soft cloth in a safe place to avoid damage to the clear plastic face plate.
9. If necessary, you can replace any burned out bulbs in the instrument cluster. From the rear of the cluster, twist the socket ¼ turn to release it, then pull the bulb straight out to replace.

To install:

10. Installation is the reverse of removal.
11. Check that all wiring and cables have been re-connected before you fasten the cluster to the dashboard with the mounting screws.
12. Road test the vehicle to ensure proper cluster and gauge function.

Gauges

REMOVAL & INSTALLATION

The gauges are an integral part of the instrument cluster and cannot be separated. If a gauge fails, the entire cluster must be replaced.

Back-up Light Switch

REMOVAL & INSTALLATION

Manual Transaxle

On vehicles equipped with manual transaxles, the back-up light switch is located on the top of the transaxle gear case. The switch looks similar to a large nut with two wires protruding from it. The switch is not adjustable.

1. Detach the electrical connector from the switch.
2. Loosen and remove the switch by turning it counterclockwise.

➡ **When replacing the switch, always use a new sealing washer.**

3. Installation is the reverse of the removal procedure.

Automatic Transaxle

On vehicles with automatic transaxles, the back-up light switch is located on the right side of the transaxle, under a protective cover. The switch is actually a combination switch for the neutral safety circuit, gear shift indicator and back-up lights. The switch is adjustable.

1. Set the parking brake and place the transaxle in Neutral.
2. Remove the protective cover for the switch.
3. Detach the electrical connector from the switch.
4. Loosen the switch mounting bolts, and remove the switch by lifting it away from the transaxle.

To install:

5. Make sure the transmission is in Neutral.
6. Set the switch such that it is in the neutral position. The switch will click when it is in the neutral position.
7. The remainder of the installation is the reverse of removal, making sure of the following:

   a. Turn the ignition switch **ON** and move the gear selector from position to position making sure all the gear indicator lights work properly.

   b. Then place the gear selector in the Reverse position and verify that the reverse lights are functioning.

   c. Next test to make sure the engine will start in the Neutral and Park positions, but will NOT start in any other position. If, necessary, adjust the switch as needed.

Fig. 50 Carefully pry around the edges of the instrument cluster trim panel . . .

Fig. 51 . . . then remove the cluster trim plate from the vehicle

Fig. 52 Unfasten the retaining screws from both sides of the instrument cluster . . .

Fig. 53 . . . then carefully pull the instrument cluster partially out from the instrument panel

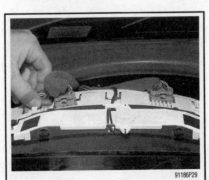

Fig. 54 With the cluster pulled out, detach all of the wiring harnesses from the rear of the cluster

Fig. 55 Once the cluster is removed, replace any burned out bulbs by twisting the bulb and socket ¼ turn, then pulling the bulb straight out of the socket

LIGHTING

Headlights

REMOVAL & INSTALLATION

♦ **See Figures 56 thru 61**

1. Locate the headlight bulb that needs to be replaced.

➡ **It may be necessary to remove a component or the composite headlight assembly to gain access to the bulbs.**

2. Turn the headlights off.
3. Detach the two prong connector from the base of the headlight bulb.
4. Twist the bulb counterclockwise to unlock it from the headlight housing, then carefully withdraw the bulb from the housing.

✳✳ WARNING

Do not touch the glass part of the bulb with your fingers. The pads of your fingers contain oils that will cause premature bulb failure.

To install:

5. Install a new bulb into the headlight housing, then turn it ¼ turn to lock it into place.
6. Attach the 2 prong connector to the bottom of the bulb.
7. Turn the headlight switch on to make sure the bulb works, then turn the switch off.

8. Install any components that were removed to get to the headlight bulb.

AIMING THE HEADLIGHTS

♦ **See Figures 62, 63 and 64**

The headlights must be properly aimed to provide the best, safest road illumination. The lights should be checked for proper aim and adjusted as necessary. Certain state and local authorities have requirements for headlight aiming; these should be checked before adjustment is made.

✳✳ CAUTION

About once a year, when the headlight assemblies are replaced or any time front end work is performed on your vehicle, the headlight should be accurately aimed by a reputable repair shop using the proper equipment. Headlights not properly aimed can make it virtually impossible to see and may blind other drivers on the road, possibly causing an accident. Note that the following procedure is a temporary fix, until you can take your vehicle to a repair shop for a proper adjustment.

Headlight adjustment may be temporarily made using a wall, as described below, or on the rear of another vehicle. When adjusted, the lights should not glare in oncoming car or truck windshields, nor

should they illuminate the passenger compartment of vehicles driving in front of you. These adjustments are rough and should always be fine-tuned by a repair shop which is equipped with headlight aiming tools. Improper adjustments may be both dangerous and illegal.

➡**Because the composite headlight assembly is bolted into position, no adjustment should be necessary or possible. Some applications, however, may be bolted to an adjuster plate or may be retained by adjusting screws. If so, follow this procedure when adjusting the lights, BUT always have the adjustment checked by a reputable shop.**

Before removing the headlight bulb or disturbing the headlamp in any way, note the current settings in order to ease headlight adjustment upon reassembly. If the high or low beam setting of the old lamp still works, this can be done using the wall of a garage or a building:

1. Park the vehicle on a level surface, with the fuel tank about ½ full and with the vehicle empty of all extra cargo (unless normally carried). The vehicle should be facing a wall which is no less than 6 feet (1.8m) high and 12 feet (3.7m) wide. The front of the vehicle should be about 25 feet from the wall.

2. If aiming is to be performed outdoors, it is advisable to wait until dusk in order to properly see the headlight beams on the wall. If done in a garage, darken the area around the wall as much as possible by closing shades or hanging cloth over the windows.

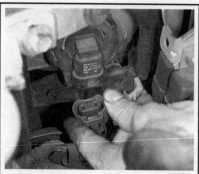

91186P60

Fig. 56 Unplug the connector from the bottom of the headlight bulb

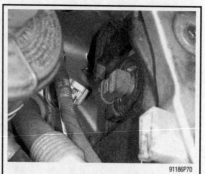

91186P70

Fig. 57 Space is limited, so once you have detached the connector push it out of the way so you have room to remove the bulb

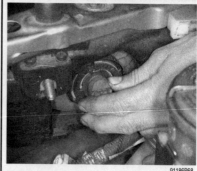

91186P68

Fig. 58 Grasp the base of the bulb and turn it counterclockwise to remove

91186P66

Fig. 59 Holding it by the base only, carefully pull the bulb from the headlight housing

91186P65

Fig. 60 Do not touch the glass part of the bulb. Your fingers contain oils that will retain heat and shorten the life of the bulb

91186P57

Fig. 61 The manufacturer's part number is usually stamped on the base of the bulb. Always make sure to get the proper part when replacing a bulb

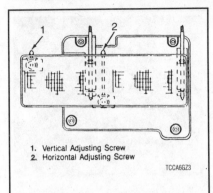

1. Vertical Adjusting Screw
2. Horizontal Adjusting Screw

TCCA6GZ3

Fig. 62 Example of headlight adjustment screw location for composite headlamps

3. Turn the headlights **ON** and mark the wall at the center of each light's low beam, then switch on the brights and mark the center of each light's high beam. A short length of masking tape which is visible from the front of the vehicle may be used. Although marking all four positions is advisable, marking one position from each light should be sufficient.

4. If neither beam on one side is working, and if another like-sized vehicle is available, park the second one in the exact spot where the vehicle was and mark the beams using the same-side light. Then switch the vehicles so the one to be aimed is back in the original spot. It must be parked no closer to or farther away from the wall than the second vehicle.

5. Perform any necessary repairs, but make sure the vehicle is not moved, or is returned to the exact spot from which the lights were marked. Turn

the headlights **ON** and adjust the beams to match the marks on the wall.

6. Have the headlight adjustment checked as soon as possible by a reputable repair shop.

Signal and Marker Lights

REMOVAL & INSTALLATION

Front Turn Signal and Parking Lights

▶ See Figures 65 thru 72

1. Remove the negative battery cable.
2. Remove the screw from the front turn signal/parking light lens.

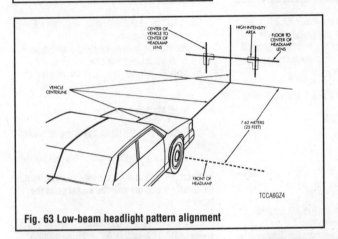

TCCA6GZ4

Fig. 63 Low-beam headlight pattern alignment

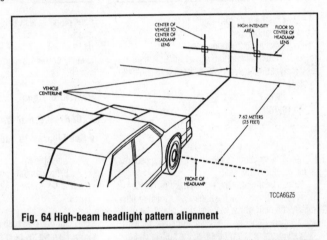

TCCA6GZ5

Fig. 64 High-beam headlight pattern alignment

91186P75

Fig. 65 Access the turn signal mounting screw through the front lower grille opening

91186P84

Fig. 66 Use a prytool to push the lens over about an inch

91186P76

Fig. 67 You must pull the lens out to access the front turn signal and parking light bulbs that are mounted in the rear of the lens

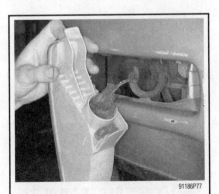

91186P77

Fig. 68 Hold the lens assembly securely . . .

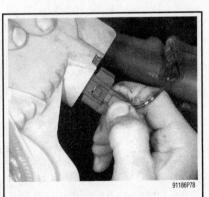

91186P78

Fig. 69 . . . then squeeze the wiring harness connector . . .

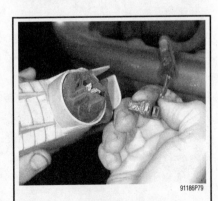

91186P79

Fig. 70 . . . and remove the wiring harness from the bulb assembly

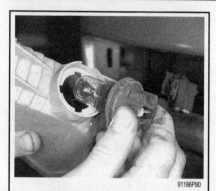

Fig. 71 Twist the bulb and socket ¼ turn, then withdraw from the lens

Fig. 72 Remove the bulb by pulling it straight out of the socket

Fig. 73 Unfasten the front turn signal/side marker light retaining screws

3. Pull the front turn signal light assembly from the front bumper.

4. Detach the 2 prong connector.

5. To remove the bulb socket from the light assembly, turn the socket 45 degrees counterclockwise.

6. Remove the bulb.

To install:

7. Inspect the bulb socket for corrosion or damage.

8. Install a new bulb into the holder.

9. The remainder of the installation procedure is the reverse of removal.

10. To ensure that the replacement bulb functions properly, activate the applicable switch to illuminate the bulb which was just replaced. If the replacement light bulb does not illuminate, either it is faulty or there is a problem in the bulb circuit or switch. Correct as necessary.

Front Turn Signal/Side Marker Light

▶ See Figures 73, 74 and 75

1. Remove the screw(s) from the front turn signal/side marker light assembly.

2. Pull the lens assembly from the front bumper.

3. Detach the two prong electrical connector from the light.

4. To remove the turn signal/side marker bulb(s), press in slightly and turn counterclockwise to release the bulb(s).

5. Installation is the reverse of the removal procedure.

6. To ensure that the replacement bulb func-

tions properly, activate the applicable switch to illuminate the bulb which was just replaced. If the replacement light bulb does not illuminate, either it is faulty or there is a problem in the bulb circuit or switch. Correct as necessary.

Rear Turn Signal, Brake and Parking Lights

EXCEPT ACCORD WAGON

▶ See Figures 76 and 77

1. Open the trunk.

2. Either carefully pry off the rear light trim covers, or unfasten the retainers then remove the trim covers.

3. If necessary, you can unplug the electrical connector from the bulb assembly.

4. Remove the bulb socket from the light assembly by turning it counterclockwise ¼ of a turn.

5. To remove the bulb, carefully pull it straight out of the socket.

6. Installation is the reverse of the removal procedure.

7. To ensure that the replacement bulb functions properly, activate the applicable switch to illuminate the bulb which was just replaced. If the replacement light bulb does not illuminate, either it is faulty or there is a problem in the bulb circuit or switch. Correct as necessary.

ACCORD WAGON

1. Open the tailgate and remove the corner panel.

2. Unplug the weather pack connector from the taillight assembly.

3. Unfasten the rear light mounting screws, then remove the light assembly.

4. Remove the bulb by pushing it while you turn it 45 degrees counterclockwise.

5. Installation is the reverse of the removal procedure.

Rear Side Marker Light(s)

1. Remove the screw from the rear side marker light.

2. Carefully pry the light out of the rear bumper.

➡When prying out the rear side marker light, be careful along the painted surfaces of the bumper.

3. Detach the 2 prong electrical connector.

4. Remove the bulb by turning it 45 degrees counterclockwise.

5. Installation is the reverse of the removal procedure.

High-mount Brake Light

▶ See Figure 78

1. Open the trunk.

2. Press in on the tabs on either side to release the cover for the high-mount brake light. Some models require removing the high-mount brake light by removing the entire lens assembly.

3. Remove the bulb socket from the light assembly by turning it counterclockwise ¼ of a turn.

4. To remove the bulb, carefully pull it straight out of the socket.

Fig. 74 Removing the side marker lens assembly

Fig. 75 The side marker bulb and sockets are accessed from the rear of the lens

Fig. 76 Detaching the wiring harness from the bulb socket first may ease removing the bulb

Fig. 77 You may have to access the rear signal bulbs through the trunk lid as shown

Fig. 78 Removing the bulb from the high-mount brake light

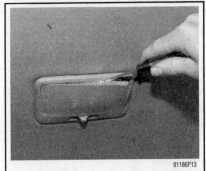

Fig. 79 Using a small prytool, carefully remove the cover lens from the dome lamp assembly

5. Installation is the reverse of the removal procedure.

Dome Light

▶ **See Figures 79, 80 and 81**

1. Using a small prytool, carefully remove the cover lens from the lamp assembly.
2. Remove the bulb from its retaining clip contacts. If the bulb has tapered ends, gently depress the spring clip/metal contact and disengage the light bulb, then pull it free of the two metal contacts.

To install:

3. Before installing the light bulb into the metal contacts, ensure that all electrical conducting surfaces are free of corrosion or dirt.
4. Position the bulb between the two metal contacts.
5. To ensure that the replacement bulb functions properly, activate the applicable switch to illuminate the bulb which was just replaced. If the replacement light bulb does not illuminate, either it is faulty or there is a problem in the bulb circuit or switch. Correct as necessary.
6. Install the cover lens until its retaining tabs are properly engaged.

Cargo or Passenger Area Lamps

1. Carefully pry the lens cover off of the light assembly.
2. Remove the bulb from the socket.
3. Installation is the reverse of the removal procedure.

License Plate Lights

▶ **See Figure 82**

1. Remove the 2 Phillips screws securing the license plate light lens assembly, the remove the lens.
2. To remove the bulb, pull it carefully straight out of the socket.
3. Installation is the reverse of the removal procedure.

Fog/Driving Lights

REMOVAL & INSTALLATION

1. Disconnect the negative battery cable.
2. Remove the mounting bolts.
3. Carefully lower the fog light assembly, detach the electrical connector, then remove the fog light from the vehicle.

To install:

4. Install the fog light in the reverse order of removal.
5. After replacing the fog light, adjust the lights to local requirements.

INSTALLING AFTERMARKET AUXILIARY LIGHTS

➡ **Before installing any aftermarket light, make sure it is legal for road use. Most acceptable lights will have a DOT approval number. Also check your local and regional inspection regu-**

lations. In certain areas, aftermarket lights must be installed in a particular manner or they may not be legal for inspection.

1. Disconnect the negative battery cable.
2. Unpack the contents of the light kit purchased. Place the contents in an open space where you can easily retrieve a piece if needed.
3. Choose a location for the lights. If you are installing fog lights, below the bumper and apart from each other is desirable. Most fog lights are mounted below or very close to the headlights. If you are installing driving lights, above the bumper and close together is desirable. Most driving lights are mounted between the headlights.
4. Drill the needed hole(s) to mount the light. Install the light, and secure using the supplied retainer nut and washer. Tighten the light mounting hardware, but not the light adjustment nut or bolt.
5. Install the relay that came with the light kit in the engine compartment, in a rigid area, such as a fender. Always install the relay with the terminals facing down. This will prevent water from entering the relay assembly.
6. Using the wire supplied, locate the ground terminal on the relay, and connect a length of wire from this terminal to a good ground source. You can drill a hole and screw this wire to an inside piece of metal; just scrape the paint away from the hole to ensure a good connection.
7. Locate the light terminal on the relay; and attach a length of wire between this terminal and the fog/driving lamps.
8. Locate the ignition terminal on the relay, and connect a length of wire between this terminal and the light switch.

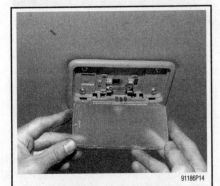

Fig. 80 Pivot the lens cover and then pull it down

Fig. 81 Carefully slide the bulb out from between the contacts

Fig. 82 Removing the license plate bulb from the socket

9. Find a suitable mounting location for the light switch and install. Some examples of mounting areas are a location close to the main light switch, auxiliary light position in the dash panel, if equipped, or in the center of the dash panel.

10. Depending on local and regional regulations, the other end of the switch can be connected to a constant power source such as the battery, an ignition opening in the fuse panel, or a parking or headlight wire.

11. Locate the power terminal on the relay, and connect a wire with an in-line fuse of at least 10 amperes between the terminal and the battery.

12. With all the wires connected and tied up neatly, connect the negative battery cable.

13. Turn the lights ON and adjust the light pattern, if necessary.

AIMING

1. Park the vehicle on level ground, so it is perpendicular to and, facing a flat wall about 25 ft. (7.6m) away.

2. Remove any stone shields, if equipped, and switch ON the lights.

3. Loosen the mounting hardware of the lights so you can aim them as follows:

a. The horizontal distance between the light beams on the wall should be the same as between the lights themselves.

b. The vertical height of the light beams above the ground should be 4 in. (10cm) less than the distance between the ground and the center of the lamp lenses for fog lights. For driving lights, the vertical height should be even with the distance between the ground and the center of the lamp.

4. Tighten the mounting hardware.

5. Test to make sure the lights work correctly, and the light pattern is even.

TRAILER WIRING

Wiring the vehicle for towing is fairly easy. There are a number of good wiring kits available and these should be used, rather than trying to design your own.

All trailers will need brake lights and turn signals as well as tail lights and side marker lights. Most areas require extra marker lights for overwide trailers. Also, most areas have recently required back-up lights for trailers, and most trailer manufacturers have been building trailers with back-up lights for several years.

Additionally, some Class I, most Class II and just about all Class III and IV trailers will have electric brakes. Add to this number an accessories wire, to operate trailer internal equipment or to charge the trailer's battery, and you can have as many as seven wires in the harness.

Determine the equipment on your trailer and buy the wiring kit necessary. The kit will contain all the wires needed, plus a plug adapter set which includes the female plug, mounted on the bumper or hitch, and the male plug, wired into, or plugged into the trailer harness.

When installing the kit, follow the manufacturer's instructions. The color coding of the wires is usually standard throughout the industry. One point to note: some domestic vehicles, and most imported vehicles, have separate turn signals. On most domestic vehicles, the brake lights and rear turn signals operate with the same bulb. For those vehicles without separate turn signals, you can purchase an isolation unit so that the brake lights won't blink whenever the turn signals are operated.

One, final point, the best kits are those with a spring loaded cover on the vehicle mounted socket. This cover prevents dirt and moisture from corroding the terminals. Never let the vehicle socket hang loosely; always mount it securely to the bumper or hitch.

CIRCUIT PROTECTION

Fuses

REPLACEMENT

▶ **See Figure 83**

Fuses are located either in the engine compartment or passenger compartment fuse and relay panels. If a fuse blows, a single component or single circuit will not function properly. Excessive current draw is what causes a fuse to blow. Observing the condition of the fuse will provide insight as to what caused this to occur.

A fuse with signs of burns, melting of the plastic shell, or little to no trace of the wire that once served as the conductor indicates that a direct short to ground exists.

1. Remove the fuse or relay box cover.

2. Inspect the fuses to determine which is faulty.

3. Unplug and discard the fuse.

4. Inspect the box terminals and clean if corroded. If any terminals are damaged, replace the terminals.

5. Plug in a new fuse of the same amperage rating.

❋❋ WARNING

Never exceed the amperage rating of a blown fuse. If the replacement fuse also blows, check for a problem in the circuit.

6. Check for proper operation of the affected component or circuit.

Maxi-Fuses

Maxi-fuses are located in the engine compartment relay box. If a maxi-fuse blows, an entire circuit or several circuits will not function properly.

REPLACEMENT

▶ **See Figure 84**

1. Remove the fuse and relay box cover.

2. Inspect the fusible links to determine which is faulty.

3. Unplug and discard the fusible link.

4. Inspect the box terminals and clean if corroded. If any terminals are damaged, replace the terminals.

5. Plug in a new fusible link of the same amperage rating.

Fig. 84 The engine compartment relay box contains the maxi-fuses

❋❋ WARNING

Never exceed the amperage rating of a blown maxi-fuse. If the replacement fuse also blows, check for a problem in the circuit(s).

6. Check for proper operation of the affected circuit(s).

Circuit Breakers

RESETTING AND/OR REPLACEMENT

Circuit breakers are located inside the fuse panel. They are automatically reset when the problem corrects itself, is repaired, or the circuit cools down to allow operation again.

Fig. 83 Remove the cover, usually located near the steering column, for access to the fuses

Fusible Link

♦ **See Figure 85**

The fusible link is a short length of wire, integral with the engine compartment wiring harness and

FUSIBLE LINK COLOR CODING

WIRE LINK SIZE	INSULATION COLOR
20 GA	Blue
18 GA	Brown or Red
16 GA	Black or Orange
14 GA	Green
12 GA	Gray

90986G89

Fig. 85 Common fusible link color coding

should not be confused with standard wire. The fusible link wire gauge is smaller than the circuit which it protects. Under no circumstances should a fusible link replacement repair be made using a length of standard wire cut from bulk stock or from another wiring harness.

Fusible link wire is covered with a special thick, non-flammable insulation. An overload condition causes the insulation to blister. If the overall condition continues, the wire will melt. To check a fusible link, look for blistering insulation. If the insulation is okay, pull gently on the wire. If the fusible link stretches, the wire has melted.

Fusible links are often identified by the color coding of the insulation. Refer to the accompanying illustration for wire link size and color.

Flashers

REPLACEMENT

Turn Signal Flasher/Hazard Warning Relay

1. Grasp and pull the flasher from the connector located near the top of the fuse panel.
2. Inspect the socket for corrosion or any other signs of a bad contact.

To install:

3. Install a new flasher in the connector.
4. Install the fuse panel cover.

WIRING DIAGRAMS

INDEX OF WIRING DIAGRAMS

91186W01

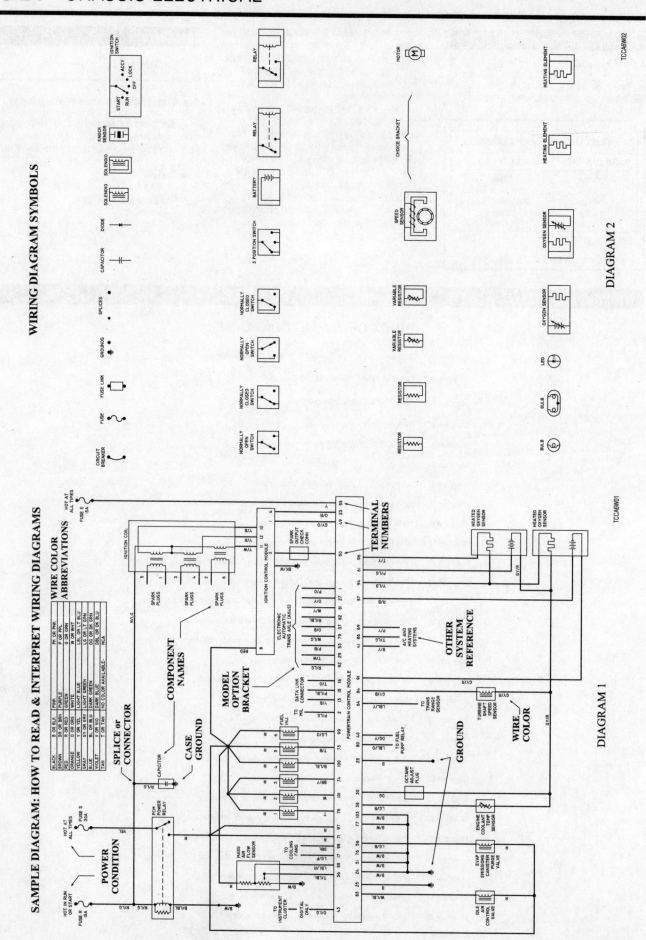

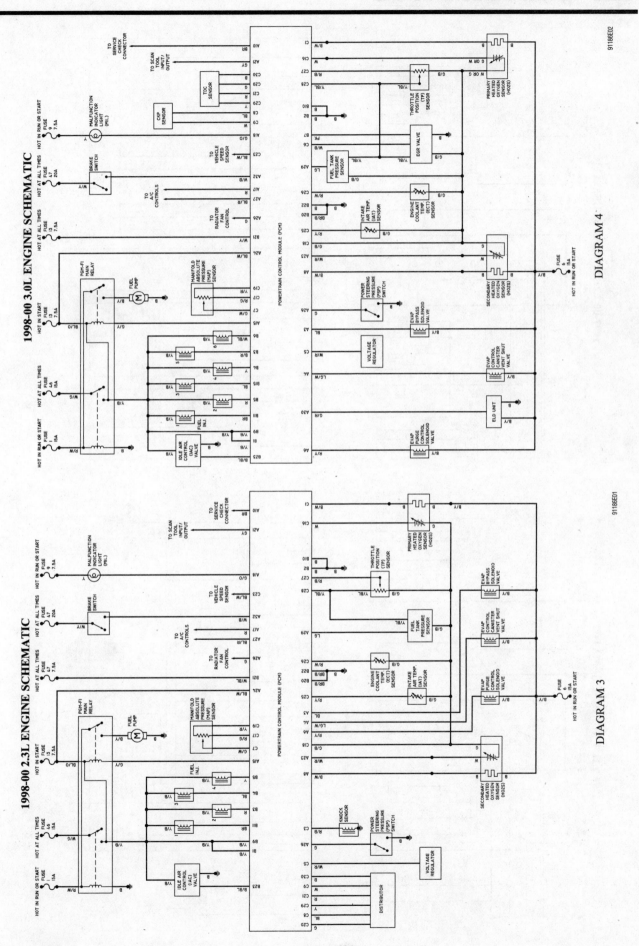

1998-00 3.0L ENGINE SCHEMATIC

DIAGRAM 4

1998-00 2.3L ENGINE SCHEMATIC

DIAGRAM 3

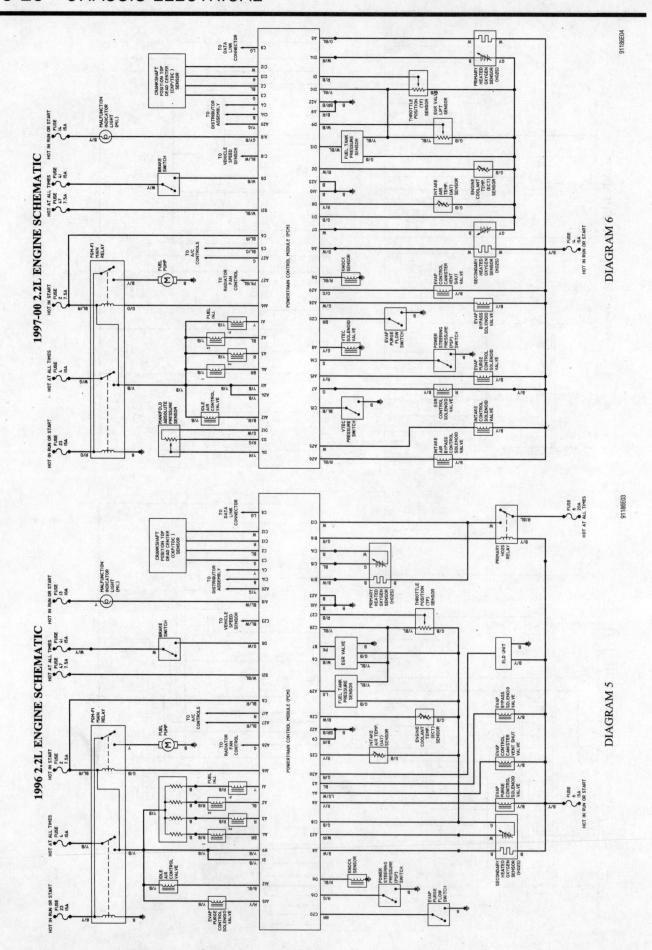

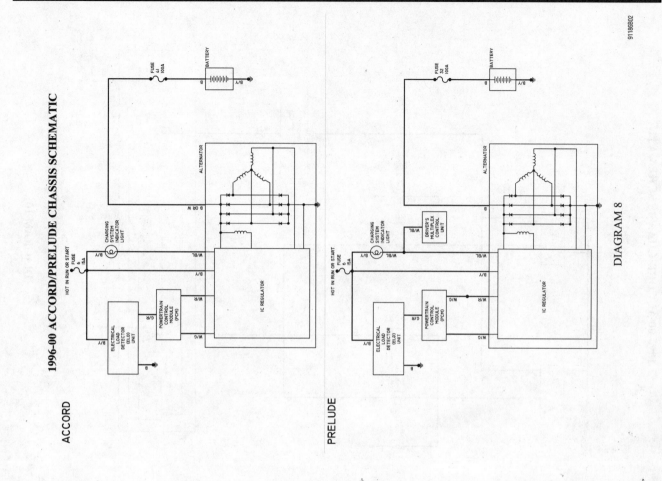

1996-00 ACCORD/PRELUDE CHASSIS SCHEMATIC

ACCORD

PRELUDE

DIAGRAM 8

1996-00 ACCORD CHASSIS SCHEMATIC

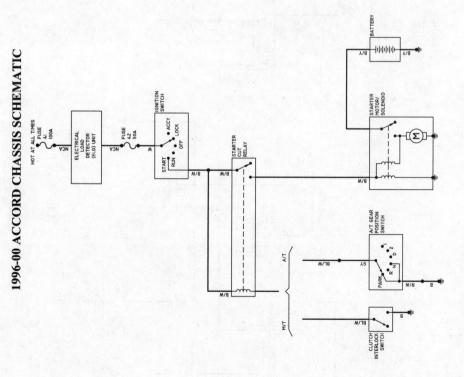

DIAGRAM 7

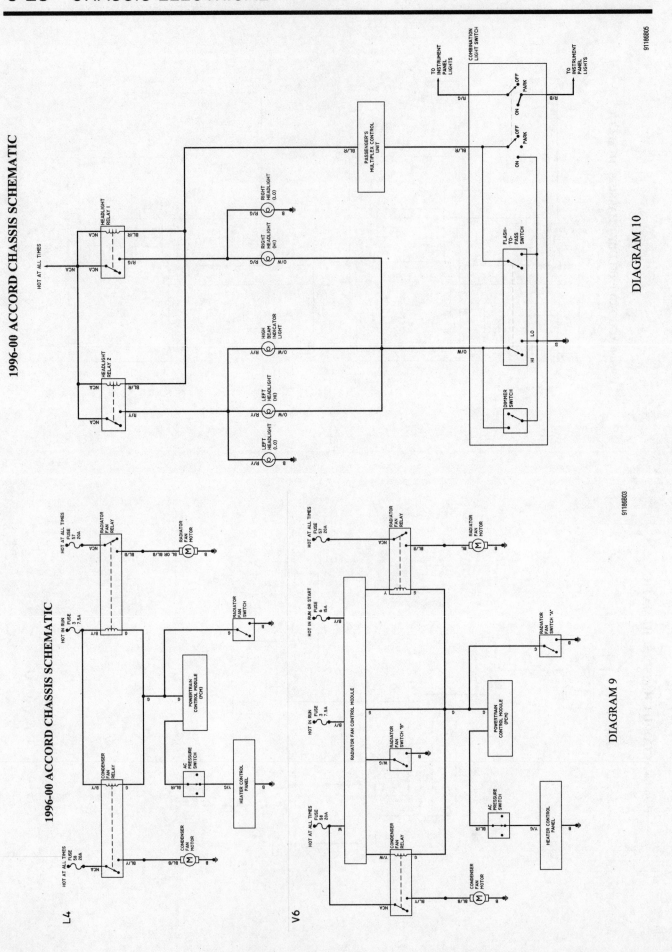

1996-00 ACCORD CHASSIS SCHEMATIC

DIAGRAM 10

1996-00 ACCORD CHASSIS SCHEMATIC

DIAGRAM 9

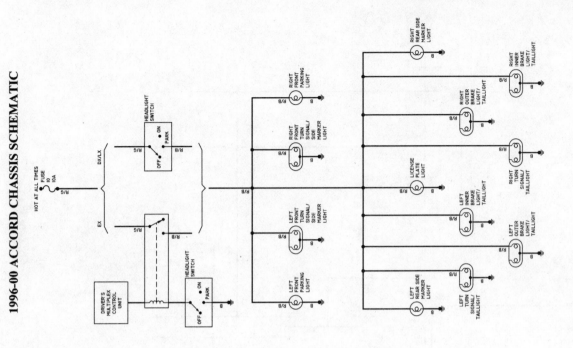

1996-00 ACCORD CHASSIS SCHEMATIC

COUPE

DIAGRAM 12

91186B07

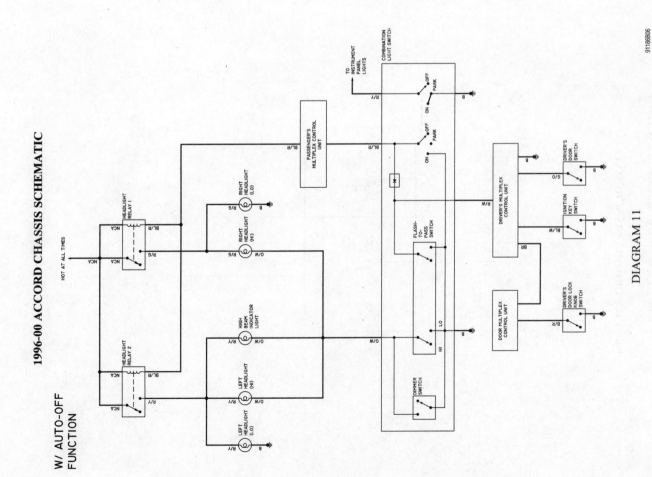

1996-00 ACCORD CHASSIS SCHEMATIC

W/ AUTO-OFF FUNCTION

DIAGRAM 11

91186B06

1996-00 ACCORD CHASSIS SCHEMATIC

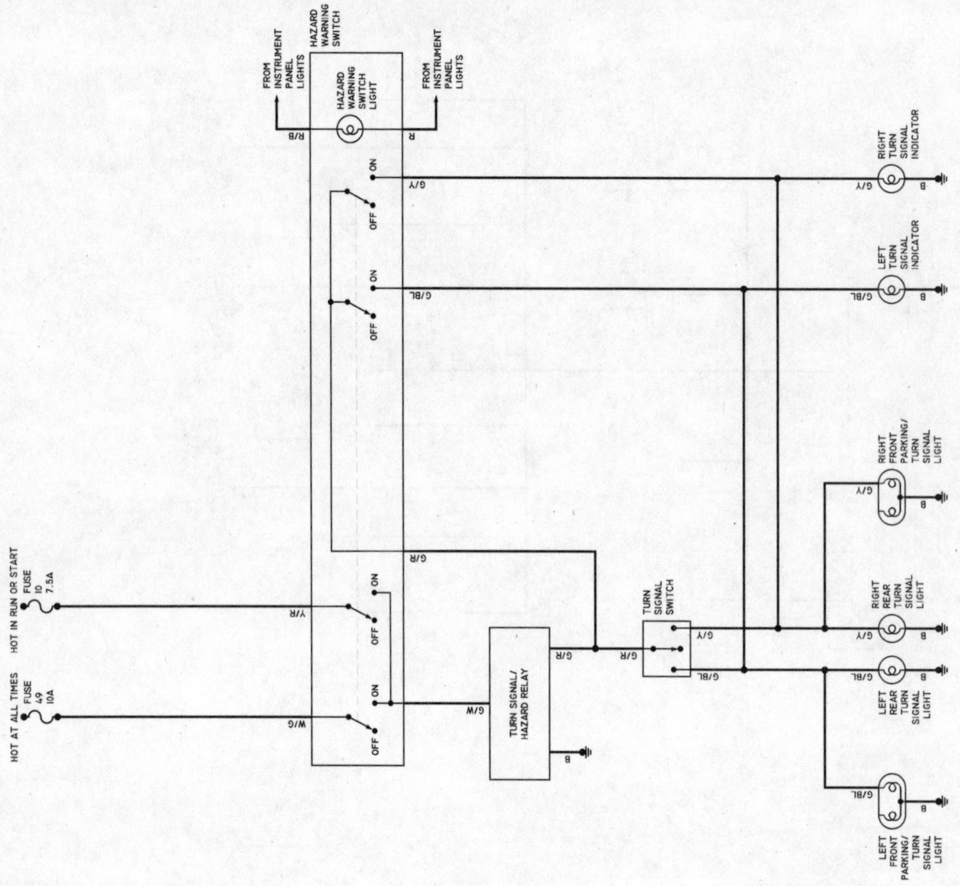

DIAGRAM 14

91186B09

1996-00 ACCORD CHASSIS SCHEMATIC

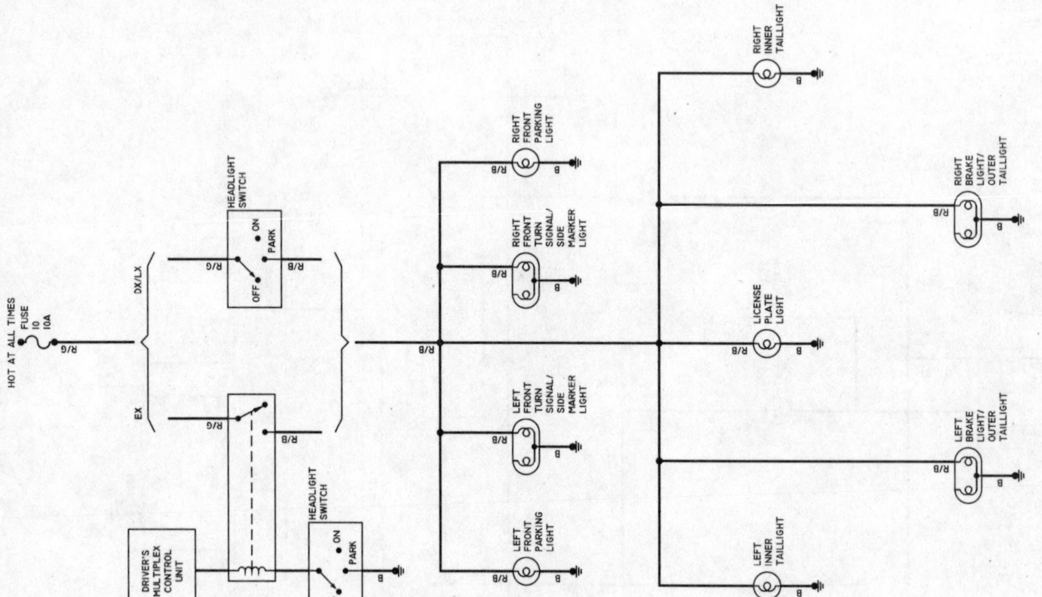

DIAGRAM 13

91186B08

SEDAN

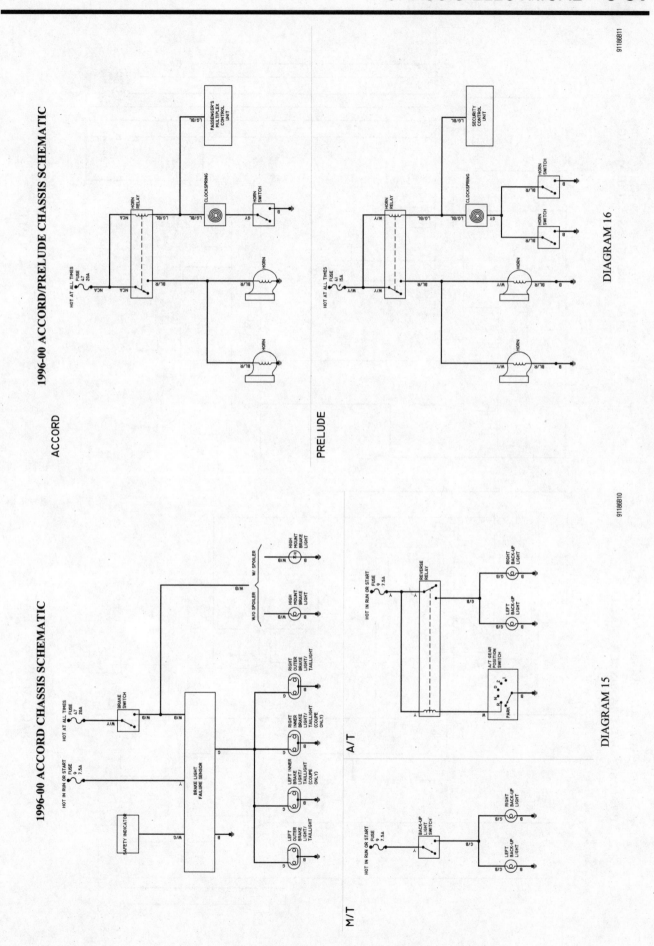

1996-00 ACCORD/PRELUDE CHASSIS SCHEMATIC

ACCORD

PRELUDE

DIAGRAM 16

1996-00 ACCORD CHASSIS SCHEMATIC

M/T

A/T

DIAGRAM 15

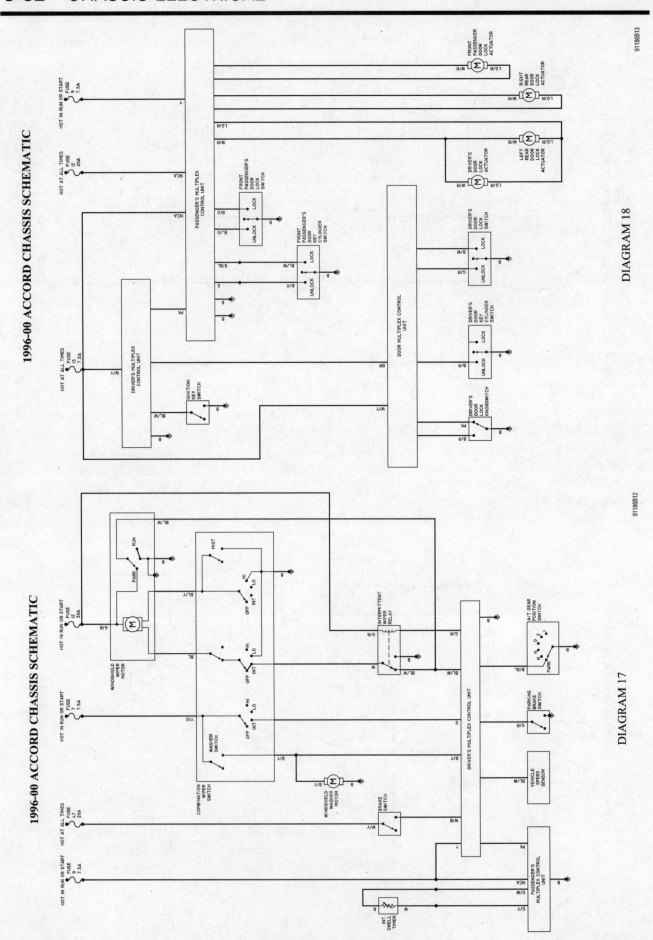

1996-00 ACCORD CHASSIS SCHEMATIC

DIAGRAM 18

1996-00 ACCORD CHASSIS SCHEMATIC

DIAGRAM 17

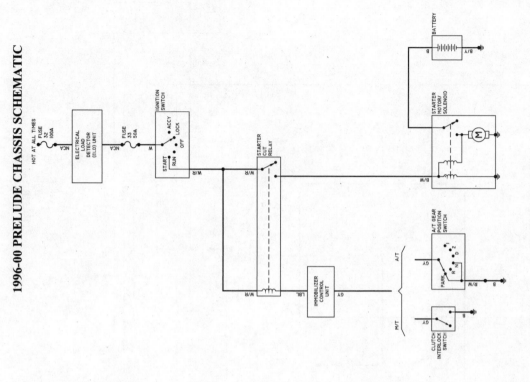

1996-00 PRELUDE CHASSIS SCHEMATIC

DIAGRAM 20

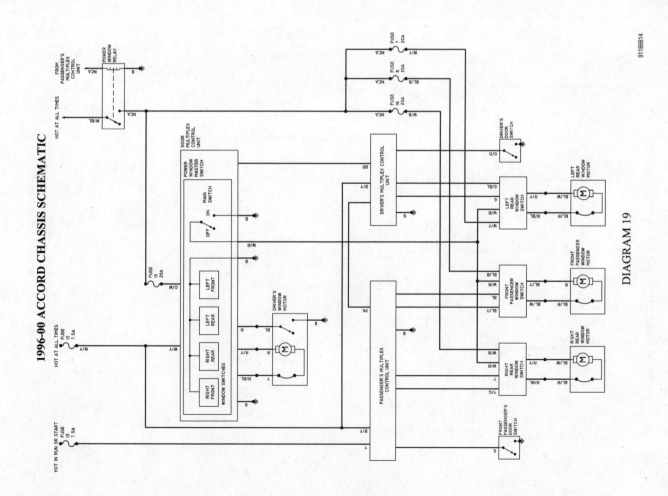

1996-00 ACCORD CHASSIS SCHEMATIC

DIAGRAM 19

1996-00 PRELUDE CHASSIS SCHEMATIC

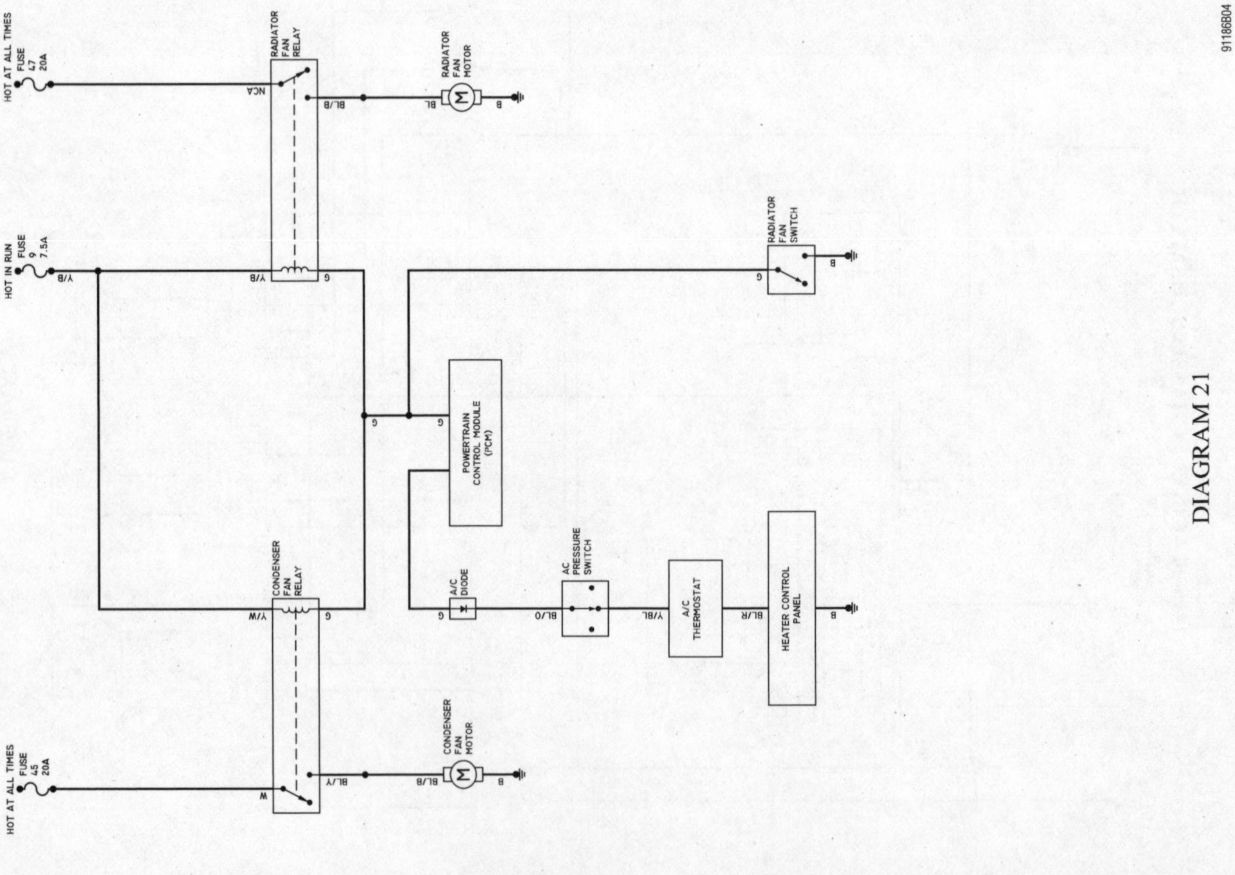

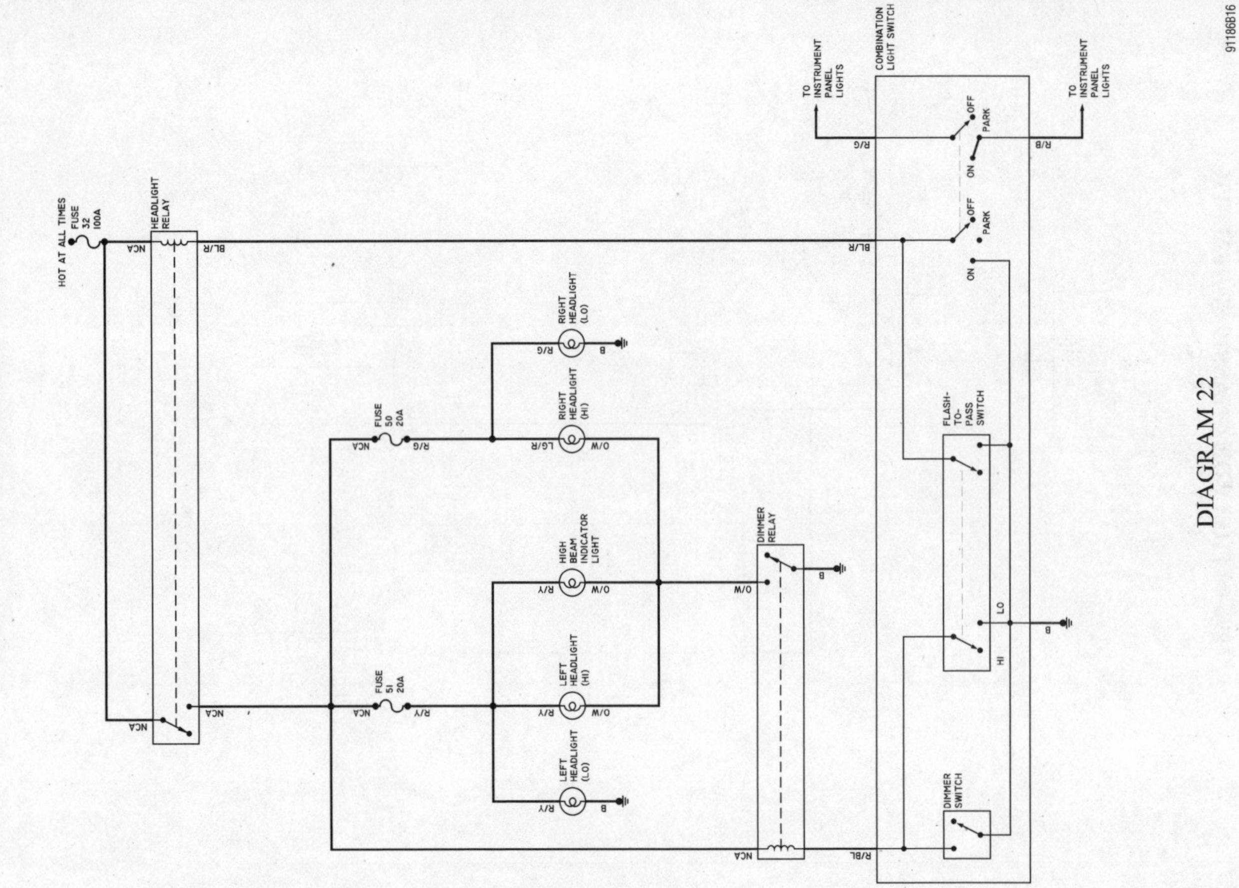

DIAGRAM 22

1996-00 PRELUDE CHASSIS SCHEMATIC

DIAGRAM 21

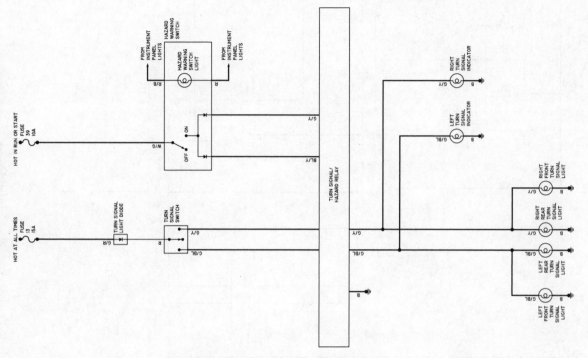

1996-00 PRELUDE CHASSIS SCHEMATIC

DIAGRAM 24

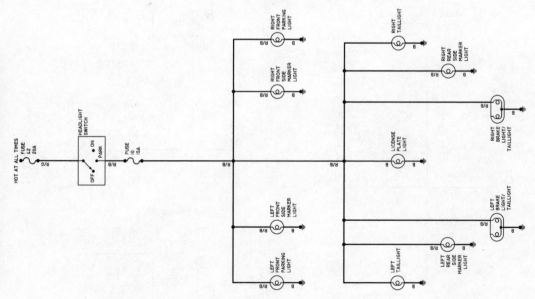

1996-00 PRELUDE CHASSIS SCHEMATIC

DIAGRAM 23

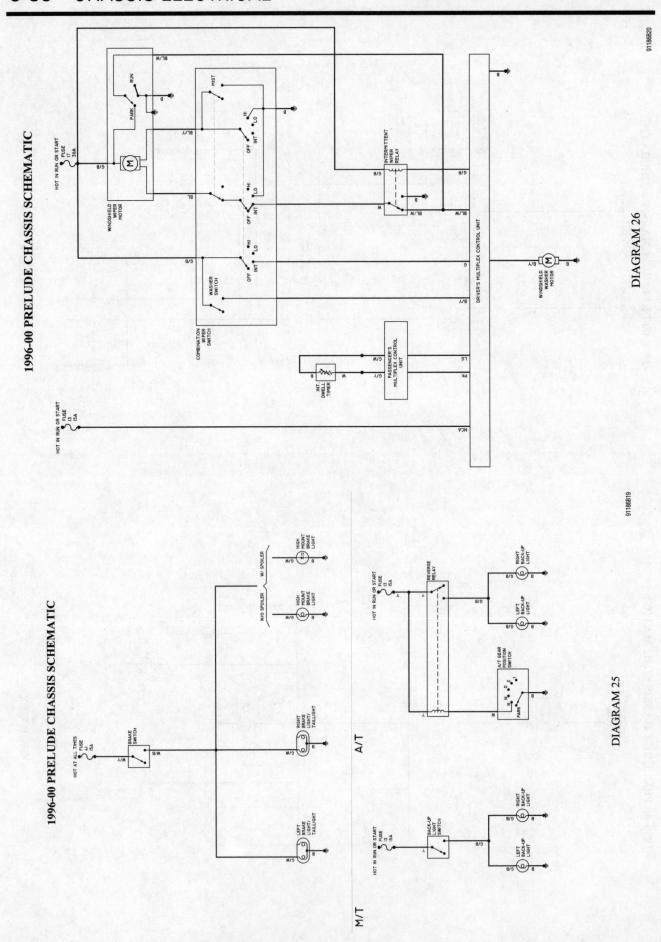

1996-00 PRELUDE CHASSIS SCHEMATIC

DIAGRAM 26

1996-00 PRELUDE CHASSIS SCHEMATIC

DIAGRAM 25

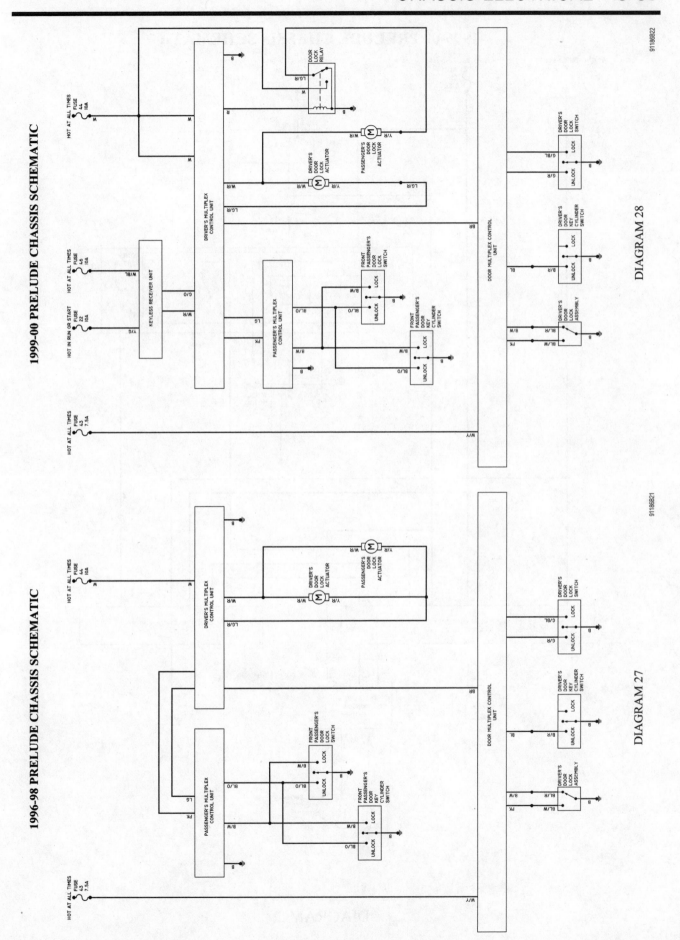

1999-00 PRELUDE CHASSIS SCHEMATIC

DIAGRAM 28

1996-98 PRELUDE CHASSIS SCHEMATIC

DIAGRAM 27

1996-00 PRELUDE CHASSIS SCHEMATIC

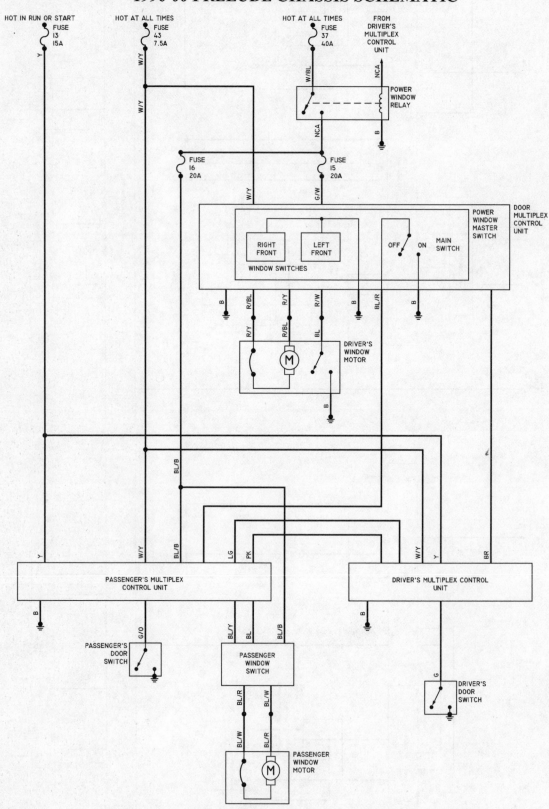

DIAGRAM 29

91186B23

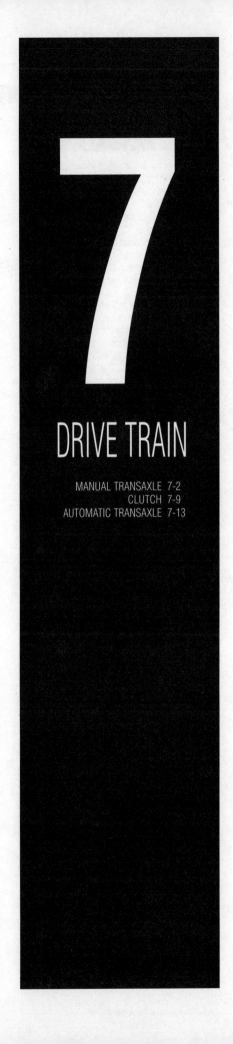

7

DRIVE TRAIN

MANUAL TRANSAXLE

Understanding the Manual Transaxle

Because of the way an internal combustion engine breathes, it can produce torque, or twisting force, only within a narrow speed range. Most modern, overhead valve pushrod engines must turn at about 2500 rpm to produce their peak torque. By 4500 rpm they are producing so little torque that continued increases in engine speed produce no power increases. The torque peak on overhead camshaft engines is generally much higher, but much narrower.

The manual transaxle and clutch are employed to vary the relationship between engine speed and the speed of the wheels so that adequate engine power can be produced under all circumstances. The clutch allows engine torque to be applied to the transaxle input shaft gradually, due to mechanical slippage. Consequently, the vehicle may be started smoothly from a full stop. The transaxle changes the ratio between the rotating speeds of the engine and the wheels by the use of gears. The gear ratios allow full engine power to be applied to the wheels during acceleration at low speeds and at highway/passing speeds.

In a front wheel drive transaxle, power is usually transmitted from the input shaft to a mainshaft or output shaft located slightly beneath and to the side of the input shaft. The gears of the mainshaft mesh with gears on the input shaft, allowing power to be carried from one to the other. All forward gears are in constant mesh and are free from rotating with the shaft unless the synchronizer and clutch is engaged. Shifting from one gear to the next causes one of the gears to be freed from rotating with the shaft and locks another to it. Gears are locked and unlocked by internal dog clutches which slide between the center of the gear and the shaft. The forward gears employ synchronizers; friction members which smoothly bring gear and shaft to the same speed before the toothed dog clutches are engaged.

Back-up Light Switch

REMOVAL & INSTALLATION

For back-up light switch replacement, please refer to the procedure located in Section 6 of this manual.

Manual Transaxle Assembly

REMOVAL & INSTALLATION

➡The radio may contain a coded theft protection circuit. Always obtain the code number before disconnecting the battery. If the vehicle is equipped with 4WS, the steering control unit is shut down when the battery is disconnected. After connecting the battery, turn the steering wheel lock-to-lock to reset the steering control unit.

Accord

◆ See Figures 1, 2, 3, 4 and 5

1. Shift the transaxle into **R**.
2. Disconnect the negative and positive battery cables. Remove the battery.
3. Detach the Idle Air Control (IAC) solenoid connector. Remove the intake duct, resonator, air cleaner case, and battery base.
4. Disconnect the starter wires and remove the starter.
5. Disconnect the transaxle ground cable and the back-up light switch wire.
6. Remove the cable stay, then disconnect the cables from the top housing of the transaxle. Remove both cables and the stay together.
7. Detach the Vehicle Speed Sensor (VSS) connector and remove the speed sensor. Leave the speed sensor hoses connected.
8. Remove the shift cable bracket. Then, disconnect the shift and select cables from the top of the transaxle case. Leave the cables and bracket together, and wire them out of the work area.
9. Remove the mounting bolts and clutch slave cylinder with the clutch pipe and pushrod.
10. Remove the mounting bolt and clutch hose joint with the clutch pipe and clutch hose.

➡Do not depress the clutch pedal once the slave cylinder has been removed. Be careful not to kink the metal hydraulic lines.

11. Remove the two upper transaxle case bolts.
12. Raise and safely support the vehicle.
13. Remove the front wheels.
14. Remove the engine splash shield.

15. Drain the transaxle fluid into a suitable container.
16. Remove the clutch damper bracket and raise it out of the way.
17. Remove the subframe center beam.
18. Remove the cotter pins and lower arm ball joint nuts. Separate the ball joints and lower arms using a press type ball joint tool.
19. Remove the right damper fork bolt. Remove the right damper pinch bolt, then separate the damper fork and damper. Remove the radius rod bolts and nut, then remove the right radius rod.
20. Use a suitable prytool to separate the right and left halfshafts from the differential and the intermediate shaft. Remove the left halfshaft.
21. Remove the intermediate shaft from the differential by removing its three bearing shaft mounting bolts.
22. Swing the right halfshaft out and wire it up inside the right fender well. Tie plastic bags over the inboard CV-joints to protect the boots and splines from damage.
23. Remove the engine stiffener and the clutch cover.
24. Remove the intake manifold bracket.
25. Remove the rear engine mount bracket. Remove and discard the three rear engine mount bracket mounting bolts.
26. Place a transaxle jack under the transaxle. Raise the transaxle just enough to take the weight off the its mounts.

➡A chain hoist may be attached the transaxle lifting hooks to steady it and aid in lowering it from the vehicle.

27. Remove the transaxle housing mounting bolt on the engine side.
28. Remove the transaxle mount bolt and loosen the mount bracket nuts.
29. Remove the three transaxle housing mounting bolts.
30. Remove the transaxle from the vehicle.
To install:

➡Use new self-locking nuts when assembling the front suspension. Install new set rings onto the inboard CV-joints. Use new self-locking bolts when installing transaxle rear mount bracket (the bolts are color coded by type). New fasteners are available from a Honda dealer.

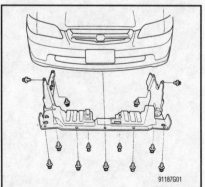

Fig. 1 Unfasten the retainers, then remove the engine splash shield

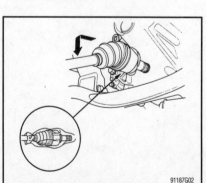

Fig. 2 Remove the halfshafts, then put plastic bags over the ends to protect the boots and shaft splines

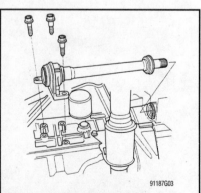

Fig. 3 Remove the retaining bolts, then remove the intermediate shaft

31. Be sure the two dowel pins are installed into the transaxle case.

32. Apply heavy duty high temperature grease (use Honda part No. 08798–9002) to the release bearing, mainshaft splines, and the release fork pawls. Install the release fork and release bearing.

33. Raise the transaxle into position.

34. Install the three lower transaxle case bolts and tighten to 47 ft. lbs. (65 Nm).

35. Install the transaxle mount and mount bracket. Install the through-bolt and tighten temporarily. Be sure the engine is level and tighten the three mount bracket nuts to 40 ft. lbs. (55 Nm). Tighten the through-bolt to 47 ft. lbs. (65 Nm).

36. Install the upper transaxle case bolts on the engine side and tighten to 47 ft. lbs. (65 Nm).

37. Install the three new rear engine bracket mounting bolts and tighten to 40 ft. lbs. (55 Nm).

38. Install the intake manifold bracket and tighten the bolts to 16 ft. lbs. (22 Nm).

39. Install the clutch cover and tighten the bolts to 9 ft. lbs. (12 Nm).

40. Install the subframe center beam with new self-locking bolts. Evenly tighten the bolts to 37 ft. lbs. (50 Nm).

41. If equipped, install the engine stiffener plate and loosely install the mounting bolts. Tighten the stiffener-to-transaxle case mounting bolt to 28 ft. lbs. (39 Nm), then tighten the two stiffener-to-engine block mounting bolts to 28 ft. lbs. (39 Nm) beginning with the bolt closest to the transaxle.

42. Install the radius rod and the damper fork. Install all the fasteners, but only hand-tighten them at this time.

43. Install the intermediate shaft and tighten its mounting bolts to 28 ft. lbs. (39 Nm).

44. Install a new set ring on the end of each halfshaft. Install the right and left halfshafts. Turn the right and left steering knuckle fully outward and slide the axle into the differential, until the set ring is felt engaging the differential side gear.

45. Reconnect the lower control arm ball joints. Tighten the castle nuts to 40 ft. lbs. (50 Nm). Then, tighten them only enough to install a new cotter pin.

46. Install the clutch damper and tighten its mounting bolts to 16 ft. lbs. (22 Nm).

47. Install the front wheels. Lower the vehicle.

48. Place a floor jack under the right front knuckle, and raise the jack until it is supporting the vehicle's weight.

49. Tighten the radius rod mounting bolts to 76 ft. lbs. (105 Nm) and the radius rod nut to 32 ft. lbs. (44 Nm). Tighten the damper fork nut while holding the damper fork bolt to 40 ft. lbs. (55 Nm). Tighten the damper pinch bolt to 32 ft. lbs. (44 Nm).

50. Coat the tip of the slave cylinder with high temperature grease. Install the clutch hose joint and clutch slave cylinder to the transaxle housing. Be sure the slave cylinders tip snaps into the release fork. Tighten the slave cylinder mounting bolts to 16 ft. lbs. (22 Nm).

51. Install the speed sensor. Tighten the mounting bolt to 13 ft. lbs. (18 Nm).

52. Install the shift cable and select cable to the shift arm lever. Tighten the cable bracket mounting bolts to 20 ft. lbs. (27 Nm). Install new cotter pins.

53. Connect the back-up light switch.

54. Install the starter. Tighten the 10mm bolt to 32 ft. lbs. (45 Nm) and the 12mm bolt to 54 ft. lbs. (75 Nm). Connect the starter wires.

55. Install the transaxle ground cable.

56. Fill the transaxle with the proper type and quantity of oil.

57. Install the air cleaner case and the resonator, then the intake duct.

58. Install the battery tray bracket and battery tray and tighten the bolts to 16 ft. lbs. (22 Nm).

59. Install the battery and connect the battery cables.

60. Check the clutch pedal free-play.

61. Check and adjust the front wheel alignment.

62. Road test the vehicle and check the transaxle for smooth operation.

63. Loosen the three front engine mount bracket mounting bolts, then retighten them to 28 ft. lbs. (38 Nm).

64. Enter the radio security code.

PRELUDE

▶ See Figures 6 thru 12

1. Shift the transaxle to **R**.

2. Disconnect the negative and positive battery cables. Remove the battery.

3. Remove the intake duct and air cleaner case. Remove the battery base.

4. Remove the vacuum tank and bracket. Do not disconnect the hoses.

5. Disconnect the starter wires and remove the starter.

6. Loosen, but do not remove the two upper transaxle mounting bolts.

7. Disconnect the transaxle ground cable and

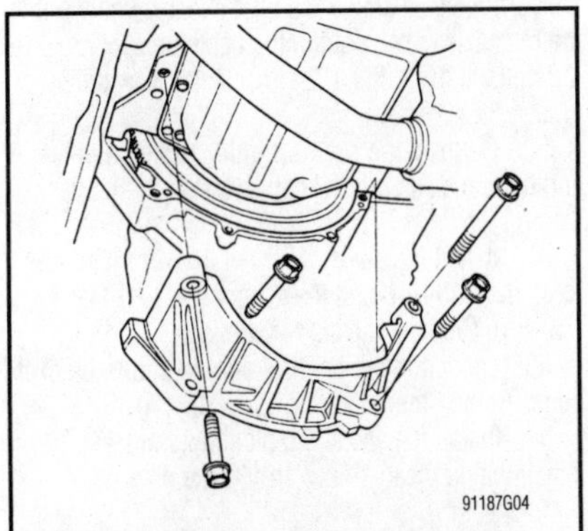

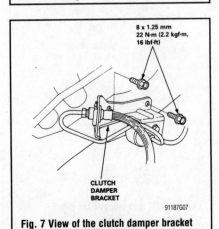

Fig. 4 Exploded view of the engine stiffener mounting

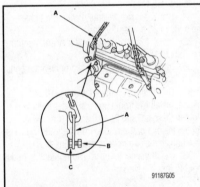

Fig. 5 Attach the chain hoist (A) using the bolts (B) and nut (C) as shown

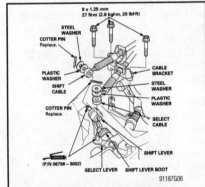

Fig. 6 Exploded view of the shift cable-to-bracket mounting

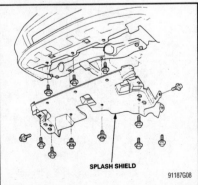

Fig. 7 View of the clutch damper bracket

Fig. 8 Unfasten the retainers, then remove the splash shield

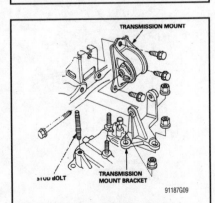

Fig. 9 Exploded view of the transaxle mount and bracket

the back-up light switch wire. Unbolt the engine harness clamp.

8. Leave both shift cables attached their bracket. Remove the shift cables from the transaxle case and wire them safely out of the work area.

9. Detach the Vehicle Speed Sensor (VSS) connector. Leave the sensor hoses connected and remove the sensor from the transaxle case.

10. Remove the slave cylinder mounting bolts. Leave the hydraulic line connected to the slave cylinder. Remove the slave cylinder from the release fork, and move it out of the work area.

➡ **Do not depress the clutch pedal once the slave cylinder has been removed. Be careful not to kink the metal hydraulic line.**

11. Raise and safely support the vehicle. Drain the transaxle fluid.

12. Remove the clutch damper mounting bolts and raise the clutch damper.

13. If equipped, remove the rear engine mount bracket stay.

14. Remove the front wheels.

15. Remove the splash shield.

16. Remove the cotter pins and lower arm ball joint nuts. Separate the ball joints and lower arms using a press-type ball joint tool.

17. Remove the damper fork bolt and the radius rod on the right side of the vehicle only.

18. Use a suitable tool to pry the right and left halfshafts out of the differential and the intermediate shaft. Pull on the inboard joint and remove the right and left halfshafts.

19. Unbolt and remove the intermediate shaft from the differential. Tie plastic bags over the halfshaft inboard joints to prevent damage to the boots and splines. Wire the halfshafts to the underbody of the vehicle so that their weight doesn't hang on their outboard joints.

20. Remove the center beam and remove the clutch cover. On vehicles with the H22A1 engine, remove the front engine stiffener plate.

21. Remove the rear beam stiffener and the intake manifold stay.

22. Remove the three rear engine mount bracket bolts.

23. Place a transaxle jack under the transaxle and raise the transaxle just enough to take its weight off the mounts.

24. Remove the transaxle mount and mount bracket.

25. Remove the two upper transaxle housing mounting bolts, the three rear engine mount bracket mounting bolts and the three lower transaxle housing bolts.

26. Pull the transaxle away from the engine to clear the mainshaft.

27. Lower the transaxle from the vehicle.

To install:

➡ **Use new self-locking nuts and set rings when assembling the front suspension components and halfshafts. Use new self-locking bolts when installing the center beam and rear engine mount bracket. These fasteners can be purchased from a Honda dealer.**

28. Be sure the dowel pins are installed into the transaxle case.

29. Apply heavy duty high temperature grease (use Honda part number 08798–9002) to the mainshaft splines, release fork bolt and paws, and the throw-out bearing. Install the bearing and release fork. Be sure the release fork snaps into place.

30. Raise the transaxle into position with a transaxle jack.

31. Install the three lower and two upper transaxle mounting bolts and evenly tighten them to 47 ft. lbs. (65 Nm).

32. Install the transaxle mount and mount bracket. Install the through-bolt and tighten temporarily. Be sure the engine is level. First tighten the three bracket-to-mount nuts and two bolts to 28 ft. lbs. (39 Nm). Then, tighten the through-bolt to 47 ft. lbs. (65 Nm).

33. Install the three new rear engine mount bracket bolts on the engine side and tighten them to 40 ft. lbs. (55 Nm).

34. Install the rear beam stiffener and tighten the bolts to 28 ft. lbs. (39 Nm).

35. Install the intake manifold stay and tighten the bolts to 16 ft. lbs. (22 Nm).

36. Install the clutch cover and tighten the bolts to 9 ft. lbs. (12 Nm).

37. On Preludes equipped with the H22A1 engine, install the front engine stiffener bolts. Tighten these bolts to 28 ft. lbs. (39 Nm). First tighten the one bolt threaded into the transaxle case, then tighten the two bolts to the engine block.

38. Install the center beam and tighten the bolts to 43 ft. lbs. (60 Nm).

39. Install the intermediate shaft. Tighten its mounting bolts to 28 ft. lbs. (39 Nm).

40. Install new set rings onto the halfshaft inboard joint splines. Install the halfshafts, making sure that they lock into place.

41. Install the radius rod and damper fork. Only hand-tighten their fasteners at this time.

42. Install the ball joint to the lower arm. Tighten the castle nut to 36–43 ft. lbs. (50–60 Nm). Then, only tighten the nut enough to install a new cotter pin.

43. If equipped, install the rear engine mount bracket stay. Tighten the nut to 15 ft. lbs. (21 Nm) and the bolt to 28 ft. lbs. (39 Nm).

44. Install the clutch damper and tighten the bolts to 16 ft. lbs. (22 Nm).

45. Install the front wheels.

46. Lower the vehicle.

47. Use a floor jack placed under the right front control arm to raise the vehicle enough so that its weight is supported by the jack. Tighten the radius rod mounting bolts to 76 ft. lbs. (105 Nm) and the radius rod nut to 32 ft. lbs. (44 Nm). Tighten the damper pinch bolt to 32 ft. lbs. (44 Nm). Tighten the damper fork bolt to 47 ft. lbs. (65 Nm). After pre-loading the suspension, lower the vehicle and remove the floor jack.

48. Coat the tip of the slave cylinder with heavy duty high temperature grease. Install the clutch hose pipe and clutch slave cylinder to the transaxle housing. Be sure the slave cylinder snaps into the release fork. Tighten the slave cylinder mounting bolts to 16 ft. lbs. (22 Nm).

49. Install the speed sensor. Tighten the mounting bolt to 14 ft. lbs. (19 Nm).

50. Install the shift cable and select cable to the shift arm lever. Install the shift cable assembly onto the transaxle case. Tighten the cable bracket mounting bolts to 16 ft. lbs. (22 Nm). Install new cotter pins.

51. Connect the back-up light switch coupler and the transaxle ground cable. Install the harness clamp.

52. Install the starter. Tighten the 10mm bolt to 32 ft. lbs. (45 Nm) and the 12mm bolt to 54 ft. lbs. (75 Nm). Connect the starter wires.

53. Loosen the three front engine mount bracket bolts. Tighten them to 28 ft. lbs. (39 Nm).

54. Install the vacuum tank and its bracket. Install the air cleaner case and intake duct.

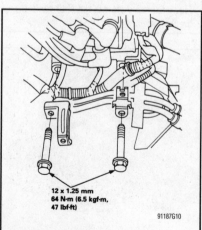

Fig. 10 Remove the 2 upper transaxle mounting bolts . . .

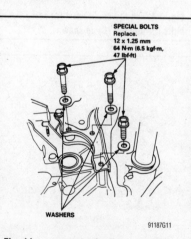

Fig. 11 . . . remove the 3 rear engine mount bracket mounting bolts . . .

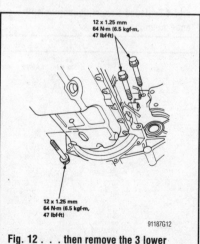

Fig. 12 . . . then remove the 3 lower transaxle housing bolts

55. Fill the transaxle with the proper type and quantity of oil.

56. Install the battery base stay and the battery base. Tighten the battery base bolts to 16 ft. lbs. (22 Nm). Install the battery and connect the battery cables.

57. Check the clutch pedal free-play.

58. Start the vehicle and check the transaxle and clutch for smooth operation.

59. On Preludes equipped with 4WS, and turn the steering wheel lock-to-lock to reset the steering control unit.

60. Check and adjust the front wheel alignment.

61. Enter the radio security code.

Halfshafts

♦ See Figure 13

All Accord and Prelude models use front half-shafts to couple the transaxle to the road wheels. This allows power to be delivered as the suspension moves up and down and while the wheels are turned side to side to negotiate turns. In order to accomplish the ability to simultaneously supply rotational power and the ability to change direction, an axle must have a component that can pivot and rotate at the same time.

On the Accord and Prelude, this is accomplished by using a halfshaft with an inner and outer Constant Velocity (CV) joint. In order to lubricate the CV-joint, the joint is assembled using an approved high temperature molybdenum disulfide grease capable of withstanding extreme pressure and heat. The grease is retained in the CV-joint by a tapered

Fig. 13 A typical halfshaft used on Accord and Prelude models

accordion boot, which is installed over the axle and the CV-joint.

The CV-boot allows the CV-joint to rotate and pivot, while retaining the lubricant and protecting the CV-joint from water and debris.

HALFSHAFT INSPECTION

When inspecting a halfshaft, it is more likely to have an outer CV-joint or CV-boot failure because the outer CV-joint pivots more when the vehicle is turning than the inner CV-joint. The outer CV-boot is more vulnerable to physical damage because of its location, unlike the inner CV-joint/boot, which is surrounded by the transaxle, engine, and the vehicle's body.

Although the CV-joint lubricant is sealed in place via the CV-boot, grease does lose its ability to lubricate with time and use. If a vehicle is used in extreme conditions under severe loads, it's likely the CV-joint lubricant could loose its ability to lubricate within 5 years or 1,000 miles (160,000 km) or less.

In these extreme cases, the CV-boots should be removed, and the CV-joints cleaned and repacked with the recommended lubricant.

To diagnose a CV-joint failure, proceed as follows:

1. Road test the vehicle and listen for a "clicking" noise from the left front or right front wheel area, especially during moderate acceleration from a stop while turning. Use a large, safe, empty parking lot and accelerate from a stop, alternately turning left and right. A clicking noise from the front of the vehicle is an indication of a worn CV-joint.

2. Apply the parking brake and put the transmission in neutral with the ignition in the **OFF** position.

3. Carefully raise and safely support the vehicle.

4. Rotate the tire/wheel assembly slowly by hand. Turn the front wheels side to side to simulate a turn to inspect the halfshaft Constant Velocity (CV) joint boots for leakage, wear, cracks, punctures or tears.

➡If an outer CV-boot is leaking, the inside portion of the road wheel and surrounding suspension components will be covered with grease. The cost of a typical CV joint is many times more expensive than a CV-boot.

✵✵ WARNING

If a CV-boot has failed, the centrifugal force of the axle spinning will cause the lubricant to leak, and allow water and other harmful

debris to enter and permanently damage the CV-joint. A failed CV-boot should be replaced immediately.

5. Wrap a suitable protective cloth around the center of the axle and securely fasten a clamping-type pliers to the axle.

6. Hold the tire/wheel assembly stationary while trying to rotate the axle back and forth while checking for excessive looseness from the outer CV-joint. Then hold the inner CV-joint and move the axle back and forth to check for excessive looseness. A slight amount of free movement is acceptable, however, if the axle can be moved ³⁄₁₆inches (5mm) or more, the CV-joint should be replaced.

Symptoms of a failed CV-joint could include:

• A clicking noise during moderate acceleration, especially when turning.

• A shuddering vibration or rumbling noise when driving, especially when accelerating.

• A clunking noise when shifting from, or moving from, forward to reverse to forward.

➡A shuddering vibration or rumbling noise can also be caused by a failed wheel bearing, severe tire imbalance, or a tire with internal belt damage. Should this symptom occur, the problem should be diagnosed immediately.

REMOVAL & INSTALLATION

♦ See Figures 14, 15 and 16

1. Loosen the front spindle nut.

2. Raise and safely support the vehicle.

3. Remove the front wheels and the spindle nut.

4. Drain the transaxle fluid and install the drain plug with a new washer. If the halfshaft to be removed is installed into the intermediate shaft, the transaxle fluid does not need to be drained.

5. Remove the damper fork nut and damper pinch bolt.

6. Remove the damper fork.

7. Remove the cotter pin and castle nut from the lower arm ball joint. Install a hex nut flush onto the ball joint stud to prevent the ball joint tool from damaging the stud threads.

8. Using a ball joint tool, separate the lower arm from the knuckle.

9. Pull the knuckle outward. Remove the halfshaft outboard joint from the hub by tapping it with a plastic hammer.

10. Carefully pry the inner CV-joint away from

Fig. 14 Use a large prytool to gently pry the halfshaft from the transaxle assembly

Fig. 15 Once the shaft has been dislodged from the transaxle, carefully lower it to the ground

Fig. 16 Close up of the splined end of a halfshaft

the transaxle case to force the halfshaft set ring out of the groove.

11. Pull on the inboard CV-joint and remove the halfshaft from the differential case or intermediate shaft.

➡**Do not pull on the halfshaft as the CV-joint may come apart. Use care when prying out the assembly and pull it straight to avoid damaging the differential oil seal or intermediate shaft oil or dust seals.**

To install:

12. Replace the differential oil seal or intermediate shaft seal if either were damaged during removal.

13. Install new set rings on the ends of the halfshafts.

14. Install the halfshafts and be sure the set ring locks in the differential gear groove and the halfshaft bottoms in the differential or intermediate shaft.

15. Install the outboard joint into the hub. Be sure the splines mesh together and the joint is fully seated into the hub.

16. Fit the ball joint stud into the lower control arm. Install the damper fork into position. Tighten the upper damper pinch bolt to 32 ft. lbs. (44 Nm) and the fork nut to 47 ft. lbs. (65 Nm).

17. Tighten the ball joint castle nut to 40 ft. lbs. (55 Nm), then tighten the nut just enough to install a new cotter pin.

18. Install the front wheels. Install a new spindle nut, but don't tighten it yet.

19. Lower the vehicle.

20. Tighten the spindle nut to 181 ft. lbs. (245

Nm) and stake its tab. Tighten the wheel nuts to 80 ft. lbs. (110 Nm).

21. Fill the transaxle with the proper type and quantity of fluid.

22. Warm the engine up, check the transaxle fluid level, and road test the vehicle.

CV-JOINT OVERHAUL

▶ **See Figures 17 thru 35**

The replacement CV-boot clamps can be one of three types, a folding double clamped band, a double loop band, or an ear clamp band. Do not

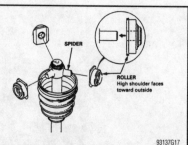

Fig. 17 Clamp the halfshaft to be overhauled securely in a vise to remove the joint and boot

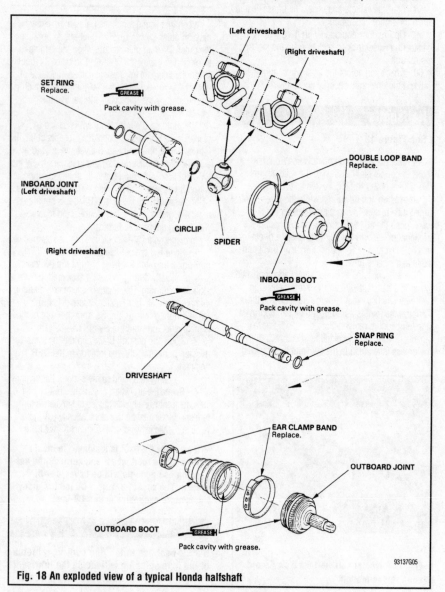

Fig. 18 An exploded view of a typical Honda halfshaft

Fig. 19 Matchmark the location of the rollers when removing them from the spider, and matchmark the location of the spider to the splined axle to ensure proper reassembly

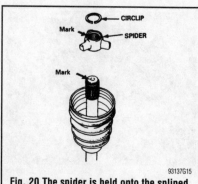

Fig. 20 The spider is held onto the splined drive axle with a circlip. Use a new circlip during reassembly

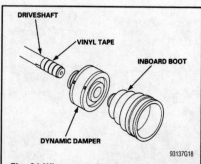

Fig. 21 When removing the components from the drive axle, wrap vinyl tape around the spines to prevent damaging the boot or damper

substitute ordinary radiator hose clamps or plastic ties in place of a CV-boot clamp.

✳✳ CAUTION

When replacing a CV-joint or CV-boot, do NOT reuse the CV-boot clamps.

➡ The Canadian and USA versions of the Accord and Prelude models produced before 1998 use different outer CV-boots and clamps. The Canadian models use outer CV-boots made of Thermoplastic Polyester Elastomer (TPE), while the USA models use rubber.

✳✳ WARNING

When removing a CV-joint, make sure to matchmark all the components before disassembly to ensure the components are installed exactly in the same location from which they were removed. If a component is to be replaced, make sure to install the replacement part in the exact location as the component being replaced. Failure to reinstall the components correctly could result in premature failure or excessive driveline vibration.

If a CV-boot has failed and is to be replaced, the CV-joint from where the failed boot was located **must** be cleaned and repacked with the appropriate lubricant.

When the outer CV-boot is to be replaced and/or the outer CV-joint serviced, if special tools are not available to remove the outer CV-joint, simply disassemble and remove the inner CV-joint and boot, then slide the outer boot off of the axle.

If the outer CV-joint has failed, on vehicles produced before 1998, the shaft and CV-joint may only be replaced as an assembly.

✳✳ WARNING

If the outer CV-joint is to be replaced, make sure to note whether or not the vehicle is equipped with ABS brakes to ensure the correct replacement parts.

Due to the popularity of halfshafts on front wheel drive and four wheel drive vehicles, axle and halfshaft rebuilding facilities have become increasingly popular. Before removing and disassembling a halfshaft, check locally to see if there is a facility available that will sell a rebuilt halfshaft, or rebuild your halfshaft. You may discover that this is more cost effective and convenient, especially if you remove the halfshaft yourself.

1. Remove the halfshaft assembly.

2. Mark the location of the dynamic damper (if installed) and the CV-boots on the drive axle.

3. Be sure to mark the inner CV-joint roller grooves during disassembly to ensure proper positioning during reassembly.

4. Remove the CV-boot clamps, then remove the boot from the inner CV-joint housing and remove the housing from the inboard spider gear rollers. If the CV-boot clamps are welded, the clamps must be cut using a pair of suitable side cutters.

5. Mark the rollers to the spider gear yoke, and the yoke to the driveshaft so they can be installed in their original positions.

6. Remove the rollers, snapring, and spider gear yoke, then remove the stopper ring.

➡ It may be necessary to use a small universal gear puller to remove the spider gear yoke from the axle.

7. On vehicles produced before 1998, the outer CV-joint cannot be removed from the shaft. Wrap the end of the axle with vinyl tape, the remove the inboard CV-joint boot, dynamic damper, then the outboard CV-joint boot.

8. If a suitable slide hammer with a ⅝ inch x 18 thread and a 24 x 1.5mm threaded adapter Tool No. 07XAC-0010200 or its equivalent are available, the outer CV-joint can be removed on 1998 and later vehicles as follows:

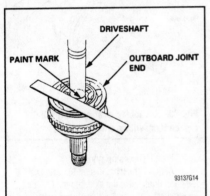

Fig. 22 If removing the outer CV-joint on a 1998 or later vehicle, lay a straight edge across the joint and make a paint mark to ensure proper reassembly

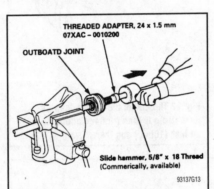

Fig. 23 Removal of an outer CV-joint on 1998–00 vehicles requires using a suitable slide hammer and an adapter. If not available, remove the inner components to replace the boot

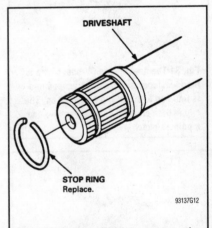

Fig. 24 If the outer CV-joint was removed, replace the stop ring

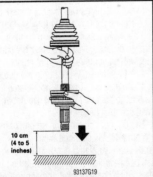

Fig. 25 When installing the outer CV-joint, tap the spindle on a hard surface, such as an oak plank, until the joint is fully seated and the paint mark made during disassembly is aligned

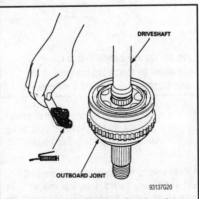

Fig. 26 Use a 2 inch (50mm) wide paint or gasket scraper, or plastic spatula to pack the outer CV-joint assembly with an approved CV-joint grease

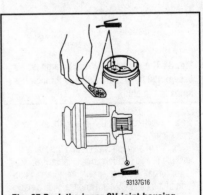

Fig. 27 Pack the inner CV-joint housing with grease before installing the spider and rollers. If the housing (A) attaches to an intermediate shaft, put a tablespoon's worth of grease in it

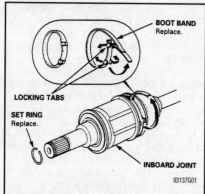

Fig. 28 The folding double clamped CV-boot clamp is removed by opening the tabs and lifting the curved section upward to release the tension

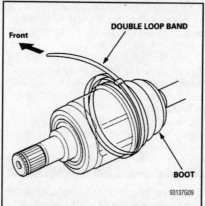

Fig. 29 The double loop CV-boot clamp wraps around the boot and through the clip two times

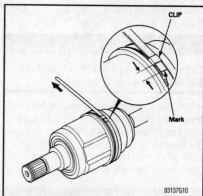

Fig. 30 The double loop CV-boot clamp is initially tensioned by hand, and while being held a line is scribed ½ of an inch (12mm) from the clip

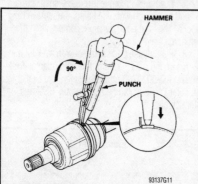

Fig. 31 The double loop CV-boot clamp is then tensioned such that the scribed line is lined up with the clip ad folded up. The clip is then crimped using a hammer and a pointed punch

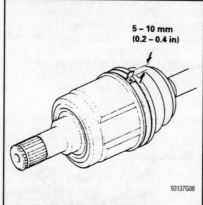

Fig. 32 The end of the double loop CV-boot clamp is then trimmed about ³/₁₆ of an inch (10mm) and then . . .

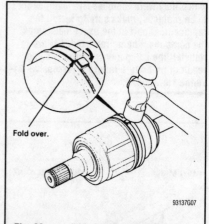

Fig. 33 . . . folded over and carefully tapped flush with a small hammer

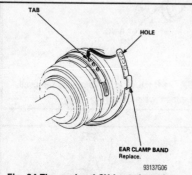

Fig. 34 The ear band CV-boot clamp is assembled by placing the tabs through the holes in the clamp

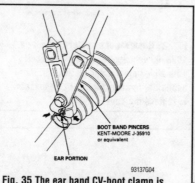

Fig. 35 The ear band CV-boot clamp is tensioned by squeezing the base of the ears together using a boot band pincher

a. Matchmark the CV-joint to the axle for reassembly.

b. Wrap a shop towel around the axle and install the axle securely in a suitable vise.

c. Install the adapter onto the threaded portion of the outer CV-joint and the slide hammer, and remove the CV-joint using the slide hammer.

d. Remove the stop ring.

e. Wrap the end of the axle with vinyl tape and remove the CV-boot.

To install:

9. Wrap the end of the axle splines with vinyl tape to prevent damage to the boots. Install the outboard boot, dynamic strut, and inboard boot, along with their small CV-joint clamps, then remove the vinyl tape.

➥**Make sure to loosely install the small CV-boot and dynamic strut clamps at this time. In some cases it may be impossible to install the small clamps once the CV-joints are reinstalled.**

10. If the outer CV-joint was removed from the axle:

a. Install a new stop ring.

b. Align the matchmarks on the axle and CV-joint and lightly seat the axle into the CV-joint until the stop ring end gap is closed.

c. Seat the axle into the CV-joint by holding the axle and CV-joint and tapping the CV-joint using 5 inch (10cm) strokes onto a hard surface while holding the axle until the stop ring is fully seated into the CV-joint.

d. Place a straight edge across the CV-joint to see if it aligns with the paint mark on the axle, to ensure the CV-joint is fully seated.

11. Using a 2 inch (50mm) paint or gasket scraper, or its equivalent, thoroughly pack the CV-joint with an approved CV-joint grease.

12. Install the CV-boot onto the outer CV-joint.

13. Install the large CV-boot clamp to secure the boot to the outer CV-joint. Do not tighten the small clamp at this time.

The CV-boot clamps can be one of three types, a folding double clamped band, a double loop band, or an ear clamp band. The folding double clamped band has thick curved portion of band that seats into a small bracket and applies tension as the curved portion is pressed downward, and held in place by two folding tabs. The double loop band wraps around the CV-boot twice and through a small clip. The ear clamp band has a series of holes and locking tabs that are locked into the holes.

14. To install a folding double clamped band, perform the following:

   a. Seat the end of the thick curved section into the small bracket.

   b. Press the thick curved section down, flush with the band.

   c. While holding the curved section down, fold over the locking tabs and seat them by tapping them lightly with a small hammer.

15. To install a double loop band CV-boot clamp, proceed as follows:

   a. Install the clamp in the direction such that if the axle were installed on the vehicle the clip of the clamp is at the top, with the end of the clamp is facing forward.

   b. Wrap the clamp around the boot 2 times, and seat the clamp into the groove of the boot.

   c. Pull the end of the clamp by hand to remove any slack in the band, and scribe a mark in the band ½ an inch (12mm) from the clip.

   d. Using a boot band tool or an equivalent device, pull the end of the clamp until the line is flush with the rear edge of the clip, and then fold the end of the clamp upward so it is at a 90° angle with the clip.

   e. While holding the end of the clamp in this position, center punch the clip using a pointed center punch and a hammer.

   f. Trim the end of the clamp ⅜ of an inch (10mm) from the end of the clip, fold the clamp end over the clip and seat the folded clamp end by tapping it with a hammer.

16. To install an ear clamp style band clamp, proceed as follows:

   a. Feed the tab of the band into the holes of the band. Sometimes a small flat blade jewelers screwdriver can be placed through the clamp's hole and the tab levered into place.

   b. Squeeze the small raised ear portion at the base of the clamp using a pair of boot band pinchers, or carefully alternate side to side with a thin pair of needle nose pliers, until the gap at the base of the clamp's ear is ⅛ of an inch (3mm) apart.

17. Install the spider gear in its original position by aligning the matchmarks.

18. Fit the snapring onto the halfshaft groove.

19. Fit the rollers to the spider gear with their high shoulders facing outward. Reinstall the rollers in their original positions on the spider gear.

20. Pack the inboard joint housing with an approved CV-joint grease. Do not use a substitute, or mix types of grease.

21. Fit the inboard joint onto the halfshaft while holding the axle with the rollers facing downward to prevent them from falling off, and place the rollers into the inboard joint housing.

22. Install the CV-boot onto the inner CV-joint.

23. Install the large CV-boot clamp to secure the boot to the inner CV-joint. Do not install the small clamp at this time.

24. With the boots installed onto the CV-joints, adjust the CV-boots on the axle in or out to place the boot ends in their original positions.

25. Tighten the new clamps on the small end of the boots and secure as necessary to ensure a good fit.

26. Always use a new set ring whenever the driveshaft is being installed. When reinstalling, be sure the driveshaft ends lock securely in place into the differential or intermediate shaft.

27. Reinstall the halfshaft into the vehicle.

28. Install a new axle nut onto the axle, tighten the axle nut to 181 ft. lbs. (245 Nm).

29. Stake the axle nut into the slot in the axle.

CLUTCH

Understanding the Clutch

▶ See Figures 36 and 37

> ※ **CAUTION**
>
> **The clutch driven disc may contain asbestos, which has been determined to be a cancer causing agent. Never clean clutch surfaces with compressed air! Avoid inhaling any dust from any clutch surface! When cleaning clutch surfaces, use a commercially available brake cleaning fluid.**

The purpose of the clutch is to disconnect and connect engine power at the transaxle. A vehicle at rest requires a lot of engine torque to get all that weight moving. An internal combustion engine does not develop a high starting torque (unlike steam engines) so it must be allowed to operate without any load until it builds up enough torque to move the vehicle. Torque increases with engine rpm. The clutch allows the engine to build up torque by physically disconnecting the engine from the transaxle, relieving the engine of any load or resistance.

The transfer of engine power to the transaxle (the load) must be smooth and gradual; if it weren't, drive line components would wear out or break quickly. This gradual power transfer is made possible by gradually releasing the clutch pedal. The clutch disc and pressure plate are the connecting link between the engine and transaxle. When the clutch pedal is released, the disc and plate contact each other (the clutch is engaged) physically joining the engine and transaxle. When the pedal is pushed inward, the disc and plate separate (the clutch is disengaged) disconnecting the engine from the transaxle.

Most clutches utilize a single plate, dry friction disc with a diaphragm-style spring pressure plate. The clutch disc has a splined hub which attaches

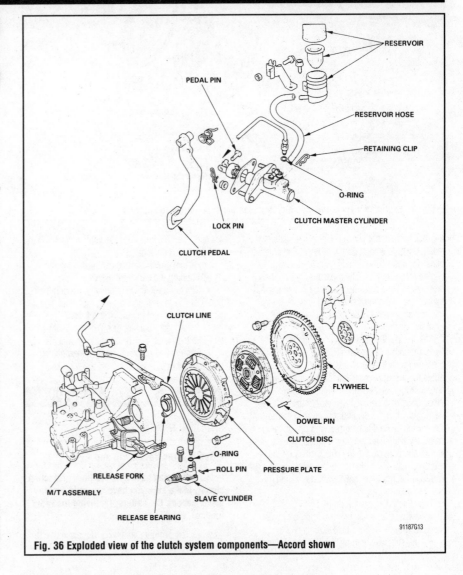

Fig. 36 Exploded view of the clutch system components—Accord shown

91187G13

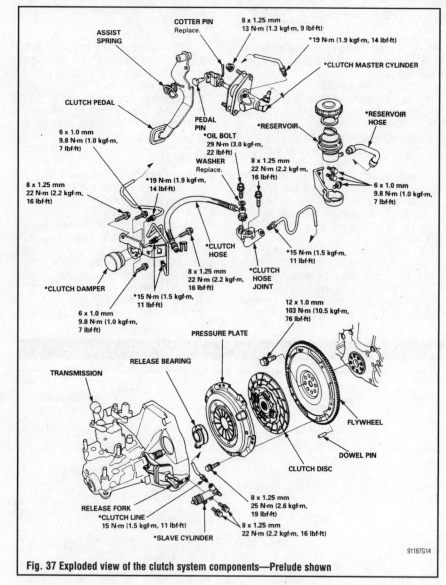

Fig. 37 Exploded view of the clutch system components—Prelude shown

the disc to the input shaft. The disc has friction material where it contacts the flywheel and pressure plate. Torsion springs on the disc help absorb engine torque pulses. The pressure plate applies pressure to the clutch disc, holding it tight against the surface of the flywheel. The clutch operating mechanism consists of a release bearing, fork and cylinder assembly.

The release fork and actuating linkage transfer pedal motion to the release bearing. In the engaged position (pedal released) the diaphragm spring holds the pressure plate against the clutch disc, so engine torque is transmitted to the input shaft. When the clutch pedal is depressed, the release bearing pushes the diaphragm spring center toward the flywheel. The diaphragm spring pivots the fulcrum, relieving the load on the pressure plate. Steel spring straps riveted to the clutch cover lift the pressure plate from the clutch disc, disengaging the engine drive from the transaxle and enabling the gears to be changed.

The clutch is operating properly if:

• It will stall the engine in second gear when released with the vehicle held stationary.

• The shift lever can be moved freely between 1st and reverse gears when the vehicle is stationary and the clutch disengaged.

Premature clutch failures can be caused by:

• Slipping the clutch excessively.

• When the vehicle is stationary, leaving the transmission in gear and keeping the clutch pedal depressed for a prolonged length of time.

• A fluid leak (coolant or oil) coming into contact with the clutch disk or related components.

• Improper adjustment, such as insufficient clutch pedal free play.

Driven Disc and Pressure Plate

REMOVAL & INSTALLATION

▶ See Figures 38, 39, 40 and 41

➡ The radio may have a coded theft protection circuit. Make sure you have the code before disconnecting the battery, removing the radio fuse, or removing the radio.

When removing the transaxle to replace the clutch disk, always replace the clutch disk, release

bearing, pilot bearing and pressure plate. Often times these components are sold more economically as a clutch kit.

If the flywheel is damaged or excessively worn, check to see if the flywheel is sold with the clutch replacement parts as a kit. Usually it is more cost effective to buy a complete kit than to purchase the parts individually.

➡ If a flywheel with surface irregularities is reused, it is very likely that when driving, the clutch will chatter as it is engaged.

Try to avoid the use of rebuilt parts, as at times, the expense saved on parts may be far less justified than the labor cost (or time) to do the job a second time.

1. Disconnect the negative battery cable.
2. Raise and safely support the vehicle.
3. Remove the transaxle from the vehicle, as outlined earlier in this section. Matchmark the flywheel and clutch for reassembly.
4. Use a flywheel ring-gear holder to lock the flywheel in position.
5. Loosen the pressure plate bolts two turns at a time working in a crisscross pattern to prevent warping the pressure plate. Remove the pressure plate and clutch disc.
6. Inspect the flywheel, disc, and pressure plate for wear, cracks, and warpage.. Light scoring of the flywheel may be polished out; gouges, warpage, burn marks, cracks, or chipped teeth require replacement of the flywheel.

➡ If the flywheel is to be removed, but is going to be reused, matchmark it to the engine block prior to removal. Aligning the matchmarks upon reassembly will preserve driveline balance.

7. Inspect the flywheel's ball bearing: turn the inner race of the bearing with your finger, and be sure it turns smoothly and quietly. If the bearing is loose or noisy, or exhibits rough motion, replace it.
8. Remove the release fork boot. Squeeze the release fork retaining spring to disengage the fork from its pivot. Remove the release fork from the clutch housing.
9. Remove the release bearing. Spin the bearing by hand to check its degree of play. Replace the release bearing if it has excessive play or is leaking grease.

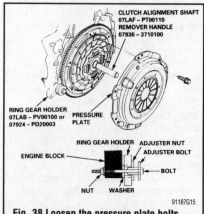

Fig. 38 Loosen the pressure plate bolts gradually, in a crisscross pattern to avoid warping the plate

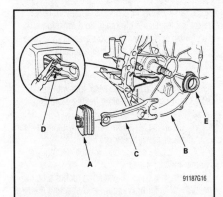

Fig. 39 Remove the release fork (C) from the clutch housing (B) by squeezing the release fork set spring (D) with pliers, then remove the release bearing (E)

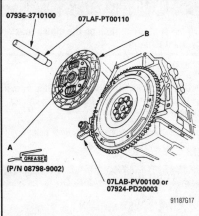

Fig. 40 Using the special tools, install the clutch disc (B) . . .

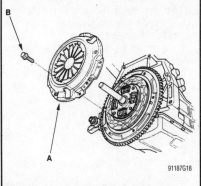

Fig. 41 . . . then install the pressure plate (A). Tighten the pressure plate bolts in a crisscross pattern two turns at a time to prevent warping the plate

10. Inspect the rear main bearing oil seal for signs of leakage. If necessary, replace the seal to prevent oil leakage onto the clutch's friction surfaces.

To install:

11. If necessary, drive out the flywheel bearing, then use a suitably-sized bearing driver to install a new one. Use a crisscross pattern to tighten the flywheel mounting bolts in several steps to 87 ft. lbs. (118 Nm).

12. Install the clutch disc and pressure plate by aligning the dowels on the flywheel with the dowel holes in the pressure plate. If a new pressure plate is not being installed, align the matchmarks that were made during removal. Install and hand-tighten the pressure plate bolts.

13. Insert a suitable clutch disc alignment tool into the splined hole in the clutch disc. Align the clutch and pressure plate.

14. Tighten the pressure plate bolts in a crisscross pattern two turns at a time to prevent warping the pressure plate. The final torque is 19 ft. lbs. (26 Nm).

15. Remove the alignment tool and ring gear holder.

16. Coat the mainshaft with heavy-duty high-temperature grease. The manufacturer recommends part No. 08798–9002, Honda super high-temp urea grease.

17. Coat the release fork pawls and the inner race of the release bearing with high temperature grease and install them into the clutch housing. Be sure the release fork retainer spring snaps into place on the pivot. The bearing and fork must fit together properly and slide back and forth smoothly.

18. Coat the tip of the slave cylinder with grease. Install the release fork boot.

19. Install the transaxle, making sure the mainshaft is properly aligned with the clutch disc splines, and the transaxle case dowels are properly aligned with the engine block.

20. Install the transaxle case bolts and sequentially tighten them to 47 ft. lbs. (65 Nm).

21. Bleed the clutch hydraulic system.

22. Adjust the clutch pedal free-play.

23. Verify that all engine and transaxle components are installed and connected properly.

24. Reconnect the negative battery cable.

25. Road test the vehicle.

ADJUSTMENTS

Clutch Pedal Free-Play

▶ **See Figure 42**

➡ **The hydraulic clutch is self-adjusting to compensate for wear.**

1. Loosen the locknut at the base of the clutch switch (or the cruise control, if equipped), or the adjusting bolt that contacts the clutch pedal when the pedal is fully released. Back off the switch or adjustment bolt until it no longer contacts the clutch pedal.

2. Loosen the locknut at the rear of the pushrod for the clutch master cylinder.

3. Turn the clutch master cylinder pushrod in or out until:

- The clutch pedal height from the floor is 7 $\frac{3}{16}$ inches (183mm).
- The clutch pedal stroke is $5\frac{5}{16}$–$5\frac{11}{16}$ inches (135–145mm).

4. Tighten the pushrod locknut.

5. Thread in the clutch switch or adjusting bolt until it contacts the clutch pedal, then thread the component an additional ¾–1 turn, and tighten the locknut.

6. Loosen the locknut on the clutch interlock switch.

7. Measure the clearance between the clutch

pedal and the floor board with the clutch pedal fully depressed.

8. Allow the clutch pedal to rise from the floor until it is $\frac{9}{16}$–$\frac{3}{4}$ inches (15–20mm) above the full bottom measurement.

9. Adjust the interlock switch so that the engine will start from this position.

10. Turn the interlock switch in an additional ¾–1 turn, and tighten the locknut.

11. Tighten the locknut to secure the clutch interlock switch in this position.

Master Cylinder

REMOVAL & INSTALLATION

▶ **See Figures 43, 44 and 45**

❊❊ **WARNING**

Do not spill brake fluid on any of the vehicles painted surfaces. It will damage the paint!

1. Use a suitable siphon or a clean turkey baster to remove the old fluid, or remove the clutch

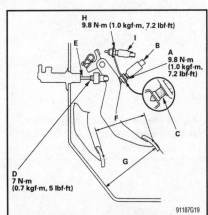

Fig. 42 Loosen the locknut (A), then back the clutch switch, or adjusting bolt, (B) off until it doesn't touch the clutch pedal

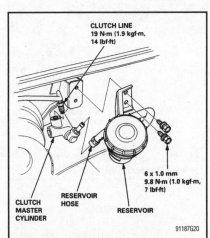

Fig. 43 Disconnect and plug the fluid line(s) from the master cylinder—Prelude shown, Accord similar

master cylinder reservoir bracket mounting bolts and pour the old fluid into a suitable container.

2. Clean the reservoir thoroughly using a clean shop cloth or paper towel.

3. Disconnect the clutch pipe from the master cylinder.

4. Remove the reservoir hose from the master cylinder reservoir.

5. If additional room is needed, remove the driver's side lower dash panel and the following items from under the dash:

   a. Remove the cotter pin on the clutch pedal rod.

   b. Remove the clutch pedal pin out of the yoke.

   c. Remove the master cylinder retaining nuts.

6. Remove the clutch master cylinder from under the hood.

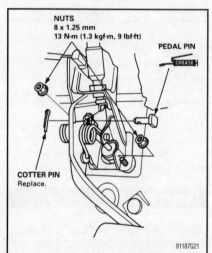

Fig. 44 Pry the cotter pin (or lock pin) out, then pull the pedal pin from the yoke. Unfasten the retaining nuts securing the master cylinder . . .

Fig. 45 . . . then, from under the hood, remove the master cylinder

✳✳ WARNING

Do not spill brake fluid on the clutch master cylinder damper.

7. Installation is the reverse of removal.

➡**Use only fresh DOT 3 or 4 brake fluid from a sealed container to refill the clutch hydraulic system.**

8. Fill and bleed the clutch system, using a suitable DOT 3 or 4 brake fluid.

Slave Cylinder

REMOVAL & INSTALLATION

▶ **See Figures 46 and 47**

1. Locate the slave cylinder mounted on the transaxle assembly, near the radiator.

2. Remove the flare fitting and steel line from the slave cylinder assembly.

3. Remove the slave cylinder from the clutch housing by removing the attaching bolts.

4. Installation is the reverse of the removal procedure

➡**Use only fresh DOT 3 or 4 brake fluid from a sealed container to refill the clutch hydraulic system.**

5. Fill, then bleed the clutch system, using a suitable DOT 3 or 4 brake fluid.

HYDRAULIC SYSTEM BLEEDING

➡**Use only DOT 3 or 4 brake fluid from a clean, sealed container, for the clutch master reservoir. As brake fluid will damage the vehicle's paint, clean up any spills immediately.**

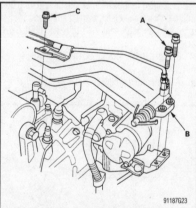

Fig. 46 The slave cylinder (B) is mounted to the transaxle with retaining bolts (A & C)—Accord shown

1. Use a suitable siphon or a clean turkey baster to remove the old brake fluid, or remove the clutch master cylinder reservoir bracket mounting bolts and pour the old fluid into a suitable container.

2. If removed, install the clutch master cylinder fluid reservoir and fill it the MAX line with suitable DOT 3 or 4 brake fluid from a fresh, sealed container.

3. Clean the reservoir thoroughly using a clean shop cloth or paper towel.

4. Fit a flare or box end wrench onto the slave cylinder bleeder screw.

5. Attach a (clear if available) rubber tube to the slave cylinder bleed screw and suspend it into a suitable clear drain container partially filled with brake fluid.

6. Make sure the clutch master cylinder is filled with brake fluid.

7. Open the bleeder screw and have an assistant press the clutch pedal to the floor.

8. While holding the clutch pedal to the floor, close the bleed screw.

9. Slowly release the clutch pedal to its fullest extension and recheck the reservoir fluid level. Top off as necessary.

10. Repeat the above steps until the fluid exiting the bleed screw is clean and free of all air bubbles.

11. Top off the clutch master cylinder reservoir as necessary.

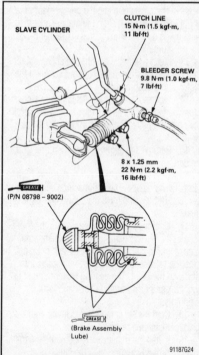

Fig. 47 Installed view of the slave cylinder—Prelude shown

AUTOMATIC TRANSAXLE

▶ **See Figure 48**

The automatic transaxle on the Accord and Prelude allows engine torque and power to be transmitted to the front wheels within a narrow range of engine operating speeds. It will allow the engine to turn fast enough to produce plenty of power and torque at very low speeds, while keeping it at a sensible rpm at high vehicle speeds (and it does this job without driver assistance). The transaxle uses a light fluid as the medium for the transmission of power. This fluid also works in the operation of various hydraulic control circuits and as a lubricant. Because the transaxle fluid performs all of these functions, trouble within the unit can easily travel from one part to another. For this reason, and because of the complexity and unusual operating principles of the transaxle, a very sound understanding of the basic principles of operation will simplify troubleshooting.

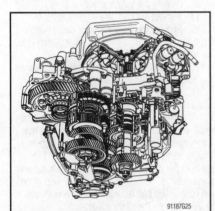

91187G25

Fig. 48 Cross-sectional view of an automatic transaxle

Fluid Pan

These vehicles do not have a fluid pan. For draining and refilling procedures please refer to Section 1.

Neutral Safety Switch

Description

The neutral safety switch is a combination switch that also controls the backup lights and gear position indicators. The switch is located on the transaxle assembly.

REMOVAL & INSTALLATION

For the removal and installation procedures, see the backup light switch procedures in Section 6.

ADJUSTMENT

See the backup light switch procedures in Section 6, for adjustment procedures.

Automatic Transaxle

REMOVAL & INSTALLATION

Accord

2.2L & 2.3L ENGINES

▶ **See Figures 49 and 50**

1. Disconnect the negative, then the positive battery cables.
2. Remove the battery from the vehicle.
3. Shift the transaxle into **N**.
4. Remove the air intake hose, air cleaner housing, and the resonator assembly.
5. Remove the battery base and the base stay.
6. Disconnect the throttle cable from the throttle control lever.
7. Disconnect the transaxle ground cable and the speed sensor connectors. Detach the solenoid valve connectors.
8. Disconnect the lock-up control solenoid valve and shift control solenoid valve connectors.
9. Disconnect the transaxle cooler hoses from the joint pipes and plug the hoses.
10. Disconnect the starter cables and remove the starter.
11. Detach the Countershaft Speed Sensor (CSS) connector.
12. Unplug the Vehicle Speed Sensor (VSS) connector.
13. Install a hoist to the engine.
14. Remove the four upper bolts attaching the transaxle to the engine block.
15. Loosen the three bolts attaching the front engine mount bracket to the engine.
16. Remove the transaxle mount.
17. Raise and safely support the vehicle. Remove the front wheels.
18. Drain the transaxle fluid and reinstall the drain plug with a new washer.
19. Remove the splash shield.
20. Remove the subframe center beam.
21. Remove the cotter pins and lower arm ball joint nuts, then separate the ball joints from the lower arms using a suitable tool.
22. Remove the right damper pinch bolt, then separate the damper fork and damper.

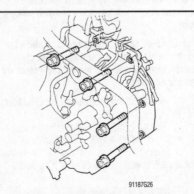

91187G26

Fig. 49 Unfasten the 4 transmission housing bolts

23. Remove the bolts and nut, then remove the right radius rod.
24. Using a small prying device, carefully pry the right and left halfshafts out of the differential. Remove the right and left halfshafts. Tie plastic bags over the halfshaft ends to prevent damage to the CV boots and splines.
25. Remove the bolts mounting the intermediate shaft, then remove the intermediate shaft from the differential.
26. Remove the torque converter cover and shift cable cover.
27. Remove the shift control cable by removing the lockbolt. Remove the shift cable lever from the control shaft. Don't disconnect the control lever from the shift cable. Wire the shift cable out of the work area and be careful not to kink it.
28. Remove the eight drive plate bolts one at a time while rotating the crankshaft pulley.
29. Place a suitable jack under the transaxle and raise the jack just enough to take weight off of the mounts.
30. Remove the intake manifold bracket.
31. Remove the transaxle housing mounting bolts.
32. Remove the mounting bolts from the rear engine mount bracket.
33. Remove the four transaxle housing mounting bolts and three mount bracket nuts.
34. Pull the transaxle away from the engine until it clears the 14mm dowel pins, then lower it using the jack.

To install:

➡**Use new self-locking nuts when assembling the front suspension components. Install new set rings onto the halfshaft inboard joint splines. Replace any color-coded self-locking bolts.**

35. Flush the transaxle cooler lines before installing the transaxle. Use a pressurized flushing unit such as Honda J38405-A or equivalent. Use only Honda biodegradable flushing fluid, Honda J35944–20. Other fluids will damage the A/T cooling system.

a. Fill the flusher with 21 ounces of fluid. Pressurize the flusher to 80–120 PSI, following the procedure on the fluid container and flusher.

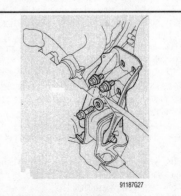

91187G27

Fig. 50 Remove the front mount bracket bolts, then remove the mount

b. Clamp the discharge hose of the flusher to the cooler return line. Clamp the drain hose to the cooler inlet line and route it into a bucket or drain tank.

c. Connect the flusher to air and water lines. Open the flusher water valve and flush the cooler for ten seconds. The air line should be equipped with a water trap to keep the system dry.

d. Depress the flusher trigger to mix flushing fluid with the water. Flush for two minutes, turning the air valve on and off for five seconds every 15–20 seconds to create a surging action.

e. After finishing one flushing cycle, reverse the hose and flush in the opposite direction following the same steps.

f. Dry the cooler lines with compressed air so that no moisture is left in the cooler system.

36. Be sure the two 14mm dowel pins are installed into the torque converter housing.

37. Install the torque converter onto the transaxle mainshaft with a new hub O-ring. Install the starter motor onto the transaxle case and tighten the mounting bolts to 33 ft. lbs. (44 Nm).

38. Raise the transaxle into position and install the transaxle housing mounting bolts. Tighten the bolts to 47 ft. lbs. (65 Nm).

39. Install the rear engine mounting bolts and tighten to 40 ft. lbs. (54 Nm).

40. Install the intake manifold bracket and tighten the bolts to 16 ft. lbs. (22 Nm).

41. Install the upper bolts attaching the transaxle to the engine and tighten the bolts to 47 ft. lbs. (64 Nm).

42. Tighten the front engine mount bracket bolts to 28 ft. lbs. (38 Nm).

43. Install the transaxle mount and loosely install the nuts and bolt that attach the mount. Tighten the nuts first to 28 ft. lbs. (38 Nm), then tighten the bolt to 47 ft. lbs. (64 Nm).

44. Remove the jack from the transaxle.

45. Attach the torque converter to the drive plate with the eight bolts. Tighten the bolts in two steps in a crisscross pattern: first to 4.5 ft. lbs. (6 Nm), and finally to 9 ft. lbs. (12 Nm). Check for free rotation after tightening the last bolt.

46. Install the shift control cable and control cable holder. Tighten the shift cable lockbolt to 10 ft. lbs. (14 Nm). Tighten the shift cable cover bolts to 13 ft. lbs. (18 Nm).

47. Install the torque converter cover and tighten the bolts to 9 ft. lbs. (12 Nm).

48. Remove the engine hoist.

49. Install the radius rod and damper fork.

50. Install the intermediate shaft into the differential and tighten the mounting bolts to 28 ft. lbs. (38 Nm).

51. Install a new set ring on the end of each halfshaft.

52. Turn the right steering knuckle fully outward and slide the axle into the differential until the set ring snaps into the differential side gear. Repeat the procedure on the left side.

53. Install the damper fork bolts and ball joint nuts to the lower arms. Tighten the ball joint nut to 40 ft. lbs. (55 Nm) and install a new cotter pin.

54. Install the subframe center beam and tighten the center beam bolts to 28 ft. lbs. (39 Nm).

55. Install the splash shield.

56. Install the front wheels and lower the vehicle.

57. Reconnect the speed sensor connector.

58. Support the right front knuckle with a floor jack until the weight of the vehicle is held by the jack. Tighten the damper fork pinch bolt to 32 ft. lbs. (44 Nm). Tighten the radius rod bolts to 76 ft. lbs. (105 Nm), and the radius rod nut to 32 ft. lbs. (44 Nm). Hold the damper fork bolt with a wrench, and tighten the nut to 40 ft. lbs. (55 Nm). Remove the floor jack.

59. Connect the cables to the starter.

60. Reconnect the throttle control cable.

61. Connect the lock-up control solenoid valve and shift control solenoid valve connectors.

62. Attach the speed sensor connectors and the transaxle ground cable.

63. Connect the transaxle cooler inlet hose to the joint pipe. Attach a drain hose to the return line.

64. Install the battery base stay and the battery base.

65. Install the resonator assembly, the air cleaner assembly, and the air intake hose.

66. Install the battery and connect the positive, then the negative battery cables to the battery.

67. Refill the transaxle with ATF. Use only Honda Premium ATF or an equivalent DEXRON® II ATF.

a. With the flusher drain hose attached to the cooler return line.

b. Place the transaxle in **P**, run the engine for 30 seconds, or until approximately one quart of fluid is discharged. Immediately shut off the engine. This completes the cooler flushing process.

c. Remove the drain hose and reconnect the cooler return line.

d. Refill the transaxle to the proper level with ATF.

68. Start the engine, set the parking brake, and shift the transaxle through all gears 3 times. Check for proper shift cable adjustment.

69. Let the engine reach operating temperature with the transaxle in **P** or **N**. Then, shut off the engine and check the fluid level.

70. Road test the vehicle.

71. After road testing the vehicle, loosen the front engine mount bracket bolts, then retighten them to 28 ft. lbs. (39 Nm).

72. Check and adjust the vehicle's front end alignment.

73. Enter the radio security code.

2.7L ENGINE

➡Several of the engine mounts must be removed during the transaxle removal procedure.

The objective of this procedure is to allow the engine to tilt so that the transaxle will clear the left shock tower. A chain host is necessary for this operation.

1. Disconnect the negative and positive battery cables.

2. Prop the hood open and remove the support struts. Secure the hood open in a vertical position.

3. Remove the battery. Remove the battery tray and bracket. Unbolt the cable holder from the battery tray.

4. Remove the intake air duct.

5. Detach the clips securing the starter cable to the strut brace. Remove the strut brace.

6. Drain the transaxle fluid. Install the drain plug with a new crush washer.

7. Uncouple the ATF cooler lines. Plug the lines, and turn them upward to lessen fluid spillage.

8. Remove the starter cables. Unbolt the starter cable clamp and the transaxle ground cable. Unbolt the engine sub-harness clamp from the transaxle case, and move the harness holder out of the way.

9. Disconnect the following electrical couplings:
- Shift control solenoid valve
- Mainshaft speed sensor connector
- Lock-up control solenoid valve
- Vehicle Speed Sensor (VSS) connector
- Linear solenoid connector
- Countershaft Speed Sensor (CSS)

10. Remove the Intake Air Bypass (IAB) vacuum tank from the transaxle. Do not disconnect its vacuum hoses.

11. Loosen the top two upper transaxle case bolts, they may not be easily accessible when the vehicle is raised.

12. Raise and safely support the vehicle. Remove the front wheels.

13. Remove the splash shield.

14. Remove the subframe center beam.

15. Remove the lower ball joint castle nuts. Separate the ball joints from the lower control arms using a suitable press type tool.

16. Remove the damper fork bolts, and separate the damper forks from the lower control arm.

17. Use a flat-bladed tool to carefully pry the half-shafts out of the differential and intermediate shaft.

18. Pull the inboard joints away from the differential and intermediate shaft. Tie plastic bags over the inboard joints to protect the boots and splines.

19. Remove the left damper pinch bolt, then separate the damper fork from the strut. Unbolt and remove the left radius rod. Use wire to support the left control arm and halfshaft out of the work area.

20. Remove the intermediate shaft.

21. Remove the shift cable holder and cover. Remove the shift cable lockbolt, and slide the cable lever off of the control rod. Be careful not to kink the shift cable.

22. Remove the torque converter cover. Remove the eight driveplate bolts one at a time while rotating the crankshaft pulley.

23. Attach a chain hoist to the transaxle. Place a jack under the engine for support.

24. Remove the rear mount stiffener, then unbolt and remove the rear mount.

25. Remove the front mount bracket, then remove the front mount.

26. Remove the four upper transaxle case bolts.

27. Remove the side transaxle mount.

28. Remove the two lower transaxle case bolts.

❋❋ CAUTION

Be sure the transaxle is securely supported before removing the rear mounting bracket bolts. Place a transaxle jack under the transaxle for additional support.

29. Remove the rear mount bolts. Raise the engine and transaxle slightly, then remove the rear mount bracket from the rear mount.

30. Carefully lower the transaxle from the vehicle. Tilt the engine just enough for the transaxle to clear the left shock tower.

➡️Do not allow the A/C compressor to hit the right shock tower when the engine is being tilted.

31. Pull the transaxle away from the engine until it clears the dowel pins, then lower it from the vehicle.

To install:

➡️Use new self-locking nuts when assembling the front suspension components. Install a new set ring onto the inboard halfshafts. Replace any color-coded self-locking nuts and bolts when installing the engine and transaxle mounts. These fasteners are available from a Honda dealer.

32. Flush the transaxle cooler lines before installing the transaxle. Use a pressurized flushing unit such as Honda J38405-A or equivalent. Use only Honda biodegradable flushing fluid, Honda J35944–20. Other fluids will damage the A/T cooling system.

   a. Fill the flusher with 21 ounces of fluid. Pressurize the flusher to 80–120 PSI, following the procedure on the fluid container and flusher.

   b. Clamp the discharge hose of the flusher to the cooler return line. Clamp the drain hose to the cooler inlet line and route it into a bucket or drain tank.

   c. Connect the flusher to air and water lines. Open the flusher water valve and flush the cooler for ten seconds. The air line should be equipped with a water trap to keep the system dry.

   d. Depress the flusher trigger to mix flushing fluid with the water. Flush for two minutes, turning the air valve on and off for five seconds every 15–20 seconds to create a surging action.

   e. After finishing one flushing cycle, reverse the hose and flush in the opposite direction following the same steps.

   f. Dry the cooler lines with compressed air so that no moisture is left in the cooler system.

33. Be sure the two 14mm dowel pins are installed into the torque converter housing.

34. Install the torque converter onto the transaxle mainshaft with a new O-ring. Install the starter motor onto the transaxle case and tighten the mounting bolts to 33 ft. lbs. (44 Nm).

35. Position the transaxle under the vehicle and attach the chain hoist to it.

36. Jack or hoist the engine into position, then lift the transaxle into place.

37. Mate the transaxle to the engine. Install the transaxle case bolts, and tighten them to 47 ft. lbs. (65 Nm). The one long bolt fits behind the starter.

38. Install the rear mount bracket onto the rear mount and hand-tighten the nut and upper bolt. Install two new rear mount bracket-to-transaxle case bolts, and tighten them to 40 ft. lbs. (55 Nm).

39. Verify that all of the transaxle case bolts have been installed.

40. Install the front mount and tighten the three bolts to 43 ft. lbs. (59 Nm). Install the front mount bracket onto the transaxle and tighten the bolts to 28 ft. lbs. (39 Nm). Install and hand-tighten the mount nut.

41. Install the side transaxle mount. Install and hand-tighten the three nuts and the through-bolt. Tighten the nuts to 28 ft. lbs. (39 Nm), then tighten the bolt to 47 ft. lbs. (65 Nm).

42. With all the engine and transaxle mounts installed, tighten the mount nuts to 40 ft. lbs. (55 Nm). Install the rear mount stiffener. Tighten the

rear stiffener bolt and upper rear mount bracket bolt to 28 ft. lbs. (39 Nm).

43. Remove the chain hoist and jacks from the engine and transaxle.

44. Install the eight driveplate bolts and tighten them to their final torque specification in two steps in a crisscross pattern. The first tightening step is 4.3–4.5 ft. lbs. (6 Nm). The second tightening step is 8.7 ft. lbs. (12 Nm). After tightening the last bolt, check the crankshaft for free rotation.

45. Install the torque converter cover and tighten its bolts to 8.7 ft. lbs. (12 Nm).

46. Use a holder tool and a torque wrench to retighten the crankshaft pulley to 181 ft. lbs. (245 Nm).

47. Reconnect the shift cable lever to the control shaft with a new lockwasher, and tighten the bolt to 10 ft. lbs. (14 Nm). Install the shift cable holder and cover. Tighten the cover bolts to 20 ft. lbs. (26 Nm).

48. Install the intermediate shaft and tighten the bolts to 16 ft. lbs. (22 Nm).

49. Install the left radius rod and damper fork. Hand-tighten the bolts.

50. Install new set rings on the halfshaft inboard CV-joints. Install the halfshafts into the differential and intermediate shaft. Be sure the set rings snap into place.

51. Reassemble the damper forks and lower control arm ball joints. Tighten the ball joint castle nuts to 36–43 ft. lbs. (49–59 Nm), then tighten them only enough to install new cotter pins.

52. Install the center beam and tighten the bolts to 37 ft. lbs. (50 Nm). Install the splash shield.

53. Install the front wheels and lower the vehicle.

54. Use a floor jack to raise the left front knuckle until it is supporting the weight of the vehicle. Tighten the damper pinch bolt to 32 ft. lbs. (43 Nm). Tighten the radius rod bolts to 76 ft. lbs. (101 Nm), and the nuts to 32 ft. lbs. (43 Nm). Tighten the damper fork nuts to 47 ft. lbs. (65 Nm). Remove the jack.

55. Install the IAB vacuum tank and the engine wiring harness clamp.

56. Reconnect the following electrical couplings:
- Shift control solenoid valve
- Mainshaft speed sensor connector
- Lock-up control solenoid valve
- VSS connector
- Linear solenoid connector
- CSS connector

57. Install and connect the starter cables and the transaxle ground cable.

58. Reconnect the ATF cooler hoses.

59. Install the strut brace and tighten the mounting bolts to 16 ft. lbs. (22 Nm). Attach the starter cable clips to the strut brace.

60. Install the intake air duct. Install the battery tray and tighten its mounting bolts to 16 ft. lbs. (22 Nm). Reconnect the cable holder and ground terminal.

61. Install the battery and reconnect the battery cables.

62. Prop the hood and install the support struts.

63. Refill the transaxle with ATF. Use only Honda Premium ATF or an equivalent DEXRON® II ATF. Connect the battery cables.

   a. Leave the flusher drain hose attached to the cooler return line.

   b. With the transaxle in **P**, run the engine for 30 seconds, or until approximately one quart of fluid is discharged. Immediately shut off the

engine. This completes the cooler flushing process.

   c. Remove the drain hose and reconnect the cooler return line.

   d. Refill the transaxle to the proper level with ATF.

64. Start the engine, set the parking brake, and shift the transaxle through all gears three times. Check for proper shift cable adjustment.

65. Let the engine reach operating temperature with the transaxle in **P** or **N**. Then, shut off the engine and check the fluid level.

66. Road test the vehicle.

67. After road testing the vehicle, loosen the front and rear engine mount nuts, then retighten them to 40 ft. lbs. (54 Nm).

68. Check and adjust the vehicle's front end alignment.

69. Enter the radio security code.

3.0L ENGINE

▶ See Figures 51 and 52

1. Disconnect the negative battery cable, then the positive cable.

2. Remove the battery and tray.

3. Remove the clamps securing the battery cables to the base.

4. Remove the intake air duct and the air cleaner assembly.

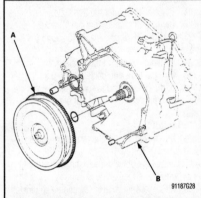

Fig. 51 Exploded view of the torque converter (A) and torque converter housing (B)

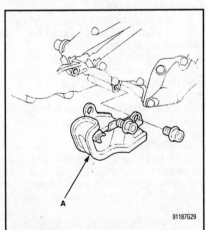

Fig. 52 Remove the transaxle lower front mount (A)

5. Raise the vehicle and drain the transaxle fluid. Replace the drain plug with a new washer.

6. Remove the starter wiring and harness clamps, remove the breather and radiator hoses from the retainer.

7. Detach the wiring connectors from the transaxle assembly.

8. Disconnect the cooler lines and point them up to prevent fluid drainage.

9. Remove the bolt and nut securing the rear stiffener and remove the stiffener.

10. Remove the bolts securing the transaxle to the engine.

11. Remove the front mounting bracket bolts.

12. Remove the engine under cover.

13. Disconnect the lower shock absorber mounting and the lower ball joints from the control arms.

14. Remove the bolts securing the radius rods to the lower arms.

15. Remove the halfshafts. Keep the splined ends of the shafts clean.

16. Mark the position of the sub-frame on the main-frame and remove it.

17. Remove the engine brace from the rear of the engine.

18. Remove the shift cable cover, bracket and cable.

19. Remove the eight bolts securing the drive plate to the torque converter.

20. Attach a chain hoist to the engine and raise it slightly.

21. Place a jack under the transaxle.

22. Remove the transaxle mount bracket.

23. Remove the intake manifold support bracket.

24. Remove the rear mount bracket.

25. Pull the transaxle back slightly until it comes off the dowels and lower it from the vehicle. Do not let the torque converter fall out of the transaxle.

To install:

26. If removed, install the torque converter using a new O-ring.

27. Install the dowel pins in the torque converter housing.

28. Raise the transaxle to the engine and install the rear mount bracket. Tighten the 8mm bolt to 16 ft. lbs. (22 Nm) and the 12mm bolts to 40 ft. lbs. (54 Nm).

29. Install the transaxle-to-engine bolts. Tighten the bolts to 47 ft. lbs. (64 Nm).

30. Connect the breather tube with the dot facing up and install the transaxle mount bracket. Tighten the nuts to 28 ft. lbs. (38 Nm) and the through-bolt to 40 ft. lbs. (54 Nm).

31. Install the driveplate-to-torque converter bolts. Tighten them to 9 ft. lbs. (12 Nm) in a criss-cross pattern.

32. Install the shift cable, bracket and cover.

33. Install the engine brace on the rear of the engine.

34. Install the halfshafts.

35. Install the sub-frame after aligning the matchmarks. Tighten the rear bolts to 47 ft. lbs. (64 Nm) and the front bolts to 76 ft. lbs. (103 Nm).

36. Install the front mount. Tighten the bolts to 28 ft. lbs. (38 Nm).

37. Connect the shock absorbers and the radius rods to the lower control arms.

38. Install the engine under cover.

39. Attach all the wiring connectors.

40. Connect the starter wiring and install harness clamps.

41. Install the battery.

42. Install the air cleaner assembly and intake duct.

43. Refill the transaxle with Genuine Honda® premium automatic transmission fluid.

Prelude

▶ **See Figures 53 and 54**

1. Disconnect the negative, then the positive battery cables from the battery.

2. Shift the transaxle into **N**.

3. Remove the battery hold-down and remove the battery.

4. Drain the transaxle fluid and reinstall the drain plug with a new crush washer.

5. Remove the air intake duct, air cleaner case, and resonator.

6. Disconnect the connector from the vacuum tank and remove the vacuum tank and tank bracket. Do not remove the vacuum tube from the vacuum tank.

7. Disconnect the transaxle-to-body ground cable.

8. Remove the battery base with the ground cable and remove the battery base stay.

9. Disconnect the lock-up control solenoid valve and shift control solenoid valve connectors.

10. Disconnect the throttle control cable from the throttle control lever.

11. Detach the Countershaft Speed Sensor (CSS) connector.

12. Unplug the Vehicle Speed Sensor (VSS) connector.

13. Remove the rear stiffener, then remove the Vehicle Speed Sensor (VSS) and Power Steering Speed (PSS) sensor.

➡**Do not disconnect the power steering pressure hoses from the VSS and PSS sensor.**

14. Disconnect the ATF cooler hoses at the joint pipes. Turn the ends of the cooler hoses upward to prevent fluid loss. Plug the joint pipes.

15. Remove the starter motor.

16. Remove the upper transaxle housing mounting bolts.

17. Loosen the front engine mount bracket bolts.

18. Remove the transaxle mount.

19. Raise and support the vehicle safely. Remove the front wheels.

20. Remove the splash shield and remove the subframe center beam and rear beam stiffener.

21. Remove the cotter pins and castle nuts from the lower ball joints. Use a press-type ball joint tool to separate the ball joints from the lower arm.

22. Remove the damper fork bolts and separate the damper fork and the damper.

23. Use a suitable prytool to separate the right and left halfshafts from the differential.

24. Pull on the inboard joint and remove the right and left halfshafts. Tie plastic bags over the halfshaft ends to protect the boots and splined shafts from damage.

25. Remove the right damper pinch bolt and separate the right damper fork from the strut.

26. Remove the right radius rod bolts and nut. Remove the radius rod.

27. Remove the torque converter cover and the shift cable cover.

28. Remove the control lever lockbolt and remove the shift cable with the lever. Do not bend the shift control cable during removal. Wire the cable to the underbody of the vehicle our of the work area.

29. Remove the driveplate bolts while rotating the crankshaft.

30. Place a transaxle jack below the transaxle and raise it enough to take the weight off the mounts.

31. Remove the intake manifold bracket.

32. Remove the lower transaxle housing mounting bolts and lower rear engine mounting bolts.

33. Pull the transaxle away from the engine until it clears the dowel pins. Lower the transaxle out of the vehicle.

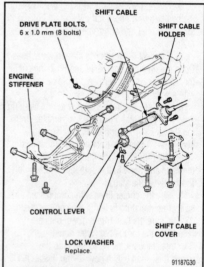

Fig. 53 Exploded view of the stiffener and related components

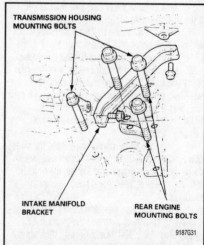

Fig. 54 Various transaxle and related components mounting bolts and brackets

To install:

➡ **Use new self-locking nuts when assembling the front suspension components. Use new set rings on the halfshaft inboard joints. Use new self-locking bolts for the subframe beams. These fasteners are available from a Honda dealer.**

34. Flush the transaxle cooling lines before installing the transaxle. Use a pressurized flushing canister, such as Honda tool No. J38405-A, or its equivalent. Use only biodegradable flushing fluid, Honda part No. J35944–20.

    a. Fill the flusher with 21 ounces of fluid. Pressurize the flusher to 80–120 PSI, following the procedure on the fluid container and flusher.

    b. Clamp the discharge hose of the flusher to the cooler return line. Clamp the drain hose to the cooler inlet line and route it into a bucket or drain tank.

    c. Connect the flusher to air and water lines. Open the flusher water valve and flush the cooler for ten seconds.

    d. Depress the flusher trigger to mix flushing fluid with the water. Flush for two minutes, turning the air valve on and off for five seconds every 15–20 seconds.

    e. After finishing one flushing cycle, reverse the hose and flush in the opposite direction.

    f. Dry the cooler lines with compressed air so that no moisture remains in the cooler lines.

35. Install the starter motor onto the transaxle case. Install the torque converter with a new hub O-ring. Tighten the starter bolts to 33 ft. lbs. (45 Nm).

36. Place the transaxle on a transaxle jack and raise it to the level of the engine.

37. Align the transaxle to the engine and install the transaxle housing mounting bolts and lower rear engine mounting bolts. Tighten the rear engine mounting bolts to 40 ft. lbs. (55 Nm) and the transaxle mounting bolts to 47 ft. lbs. (65 Nm). Install the intake manifold bracket and tighten the bolts to 16 ft. lbs. (22 Nm).

38. Tighten the front engine mount bracket bolts to 28 ft. lbs. (39 Nm).

39. Install the transaxle mount. Tighten the bolt to 47 ft. lbs. (65 Nm) and the nuts to 28 ft. lbs. (39 Nm).

40. Remove the transaxle jack.

41. Attach the torque converter to the driveplate and install the mounting bolts. Turn the crankshaft to rotate the driveplate. Tighten the bolts in 2 steps, first to 4.5 ft. lbs. (6 Nm) in a crisscross pattern and finally to 9 ft. lbs. (12 Nm). (75 Nm). Check for free rotation after tightening the last bolt.

42. Install the shift cable onto the control shaft and tighten the lockbolt to 10 ft. lbs. (14 Nm).

43. Install the torque converter cover and the shift cable cover.

44. Install a new set ring onto the inboard joint of each halfshaft.

45. Install the damper fork bolts and ball joint nuts to the lower arms. Tighten the ball joint nut to 47 ft. lbs. (65 Nm) and install a new cotter pin. Install the radius rod and connect the damper fork. Only hand-tighten the radius rod and damper fork fasteners at this point.

46. Turn the right steering knuckle fully outward and slide the axle into the differential until the spring clip is felt engaging the differential side gear. Repeat the procedure on the left side.

47. Install the subframe rear beam stiffener and the center beam. Tighten the stiffener bolts to 28 ft. lbs. (39 Nm). Tighten the subframe center beam bolts to 43 ft. lbs. (60 Nm).

48. Install the front wheels and lower the vehicle.

49. Use a floor jack to place the weight of the vehicle onto the right front knuckle. Tighten the radius rod bolts to 76 ft. lbs. (105 Nm) and the nut to 40 ft. lbs. (55 Nm). Tighten the damper pinch bolt to 32 ft. lbs. (44 Nm). Tighten the nut to 47 ft. lbs. (65 Nm) while holding the damper fork bolt. Remove the floor jack.

50. Install the speedometer sensor. Tighten the sensor bolt to 9 ft. lbs. (12 Nm).

51. Connect the ATF cooler hoses to the joint pipes.

52. Connect the lock-up control solenoid and shift control solenoid valve connectors.

53. Attach the VSS and PSS sensor connectors.

54. Connect the starter motor cables and install the battery base and base stay.

55. Connect the ground cables on the body and on the transaxle.

56. Install the vacuum tank, tank bracket, and connect the tank connector.

57. Install the resonator, air cleaner case, and air intake duct.

58. Refill the transaxle with ATF. Use only Honda Premium ATF or an equivalent DEXRON® II ATF. Connect the negative and positive battery cables.

    a. Leave the flusher drain hose attached to the cooler return line.

    b. With the transaxle in park, run the engine for 30 seconds, or until approximately one quart of fluid is discharged. This completes the cooler flushing process.

    c. Remove the drain hose and reconnect the cooler return line.

    d. Refill the transaxle to the proper level with ATF.

59. Start the engine, set the parking brake, and shift the transaxle through all gears 3 times. Check for proper control cable adjustment.

60. On Preludes equipped with 4WS, turn the steering wheel lock-to-lock to reset the steering control unit.

61. Check and adjust the front wheel alignment.

62. Let the engine reach operating temperature with the transaxle in **N** or **P**, then turn the engine OFF and check the fluid level

63. After road testing the vehicle, loosen the front engine mount bolts, and tighten them to 28 ft. lbs. (39 Nm).

64. Enter the radio security code.

ADJUSTMENTS

Shift Linkage

To adjust the shift cable proceed as follows:

1. Remove the lower right steering column access hole cover.

2. Shift the transmission to the **N** position.

3. Remove the shift cable end lock pin from the adjustable cable end.

4. Check the alignment of the hole in the cable end to see if it is perfectly aligned with the linkage adjusting rod.

5. If the holes are not aligned, loosen the cable end lock nut and adjust the cable end until the hole in the cable end and the adjusting rod are perfectly aligned.

6. Reinstall the lock pin. If any resistance is felt when inserting the lock pin, re-adjust the cable end.

7. Make sure the lock pin snaps firmly into place. If the lock pin is not secure, it must be replaced.

8. Move the gear selector through each gear position and verify the operation of the gear position indicators.

9. Insert the ignition key into the key cylinder on the upper steering column cover and check to see that the shift lock lever releases.

Throttle Linkage

1. Start the engine and allow the engine to run in **P** at 3,000 RPM until the radiator fan comes on, then allow the engine to idle.

2. Check the throttle cable side-to-side deflection. The total deflection should be ⅜–½ inches (10–12mm).

3. If the deflection is not within specification, loosen the locknut and adjust the throttle cable as necessary.

Halfshafts

REMOVAL & INSTALLATION

Please refer to the halfshaft removal procedures under Manual Transaxle in this section for specific details.

TORQUE SPECIFICATIONS

Components	ft. lbs.	Nm
Accord		
Battery tray bracket bolts	16 ft. lbs.	22 Nm
Clutch cover bolts	9 ft. lbs.	12 Nm
Clutch damper mounting bolts	16 ft. lbs.	22 Nm
Damper fork nut	40 ft. lbs.	55 Nm
Damper pinch bolt	32 ft. lbs.	44 Nm
Engine stiffener plate mounting bolts	28 ft. lbs.	39 Nm
Front engine mount bracket mounting bolts	28 ft. lbs.	38 Nm
Intake manifold bracket bolts	16 ft. lbs.	22 Nm
Intermediate shaft mounting bolts	28 ft. lbs.	39 Nm
Lower control arm ball joint castle nuts	40 ft. lbs.	50 Nm
Lower transaxle case bolts	47 ft. lbs.	65 Nm
Radius rod mounting bolts	76 ft. lbs.	105 Nm
Radius rod nut	32 ft. lbs.	44 Nm
Rear engine bracket mounting bolts	40 ft. lbs.	55 Nm
Shift cable bracket mounting bolts	20 ft. lbs.	27 Nm
Speed sensor mounting bolt	13 ft. lbs.	18 Nm
Starter 10mm bolt	32 ft. lbs.	45 Nm
Starter 12mm bolt	54 ft. lbs.	75 Nm
Stiffener-to-engine block mounting bolts	28 ft. lbs.	39 Nm
Subframe center beam bolts	37 ft. lbs.	50 Nm
Transaxle mount bracket through-bolt	40 ft. lbs.	55 Nm
Upper transaxle case bolts on the engine side	47 ft. lbs.	65 Nm
Prelude		
Ball joint to the lower arm castle nut	36–43 ft. lbs.	50–60 Nm
Battery base stay bolts	16 ft. lbs.	22 Nm
Center beam bolts	43 ft. lbs.	60 Nm
Clutch cover bolts	9 ft. lbs.	12 Nm
Clutch damper bolts	16 ft. lbs.	22 Nm
Front engine mount bracket bolts	28 ft. lbs.	39 Nm
Front engine stiffener bolts	28 ft. lbs.	39 Nm
Intake manifold stay bolts	16 ft. lbs.	22 Nm
Intermediate shaft mounting bolts	28 ft. lbs.	39 Nm
Lower and upper transaxle mounting bolts	47 ft. lbs.	65 Nm
Rear beam stiffener bolts	28 ft. lbs.	39 Nm
Rear engine mount bracket bolts on the engine side	40 ft. lbs.	55 Nm
Rear engine mount bracket stay bolt	28 ft. lbs.	39 Nm
Rear engine mount bracket stay bolt	15 ft. lbs.	21 Nm
Shift cable bracket mounting bolts	16 ft. lbs.	22 Nm
Speed sensor mounting bolt	14 ft. lbs.	19 Nm
Starter 10mm bolt	32 ft. lbs.	45 Nm
Starter 12mm bolt	54 ft. lbs.	75 Nm
Transaxle mount and mount bracket nuts/bolts	28 ft. lbs.	39 Nm
Transaxle mount through-bolt	47 ft. lbs.	65 Nm

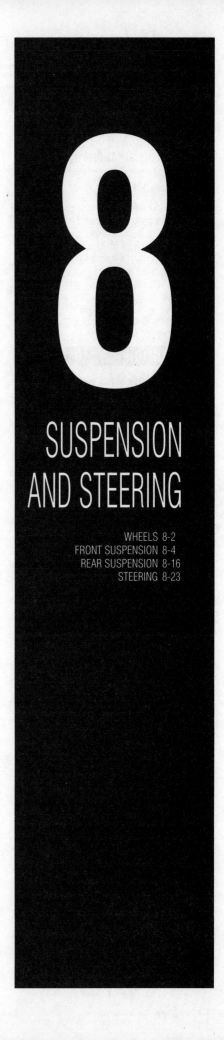

8

SUSPENSION AND STEERING

WHEELS

Front And Rear Wheels

REMOVAL & INSTALLATION

▶ **See Figures 1 thru 7**

There are four reinforced jacking points located along the lower seam of the Accord and Prelude's rocker panel. The two jack points per side are located behind the front wheel opening, for accessing a front wheel and forward of the rear wheel opening to access a rear wheel.

These jack points can be used to lift the vehicle with the supplied scissors-style jack, or a suitable hydraulic floor jack. If lifting the vehicle using a suitable lift, the lift arms can be placed under the four jack points.

✳✳ CAUTION

Never compromise safety when lifting and supporting a vehicle. Make sure the equipment being used is rated for the vehicle's weight. Never work underneath a vehicle supported by a jack. Always use a suitable jackstand to support the vehicle's weight. As an added measure of safety, if tire/wheel assembly is being removed from the vehicle to allow a repair procedure to be performed, place the tire/wheel assembly under the vehicle. If the vehicle were accidentally knocked off it's support by an external force, the tire/wheel assembly could protect the vehicle from coming into contact with the ground. When placing a jack or jackstand under a vehicle, never place a finger, hand or other body part between the vehicle and the support or lifting tool. When lifting only one side (left, right, front, or rear) of a vehicle, always set the parking brake and block the wheels remaining in contact with the ground.

1. Park the vehicle on a hard level surface.
2. Remove the jack, tire iron and, if necessary, the spare tire from their storage compartments.
3. Locate the reinforced jack point located along the lower seam of the vehicle's rocker panel for the part of the vehicle that is to be lifted.

➡ **This procedure is also covered in the vehicle's owner's manual.**

4. Place the jack in the proper position.
5. Apply the parking brake and block the diagonally opposite wheel with a wheel chock or two.

➡ **Wheel chocks may be purchased at your local auto parts store, or a block of wood cut into wedges may be used. If possible, keep one or two of the chocks in your tire storage compartment, in case any of the tires has to be removed on the side of the road.**

6. If equipped with an automatic transaxle, place the selector lever in **P** or Park; with a manual transaxle, place the shifter in first gear.
7. With the tires still on the ground, use the wheel nut tool to loosen the wheel nuts ½ turn.

➡ **If a nut is stuck, never use heat to loosen it. Damage to the wheel and/or bearings may occur. If the nuts are seized, spray the seized nut with a penetrating lubricant and give it one or two heavy hammer blows directly on the end of the bolt to loosen the corrosion. Be careful, as continued pounding will likely damage the nut, wheel stud, brake drum or rotor. Use a large ½ inch breaker bar and a six sided 19mm (¾ inch) deep well socket if available to increase the mechanical advantage.**

8. Using the jack, raise the vehicle until the tire is clear of the ground. Support the vehicle safely using suitable jackstands.
9. Remove the lug nuts, then remove the tire and wheel assembly.

To install:

10. Make sure the wheel, hub mating surfaces, and wheel lug studs, are clean and free of all foreign material. Always remove corrosion from the wheel mounting surface and the brake rotor or drum. Failure to do so may cause the wheel to cor-

TCCA8P00

Fig. 1 Place the jack at the proper lifting point on your vehicle

TCCA8P01

Fig. 2 Before jacking the vehicle, block the diagonally opposite wheel with one or, preferably, two chocks

TCCA8P02

Fig. 3 With the vehicle still on the ground, break the lug nuts loose using the wrench end of the tire iron

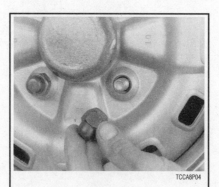

TCCA8P03

Fig. 4 After the lug nuts have been loosened, raise the vehicle using the jack until the tire is clear of the ground

TCCA8P04

Fig. 5 Remove the lug nuts from the studs

TCCA8P05

Fig. 6 Remove the wheel and tire assembly from the vehicle

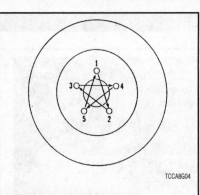

Fig. 7 Typical wheel lug tightening sequence

rode onto the mounting surface or the lug nuts to either seize in place or loosen in service.

11. Apply an anti-seize compound the wheel studs.

12. Install the tire/wheel assembly, and if equipped install the wheel covers making sure the valve stem protrudes through the proper opening in the cover. Install then hand-tighten the lug nuts.

13. Using the lug nut tool, tighten all the lug nuts, in a star shaped crisscross pattern, until they are snug.

14. Raise the vehicle and withdraw the jackstand, then lower the vehicle until the tire contacts the ground.

15. Using a torque wrench, tighten the lug nuts in a star shaped crisscross pattern to 80 ft. lbs. (108 Nm).

❊❊❊ WARNING

Do not overtighten the lug nuts, as this may cause the wheel studs to stretch, break or crossthread and/or cause a brake pulsation due to component warpage.

16. Remove the jack from under the vehicle, and place the jack and tire tool in their storage compartments. Remove the wheel chock(s).

17. If you have removed a flat or damaged tire, place it in the storage compartment of the vehicle and take it to your local repair station to have it fixed or replaced as soon as possible.

INSPECTION

Inspect the tires for proper inflation, lacerations, puncture marks, nails and other sharp objects. Repair or replace as necessary. Remove any debris that is wedged into the tire's tread, as this could cause an annoying clicking noise when driving. Periodically check the tire treadwear. Uneven wear could be a sign of an alignment related condition. As the treadwear approaches the wear bars on the tire, the tire looses its ability to disperse water when driven in wet weather conditions and could compromise the vehicle's handling and safety.

Check the wheel assemblies for dents, cracks, rust and metal fatigue. Repair or replace as necessary. If a wheel vibration is felt, check the wheel

axial and radial runout and tire balance. A tire which has aged, or has had a severe impact such as from a pot hole, may have an internal belt damage and must be replaced immediately.

To inspect the wheel axial runout proceed as follows:

1. Raise and safely support the vehicle.

2. To measure the axial runout, place a sturdy object near the wheel that will allow a dial indicator to be attached to it and zero the dial indicator to the side of the rim. To check the axial runout without a dial indicator use a strong wooden dowel and attach it to a sturdy object and adjust it so that it is almost touching the side of the wheel rim.

3. Rotate the wheel and read the dial indicator, or if using the wooden dowel:

a. Watch to see if the wheel moves in and out from the dowel.

b. If it does move in and out, adjust the dowel such that it is just barely touching the side of the wheel.

c. Rotate the wheel until the wheel moves furthest away from the dowel.

d. Measure the distance with a feeler gauge or a small ruler. The maximum movement (service limit) allowed is 0.080 inches (2.0mm). Note 0.080 inches is just a little over ⅟₁₆ of an inch.

4. Next measure the radial runout. Zero the dial indicator downward on the rim, or adjust the dowel such that it is just above the inside of the rim.

5. Rotate the wheel and read the dial indicator, or if using the wooden dowel:

a. Watch to see if the wheel moves up and down from the dowel.

b. If it does move up and down, adjust the dowel such that it is just barely touching the inside of the wheel.

c. Rotate the wheel until the wheel moves furthest away from the dowel.

d. Measure the distance with a feeler gauge or a small ruler. The maximum movement (service limit) allowed is 0.060 inches (1.5mm). Note 0.060 inches is just a less than ⅟₁₆ of an inch.

6. If the wheel is beyond the service limit, replace the wheel, or have it straightened.

Wheel Lug Studs

REPLACEMENT

Front

Replacing a front wheel lug stud will require removal of the front steering knuckle from the vehicle and replacement of the axle nut. In addition to replacing the axle nut, on some Accord models, the front wheel bearing must be replaced, as the front hub is pressed into the bearing. On these models, the hub must be pressed out of the bearing to allow enough room for the wheel lug stud to be removed from and installed into the hub.

To replace a front wheel lug stud proceed as follows:

1. Remove the front knuckle assembly. For specific details, refer to the procedure in this section.

2. On 1996–97 Accord models, press the front hub out of the wheel bearing assembly.

➥**On some models of the Accord you may have to unbolt the hub sub-assembly from the knuckle.**

3. Place the back side of the hub squarely over a suitable deep well impact socket just large enough to clear the button head of the stud.

4. Using a hydraulic press, or a suitable ball peen hammer, drive the stud out of the hub into the socket.

To install:

5. Place the front side of the hub flush with the deep well socket used for removal. Make sure the socket is deep enough to ensure that the threaded portion of the stud will not contact the bottom of the socket when it is fully installed.

6. Drive the threaded portion of the stud though the back of the hub until the button head portion of the stud bottoms on the hub.

7. On 1996–97 Accord models:

a. Replace the wheel bearing. For specific details, follow the bearing removal and installation procedures in this section.

b. Press the hub into the wheel bearing assembly.

8. If the hub sub-assembly was removed, install it onto the knuckle.

9. The balance of the installation procedure is the reverse of removal, noting the following points:

- For every stud replaced, use a new wheel lug nut. Torque the lug nuts to 80 ft. lbs. (108 Nm).
- Install a new axle nut and torque the nut to 181 ft. lbs. (245 Nm), then stake the nut.

Rear

1. Remove the rear hub assembly. For specific details follow the hub removal and installation procedures in this section.

2. Place the back side of the hub squarely over a suitable deep well impact socket just large enough to clear the button head of the stud.

3. Using a hydraulic press, or a suitable ball peen hammer, drive the stud out of the hub into the socket.

To install:

4. Place the front side of the hub flush with the deep well socket used for removal. Make sure the socket is deep enough to ensure that the threaded portion of the stud will not contact the bottom of the socket when it is fully installed.

5. Drive the threaded portion of the stud though the back of the hub until the button head portion of the stud bottoms on the hub.

6. The balance of installation is the reverse of the removal procedure, noting the following points:

- For every stud replaced, use a new wheel lug nut. Torque the lug nuts to 80 ft. lbs. (108 Nm).
- Install a new axle nut and torque the nut to 181 ft. lbs. (245 Nm), then stake the nut.

FRONT SUSPENSION

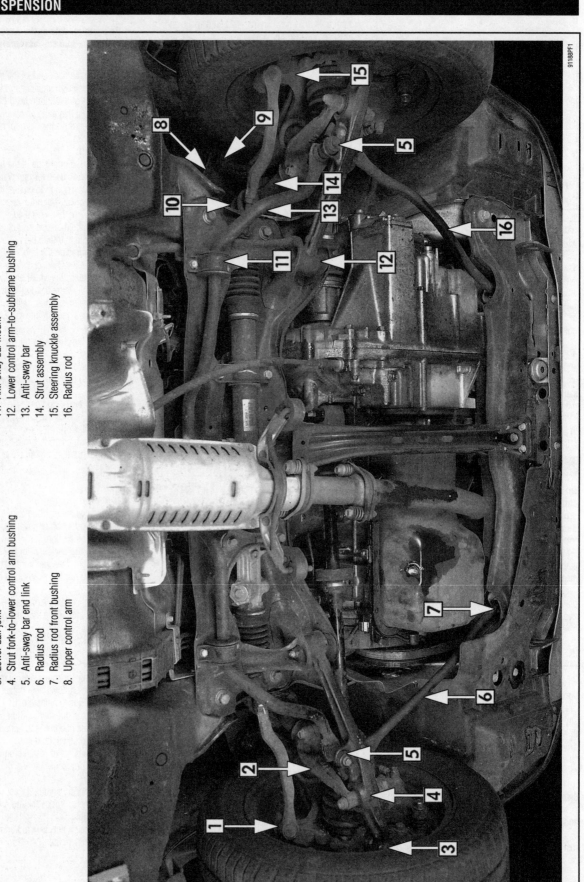

FRONT SUSPENSION COMPONENT LOCATIONS—EARLY MODEL ACCORD

1. Tie rod end
2. Strut fork
3. Lower ball joint
4. Strut fork-to-lower control arm bushing
5. Anti-sway bar end link
6. Radius rod
7. Radius rod front bushing
8. Upper control arm
9. Upper ball joint
10. Coil spring
11. Anti-sway bar mount
12. Lower control arm-to-subframe bushing
13. Anti-sway bar
14. Strut assembly
15. Steering knuckle assembly
16. Radius rod

FRONT SUSPENSION COMPONENT LOCATIONS—LATE MODEL ACCORD

1. Tie rod end
2. Upper control arm
3. Upper ball joint
4. Strut fork
5. Lower ball joint
6. Lower control arm
7. Radius arm-to-control arm bushing
8. Anti-sway bar mount
9. Radius rod front bushing
10. Radius rod
11. Lower control arm bushing
12. Strut fork-to-control arm bushing
13. Strut assembly
14. Coil spring
15. Tie rod
16. Anti-sway bar

FRONT SUSPENSION COMPONENT LOCATIONS—PRELUDE

1. Tie rod end
2. Lower ball joint
3. Radius rod ball joint
4. Lower control arm bushing
5. Radius rod
6. Anti-sway bar end link
7. Strut assembly
8. Anti-sway bar mount
9. Anti-sway bar
10. Lower control arm-to-subframe bushing
11. Radius rod front bushing
12. Lower control arm
13. Strut fork
14. Steering knuckle assembly
15. Coil spring
16. Upper ball joint

9188PF3

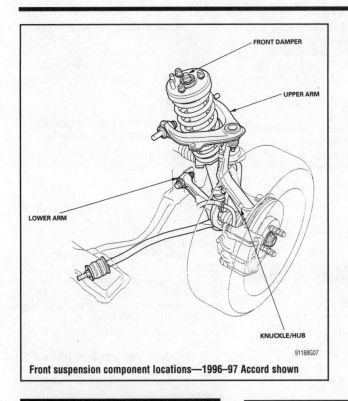

Front suspension component locations—1996–97 Accord shown

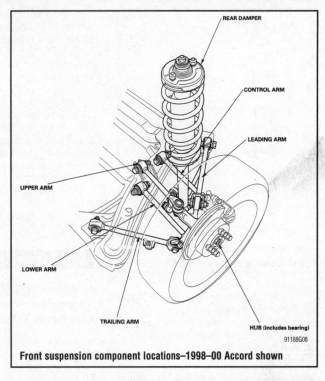

Front suspension component locations–1998–00 Accord shown

Coil Springs

REMOVAL & INSTALLATION

▶ **See Figures 8, 9 and 10**

1. Raise and safely support the vehicle.
2. Remove the front wheels.
3. Unbolt the brake hose clamp from the strut.
4. Unfasten the damper fork bolts, then remove the damper fork.
5. Remove the three strut mounting nuts, then remove the strut from the vehicle.
6. Place the strut in vice and install a suitable spring compressor onto the coil spring. Follow the spring compressor manufacturer's instructions.
7. Compress the spring and remove the self-locking nut from the top of the strut. Disassemble the strut mounts and remove the coil spring.

➡The left and right front coil springs on 1996–97 Accords equipped with the 2.2L VTEC (F22B1) engine are not interchangeable. Remember this when ordering parts or reassembling the strut.

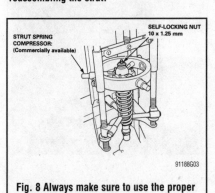

Fig. 8 Always make sure to use the proper tool when removing the coil spring

Fig. 9 Coil spring, strut cartridge, and strut mount components—Accord and Prelude

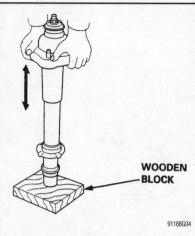

Fig. 10 Place a wooden block under the strut assembly before you test it

8. Inspect the strut mounts for wear and damage. Replace any damaged or worn parts.

9. While the coil spring is removed, you can test the damper as shown in the accompanying illustration.

To install:

➡Use new self-locking nuts when assembling and installing the struts.

10. Install the spring compressor onto the coil spring. Set the spring onto the strut cartridge. The flat part of the coil spring is its top.

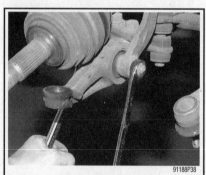

Fig. 11 With one wrench holding the nut, break the damper fork flange bolt loose using another wrench

Fig. 14 From the engine compartment, remove the upper strut flange nuts

11. Assemble the strut mount and washer onto the strut. Tighten the self-locking nut to 22 ft. lbs. (29 Nm). Remove the spring compressor.

12. Install the strut into the damper fork. The alignment mark on the strut tube fits into the groove on the damper fork.

13. Install the pinch bolt and damper fork bolt. Only hand-tighten these bolts.

14. Install the front wheels and lower the vehicle.

15. With all four of the vehicle's wheels on the ground, tighten the damper fork nut to 47 ft. lbs. (65 Nm) while holding the damper fork bolt. Tighten the damper fork pinch bolt to 32 ft. lbs. (44 Nm). Tighten the strut mounting nuts to 28 ft. lbs. (39 Nm).

16. Tighten the wheel nuts to 80 ft. lbs. (108 Nm).

17. Check and adjust the vehicle's front wheel alignment.

Strut Assembly

REMOVAL & INSTALLATION

◆ **See Figures 11 thru 17**

1. Raise and safely support the vehicle.
2. Remove the front wheels.
3. Remove the brake hose clamp bolts from the strut.

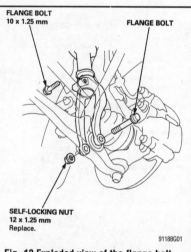

Fig. 12 Exploded view of the flange bolt and fork

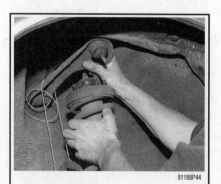

Fig. 15 Lower the strut and guide it past the upper control arm . . .

4. Unfasten the damper fork bolts, then remove the damper fork.

5. From the engine compartment, remove the three upper strut mounting nuts, then remove the strut from the vehicle.

To install:

➡Use new self-locking bolts when installing the struts and assembling the damper forks.

6. Install the strut into the vehicle. Hand-tighten the upper mounting nuts.

7. Install the strut into the damper fork. The alignment mark on the strut tube fits into the groove on the damper fork.

8. Install the pinch bolt and damper fork bolt. Only hand-tighten these bolts.

9. Install the front wheels and lower the vehicle.

10. With all four of the vehicle's wheels on the ground, tighten the damper fork nut to 47 ft. lbs. (65 Nm) while holding the damper fork bolt. Tighten the damper fork pinch bolt to 32 ft. lbs. (44 Nm). Tighten the upper strut mounting nuts to 28 ft. lbs. (39 Nm).

11. Tighten the wheel lug nuts to 80 ft. lbs. (108 Nm).

12. Check and adjust the vehicle's front end alignment.

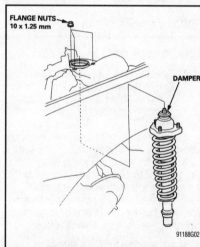

Fig. 13 The strut is also secured with 3 upper flange nuts

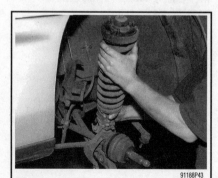

Fig. 16 . . . then remove the strut from the vehicle

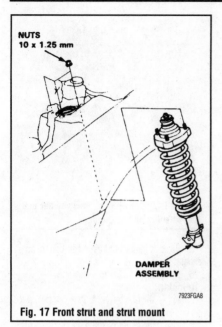

Fig. 17 Front strut and strut mount

OVERHAUL

The strut assemblies are sealed units. If worn or damaged, they must be replaced. The only component that can be removed is the coil spring. For more information, please refer to that procedure in this section.

Upper Ball Joint

INSPECTION

♦ See Figure 18

The ball joint is part of the upper control arm. If the ball joint has failed, the entire control arm assembly must be replaced.

1. Raise and safely support the vehicle.
2. Place a suitable jack under the lower control arm and lift the arm upward 2 inches (50mm).
3. Carefully grasp the upper and lower portion of the front tires and attempt to rock back and forth.
4. If looseness is felt at the upper portion of the tire:
    a. Remove the tire/wheel assembly and inspect the upper control arm bushings using a suitable prytool to check for looseness. If looseness is felt, replace the upper control arm.

Fig. 19 Installed view of a typical Honda sway bar end link

Fig. 18 The upper ball joint is mounted in the upper control arm. If the ball joint fails, the control arm assembly must be replaced

    b. Using a suitable prytool pry between the steering knuckle and the upper control arm. If looseness is present, replace the control arm assembly.

REMOVAL & INSTALLATION

The upper ball joints cannot be replaced separately. If the ball joints become worn or damaged, the upper control arm must be replaced.

Lower Ball Joint

INSPECTION

1. Raise and safely support the vehicle.
2. Place a suitable jack under the lower control arm and lift the arm upward 2 inches (50mm).
3. Carefully grasp the upper and lower portion of the front tires and attempt to rock back and forth.
4. If looseness is felt at the lower portion of the tire proceed as follows:
    a. Using a suitable prytool pry between the steering knuckle and the lower control arm.
    b. If looseness is present replace the lower joint.

REMOVAL & INSTALLATION

➡This procedure is performed after the removal of the steering knuckle and requires the use of special press tools to press the ball joint out of the knuckle. In addition, a large,

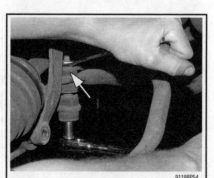

Fig. 20 You may need to use an additional wrench to keep the end link bolt from spinning during removal

sturdy vise is needed. After replacement of the ball joint, the ball joint retaining clip is installed onto the boot using a Clip Guide Tool or equivalent tool.

1. Remove the brake caliper, and brake rotor from the steering knuckle assembly. For more information, refer to Section 9 of this manual.
2. Remove the steering knuckle assembly from the vehicle, as outlined later in this section.
3. Pry the ball joint boot snapping off, then remove the boot.
4. Check the boot condition and replace if damaged or deteriorated.
5. Install the ball joint removal/installer around the ball joint spindle with the large end facing out. Install and tighten the ball joint castle nut to hold the tool in position.
6. Position the knuckle with the installed tool into a suitable vise, with the ball joint removal base tool installed over the ball joint base.
7. Tighten the vise to press the ball joint out of the steering knuckle.
    To install:
8. Position the new ball joint into the hole of the steering knuckle.
9. Install the ball joint removal/installer on the ball joint spindle side of the steering knuckle with the small end facing out.
10. Position the installation base on the ball joint base and set the assembly in a large vise. Tighten the vise to press the ball joint into the steering knuckle.
11. Pack the interior of the ball joint boot with grease.
12. Adjust the boot clip guide tool with its adjusting bolt until the end of the tool aligns with the groove on the boot. Slide the clip over the installed onto the boot using the clip guide tool and into position on the ball joint boot and seat the ball joint boot snapping in the groove of the ball joint.
13. The remainder of installation is the reverse of the removal procedure.

Sway Bar

REMOVAL & INSTALLATION

♦ See Figures 19 thru 24

1. Raise and safely support the vehicle.
2. Matchmark the sway bar for proper reinstallation.

Fig. 21 Note the positions of the nut, washer and bushing as you remove them

91188P50

Fig. 22 Sway bar bracket mounting

91188P55

Fig. 23 View of the sway bar end link and bushings, once removed from the vehicle

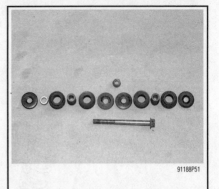

91188P51

Fig. 24 Exploded view of the sway bar end link washers and bushings

3. Disconnect the sway bar links from the end of the sway bar.

4. Remove the sway bar bushing brackets from the vehicle's underbody.

5. Remove the sway bar.

6. If necessary you can disassemble the sway bar end link and bushings.

To install:

7. If necessary, assemble the sway bar end link and bushings.

8. Installation is the reverse of removal, noting the following steps:

9. Apply silicone grease between the sway bar bracket bushing and sway bar.

10. Tighten the sway bar retainers, as follows:
  • Sway bar bracket-to-body bolts: 16 ft. lbs. (22 Nm)

  • Sway bar end link nut and bolt for Prelude: 13 ft. lbs. (18 Nm)
  • Sway bar end link nut and bolt for Accord: 14 ft. lbs. (19 Nm)

Radius Rod

REMOVAL & INSTALLATION

▶ See Figures 25 thru 32

1. Loosen the front wheel lug nuts ½ turn.
2. Raise and safely support the vehicle.
3. Remove the wheel and tire assembly.
4. Remove the radius rod self-locking nut from the front subframe.

5. Remove the two radius rod-to-control arm fasteners.

6. Remove the radius rod assembly.

To install:

7. Apply silicone grease to the front radius rod bushings.

8. Install the larger bushing on the front of the subframe, and the smaller bushing on the rear of the subframe both with the small end of the bushing facing out.

9. Install the washer onto the radius rod then the sleeve, and install the radius rod through the bushings in the lower subframe.

10. Install the front radius rod washer, then install and hand-tighten a new self-locking radius rod nut.

11. Install the radius rod-to-control arm flange bolts and tighten to 76 ft. lbs. (103 Nm).

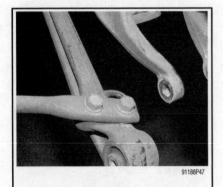

91188P47

Fig. 25 View of the radius rod-to-lower control arm bolts–1996 Accord shown

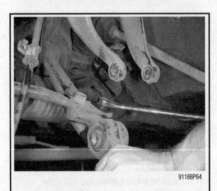

91188P64

Fig. 26 Use a wrench to remove the radius rod-to-control arm mounting bolts

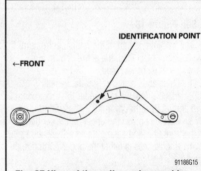

91188G15

Fig. 27 View of the radius rod assembly—Prelude with Active Torque Transfer System (ATTS)

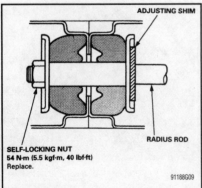

91188G09

Fig. 28 View of a typical Honda radius rod bushing

91188P68

Fig. 29 Use a wrench to break the radius rod bushing nut loose

91188P66

Fig. 30 Note the position of the nut, washer and bushing upon removal

Fig. 31 View of the radius rod and bushings

Fig. 32 A ratchet and a socket can speed installation

Fig. 33 Installed view of the upper control arm with integral ball joint (strut removed for photo only)

Fig. 34 Use needlenose pliers to remove the cotter pin from the ball joint. Discard the cotter pin

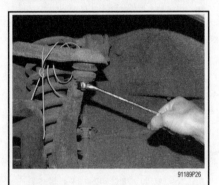

Fig. 35 Remove the castle nut with a wrench . . .

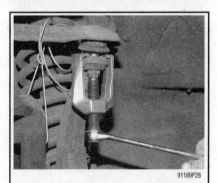

Fig. 36 . . . then separate the upper ball joint with a suitable 2-jawed puller

Fig. 37 You may have to move the engine compartment fuse box to gain access to the upper control arm bolts on the passenger side of the vehicle

Fig. 38 Use a closed-end wrench to remove the upper control arm bolts . . .

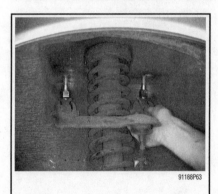

Fig. 39 . . . then remove the upper control arm

12. Tighten the radius rod bushing bolt to 40 ft. lbs. (54 Nm).

13. The balance of assembly is the reverse of the removal procedure. Make sure to tighten the lugnuts to 80 ft. lbs. (108 Nm).

Upper Control Arm

REMOVAL & INSTALLATION

▶ See Figures 33 thru 39

➡Do not disassemble the upper arm. If the ball joint or bushings are faulty, or the upper arm is damaged, the entire upper arm must be replaced.

1. Raise and support the vehicle safely.
2. Remove the front wheels. Support the lower control arm assembly with a floor jack.
3. Use needlenose pliers to remove the cotter pin from the ball joint. Discard the cotter pin.
4. Remove the castle nut.
5. Separate the upper ball joint from the steering knuckle using a ball joint separator tool.
6. Remove the self-locking nuts from the upper arm anchor bolts. Remove the upper arm from the vehicle.

➡Do not disassemble the upper arm. If the ball joint or bushings are faulty, or the upper arm is damaged, the entire upper arm must be replaced.

To install:

➡Use new self-locking nuts when installing the upper arm and strut.

7. Install the upper control arm assembly into the strut tower.
8. Connect the upper ball joint.
9. Install the front wheels and lower the vehicle.
10. With all four of the vehicle's wheels on the ground, torque the upper control arm nuts to 47 ft. lbs. (65 Nm). Torque the castle nut to 32 ft. lbs. (44 Nm); then, only tighten it only enough to install a new cotter pin.
11. Tighten the wheel nuts to 80 ft. lbs. (108 Nm).
12. Check and adjust the vehicle's front end alignment.

Lower Control Arm

REMOVAL & INSTALLATION

▶ **See Figures 40, 41, 42 and 43**

1. Loosen the front wheel nuts ½ turn.
2. Raise and safely support the vehicle.
3. Remove the front tire/wheel assembly
4. Disconnect the lower sway bar link.
5. Remove the strut fork through bolt.
6. Remove the radius rod-to-control arm fasteners.
7. Loosen the lower ball joint flange nut.
8. Using a suitable ball joint removal tool, separate the ball joint from the control arm.
9. Remove the lower control arm bushing fasteners, then remove the control arm.

To install:

10. Installation is the reverse of the removal procedure, noting the following steps and tightening specifications:

➡ **Lubricate the lower control arm bushings with silicone grease**

a. Replace the strut fork-to-control arm flange nut, then torque the nut and through bolt to 47 ft. lbs. (64 Nm)

b. Install the lower ball joint castle nut using a new cotter pin, then torque to 36–43 ft. lbs. (49–59 Nm)

c. Tighten the control arm retainers, as follows:

- Front flange bolt: 76 ft. lbs. (103 Nm)

- Rear bushing bolts: 40 ft. lbs. (54 Nm)

d. Torque the lug nuts to 80 ft. lbs. (108 Nm)

CONTROL ARM BUSHING REPLACEMENT

▶ **See Figures 44 and 45**

✳✳ CAUTION

When replacing control arm bushings, use caution, stay alert at all times and wear proper eye protection to avoid an accident.

The bushings on the front lower control arms are replaceable on most models.

➡ **This procedure requires the use of a press and may be above the skill range of the average driveway enthusiast. It is recommended that this procedure be done by a qualified machine shop if you are not skilled in the proper use of a press.**

1. Remove the lower control arm that is in need of new bushings.

➡ **It is recommended that both the left and right lower control arm bushings be replaced at the same time. The vehicle's handling may become unstable if there are new bushings on one side of the car and worn ones on the other.**

2. Set up the control arm in a suitable shop press.

3. Using an impact socket of the correct length and size, press out the old bushing.

4. Install the new bushing by slowly using the press to push it into the control arm.

✳✳ WARNING

Excessive force could cause the bushing to bend or tear so be careful.

5. Once the bushing is properly seated in the control arm, remove the arm from the press and install it on the vehicle.

Knuckle/Hub Assembly

REMOVAL & INSTALLATION

▶ **See Figures 46 and 47**

➡ **Once the hub has been removed, the wheel bearings must be replaced. A hydraulic press and bearing drivers must be used to remove and install the bearing.**

1. Loosen the wheel lug nuts slightly.
2. Using a suitable sized chisel, lift the lock tab of the front axle spindle nut from the groove in the spindle.
3. Break the axle spindle nut loose using an impact socket and breaker bar..
4. Raise the front of the vehicle and support the vehicle securely with jackstands.
5. Remove the lug nuts and then the wheel.
6. Unscrew the brake hose mounting bolts.
7. Remove the brake hose and caliper mounting bolts, then place the caliper assembly aside

Fig. 40 Loosen the lower control arm-to-chassis bolt

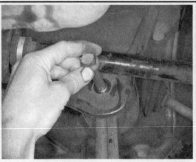

Fig. 41 Once loosened, pull the bolt out with you fingers

Fig. 42 After the bolt is removed, you can remove the lower control arm

Fig. 43 View of the lower control arm, once removed from the vehicle

Fig. 44 Using an industrial press to remove the control arm bushings

Fig. 45 Some ball joint removal tools are equipped to also press control arm bushings out

supported by mechanic's wire to prevent the hydraulic hose from being damaged.

8. On cars with ABS, remove the ABS wheel sensor bolts, then remove the wheel sensor.

➡Do not remove the wheel sensor connector.

9. Remove the cotter key from the tie rod end spindle, and remove the castle nut, then using a tie rod end removal tool, separate the tie rod end from the knuckle.

10. Remove the cotter key from the lower ball joint spindle, then loosen and remove the castle nut and release the ball joint from the lower control arm.

➡A penetrating lubricant may be used if the ball joint is difficult to remove.

11. Remove the cotter key from the upper ball joint spindle, then loosen and remove the castle nut and release the ball joint from the upper control arm.

12. Pull the knuckle away from the vehicle. If necessary, use a plastic hammer to tap on the spindle to help release it from the hub splines.

13. On late models of the Accord and Prelude, use a hydraulic press and suitable press tools to remove the front hub/bearing assembly. For specific details, refer to the hub/bearing removal and installation procedures in this section.

14. On early models, you can remove the hub by extracting the flange bolts securing the hub unit to the knuckle.

➡Carefully inspect the lug bolt studs. If they have been damaged, replace them while the hub is removed from the knuckle.

To install:

15. On late model vehicles, install the wheel bearing, snapring and hub.

16. On early model vehicles, install the wheel bearing/hub assembly and tighten the flange bolts to 33 ft. lbs. (44 Nm)

17. The balance of installation is the reverse of the removal procedure, making note of the following points and tightening specifications:

- Upper ball joint: 29–35 ft. lbs. (39–47 Nm), install using a new cotter pin
- Lower ball joint: 36–43 ft. lbs. (49–59 Nm), install using a new cotter pin
- Tie rod end: 32 ft. lbs. (43 Nm), install using a new cotter pin
- ABS sensor fasteners: 16 ft. lbs. (22 Nm)
- Hub unit flange bolts: 33 ft. lbs. (44 Nm)
- Brake rotor mounting screws: 82 inch lbs. (9.3 Nm)
- Brake caliper bolt: 80 ft. lbs. (108 Nm)
- Lug nuts: 80 ft. lbs. (108 Nm)
- Axle spindle nut: 181 ft. lbs. (245 Nm); stake nut afterwards

Front Hub & Bearings

ADJUSTMENT

The wheel bearings are not adjustable or repairable and should be replaced if found defective.

REMOVAL & INSTALLATION

♦ See Figures 48, 49, 50, 51, 52, 53

➡Once the hub has been removed, the wheel bearings must be replaced. A hydraulic press

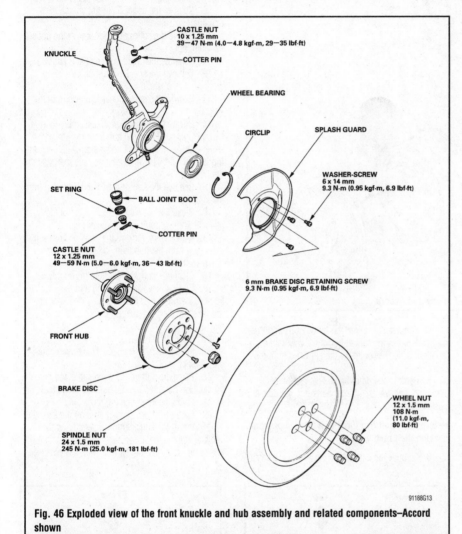

Fig. 46 Exploded view of the front knuckle and hub assembly and related components—Accord shown

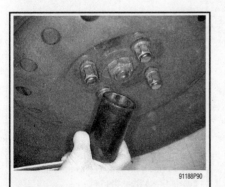

Fig. 47 Use an impact socket and a breaker bar to remove the spindle nut

Fig. 48 With the vehicle on the ground, remove the spindle nut

Fig. 49 Removing the rotor/hub assembly—1996 Accord shown

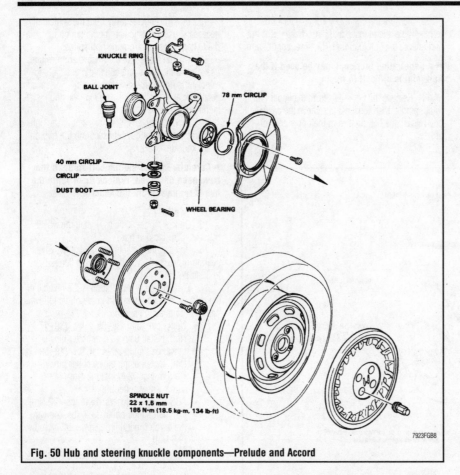

KNUCKLE RING

BALL JOINT

78 mm CIRCLIP

40 mm CIRCLIP

CIRCLIP

DUST BOOT

WHEEL BEARING

SPINDLE NUT
22 x 1.5 mm
185 N·m (18.5 kg-m, 134 lb-ft)

7923FGB8

Fig. 50 Hub and steering knuckle components—Prelude and Accord

and bearing drivers must be used to remove and install the bearing.

1. Pry the spindle nut stake away from the spindle and loosen the nut. Do not tighten or loosen a spindle nut unless the vehicle is sitting on all four wheels. The torque required is high enough to cause the vehicle to fall off the stands even when properly supported.

2. Raise and safely support the vehicle.

3. Remove the wheel and the spindle nut.

4. Remove the caliper mounting bolts and the caliper. Support the caliper out of the way with a length of wire. Do not let the caliper hang from the brake hose.

5. Remove the 6mm brake disc retaining screws. Screw two 8x1.25mm bolts into the disc to push it away from the hub.

➡**Turn each bolt two turns at a time to prevent cocking the brake disc.**

6. Remove the cotter pin from the tie rod castle

nut, then remove the nut. Separate the tie rod ball joint using a ball joint remover, then lift the tie rod out of the knuckle.

7. Remove the cotter pin and loosen the lower arm ball joint nut half the length of the joint threads. The nut will retain the arm when the joint comes loose.

8. Separate the ball joint and lower arm using a puller with the pawls applied to the lower arm. Avoid damaging the ball joint boot. If necessary, apply penetrating lubricant to loosen the ball joint.

9. Remove the upper ball joint shield, if equipped.

10. Pry off the cotter pin and remove the upper ball joint nut.

11. Separate the upper ball joint and knuckle.

12. Remove the knuckle and hub by sliding them off the halfshaft.

13. Remove the splash guard screws from the knuckle.

14. Position the knuckle/hub assembly in a hydraulic press. Press the hub from the knuckle using a driver of the proper diameter while supporting the knuckle. The inner bearing race may stay on the hub.

15. Remove the splash guard and snapring from the knuckle.

16. Press the hub/wheel bearing out of the knuckle while supporting the knuckle.

17. If necessary, remove the outboard bearing inner race from the hub using a bearing puller.

To install:

18. Clean the knuckle and hub thoroughly.

19. Press a new wheel bearing into the knuckle. Be sure the press tool contacts only the outer bearing race and properly support the knuckle so it is stable.

20. Install the snapring.

21. Install the splash shield. Don't overtighten the screws.

22. Place the hub on the press table and press the knuckle onto the hub. Be sure the press tool contacts only the inner bearing race.

23. Install the front knuckle ring on the knuckle.

24. Install the knuckle/hub assembly on the vehicle. Tighten the upper ball joint nut and tie rod end nut to 32 ft. lbs. (44 Nm). Install new cotter

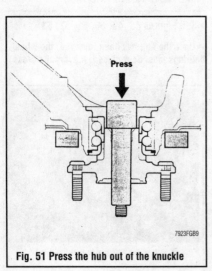

Press

7923FGB9

Fig. 51 Press the hub out of the knuckle

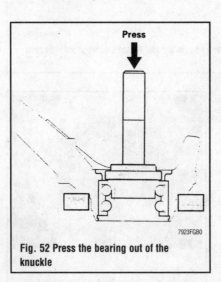

Press

7923FGB0

Fig. 52 Press the bearing out of the knuckle

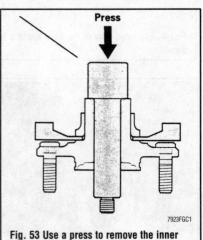

Press

7923FGC1

Fig. 53 Use a press to remove the inner bearing race from the hub

pins. Tighten the lower ball joint nut to 40 ft. lbs. (55 Nm) and install a new cotter pin.

25. Install the brake disc and caliper. Tighten the caliper bracket bolts to 80 ft. lbs. (108 Nm).

26. Install the front wheels and lower the vehicle.

27. Tighten the spindle nut to 181 ft. lbs. (245 Nm). Tighten the wheel nuts to 80 ft. lbs. (108 Nm).

28. Check and adjust the vehicle's front wheel alignment.

Wheel Alignment

If the tires on your Accord or Prelude are worn unevenly, if the vehicle is not stable on the highway or if the handling seems uneven in spirited driving, the wheel alignment should be checked. If an alignment problem is suspected, first check for improper tire inflation and other possible causes. These can be worn suspension or steering components, accident damage or even unmatched tires. If any worn or damaged components are found, they must be replaced before the wheels can be properly aligned. Wheel alignment requires very expensive equipment and involves minute adjustments which must be accurate; it should only be performed by a trained technician. Take your vehicle to a properly equipped shop.

Following is a description of the alignment angles which are adjustable on most vehicles and how they affect vehicle handling. Although these angles can apply to both the front and rear wheels, usually only the front suspension is adjustable.

CASTER

▶ See Figure 54

Looking at a vehicle from the side, caster angle describes the steering axis rather than a wheel angle. The steering knuckle is attached to a control arm or strut at the top and a control arm at the bottom. The wheel pivots around the line between these points to steer the vehicle. When the upper point is tilted back, this is described as positive caster. Having a positive caster tends to make the wheels self-centering, increasing directional stability. Excessive positive caster makes the wheels hard to steer, while an uneven caster will cause a pull to one side. Overloading the vehicle or sagging rear springs will affect caster, as will raising the rear of the vehicle. If the rear of the vehicle is lower than normal, the caster becomes more positive.

CAMBER

▶ See Figure 55

Looking from the front of the vehicle, camber is the inward or outward tilt of the top of wheels. When the tops of the wheels are tilted in, this is negative camber; if they are tilted out, it is positive. In a turn, a slight amount of negative camber helps maximize contact of the tire with the road. However, too much negative camber compromises straight-line stability, increases bump steer and torque steer.

TOE

▶ See Figure 56

Looking down at the wheels from above the vehicle, toe angle is the distance between the front of the wheels, relative to the distance between the back of the wheels. If the wheels are closer at the front, they are said to be toed-in or to have negative toe. A small amount of negative toe enhances directional stability and provides a smoother ride on the highway.

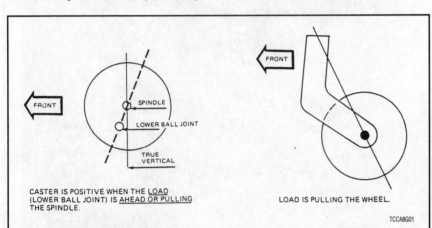

Fig. 54 Caster affects straight-line stability. Caster wheels used on shopping carts, for example, employ positive caster

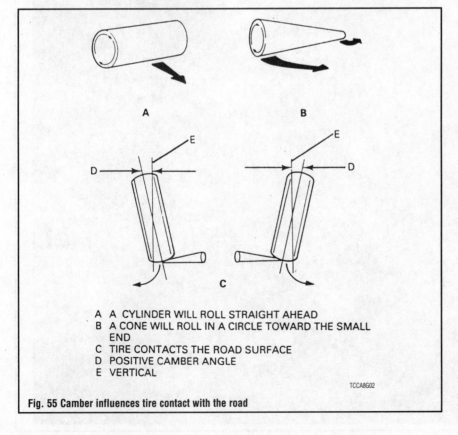

A   A CYLINDER WILL ROLL STRAIGHT AHEAD
B   A CONE WILL ROLL IN A CIRCLE TOWARD THE SMALL END
C   TIRE CONTACTS THE ROAD SURFACE
D   POSITIVE CAMBER ANGLE
E   VERTICAL

Fig. 55 Camber influences tire contact with the road

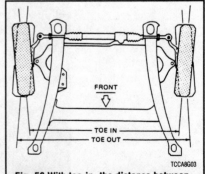

Fig. 56 With toe-in, the distance between the wheels is closer at the front than at the rear

REAR SUSPENSION

REAR SUSPENSION COMPONENT LOCATIONS—EARLY MODEL ACCORD

1. Lower control arm bushing
2. Lower strut bushing
3. Lower control arm
4. Lower control arm-to-subframe bushing
5. Coil spring
6. Strut assembly
7. Knuckle assembly
8. Upper control arm ball joint
9. Upper control arm

REAR SUSPENSION COMPONENT LOCATIONS—LATE MODEL ACCORD

1. Lower control arm bushing
2. Anti-sway bar
3. Anti-sway bar mount
4. Upper control arm
5. Lower control arm-to-knuckle housing
6. Trailing arm bushing
7. Lower control arm
8. Leading arm
9. Strut assembly
10. Lower control arm-to-subframe bushing
11. Anti-sway bar end link
12. Strut bushing
13. Steering knuckle assembly
14. Trailing arm-to-subframe bushing

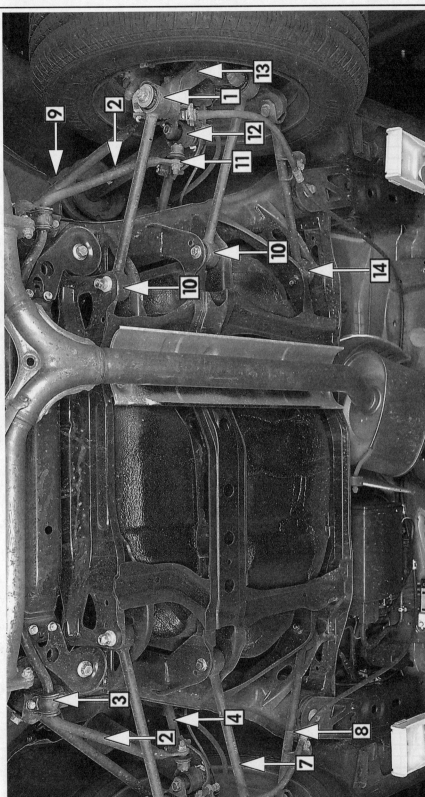

REAR SUSPENSION COMPONENT LOCATIONS—PRELUDE

1. Upper control arm ball joint
2. Lower control arm ball joint
3. Strut bushing
4. Anti-sway bar mount
5. Lower control arm
6. Trailing arm bushing
7. Anti-sway bar
8. Lower control arm-to-subframe bushing
9. Lower control arm
10. Coil spring
11. Strut assembly
12. Trailing arm

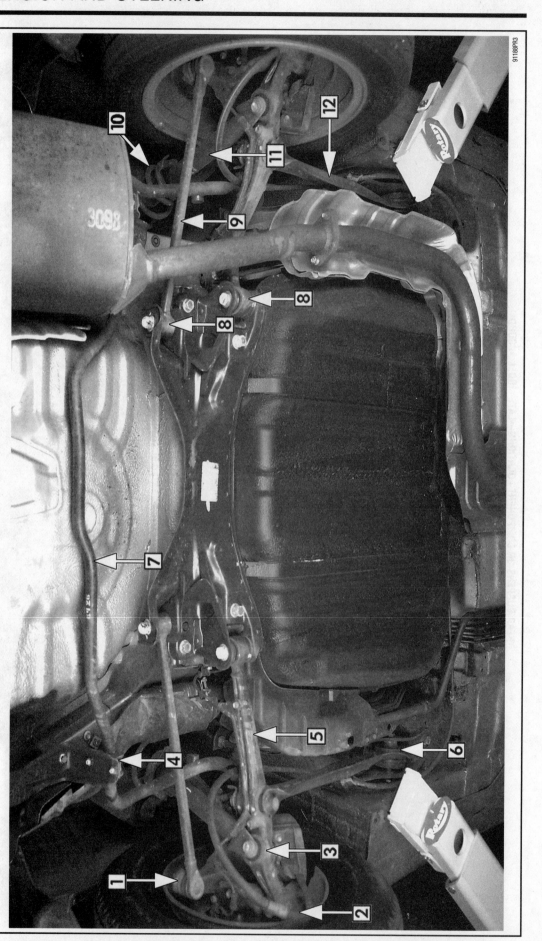

9118PR3

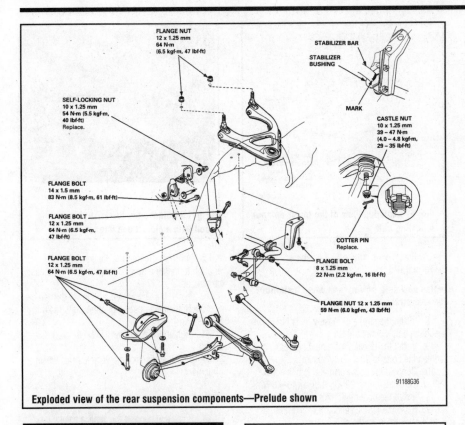

FLANGE NUT
12 x 1.25 mm
64 N·m
(6.5 kgf·m, 47 lbf·ft)

STABILIZER BAR

STABILIZER
BUSHING

MARK

SELF-LOCKING NUT
10 x 1.25 mm
54 N·m (5.5 kgf·m,
40 lbf·ft)
Replace.

CASTLE NUT
10 x 1.25 mm
39 – 47 N·m
(4.0 – 4.8 kgf·m,
29 – 35 lbf·ft)

FLANGE BOLT
14 x 1.5 mm
83 N·m (8.5 kgf·m, 61 lbf·ft)

FLANGE BOLT
12 x 1.25 mm
64 N·m (6.5 kgf·m,
47 lbf·ft)

FLANGE BOLT
12 x 1.25 mm
64 N·m (6.5 kgf·m, 47 lbf·ft)

COTTER PIN
Replace.

FLANGE BOLT
8 x 1.25 mm
22 N·m (2.2 kgf·m, 16 lbf·ft)

FLANGE NUT 12 x 1.25 mm
59 N·m (6.0 kgf·m, 43 lbf·ft)

91188G36

Exploded view of the rear suspension components—Prelude shown

Coil Springs

REMOVAL & INSTALLATION

Accord

▶ See Figure 57

1. Remove the strut, as outlined later in this section.

2. Place the strut in a vice and install a spring compressor onto the coil spring. Follow the spring compressor manufacturer's instructions.

3. Compress the spring and remove the self-locking nut from the strut. Disassemble the strut mounts and remove the coil spring.

4. Inspect the strut mounts for wear and damage. Replace any damaged or worn parts.

To install:

➡ Use new self-locking nuts when assembling and installing the struts.

5. Install the spring compressor onto the coil spring. Set the spring onto the strut cartridge. The flat part of the coil spring is its top.

6. Assemble the strut mount and washer onto the strut. Tighten the self-locking nut to 22 ft. lbs. (29 Nm). Remove the spring compressor.

7. Install the strut into the vehicle. Hand-tighten the mounting nuts.

8. Fit the strut into position on the knuckle. Install the mounting bolt.

9. Place a jack under the lower strut mount. Raise the jack until the weight of the vehicle is on the jack.

10. With the suspension under load, tighten the lower mount bolt to 40 ft. lbs. (55 Nm). Tighten the upper nuts to 28 ft. lbs. (39 Nm).

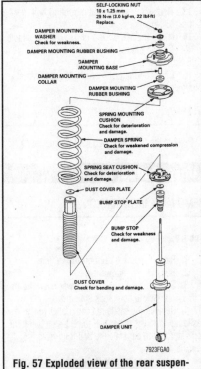

SELF-LOCKING NUT
10 x 1.25 mm
29 N·m (3.0 kgf·m, 22 lbf·ft)
Replace.

DAMPER MOUNTING
WASHER
Check for weakness.

DAMPER MOUNTING RUBBER BUSHING

DAMPER
MOUNTING BASE

DAMPER MOUNTING
COLLAR

DAMPER MOUNTING
RUBBER BUSHING

SPRING MOUNTING
CUSHION
Check for deterioration
and damage.

DAMPER SPRING
Check for weakened compression
and damage.

SPRING SEAT CUSHION
Check for deterioration
and damage.

DUST COVER PLATE

BUMP STOP PLATE

BUMP STOP
Check for weakness
and damage.

DUST COVER
Check for bending and damage.

DAMPER UNIT

7923FGA0

Fig. 57 Exploded view of the rear suspension strut assembly—Accord

11. Install the rear wheel. Lower the vehicle to the ground.

12. Tighten the wheel nuts to 80 ft. lbs. (108 Nm).

13. Install the rear seat side bolsters and fold the seat back into place.

14. Check and adjust the vehicle's rear wheel alignment.

Prelude

1. Raise and safely support the vehicle.

2. Remove the trunk side trim and remove the two strut mounting nuts.

3. Remove the upper ball joint cover.

4. Remove the cotter pin and upper ball joint nut.

5. Fit a 10mm nut on the ball joint and separate the ball joint and the knuckle by using a ball joint removal tool.

6. Remove the lower strut mounting bolt and lower the suspension.

7. Remove the strut from the vehicle.

8. Place the strut in vice and install a spring compressor onto the coil spring. Follow the spring compressor manufacturer's instructions.

9. Compress the spring and remove the self-locking nut from the strut. Disassemble the strut mounts and remove the coil spring.

10. Inspect the strut mounts for wear and damage. Replace any damaged or worn parts.

To install:

➡ Use new self-locking nuts when installing the rear struts.

11. Install the spring compressor onto the coil spring. Set the spring onto the strut cartridge. The flat part of the coil spring is its top.

12. Assemble the strut mount and washer onto the strut. Tighten the self-locking nut to 22 ft. lbs. (29 Nm). Remove the spring compressor.

13. Install the strut to the vehicle and loosely install the lower mounting bolt. Do not tighten at this time.

14. Install the upper strut mounting bolts. Tighten the bolts to 28 ft. lbs. (39 Nm).

15. Connect the upper arm and knuckle and tighten the castle nut to 29–35 ft. lbs. (40–48 Nm).

16. Install the upper ball joint cover.

17. Raise the rear suspension with a floor jack until the weight is on the strut.

18. Tighten the lower strut mounting bolt to 47 ft. lbs. (65 Nm).

19. Install the rear wheels and lower the vehicle.

20. Tighten the rear wheel nuts to 80 ft. lbs. (108 Nm).

21. Install the trunk trim.

22. Check and adjust the vehicle's rear wheel alignment.

Struts

REMOVAL & INSTALLATION

Accord

▶ See Figures 58, 59, 60 and 61

1. Fold the rear seat forward and remove the side bolster cushions. The side bolster cushions are secured by a screw at the bottom and two clips at the top.

2. Remove the strut mount cap. Remove the upper strut mounting nuts.

3. Raise and safely support the vehicle.

4. Remove the rear wheels.

5. Support the knuckle with a floor jack.

6. Remove the strut mounting bolt, carefully lower the jack, and remove the strut.

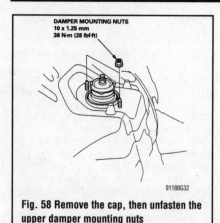

Fig. 58 Remove the cap, then unfasten the upper damper mounting nuts

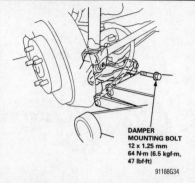

Fig. 59 Exploded view of the lower damper mounting bolt

Fig. 60 Remove the lower strut mounting bolt with a closed end wrench

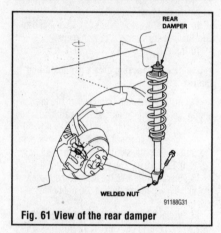

Fig. 61 View of the rear damper

To install:

→Use new self-locking nuts when installing the strut.

7. Fit the strut into the upper mount. Only hand-tighten the upper mounting nuts.

8. Fit the strut into position on the knuckle. Install the mounting bolt.

9. Place a jack under the lower strut mount. Raise the jack until the weight of the vehicle is on the jack.

10. With the suspension under load, tighten the lower mount bolt to 40 ft. lbs. (55 Nm). Tighten the upper nuts to 28 ft. lbs.(39 Nm).

11. Install the rear wheel. Lower the vehicle to the ground.

12. Tighten the wheel nuts to 80 ft. lbs. (108 Nm).

13. Install the rear seat side bolsters and fold the seat back into place.

14. Check and adjust the vehicle's rear wheel alignment.

Prelude

1. Raise and safely support the vehicle.

2. Remove the trunk side trim and remove the 2 top strut nuts.

3. Remove the upper ball joint cover.

4. Remove the cotter pin and upper ball joint nut.

5. Fit a 10mm nut on the ball joint and separate the ball joint and the knuckle by using a ball joint removal tool.

6. Remove the lower strut mounting bolt and lower the suspension.

7. Remove the strut from the vehicle.

To install:

→Use new self-locking nuts when installing the rear struts.

8. Install the strut and loosely install the lower mounting bolt. Do not tighten.

9. Install the upper strut mounting bolts. Tighten the bolts to 28 ft. lbs. (39 Nm).

10. Connect the upper arm and knuckle and tighten the castle nut to 29–35 ft. lbs. (40–48 Nm).

11. Install the upper ball joint cover.

12. Raise the rear suspension with a floor jack until the weight is on the strut.

13. Tighten the lower strut mounting bolt to 47 ft. lbs. (65 Nm).

14. Install the rear wheels and lower the vehicle.

15. Tighten the rear wheel nuts to 80 ft. lbs. (108 Nm).

16. Check and adjust the vehicle's rear wheel alignment.

OVERHAUL

Refer to the front strut overhaul procedure.

Upper Control Arms

REMOVAL & INSTALLATION

Accord

1. Raise and safely support the vehicle.

2. Remove the rear wheels.

3. Support the knuckle and lower control arm with a floor jack to compress the strut.

4. Remove the castle nut cap, cotter pin, and castle nut from the upper ball joint. Use a ball joint separator tool to separate the ball joint from the knuckle.

5. Unbolt and remove the upper control arm.

6. Check upper control arm and bushing for signs of wear and damage. Replace the upper control arm if the ball joint is faulty.

To install:

→Use new self-locking nuts when assembling the suspension components.

7. Install the upper arm into the vehicle. Install the mounting bolts and only hand–tighten them. Reconnect the upper arm to the knuckle.

8. Tighten the castle nut at the ball joint to 32

ft. lbs. (44 Nm). Tighten the castle nut only enough to install a new cotter pin. Install the castle nut cap.

9. Install the rear wheels and lower the vehicle.

10. Tighten the upper mounting bolts to 28 ft. lbs. (39 Nm).

11. Tighten the wheel nuts to 80 ft. lbs. (108 Nm).

12. Check and adjust the vehicle's rear wheel alignment.

Prelude

1. Raise and support the vehicle safely.

2. Remove the rear wheels. Support the knuckle and lower control arm assembly with a jack.

3. Separate the upper ball joint from the knuckle using a ball joint separator tool.

4. Pull back the trunk side trim and remove the two strut mounting nuts.

5. Remove the self-locking nuts from the upper arm anchor bolts. Remove the upper arm from the vehicle.

→Do not disassemble the upper arm. If the ball joint or bushings are faulty, or the upper arm is damaged, the entire upper arm must be replaced.

To install:

→Use new self-locking nuts when installing the upper arm and strut.

6. Install the upper control arm assembly into the strut tower.

7. Connect the upper ball joint.

8. Install the rear wheels and lower the vehicle.

9. With all four of the vehicle's wheels on the ground, torque the upper control arm nuts to 47 ft. lbs. (65 Nm). Torque the castle nut to 32 ft. lbs. (44 Nm); then, only tighten it only enough to install a new cotter pin.

10. Tighten the wheel nuts to 80 ft. lbs. (108 Nm).

11. Put the trunk side trim back into position.

12. Check and adjust the vehicle's rear end wheel alignment.

CONTROL ARM BUSHING REPLACEMENT

The upper control arm bushings are part of the control arm. If the bushings are worn or damaged, the control arm must be replaced as an assembly

Lower Control Arms

REMOVAL & INSTALLATION

Accord

▶ See Figures 62, 63, 64 and 65

1. Raise and safely support the vehicle.
2. Remove the rear tire/wheel assembly.
3. Remove the inner and outer bushing flanged through bolts.
4. Remove the stabilizer bar link flange nut.
5. Remove the lower arm.

To install:

6. Installation is the reverse of removal, noting the following steps:
   - Lubricate the outer arm bushing with silicone grease.
   - Tighten the stabilizer bar link flange nut to 22 ft lbs. (29 Nm)
   - Tighten the bushing through bolts to 40–43 ft. lbs. (54–59 Nm)
   - Tighten the lug nuts to 80 ft. lbs. (108 Nm)

Prelude

LOWER ARM A

▶ See Figure 66

1. Raise and safely support the vehicle.
2. Remove the rear tire/wheel assembly.
3. Remove the inner bushing flanged through bolt.
4. Remove the flange nut, then remove the lower arm.

To install:

5. Installation is the reverse of removal, noting the following steps:
   - Lubricate the inner arm bushing with silicone grease.
   - Tighten the flange nut to 47 ft lbs. (64 Nm)
   - Tighten the bushing through bolts to 69 ft. lbs. (93 Nm)
   - Tighten the lug nuts to 80 ft. lbs. (108 Nm)

LOWER ARM B

▶ See Figure 66

1. Raise and safely support the vehicle.
2. Remove the rear wheels.
3. Place a floor jack under the lower control arm spring perch and raise it slightly.
4. Remove the strut flange through bolt and the knuckle flange through bolt from the lower control arm.
5. Remove and the strut assembly. For specific details, see the strut removal procedures in this section.
6. Remove the coil spring.
7. Remove the upper and lower spring seats.
8. Matchmark the inner bushing concentric washer location for reassembly.
9. Remove the inner arm bushing through bolt.
10. Remove the lower arm.

To install:

11. Lubricate the inner busing with silicone grease.
12. Install the lower arm and it's through bolt using a new flange nut. Do not tighten it at this time.

13. Replace the upper and lower spring seats if they are distorted or have disintegrated.
14. Install the spring seats into position.
15. Raise the floor jack under the lower control arm to compress the spring.
16. Install the shock absorber and knuckle flange bolts and hand tighten them only at this point.
17. Lower the jack and move it under the knuckle. Raise the jack under the knuckle until it is supporting the weight of the vehicle. Tighten each of the inner bushing flange nut to 40 ft. lbs. (54 Nm), the three flange bolts to 47 ft. lbs. (64 Nm) and the strut flange nuts also to 47 ft lbs. (64 Nm).
18. Lower the floor jack. Install the rear wheels. Lower the vehicle.
19. Tighten the wheel nuts to 80 ft. lbs. (108 Nm).
20. Check and adjust the rear wheel alignment as necessary.

Fig. 62 View of the rear lower control arm—1996 Accord

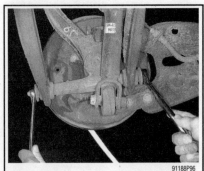

Fig. 63 Breaking the rear lower control arm nut loose may require the use of two closed end wrenches

Fig. 64 Note the position of the nut and washer when removing them

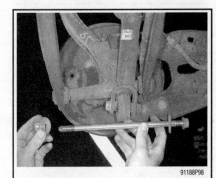

Fig. 65 Lower control arm-to-knuckle mounting bolt

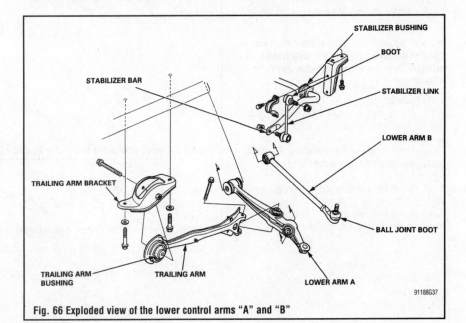

Fig. 66 Exploded view of the lower control arms "A" and "B"

Sway Bar

REMOVAL & INSTALLATION

1. Raise and safely support the vehicle.
2. Matchmark the sway bar for proper reinstallation.
3. Disconnect the sway bar links from the end of the sway bar.
4. Remove the sway bar bushing brackets from the vehicle's underbody.
5. Remove the sway bar.

To install:

6. Installation is the reverse of removal, noting the following steps:
7. Tighten the sway bar retainers, as follows:
   - Sway bar bracket-to-body bolts: 16 ft. lbs. (22 Nm)
   - Sway bar end link nut and bolt: 13 ft. lbs. (18 Nm) for Prelude, 14 ft. lbs. (19 Nm) for 1996–97 Accord and 43 ft. lbs. (59 Nm) for 1998–00 Accord.

Hub & Bearings

REMOVAL & INSTALLATION

▶ **See Figures 67, 68, 69 and 70**

➡ **The rear wheel bearing and hub unit are replaced as a unit.**

1. With the vehicle on the ground, loosen the spindle nut.
2. Raise the vehicle and support it safely.
3. Remove the rear wheels.
4. Remove the brake disc retaining screws.
5. Unbolt the brake hose brackets from the knuckle.
6. Remove the caliper bracket mounting bolts and hang the caliper out of the way with a piece of wire.
7. Remove the brake disc. If the disc is frozen on the hub, screw two 8 x 1.25mm bolts evenly into the disc to push it away from the hub.
8. Remove the spindle nut and pull the hub unit off of the spindle.

➡ **Clean the backing plate and the mating surfaces of the brake disc and hub with brake cleaner. Clean the spindle, washer, and hub with solvent.**

To install:

9. Inspect the hub unit for signs of damage or wear. If the bearings are worn, the entire unit must be replaced.
10. Install the hub unit and spindle washer onto the spindle. Install the spindle nut but do not tighten it.
11. Install the brake disc and tighten the retaining screws to 7 ft. lbs. (10 Nm).
12. Install the brake caliper and tighten the mounting bolts to 28 ft. lbs. (39 Nm). Install the

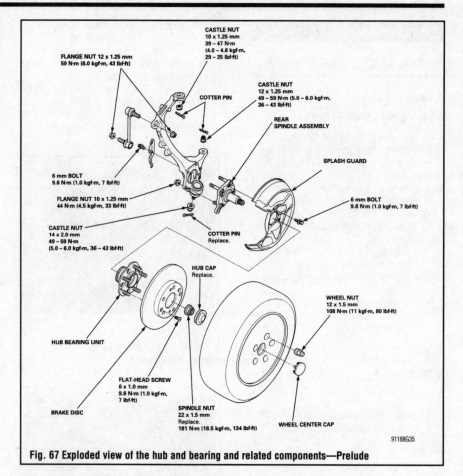

Fig. 67 Exploded view of the hub and bearing and related components—Prelude

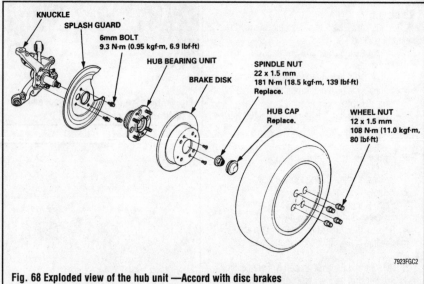

Fig. 68 Exploded view of the hub unit —Accord with disc brakes

brake hose brackets onto the knuckle and tighten the bolts to 16 ft. lbs. (22 Nm).

13. Install the rear wheels and lower the vehicle.
14. With the vehicle on the ground, tighten the

new spindle nut to 181 ft. lbs. (245 Nm), then stake the nut with a punch.

15. Tighten the wheel nuts to 80 ft. lbs. (108 Nm).
16. Test the operation of the brakes.

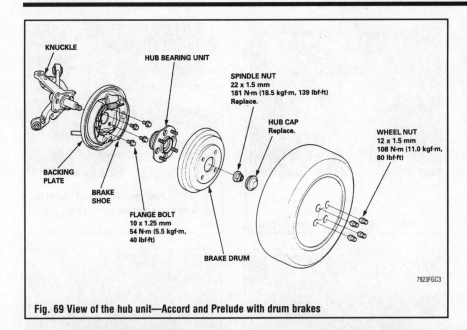

Fig. 69 View of the hub unit—Accord and Prelude with drum brakes

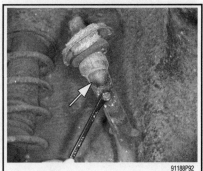

Fig. 70 You may have to remove the dust cap from the upper rear control arm to gain access to the castle nut

ADJUSTMENT

The wheel bearings are not adjustable or repairable and should be replaced if found defective.

STEERING

Steering Wheel

REMOVAL & INSTALLATION

▶ See Figures 71 thru 85

✳✳ CAUTION

The models covered by this manual are equipped with a Supplemental Restraint System (SRS), which uses an air bag. Whenever working near any of the SRS components, such as the impact sensors, the air bag module, steering column and instrument panel, disable the SRS, as described in Section 6.

Several precautions must be observed when handling the inflator module to avoid accidental deployment and possible personal injury.

• Never carry the inflator module by the wires or connector on the underside of the module.

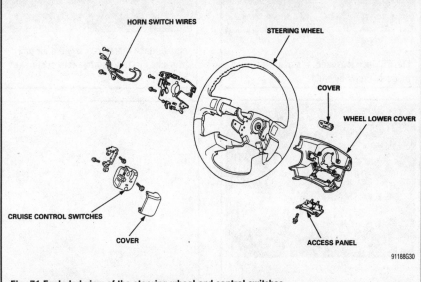

Fig. 71 Exploded view of the steering wheel and control switches

Fig. 72 Detach the wiring from the steering wheel mounted switches

Fig. 73 Remove the cover plate from the rear of the steering column

Fig. 74 Grasp the yellow air bag connector with both hands

Fig. 75 Depress the connector as shown to release it . . .

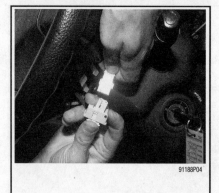

Fig. 76 . . . then pull the connector apart

Fig. 77 On most models, a Torx® socket is required to remove the air bag retaining screws

Fig. 78 Once loosened, remove the air bag module screws by hand

Fig. 79 Once removed, carry the air bag, trim side up, to a nearby table or storage area

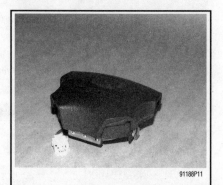

Fig. 80 Position the air bag on a table, with the trim/cosmetic side up

Fig. 81 View of steering wheel with the air bag removed

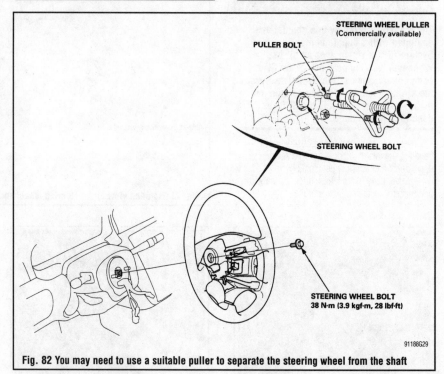

Fig. 82 You may need to use a suitable puller to separate the steering wheel from the shaft

• When carrying a live inflator module, hold securely with both hands, and ensure that the bag and trim cover are pointed away.

• Place the inflator module on a bench or other surface with the bag and trim cover facing up.

• With the inflator module on the bench, never place anything on or close to the module which may be thrown in the event of an accidental deployment.

1. Disconnect the negative, then the positive battery cables.

2. Disable the air bag system, as outlined in Section 6 of this manual.

3. Remove the access panel from the steering wheel bottom to get to the electrical connector.

4. Remove the connector from its holder, then detach the electrical connector between the air bag and the cable reel.

5. Remove the steering wheel side access panels and remove the fasteners that mount the air bag to the steering wheel using a T-30 Torx® bit.

6. Carefully remove the air bag assembly, holding the padded surface away from your body in case of accidental deployment.

7. Place the air bag unit in a safe area with the padded surface facing UP.

8. Remove the electrical connectors for the horn.

9. If equipped, unplug the electrical connector for the cruise control.

Fig. 83 Remove the steering wheel from the splined shaft

Fig. 84 As you remove the steering wheel, guide the air bag wiring through the wheel to prevent damage to the connectors

Fig. 85 Use a torque wrench to tighten the steering wheel fastener to the proper specifications

10. Remove the steering wheel mounting fastener.

11. Turn the steering wheel to the straight ahead position, so the steering wheel is properly centered.

12. Matchmark the steering wheel to the splined steering shaft for proper alignment during reassembly.

13. Remove the steering wheel by rocking it slowly from side to side while pulling steadily with both hands, or if necessary, use a commercially available steering wheel puller.

✳✳ WARNING

If using a steering wheel puller, use care to not thread the puller-to-steering wheel

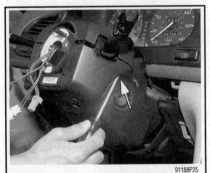

Fig. 86 A Phillips screwdriver may be required to remove the steering column covers

Fig. 87 Removal of the combination switch

attachment bolts in more than 5 turns, otherwise the air bag cable reel could be damaged.

To install:

14. Before installing the steering wheel, center the cable reel by pointing the arrow up. This can be done by rotating the cable reel clockwise until it stops. Then rotate the cable reel about two turns counterclockwise, and the arrow should face up.

15. Install the steering wheel and make sure the wheel shaft engages the cable reel and the turn signal canceling sleeve.

16. Tighten the steering wheel fastener to 29 ft. lbs. (39 Nm).

17. Attach all wires and harnesses.

18. Install the air bag assembly using new air bag mounting fasteners, then torque the fasteners to 86 inch lbs. (9.8 Nm).

19. Install all covers.

20. Connect the positive battery cable first and then the negative.

21. After installation, confirm normal system operation of all related equipment, and that all controls are working properly.

Turn Signal (Combination) Switch

REMOVAL & INSTALLATION

♦ **See Figures 86, 87 and 88**

✳✳ CAUTION

The models covered by this manual are equipped with a Supplemental Restraint System (SRS), which uses an air bag. Whenever working near any of the SRS components, such as the impact sensors, the air bag module, steering column and instrument panel, disable the SRS, as described in Section 6.

1. Disable the air bag system, as outlined in Section 6 of this manual.

2. Disconnect the negative battery cable.

3. Remove the driver's side lower dashboard cover and knee bolster.

4. Remove the steering column covers.

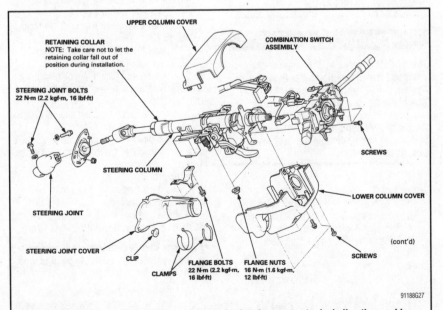

Fig. 88 Exploded view of the steering column and related components, including the combination switch

5. Remove the steering wheel, as outlined earlier in this section.

6. Disconnect the harness by gently depressing the tab on the connector and pulling.

7. Remove the combination switch mounting screws, then remove the switch.

8. Installation is the reverse of the removal procedure.

Windshield Wiper Switch

REMOVAL & INSTALLATION

✳✳ CAUTION

The models covered by this manual are equipped with a Supplemental Restraint System (SRS), which uses an air bag. Whenever working near any of the SRS components, such as the impact sensors, the air bag module, steering column and instrument panel, disable the SRS, as described in Section 6.

1. Disable the air bag system, as outlined in Section 6 of this manual.

2. Disconnect the negative battery cable.

3. Remove the driver's side lower dashboard cover and knee bolster.

4. Remove the steering column covers.

5. Remove the steering wheel, as outlined earlier in this section.

6. Disconnect the harness by gently depressing the tab on the connector and pulling.

7. Remove the combination switch mounting screws.

8. Remove the switch.

9. Installation is the reverse of the removal procedure.

Ignition Switch

REMOVAL & INSTALLATION

✳✳ CAUTION

The models covered by this manual are equipped with a Supplemental Restraint System (SRS), which uses an air bag. Whenever working near any of the SRS components, such as the impact sensors, the air bag module, steering column and instrument panel, disable the SRS, as described in Section 6.

1. Disable the air bag system, as outlined in Section 6 of this manual.

2. Disconnect the negative battery cable.

3. Remove the lower panel of the dashboard.

4. Remove the knee bolster.

5. Remove the steering column covers.

6. Unplug the connectors from the underdash fuse block.

7. Remove the steering column upper and lower covers.

8. Position the ignition switch to the **"0"** position.

9. Remove the two screws that secure the switch to the mount.

10. Pull the ignition switch away from the mount.

11. Installation is the reverse of the removal procedure.

Ignition Lock Cylinder

REMOVAL & INSTALLATION

▶ **See Figure 88**

✳✳ CAUTION

The models covered by this manual are equipped with a Supplemental Restraint System (SRS), which uses an air bag. Whenever working near any of the SRS components, such as the impact sensors, the air bag module, steering column and instrument panel, disable the SRS, as described in Section 6.

1. Disable the air bag system, as outlined in Section 6 of this manual.

2. Disconnect the negative battery cable.

3. Remove the steering column as follows:

   a. Remove the steering wheel, as outlined earlier in this section.

   b. Remove the driver's side dash lower covers and knee bolster.

   c. Remove the steering column covers.

   d. If equipped with an automatic transaxle, place the gear selector to **N** and disconnect the selector cable.

   e. Remove the combination switches from the steering column.

   f. Matchmark and disconnect the steering joint in the engine compartment.

   g. Remove the steering column mounting fasteners.

   h. Remove the lower dash cover.

   i. Remove the steering column covers.

   j. Detach the electrical connectors.

   k. Remove the steering column mounting nuts and bolts.

   l. Lower the steering column assembly.

4. Center punch the shear bolt(s).

5. Use a ³⁄₁₆ inch (5mm) drill bit to drill out the head(s) of the bolt(s), then remove the shear bolt(s).

6. Insert the ignition key and turn the ignition switch to the **"I"** position.

7. Press down the lock pin at the service hole in the top of the clamp and remove the lock assembly from the column.

To install:

8. Insert the ignition key and turn the ignition switch to the **"I"** position.

9. Press down the lock key and install the lock assembly onto the column until it clicks in place.

➡ **You may have to install the lock body without the key installed in order to get it to properly fit in.**

10. Finger-tighten the new shear bolts.

11. Insert the key into the new lock cylinder and check for proper switch operation.

12. Tighten the shear bolt(s) until the head(s) can be snapped off.

13. Align the steering column and tighten the bolts.

14. Plug the harness into the ignition switch.

15. Install the steering column covers.

16. Install the dashboard panel and knee bolster.

17. Connect the negative battery cable.

18. Enable the air bag system, as outlined in Section 6.

Steering Linkage

REMOVAL & INSTALLATION

Inner Steering Rods (Tie Rods)

▶ **See Figure 89**

1. Raise and safely support the vehicle.

2. Remove the front wheel/tire assembly.

3. Clean the steering rod between the steering boot and outer tie rod end lock nut with a suitable penetrating lubricant and a clean cloth or shop towel.

4. Loosen the outer tie rod end locking nut ⅛ turn.

5. Loosen the steering boot clamp(s), and slide the small clamp off the boot.

6. Carefully loosen the boot and slide outward off the steering rack and onto the shaft to expose the inner steering rod mounting fastener.

7. If necessary, position the inner steering rack shaft in or out to allow for additional access.

8. Relieve the steering rod nut locking tab from the inner steering rack shaft, then loosen the steering rod ball socket nut 1 turn.

9. Matchmark the tie rod end to the threaded shaft.

10. Remove the cotter key and castle nut from the outer tie rod end threaded spindle, and using a tie rod end removal tool, remove the tie rod from the steering knuckle.

11. Hold the tie rod with a wrench, and remove the outer tie rod end from the threaded rod, counting the number of complete turns it takes to remove the tie rod end from the shaft. Write the number of turns on a piece of note paper.

12. Remove the tie rod end lock nut from the threaded steering shaft.

13. Slide the steering rack boot off the shaft.

14. Remove the inner steering rod ball socket nut from the inner steering rack shaft.

To install:

15. Inspect the tie rod end for looseness, and the steering rack boot and tie rod end boot for cracks deterioration or damage and replace as necessary.

16. Clean steering rack shaft and apply a light coating of Genuine Honda Power steering fluid as necessary.

17. Apply a medium strength locking agent to the threads where the inner steering rod ball socket mounts. Use a new locking washer and a new stop washer, and install the inner tie rod onto the steering rack shaft.

18. Tighten the inner tie rod end fastener to 40 ft. lbs. (54 Nm)

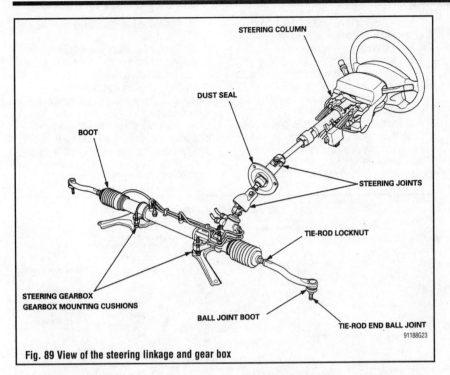

Fig. 89 View of the steering linkage and gear box

22. Apply a light film of an anti-seize compound onto the threaded tie rod end, and install the tie rod end lock nut.

23. Install the tie rod end onto the tie rod, turning it in exactly the number of turns it took to remove it.

24. Install the tie rod end following the tie rod end installation procedures in this section

25. The balance of installation is the reverse of the removal procedure.

26. Check the front end alignment and adjust as necessary.

Outer Tie Rod Ends

▶ See Figures 90 thru 95

1. Raise and safely support the vehicle.
2. Remove the front wheel/tire assembly.
3. Loosen the outer tie rod end locking nut 1/8 turn.
4. Matchmark the tie rod end to the threaded shaft.
5. Remove the cotter key and castle nut from the outer tie rod end threaded spindle, and using a tie rod end removal tool, separate the tie rod end from the steering knuckle.
6. Hold the tie rod with a wrench, and remove the outer tie rod end from the threaded rod, counting the number of complete turns it takes to remove the tie rod end from the shaft. Write the number of turns on a piece of note paper.

To install:

7. Apply a light film of an anti-seize compound onto the threaded tie rod end, and install the tie rod end lock nut.

19. Peen the lock washer over the nut or onto the flat surface of the steering rack shaft.

20. Apply silicone grease to the outer circumference of the inner tie rod end ball socket, and onto the groove just outside of the socket.

21. Apply silicone grease to the inside of the small end of the steering rack boot, and slide the boot over the steering shaft and onto the rack and install the boot clamps. If the boot has air hose fittings make sure they are installed as removed.

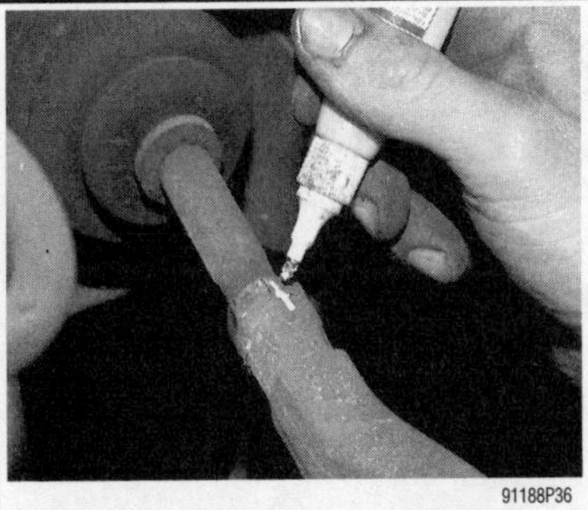

Fig. 90 Use a paint marker to matchmark the outer tie rod end to the tie rod before you remove it

Fig. 91 Also, matchmark the location of the jam nut on the threads of the tie rod

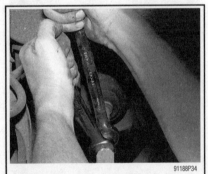

Fig. 92 Hold the tie rod stationary with one wrench and break the jam nut free with another wrench

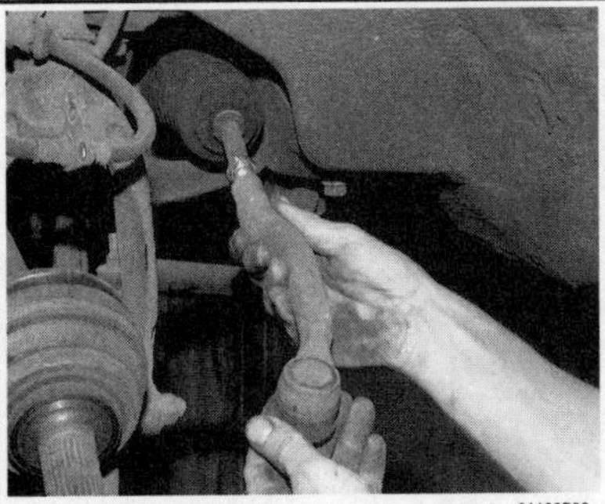

Fig. 93 Remove the outer tie rod end by turning . . .

Fig. 94 . . . the outer tie rod end counterclockwise. . .

Fig. 95 . . . until it is free of the tie rod

8. Install the tie rod end onto the tie rod, turning it exactly the number of turns it took to remove it.

9. Install the tapered spindle of the tie rod end into the knuckle and tighten the castle head nut to:
- Models using a castle nut: 29–35 ft. lbs. (39–47 Nm)
- Models using a non-castle nut: 32 ft. lbs. (43 Nm)

10. Install a new cotter pin in the tie rod end threaded spindle.

11. Tighten the tie rod end lock nut.

12. The balance of installation is the reverse of the removal procedure.

13. Have the front end alignment checked and adjusted as necessary.

Rack and Pinion Steering Gear

REMOVAL & INSTALLATION

Accord

▶ **See Figures 96 thru 105**

1. Lift the power steering reservoir off of its mount and disconnect the inlet hose.

2. Insert a length of tubing into the inlet hose and route the tubing into a drain container.

3. With the engine running at idle, turn the steering wheel lock-to-lock several times until fluid stops running out of the hose. Immediately shut off the engine.

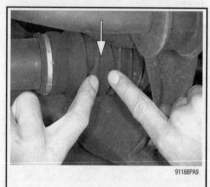

Fig. 96 Checking the steering gear dust boot for cracks or tears

4. Position the front wheels straight ahead. Lock the steering column with the ignition key. Reconnect the reservoir inlet hose.

5. Disconnect the negative battery cable.

6. Remove the steering joint cover and remove the upper and lower steering joint bolts.

7. Raise and support the vehicle safely.

8. Remove the front wheels.

9. Remove the tie rod end cotter pins and castle nuts. Using a ball joint tool, disconnect the tie rod ends from the steering knuckles.

10. Remove the left tie rod end and slide the rack all the way to the right.

11. Disconnect the Heated Oxygen Sensor (HO2S).

12. Remove the self-locking nuts and separate the catalytic converter from the exhaust pipe. Remove the catalytic converter.

13. On vehicles equipped with manual transaxles, disconnect the shift linkage from the transaxle case.

14. On vehicles equipped with automatic transaxles, remove the shift cable cover, disconnect the cable, and wire it up and out of the way.

15. Use a flare nut wrench to disconnect the two hydraulic lines from the rack valve body. Plug the

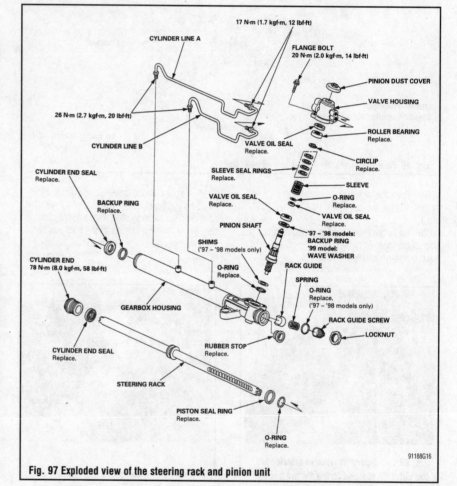

Fig. 97 Exploded view of the steering rack and pinion unit

Fig. 98 Move the steering gear to the right, then down and out of the vehicle

Fig. 99 Location of the air vent tube on the steering gear

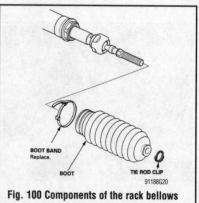

Fig. 100 Components of the rack bellows boot

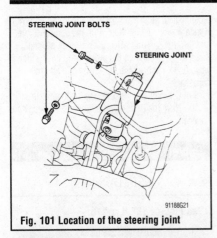

Fig. 101 Location of the steering joint

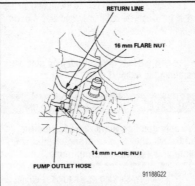

Fig. 102 View of the pump outlet hose and the return line

Fig. 103 Use a flare nut wrench to disconnect the lines from the rack and pinion unit

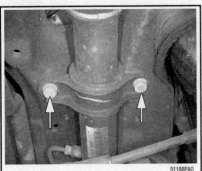

Fig. 104 Location of the rack and pinion mounting bolts

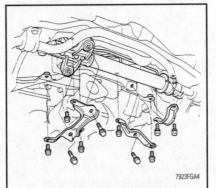

Fig. 105 Power rack and pinion steering gear mounting—Accord

lines to keep dirt and moisture out. Carefully move the disconnected lines to the rear of the rack assembly so that they are not damaged when the rack is removed.

16. Remove the rack stiffener plate, then remove the steering rack mounting bolts.

17. Pull the steering rack down to release it from the pinion shaft.

18. Drop the steering rack far enough to permit the end of the pinion shaft to come out of the hole in the frame channel.

19. Slide the steering rack to the right until the left tie rod clears the subframe, then drop it down and out of the vehicle to the left.

To install:

➡Use new gaskets and self-locking nuts when installing the catalytic converter.

❊❊ WARNING

Use only genuine Honda power steering fluid. Any other type or brand of fluid will damage the power steering pump.

20. Before installing the rack and pinion, slide the ends all the way to the right. Install the pinion shaft grommet. The lug on the pinion shaft grommet aligns with the slot on the valve body.

21. Install the steering rack into position. Install the pinion shaft grommet and insert the pinion through the hole in the bulkhead.

22. Install the rack mounting bolts. Tighten the

bracket bolts to 28 ft. lbs. (39 Nm). Tighten the stiffener plate mounting bolts to 32 ft. lbs. (43 Nm).

23. Center the rack ends within their steering strokes.

24. Center the air bag cable reel, as follows:

a. Turn the steering wheel left approximately 150°, to check the cable reel position with the indicator.

b. If the cable reel is centered, the yellow gear tooth lines up with the alignment mark on the cover.

c. Return the steering wheel right approximately 150° to position the steering wheel in the straight ahead position.

25. Line up the bolt hole in the steering joint with the groove in the pinion shaft. Slip the joint onto the pinion shaft. Pull the joint up and down to be sure the splines are fully seated. Tighten the joint bolts to 16 ft. lbs. (22 Nm).

➡Connect the steering joint and pinion shaft with the cable reel and steering rack centered. Verify that the lower joint bolt is securely seated in the pinion shaft groove. If the steering wheel and rack are not centered, reposition the serrations at the lower end of the steering joint.

26. Install the steering joint cover and the rack and pinion cover.

27. Reconnect the two hydraulic lines to the rack valve body. Carefully tighten the 14mm inlet fitting to 27 ft. lbs. (37 Nm) and the 16mm outlet fitting to 21 ft. lbs. (28 Nm).

28. If equipped with a manual transaxle, connect the shift cable and the select cable to the transaxle with new cotter pins.

29. If equipped with an automatic transaxle, connect the shift cable to the transaxle using a new lockwasher. Tighten the lockbolt to 10 ft. lbs. (14 Nm).

30. Install the catalytic converter using new gaskets and self-locking nuts. Tighten the front nuts to 16 ft. lbs. (22 Nm), and the rear nuts to 25 ft. lbs. (34 Nm).

31. Reconnect the HO$_2$S sensor.

32. Install the tie rod ends onto the rack ends. Connect the tie rod ends to the steering knuckles and install the castle nuts.

33. Tighten the ball joint castle nuts to 29–35 ft. lbs. (40–48 Nm). Then, tighten them only enough to install new cotter pins.

34. Install the front wheels.

35. Lower the vehicle.

36. Reconnect the negative battery cable.

37. Be sure the reservoir inlet line has been reconnected. Fill the reservoir to the upper line with Honda power steering fluid. Run the engine at idle and turn the steering wheel lock-to-lock several times to bleed air from the system and fill the rack valve body. Recheck the fluid level and add more if necessary.

38. Check the power steering system for leaks.

39. Check the front wheel alignment and steering wheel spoke angle. Make adjustments by turning the left and right tie rod ends equally.

40. Road test the vehicle.

Prelude

◆ See Figures 96, 98, 106 and 107

1. Lift the power steering reservoir off of its mount and disconnect the inlet hose.

2. Insert a length of tubing into the inlet hose and route the tubing into a drain container.

3. With the engine running at idle, turn the steering wheel lock-to-lock several times until fluid stops running out of the hose. Shut off the engine.

4. Position the front wheels straight ahead. Lock the steering column with the ignition key. Reconnect the reservoir inlet hose.

5. Disconnect the negative battery cable.

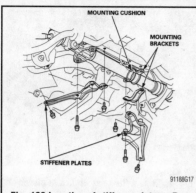

Fig. 106 Location of stiffener plates—Prelude

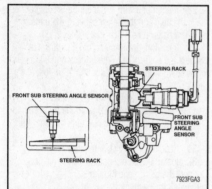

Fig. 107 Front sub-steering angle sensor, harness, and steering rack—Prelude

6. Remove the steering joint cover and remove the upper and lower steering joint bolts.

7. Raise and support the vehicle safely.

8. Remove the front wheels.

9. Remove the tie rod end cotter pins and castle nuts. Install a 12mm nut onto the end of the ball joint stud to protect the threads from damage. Using a ball joint tool, disconnect the tie rod ends from the steering knuckles.

10. Disconnect the Heated Oxygen Sensor (HO$_2$S).

11. Remove the self-locking nuts and separate the catalytic converter from the exhaust pipe. Unbolt the exhaust pipe from the intake manifold, and remove it from the vehicle.

12. On vehicles equipped with automatic transaxles, remove the shift cable cover, disconnect the shift cable, and wire it up and out of the way.

13. Clean any oil or dirt off of the valve body with solvent.

14. Remove the center beam from the subframe.

15. Remove the valve body shield.

16. Use a flare nut wrench to disconnect the four hydraulic lines from the rack valve body. Plug the lines to keep dirt and moisture out.

17. Remove the steering joint bolt and slide the pinion shaft out of the joint.

18. Remove the left mounting bracket, then remove the right mounting brackets.

19. Remove the left tie rod end and slide the rack all the way to the right.

20. Pull the steering rack down to release it from the pinion shaft.

21. Slide the steering rack to the right until the left tie rod clears the subframe, then drop it down and out of the vehicle to the left.

To install:

➡ Use new gaskets and self-locking nuts when installing the exhaust pipe.

✳✳ WARNING

Use only genuine Honda power steering fluid. Any other type or brand of fluid will damage the power steering pump.

22. Install the steering rack into position. Install the pinion shaft grommet and insert the pinion through the hole in the firewall.

23. Install the right and left mounting brackets. Tighten the short bolts to 28 ft. lbs. (39 Nm), and the long bolts to 32 ft. lbs. (44 Nm).

24. Center the rack ends within their steering strokes.

25. Center the air bag cable reel as follows:
- Turn the steering wheel clockwise until it stops.
- Turn the steering wheel counterclockwise until the yellow gear tooth lines up with the alignment mark on the lower column cover.

26. Line up the bolt hole in the steering joint with the groove in the pinion shaft. Slip the joint onto the pinion shaft. Pull the joint up and down to be sure the splines are fully seated. Tighten the joint bolts to 16 ft. lbs. (22 Nm).

➡ Connect the steering joint and pinion shaft with the cable reel and steering rack centered. Verify that the lower joint bolt is securely seated in the pinion shaft groove. If the steering wheel and rack are not centered, reposition the serrations at the lower end of the steering joint.

27. Reconnect the four hydraulic lines to the rack valve body. Carefully tighten the 12mm fittings to 9 ft. lbs. (13 Nm), the 14mm inlet fitting to 28 ft. lbs. (37 Nm), and the 17mm oil cooler fitting to 21 ft. lbs. (29 Nm).

28. Install the valve body shield.

29. Install the center beam. Use new self-locking bolts and tighten them to 43 ft. lbs. (60 Nm).

30. On automatic transaxle equipped vehicles, reconnect the shift cable and tighten the locknut to 10 ft. lbs. (14 Nm). Install the cable holder and tighten its bolts to 13 ft. lbs. (18 Nm).

31. Install the catalytic converter using new gaskets and self-locking nuts. Tighten the exhaust manifold nuts to 40 ft. lbs. (55 Nm), and the rear nuts to 25 ft. lbs. (34 Nm).

32. Reconnect the HO$_2$S.

33. Install the tie rod ends onto the rack ends. Connect the tie rod ends to the steering knuckles and install the castle nuts. Install the front wheels.

34. Verify that the rack is centered within its strokes. Lower the vehicle.

35. Install the steering joint cover.

36. Tighten the ball joint castle nuts to 36–43 ft. lbs. (50–60 Nm). Then, tighten them only enough to install new cotter pins.

37. Reconnect the negative battery cable.

38. Be sure the reservoir inlet line has been reconnected. Fill the reservoir to the upper line with Honda power steering fluid. Run the engine at idle and turn the steering wheel lock-to-lock several times to bleed air from the system and fill the rack valve body. Recheck the fluid level and add more if necessary.

39. Check the power steering system for leaks.

40. Have the front wheel alignment checked and adjusted.

Power Steering Pump

REMOVAL & INSTALLATION

▶ **See Figures 108 thru 115**

1. Remove the negative battery cable.

2. Place a suitable container/catch pan under the vehicle.

3. Loosen the adjusting bolt.

4. Break loose the mounting bolts and nuts and remove the power steering belt, or release the tension from the belt auto tensioner and remove the serpentine drive belt.

5. Cover the A/C compressor for Accord or alternator for Prelude, with shop rags to prevent any fluid from spilling into it.

➡ Spilling power steering fluid into the alternator assembly can damage the unit.

6. Detach the pump inlet and outlet hoses, then plug them to avoid getting debris in the system.

➡ Power steering fluid will destroy your vehicle's paint. Use caution and clean up all spills immediately.

7. Remove the power steering pump mounting bolts, then pull the pump from the vehicle.

✳✳ WARNING

On Prelude models, do not turn the steering wheel with the pump removed.

8. Cover the open ends of the pump, with tape, to prevent foreign material from entering the openings.

To install:

9. Installation is the reverse of removal, noting the following steps and specifications.

Fig. 108 Installed view of the power steering pump

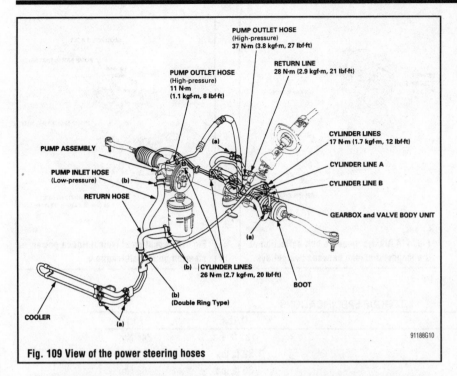

Fig. 109 View of the power steering hoses

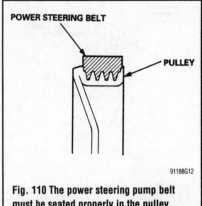

Fig. 110 The power steering pump belt must be seated properly in the pulley

Fig. 111 Note the length and position of each pump bolt removed

10. Please refer to the following fastener tightening specifications:
   - Power steering pump mounting bolt(s): 17 ft. lbs. (24 Nm)
   - Power steering pump outlet hose fasteners: 8 ft. lbs. (11 Nm)
   - Power steering pump mounting nut: 17 ft. lbs. (24 Nm)
11. Make note of the following points:
   - Make sure all fasteners, hose clamps and fittings are properly installed and tightened.
   - If equipped with a power steering v-belt, properly adjust the belt tension. For more information, refer to Section 1.

➡ **Always follow the belt manufacturers tension recommendation if you are not using a genuine Honda belt.**

   - When topping off the system use only Genuine Honda Power Steering Fluid.

✹✹ WARNING

Substituting another brand may damage internal components.

   - Clean any spilled fluid before starting the vehicle.
   - Bleed the system and top off as necessary.

BLEEDING

1. Fill the reservoir to the upper line with Genuine Honda Power Steering Fluid-V or S.

2. Run the engine at idle and turn the steering wheel lock-to-lock several times to bleed air from the system and fill the rack valve body.
3. Recheck the fluid level and add more if necessary. Don't overfill the reservoir.
4. Check the power steering system for leaks.

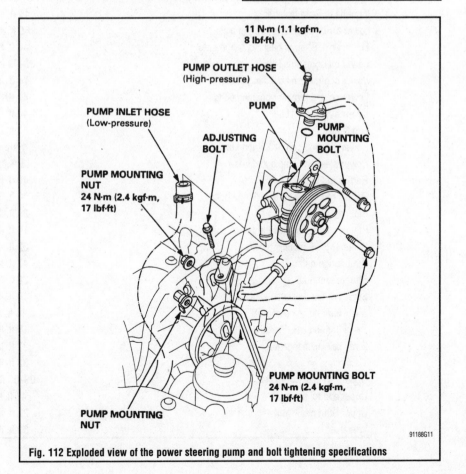

Fig. 112 Exploded view of the power steering pump and bolt tightening specifications

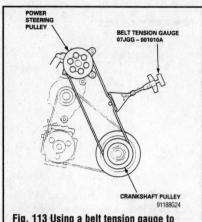

Fig. 113 Using a belt tension gauge to properly adjust the power steering belt after pump installation

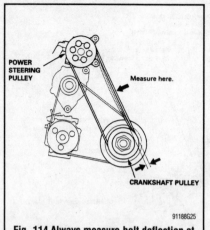

Fig. 114 Always measure belt deflection at the longest distance between two pulleys

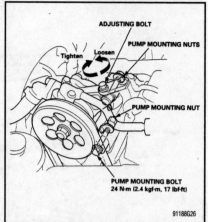

Fig. 115 Location of typical Honda power steering pump bolt locations

TORQUE SPECIFICATIONS

Components	ft. lbs.	Nm
Axle spindle nut	181 ft. lbs.	245 Nm
Ball joint castle nut	32 ft. lbs.	44 Nm
Brake caliper bolts	80 ft. lbs.	108 Nm
Brake rotor mounting screws	82 inch. lbs.	9.3 Nm
Damper fork nut	47 ft. lbs.	65 Nm
Damper fork pinch bolt	32 ft. lbs.	44 Nm
Hub unit flange bolts	33 ft. lbs	44 Nm
Hydraulic fittings to the steering valve body	21–27 ft. lbs	28–37 Nm
Inner tie rod end fastener	40 ft. lbs.	54 Nm
Lower arm "A" bushing through bolts	69 ft. lbs.	93 Nm
Lower arm "B" inner bushing flange nuts	40 ft. lbs.	54 Nm
Lower ball joint nuts/bolts	36–43 ft. lbs	49–59 Nm
Lower control arm front flange bolts	76 ft. lbs.	103 Nm
Lower control arm rear bushing bolts	40 ft. lbs.	54 Nm
Lower strut mount bolt	40 ft. lbs.	55 Nm
Lug Nuts	80 ft. lbs.	108 Nm
Power steering pump mounting bolt	17 ft. lbs	24 Nm
Power steering pump outlet hose	8 ft. lbs.	11 Nm
Radius rod bushing bolt	40 ft. lbs.	54 Nm
Radius rod to control arm flange bolts	76 ft. lbs.	103 Nm
Steering wheel nut	29 ft. lbs.	39 Nm
Steering wheel slip joint to pinion shaft	16 ft. lbs.	22 Nm
Stiffener plate mounting bolts	32 ft. lbs.	43 Nm
Strut flange nuts	47 ft. lbs.	64 Nm
Strut mount nuts	28 ft. lbs.	39 Nm
Sway bar bracket to body bolts	16 ft. lbs.	22 Nm
Sway bar end link (Accord)	14 ft. lbs	19 Nm
Sway bar end link (Prelude)	13 ft. lbs.	18 Nm
Sway bar link flange nut	22 ft. lbs.	29 Nm
Tie rod end	32 ft. lbs.	43 Nm
Upper ball joint nuts/bolts	29–35 ft. lbs	39–47 Nm
Upper control arm nuts	47 ft. lbs	65 Nm
Upper Strut mount nuts	28 ft. lbs.	39 Nm
Wheel lug nuts	80 ft. lbs.	108 Nm

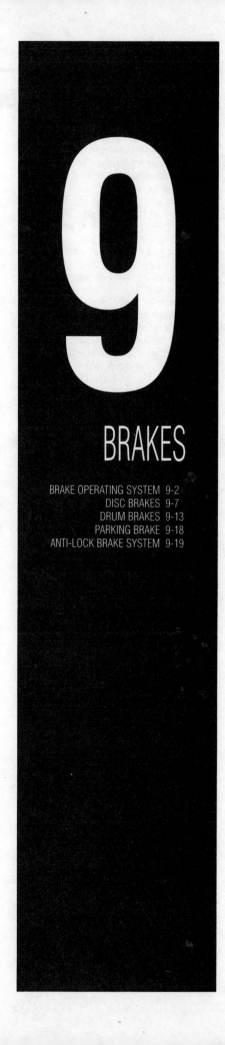

9

BRAKES

BRAKE OPERATING SYSTEM

Hydraulic systems are used to actuate the brakes of all modern automobiles. The system transports the power required to force the frictional surfaces of the braking system together from the pedal to the individual brake units at each wheel. A hydraulic system is used for two reasons.

First, fluid under pressure can be carried to all parts of an automobile by small pipes and flexible hoses without taking up a significant amount of room or posing routing problems.

Second, a great mechanical advantage can be given to the brake pedal end of the system, and the foot pressure required to actuate the brakes can be reduced by making the surface area of the master cylinder pistons smaller than that of any of the pistons in the wheel cylinders or calipers.

The master cylinder consists of a fluid reservoir along with a double cylinder and piston assembly. Double type master cylinders are designed to separate the front and rear braking systems hydraulically in case of a leak. The master cylinder coverts mechanical motion from the pedal into hydraulic pressure within the lines. This pressure is translated back into mechanical motion at the wheels by either the wheel cylinder (drum brakes) or the caliper (disc brakes).

Steel lines carry the brake fluid to a point on the vehicle's frame near each of the vehicle's wheels. The fluid is then carried to the calipers and wheel cylinders by flexible tubes in order to allow for suspension and steering movements.

In drum brake systems, each wheel cylinder contains two pistons, one at either end, which push outward in opposite directions and force the brake shoe into contact with the drum.

In disc brake systems, the cylinders are part of the calipers. At least one cylinder in each caliper is used to force the brake pads against the disc.

All pistons employ some type of seal, usually made of rubber, to minimize fluid leakage. A rubber dust boot seals the outer end of the cylinder against dust and dirt. The boot fits around the outer end of the piston on disc brake calipers, and around the brake actuating rod on wheel cylinders.

The hydraulic system operates as follows: When at rest, the entire system, from the piston(s) in the master cylinder to those in the wheel cylinders or calipers, is full of brake fluid. Upon application of the brake pedal, fluid trapped in front of the master cylinder piston(s) is forced through the lines to the wheel cylinders. Here, it forces the pistons outward, in the case of drum brakes, and inward toward the disc, in the case of disc brakes. The motion of the pistons is opposed by return springs mounted outside the cylinders in drum brakes, and by spring seals, in disc brakes.

Upon release of the brake pedal, a spring located inside the master cylinder immediately returns the master cylinder pistons to the normal position. The pistons contain check valves and the master cylinder has compensating ports drilled in it. These are uncovered as the pistons reach their normal position. The piston check valves allow fluid to remain in the fluid lines for the wheel cylinders or calipers as the master cylinder piston withdraws. Then, as the return springs force the brake pads or shoes into the released position, the excess fluid enters the reservoir through the compensating ports. It is during the time the pedal is in the released position

that any fluid that has leaked out of the system will be replaced through the compensating ports.

Dual circuit master cylinders employ two pistons, located one behind the other, in the same cylinder. The primary piston is actuated directly by mechanical linkage from the brake pedal through the power booster. The secondary piston is actuated by fluid trapped between the two pistons. If a leak develops in front of the secondary piston, it moves forward until it bottoms against the front of the master cylinder, and the fluid trapped between the pistons will operate the rear brakes. If the rear brakes develop a leak, the primary piston will move forward until direct contact with the secondary piston takes place, and it will force the secondary piston to actuate the front brakes. In either case, the brake pedal moves farther when the brakes are applied, and less braking power is available.

All dual circuit systems use a switch to warn the driver when only half of the brake system is operational. This switch is usually located in a valve body which is mounted on the firewall or the frame below the master cylinder. A hydraulic piston receives pressure from both circuits, each circuit's pressure being applied to one end of the piston. When the pressures are in balance, the piston remains stationary. When one circuit has a leak, however, the greater pressure in that circuit during application of the brakes will push the piston to one side, closing the switch and activating the brake warning light.

In disc brake systems, this valve body also contains a metering valve and, in some cases, a proportioning valve. The metering valve keeps pressure from traveling to the disc brakes on the front wheels until the brake shoes on the rear wheels have contacted the drums, ensuring that the front brakes will never be used alone. The proportioning valve controls the pressure to the rear brakes to lessen the chance of rear wheel lock-up during very hard braking.

Warning lights may be tested by depressing the brake pedal and holding it while opening one of the wheel cylinder bleeder screws. If this does not cause the light to go on, substitute a new lamp, make continuity checks, and, finally, replace the switch as necessary:

The hydraulic system may be checked for leaks by applying pressure to the pedal gradually and steadily. If the pedal sinks very slowly to the floor, the system has a leak. This is not to be confused with a springy or spongy feel due to worn flexible brake lines or the compression of air within the lines. If the system leaks, there will be a gradual change in the position of the pedal with a constant pressure.

Check for leaks along all lines and at the master and wheel cylinders. If no external leaks are apparent, the problem is inside the master cylinder. Either the check valve is contaminated with debris and/or the seals are worn.

The typical cause of a brake pulsation is an irregular surface or a worn mechanical component. Possible causes include:

• Bent suspension hub
• Improper wheel lug nut torque
• Worn or damaged wheel bearing
• Improper machined surfaces of a brake drum or rotor
• Thickness variations and/or warpage of a brake drum or rotor

DISC BRAKES

Instead of the traditional expanding brakes that press outward against a circular drum, disc brake systems utilize a disc (rotor) with brake pads positioned on either side of it. An easily-seen analogy is the hand brake arrangement on a bicycle. The pads squeeze onto the rim of the bike wheel, slowing its motion. Automobile disc brakes use the identical principle but apply the braking effort to a separate disc instead of the wheel.

The disc (rotor) is a casting, usually equipped with cooling fins between the two braking surfaces. This enables air to circulate between the braking surfaces making them less sensitive to heat buildup and more resistant to fade. Dirt and water do not drastically affect braking action since contaminants are thrown off by the centrifugal action of the rotor or scraped off the by the pads. Also, the equal clamping action of the two brake pads tends to ensure uniform, straight line stops. Disc brakes are inherently self-adjusting. There are three general types of disc brake:

1. A fixed caliper.
2. A floating caliper.
3. A sliding caliper.

The fixed caliper design uses two hydraulic pistons mounted on either side of the rotor (on each side of the caliper). The caliper is mounted rigidly and does not move.

The sliding and floating designs are quite similar. In fact, these two types are often lumped together. In both designs, the pad on the inside of the rotor is moved into contact with the rotor by hydraulic force. The caliper, which is not held in a fixed position, moves slightly, bringing the outside pad into contact with the rotor. There are various methods of attaching floating calipers. Some pivot at the bottom or top, and some slide on mounting bolts. In any event, the end result is the same.

DRUM BRAKES

Drum brakes employ two brake shoes mounted on a stationary backing plate. These shoes are positioned inside a circular drum which rotates with the wheel assembly. The shoes are held in place by springs. This allows them to slide toward the drums (when they are applied) while keeping the linings and drums in alignment. The shoes are actuated by a wheel cylinder which is mounted at the top of the backing plate. When the brakes are applied, hydraulic pressure forces the wheel cylinder's actuating links outward. Since these links bear directly against the top of the brake shoes, the tops of the shoes are then forced against the inner side of the drum. This action forces the bottoms of the two shoes to contact the brake drum by rotating the entire assembly slightly (known as servo action). When pressure within the wheel cylinder is relaxed, return springs pull the shoes back away from the drum.

Most modern drum brakes are designed to self-adjust themselves during application when the vehicle is moving in reverse. This motion causes both shoes to rotate very slightly with the drum, rocking an adjusting lever, thereby causing rotation of the adjusting screw. Some drum brake systems are designed to self-adjust during application whenever the brakes are applied. This on-board adjustment system reduces the need for maintenance adjustments and keeps both the brake function and pedal feel satisfactory.

PARKING BRAKES

Parking brakes are most often actuated by a mechanical linkage. Typically a cable moves a linkage to actuate the brake lining as the cable is pulled via a foot pedal or hand lever. The parking brake can be either a disc or a drum design. A drum parking brake is engaged by mechanically forcing the brake shoes outward into the brake drum. The parking brake may use the same brake shoes as the hydraulic brake system, or it could be a completely separate system.

Such is the case where a disc brake rotor also incorporates a drum brake on the inside area of the brake rotor. In this instance, the hydraulic brake is a disc brake, while the parking brake is a mechanically operated drum brake. On a combination system of this type, the parking brake functions separately from the hydraulic brake and shares no common parts with exception of the combination brake disc/drum.

Some manufactures use a disc brake caliper with an internal mechanical linkage. On this system, the parking brake and the hydraulic brake share the same brake linings.

POWER BRAKE BOOSTER

Virtually all modern vehicles use a vacuum assisted power brake system to multiply the braking force and reduce pedal effort. Since vacuum is always available when the engine is operating, the system is simple and efficient. A vacuum diaphragm is located on the front of the master cylinder and assists the driver in applying the brakes, reducing both the effort and travel he must put into moving the brake pedal.

The vacuum diaphragm housing is normally connected to the intake manifold by a vacuum hose. A check valve is placed at the point where the hose enters the diaphragm housing, so that during periods of low manifold vacuum brakes assist will not be lost.

Depressing the brake pedal closes off the vacuum source and allows atmospheric pressure to enter on one side of the diaphragm. This causes the master cylinder pistons to move and apply the brakes. When the brake pedal is released, vacuum is applied to both sides of the diaphragm and springs return the diaphragm and master cylinder pistons to the released position.

If the vacuum supply fails, the brake pedal rod will contact the end of the master cylinder actuator rod and the system will apply the brakes without any power assistance. The driver will notice that much higher pedal effort is needed to stop the car and that the pedal feels harder than usual.

Vacuum Leak Test

1. Operate the engine at idle without touching the brake pedal for at least one minute.
2. Turn off the engine and wait one minute.
3. Test for the presence of assist vacuum by depressing the brake pedal and releasing it several times. If vacuum is present in the system, light application will produce less and less pedal travel. If there is no vacuum, air is leaking into the system.

System Operation Test

1. With the engine **OFF**, pump the brake pedal until the supply vacuum is entirely gone.
2. Put light, steady pressure on the brake pedal.
3. Start the engine and let it idle. If the system is operating correctly, the brake pedal should fall toward the floor if the constant pressure is maintained.

Power brake systems may be tested for hydraulic leaks just as ordinary systems are tested.

❊❊ WARNING

Clean, high quality brake fluid is essential to the safe and proper operation of the brake system. You should always buy the highest quality brake fluid that is available. If the brake fluid becomes contaminated, drain and flush the system, then refill the master cylinder with new fluid. Never reuse any brake fluid. Any brake fluid that is removed from the system should be discarded.

Brake Light Switch

REMOVAL & INSTALLATION

1. Detach the brake light switch electrical connector.
2. Loosen the locknut.
3. Remove the brake light switch by unthreading it in a counter-clockwise direction.
To install:
4. Thread the brake light switch into its mounting bracket until the threaded end of the switch contacts the pad on the brake pedal. The switch plunger should be fully depressed and not visible at this time.
5. Back off the switch ¼ turn to allow 0.01 in (0.3mm) of clearance between the threaded portion of the switch and the pedal pad.
6. Attach the brake light switch electrical connector.
7. Connect the negative battery cable.

Master Cylinder

REMOVAL & INSTALLATION

▶ **See Figures 1 and 2**

❊❊ CAUTION

The Honda Anti-lock Brake System (ABS) contains brake fluid under extremely high pressure within the pump, accumulator and modulator assembly. Do not disconnect or loosen any lines, hoses, fittings or components without properly relieving the system pressure. Use only a bleeder T-wrench

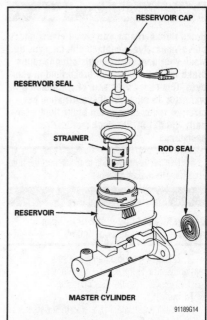

91189G14

Fig. 1 Exploded view of the master cylinder, cap and strainer

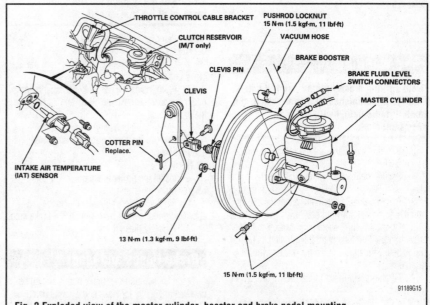

91189G15

Fig. 2 Exploded view of the master cylinder, booster and brake pedal mounting

07HAA-SG00100, or equivalent, to relieve pressure. Improper procedures or failure to discharge the system pressure may result in severe personal injury and/or property damage.

Honda vehicles have a tandem master cylinder that is used to improve the safety of the vehicle. The master cylinder has one reservoir tank with two feed holes at the bottom of the tank to feed both the primary and secondary circuit.

1. Disconnect the negative battery cable.
2. Detach the electrical connectors from the master cylinder.
3. Remove the master cylinder reservoir cap.
4. Remove the brake fluid from the master cylinder using a siphon or clean turkey baster.

❉❉ CAUTION

Brake fluid contains polyglycol ethers and polyglycols. Avoid contact with the eyes and wash your hands thoroughly after handling brake fluid. If you do get brake fluid in your eyes, flush your eyes with clean, running water for 15 minutes. If eye irritation persists, or if you have taken brake fluid internally, IMMEDIATELY seek medical assistance.

5. Use a flare nut wrench to disconnect the fluid lines from the master cylinder.

❉❉ WARNING

Be careful not to bend the lines upon removal of the master cylinder.

6. Unfasten the mounting nuts that attach the master cylinder to the booster, then remove the master cylinder from the brake booster.
To install:
7. Install the master cylinder in the reverse order of removal.
8. Fill the master cylinder with an approved DOT 3 or DOT 4 brake fluid.
9. Properly bleed the master cylinder, as outlined in this section.

BENCH BLEEDING

❉❉ WARNING

Avoid spilling brake fluid on paint. It will damage most finishes. If a spill does occur, wash it immediately with water and absorbent cloth.

If the master cylinder is off the vehicle, it can be bench bled.
1. Secure the master cylinder in a bench vise.
2. Place a suitable catch pan under the master cylinder, to collect any fluid seepage.
3. Connect 2 short sections of brake line to the outlet fittings. Carefully bend them until the open end is below the fluid level in the master cylinder reservoirs.
4. Fill the reservoir with fresh DOT 3 or DOT 4 type brake fluid.
5. Using a wooden dowel, or equivalent, pump

the piston slowly several times until no more air bubbles appear in the reservoirs.
6. Disconnect the 2 short lines, refill the master cylinder and securely install the cylinder cap.
7. If the master cylinder is on the vehicle, it can still be bled as follows:
   a. Using a flare nut wrench open one brake line at a time ¼ turn with a flare nut wrench.
   b. Have an assistant press the brake pedal to the floor and hold it there, then tighten the brake line and have the assistant slowly release the brake pedal.
   c. Check the reservoir fluid level and top off as necessary.
   d. Repeat the above procedures on all of the lines until the dispersed fluid is free of all air bubbles.

➡**Always tighten the line before the brake pedal is released.**

8. Once the master cylinder is bled, flush the surrounding area with water to neutralize the brake fluid.
9. Bleed the complete brake system, if necessary.

➡**If the master cylinder has been thoroughly bled and filled to the proper level upon installation into the vehicle, it should not be necessary to bleed the entire hydraulic system.**

Power Brake Booster

REMOVAL & INSTALLATION

◆ **See Figure 2**

1. Disconnect the negative battery cable.
2. Detach all electrical connectors from the master cylinder.
3. Remove the brake fluid from the master cylinder, then use a flare nut wrench to disconnect the metal fluid lines.

❉❉ WARNING

Be careful not to bend the lines upon removal of the master cylinder.

4. Remove the master cylinder from the brake booster.
5. Disconnect the vacuum hoses from the brake booster.
6. From inside the passenger compartment, under the dash, remove the clevis and its pin from the brake pedal.
7. Remove the booster mounting bolts.
8. Remove the brake booster from the engine compartment.
To install:
9. Install the power brake booster in the reverse order of removal.
10. Fill the master cylinder with Honda approved or equivalent DOT 3 or DOT 4 brake fluid.
11. Properly bleed the master cylinder.

Brake Hoses and Lines

Metal lines and rubber brake hoses should be checked frequently for leaks and external damage. Metal lines are particularly prone to crushing and

kinking under the vehicle. Any such deformation can restrict the proper flow of fluid and therefore impair braking at the wheels. Rubber hoses should be checked for cracking or scraping; such damage can create a weak spot in the hose and it could fail under pressure.

Any time the lines are removed or disconnected, extreme cleanliness must be observed. Clean all joints and connections before disassembly (use a stiff bristle brush and clean brake fluid); be sure to plug the lines and ports as soon as they are opened. New lines and hoses should be flushed clean with brake fluid before installation to remove any contamination.

REMOVAL & INSTALLATION

◆ **See Figures 3 thru 13**

1. Disconnect the negative battery cable.
2. Raise and safely support the vehicle on jackstands.
3. Remove any wheel and tire assemblies necessary for access to the particular line you are removing.
4. Thoroughly clean the surrounding area at the joints to be disconnected.
5. Place a suitable catch pan under the joint to be disconnected.
6. Using two wrenches (one to hold the joint and one to turn the fitting), disconnect the hose or line to be replaced.
7. Disconnect the other end of the line or hose, moving the drain pan if necessary. Always use a back-up wrench to avoid damaging the fitting.
8. Disconnect any retaining clips or brackets holding the line and remove the line from the vehicle.

➡**If the brake system is to remain open for more time than it takes to swap lines, tape or plug each remaining clip and port to keep contaminants out and fluid in.**

To install:
9. Install the new line or hose, starting with the end farthest from the master cylinder. Connect the other end, then confirm that both fittings are correctly threaded and turn smoothly using finger pressure. Make sure the new line will not rub against any other part. Brake lines must be at least 1/2 in. (13mm) from the steering column and other moving parts. Any protective shielding or insulators must be reinstalled in the original location.

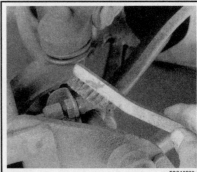

TCCA9P09

Fig. 3 Use a brush to clean the fittings of any debris

⁂ WARNING

Make sure the hose is NOT kinked or touching any part of the frame or suspension

after installation. These conditions may cause the hose to fail prematurely.

10. Using two wrenches as before, tighten each fitting.

11. Install any retaining clips or brackets on the lines.

12. If removed, install the wheel and tire assemblies, then carefully lower the vehicle to the ground.

13. Refill the brake master cylinder reservoir with clean, fresh brake fluid, meeting DOT 3 specifications. Properly bleed the brake system.

14. Connect the negative battery cable.

Bleeding Brake System

➡The brake fluid should be replaced at least every 3 years or 45,000 miles (72,000 km).

⁂ WARNING

Avoid spilling brake fluid on the vehicle's paint. It will damage the finish. If a spill does occur, wash it immediately with water.

The purpose of bleeding the brakes is to expel air trapped in the hydraulic system. The system should be checked for fluid condition, brake hose condition and air whenever the pedal feels spongy. The system must be bled whenever it has been opened, repaired, or a hydraulic component replaced. If you are not using a pressure bleeder, you will need an assistant for this job.

⁂ WARNING

Never reuse brake fluid which has been bled from the brake system. Brake fluid absorbs moisture which can lower its boil-

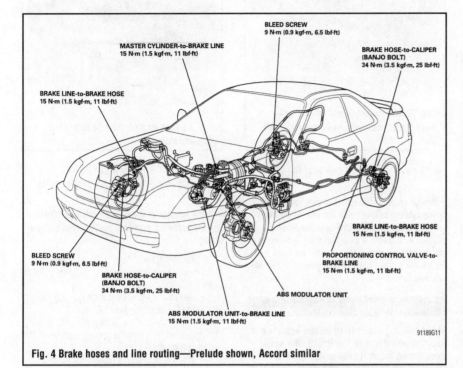

BLEED SCREW
9 N·m (0.9 kgf·m, 6.5 lbf·ft)

MASTER CYLINDER-to-BRAKE LINE
15 N·m (1.5 kgf·m, 11 lbf·ft)

BRAKE HOSE-to-CALIPER
(BANJO BOLT)
34 N·m (3.5 kgf·m, 25 lbf·ft)

BRAKE LINE-to-BRAKE HOSE
15 N·m (1.5 kgf·m, 11 lbf·ft)

BLEED SCREW
9 N·m (0.9 kgf·m, 6.5 lbf·ft)

BRAKE HOSE-to-CALIPER
(BANJO BOLT)
34 N·m (3.5 kgf·m, 25 lbf·ft)

ABS MODULATOR UNIT-to-BRAKE LINE
15 N·m (1.5 kgf·m, 11 lbf·ft)

ABS MODULATOR UNIT

PROPORTIONING CONTROL VALVE-to-BRAKE LINE
15 N·m (1.5 kgf·m, 11 lbf·ft)

BRAKE LINE-to-BRAKE HOSE
15 N·m (1.5 kgf·m, 11 lbf·ft)

91189G11

Fig. 4 Brake hoses and line routing—Prelude shown, Accord similar

91189P43

Fig. 5 To remove the brake hose, you must first unscrew all of the fasteners from the mounting brackets that suspend the hoses

91189P11

Fig. 6 Remove the banjo bolt from the brake line

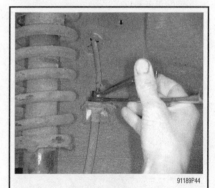

91189P44

Fig. 7 Use two line wrenches to remove the brake hose from the line

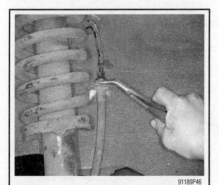

91189P46

Fig. 8 Remove the brake hose retaining clip

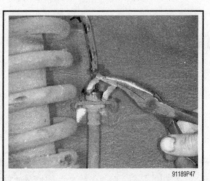

91189P47

Fig. 9 Once the brake hose retaining clip is removed, check it's condition and replace if necessary

91189P48

Fig. 10 Once loosened, disconnect the brake hose from the line

Fig. 11 Close up of a brake hose line fitting

Fig. 12 Any gaskets/crush washers should be replaced with new ones during installation

Fig. 13 Tape or plug the line to prevent contamination

ing point, therefore re-using old, used, or contaminated fluid can decrease the effectiveness of the braking system.

BLEEDING

▶ See Figures 14, 15, 16, 17 and 18

➥If the ABS modulator has been opened or replaced, it may be necessary to bleed each line at the modulator unit.

When bleeding the brakes, air may be trapped in the brake lines or valves far upstream, as much as 10 feet from the bleeder screw. Therefore, it is very important to have a fast flow of a large volume of brake fluid when bleeding the brakes, to

make sure all of the air is expelled from the system.

➥Proper manual bleeding of the hydraulic brake system will require the use of an assistant unless a suitable self-bleeding tool is available. If using a self-bleeding tool, refer to the manufacturer's directions for tool use and follow the proper bleeding sequence listed in this section.

✳✳ WARNING

Avoid spilling brake fluid on the vehicle's paint. It will damage the finish. If a spill does occur, wash it with water immediately.

1. To bleed the brakes, if the ABS modulator has not been opened or replaced, proceed as follows.

➥If the master cylinder reservoir runs dry during the bleeding process, restart from the first fitting.

2. Remove the old brake fluid and clean the brake master cylinder reservoir with a clean lint-free cloth.

3. Bleed the brake system at each fitting. Do not proceed to the next fitting until all air bubbles are removed from the previous fitting. Bleed the brakes, making sure to following the sequence shown in the accompanying figures.

4. Attach a clear plastic hose to the bleeder screw, then place the hose into a clean jar that has

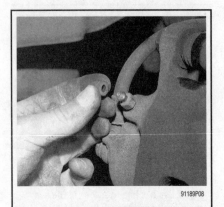

Fig. 14 Remove the bleeder screw cap

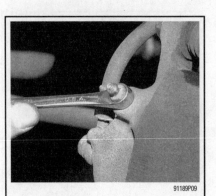

Fig. 15 Position a closed-end wrench over the bleeder screw

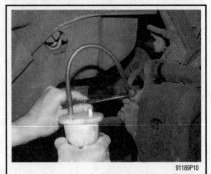

Fig. 16 Use an approved container to collect the brake fluid during the bleeding process

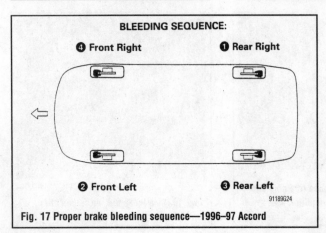

BLEEDING SEQUENCE:

❹ Front Right   ❶ Rear Right

❷ Front Left   ❸ Rear Left

Fig. 17 Proper brake bleeding sequence—1996–97 Accord

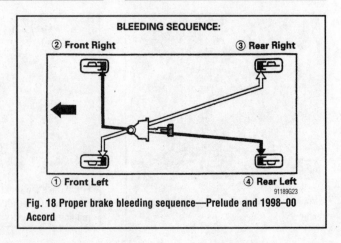

BLEEDING SEQUENCE:

② Front Right   ③ Rear Right

① Front Left   ④ Rear Left

Fig. 18 Proper brake bleeding sequence—Prelude and 1998–00 Accord

enough fresh brake fluid to submerge the end of the hose.

5. Have an assistant pump the brake pedal 3–4 times, and hold pressure on it, then open the bleeder screw at least ¼ turn. When the bleeder screw opens, the brake pedal will drop. Have the assistant hold it there until the bleed valve is closed.

6. Close the bleeder screw and have the assis-

tant slowly release the brake pedal only AFTER the bleeder screw is closed, then check the master cylinder fluid level and top off as necessary.

7. Repeat the bleeding procedure until all there are no air bubbles, or a minimum of 4 or 5 times at each bleeder screw, then check the pedal for travel and feel. If the pedal travel is excessive, or feels spongy, it's possible enough fluid has not passed through the system to expel all of the trapped air.

➡**Constantly check and top off the master cylinder. Do not allow the master cylinder to run dry, otherwise air will re-enter the brake system.**

8. Once completed, test drive the vehicle to be sure the brakes are operating correctly and that the pedal feel is firm.

DISC BRAKES

❊❊ CAUTION

Older brake pads or shoes may contain asbestos, which has been determined to be a cancer causing agent. Never clean the brake surfaces with compressed air! Avoid inhaling any dust from any brake surface! When cleaning brake surfaces, use a commercially available brake cleaning fluid.

The brake pads should be inspected during every oil change. Brake wear varies with vehicle use and driving habits. Constant stop and go driving is likely to wear the linings much more quickly than highway driving. Vehicles equipped with an automatic transaxle are more likely to wear the linings more quickly than those equipped with a manual transaxle.

Driving habits also affect brake wear. Aggressive braking from high speeds is likely to wear the linings more quickly than slow gradual stops. Aggressive braking also generates much more heat which could result in premature brake rotor wear, potential rotor warpage and wheel bearing damage, as the heat generated can decrease the ability of the grease to adequately lubricate the sealed wheel bearing.

Some brake pads are equipped with audible wear sensors. When the brake linings reach their wear limit, a small metal tab begins to contact the brake rotor, making an audible, but light scraping noise which initially occurs when the brakes are used. Eventually it will make a high pitched scraping noise any time the vehicle is moving, being most noticeable at slow speeds.

❊❊ WARNING

If a scraping noise is heard when applying the brakes, inspect the brake linings immediately.

Sometimes brakes do squeal even though the brake linings are not worn. In this instance, the brake squeal usually diminishes when the brakes are used hard.

Causes of brake squeal include the following:
• Rust or debris built up between the brake pad backing and caliper bracket
• Insufficient lubricant on the sliding pins
• Loose brake pad shims
• Brake rotor surface wear and/or a ridge on the outer circumference of the brake rotor
• Glazed, contaminated or improper brake linings

Brake Pads

REMOVAL & INSTALLATION

◗ **See Figures 19 thru 25**

1. Use a siphon or clean turkey baster to remove about half of the brake fluid from the master cylinder. Or remove all of the fluid, clean the reservoir with an approved brake cleaner and a clean lint-free cloth and fill ½ full with fresh brake fluid.

2. Raise and safely support the vehicle with jackstands.

3. Remove the front tire and wheel assemblies.

4. If necessary, remove the brake hose mounting bolts from the steering knuckle.

➡**Regardless of their wear pattern, when brake pads are replaced on one side of the vehicle, they must also be replaced on the other side. It is advisable, however, to complete one side before beginning the other.**

5. Working on one brake caliper at a time, remove the lower brake caliper bolt and pivot the caliper up and out of the way.

❊❊ WARNING

Once a brake caliper has been lifted away from the brake pads, do not press the brake pedal.

6. Remove the brake pads, shims and retainers.

To install:

7. Inspect the brake pads, as outlined later in this section. If the pad thickness is less than the service requirement, replace them.

8. Clean and check the brake rotor for cracks and uneven wear, or an excessive ridge on the outer circumference. Measure the brake rotor thickness with a micrometer and replace the rotor if the mea-

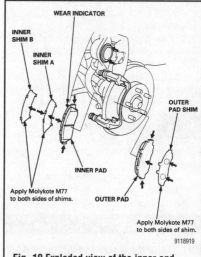

Fig. 19 Exploded view of the inner and outer disc brake pads and shims

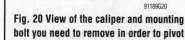

Fig. 20 View of the caliper and mounting bolt you need to remove in order to pivot the caliper up and replace the brake pads

Fig. 21 Once the caliper is pivoted upward and out of the way, you can access the brake pads . . .

Fig. 22 . . . and remove them from the caliper

Fig. 23 Some brake pads may have a wear indicator such as this one. When the friction material wears to an unsafe level, the metal tab will make contact with the rotor to alert the driver

Fig. 24 Remove the brake pad retainers—Accord shown

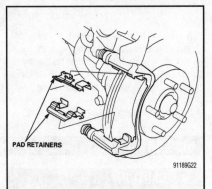

Fig. 25 View of the brake pad retainers—Prelude shown

sured thickness is less than the minimum thickness specification stamped into the rotor. For more information, refer to the procedure in this section.

9. Clean the caliper brackets, and lubricate the bracket sliding pins with a high temperature brake grease.

10. Apply a light coat of an anti-seizing compound to the brake pad backing tabs and the slots the tabs are installed into on the brake caliper bracket.

11. Make sure all the brake pad retainers and shims are properly and securely installed. If equipped with wear indicators, install the brake pad such that the wear indicator is at the top of the inside brake pad.

12. If the brake pads are being replaced, the brake caliper piston must be pressed back into the caliper body as follows:

a. Clean the exposed portion of the brake caliper piston with an approved brake cleaner, and wipe off any residual debris using a clean lint-free cloth.

b. Using a tool designed for retracting brake caliper pistons or a suitable C-clamp, press on the center of the brake piston using a slow, light, even pressure to press the piston into the caliper. If necessary, place a suitable sized socket in the center cavity of the piston to act as a spacer, or, use an old brake pad to lay across the piston.

✳✳ WARNING

Do not force the brake caliper piston back into the caliper. If the piston begins to bind, stop immediately until the cause can be determined.

Possible causes for a brake caliper piston to bind include:
- An out of round brake caliper piston
- An excessively worn brake caliper bore and/or brake piston
- Excessive corrosion or debris built up on the brake piston surface or caliper bore

✳✳ WARNING

When reusing the old brake pads, be sure to install them in the same positions to prevent an increase in stopping distance.

13. Install the brake pads.
14. Pivot the caliper down to its installed position, then install the mounting bolts.

15. Check the master cylinder brake reservoir fluid level and top off as necessary.

16. Once the brake calipers are completely installed, press the brake pedal in short 2 inch (50mm) strokes until the brake pedal is firm. Avoid pressing the brake pedal more than 2 inches because the wear in the master cylinder bore could damage the internal seals. Depress and hold the brake several times to ensure they work.

17. Carefully road test the vehicle. Allow approximately 200 miles (320km) of driving for new brake pads to fully seat.

INSPECTION

◆ See Figure 26

You should check the brake pads every 6,000 miles (9,600km), any time the oil is changed or wheels are removed. Inspect both ends of the outer brake pad by looking in at each end of the caliper. These are the points at which the highest rate of wear normally occurs. Also, check the thickness on the inner brake pad to make sure it is not wearing prematurely. Some inboard pads have a thermal layer against the steel backing surface which is integrally molded with the pad. Do not confuse this extra layer with uneven inboard/outboard brake pad wear.

Look down through inspection hole in the top of the caliper to view the inner brake pad. Replace the pads whenever the thickness of any pad is worn within 0.030 in. (0.76mm) of the steel backing surface. For riveted brake pads, they must be replaced if the pad is worn to 0.030 (0.76mm) of any rivet head. The disc brake pads MUST be replaced in axle sets, for example, if you replace the driver's

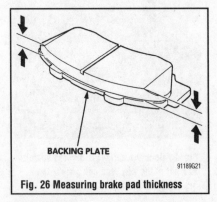

Fig. 26 Measuring brake pad thickness

side front brake pads, you must also replace the passenger's side front brake pads. This will prevent uneven wear and other brake system problems.

1. Remove the brake pads and observe their condition.

2. Measure the thickness of the brake pad's lining material at the thinnest portion of the assembly. Do not include the pad's metal backing plate in the measurement.

3. If you can't accurately determine the condition of the brake pads by visual inspection, you must remove the caliper, then remove the brake pads.

Brake Caliper

REMOVAL & INSTALLATION

◆ See Figures 27 thru 33

➡**Do not allow the master cylinder reservoir to empty. An empty reservoir will allow air to enter the brake system and complete system bleeding will be required.**

1. Use a siphon or clean turkey baster to remove about half of the brake fluid from the master cylinder.

2. Raise and safely support the vehicle, then remove the tire and wheel assembly.

3. Unfasten the caliper mounting bolts, then remove the caliper assembly from the rotor and bracket. If the caliper is only being removed for access to other components or for pad replacement, support the caliper from the suspension using mechanic's wire so that there is no strain on the brake hose, and leave the brake hose attached.

4. If the caliper is to be completely removed from the vehicle for replacement or overhaul, remove the brake hose attaching bolt, then disconnect the brake hose from the caliper and plug the hose to prevent fluid contamination or loss.

5. Remove the caliper mounting bracket bolts, then remove the bracket from the rotor.

To install:

6. Completely retract the piston into the caliper using a large C-clamp or other suitable tool. Refer to the brake pad procedure for more information on retracting the caliper piston.

7. Clean and lubricate both steering knuckle abutments or support brackets with a coating of multi-purpose grease.

8. Install the caliper bracket and secure with the mounting bolts.

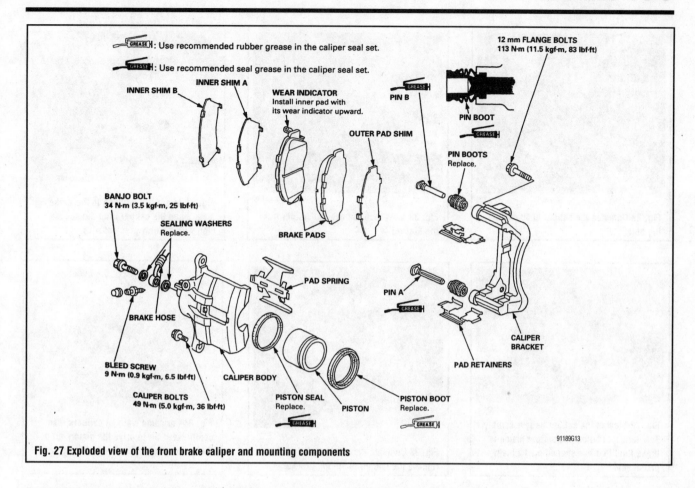

Fig. 27 Exploded view of the front brake caliper and mounting components

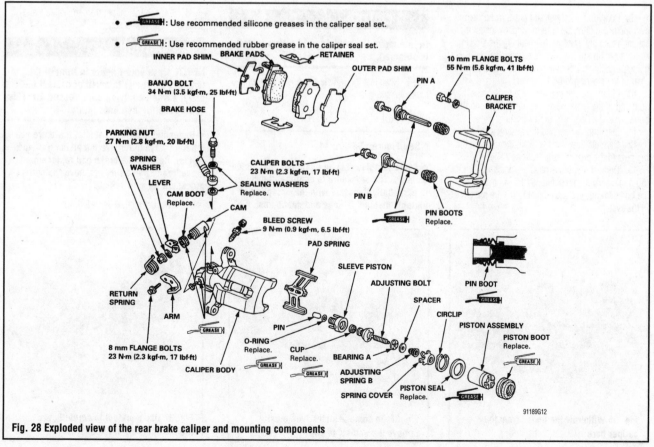

Fig. 28 Exploded view of the rear brake caliper and mounting components

Fig. 29 Unfasten the caliper body mounting bolts . . .

Fig. 30 . . . then remove the caliper from the bracket

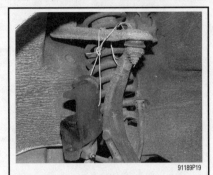

Fig. 31 To prevent damage to the brake hose, hang the caliper from the suspension with a sturdy piece of wire

Fig. 32 View of the caliper body assembly. The dark spot below the caliper piston is brake fluid that has seeped past a leaky piston seal

Fig. 33 Unfasten the retaining bolts, then remove the caliper mounting bracket

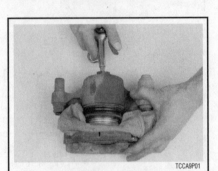

Fig. 34 For some types of calipers, use compressed air to drive the piston out of the caliper, but make sure to keep your fingers clear

9. Position the caliper and brake pad assembly over the brake rotor. Be sure to properly install the caliper assembly into the abutments of the steering knuckle or support bracket. Be sure the caliper guide pin bolts, rubber bushings and sleeves are clear of the steering knuckle bosses.

10. Fill the master cylinder with fresh brake fluid and, if the brake hose was removed, bleed the brake system as outlined in this section.

11. Install the wheel and tire assembly.

12. Carefully lower the vehicle, then tighten the lug nuts to the proper specifications.

13. Depress the brake pedal using short 2 inch (50 mm) strokes, in repetitions of 3–4 times until the brake linings are seated and to restore pressure in the system.

✳✳ CAUTION

Do not move the vehicle until a firm pedal is obtained.

14. Road test the vehicle and check for proper brake operation.

OVERHAUL

◆ **See Figures 34 thru 41**

➡Some vehicles may be equipped dual piston calipers. The procedure to overhaul the caliper is essentially the same with the exception of multiple pistons, O-rings and dust boots.

1. Remove the caliper from the vehicle and place on a clean workbench.

✳✳ CAUTION

NEVER place your fingers in front of the pistons in an attempt to catch or protect the pistons when applying compressed air. This could result in personal injury!

➡Depending upon the vehicle, there are two different ways to remove the piston from the caliper. Refer to the brake pad replacement procedure to make sure you have the correct procedure for your vehicle.

2. The first method is as follows:

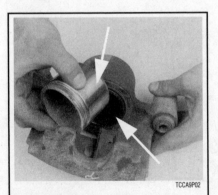

Fig. 35 Withdraw the piston from the caliper bore

Fig. 36 On some vehicles, you must remove the anti-rattle clip

Fig. 37 Use a prytool to carefully pry around the edge of the boot . . .

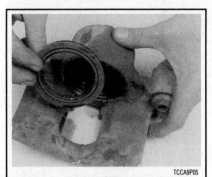

Fig. 38 . . . then remove the boot from the caliper housing, taking care not to score or damage the bore

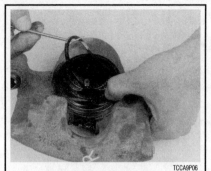

Fig. 39 Use extreme caution when removing the piston seal; DO NOT scratch the caliper bore

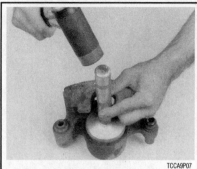

Fig. 40 Use the proper size driving tool and a mallet to properly seal the boots in the caliper housing

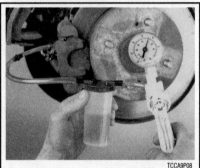

Fig. 41 Tools, such as this Mighty-Vac, are available to assist in proper brake system bleeding

a. Stuff a shop towel or a block of wood into the caliper to catch the piston.

b. Remove the caliper piston using compressed air applied into the caliper inlet hole. Inspect the piston for scoring, nicks, corrosion and/or worn or damaged chrome plating. The piston must be replaced if any of these conditions are found.

3. For the second method, you must rotate the piston to retract it from the caliper.

4. If equipped, remove the anti-rattle clip.

5. Use a prytool to remove the caliper boot, being careful not to scratch the housing bore.

6. Remove the piston seals from the groove in the caliper bore.

7. Carefully loosen the brake bleeder valve cap and valve from the caliper housing.

8. Inspect the caliper bores, pistons and mounting threads for scoring or excessive wear.

9. Use crocus cloth to polish out light corrosion from the piston and bore.

10. Clean all parts with denatured alcohol and dry with compressed air.

To install:

11. Lubricate and install the bleeder valve and cap.

12. Install the new seals into the caliper bore grooves, making sure they are not twisted.

13. Lubricate the piston bore.

14. Install the pistons and boots into the bores of the calipers and push to the bottom of the bores.

15. Use a suitable driving tool to seat the boots in the housing.

16. Install the caliper in the vehicle.

17. Install the wheel and tire assembly, then carefully lower the vehicle.

18. Properly bleed the brake system.

Brake Disc (Rotor)

REMOVAL & INSTALLATION

Except 1996–97 Accord

▶ See Figure 42

1. Use a siphon or clean turkey baster to remove about half of the brake fluid from the master cylinder.

2. Raise and safely support the vehicle and remove the tire/wheel assembly.

3. Remove the caliper mounting bolts, then lift the caliper assembly away from the brake rotor.

4. Use a suitable piece of wire to suspend the caliper assembly. This will prevent the weight of the caliper from being supported by the brake flex hose which will damage the hose.

5. Once the caliper body and brake pads are removed, unfasten the caliper bracket mounting bolts, then remove the bracket from the rotor.

6. Remove the rotor retaining screws.

7. Remove the brake rotor by pulling it straight off the wheel mounting studs or if seized in place, remove the stubborn brake rotor by threading in two 8 x 1.25mm bolts, two turns at a time until the brake rotor is released.

Fig. 42 After removing the caliper body, unfasten the retaining bolts and remove the caliper mounting bracket, in order to remove the rotor

To install:

8. If necessary, completely retract the piston into the caliper using a large C-clamp or other suitable tool as provided in the front disc brake pad replacement procedures in this section.

9. Install the brake rotor onto the wheel hub and tighten the mounting screws.

10. Install the caliper mounting bracket and secure with the retaining bolts.

11. Install the caliper and pad assembly over the brake rotor and mounting bracket and install the mounting bolts.

12. Fill the master cylinder to the proper level with fresh brake fluid.

13. Install the tire/wheel assembly and lower the vehicle.

14. Pump the brake pedal until the brake pads are seated and a firm pedal is achieved before attempting to move the vehicle.

❊❊ CAUTION

Do not move the vehicle until a firm pedal is obtained.

15. Road test the vehicle to check for proper brake operation.

1996–97 Accord

▶ See Figures 42, 43 and 44

1. Remove the knuckle/hub assembly from the vehicle. See Section 8 for this procedure.

2. Detach the hub from the unit.

Fig. 43 Use a prybar to hold the rotor while removing the attaching bolts

Fig. 44 Once all of the bolts have been removed, pull the hub from the rotor

3. Remove the splash guard from the knuckle.

4. Remove the four flange bolts

5. Pull the hub from the brake rotor.

To install:

6. Installation is the reverse of removal. Refer to Section 8 for knuckle/hub assembly procedures.

7. Tighten the spindle nut to 181 ft. lbs. (245 Nm).

8. Torque the wheel lug nuts to 80 ft. lbs. (108 Nm).

INSPECTION

▶ **See Figures 45 and 46**

Whenever the brake calipers or pads are removed, inspect the rotors for defects. The brake rotor is an extremely important component of the brake system. Cracks, large scratches or warpage can adversely affect the braking system, at times to the point of becoming very dangerous.

Light scoring is acceptable. Heavy scoring or warping will necessitate refinishing or replacement of the disc. The brake disc must be replaced if cracks or burned marks are evident.

If the rotor needs to be replaced with a new part, the protective coating on the braking surface of the rotor must be removed with an appropriate solvent before installing the rotor to the vehicle.

Check the run-out of the hub (disc removed). It should not be more than 0.002 inch (0.050mm). If so, the hub should be replaced.

All brake discs or rotors have markings for MINIMUM allowable thickness cast on an unmachined surface or an alternate surface. Always use this specification as the **minimum** allowable thickness or refinishing limit. Refer to a local auto parts store or machine shop, if necessary, where rotors are resurfaced.

If the rotor needs to be replaced with a new part, the protective coating on the braking surface of the rotor must be removed with an appropriate solvent before installing the rotor to the vehicle.

To properly check a brake rotor, the disc runout, thickness and parallelism should be measured. To perform these measurements proceed as follows:

1. Raise and safely support the vehicle.

2. Remove the tire/wheel assembly for the brake rotor to be inspected.

3. Reinstall the lug nuts and torque to 80 ft. lbs. (108 Nm).

4. Remove the brake pads as outlined in this section.

5. Inspect the brake surface for cracks and damage, then thoroughly clean the brake surface.

6. To measure runout:

a. Attach a dial indicator to a solid portion of the suspension.

b. Set and zero the dial indicator plunger 0.40 inches (10mm) inside the outer circumference of the brake rotor.

c. Rotate the brake rotor and note the amount of runout by reading the dial indicator. If the runout exceeds 0.004 inches (0.10mm), measure the minimum thickness. If rotor thickness is within specification, use an approved on-car brake lathe and machine the brake rotor.

7. To measure the brake rotor thickness and parallelism proceed as follows:

a. Use a micrometer and measure the brake rotor thickness 0.40 inches (10mm) inside the outer circumference of the brake rotor every 45° (⅛ of a rotation).

b. Compare the smallest value measured to the minimum thickness specifications stamped on the brake rotor. If the rotor is below the minimum thickness, the rotor must be replaced. If within specification, measure the parallelism.

c. To measure parallelism, subtract the smallest value measured from the largest value measured. If the parallelism is greater than 0.0006 inches (0.015mm), use an approved on car brake lathe and machine the brake rotor.

➡ **If after machining the brake rotor is below minimum thickness, it must be replaced.**

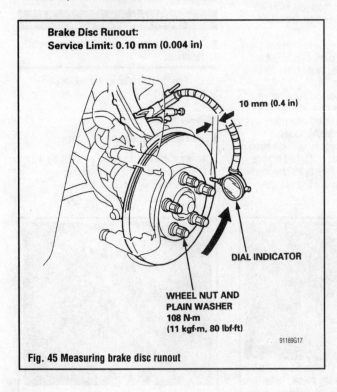

Brake Disc Runout:
Service Limit: 0.10 mm (0.004 in)

10 mm (0.4 in)

DIAL INDICATOR

WHEEL NUT AND
PLAIN WASHER
108 N·m
(11 kgf·m, 80 lbf·ft)

Fig. 45 Measuring brake disc runout

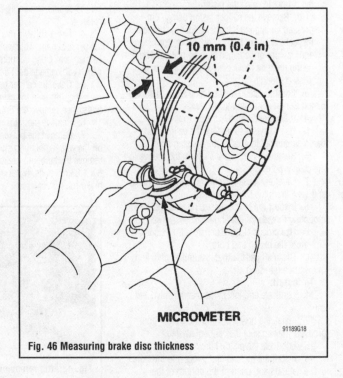

10 mm (0.4 in)

MICROMETER

Fig. 46 Measuring brake disc thickness

DRUM BRAKES

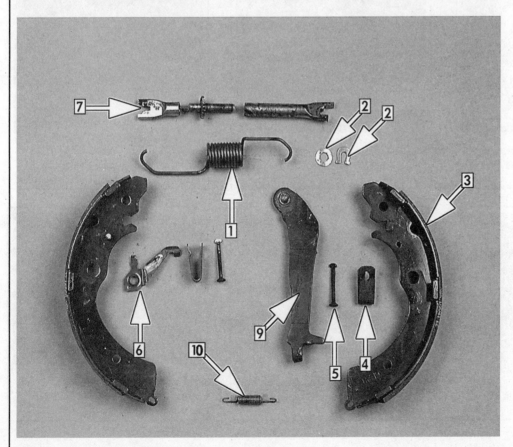

REAR DRUM BRAKE COMPONENT LOCATIONS

1. Upper return spring
2. U-clip and wave washer
3. Brake shoe lining
4. Retainer spring
5. Tension pins
6. Adjuster lever
7. Self-adjuster
8. Adjuster spring
9. Parking brake lever
10. Lower return spring
11. Parking brake cable

91189PB1

Brake Drums

REMOVAL & INSTALLATION

▶ **See Figures 47, 48 and 49**

1. Raise and safely support the rear of the vehicle.
2. Remove the rear tire/wheel assemblies.
3. Thread two 8 x 1.25mm bolts into the threaded holes two turns at a time to lift the drum off the hub.

⁕⁑ WARNING

Do not press the brake pedal with the brake drum removed.

4. Installation is in reverse order of removal.

INSPECTION

▶ **See Figures 50 and 51**

Inspect the drum for cracks, uneven surface wear, scoring, grooves, excessive ridge wear and out of round conditions. If necessary and within wear limits, resurface the brake drum. Otherwise replace it.

Inspect the rear bearing condition with the drum removed. Rotate the rear hub bearings and check for smooth operation.

The maximum allowable inside diameter should be stamped into the brake drum. Measure the inside diameter of the drum to determine if it is within the service limit. If resurfaced, recheck the inside diameter. If the drum exceeds the specification, replace the drum. Compare the measured brake drum inside diameter to the following specifications:

- Standard: 8.657–8.661 inches (219.9–220.0mm)
  - Service Limit: 8.700 inches (221.0mm)
  - Standard: 9.996–10.000 inches (253.9–254.0mm)
  - Service Limit: 10.04 inches (255.0mm)

Brake Shoes

INSPECTION

Inspect the brake linings for cracking, glazing, contamination and wear. If any one shoe is dam-

aged or beyond specification, replace the shoes as a set. Brake shoe lining thickness specifications:

- Standard: 0.15–0.18 inches (3.9–4.5mm)
- Service Limit: 0.08 inches (2.0mm)

REMOVAL & INSTALLATION

▶ **See Figures 52 thru 67**

1. Raise and safely support the rear of the vehicle.
2. Remove the rear tire/wheel assemblies.
3. Remove the brake drums.

⁕⁑ WARNING

Do not press the brake pedal when the brake drum is removed.

4. Place a small paint stick or ruler between the wheel cylinder and rear brake shoe.
5. Clamp a pair of locking pliers securely onto the backing plate at the center of the rear brake shoe.
6. Using locking needle-nose pliers, clamp onto the upper brake spring where the brake adjuster meets the rear shoe. Pull back on the spring and remove it.
7. Remove the lower return spring.
8. Support the back of the brake shoe retainer pin with a finger, and using the special brake tool, or clamping needle-nose pliers, grasp the top of the

Fig. 47 To remove the drum, thread two 8 x 1.25mm bolts into the threaded holes in the front surface of the drum

Fig. 48 Once the bolts are started by hand you may use a small ratchet to speed the process up

Fig. 49 Using both hands, remove the drum by pulling it straight off the lug studs

Fig. 50 Inspect the drum for signs of cracking

Fig. 51 The maximum drum diameter is usually stamped on the outside of the drum

Fig. 52 Brake cleaning machines are commercially available and help avoid some of the mess of cleaning your brakes

Fig. 53 View of the shoes as they appear on the backing plate

Fig. 54 Removing the hub first will ease brake shoe removal

Fig. 55 Use a suitable brake spring tool to remove the upper return spring

Fig. 56 There's a special tool available to remove the retainer springs

Fig. 57 Close up of the retainer spring

Fig. 58 Withdraw the tension pins from the rear of the brake backing plate

Fig. 59 Slide the adjuster from the brake shoe assembly

Fig. 60 View of the adjusting spring and adjuster

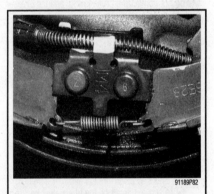

Fig. 61 The lower return spring attaches the bottom of the brake shoes

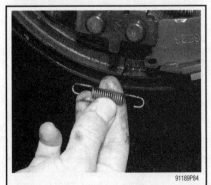

Fig. 62 Unhook and remove the lower return spring

Fig. 63 Hold the cable with a pair of locking pliers and then push back on the parking brake lever to remove it

Fig. 64 Removing the parking brake cable from the parking brake lever

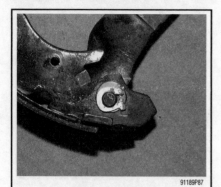

Fig. 65 The U-clip and wave washer hold the parking brake lever to the shoe

Fig. 66 Close up of the U-clip and wave washer

Fig. 67 View of the parking brake lever removed from the brake shoe

Fig. 68 The wheel cylinder is mounted to the brake backing plate

retainer spring, press inward and turn 90° to release it from the pin.

9. Place a suitable elastic band around the wheel cylinder to keep the pistons in place.

❈❈ WARNING

If the wheel cylinder pistons are not held in place when the brake shoes are removed, they may fall out causing fluid loss and component damage. Brake bleeding is necessary if this occurs.

10. Remove the front brake shoe, brake adjuster and related components, then use a pair of suitable pliers to pull the parking brake cable out of the bracket for the rear brake shoe.

11. Place the brake shoe in a vise so that the jaws do not contact the brake lining, and the pivot pin head and the lever arm are supported.

12. Use a hammer and chisel to drive the U-clip off the pin, then remove the lever arm.

13. Inspect the wheel cylinder for seepage, leaks or damage and replace as necessary.

To install:

14. Clean the lever arm and lubricate the pivot point and transfer to the replacement brake shoe.

15. Install the lever arm and brake shoe into the vise, install an new washer, and U-clip, bending the open end of the U-clip closed with flat-nosed pliers.

16. Clean and lubricate the following with an approved high temperature brake grease:
- Brake adjuster threads and clevis pivot
- All raised areas on the brake shoe backing plate that contact the metal portion of the brake shoe.
- The grooves in the wheel cylinder and lower brake shoe resting blocks.

17. Install the brake cable into the rear shoe lever arm, then install the rear shoe onto the backing plate with new retaining pins and springs.

18. Install the paint stick, or suitable ruler, between the rear shoe and the wheel cylinder.

19. Clamp locking pliers securely onto the backing plate at the center of the rear brake shoe.

20. Install the brake adjuster along with the upper and lower springs onto the front shoe, then hook the lower spring into the rear shoe as the front shoe is installed onto the backing plate. Secure the front shoe to the backing plate using a new retaining pin and spring.

21. Remove the elastic band used around the wheel cylinder to keep the pistons in place.

22. Using locking needle-nose pliers, clamp onto the upper brake spring where the brake adjuster meets the rear shoe. Pull back on the spring and install it onto the rear shoe.

23. Remove the locking pliers, and paint stick or ruler. Clean and install the brake drum, and hold in place with two lug nuts.

24. Rotate the brake drum and using a flat blade screwdriver, adjust the brake adjuster until a very light scuffing noise is heard when rotating the drum. If necessary, remove the drum to rotate the adjustment star wheel.

25. Install the wheel/tire assemblies, carefully lower the vehicle and torque the lug nuts to specification.

26. Pump the brake pedal repeatedly several times to set the brake adjusters. If brake pedal pressure is acceptable, test drive the vehicle slowly for approximately 5 minutes and press the brake pedal several times while backing up and pulling forward to set the adjusters and seat the brake shoes.

❈❈ WARNING

Overtightening or over-adjusting the parking brake cable may cause the brakes to drag causing excessive heat build up and brake failure.

27. Check and top off the brake fluid reservoir as necessary.

28. Check the parking brake adjustment and adjust as necessary.

Wheel Cylinders

Inspect the brake backing plate for signs of fluid stains. Remove the brake drums, then pull back the wheel cylinder dust boot and check for signs of brake fluid seepage. If fluid leakage is found in these areas, replace the wheel cylinder.

REMOVAL & INSTALLATION

◆ See Figure 68

1. Raise and safely support the rear of the vehicle.

2. Remove the rear tire/wheel assemblies.

3. Remove the brake drums and brake shoes, as outlined in this section.

4. Install a suitable brake line clamp on the flexible brake line to seal the brake fluid in the system. If the proper tool is not available, do NOT use a pair of locking pliers to clamp the brake line shut.

Instead, drain the fluid from the disconnected brake line into a suitable container, then plug the fitting to avoid contaminating the system.

5. Place a suitable drain pan directly underneath the wheel cylinder. If necessary wash the residual brake fluid away with cold water.

6. Using a brake line wrench, loosen the flare nut 1/8–1/4 turn while watching the metal brake line. If the flare nut moves freely, remove the flare nut and brake line.

❈❈ WARNING

Do not bend or kink the metal hydraulic brake lines

If the metal line moves as the flare nut turns, the line is seized to the flare nut. To overcome this condition, remove the two wheel cylinder mounting bolts, then remove the brake bleeder and carefully pull the wheel cylinder outward until the wheel cylinder can be rotated while holding the flare nut. Install the wheel cylinder in reverse order if necessary.

7. Remove the wheel cylinder mounting bolt(s), and remove the wheel cylinder.

❈❈ WARNING

Use only original grade wheel cylinder mounting bolts when replacing the bolt.

8. Installation is in reverse order of removal, making sure to remove the brake line clamp, properly torque all fasteners and bleed the brake hydraulic system.

OVERHAUL

▶ **See Figures 69 thru 78**

Wheel cylinder overhaul kits may be available, but often at little or no savings over a reconditioned wheel cylinder. It often makes sense with these components to substitute a new or reconditioned part instead of attempting an overhaul.

If no replacement is available, or you would prefer to overhaul your wheel cylinders, the following procedure may be used. When rebuilding and installing wheel cylinders, avoid getting any contaminants into the system. Always use clean, new, high quality brake fluid. If dirty or improper fluid has been used, it will be necessary to drain the entire system, flush the system with proper brake fluid, replace all rubber components, then refill and bleed the system.

1. Remove the wheel cylinder from the vehicle and place on a clean workbench.

2. First remove and discard the old rubber boots, then withdraw the pistons. Piston cylinders are equipped with seals and a spring assembly, all located behind the pistons in the cylinder bore.

3. Remove the remaining inner components, seals and spring assembly. Compressed air may be useful in removing these components. If no compressed air is available, be VERY careful not to score the wheel cylinder bore when removing parts from it. Discard all components for which replacements were supplied in the rebuild kit.

4. Wash the cylinder and metal parts in denatured alcohol or clean brake fluid.

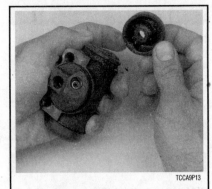

Fig. 69 Remove the outer boots from the wheel cylinder

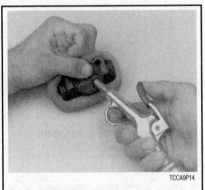

Fig. 70 Compressed air can be used to remove the pistons and seals

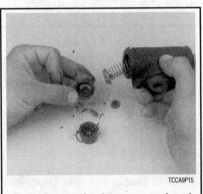

Fig. 71 Remove the pistons, cup seals and spring from the cylinder

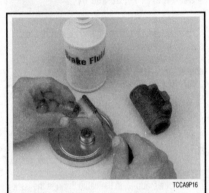

Fig. 72 Use brake fluid and a soft brush to clean the pistons . . .

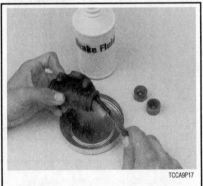

Fig. 73 . . . and the bore of the wheel cylinder

Fig. 74 Once cleaned and inspected, the wheel cylinder is ready for assembly

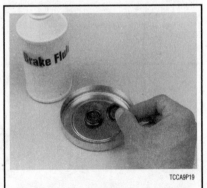

Fig. 75 Lubricate the cup seals with brake fluid

Fig. 76 Install the spring, then the cup seals in the bore

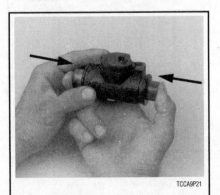

Fig. 77 Lightly lubricate the pistons, then install them

Fig. 78 The boots can now be installed over the wheel cylinder ends

❄ WARNING

Never use a mineral-based solvent such as gasoline, kerosene or paint thinner for cleaning purposes. These solvents will swell rubber components and quickly deteriorate them.

5. Allow the parts to air dry or use compressed air. Do not use rags for cleaning, since lint will remain in the cylinder bore.

6. Inspect the piston and replace it if it shows scratches.

7. Lubricate the cylinder bore and seals using clean brake fluid.

8. Position the spring assembly.

9. Install the inner seals, then the pistons.

10. Insert the new boots into the counterbores by hand. Do not lubricate the boots.

11. Install the wheel cylinder.

PARKING BRAKE

Cable(s)

REMOVAL & INSTALLATION

▶ **See Figures 79, 80 and 81**

1. Disconnect the negative battery cable.
2. Loosen the lug nuts, then raise and safely support the vehicle.
3. Detach the parking brake switch electrical connector.
4. Release the parking brake lever, then disconnect the parking brake cable.
5. Remove the parking brake lever assembly.
6. Remove the brake shoes as necessary to access the cable attached to the brake shoe bracket, and disconnect the cable.
7. Slide a 12mm offset boxed end wrench onto the brake cable to compress the cable-to-backing plate retainer, and slide the cable through the backing plate.
8. Remove the parking brake cable guide brackets attached to the vehicle's underbody and remove the cable.
9. Installation is in reverse order of the removal procedure, making sure upon completion the parking brake is properly adjusted.

ADJUSTMENT

❄ CAUTION

An over-adjusted parking brake cable may not allow the rear brake self-adjusters to function properly.

The parking brake shares the brake shoes with the hydraulic brake. If the shoes are worn and the hydraulic brake shoe adjustment is not functioning properly, they should be checked and adjusted before proceeding with the parking brake adjustment. A typical symptom of a brake system that may need adjustment is when the parking brake is released, the hydraulic brake pedal is pumped repetitively 3 times and the pedal height and/or pedal pressure increases.

❄ WARNING

Overtightening the parking brake cable may cause the brakes to drag causing excessive heat build up and brake failure.

1. Remove the screw covers, screws and parking brake trim cover.

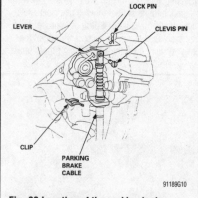

Fig. 80 Location of the parking brake cable-to-rear caliper attachment

Fig. 81 View of the parking brake cable adjusting mechanism

2. Turn the adjuster as needed to attain the proper adjustment.

➡ **Make sure the brakes do not drag when the parking brake lever is released.**

3. Reinstall the trim cover.
4. Lift the parking brake so it engages 2 notches.
5. Tighten the adjusting nut at the lever assembly until the rear brakes just begin to drag when rotated.
6. Release the parking brake lever and check that the wheels do not drag when turned. The parking brake should engage in 3–5 notches when a force of 66 lbs. (294N) is applied to the parking brake pedal.
7. Lower the vehicle.

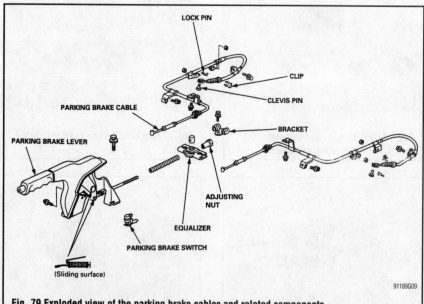

Fig. 79 Exploded view of the parking brake cables and related components

ANTI-LOCK BRAKE SYSTEM

General Information

▶ See Figures 82 and 83

When conventional brakes are applied in an emergency stop or on ice, one or more wheels may lock. This may result in loss of steering control and vehicle stability. The purpose of the Anti-lock Brake System (ABS) is to prevent lock up when traction is marginal or under heavy braking conditions. This system offers many benefits allowing the driver increased safety and control during braking. Anti-lock braking operates only at speeds above 3 mph (5 km/h).

Under normal braking conditions, the ABS functions the same as a standard brake system with a diagonally split master cylinder and conventional vacuum assist.

If wheel lock is detected during the brake application, the system will enter anti-lock mode. During anti-lock mode, hydraulic pressure in the four wheel circuits is modulated to prevent any one wheel from locking. Each wheel circuit is designed with a set of electrical valves and hydraulic line to provide modulation, although for vehicle stability, both rear wheel valves receive the same electrical signal. The system can build or reduce pressure at each wheel, depending on signals generated by the Wheel Speed Sensors (WSS) at each wheel and received at the Controller Anti-lock Brake (CAB).

Anti-lock Braking Systems (ABS) are available on all Honda models. When this system engages, some audible noise as well as pulses in the brake pedal may occur. Do not be alarmed; this is normal system operation.

PRECAUTIONS

Failure to observe the following precautions may result in system damage:
• Before performing electric arc welding on the vehicle, disconnect the control module and the hydraulic unit connectors.
• When performing painting work on the vehicle, do not expose the control module to temperatures in excess of 185°F (85°C) for longer than 2 hours. The system may be exposed to temperatures up to 200°F (95°C) for less than 15 minutes.
• Never disconnect or connect the control module or hydraulic modulator connectors with the ignition switch **ON**.
• Never disassemble any component of the Anti-Lock Brake System (ABS) which is designated unserviceable; the component must be replaced as an assembly.
• When filling the master cylinder, always use brake fluid which meets DOT-3 specifications; petroleum-based fluid will destroy the rubber parts.
• Working on ABS system requires extreme amount of mechanical ability, training and special tools. If you are not familiar, have your vehicle repaired by a certified mechanic.

Diagnosis and Testing

▶ See Figure 84

Much like the Powertrain Control Module (PCM), the ABS system is capable of storing Diagnostic Trouble Codes (DTCs) which can be

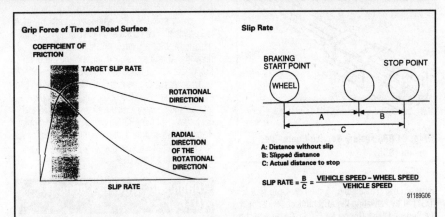

Fig. 82 The ABS computer uses information from the wheel speed sensors to determine the maximum possible braking on any type of road surface

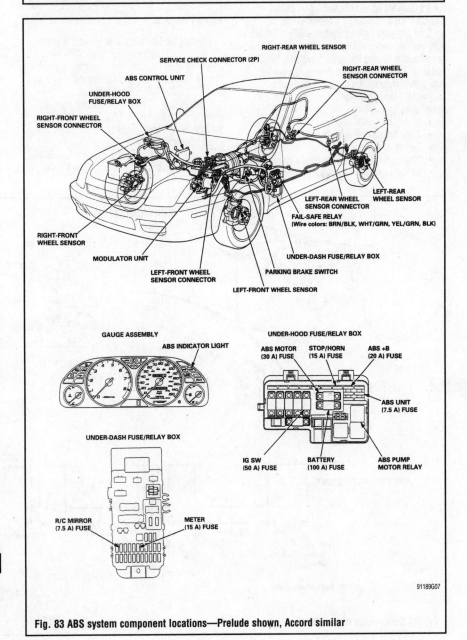

Fig. 83 ABS system component locations—Prelude shown, Accord similar

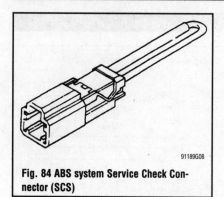

Fig. 84 ABS system Service Check Connector (SCS)

accessed using a suitable 16-pin Data Scan Tool (DST) or by activating the ABS blink codes using the Service Check Connector (SCS). Because of the complexity of the ABS system and the importance of correct system operation, it is a good idea to have a qualified automotive technician inspect the system if any problems have been detected.

If the Anti-lock Braking System (ABS) is OK, the ABS indicator lamp will light and then go out two seconds after turning the ignition switch to the **ON** position. The ABS lamp may illuminate a second time and then go off again. This is also normal.

The ABS lamp may illuminate under the below conditions.

- When only the drive wheels spin.
- If one drive wheel is stuck.
- During vehicle spin.
- If the ABS continues to operate for a long time.
- If there is signal disturbance is detected.

The ABS lamp may or may not stay illuminated continuously if a fault is detected. It depends which DTC was detected and if the system corrected the problem or not. The ABS lamp may go off only after the problem is corrected and the vehicle has been restarted and driven a few miles. Remember it depends on which code was thrown and the duration or number of times that the code was detected.

This system can perform an initial diagnosis and a regular diagnosis. The initial diagnosis is performed immediately after the engine is started and continues until the ABS lamp goes out. The regular diagnosis is performed after the initial system check and monitors the system constantly until the ignition switch is turned **OFF**.

Diagnostic Trouble Codes (DTCs)

READING DIAGNOSTIC TROUBLE CODES

♦ **See Figure 85**

Reading the control module memory is one of the first steps in system diagnostics. This step should be initially performed to determine the general nature of the fault. Subsequent readings will determine if the fault has been cleared.

Reading codes can be performed using a suitable 16-pin Data Scan Tool (DST) or by activating the ABS system blink codes using the SCS service check connector.

To read the fault codes, connect the 16-pin DST scan tool according to the manufacturer's instruc-

tions. Follow the manufacturer's specified procedure for accessing and reading the codes.

To activate the self check ABS blink code, the vehicle must be turned **OFF**, not moving, SCS service connector installed, and the brake pedal released. Then proceed as follows:

1. Block the wheels as necessary to prevent moving.

2. With the ignition in the **OFF** position, locate the SCS service check cable connection under the vehicle's dash, and install the shunting tool, SCS Service Connector Tool No. 07PAZ-0010100 or its equivalent.

3. Once the SCS tool is installed, make sure the brake pedal is released, turn the ignition **ON** and record the ABS indicator light blinking frequency.

4. The ABS indicator should light for 2 seconds, then shut off for 3.6 seconds and begin to flash the stored DTCs. The ABS indicator light shuts off for 3.6 seconds between flashing each stored DTC. The DTC is a two digit code. The first digit is displayed by the ABS indicator light staying on in 1.3 second increments, then a 0.5 second pause, and the second digit flashed in 0.3 of a second increments. Hence code 32 would be displayed as three long flashes followed by two short flashes of the ABS indicator light.

5. Turn the ignition switch **OFF**, clear the stored DTCs and remove the SCS connector.

Following are the ABS trouble codes for Accord and Prelude models.

- Code 11: Front right wheel sensor has an open or short to the body ground or a short to power.
- Code 12: Front left wheel sensor electrical noise or an intermittent interruption.

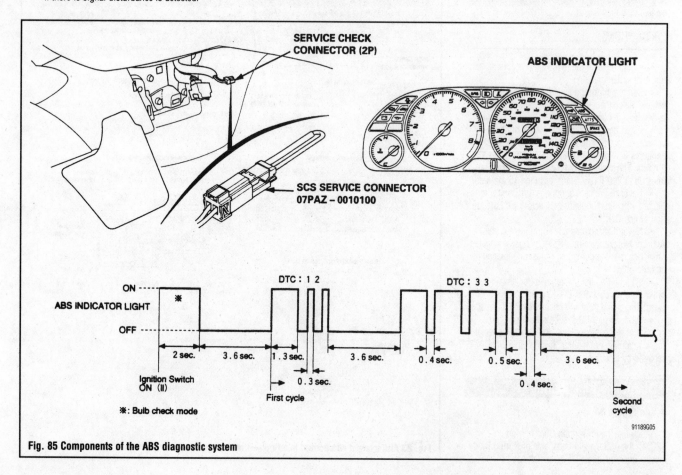

Fig. 85 Components of the ABS diagnostic system

- Code 13: Rear right wheel sensor has an open or short to the body ground or a short to power.
- Code 14: Rear left wheel sensor electrical noise or an intermittent interruption.
- Code 15: Front right wheel sensor has an open or short to the body ground or a short to power.
- Code 16: Front left wheel sensor electrical noise or an intermittent interruption.
- Code 17: Rear right wheel sensor has an open or short to the body ground or a short to power.
- Code 18: Rear left wheel sensor electrical noise or an intermittent interruption.
- Code 21: Pulser
- Code 22: Pulser
- Code 23: Pulser
- Code 24: Pulser
- Code 31: Front right input solenoid has a short to ground or a short to wire.
- Code 32: Front right output solenoid has a short to ground or a short to wire.
- Code 33: Front left input solenoid has a short to ground or a short to wire.
- Code 34: Front left output solenoid has a short to ground or a short to wire.
- Code 35: Rear right input solenoid has a short to ground or a short to wire.
- Code 36: Rear right output solenoid has a short to ground or a short to wire.
- Code 37: Rear left input solenoid has a short to ground or a short to wire.
- Code 38: Rear left output solenoid has a short to ground or a short to wire.
- Code 41: Front right wheel lock.
- Code 42: Front left wheel lock.
- Code 43: Right rear wheel lock.
- Code 44: Left rear wheel lock.
- Code 51: Motor lock.
- Code 52: Motor stuck off.
- Code 53: Motor stuck on.
- Code 54: Fail safe relay.
- Code 61: Ignition voltage.
- Code 62: Ignition voltage.
- Code 71: Different diameter tire.
- Code 81: Central Processing Unit (CPU)

CLEARING DIAGNOSTIC TROUBLE CODES

The Diagnostic Trouble Codes (DTCs) are cleared using a 16-pin Diagnostic Scan Tool (DST), a vehicle manufacturer's specific tester, or by using the shunting tool, SCS Service Connector Tool No. 07PAZ-0010100 or its equivalent.

Follow the tool manufacturer's instructions when using a 16-pin DST to erase the DTCs. To use the SCS shunting tool proceed as follows:

1. Block the wheels as necessary to prevent moving.
2. With the ignition in the OFF position, locate the SCS service check cable connection under the vehicle's dash as illustrated in Section 4, and install the SCS shunting tool or its equivalent.
3. Once the SCS tool is installed, press and hold the brake pedal, then turn the ignition ON while holding the brake pedal pressed.
4. The ABS indicator should light for 2 seconds, then shut off, then the brake pedal is released.
5. The ABS indicator lights again within 4 seconds, when the indicator light comes on, press and

hold the brake pedal until the light goes out, then release the brake pedal.
6. If the ABS indicator shuts off for 4 seconds, then quickly blinks 2 times, the DTCs are erased.
7. Turn the ignition switch OFF, remove the SCS connector.
8. Start the engine and check that the ABS indicator lamp goes out. Test drive the vehicle to allow the ABS system to perform a dynamic check.
9. If the ABS indicator light comes on while operating the vehicle, recheck the DTCs, diagnose and repair as necessary.

ABS Modulator

♦ See Figure 86

The ABS Modulator Unit contains solenoid valves for each wheel. These valves are independent of each other and are positioned vertically for improved maintainability. The modulators for the rear wheels act as proportioning control valves to prevent the rear wheels from locking up in the event the anti-lock braking system is malfunctioning or not activated.

The ABS Modulator Unit consists of the inlet solenoid valve, reservoir, pump, pump motor and the damping chamber. The modulator controls pressure reduction, pressure retaining, and pressure intensifying for each wheel.

REMOVAL & INSTALLATION

♦ See Figure 86

1. Disconnect the negative battery cable.
2. Remove the modular unit mounting bolts.
3. Detach the pump motors connectors.

♦ See Figure 87

WARNING

Always use a flare nut wrench on the fittings, to prevent stripping of the flare nuts.

4. Disconnect the brake lines using a flare nut wrench.
5. Remove the modular unit from the bracket assembly.
   To install:
6. Install the modulator unit.
7. Connect the brake lines, using a flare nut wrench. Tighten the fittings to 11 ft. lbs. (15 Nm).
8. Connect the modulator unit.
9. Attach the pump motor connectors.
10. Bleed the brake system beginning with the left front brake caliper. Bleed each fitting until all air is removed. Proceed in the order given in the procedure earlier in this section.
11. Connect the negative battery cable.
12. After starting the engine, check to make sure the ABS lamp is not illuminated.
13. Drive the vehicle and check that the ABS light does not come on.
14. Check and clear codes as necessary.

ABS Control Unit

♦ See Figure 87

The ABS control unit and Powertrain Control Module (PCM) manage the entire system via inputs from various sensors and programmed decisions which are stored within the unit. This management system includes the Vehicle Speed Sensor (VSS), pump motor, various electronic solenoids, ABS wheel sensors and an internal self-diagnostic mode. The main function of the ABS control unit is to per-

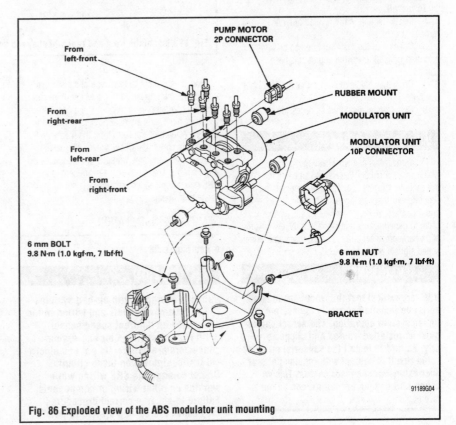

Fig. 86 Exploded view of the ABS modulator unit mounting

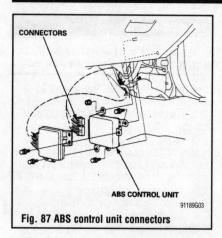

Fig. 87 ABS control unit connectors

form calculations on the signals received from each one of the sensors at the wheels. This will enable it to control the system by actuating solenoid valves that regulate the flow and pressure of the brake fluid to each wheel. The system was designed with a sub-function that gives driving signals to the pump motor as well as signals the self-diagnostic mode which is a necessity for backing up the anti-lock braking system.

REMOVAL & INSTALLATION

▶ See Figure 87

1. Disconnect the negative battery cable.
2. Remove the passenger's right kick panel.
3. Detach the ABS control unit electrical connectors.
4. Remove the ABS control unit by removing the mounting fasteners.

To install:

5. Install the unit in the reverse order of removal.
6. Check that the ABS light comes on briefly and then goes off once the engine has been started.
7. Drive the vehicle to ensure that the ABS light does not come on.
8. Check and clear codes as necessary.

Wheel Speed Sensor

Each wheel has its own wheel speed sensor which sends a small AC electrical signal to the control module. Correct ABS operation depends on accurate wheel speed signals. The vehicle's wheels and tires must all be the same size and type in order to generate accurate signals. If there is a variation between wheel and tire sizes, inaccurate wheel speed signals will be produced.

✲✲ WARNING

It is very critical that the wheel speed sensor(s) be installed correctly to ensure continued system operation. The sensor cables must be installed, routed and clipped properly. Failure to install the sensor(s) properly could result in contact with moving parts or over extension of sensor cables. This will cause ABS component failure and an open circuit.

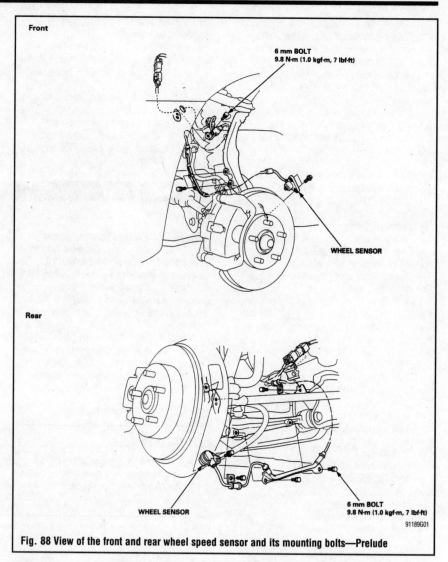

Fig. 88 View of the front and rear wheel speed sensor and its mounting bolts—Prelude

Honda uses a contactless type of sensor that detects the rotating speed of the wheel. It is constructed of a permanent magnet and a coil. Attached to the rotating parts are gear pulsers (a.k.a. Tone Rings). When these pulsers turn, the magnetic flux around the coil in the wheel sensor alternates its current. This generates voltages in a frequency or wave pattern. These wave pulses are sent to the ABS control unit which identifies the speed of each of the four wheels.

REMOVAL & INSTALLATION

▶ See Figure 88

✲✲ CAUTION

Vehicles equipped with air bag systems (SRS) have components and wiring in the same area as the front speed sensor wiring harnesses. The air bag system connectors are yellow. Do not use electrical test equipment on these circuits. Do not damage the SRS wiring while working on other wiring or components. Failure to observe correct procedures may cause the air bag system to inflate

unexpectedly or render the system totally inoperative.

1. Raise and safely support the vehicle as necessary for access.
2. Make certain the ignition switch is **OFF**.
3. Detach the sensor harness connector.
4. Beginning at the connector end, remove grommets, clips or retainers as necessary to free the harness. Take careful note of the placement and routing of the harness; it must be reinstalled in the exact original position.
5. Remove the bolt holding the speed sensor to its mounting, then remove the sensor. If it is stuck in place, gently tap on the side of the mounting flange with a hammer and small punch; do not tap on the sensor.

To install:

6. Place the sensor in position; install the retaining bolts loosely. Route the harness correctly. Avoid twisting or crimping the harness; use the white line on the wires as a guide.
7. Once the harness and sensor are correctly but loosely placed, tighten the sensor mounting bolts. Tighten bolts to 16 ft. lbs. (22 Nm).
8. Working from the sensor end to the connector, install each clip, retainer, bracket or grommet

holding the sensor harness. The harness must not be twisted. Tighten any bolt holding brackets to 84 inch lbs. (10 Nm).

9. Attach the wiring connector.

10. Use the ABS checker to check for proper signal from the wheel speed sensor.

11. Carefully lower the vehicle to the ground.

INSPECTION

▶ See Figure 89

1. Use a non-metallic feeler gauge to measure the gap between the sensor and the pulser.

2. Rotate the hub or axle slowly by hand, taking measurements at several locations and compare with the following specifications:

- Front and Rear: 0.020–0.040 in. (0.5–1.0mm)

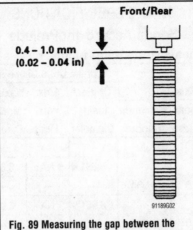

Fig. 89 Measuring the gap between the tone wheel and the wheel speed sensor

Tone Ring (Pulser)

Inspect the tone ring for any built up debris and clean as necessary. If any one tooth is damaged, it must be replaced.

The ABS tone ring on the front of all vehicles is an integral component of the halfshaft assemblies and cannot be serviced separately, therefore if the tone ring requires service, the halfshaft assembly must be replaced.

Bleeding the ABS System

The ABS brake system is bled in the usual fashion with no special procedures required. Refer to the bleeding procedure located earlier in this section. Make certain the master cylinder reservoir is filled before the bleeding is begun and check the level frequently.

BRAKE SPECIFICATIONS
Honda Accord and Prelude
All measurements in inches unless noted

Year	Model		Brake Disc Original Thickness	Brake Disc Minimum Thickness	Brake Disc Maximum Runout	Brake Drum Diameter Original Inside Diameter	Max. Wear Limit	Maximum Machine Diameter	Minimum Lining Thickness Front	Minimum Lining Thickness Rear	Brake Caliper Bracket Bolts (ft. lbs.)	Mounting Bolts (ft. lbs.)
1996	Accord	F	0.910	0.830	0.004	—	—	—	0.060	—	80	54
		R	—	—	—	8.661	NA	8.071	—	0.080	—	—
	Accord Wagon	F	0.990	0.910	0.004	—	—	—	0.060	—	80	54
		R	—	—	—	8.661	NA	8.071	—	0.080	—	—
	Accord V6	F	0.990	0.910	0.004	—	—	—	0.060	—	80	54
		R	—	—	—	8.661	NA	8.071	—	0.080	—	—
	Accord w/rear disc	F	—	—	—	—	—	—	—	—	—	—
		R	0.358	0.310	0.004	—	—	—	—	0.060	28	17
	Prelude	F	0.910	0.830	0.004	—	—	—	0.060	—	80	36
		R	0.390	0.320	0.004	—	—	—	—	0.060	28	17
1997	Accord	F	0.910	0.830	0.004	—	—	—	0.060	—	80	54
		R	—	—	—	8.661	NA	8.071	—	0.080	—	—
	Accord Wagon	F	0.990	0.910	0.004	—	—	—	0.060	—	80	54
		R	—	—	—	8.661	NA	8.071	—	0.080	—	—
	Accord V6	F	0.990	0.910	0.004	—	—	—	0.060	—	80	54
		R	—	—	—	8.661	NA	8.071	—	0.080	—	—
	Accord w/rear disc	F	—	—	—	—	—	—	—	—	—	—
		R	0.358	0.310	0.004	—	—	—	—	0.060	28	17
	Prelude	F	0.910	0.830	0.004	—	—	—	0.060	—	80	36
		R	0.390	0.320	0.004	—	—	—	—	0.060	28	17
1998	Accord	F	0.910	0.830	0.004	—	—	—	0.060	—	80	54
		R	—	—	—	8.661	NA	8.071	—	0.080	—	—
	Accord w/rear disc	F	—	—	—	—	—	—	—	—	—	—
		R	0.358	0.310	0.004	—	—	—	—	0.060	28	17
	Prelude	F	0.910	0.830	0.004	—	—	—	0.060	—	80	36
		R	0.390	0.320	0.004	—	—	—	—	0.060	28	17
1999	Accord	F	0.910	0.830	0.004	—	—	—	0.060	—	80	54
		R	—	—	—	8.661	NA	8.071	—	0.080	—	—
	Accord w/rear disc	F	—	—	—	—	—	—	—	—	—	—
		R	0.358	0.310	0.004	—	—	—	—	0.060	28	17
	Prelude	F	0.910	0.830	0.004	—	—	—	0.060	—	80	36
		R	0.390	0.320	0.004	—	—	—	—	0.060	28	17
2000	Accord	F	0.910	0.830	0.004	—	—	—	0.060	—	80	54
		R	—	—	—	8.661	NA	8.071	—	0.080	—	—
	Accord w/rear disc	F	—	—	—	—	—	—	—	—	—	—
		R	0.358	0.310	0.004	—	—	—	—	0.060	28	17
	Prelude	F	0.910	0.830	0.004	—	—	—	0.060	—	80	36
		R	0.390	0.320	0.004	—	—	—	—	0.060	28	17

F - Front   NA - Not Available
R - Rear

91189C01

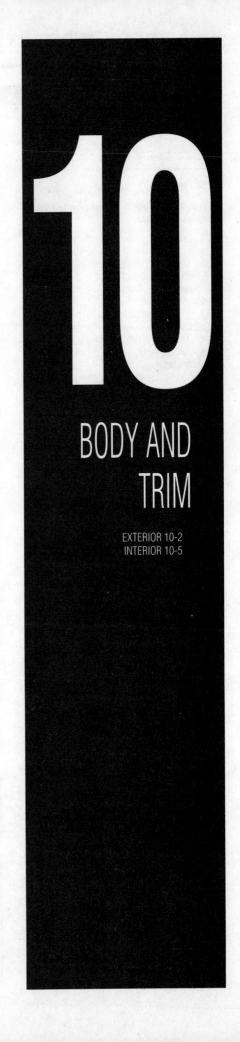

10

BODY AND
TRIM

EXTERIOR 10-2
INTERIOR 10-5

EXTERIOR

Doors

REMOVAL & INSTALLATION

▶ See Figure 1

➡Front and rear doors may be removed using the same procedure.

1. Disconnect the negative battery cable.
2. Protect the door and surrounding trim and painted areas using cardboard and masking tape. A thick masking tape is available at local body and paint supply stores. Cover and protect any corners, sharp edges or protruding objects.
3. Support the door, by placing a floor jack and a piece of wood underneath the door.
4. Remove the bolts from the door stop arm.
5. Remove the door panel, detach the wiring connectors, and guide clips.
6. Remove the wiring harness from the door frame. If necessary, use tape to keep the wiring pulled aside.
7. Inspect and make sure all applicable wiring connectors are disconnected and removed.
8. Matchmark the location of the hinges on the door and/or vehicle frame.
9. Unfasten the hinge bolts, then remove the door assembly.

To install:

➡If necessary, make shims out of scrap sheet metal, paint stirring sticks or cardboard and tape in place with masking tape to the area to be aligned or shimmed.

10. Position the door into place and finger tighten the hinge bolts.
11. Align the door with the hinge marks made earlier and tighten the bolts.
12. Attach the wiring connectors.

13. Attach the door stop arm and tighten the bolts to 89 inch lbs. (10 Nm).
14. Remove the supporting jack.
15. Install the door panel.
16. Connect the negative battery cable.

ADJUSTMENT

▶ See Figures 2 and 3

When checking door alignment, look carefully at each seam between the door and body. The gap should be constant and even all the way around the door. Pay particular attention to the door seams at the corners farthest from the hinges; this is the area where errors will be most evident. Additionally, the door should pull in against the weatherstrip when latched to seal out wind and water. The contact should be even all the way around and the stripping should be about half compressed.

The position of the door can be adjusted in three dimensions: fore and aft, up and down, in and out. The primary adjusting points are the hinge-to-body bolts. Apply tape to the fender and door edges to protect the paint. Two layers of common masking tape works well. Loosen the bolts just enough to allow the hinge to move in place. With the help of an assistant, position the door and retighten the bolts. Inspect the door seams carefully and repeat the adjustment until correctly aligned.

The in-out adjustment (how far the door "sticks out" from the body) is adjusted by loosening the hinge-to-door bolts. Again, move the door into place, then retighten the bolts. This dimension affects both the amount of crush on the weatherstrips and the amount of "bite" on the striker.

The door should be adjusted such that the leading edge of the door just below or no more than level with the adjoining body panel. The trailing edge of the door should be adjusted such the edge of the panel is slightly above the adjoining body panel. If not properly adjusted, the doors are likely to cause a wind noise.

Further adjustment for closed position and smoothness of latching is made at the latch plate or striker. This piece is located at the rear edge of the door and is attached to the bodywork; it is the piece the latch engages when the door is closed. Although the striker size and style may vary between models or from front to rear, the method of adjusting it is the same:

1. Loosen the large cross-point screw(s) holding the striker. Know in advance that these bolts will be very tight; an impact screwdriver is a handy tool to have for this job. Make sure you are using the proper size bit.
2. With the bolts just loose enough to allow the striker to move if necessary, hold the outer door handle in the released position and close the door. The striker will move into the correct location to match the door latch. Open the door and tighten the mounting bolts. The striker may be adjusted towards or away from the center of the car, thereby tightening or loosening the door fit.
3. The striker can be moved up and down to compensate for door position, but if the door is correctly mounted at the hinges this should not be necessary.

➡Do not attempt to correct height variations (sag) by adjusting the striker.

Additionally, some models may use one or more spacers or shims behind the striker or at the hinges. These shims may be removed or added in combination to adjust the reach of the striker or hinge.

4. After the striker bolts have been tightened, open and close the door several times. Observe the motion of the door as it engages the striker; it should continue its straight-in motion and not deflect up or down as it hits the striker.
5. Check the feel of the latch during opening and closing. It must be smooth and linear, without any trace of grinding or binding during engagement and release.

It may be necessary to repeat the striker adjustment several times (and possibly re-adjust the hinges) before the correct door to body match is produced. This can be a maddening process of loosen and tighten, check and readjust; have patience.

If a door makes a knocking noise over bumps, it's likely the striker is not centered in the door latch. Inspect, loosen and lightly tap the striker up or down as necessary.

Hood

REMOVAL & INSTALLATION

▶ See Figures 4 and 5

➡The help of an assistant is recommended when removing or installing the hood.

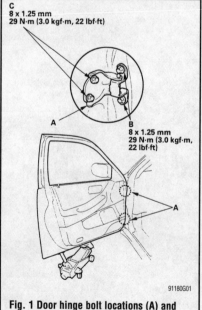

C
8 x 1.25 mm
29 N·m (3.0 kgf·m, 22 lbf·ft)

B
8 x 1.25 mm
29 N·m (3.0 kgf·m, 22 lbf·ft)

A

91180G01

Fig. 1 Door hinge bolt locations (A) and tightening specifications (B & C)

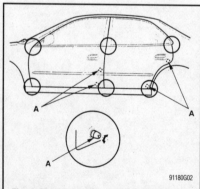

91180G02

Fig. 2 Check the areas shown to make sure the door and body edges are parallel

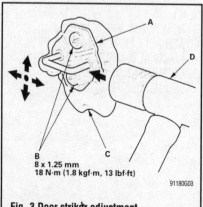

A

D

B
8 x 1.25 mm
18 N·m (1.8 kgf·m, 13 lbf·ft)

C

91180G03

Fig. 3 Door striker adjustment

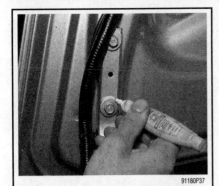

Fig. 4 Matchmark the installed position of each hood bolt

Fig. 5 Remove the fasteners using a closed end wrench

1. Open and support the hood.
2. Disconnect the negative battery cable.
3. Protect the body with covers to prevent damage to the paint.
4. Use a suitable marker, or scribe marks around the hinge locations for reference during installation.
5. Unplug any electrical connections and windshield washer hoses that would interfere with hood removal.
6. While an assistant helps secure the hood, unfasten the attaching bolts, then remove the hood from the vehicle.

To install:
7. Place the hood into position. Install and partially tighten attaching bolts.
8. Adjust the hood with the reference marks and tighten the attaching bolts.
9. Check the hood for an even fit between the fenders and for flush fit with the front of the fenders. Also, check for a flush fit with the top of the cowl and fenders. If necessary, adjust the hood latch.
10. Attach any electrical connections or windshield washer hoses that were disconnected during hood removal.

ALIGNMENT

Once the hood is installed, tighten the hood-to-hinge bolts just snug. Close the hood and check for perfect seam alignment. The hood seams are one of the most visible on the car; the slightest error will be plainly obvious to an observer.

Loosen the bolts and position the hood as necessary, then snug the nuts and recheck. Continue the process until the hood latches smoothly and aligns evenly at all the seams.

➡️**Do not adjust hood position by moving the latch.**

The hood bolts and the hinge mount bolts may be loosened to adjust their positions. Shims may be used behind the hinge mounts if necessary. When everything aligns correctly, tighten the bolts securely.

The elevation of the hood at the latch end may be adjusted by turning the rubber stops or cushions. These bumpers have threaded bottoms and move up or down when turned. An annoying hood rattle on bumps may be caused by missing cushions, or misalignment of the hood.

Trunk Lid

REMOVAL & INSTALLATION

1. Disconnect the negative battery cable.
2. Protect the trunk and surrounding trim and painted areas using cardboard and masking tape. A thick masking tape is available at local body and paint supply stores. Cover and protect any corners, sharp edges or protruding objects.
3. Open the trunk and support it in the open position.
4. If necessary, remove any trim panels for access to the trunk retaining bolts.
5. Detach any necessary wiring from the trunk. If necessary, use tape to keep the wiring pulled aside.
6. Inspect and make sure all applicable wiring connectors are disconnected and removed.
7. Matchmark the location of the hinges/bolts on the trunk and/or vehicle frame.
8. Remove the bolts and remove the trunk assembly.

➡️**If necessary, make shims out of scrap sheet metal, paint stirring sticks or cardboard and tape in place with masking tape to the area to be aligned or shimmed.**

9. Installation is the reverse of the removal procedure. Make sure to align the trunk with the marks made earlier and tighten the bolts.

Tailgate

REMOVAL & INSTALLATION

Accord Wagon

1. Disconnect the negative battery cable.
2. Protect the tailgate and surrounding trim and painted areas using cardboard and masking tape. A thick masking tape is available at local body and paint supply stores. Cover and protect any corners, sharp edges or protruding objects.
3. Support the tailgate, by placing a floor jack and a piece of wood underneath the tailgate.
4. Remove the bolts from the tailgate stop arm.
5. Remove the tailgate interior trim panel, detach the wiring connectors, and guide clips.

6. Remove the wiring harness from the tailgate frame. If necessary, use tape to keep the wiring pulled aside.
7. Inspect and make sure all applicable wiring connectors are disconnected and removed.
8. Matchmark the location of the hinges on the tailgate and/or vehicle frame.
9. Remove the hinge bolts and remove the tailgate assembly.

To install:

➡️**If necessary, make shims out of scrap sheet metal, paint stirring sticks or cardboard and tape in place with masking tape to the area to be aligned or shimmed.**

10. Position the tailgate into place and finger tighten the hinge bolts.
11. Align the tailgate with the hinge marks made earlier and tighten the bolts.
12. Attach the wiring connectors.
13. Attach the tailgate stop arm.
14. Remove the supporting jack.
15. Install the tailgate interior trim panel.
16. Connect the negative battery cable.

Grille

REMOVAL & INSTALLATION

▶ **See Figures 6 and 7**

➡️**Use caution not to scratch the front grille.**

1. On 1998–00 Accord models, remove the front bumper.

Fig. 6 Remove the fasteners from the front grille . . .

Fig. 7 . . . then pull the grille from the vehicle as shown

2. Remove the front grill mounting screws.

3. Depress the front clips on each side with a flat-tip screwdriver.

4. Remove the grille from the vehicle

5. Installation is the reverse of removal.

Outside Mirrors

REMOVAL & INSTALLATION

Mirror Assembly

▶ See Figure 8

1. Disconnect the negative battery cable.

2. Lower the door glass and unsnap the inside triangular mirror trim by hand.

3. If equipped with power mirrors, detach the electrical connector.

4. Remove the mirror mounting bolts/screws, and remove the mirror assembly.

5. Installation is the reverse of the removal procedure.

Mirror Glass

✳✳ CAUTION

Wear gloves and eye protection when removing the mirror glass.

1. Carefully pull out the bottom edge of the mirror holder by hand.

2. Carefully and evenly, pull the lower edge of the mirror holder slowly, until it unsnaps from the actuator.

To install:

3. If the hooks stuck to the mirror holder, remove them and reinstall them onto the actuator base.

4. Carefully align the clips and hooks, and using even pressure, snap the mirror holder onto the actuator base.

5. Check the mirror operation.

Antenna

REPLACEMENT

Pillar Mount

On later model vehicles, the radio antenna may be an integral part of the rear window. The window and the antenna must be replaced as a unit. If your vehicle has a pillar or trunk mounted antenna, follow the below procedure.

1. Detach the negative battery cable.

2. Remove the two antenna-to-windshield pillar mounting screws.

3. Pull up on the antenna's base to break it free from the pillar.

4. Slightly feed the antenna cable out of the a pillar

5. Detach the antenna cable from the underside of the antenna's base plate.

6. Remove the antenna.

7. Installation is the reverse of removal.

Trunk Mount

➡ **Before beginning this procedure, check with your local parts supplier as to the availability of the antenna. This part may only be sold at your local Honda dealer.**

1. Gain access to the antenna motor.

2. Remove the trim panel.

3. Detach the connector from the motor.

4. Disconnect the antenna lead.

5. Remove the antenna nut from the top of the fender.

6. Remove the motor bracket nut.

7. Remove the motor and antenna as an assembly.

8. Remove the antenna nut spacer.

9. Connect the wiring harness to the antenna assembly.

10. Carefully pull out the antenna while an assistant turns on the radio.

To install:

11. Carefully steer the teeth of the new antenna mast cable into the antenna housing.

12. Check the engagement by gently moving the cable up and down a few times.

13. Clean and lubricate the antenna mast housing threads with a light penetrating oil.

14. Turn the radio switch off and let the power antenna's motor pull the cable down into the housing.

15. Install the bushing, spacer, and the nut.

16. The remaining steps are the reverse of the removal procedure.

Fenders

REMOVAL & INSTALLATION

1. Disconnect the negative battery cable.

2. Open and support the hood with the prop rod.

3. Remove the grille and front bumper.

4. Remove the two piece pin and clips from the inner fender liner, then remove the self-tapping screws and remove the inner fender liner.

5. Detach the electrical connectors for the headlights, remove the headlight mounting bolts and the headlight assembly.

6. Protect the edges of the fender and door with masking tape as necessary.

7. Matchmark the fender to the inner fender for reassembly. Trace the outline of the fender to inner fender with a sharpened No. 2 pencil.

8. Open the front doors as necessary to access and remove the rear fender mounting bolts.

9. Remove the fender mounting bolts at the front cowl, headlight opening and along the top of the fender in the engine compartment.

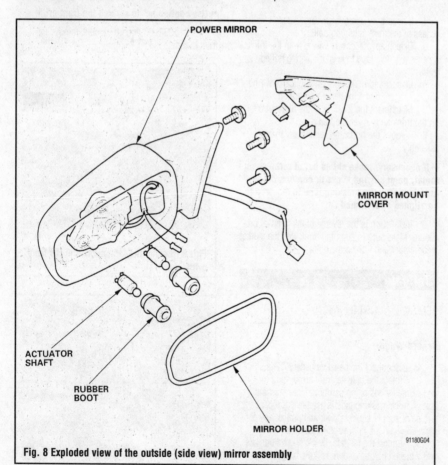

POWER MIRROR

MIRROR MOUNT COVER

ACTUATOR SHAFT

RUBBER BOOT

MIRROR HOLDER

91180G04

Fig. 8 Exploded view of the outside (side view) mirror assembly

10. Have an assistant help remove the fender from the vehicle.

11. Installation is the reverse of the removal procedure.

Power Sunroof

REMOVAL & INSTALLATION

SUNROOF PANEL

1. Open the sunroof halfway.
2. Carefully unsnap the front of the liner by pulling it downward.
3. Slide the liner toward the back to release the pins from the holder and remove the liner.
4. Remove the panel mounting bolts from the panel bracket, then carefully lift the sunroof from the vehicle.

To install:

5. Inspect the sunroof liner clips and replace as necessary.
6. Install the sunroof in reverse order of removal.

7. Adjust the sunroof such that the panel is level with the sunroof seal and not more than ³⁄₃₂ inches (2mm) above the roof of the vehicle.

MOTOR REPLACEMENT

▶ **See Figure 9**

➡ **If the sunroof motor fails, the sunroof can be closed by removing the slotted plug between the sun visors and using the tool provided in the tool kit to manually wind the sunroof shut.**

1. Remove the headliner to access the motor.
2. Detach the motor electrical connector.
3. Remove the screws holding the motor in place, then remove the motor from the bracket assembly.
4. Installation is the reverse of the removal procedure.

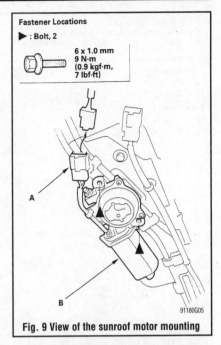

Fastener Locations

▶ : Bolt, 2

6 x 1.0 mm
9 N·m
(0.9 kgf·m,
7 lbf·ft)

91180G05

Fig. 9 View of the sunroof motor mounting

INTERIOR

Instrument Panel and Pad

REMOVAL & INSTALLATION

1. Remove the console, as outlined in this section.
2. Detach the glove box, as outlined in this section.
3. Remove the radio, as outlined in Section 6.
4. Detach all necessary switches and connectors such as the cruise control master switch, panel brightness controller, or the rear window defogger switch.
5. Remove the heater air vent.
6. Detach the mixture control cables.
7. Lower the steering column.
8. Remove the screws and then carefully pull out the instrument panel.
9. Installation is the reverse of removal.

Console

REMOVAL & INSTALLATION

▶ **See Figures 10, 11 and 12**

1. Detach the negative battery cable.
2. Open the arm rest.
3. Remove the inner cover panel.
4. Remove the access lid and screws.
5. Remove the cup holder.
6. Lift up the parking brake.
7. Lift the front of the console and slide it rearward. This will detach it from the mounting hooks below.
8. Remove the rear console by sliding it over the parking brake.
9. Detach the ashtray.
10. Lift up the console and detach any electrical connectors.

➡ **Use caution not to scratch the automatic transaxle shift lever.**

11. Remove the shift knob vehicles equipped with manual transaxles.
12. Remove the radio.

91180P16

Fig. 10 Remove the rear console . . .

91180P17

Fig. 11 . . . to gain access to the two front fasteners

13. Remove the dashboard lower cover.
14. Glove box.
15. Remove the front console.

➡ **Wrap a clean shop towel around the gear selector to prevent damage during removal and installation of the console.**

16. Installation is the reverse of removal.

Dashboard

REMOVAL & INSTALLATION

▶ **See Figure 13**

➡ **Before disconnecting the battery cable(s) or the radio electrical connectors, make sure to note the radio security code. Once disconnected, the radio will not function until the code is entered.**

✳ CAUTION

The models covered by this manual are equipped with a Supplemental Restraint System (SRS), which uses an air bag. Whenever working near any of the SRS components, such as the impact sensors, the air bag module, steering column and instrument panel, disable the SRS, as described in Section 6.

1. Note the radio security code and disconnect the negative battery cable.
2. Disable the Supplemental Restraint System (SRS) as outlined in Section 6.
3. Remove the following components, most of which are outlined in this section:
   - Console
   - Glove box
   - Driver's side lower dash cover

- Replace any damaged clips.
- Make sure the connectors are plugged in properly.
- Readjust the parking brake cable, if necessary (see page 19-6).

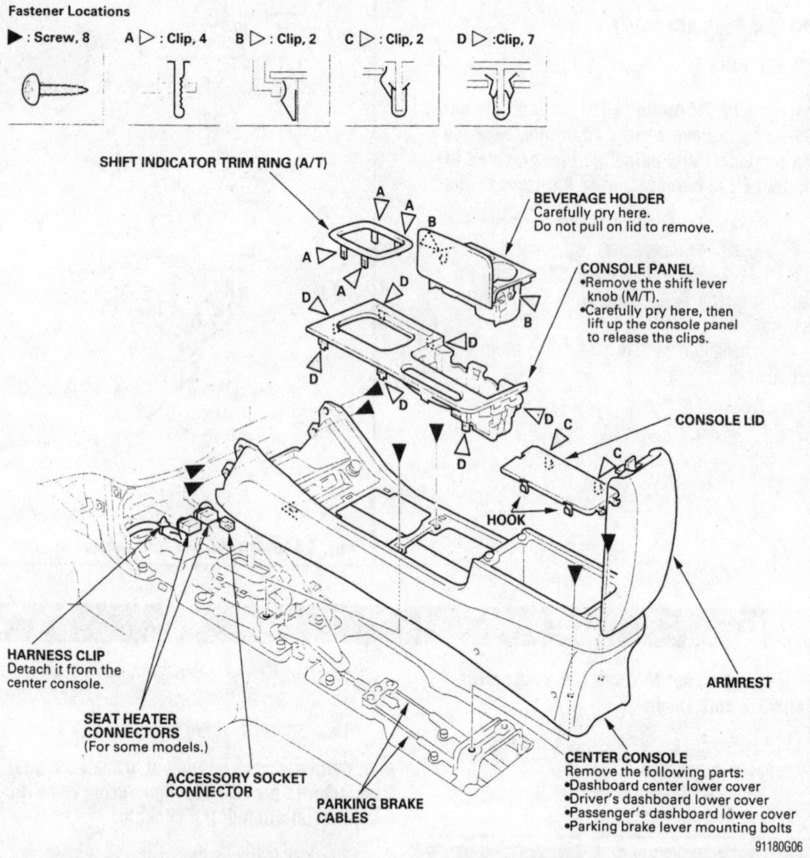

Fastener Locations

▶ : Screw, 8   A ▷ : Clip, 4   B ▷ : Clip, 2   C ▷ : Clip, 2   D ▷ : Clip, 7

SHIFT INDICATOR TRIM RING (A/T)

BEVERAGE HOLDER
Carefully pry here.
Do not pull on lid to remove.

CONSOLE PANEL
•Remove the shift lever knob (M/T).
•Carefully pry here, then lift up the console panel to release the clips.

CONSOLE LID

HOOK

ARMREST

HARNESS CLIP
Detach it from the center console.

SEAT HEATER CONNECTORS
(For some models.)

ACCESSORY SOCKET CONNECTOR

PARKING BRAKE CABLES

CENTER CONSOLE
Remove the following parts:
•Dashboard center lower cover
•Driver's dashboard lower cover
•Passenger's dashboard lower cover
•Parking brake lever mounting bolts

91180G06

Fig. 12 Exploded view of the center console assembly

91186P35

Fig. 13 Unscrew all fasteners and remove the dashboard cover

- Driver's side lower knee bolster
- Lower center console trim (automatic transaxle)
- Center pocket/beverage holder (automatic transaxle)
- Center console (manual transaxle)
- Center dashboard lower cover
- Dashboard center panel
- Driver's side electric switch panel

4. Remove the instrument cluster, as outlined in Section 6.

5. Detach the driver's air bag electrical connector and lower the steering column.

6. Unsnap the driver's side dash cover. Remove the screw in the passenger's lower side cover and unsnap to remove.

7. Detach the dash electrical connectors from the upper portion of the left side under dash fuse/relay panel. Remove the two fasteners, then move the left side under dash fuse/relay panel aside.

8. Disconnect the antenna lead, and disconnect the harness clips.

9. Remove the electrical connector holder from the dashboard frame.

10. Unbolt the control unit/relay bracket from the behind the center of the dash.

11. Remove the dash panel bolts.

12. Cover the lower inside of the windshield trim with protective tape.

13. Verify that all electrical connectors, brackets and clips have been disconnected.

14. Carefully lift and remove the dashboard assembly.

15. Installation is in reverse order of removal, making sure to properly activate the SRS and enter the radio security code.

Dash Panels, Covers and Vents

REMOVAL & INSTALLATION

➡Before disconnecting the battery cable(s) or the radio electrical connectors, make sure to

note the radio security code. Once disconnected, the radio will not function until the code is entered.

✳✳ CAUTION

The models covered by this manual are equipped with a Supplemental Restraint System (SRS), which uses an air bag. Whenever working near any of the SRS components, such as the impact sensors, the air bag module, steering column and instrument panel, disable the SRS, as described in Section 6.

Perform the following procedures BEFORE working on the interior components.

1. Note the radio security code and disconnect the negative battery cable.

2. Disable the Supplemental Restraint System (SRS) as outlined in Section 6.

✳✳ CAUTION

Failure to observe the previously stated repair procedures could result in severe physical injury.

Glove box

1. Open the glove box and release the two limiting stops from both sides of the glove box.

2. Remove the two Phillips screws that secure the glove box hinges, and remove the glove box.

3. Installation is the reverse of the removal procedure.

Driver's Side Lower Dash Cover

1. Remove the Phillips screws from the lower left and right corners.

2. Carefully pull the panel to release the clips on the upper portion of the panel. There are 3 clips on the left, and one on the right.

3. Installation is the reverse of the removal procedure.

Driver's Side Lower Knee Bolster

1. Remove the driver's lower dash cover.

2. Remove the knee bolster mounting bolts and release the bolster from the hooks to remove.

3. Installation is the reverse of the removal procedure.

Door Panels

REMOVAL & INSTALLATION

▶ See Figures 14, 15, 16 and 17

1. Remove the outside (side view) mirror.

2. If equipped with manual windows, remove the regulator handle by pulling the clip out with a small wire hook.

3. Remove the screw from the door handle trim.

4. Slide the handle assembly forward and out to access the lock rod clip.

5. Release the clip

6. Disconnect the door lock switch

7. Remove the inner door handle assembly.

8. Carefully pry at the small opening on the bottom of the speaker grill.

9. Remove the speaker grille.

10. Remove the speaker mounting screws.

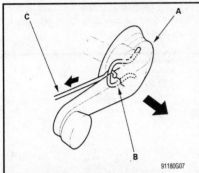

Fig. 14 Remove the window regulator handle (A) by using a small hook (C) to remove the retaining clip (B)

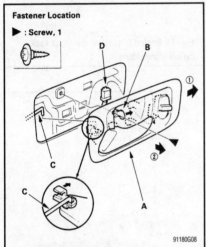

Fig. 15 To remove the inner handle, pry the cap out (B) and remove the screw. Pull the handle forward and halfway out, then detach the rod (C) and power door lock connector (D)

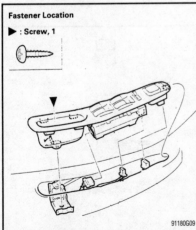

Fig. 16 Exploded view of the armrest (also called the door pull pocket panel)—model equipped with power windows shown

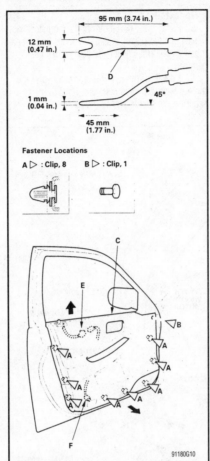

Fig. 17 Location of the door trim retaining clips. Also, note the trim pad removal tool which makes releasing the clips much easier

11. Detach the electrical connector and remove the speaker.

12. Remove the caps screws in the armrest (pull pocket panel), then remove the armrest.

13. Remove the center from the trim clip at the upper front of the door panel and remove the clip.

14. Using a suitable trim panel removal tool, unsnap the door panel from the door frame and detach any necessary electrical connectors.

15. Carefully lift the door panel up and away from the door frame.

16. Installation is the reverse of the removal procedure.

Door Locks

REMOVAL & INSTALLATION

▶ See Figure 18

1. Remove the door panel.
2. Remove the plastic vapor barrier.
3. Remove the lock cylinder and outer door handle.
4. Remove the bolt from the rear window channel guide.
5. Unplug the electrical connectors, wire harness clips and inner handle rod.

6. Remove the latch mounting screws, using a hand impact driver if necessary.

7. Installation is the reverse of the removal procedure.

Tailgate/Trunk Lock

REMOVAL & INSTALLATION

▶ See Figure 19

1. Remove the door panel.
2. Remove the plastic vapor barrier.
3. Release the lock cylinder rod retainer clip and disconnect the rod.
4. Remove the U-shaped retainer clip, then remove the lock cylinder.
5. Remove the outer door handle retainer bolts, and pull the handle out.
6. Wrap a clean soft shop towel around the handle to protect the door from damage and use a pair of diagonal cutting pliers to gently pry the release rod clip out of the handle. Replace the door handle-to-release rod clip.
7. Installation is the reverse of the removal procedure.

➡ Making sure to use a new release rod clip.

Door Glass and Regulator

REMOVAL & INSTALLATION

▶ See Figures 18, 20 and 21

1. Remove the door trim panel.
2. Remove the screws securing the pull pocket bracket. If equipped with power windows, remove the nut securing the center stiffener.
3. Remove the plastic cover (vapor barrier).

❈❈ CAUTION

When removing the window, be very careful not the drop the glass inside the door!

4. Carefully raise the glass until the bolts are visible, then remove the bolts. Carefully pull the glass out through the window slot.
5. Refer to the accompanying figure, then disconnect and detach the connector (A) and harness clip (B) from the door. Remove the bolts (C & D), then remove the regulator (F) through the hole in the door.
6. Installation is the reverse of the removal procedure.

Electric Window Motor

REMOVAL & INSTALLATION

▶ See Figures 22 and 23

1. Remove the regulator from the door assembly. Refer to the procedure in this section.
2. Except for the rear doors, drill a hole through the regulator sector gear and backplate. Install the bolt and nut to lock the sector gear in position. Be careful not to drill a hole closer than 7/16 in. (11mm) from the edge of the sector. Also, do not drill

through the lift arm attaching portion of the sector gear, or the joint integrity will be jeopardized.

3. Drill out the ends of the motor attaching rivets using a ¼ in. (6mm) bit.

4. Remove the motor and the remaining portions of the rivets from the regulator. Except for the rear doors, one rivet will not be accessible until assembly.

To install:

5. Position the new motor to the regulator. With the aid of an assistant, install new rivets by collapsing or crushing the rivet ends using a ball peen hammer.

6. Except for the rear doors, once two of the three rivets have been installed, remove the bolt securing the sector gear to the backplate, then

use an appropriate electrical source (such as the vehicle's window motor harness) to rotate the regulator, providing access to the remaining rivet.

7. Except for the rear doors, use a flat nosed rotary file to grind off one sector gear tooth from the side which does not contact the driven gear. This is

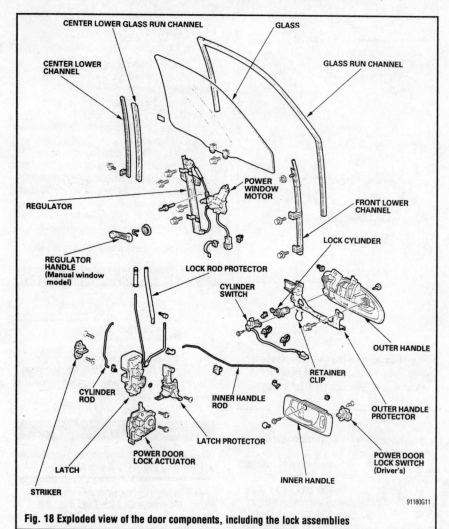

Fig. 18 Exploded view of the door components, including the lock assemblies

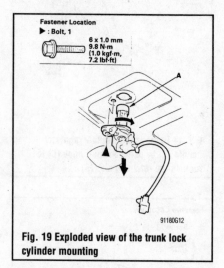

Fig. 19 Exploded view of the trunk lock cylinder mounting

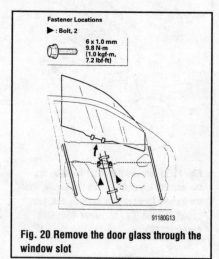

Fig. 20 Remove the door glass through the window slot

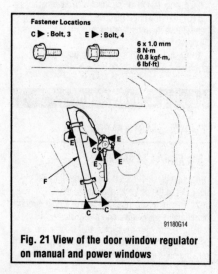

Fig. 21 View of the door window regulator on manual and power windows

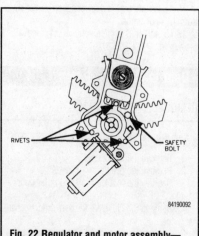

Fig. 22 Regulator and motor assembly—except rear doors

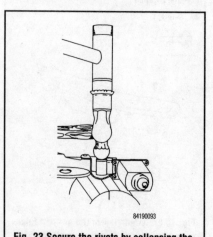

Fig. 23 Secure the rivets by collapsing the rivet ends using a ball peen hammer

necessary to reach the remaining rivet. Remove the old rivet, then install the remaining new rivet.

8. Install the regulator to the door assembly.

Windshield and Fixed Glass

REMOVAL & INSTALLATION

If your windshield, or other fixed window, is cracked or chipped, you may decide to replace it with a new one yourself. However, there are two main reasons why replacement windshields and other window glass should be installed only by a professional automotive glass technician: safety and cost.

The most important reason a professional should install automotive glass is for safety. The glass in the vehicle, especially the windshield, is designed with safety in mind in case of a collision. The windshield is specially manufactured from two panes of specially-tempered glass with a thin layer of transparent plastic between them. This construction allows the glass to "give" in the event that a part of your body hits the windshield during the collision, and prevents the glass from shattering, which could cause lacerations, blinding and other harm to passengers of the vehicle. The other fixed windows are designed to be tempered so that if they break during a collision, they shatter in such a way that there are no large pointed glass pieces. The professional automotive glass technician knows how to install the glass in a vehicle so that it will function optimally during a collision. Without the proper experi-

ence, knowledge and tools, installing a piece of automotive glass yourself could lead to additional harm if an accident should ever occur.

Cost is also a factor when deciding to install automotive glass yourself. Performing this could cost you much more than a professional may charge for the same job. Since the windshield is designed to break under stress, an often life saving characteristic, windshields tend to break VERY easily when an inexperienced person attempts to install one. Do-it-yourselfers buying two, three or even four windshields from a salvage yard because they have broken them during installation are common stories. Also, since the automotive glass is designed to prevent the outside elements from entering your vehicle, improper installation can lead to water and air leaks. Annoying whining noises at highway speeds from air leaks or inside body panel rusting from water leaks can add to your stress level and subtract from your wallet. After buying two or three windshields, installing them and ending up with a leak that produces a noise while driving and water damage during rainstorms, the cost of having a professional do it correctly the first time may be much more alluring. We here at Chilton, therefore, advise that you have a professional automotive glass technician service any broken glass on your vehicle.

WINDSHIELD CHIP REPAIR

◗ See Figures 24 thru 38

➥Check with your state and local authorities on the laws for state safety inspection. Some

states or municipalities may not allow chip repair as a viable option for correcting stone damage to your windshield.

Although severely cracked or damaged windshields must be replaced, there is something that you can do to prolong or even prevent the need for replacement of a chipped windshield. There are many companies which offer windshield chip repair products, such as Loctite's® Bullseye™ windshield repair kit. These kits usually consist of a syringe, pedestal and a sealing adhesive. The syringe is mounted on the pedestal and is used to create a vacuum which pulls the plastic layer against the glass. This helps make the chip transparent. The adhesive is then injected which seals the chip and helps to prevent further stress cracks from developing. Refer to the sequence of photos to get a general idea of what windshield chip repair involves.

➥Always follow the specific manufacturer's instructions.

Inside Rear View Mirror

REPLACEMENT

◗ See Figure 39

1. Carefully pry the cover off using a suitable prytool.
2. Remove the rubber damper from the mirror stalk.
3. If secured with screws, remove the machine screws from the base and remove the mirror.

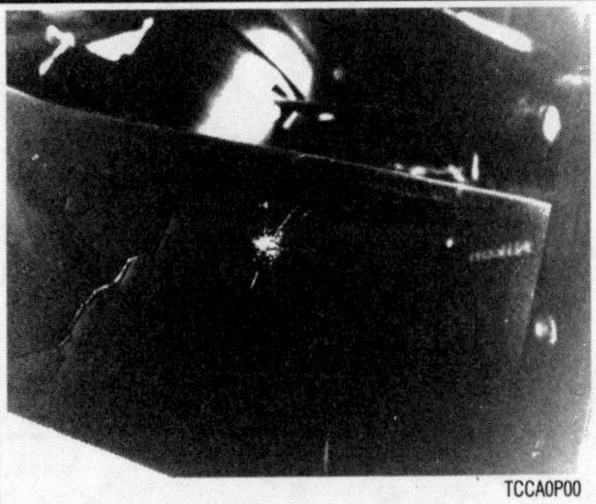

Fig. 24 Small chips on your windshield can be fixed with an aftermarket repair kit, such as the one from Loctite®

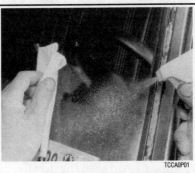

Fig. 25 To repair a chip, clean the windshield with glass cleaner and dry it completely

Fig. 26 Remove the center from the adhesive disc and peel off the backing from one side of the disc . . .

Fig. 27 . . . then press it on the windshield so that the chip is centered in the hole

Fig. 28 Be sure that the tab points upward on the windshield

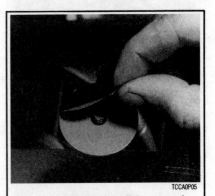

Fig. 29 Peel the backing off the exposed side of the adhesive disc . . .

Fig. 30 . . . then position the plastic pedestal on the adhesive disc, ensuring that the tabs are aligned

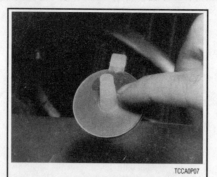

Fig. 31 Press the pedestal firmly on the adhesive disc to create an adequate seal . . .

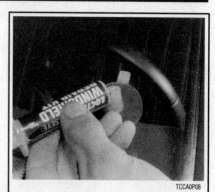

Fig. 32 . . . then install the applicator syringe nipple in the pedestal's hole

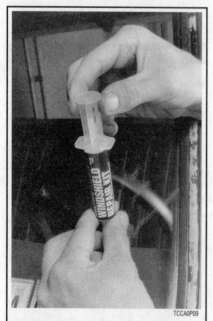

Fig. 33 Hold the syringe with one hand while pulling the plunger back with the other hand

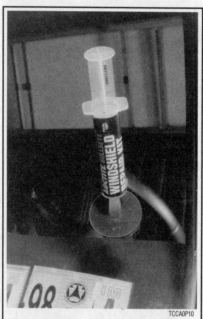

Fig. 34 After applying the solution, allow the entire assembly to sit until it has set completely

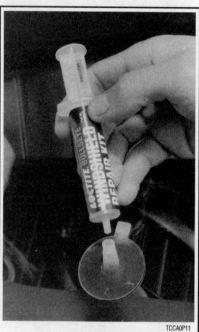

Fig. 35 After the solution has set, remove the syringe from the pedestal . . .

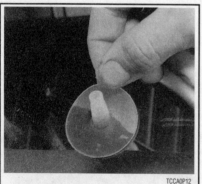

Fig. 36 . . . then peel the pedestal off of the adhesive disc . . .

Fig. 37 . . . and peel the adhesive disc off of the windshield

Fig. 38 The chip will still be slightly visible, but it should be filled with the hardened solution

4. If not secured with screws, slide the rearview mirror down toward the bottom of the windshield, and detach it from spring in the mount. Be careful not to scratch the mirror base.

5. Installation is the reverse of the removal procedure. If equipped with a mirror that does not have mounting screws, fit the mirror base over the mount, then secure the mirror by turning the base 90 degrees.

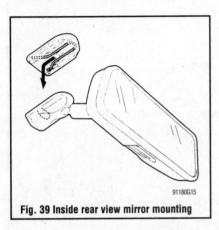

Fig. 39 Inside rear view mirror mounting

Seats

REMOVAL & INSTALLATION

Front Seats

▶ **See Figures 40 and 41**

1. Slide the seat forward.
2. Detach the seat track end/bolt covers.
3. Remove the attaching bolts.
4. Slide the seat rearward.

Fig. 40 Removing the mounting bolts that attach the front seat to the floor

5. Remove the seat track end covers.
6. Remove the attaching bolts.
7. Lift the seat and then detach the seat electrical connectors and wiring harness clips.
8. Carefully remove the seat through the front door.
9. Installation is the reverse of the removal procedure.

Rear Seats

▶ **See Figures 42 and 43**

For rear seat removal & installation, please refer to the accompanying illustrations.

Power Seat Motor

REMOVAL & INSTALLATION

1. Remove the negative battery cable.
2. Remove the seat.
3. Remove the connector from the power seat motor.
4. Remove the bolts that secure the power seat motor to the seat frame.
5. Remove the seat motor.
6. Installation is the reverse of the removal procedure.

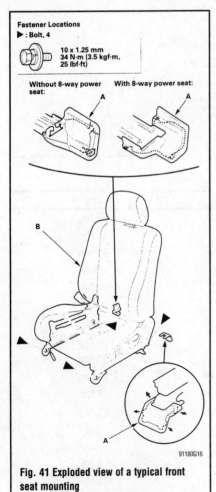

Fig. 41 Exploded view of a typical front seat mounting

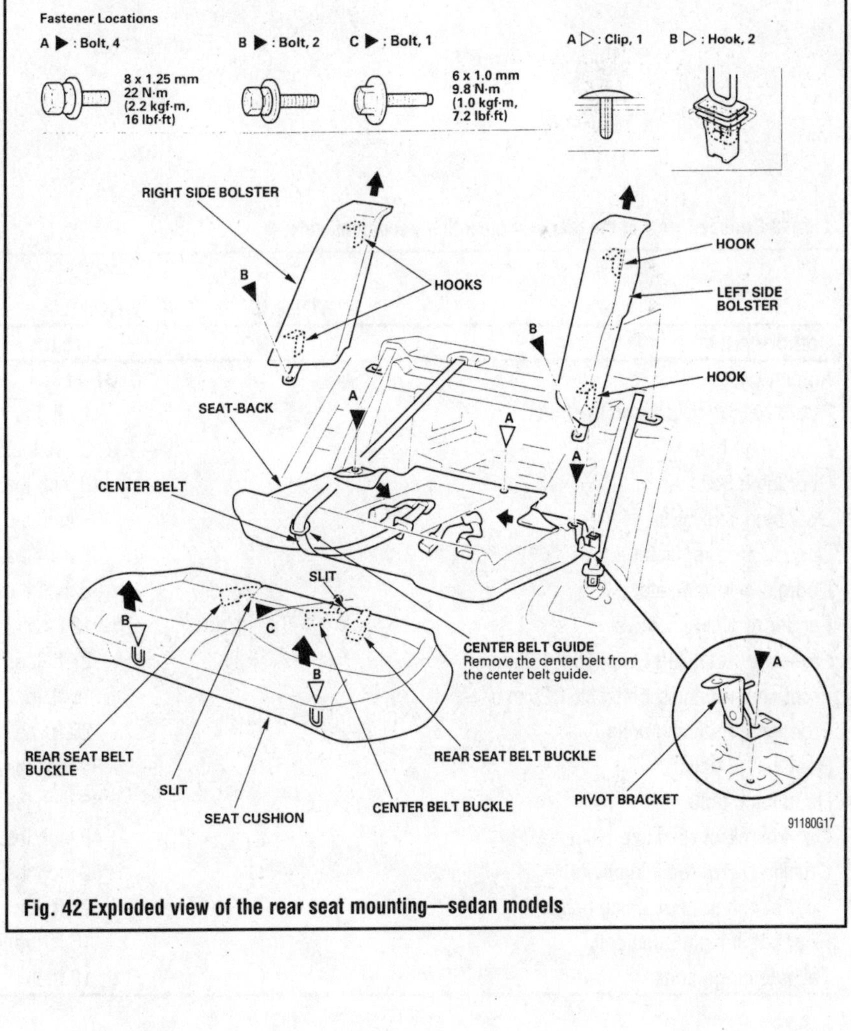

Fastener Locations
▶ : Bolt, 4

10 x 1.25 mm
34 N·m (3.5 kgf·m,
25 lbf·ft)

Without 8-way power seat: With 8-way power seat:

Fig. 42 Exploded view of the rear seat mounting—sedan models

Fastener Locations

A ▶ : Bolt, 4   B ▶ : Bolt, 2   C ▶ : Bolt, 1   A ▷ : Clip, 1   B ▷ : Hook, 2

8 x 1.25 mm
22 N·m
(2.2 kgf·m,
16 lbf·ft)

6 x 1.0 mm
9.8 N·m
(1.0 kgf·m,
7.2 lbf·ft)

RIGHT SIDE BOLSTER

HOOKS

HOOK

LEFT SIDE BOLSTER

HOOK

SEAT-BACK

CENTER BELT

SLIT

CENTER BELT GUIDE
Remove the center belt from
the center belt guide.

REAR SEAT BELT BUCKLE

REAR SEAT BELT BUCKLE

SLIT

SEAT CUSHION

CENTER BELT BUCKLE

PIVOT BRACKET

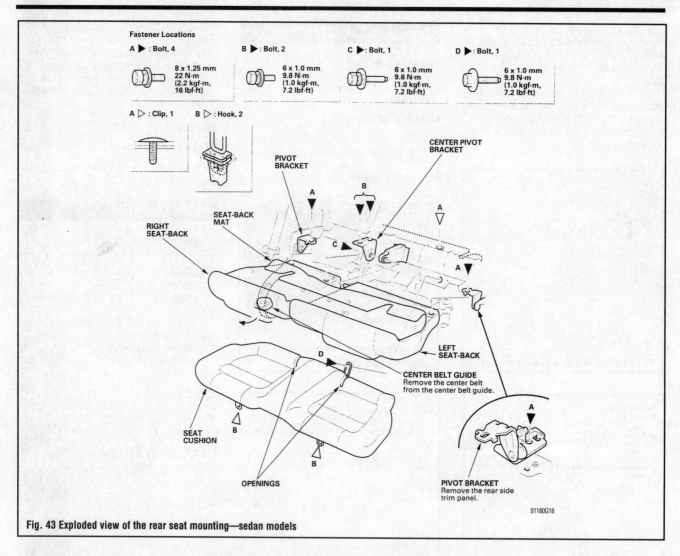

Fig. 43 Exploded view of the rear seat mounting—sedan models

TORQUE SPECIFICATIONS

Components	ft. lbs.	Nm
Antenna nut	31-44 inch lbs.	4-5 Nm
Door / hatch / tailgate striker bolts	13 ft. lbs.	18 Nm
Door hinge bolts	22 ft. lbs.	29 Nm
Door latch bolts	48 inch lbs.	6 Nm
Door stop arm bolts	89 inch lbs.	10 Nm
Doorglass-to-regulator	60 inch lbs.	7 Nm
Doorglass-to-regulator	86 inch lbs.	9.8 Nm
Fender retaining screws	89-124 inch lbs.	10-14 Nm
Front seat retaining bolts, 10 x 1.25 mm	27 ft. lbs.	37 Nm
Front seat retaining bolts, 8x 1.25 mm	16 ft. lbs.	22 Nm
Front seat retaining bolts	25 ft. lbs.	34 Nm
Hood hinge bolts	86 inch lbs.	9.8 Nm
Hood latch bolts	86 inch lbs.	9.8 Nm
Outside mirror retaining bolts	48 inch lbs.	6 Nm
Outside mirror retaining bolts	86 inch lbs.	9.8 Nm
Rear bench seat retaining bolts	25 ft. lbs.	34 Nm
Rear hatch hinge nuts/bolts	16 ft. lbs.	22 Nm
Tailgate hinge bolts	19 ft. lbs.	26 Nm

91180C01

11

TROUBLE-SHOOTING

Condition	Section/Item Number

The following troubleshooting charts are divided into 7 sections covering engine, drive train, brakes, wheels/tires/steering/suspension, electrical accessories, instruments and gauges, and climate control. The first portion (or index) consists of a list of symptoms, along with section and item numbers. After selecting the appropriate condition, refer to the corresponding diagnostic procedure in the second portion's specified location.

INDEX

SECTION 1. ENGINE

A. Engine Starting Problems

Gasoline Engines

Engine turns over, but will not start	1-A, 1
Engine does not turn over when attempting to start	1-A, 2
Engine stalls immediately when started	1-A, 3
Starter motor spins, but does not engage	1-A, 4
Engine is difficult to start when cold	1-A, 5
Engine is difficult to start when hot	1-A, 6

Diesel Engines

Engine turns over but won't start	1-A, 1
Engine does not turn over when attempting to start	1-A, 2
Engine stalls after starting	1-A, 3
Starter motor spins, but does not engage	1-A, 4
Engine is difficult to start	1-A, 5

B. Engine Running Conditions

Gasoline Engines

Engine runs poorly, hesitates	1-B, 1
Engine lacks power	1-B, 2
Engine has poor fuel economy	1-B, 3
Engine runs on (diesels) when turned off	1-B, 4
Engine knocks and pings during heavy acceleration, and on steep hills	1-B, 5
Engine accelerates but vehicle does not gain speed	1-B, 6

Diesel Engines

Engine runs poorly	1-B, 1
Engine lacks power	1-B, 2

C. Engine Noises, Odors and Vibrations

Engine makes a knocking or pinging noise when accelerating	1-C, 1
Starter motor grinds when used	1-C, 2
Engine makes a screeching noise	1-C, 3
Engine makes a growling noise	1-C, 4
Engine makes a ticking or tapping noise	1-C, 5
Engine makes a heavy knocking noise	1-C, 6
Vehicle has a fuel odor when driven	1-C, 7
Vehicle has a rotten egg odor when driven	1-C, 8
Vehicle has a sweet odor when driven	1-C, 9
Engine vibrates when idling	1-C, 10
Engine vibrates during acceleration	1-C, 11

D. Engine Electrical System

Battery goes dead while driving	1-D, 1
Battery goes dead overnight	1-D, 2

E. Engine Cooling System

Engine overheats	1-E, 1
Engine loses coolant	1-E, 2
Engine temperature remains cold when driving	1-E, 3
Engine runs hot	1-E, 4

Condition	Section/Item Number

SECTION 1. ENGINE (continued)

F. Engine Exhaust System

Exhaust rattles at idle speed	1-F, 1
Exhaust system vibrates when driving	1-F, 2
Exhaust system seems too low	1-F, 3
Exhaust seems loud	1-F, 4

SECTION 2. DRIVE TRAIN

A. Automatic Transmission

Transmission shifts erratically	2-A, 1
Transmission will not engage	2-A, 2
Transmission will not downshift during heavy acceleration	2-A, 3

B. Manual Transmission

Transmission grinds going into forward gears while driving	2-B, 1; 2-C, 2
Transmission jumps out of gear	2-B, 2
Transmission difficult to shift	2-B, 3; 2-C, 2
Transmission leaks fluid	2-B, 4

C. Clutch

Clutch slips on hills or during sudden acceleration	2-C, 1
Clutch will not disengage, difficult to shift	2-C, 2
Clutch is noisy when the clutch pedal is pressed	2-C, 3
Clutch pedal extremely difficult to press	2-C, 4
Clutch pedal remains down when pressed	2-C, 5
Clutch chatters when engaging	2-C, 6

D. Differential and Final Drive

Differential makes a low pitched rumbling noise	2-D, 1
Differential makes a howling noise	2-D, 2

E. Transfer Assembly

All Wheel and Four Wheel Drive Vehicles

Leaks fluid from seals or vent after being driven	2-E, 1
Makes excessive noise while driving	2-E, 2
Jumps out of gear	2-E, 3

F. Driveshaft

Rear Wheel, All Wheel and Four Wheel Drive Vehicles

Clunking noise from center of vehicle shifting from forward to reverse	2-F, 1
Excessive vibration from center of vehicle when accelerating	2-F, 2

G. Axles

All Wheel and Four Wheel Drive Vehicles

Front or rear wheel makes a clicking noise	2-G, 1
Front or Rear wheel vibrates with increased speed	2-G, 2

Front Wheel Drive Vehicles

Front wheel makes a clicking noise	2-G, 3
Rear wheel makes a clicking noise	2-G, 4

Condition	Section/Item Number

SECTION 2. DRIVE TRAIN (continued)

Rear Wheel Drive Vehicles

Front or rear wheel makes a clicking noise	2-G, 5
Rear wheel shudders or vibrates	2-G, 6

H. Other Drive Train Conditions

Burning odor from center of vehicle when accelerating	2-H, 1; 2-C, 1; 3-A, 9
Engine accelerates, but vehicle does not gain speed	2-H, 2; 2-C, 1; 3-A, 9

SECTION 3. BRAKE SYSTEM

Brakes pedal pulsates or shimmies when pressed	3-A, 1
Brakes make a squealing noise	3-A, 2
Brakes make a grinding noise	3-A, 3
Vehicle pulls to one side during braking	3-A, 4
Brake pedal feels spongy or has excessive brake pedal travel	3-A, 5
Brake pedal feel is firm, but brakes lack sufficient stopping power or fade	3-A, 6
Vehicle has excessive front end dive or locks rear brakes too easily	3-A, 7
Brake pedal goes to floor when pressed and will not pump up	3-A, 8
Brakes make a burning odor	3-A, 9

SECTION 4. WHEELS, TIRES, STEERING AND SUSPENSION

A. Wheels and Wheel Bearings

All Wheel and Four Wheel Drive Vehicles

Front wheel or wheel bearing loose	4-A, 1
Rear wheel or wheel bearing loose	4-A, 2

Front Wheel Drive Vehicles

Front wheel or wheel bearing loose	4-A, 1
Rear wheel or wheel bearing loose	4-A, 2

Rear Wheel Drive Vehicles

Front wheel or wheel bearing loose	4-A, 1
Rear wheel or wheel bearing loose	4-A, 2

B. Tires

Tires worn on inside tread	4-B, 1
Tires worn on outside tread	4-B, 2
Tires worn unevenly	4-B, 3

C. Steering

Excessive play in steering wheel	4-C, 1
Steering wheel shakes at cruising speeds	4-C, 2
Steering wheel shakes when braking	3-A, 1
Steering wheel becomes stiff when turned	4-C, 4

D. Suspension

Vehicle pulls to one side	4-D, 1
Vehicle is very bouncy over bumps	4-D, 2
Vehicle seems to lean excessively in turns	4-D, 3
Vehicle ride quality seems excessively harsh	4-D, 4
Vehicle seems low or leans to one side	4-D, 5

Condition	Section/Item Number

SECTION 4. WHEELS, TIRES, STEERING AND SUSPENSION (continued)

E. Driving Noises and Vibrations

Noises

Vehicle makes a clicking noise when driven	4-E, 1
Vehicle makes a clunking or knocking noise over bumps	4-E, 2
Vehicle makes a low pitched rumbling noise when driven	4-E, 3
Vehicle makes a squeaking noise over bumps	4-E, 4

Vibrations

Vehicle vibrates when driven	4-E, 5

SECTION 5. ELECTRICAL ACCESSORIES

A. Headlights

One headlight only works on high or low beam	5-A, 1
Headlight does not work on high or low beam	5-A, 2
Headlight(s) very dim	5-A, 3

B. Tail, Running and Side Marker Lights

Tail light, running light or side marker light inoperative	5-B, 1
Tail light, running light or side marker light works intermittently	5-B, 2
Tail light, running light or side marker light very dim	5-B, 3

C. Interior Lights

Interior light inoperative	5-C, 1
Interior light works intermittently	5-C, 2
Interior light very dim	5-C, 3

D. Brake Lights

One brake light inoperative	5-D, 1
Both brake lights inoperative	5-D, 2
One or both brake lights very dim	5-D, 3

E. Warning Lights

Ignition, Battery and Alternator Warning Lights, Check Engine Light, Anti-Lock Braking System (ABS) Light, Brake Warning Light, Oil Pressure Warning Light, and Parking Brake Warning Light

Warning light(s) remains on after the engine is started	5-E, 1
Warning light(s) flickers on and off when driving	5-E, 2
Warning light(s) inoperative with ignition on, and engine not started	5-E, 3

F. Turn Signal and 4-Way Hazard Lights

Turn signals or hazard lights come on, but do not flash	5-F, 1
Turn signals or hazard lights do not function on either side	5-F, 2
Turn signals or hazard lights only work on one side	5-F, 3
One signal light does not work	5-F, 4
Turn signals flash too slowly	5-F, 5
Turn signals flash too fast	5-F, 6
Four-way hazard flasher indicator light inoperative	5-F, 7
Turn signal indicator light(s) do not work in either direction	5-F, 8
One turn signal indicator light does not work	5-F, 9

Condition	Section/Item Number

SECTION 5. ELECTRICAL ACCESSORIES (continued)

G. Horn

Horn does not operate	5-G, 1
Horn has an unusual tone	5-G, 2

H. Windshield Wipers

Windshield wipers do not operate	5-H, 1
Windshield wiper motor makes a humming noise, gets hot or blows fuses	5-H, 2
Windshield wiper motor operates but one or both wipers fail to move	5-H, 3
Windshield wipers will not park	5-H, 4

SECTION 6. INSTRUMENTS AND GAUGES

A. Speedometer (Cable Operated)

Speedometer does not work	6-A, 1
Speedometer needle fluctuates when driving at steady speeds	6-A, 2
Speedometer works intermittently	6-A, 3

B. Speedometer (Electronically Operated)

Speedometer does not work	6-B, 1
Speedometer works intermittently	6-B, 2

C. Fuel, Temperature and Oil Pressure Gauges

Gauge does not register	6-C, 1
Gauge operates erratically	6-C, 2
Gauge operates fully pegged	6-C, 3

SECTION 7. CLIMATE CONTROL

A. Air Conditioner

No air coming from air conditioner vents	7-A, 1
Air conditioner blows warm air	7-A, 2
Water collects on the interior floor when the air conditioner is used	7-A, 3
Air conditioner has a moldy odor when used	7-A, 4

B. Heater

Blower motor does not operate	7-B, 1
Heater blows cool air	7-B, 2
Heater steams the windshield when used	7-B, 3

DIAGNOSTIC PROCEDURES

1. ENGINE

1-A. Engine Starting Problems

Gasoline Engines

1. Engine turns over, but will not start
a. Check fuel level in fuel tank, add fuel if empty.
b. Check battery condition and state of charge. If voltage and load test below specification, charge or replace battery.
c. Check battery terminal and cable condition and tightness. Clean terminals and replace damaged, worn or corroded cables.
d. Check fuel delivery system. If fuel is not reaching the fuel injectors, check for a loose electrical connector or defective fuse, relay or fuel pump and replace as necessary.
e. Engine may have excessive wear or mechanical damage such as low cylinder cranking pressure, a broken camshaft drive system, insufficient valve clearance or bent valves.
f. Check for fuel contamination such as water in the fuel. During winter months, the water may freeze and cause a fuel restriction. Adding a fuel additive may help, however the fuel system may require draining and purging with fresh fuel.
g. Check for ignition system failure. Check for loose or shorted wires or damaged ignition system components. Check the spark plugs for excessive wear or incorrect electrode gap. If the problem is worse in wet weather, check for shorts between the spark plugs and the ignition coils.
h. Check the engine management system for a failed sensor or control module.

2. Engine does not turn over when attempting to start
a. Check the battery state of charge and condition. If the dash lights are not visible or very dim when turning the ignition key on, the battery has either failed internally or discharged, the battery cables are loose, excessively corroded or damaged, or the alternator has failed or internally shorted, discharging the battery. Charge or replace the battery, clean or replace the battery cables, and check the alternator output.
b. Check the operation of the neutral safety switch. On automatic transmission vehicles, try starting the vehicle in both Park and Neutral. On manual transmission vehicles, depress the clutch pedal and attempt to start. On some vehicles, these switches can be adjusted. Make sure the switches or wire connectors are not loose or damaged. Replace or adjust the switches as necessary.
c. Check the starter motor, starter solenoid or relay, and starter motor cables and wires. Check the ground from the engine to the chassis. Make sure the wires are not loose, damaged, or corroded. If battery voltage is present at the starter relay, try using a remote starter to start the vehicle for test purposes only. Replace any damaged or corroded cables, in addition to replacing any failed components.
d. Check the engine for seizure. If the engine has not been started for a long period of time, internal parts such as the rings may have rusted to the cylinder walls. The engine may have suffered internal damage, or could be hydro-locked from ingesting water. Remove the spark plugs and carefully attempt to rotate the engine using a suitable breaker bar and socket on the crankshaft pulley. If the engine is resistant to moving, or moves slightly and then binds, do not force the engine any further before determining the problem.

3. Engine stalls immediately when started
a. Check the ignition switch condition and operation. The electrical contacts in the run position may be worn or damaged. Try restarting the engine with all electrical accessories in the off position. Sometimes turning the key on an off will help in emergency situations, however once the switch has shown signs of failure, it should be replaced as soon as possible.
b. Check for loose, corroded, damaged or shorted wires for the ignition system and repair or replace.
c. Check for manifold vacuum leaks or vacuum hose leakage and repair or replace parts as necessary.
d. Measure the fuel pump delivery volume and pressure. Low fuel pump pressure can also be noticed as a lack of power when accelerating. Make sure the fuel pump lines are not restricted. The fuel pump output is not adjustable and requires fuel pump replacement to repair.
e. Check the engine fuel and ignition management system. Inspect the sensor wiring and electrical connectors. A dirty, loose or damaged sensor or control module wire can simulate a failed component.
f. Check the exhaust system for internal restrictions.

4. Starter motor spins, but does not engage
a. Check the starter motor for a seized or binding pinion gear.
b. Remove the flywheel inspection plate and check for a damaged ring gear.

5. Engine is difficult to start when cold
a. Check the battery condition, battery state of charge and starter motor current draw. Replace the battery if marginal and the starter motor if the current draw is beyond specification.
b. Check the battery cable condition. Clean the battery terminals and replace corroded or damaged cables.
c. Check the fuel system for proper operation. A fuel pump with insufficient fuel pressure or clogged injectors should be replaced.
d. Check the engine's tune-up status. Note the tune-up specifications and check for items such as severely worn spark plugs; adjust or replace as needed. On vehicles with manually adjusted valve clearances, check for tight valves and adjust to specification.
e. Check for a failed coolant temperature sensor, and replace if out of specification.
f. Check the operation of the engine management systems for fuel and ignition; repair or replace failed components as necessary.

6. Engine is difficult to start when hot

a. Check the air filter and air intake system. Replace the air filter if it is dirty or contaminated. Check the fresh air intake system for restrictions or blockage.

b. Check for loose or deteriorated engine grounds and clean, tighten or replace as needed.

c. Check for needed maintenance. Inspect tune-up and service related items such as spark plugs and engine oil condition, and check the operation of the engine fuel and ignition management system.

Diesel Engines

1. Engine turns over but won't start

a. Check engine starting procedure and restart engine.

b. Check the glow plug operation and repair or replace as necessary.

c. Check for air in the fuel system or fuel filter and bleed the air as necessary.

d. Check the fuel delivery system and repair or replace as necessary.

e. Check fuel level and add fuel as needed.

f. Check fuel quality. If the fuel is contaminated, drain and flush the fuel tank.

g. Check engine compression. If compression is below specification, the engine may need to be renewed or replaced.

h. Check the injection pump timing and set to specification.

i. Check the injection pump condition and replace as necessary.

j. Check the fuel nozzle operation and condition or replace as necess-ary.

2. Engine does not turn over when attempting to start

a. Check the battery state of charge and condition. If the dash lights are not visible or very dim when turning the ignition key on, the battery has either failed internally or discharged, the battery cables are loose, excessively corroded or damaged, or the alternator has failed or internally shorted, discharging the battery. Charge or replace the battery, clean or replace the battery cables, and check the alternator output.

b. Check the operation of the neutral safety switch. On automatic transmission vehicles, try starting the vehicle in both Park and Neutral. On manual transmission vehicles, depress the clutch pedal and attempt to start. On some vehicles, these switches can be adjusted. Make sure the switches or wire connectors are not loose or damaged. Replace or adjust the switches as necessary.

c. Check the starter motor, starter solenoid or relay, and starter motor cables and wires. Check the ground from the engine to the chassis. Make sure the wires are not loose, damaged, or corroded. If battery voltage is present at the starter relay, try using a remote starter to start the vehicle for test purposes only. Replace any damaged or corroded cables, in addition to replacing any failed components.

d. Check the engine for seizure. If the engine has not been started for a long period of time, internal parts such as the rings may have rusted to the cylinder walls. The engine may have suffered internal damage, or could be hydro-locked from ingesting water. Remove the injectors and carefully attempt to rotate the engine

using a suitable breaker bar and socket on the crankshaft pulley. If the engine is resistant to moving, or moves slightly and then binds, do not force the engine any further before determining the cause of the problem.

3. Engine stalls after starting

a. Check for a restriction in the fuel return line or the return line check valve and repair as necessary.

b. Check the glow plug operation for turning the glow plugs off too soon and repair as necessary.

c. Check for incorrect injection pump timing and reset to specification.

d. Test the engine fuel pump and replace if the output is below specification.

e. Check for contaminated or incorrect fuel. Completely flush the fuel system and replace with fresh fuel.

f. Test the engine's compression for low compression. If below specification, mechanical repairs are necessary to repair.

g. Check for air in the fuel. Check fuel tank fuel and fill as needed.

h. Check for a failed injection pump. Replace the pump, making sure to properly set the pump timing.

4. Starter motor spins, but does not engage

a. Check the starter motor for a seized or binding pinion gear.

b. Remove the flywheel inspection plate and check for a damaged ring gear.

1-B. Engine Running Conditions

Gasoline Engines

1. Engine runs poorly, hesitates

a. Check the engine ignition system operation and adjust if possible, or replace defective parts.

b. Check for restricted fuel injectors and replace as necessary.

c. Check the fuel pump output and delivery. Inspect fuel lines for restrictions. If the fuel pump pressure is below specification, replace the fuel pump.

d. Check the operation of the engine management system and repair as necessary.

2. Engine lacks power

a. Check the engine's tune-up status. Note the tune-up specifications and check for items such as severely worn spark plugs; adjust or replace as needed. On vehicles with manually adjusted valve clearances, check for tight valves and adjust to specification.

b. Check the air filter and air intake system. Replace the air filter if it is dirty or contaminated. Check the fresh air intake system for restrictions or blockage.

c. Check the operation of the engine fuel and ignition management systems. Check the sensor operation and wiring. Check for low fuel pump pressure and repair or replace components as necessary.

d. Check the throttle linkage adjustments. Check to make sure the linkage is fully opening the throttle. Replace any worn or defective bushings or linkages.

e. Check for a restricted exhaust system. Check for bent or crimped exhaust pipes, or internally restricted mufflers or catalytic converters. Compare inlet and outlet temperatures for the converter or muffler. If the inlet is hot, but outlet cold, the component is restricted.

f. Check for a loose or defective knock sensor. A loose, improperly torqued or defective knock sensor will decrease spark advance and reduce power. Replace defective knock sensors and install using the recommended torque specification.

g. Check for engine mechanical conditions such as low compression, worn piston rings, worn valves, worn camshafts and related parts. An engine which has severe mechanical wear, or has suffered internal mechanical damage must be rebuilt or replaced to restore lost power.

h. Check the engine oil level for being overfilled. Adjust the engine's oil level, or change the engine oil and filter, and top off to the correct level.

i. Check for an intake manifold or vacuum hose leak. Replace leaking gaskets or worn vacuum hoses.

j. Check for dragging brakes and replace or repair as necessary.

k. Check tire air pressure and tire wear. Adjust the pressure to the recommended settings. Check the tire wear for possible alignment problems causing increased rolling resistance, decreased acceleration and increased fuel usage.

l. Check the octane rating of the fuel used during refilling, and use a higher octane rated fuel.

3. Poor fuel economy

a. Inspect the air filter and check for any air restrictions going into the air filter housing. Replace the air filter if it is dirty or contaminated.

b. Check the engine for tune-up and related adjustments. Replace worn ignition parts, check the engine ignition timing and fuel mixture, and set to specifications if possible.

c. Check the tire size, tire wear, alignment and tire pressure. Large tires create more rolling resistance, smaller tires require more engine speed to maintain a vehicle's road speed. Excessive tire wear can be caused by incorrect tire pressure, incorrect wheel alignment or a suspension problem. All of these conditions create increased rolling resistance, causing the engine to work harder to accelerate and maintain a vehicle's speed.

d. Inspect the brakes for binding or excessive drag. A sticking brake caliper, overly adjusted brake shoe, broken brake shoe return spring, or binding parking brake cable or linkage can create a significant drag, brake wear and loss of fuel economy. Check the brake system operation and repair as necessary.

4. Engine runs on (diesels) when turned off

a. Check for idle speed set too high and readjust to specification.

b. Check the operation of the idle control valve, and replace if defective.

c. Check the ignition timing and adjust to recommended settings. Check for defective sensors or related components and replace if defective.

d. Check for a vacuum leak at the intake manifold or vacuum hose and replace defective gaskets or hoses.

e. Check the engine for excessive carbon build-up in the combus-

tion chamber. Use a recommended decarbonizing fuel additive or disassemble the cylinder head to remove the carbon.

f. Check the operation of the engine fuel management system and replace defective sensors or control units.

g. Check the engine operating temperature for overheating and repair as necessary.

5. Engine knocks and pings during heavy acceleration, and on steep hills

a. Check the octane rating of the fuel used during refilling, and use a higher octane rated fuel.

b. Check the ignition timing and adjust to recommended settings. Check for defective sensors or related components and replace if defective.

c. Check the engine for excessive carbon build-up in the combustion chamber. Use a recommended decarbonizing fuel additive or disassemble the cylinder head to remove the carbon.

d. Check the spark plugs for the correct type, electrode gap and heat range. Replace worn or damaged spark plugs. For severe or continuous high speed use, install a spark plug that is one heat range colder.

e. Check the operation of the engine fuel management system and replace defective sensors or control units.

f. Check for a restricted exhaust system. Check for bent or crimped exhaust pipes, or internally restricted mufflers or catalytic converters. Compare inlet and outlet temperatures for the converter or muffler. If the inlet is hot, but outlet cold, the component is restricted.

6. Engine accelerates, but vehicle does not gain speed

a. On manual transmission vehicles, check for causes of a slipping clutch. Refer to the clutch troubleshooting section for additional information.

b. On automatic transmission vehicles, check for a slipping transmission. Check the transmission fluid level and condition. If the fluid level is too high, adjust to the correct level. If the fluid level is low, top off using the recommended fluid type. If the fluid exhibits a burning odor, the transmission has been slipping internally. Changing the fluid and filter may help temporarily, however in this situation a transmission may require overhauling to ensure long-term reliability.

Diesel Engines

1. Engine runs poorly

a. Check the injection pump timing and adjust to specification.

b. Check for air in the fuel lines or leaks, and bleed the air from the fuel system.

c. Check the fuel filter, fuel feed and return lines for a restriction and repair as necessary.

d. Check the fuel for contamination, drain and flush the fuel tank and replenish with fresh fuel.

2. Engine lacks power

a. Inspect the air intake system and air filter for restrictions and, if necessary, replace the air filter.

b. Verify the injection pump timing and reset if out of specification.

c. Check the exhaust for an internal restriction and replace failed parts.

d. Check for a restricted fuel filter and, if restricted, replace the filter.

e. Inspect the fuel filler cap vent . When removing the filler cap, listen for excessive hissing noises indicating a blockage in the fuel filler cap vents. If the filler cap vents are blocked, replace the cap.

f. Check the fuel system for restrictions and repair as necessary.

g. Check for low engine compression and inspect for external leakage at the glow plugs or nozzles. If no external leakage is noted, repair or replace the engine.

ENGINE PERFORMANCE TROUBLESHOOTING HINTS

When troubleshooting an engine running or performance condition, the mechanical condition of the engine should be determined *before* lengthy troubleshooting procedures are performed.

The engine fuel management systems in fuel injected vehicles rely on electronic sensors to provide information to the engine control unit for precise fuel metering. Unlike carburetors, which use the incoming air speed to draw fuel through the fuel metering jets in order to provide a proper fuel-to-air ratio, a fuel injection system provides a specific amount of fuel which is introduced by the fuel injectors into the intake manifold or intake port, based on the information provided by electronic sensors.

The sensors monitor the engine's operating temperature, ambient temperature and the amount of air entering the engine, engine speed and throttle position to provide information to the engine control unit, which, in turn, operates the fuel injectors by electrical pulses. The sensors provide information to the engine control unit using low voltage electrical signals. As a result, an unplugged sensor or a poor electrical contact could cause a poor running condition similar to a failed sensor.

When troubleshooting a fuel related engine condition on fuel injected vehicles, carefully inspect the wiring and electrical connectors to the related components. Make sure the electrical connectors are fully connected, clean and not physically damaged. If necessary, clean the electrical contacts using electrical contact cleaner. The use of cleaning agents not specifically designed for electrical contacts should not be used, as they could leave a surface film or damage the insulation of the wiring.

The engine electrical system provides the necessary electrical power to operate the vehicle's electrical accessories, electronic control units and sensors. Because engine management systems are sensitive to voltage changes, an alternator which over or undercharges could cause engine running problems or component failure. Most alternators utilize internal voltage regulators which cannot be adjusted and must be replaced individually or as a unit with the alternator.

Ignition systems may be controlled by, or linked to, the engine fuel management system. Similar to the fuel injection system, these ignition systems rely on electronic sensors for information to determine the optimum ignition timing for a given engine speed and load. Some ignition systems no longer allow the ignition timing to be adjusted. Feedback from low voltage electrical sensors provide information to the control unit to determine the amount of ignition advance. On these systems, if a failure occurs the failed component must be replaced. Before replacing suspected failed electrical com-

ponents, carefully inspect the wiring and electrical connectors to the related components. Make sure the electrical connectors are fully connected, clean and not physically damaged. If necessary, clean the electrical contacts using electrical contact cleaner. The use of cleaning agents not specifically designed for electrical contacts should be avoided, as they could leave a surface film or damage the insulation of the wiring.

1-C. Engine Noises, Odors and Vibrations

1. Engine makes a knocking or pinging noise when accelerating

a. Check the octane rating of the fuel being used. Depending on the type of driving or driving conditions, it may be necessary to use a higher octane fuel.

b. Verify the ignition system settings and operation. Improperly adjusted ignition timing or a failed component, such as a knock sensor, may cause the ignition timing to advance excessively or prematurely. Check the ignition system operation and adjust, or replace components as needed.

c. Check the spark plug gap, heat range and condition. If the vehicle is operated in severe operating conditions or at continuous high speeds, use a colder heat range spark plug. Adjust the spark plug gap to the manufacturer's recommended specification and replace worn or damaged spark plugs.

2. Starter motor grinds when used

a. Examine the starter pinion gear and the engine ring gear for damage, and replace damaged parts.

b. Check the starter mounting bolts and housing. If the housing is cracked or damaged replace the starter motor and check the mounting bolts for tightness.

3. Engine makes a screeching noise

a. Check the accessory drive belts for looseness and adjust as necessary.

b. Check the accessory drive belt tensioners for seizing or excessive bearing noises and replace if loose, binding, or excessively noisy.

c. Check for a seizing water pump. The pump may not be leaking; however, the bearing may be faulty or the impeller loose and jammed. Replace the water pump.

4. Engine makes a growling noise

a. Check for a loose or failing water pump. Replace the pump and engine coolant.

b. Check the accessory drive belt tensioners for excessive bearing noises and replace if loose or excessively noisy.

5. Engine makes a ticking or tapping noise

a. On vehicles with hydraulic lash adjusters, check for low or dirty engine oil and top off or replace the engine oil and filter.

b. On vehicles with hydraulic lash adjusters, check for collapsed lifters and replace failed components.

c. On vehicles with hydraulic lash adjusters, check for low oil pressure caused by a restricted oil filter, worn engine oil pump, or oil pressure relief valve.

d. On vehicles with manually adjusted valves, check for excessive valve clearance or worn valve train parts. Adjust the valves to specification or replace worn and defective parts.

e. Check for a loose or improperly tensioned timing belt or timing chain and adjust or replace parts as necessary.

f. Check for a bent or sticking exhaust or intake valve. Remove the engine cylinder head to access and replace.

6. Engine makes a heavy knocking noise

a. Check for a loose crankshaft pulley or flywheel; replace and torque the mounting bolt(s) to specification.

b. Check for a bent connecting rod caused by a hydro-lock condition. Engine disassembly is necessary to inspect for damaged and needed replacement parts.

c. Check for excessive engine rod bearing wear or damage. This condition is also associated with low engine oil pressure and will require engine disassembly to inspect for damaged and needed replacement parts.

7. Vehicle has a fuel odor when driven

a. Check the fuel gauge level. If the fuel gauge registers full, it is possible that the odor is caused by being filled beyond capacity, or some spillage occurred during refueling. The odor should clear after driving an hour, or twenty miles, allowing the vapor canister to purge.

b. Check the fuel filler cap for looseness or seepage. Check the cap tightness and, if loose, properly secure. If seepage is noted, replace the filler cap.

c. Check for loose hose clamps, cracked or damaged fuel delivery and return lines, or leaking components or seals, and replace or repair as necessary.

d. Check the vehicle's fuel economy. If fuel consumption has increased due to a failed component, or if the fuel is not properly ignited due to an ignition related failure, the catalytic converter may become contaminated. This condition may also trigger the check engine warning light. Check the spark plugs for a dark, rich condition or verify the condition by testing the vehicle's emissions. Replace fuel fouled spark plugs, and test and replace failed components as necessary.

8. Vehicle has a rotten egg odor when driven

a. Check for a leaking intake gasket or vacuum leak causing a lean running condition. A lean mixture may result in increased exhaust temperatures, causing the catalytic converter to run hotter than normal. This condition may also trigger the check engine warning light. Check and repair the vacuum leaks as necessary.

b. Check the vehicle's alternator and battery condition. If the alternator is overcharging, the battery electrolyte can be boiled from the battery, and the battery casing may begin to crack, swell or bulge, damaging or shorting the battery internally. If this has occurred, neutralize the battery mounting area with a suitable baking soda and water mixture or equivalent, and replace the alternator or voltage regulator. Inspect, service, and load test the battery, and replace if necessary.

9. Vehicle has a sweet odor when driven

a. Check for an engine coolant leak caused by a seeping radiator cap, loose hose clamp, weeping cooling system seal, gasket or cooling system hose and replace or repair as needed.

b. Check for a coolant leak from the radiator, coolant reservoir, heater control valve or under the dashboard from the heater core, and replace the failed part as necessary.

c. Check the engine's exhaust for white smoke in addition to a sweet odor. The presence of white, steamy smoke with a sweet odor indicates coolant leaking into the combustion chamber. Possible causes include a failed head gasket, cracked engine block or cylinder head. Other symptoms of this condition include a white paste build-up on the inside of the oil filler cap, and softened, deformed or bulging radiator hoses.

10. Engine vibrates when idling

a. Check for loose, collapsed, or damaged engine or transmission mounts and repair or replace as necessary.

b. Check for loose or damaged engine covers or shields and secure or replace as necessary.

11. Engine vibrates during acceleration

a. Check for missing, loose or damaged exhaust system hangers and mounts; replace or repair as necessary.

b. Check the exhaust system routing and fit for adequate clearance or potential rubbing; repair or adjust as necessary.

1-D. Engine Electrical System

1. Battery goes dead while driving

a. Check the battery condition. Replace the battery if the battery will not hold a charge or fails a battery load test. If the battery loses fluid while driving, check for an overcharging condition. If the alternator is overcharging, replace the alternator or voltage regulator. (A voltage regulator is typically built into the alternator, necessitating alternator replacement or overhaul.)

b. Check the battery cable condition. Clean or replace corroded cables and clean the battery terminals.

c. Check the alternator and voltage regulator operation. If the charging system is over or undercharging, replace the alternator or voltage regulator, or both.

d. Inspect the wiring and wire connectors at the alternator for looseness, a missing ground or defective terminal, and repair as necessary.

e. Inspect the alternator drive belt tension, tensioners and condition. Properly tension the drive belt, replace weak or broken tensioners, and replace the drive belt if worn or cracked.

2. Battery goes dead overnight

a. Check the battery condition. Replace the battery if the battery will not hold a charge or fails a battery load test.

b. Check for a voltage draw, such as a trunk light, interior light or glove box light staying on. Check light switch position and operation, and replace if defective.

c. Check the alternator for an internally failed diode, and replace the alternator if defective.

1-E. Engine Cooling System

1. Engine overheats

a. Check the coolant level. Set the heater temperature to full hot and check for internal air pockets, bleed the cooling system and inspect for leakage. Top off the cooling system with the correct coolant mixture.

b. Pressure test the cooling system and radiator cap for leaks. Check for seepage caused by loose hose clamps, failed coolant hoses, and cooling system components such as the heater control valve, heater core, radiator, radiator cap, and water pump. Replace defective parts and fill the cooling system with the recommended coolant mixture.

c. On vehicles with electrically controlled cooling fans, check the cooling fan operation. Check for blown fuses or defective fan motors, temperature sensors and relays, and replace failed components.

d. Check for a coolant leak caused by a failed head gasket, or a porous water jacket casting in the cylinder head or engine block. Replace defective parts as necessary.

e. Check for an internally restricted radiator. Flush the radiator or replace if the blockage is too severe for flushing.

f. Check for a damaged water pump. If coolant circulation is poor, check for a loose water pump impeller. If the impeller is loose, replace the water pump.

2. Engine loses coolant

a. Pressure test the cooling system and radiator cap for leaks. Check for seepage caused by loose hose clamps, failed coolant hoses, and cooling system components such as the heater control valve, heater core, radiator, radiator cap, and water pump. Replace defective parts and fill the cooling system with the recommended coolant mixture.

b. Check for a coolant leak caused by a failed head gasket, or a porous water jacket casting in the cylinder head or engine block. Replace defective parts as necessary.

3. Engine temperature remains cold when driving

a. Check the thermostat operation. Replace the thermostat if it sticks in the open position.

b. On vehicles with electrically controlled cooling fans, check the cooling fan operation. Check for defective temperature sensors and stuck relays, and replace failed components.

c. Check temperature gauge operation if equipped to verify proper operation of the gauge. Check the sensors and wiring for defects, and repair or replace defective components.

4. Engine runs hot

a. Check for an internally restricted radiator. Flush the radiator or replace if the blockage is too severe for flushing.

b. Check for a loose or slipping water pump drive belt. Inspect the drive belt condition. Replace the belt if brittle, cracked or damaged. Check the pulley condition and properly tension the belt.

c. Check the cooling fan operation. Replace defective fan motors, sensors or relays as necessary.

d. Check temperature gauge operation if equipped to verify proper operation of the gauge. Check the sensors and wiring for defects, and repair or replace defective components.

e. Check the coolant level. Set the heater temperature to full hot, check for internal air pockets, bleed the cooling system and inspect for leakage. Top off the cooling system with the correct coolant mixture. Once the engine is cool, recheck the fluid level and top off as needed.

NOTE: The engine cooling system can also be affected by an engine's mechanical condition. A failed head gasket or a porous casting in the engine block or cylinder head could cause a loss of coolant and result in engine overheating.

Some cooling systems rely on electrically driven cooling fans to cool the radiator and use electrical temperature sensors and relays to operate the cooling fan. When diagnosing these systems, check for blown fuses, damaged wires and verify that the electrical connections are fully connected, clean and not physically damaged. If necessary, clean the electrical contacts using electrical contact cleaner. The use of cleaning agents not specifically designed for electrical contacts could leave a film or damage the insulation of the wiring.

1-F. Engine Exhaust System

1. Exhaust rattles at idle speed

a. Check the engine and transmission mounts and replace mounts showing signs of damage or wear.

b. Check the exhaust hangers, brackets and mounts. Replace broken, missing or damaged mounts.

c. Check for internal damage to mufflers and catalytic converters. The broken pieces from the defective component may travel in the direction of the exhaust flow and collect and/or create a blockage in a component other than the one which failed, causing engine running and stalling problems. Another symptom of a restricted exhaust is low engine manifold vacuum. Remove the exhaust system and carefully remove any loose or broken pieces, then replace any failed or damaged parts as necessary.

d. Check the exhaust system clearance, routing and alignment. If the exhaust is making contact with the vehicle in any manner, loosen and reposition the exhaust system.

2. Exhaust system vibrates when driving

a. Check the exhaust hangers, brackets and mounts. Replace broken, missing or damaged mounts.

b. Check the exhaust system clearance, routing and alignment. If the exhaust is making contact with the vehicle in any manner, check for bent or damaged components and replace, then loosen and reposition the exhaust system.

c. Check for internal damage to mufflers and catalytic converters. The broken pieces from the defective component may travel in the direction of the exhaust flow and collect and/or create a blockage in a component other than the one which failed, causing engine running and stalling problems. Another symptom of a restricted exhaust is low engine manifold vacuum. Remove the exhaust system and carefully remove any loose or broken pieces, then replace any failed or damaged parts as necessary.

3. Exhaust system hangs too low

a. Check the exhaust hangers, brackets and mounts. Replace broken, missing or damaged mounts.

b. Check the exhaust routing and alignment. Check and replace bent or damaged components. If the exhaust is not routed properly, loosen and reposition the exhaust system.

4. Exhaust sounds loud

a. Check the system for looseness and leaks. Check the exhaust pipes, clamps, flange bolts and manifold fasteners for tightness. Check and replace any failed gaskets.

b. Check and replace exhaust silencers that have a loss of efficiency due to internally broken baffles or worn packing material.

c. Check for missing mufflers and silencers that have been replaced with straight pipes or with non-original equipment silencers.

NOTE: Exhaust system rattles, vibration and proper alignment should not be overlooked. Excessive vibration caused by collapsed engine mounts, damaged or missing exhaust hangers and misalignment may cause surface cracks and broken welds, creating exhaust leaks or internal damage to exhaust components such as the catalytic converter, creating a restriction to exhaust flow and loss of power.

2. DRIVE TRAIN

2-A. Automatic Transmission

1. Transmission shifts erratically

a. Check and if not within the recommended range, add or remove transmission fluid to obtain the correct fluid level. Always use the recommended fluid type when adding transmission fluid.

b. Check the fluid level condition. If the fluid has become contaminated, fatigued from excessive heat or exhibits a burning odor, change the transmission fluid and filter using the recommended type and amount of fluid. A fluid which exhibits a burning odor indicates that the transmission has been slipping internally and may require future repairs.

c. Check for an improperly installed transmission filter, or missing filter gasket, and repair as necessary.

d. Check for loose or leaking gaskets, pressure lines and fittings, and repair or replace as necessary.

e. Check for loose or disconnected shift and throttle linkages or vacuum hoses, and repair as necessary.

2. Transmission will not engage

a. Check the shift linkage for looseness, wear and proper adjustment, and repair as necessary.

b. Check for a loss of transmission fluid and top off as needed with the recommended fluid.

c. If the transmission does not engage with the shift linkage correctly installed and the proper fluid level, internal damage has likely occurred, requiring transmission removal and disassembly.

3. Transmission will not downshift during heavy acceleration

a. On computer controlled transmissions, check for failed sensors or control units and repair or replace defective components.

b. On vehicles with kickdown linkages or vacuum servos, check for proper linkage adjustment or leaking vacuum hoses or servo units.

NOTE: Many automatic transmissions use an electronic control module, electrical sensors and solenoids to control transmission shifting. When troubleshooting a vehicle with this type of system, be sure the electrical connectors are fully connected, clean and not physically damaged. If necessary, clean the electrical contacts using electrical contact cleaner. The use of cleaning agents not specifically designed for electrical contacts could leave a film or damage the insulation of the wiring.

2-B. Manual Transmission

1. Transmission grinds going into forward gears while driving

a. Check the clutch release system. On clutches with a mechanical or cable linkage, check the adjustment. Adjust the clutch pedal to have 1 inch (25mm) of free-play at the pedal.

b. If the clutch release system is hydraulically operated, check the fluid level and, if low, top off using the recommended type and amount of fluid.

c. Synchronizers worn. Remove transmission and replace synchronizers.

d. Synchronizer sliding sleeve worn. Remove transmission and replace sliding sleeve.

e. Gear engagement dogs worn or damaged. Remove transmission and replace gear.

2. Transmission jumps out of gear

a. Shift shaft detent springs worn. Replace shift detent springs.

b. Synchronizer sliding sleeve worn. Remove transmission and replace sliding sleeve.

c. Gear engagement dogs worn or damaged. Remove transmission and replace gear.

d. Crankshaft thrust bearings worn. Remove engine and crankshaft, and repair as necessary.

3. Transmission difficult to shift

a. Verify the clutch adjustment and, if not properly adjusted, adjust to specification.

b. Synchronizers worn. Remove transmission and replace synchronizers.

c. Pilot bearing seized. Remove transmission and replace pilot bearing.

d. Shift linkage or bushing seized. Disassemble the shift linkage, replace worn or damaged bushings, lubricate and reinstall.

4. Transmission leaks fluid

a. Check the fluid level for an overfilled condition. Adjust the fluid level to specification.

b. Check for a restricted transmission vent or breather tube. Clear the blockage as necessary and check the fluid level. If necessary, top off with the recommended lubricant.

c. Check for a porous casting, leaking seal or gasket. Replace defective parts and top off the fluid level with the recommended lubricant.

2-C. Clutch

1. Clutch slips on hills or during sudden acceleration

a. Check for insufficient clutch pedal free-play. Adjust clutch linkage or cable to allow about 1 inch (25mm) of pedal free-play.

b. Clutch disc worn or severely damaged. Remove engine or transmission and replace clutch disc.

c. Clutch pressure plate is weak. Remove engine or transmission and replace the clutch pressure plate and clutch disc.

d. Clutch pressure plate and/or flywheel incorrectly machined. If the clutch system has been recently replaced and rebuilt, or refurbished parts have been used, it is possible that the machined surfaces decreased the clutch clamping force. Replace defective parts with new replacement parts.

2. Clutch will not disengage, difficult to shift

a. Check the clutch release mechanism. Check for stretched cables, worn linkages or failed clutch hydraulics and replace defective parts. On hydraulically operated clutch release mechanisms, check for air in the hydraulic system and bleed as necessary.

b. Check for a broken, cracked or fatigued clutch release arm or release arm pivot. Replace defective parts and properly lubricate upon assembly.

c. Check for a damaged clutch hub damper or damper spring. The broken parts tend to become lodged between the clutch disc and the pressure plate. Disassemble clutch system and replace failed parts.

d. Check for a seized clutch pilot bearing. Disassemble the clutch assembly and replace the defective parts.

e. Check for a defective clutch disc. Check for warpage or lining thicknesses larger than original equipment.

3. Clutch is noisy when the clutch pedal is pressed

a. Check the clutch pedal stop and pedal free-play adjustment for excessive movement and adjust as necessary.

b. Check for a worn or damaged release bearing. If the noise ceases when the pedal is released, the release bearing should be replaced.

c. Check the engine crankshaft axial play. If the crankshaft thrust bearings are worn or damaged, the crankshaft will move when pressing the clutch pedal. The engine must be disassembled to replace the crankshaft thrust bearings.

4. Clutch pedal extremely difficult to press

a. Check the clutch pedal pivots and linkages for binding. Clean and lubricate linkages.

b. On cable actuated clutch systems, check the cable routing and condition. Replace kinked, frayed, damaged or corroded cables and check cable routing to avoid sharp bends. Check the engine ground strap for poor conductivity. If the ground strap is marginal, the engine could try to ground itself via the clutch cable, causing premature failure.

c. On mechanical linkage clutches, check the linkage for binding or misalignment. Lubricate pivots or linkages and repair as necessary.

d. Check the release bearing guide tube and release fork for a lack of lubrication. Install a smooth coating of high temperature grease to allow smooth movement of the release bearing over the guide tube.

5. Clutch pedal remains down when pressed

a. On mechanical linkage or cable actuated clutches, check for a loose or disconnected link.

b. On hydraulically actuated clutches, check the fluid level and check for a hydraulic leak at the clutch slave or master cylinder, or hydraulic line. Replace failed parts and bleed clutch hydraulic system. If no leakage is noted, the clutch master cylinder may have failed internally. Replace the clutch master cylinder and bleed the clutch hydraulic system.

6. Clutch chatters when engaging

a. Check the engine flywheel for warpage or surface variations and replace or repair as necessary.

b. Check for a warped clutch disc or damaged clutch damper hub. Remove the clutch disc and replace.

c. Check for a loose or damaged clutch pressure plate and replace defective components.

NOTE: The clutch is actuated either by a mechanical linkage, cable or a clutch hydraulic system. The mechanical linkage and cable systems may require the clutch pedal free-play to be adjusted as the clutch disc wears. A hydraulic clutch system automatically adjusts as the clutch wears and, with the exception of the clutch pedal height, no adjustment is possible.

2-D. Differential and Final Drive

1. Differential makes a low pitched rumbling noise

a. Check fluid level type and amount. Replace the fluid with the recommended type and amount of lubricant.

b. Check the differential bearings for wear or damage. Remove the bearings, inspect the drive and driven gears for wear or damage, and replace components as necessary.

2. Differential makes a howling noise

a. Check fluid level type and amount. Replace the fluid with the recommended type and amount of lubricant.

b. Check the differential drive and driven gears for wear or damage, and replace components as necessary.

2-E. Transfer Assembly

All Wheel and Four Wheel Drive Vehicles

1. Leaks fluid from seals or vent after being driven
a. Fluid level overfilled. Check and adjust transfer case fluid level.
b. Check for a restricted breather or breather tube, clear and check the fluid level and top off as needed.
c. Check seal condition and replace worn, damaged, or defective seals. Check the fluid level and top off as necessary.

2. Makes excessive noise while driving
a. Check the fluid for the correct type of lubricant. Drain and refill using the recommended type and amount of lubricant.
b. Check the fluid level. Top off the fluid using the recommended type and amount of lubricant.
c. If the fluid level and type of lubricant meet specifications, check for internal wear or damage. Remove assembly and disassemble to inspect for worn, damaged, or defective components.

3. Jumps out of gear
a. Stop vehicle and make sure the unit is fully engaged.
b. Check for worn, loose or an improperly adjusted linkage. Replace and/or adjust linkage as necessary.
c. Check for internal wear or damage. Remove assembly and disassemble to inspect for worn, damaged, or defective components.

2-F. Driveshaft

Rear Wheel, All Wheel and Four Wheel Drive Vehicles

1. Clunking noise from center of vehicle shifting from forward to reverse
a. Worn universal joint. Remove driveshaft and replace universal joint.

2. Excessive vibration from center of vehicle when accelerating
a. Worn universal joint. Remove driveshaft and replace universal joint.
b. Driveshaft misaligned. Check for collapsed or damaged engine and transmission mounts, and replace as necessary.
c. Driveshaft bent or out of balance. Replace damaged components and reinstall.
d. Driveshaft out of balance. Remove the driveshaft and have it balanced by a competent professional, or replace the driveshaft assembly.

NOTE: Most driveshafts are linked together by universal joints; however, some manufacturers use Constant Velocity (CV) joints or rubber flex couplers.

2-G. Axles

All Wheel and Four Wheel Drive Vehicles

1. Front or rear wheel makes a clicking noise
a. Check for debris such as a pebble, nail or glass in the tire or tire tread. Carefully remove the debris. Small rocks and pebbles rarely cause a puncture; however, a sharp object should be removed carefully at a facility capable of performing tire repairs.
b. Check for a loose, damaged or worn Constant Velocity (CV) joint and replace if defective.

2. Front or rear wheel vibrates with increased speed
a. Check for a bent rim and replace, if damaged.
b. Check the tires for balance or internal damage and replace if defective.
c. Check for a loose, worn or damaged wheel bearing and replace if defective.
d. Check for a loose, damaged or worn Constant Velocity (CV) joint and replace if defective.

Front Wheel Drive Vehicles

3. Front wheel makes a clicking noise
a. Check for debris such as a pebble, nail or glass in the tire or tire tread. Carefully remove the debris. Small rocks and pebbles rarely cause a puncture; however, a sharp object should be removed carefully at a facility capable of performing tire repairs.
b. Check for a loose, damaged or worn Constant Velocity (CV) joint and replace if defective.

4. Rear wheel makes a clicking noise
a. Check for debris such as a pebble, nail or glass in the tire or tire tread. Carefully remove the debris. Small rocks and pebbles rarely cause a puncture; however, a sharp object should be removed carefully at a facility capable of performing tire repairs.

Rear Wheel Drive Vehicles

5. Front or rear wheel makes a clicking noise
a. Check for debris such as a pebble, nail or glass in the tire or tire tread. Carefully remove the debris. Small rocks and pebbles rarely cause a puncture; however, a sharp object should be removed carefully at a facility capable of performing tire repairs.

6. Rear wheel shudders or vibrates
a. Check for a bent rear wheel or axle assembly and replace defective components.
b. Check for a loose, damaged or worn rear wheel bearing and replace as necessary.

2-H. Other Drive Train Conditions

1. Burning odor from center of vehicle when accelerating
a. Check for a seizing brake hydraulic component such as a brake caliper. Check the caliper piston for surface damage such as rust, and measure for out-of-round wear and caliper-to-piston clearance. For additional information on brake related odors, refer to section 3-A, condition number 9.
b. On vehicles with a manual transmission, check for a slipping clutch. For possible causes and additional information, refer to section 2-C, condition number 1.

c. On vehicles with an automatic transmission, check the fluid level and condition. Top off or change the fluid and filter using the recommended replacement parts, lubricant type and amount. If the odor persists, transmission removal and disassembly will be necessary.

2. Engine accelerates, but vehicle does not gain speed

a. On vehicles with a manual transmission, check for a slipping or damaged clutch. For possible causes and additional information refer to section 2-C, condition number 1.

b. On vehicles with an automatic transmission, check the fluid level and condition. Top off or change the fluid and filter using the recommended replacement parts, lubricant type and amount. If the slipping continues, transmission removal and disassembly will be necessary.

3. BRAKE SYSTEM

3-A. Brake System Troubleshooting

1. Brake pedal pulsates or shimmies when pressed

a. Check wheel lug nut torque and tighten evenly to specification.

b. Check the brake rotor for trueness and thickness variations. Replace the rotor if it is too thin, warped, or if the thickness varies beyond specification. Some rotors can be machined; consult the manufacturer's specifications and recommendations before using a machined brake rotor.

c. Check the brake caliper or caliper bracket mounting bolt torque and inspect for looseness. Torque the mounting bolts and inspect for wear or any looseness, including worn mounting brackets, bushings and sliding pins.

d. Check the wheel bearing for looseness. If the bearing is loose, adjust if possible, otherwise replace the bearing.

2. Brakes make a squealing noise

a. Check the brake rotor for the presence of a ridge on the outer edge; if present, remove the ridge or replace the brake rotor and brake pads.

b. Check for debris in the brake lining material, clean and reinstall.

c. Check the brake linings for wear and replace the brake linings if wear is approaching the lining wear limit.

d. Check the brake linings for glazing. Inspect the brake drum or rotor surface and replace, along with the brake linings, if the surface is not smooth or even.

e. Check the brake pad or shoe mounting areas for a lack of lubricant or the presence of surface rust. Clean and lubricate with a recommended high temperature brake grease.

3. Brakes make a grinding noise

a. Check the brake linings and brake surface areas for severe wear or damage. Replace worn or damaged parts.

b. Check for a seized or partially seized brake causing premature or uneven brake wear, excessive heat and brake rotor or drum damage. Replace defective parts and inspect the wheel bearing condition, which could have been damaged due to excessive heat.

4. Vehicle pulls to one side during braking

a. Check for air in the brake hydraulic system. Inspect the brake hydraulic seals, fluid lines and related components for fluid leaks. Remove the air from the brake system by bleeding the brakes. Be sure to use fresh brake fluid that meets the manufacturer's recommended standards.

b. Check for an internally restricted flexible brake hydraulic hose. Replace the hose and flush the brake system.

c. Check for a seizing brake hydraulic component such as a brake caliper. Check the caliper piston for surface damage such as rust, and measure for out-of-round wear and caliper-to-piston clearance. Overhaul or replace failed parts and flush the brake system.

d. Check the vehicle's alignment and inspect for suspension wear. Replace worn bushings, ball joints and set alignment to the manufacturer's specifications.

e. If the brake system uses drum brakes front or rear, check the brake adjustment. Inspect for seized adjusters and clean or replace, then properly adjust.

5. Brake pedal feels spongy or has excessive travel

a. Check the brake fluid level and condition. If the fluid is contaminated or has not been flushed every two years, clean the master cylinder reservoir, and bleed and flush the brakes using fresh brake fluid that meets the manufacturer's recommended standards.

b. Check for a weak or damaged flexible brake hydraulic hose. Replace the hose and flush the brake system.

c. If the brake system uses drum brakes front or rear, check the brake adjustment. Inspect for seized adjusters and clean or replace, then properly adjust.

6. Brake pedal feel is firm, but brakes lack sufficient stopping power or fade

a. Check the operation of the brake booster and brake booster check valve. Replace worn or failed parts.

b. Check brake linings and brake surface areas for glazing and replace worn or damaged parts.

c. Check for seized hydraulic parts and linkages, and clean or replace as needed.

7. Vehicle has excessive front end dive or locks rear brakes too easily

a. Check for worn, failed or seized brake proportioning valve and replace the valve.

b. Check for a seized, disconnected or missing spring or linkage for the brake proportioning valve. Replace missing parts or repair as necessary.

8. Brake pedal goes to floor when pressed and will not pump up

a. Check the brake hydraulic fluid level and inspect the fluid lines and seals for leakage. Repair or replace leaking components, then bleed and flush the brake system using fresh brake fluid that meets the manufacturer's recommended standards.

b. Check the brake fluid level. Inspect the brake fluid level and brake hydraulic seals. If the fluid level is ok, and the brake hydraulic system is free of hydraulic leaks, replace the brake master cylinder, then bleed and flush the brake system using fresh brake fluid that meets the manufacturer's recommended standards.

9. Brakes produce a burning odor

a. Check for a seizing brake hydraulic component such as a brake caliper. Check the caliper piston for surface damage such as rust, and measure for out-of-round wear and caliper-to-piston clearance. Overhaul or replace failed parts and flush the brake system.

b. Check for an internally restricted flexible brake hydraulic hose. Replace the hose and flush the brake system.

c. Check the parking brake release mechanism, seized linkage or cable, and repair as necessary.

BRAKE PERFORMANCE TROUBLESHOOTING HINTS

Brake vibrations or pulsation can often be diagnosed on a safe and careful test drive. A brake vibration which is felt through the brake pedal while braking, but not felt in the steering wheel, is most likely caused by brake surface variations in the rear brakes. If both the brake pedal and steering wheel vibrate during braking, a surface variation in the front brakes, or both front and rear brakes, is very likely.

A brake pedal that pumps up with repeated use can be caused by air in the brake hydraulic system or, if the vehicle is equipped with rear drum brakes, the brake adjusters may be seized or out of adjustment. A quick test for brake adjustment on vehicles with rear drum brakes is to pump the brake pedal several times with the vehicle's engine not running and the parking brake released. Pump the brake pedal several times and continue to apply pressure to the brake pedal. With pressure being applied to the brake pedal, engage the parking brake. Release the brake pedal and quickly press the brake pedal again. If the brake pedal pumped up, the rear brakes are in need of adjustment. Do not compensate for the rear brake adjustment by adjusting the parking brake, this will cause premature brake lining wear.

To test a vacuum brake booster, pump the brake pedal several times with the vehicle's engine off. Apply pressure to the brake pedal and then start the engine. The brake pedal should move downward about one inch (25mm).

4. WHEELS, TIRES, STEERING AND SUSPENSION

4-A. Wheels and Wheel Bearings

1. Front wheel or wheel bearing loose

All Wheel and Four Wheel Drive Vehicles

a. Torque lug nuts and axle nuts to specification and recheck for looseness.

b. Wheel bearing worn or damaged. Replace wheel bearing.

Front Wheel Drive Vehicles

a. Torque lug nuts and axle nuts to specification and recheck for looseness.

b. Wheel bearing worn or damaged. Replace wheel bearing.

c. Wheel bearing out of adjustment. Adjust wheel bearing to specification; if still loose, replace.

Rear Wheel Drive Vehicles

a. Wheel bearing out of adjustment. Adjust wheel bearing to specification; if still loose, replace.

b. Torque lug nuts to specification and recheck for looseness.

c. Wheel bearing worn or damaged. Replace wheel bearing.

2. Rear wheel or wheel bearing loose

All Wheel and Four Wheel Drive Vehicles

a. Torque lug nuts and axle nuts to specification and recheck for looseness.

b. Wheel bearing worn or damaged. Replace wheel bearing.

Front Wheel Drive Vehicles

a. Wheel bearing out of adjustment. Adjust wheel bearing to specification; if still loose, replace.

b. Torque lug nuts to specification and recheck for looseness.

c. Wheel bearing worn or damaged. Replace wheel bearing.

Rear Wheel Drive Vehicles

a. Torque lug nuts to specification and recheck for looseness.

b. Wheel bearing worn or damaged. Replace wheel bearing.

4-B. Tires

1. Tires worn on inside tread

a. Check alignment for a toed-out condition. Check and set tire pressures and properly adjust the toe.

b. Check for worn, damaged or defective suspension components. Replace defective parts and adjust the alignment.

2. Tires worn on outside tread

a. Check alignment for a toed-in condition. Check and set tire pressures and properly adjust the toe.

b. Check for worn, damaged or defective suspension components. Replace defective parts and adjust the alignment.

3. Tires worn unevenly

a. Check the tire pressure and tire balance. Replace worn or defective tires and check the alignment; adjust if necessary.

b. Check for worn shock absorbers. Replaced failed components, worn or defective tires and check the alignment; adjust if necessary.

c. Check the alignment settings. Check and set tire pressures and properly adjust the alignment to specification.

d. Check for worn, damaged or defective suspension components. Replace defective parts and adjust the alignment to specification.

4-C. Steering

1. Excessive play in steering wheel

a. Check the steering gear free-play adjustment and properly adjust to remove excessive play.

b. Check the steering linkage for worn, damaged or defective parts. Replace failed components and perform a front end alignment.

c. Check for a worn, damaged, or defective steering box, replace the steering gear and check the front end alignment.

2. Steering wheel shakes at cruising speeds

a. Check for a bent front wheel. Replace a damaged wheel and check the tire for possible internal damage.

b. Check for an unevenly worn front tire. Replace the tire, adjust tire pressure and balance.

c. Check the front tires for hidden internal damage. Tires which have encountered large pot holes or suffered other hard blows may have sustained internal damage and should be replaced immediately.

d. Check the front tires for an out-of-balance condition. Remove, spin balance and reinstall. Torque all the wheel bolts or lug nuts to the recommended specification.

e. Check for a loose wheel bearing. If possible, adjust the bearing, or replace the bearing if it is a non-adjustable bearing.

3. Steering wheel shakes when braking

a. Refer to section 3-A, condition number 1.

4. Steering wheel becomes stiff when turned

a. Check the steering wheel free-play adjustment and reset as needed.

b. Check for a damaged steering gear assembly. Replace the steering gear and perform a front end alignment.

c. Check for damaged or seized suspension components. Replace defective components and perform a front end alignment.

4-D. Suspension

1. Vehicle pulls to one side

a. Tire pressure uneven. Adjust tire pressure to recommended settings.

b. Tires worn unevenly. Replace tires and check alignment settings.

c. Alignment out of specification. Align front end and check thrust angle.

d. Check for a dragging brake and repair or replace as necessary.

2. Vehicle is very bouncy over bumps

a. Check for worn or leaking shock absorbers or strut assemblies and replace as necessary.

b. Check for seized shock absorbers or strut assemblies and replace as necessary.

NOTE: When one shock fails, it is recommended to replace front or rear units as pairs.

3. Vehicle leans excessively in turns

a. Check for worn or leaking shock absorbers or strut assemblies and replace as necessary.

b. Check for missing, damaged, or worn stabilizer links or bushings, and replace or install as necessary.

4. Vehicle ride quality seems excessively harsh

a. Check for seized shock absorbers or strut assemblies and replace as necessary.

b. Check for excessively high tire pressures and adjust pressures to vehicle recommendations.

5. Vehicle seems low or leans to one side

a. Check for a damaged, broken or weak spring. Replace defective parts and check for a needed alignment.

b. Check for seized shock absorbers or strut assemblies and replace as necessary.

c. Check for worn or leaking shock absorbers or strut assemblies and replace as necessary.

4-E. Driving Noises and Vibrations

Noises

1. Vehicle makes a clicking noises when driven

a. Check the noise to see if it varies with road speed. Verify if the noise is present when coasting or with steering or throttle input. If the clicking noise frequency changes with road speed and is not affected by steering or throttle input, check the tire treads for a stone, piece of glass, nail or another hard object imbedded into the tire or tire tread. Stones rarely cause a tire puncture and are easily removed. Other objects may create an air leak when removed. Consider having these objects removed immediately at a facility equipped to repair tire punctures.

b. If the clicking noise varies with throttle input and steering, check for a worn Constant Velocity (CV-joint) joint, universal (U- joint) or flex joint.

2. Vehicle makes a clunking or knocking noise over bumps

a. A clunking noise over bumps is most often caused by excessive movement or clearance in a suspension component. Check the suspension for soft, cracked, damaged or worn bushings. Replace the bushings and check the vehicle's alignment.

b. Check for loose suspension mounting bolts. Check the tightness on subframe bolts, pivot bolts and suspension mounting bolts, and torque to specification.

c. Check the vehicle for a loose wheel bearing. Some wheel bearings can be adjusted for looseness, while others must be replaced if loose. Adjust or replace the bearings as recommended by the manufacturer.

d. Check the door latch adjustment. If the door is slightly loose, or the latch adjustment is not centered, the door assembly may create noises over bumps and rough surfaces. Properly adjust the door latches to secure the door.

3. Vehicle makes a low pitched rumbling noise when driven

a. A low pitched rumbling noise is usually caused by a drive train related bearing and is most often associated with a wheel bearing which has been damaged or worn. The damage can be caused by excessive brake temperatures or physical contact with a pot hole or curb. Sometimes the noise will vary when turning. Left hand turns increase the load on the vehicle's right side, and right turns load the left side. A failed front wheel bearing may also cause a slight steering wheel vibration when turning. A bearing which exhibits noise must be replaced.

b. Check the tire condition and balance. An internally damaged tire may cause failure symptoms similar to failed suspension parts. For diagnostic purposes, try a known good set of tires and replace defective tires.

4. Vehicle makes a squeaking noise over bumps

a. Check the vehicle's ball joints for wear, damaged or leaking boots. Replace a ball joint if it is loose, the boot is damaged and leaking, or the ball joint is binding. When replacing suspension parts, check the vehicle for alignment.

b. Check for seized or deteriorated bushings. Replace bushings that are worn or damaged and check the vehicle for alignment.

c. Check for the presence of sway bar or stabilizer bar bushings which wrap around the bar. Inspect the condition of the bushings and replace if worn or damaged. Remove the bushing bracket and apply a thin layer of suspension grease to the area where the bushings wrap around the bar and reinstall the bushing brackets.

Vibrations

5. Vehicle vibrates when driven

a. Check the road surface. Roads which have rough or uneven surfaces may cause unusual vibrations.

b. Check the tire condition and balance. An internally damaged tire may cause failure symptoms similar to failed suspension parts. For diagnostic purposes, try a known good set of tires and replace defective tires immediately.

c. Check for a worn Constant Velocity (CV-joint) joint, universal (U- joint) or flex joint and replace if loose, damaged or binding.

d. Check for a loose, bent, or out-of-balance axle or drive shaft. Replace damaged or failed components.

NOTE: Diagnosing failures related to wheels, tires, steering and the suspension system can often times be accomplished with a careful and thorough test drive. Bearing noises are isolated by noting whether the noises or symptoms vary when turning left or right, or occur while driving a straight line. During a left hand turn, the vehicle's weight shifts to the right, placing more force on the right side bearings, such that if a right side wheel bearing is worn or damaged, the noise or vibration should increase during light-to-heavy acceleration. Conversely, on right hand turns, the vehicle tends to lean to the left, loading the left side bearings.

Knocking noises in the suspension when the vehicle is driven over rough roads, railroad tracks and speed bumps indicate worn suspension components such as bushings, ball joints or tie rod ends, or a worn steering system.

5. ELECTRICAL ACCESSORIES

5-A. Headlights

1. One headlight only works on high or low beam

a. Check for battery voltage at headlight electrical connector. If battery voltage is present, replace the headlight assembly or bulb if available separately. If battery voltage is not present, refer to the headlight wiring diagram to troubleshoot.

2. Headlight does not work on high or low beam

a. Check for battery voltage and ground at headlight electrical connector. If battery voltage is present, check the headlight connector ground terminal for a proper ground. If battery voltage and ground are present at the headlight connector, replace the headlight assembly or bulb if available separately. If battery voltage or ground is not present, refer to the headlight wiring diagram to troubleshoot.

b. Check the headlight switch operation. Replace the switch if the switch is defective or operates intermittently.

3. Headlight(s) very dim

a. Check for battery voltage and ground at headlight electrical connector. If battery voltage is present, trace the ground circuit for the headlamp electrical connector, then clean and repair as necessary.

If the voltage at the headlight electrical connector is significantly less than the voltage at the battery, refer to the headlight wiring diagram to troubleshoot and locate the voltage drop.

5-B. Tail, Running and Side Marker Lights

1. Tail light, running light or side marker light inoperative

a. Check for battery voltage and ground at light's electrical connector. If battery voltage is present, check the bulb socket and electrical connector ground terminal for a proper ground. If battery voltage and ground are present at the light connector, but not in the socket, clean the socket and the ground terminal connector. If battery voltage and ground are present in the bulb socket, replace the bulb. If battery voltage or ground is not present, refer to the wiring diagram to troubleshoot for an open circuit.

b. Check the light switch operation and replace if necessary.

2. Tail light, running light or side marker light works intermittently

a. Check the bulb for a damaged filament, and replace if damaged.

b. Check the bulb and bulb socket for corrosion, and clean or replace the bulb and socket.

c. Check for loose, damaged or corroded wires and electrical terminals, and repair as necessary.

d. Check the light switch operation and replace if necessary.

3. Tail light, running light or side marker light very dim

a. Check the bulb and bulb socket for corrosion and clean or replace the bulb and socket.

b. Check for low voltage at the bulb socket positive terminal or a poor ground. If voltage is low, or the ground marginal, trace the wiring to, and check for loose, damaged or corroded wires and electrical terminals; repair as necessary.

c. Check the light switch operation and replace if necessary.

5-C. Interior Lights

1. Interior light inoperative

a. Verify the interior light switch location and position(s), and set the switch in the correct position.

b. Check for battery voltage and ground at the interior light bulb socket. If battery voltage and ground are present, replace the bulb. If voltage is not present, check the interior light fuse for battery voltage. If the fuse is missing, replace the fuse. If the fuse has blown, or if battery voltage is present, refer to the wiring diagram to troubleshoot the cause for an open or shorted circuit. If ground is not present, check the door switch contacts and clean or repair as necessary.

2. Interior light works intermittently

a. Check the bulb for a damaged filament, and replace if damaged.

b. Check the bulb and bulb socket for corrosion, and clean or replace the bulb and socket.

c. Check for loose, damaged or corroded wires and electrical terminals; repair as necessary.

d. Check the door and light switch operation, and replace if necessary.

3. Interior light very dim

a. Check the bulb and bulb socket for corrosion, and clean or replace the bulb and socket.

b. Check for low voltage at the bulb socket positive terminal or a poor ground. If voltage is low, or the ground marginal, trace the wiring to, and check for loose, damaged or corroded wires and electrical terminals; repair as necessary.

c. Check the door and light switch operation, and replace if necessary.

5-D. Brake Lights

1. One brake light inoperative

a. Press the brake pedal and check for battery voltage and ground at the brake light bulb socket. If present, replace the bulb. If either battery voltage or ground is not present, refer to the wiring diagram to troubleshoot.

2. Both brake lights inoperative

a. Press the brake pedal and check for battery voltage and ground at the brake light bulb socket. If present, replace both bulbs. If battery voltage is not present, check the brake light switch adjustment and adjust as necessary. If the brake light switch is properly adjusted, and battery voltage or the ground is not present at the bulb sockets, or at the bulb electrical connector with the brake pedal pressed, refer to the wiring diagram to troubleshoot the cause of an open circuit.

3. One or both brake lights very dim

a. Press the brake pedal and measure the voltage at the brake light bulb socket. If the measured voltage is close to the battery voltage, check for a poor ground caused by a loose, damaged, or corroded wire, terminal, bulb or bulb socket. If the ground is bolted to a painted surface, it may be necessary to remove the electrical connector and clean the mounting surface, so the connector mounts on bare metal. If battery voltage is low, check for a poor connection caused by either a faulty brake light switch, a loose, damaged, or corroded wire, terminal or electrical connector. Refer to the wiring diagram to troubleshoot the cause of a voltage drop.

5-E. Warning Lights

1. Warning light(s) stay on when the engine is started

Ignition, Battery or Alternator Warning Light

a. Check the alternator output and voltage regulator operation, and replace as necessary.

b. Check the warning light wiring for a shorted wire.

Check Engine Light

a. Check the engine for routine maintenance and tune-up status. Note the engine tune-up specifications and verify the spark plug, air filter and engine oil condition; replace and/or adjust items as necessary.

b. Check the fuel tank for low fuel level, causing an intermittent lean fuel mixture. Top off fuel tank and reset check engine light.

c. Check for a failed or disconnected engine fuel or ignition component, sensor or control unit and repair or replace as necessary.

d. Check the intake manifold and vacuum hoses for air leaks and repair as necessary.

e. Check the engine's mechanical condition for excessive oil consumption.

Anti-Lock Braking System (ABS) Light

a. Check the wheel sensors and sensor rings for debris, and clean as necessary.

b. Check the brake master cylinder for fluid leakage or seal failure and replace as necessary.

c. Check the ABS control unit, pump and proportioning valves for proper operation; replace as necessary.

d. Check the sensor wiring at the wheel sensors and the ABS control unit for a loose or shorted wire, and repair as necessary.

Brake Warning Light

a. Check the brake fluid level and check for possible leakage from the hydraulic lines and seals. Top off brake fluid and repair leakage as necessary.

b. Check the brake linings for wear and replace as necessary.

c. Check for a loose or shorted brake warning light sensor or wire, and replace or repair as necessary.

Oil Pressure Warning Light

a. Stop the engine immediately. Check the engine oil level and oil filter condition, and top off or change the oil as necessary.

b. Check the oil pressure sensor wire for being shorted to ground. Disconnect the wire from the oil pressure sensor and with the ignition in the ON position, but not running, the oil pressure light should not be working. If the light works with the wire disconnected, check the sensor wire for being shorted to ground. Check the wire routing to make sure the wire is not pinched and check for insulation damage. Repair or replace the wire as necessary and recheck before starting the engine.

c. Remove the oil pan and check for a clogged oil pick-up tube screen.

d. Check the oil pressure sensor operation by substituting a known good sensor.

e. Check the oil filter for internal restrictions or leaks, and replace as necessary.

WARNING: If the engine is operated with oil pressure below the manufacturer's specification, severe (and costly) engine damage could occur. Low oil pressure can be caused by excessive internal wear or damage to the engine bearings, oil pressure relief valve, oil pump or oil pump drive mechanism.

Before starting the engine, check for possible causes of rapid oil loss, such as leaking oil lines or a loose, damaged, restricted, or leaking oil filter or oil pressure sensor. If the engine oil level and condition are acceptable, measure the engine's oil pressure using a pressure gauge, or determine the cause for the oil pressure warning light to function when the engine is running, before operating the engine for an extended period of time. Another symptom of operating an engine with low oil pressure is the presence of severe knocking and tapping noises.

Parking Brake Warning Light

a. Check the brake release mechanism and verify the parking brake has been fully released.

b. Check the parking brake light switch for looseness or misalignment.

c. Check for a damaged switch or a loose or shorted brake light switch wire, and replace or repair as necessary.

2. Warning light(s) flickers on and off when driving

Ignition, Battery or Alternator Warning Light

a. Check the alternator output and voltage regulator operation. An intermittent condition may indicate worn brushes, an internal short, or a defective voltage regulator. Replace the alternator or failed component.

b. Check the warning light wiring for a shorted, pinched or damaged wire and repair as necessary.

Check Engine Light

a. Check the engine for required maintenance and tune-up status. Verify engine tune-up specifications, as well as spark plug, air filter and engine oil condition; replace and/or adjust items as necessary.

b. Check the fuel tank for low fuel level causing an intermittent lean fuel mixture. Top off fuel tank and reset check engine light.

c. Check for an intermittent failure or partially disconnected engine fuel and ignition component, sensor or control unit; repair or replace as necessary.

d. Check the intake manifold and vacuum hoses for air leaks, and repair as necessary.

e. Check the warning light wiring for a shorted, pinched or damaged wire and repair as necessary.

Anti-Lock Braking System (ABS) Light

a. Check the wheel sensors and sensor rings for debris, and clean as necessary.

b. Check the brake master cylinder for fluid leakage or seal failure and replace as necessary.

c. Check the ABS control unit, pump and proportioning valves for proper operation, and replace as necessary.

d. Check the sensor wiring at the wheel sensors and the ABS control unit for a loose or shorted wire and repair as necessary.

Brake Warning Light

a. Check the brake fluid level and check for possible leakage from the hydraulic lines and seals. Top off brake fluid and repair leakage as necessary.

b. Check the brake linings for wear and replace as necessary.

c. Check for a loose or shorted brake warning light sensor or wire, and replace or repair as necessary.

Oil Pressure Warning Light

a. Stop the engine immediately. Check the engine oil level and check for a sudden and rapid oil loss, such as a leaking oil line or oil pressure sensor, and repair or replace as necessary.

b. Check the oil pressure sensor operation by substituting a known good sensor.

c. Check the oil pressure sensor wire for being shorted to ground. Disconnect the wire from the oil pressure sensor and with the ignition in the ON position, but not running, the oil pressure light should not be working. If the light works with the wire disconnected, check the sensor wire for being shorted to ground. Check the wire routing to make sure the wire is not pinched and check for insulation damage. Repair or replace the wire as necessary and recheck before starting the engine.

d. Remove the oil pan and check for a clogged oil pick-up tube screen.

Parking Brake Warning Light

a. Check the brake release mechanism and verify the parking brake has been fully released.

b. Check the parking brake light switch for looseness or misalignment.

c. Check for a damaged switch or a loose or shorted brake light switch wire, and replace or repair as necessary.

3. Warning light(s) inoperative with ignition on, and engine not started

a. Check for a defective bulb by installing a known good bulb.

b. Check for a defective wire using the appropriate wiring diagram(s).

c. Check for a defective sending unit by removing and then grounding the wire at the sending unit. If the light comes on with the ignition on when grounding the wire, replace the sending unit.

5-F. Turn Signal and 4-Way Hazard Lights

1. Turn signals or hazard lights come on, but do not flash

a. Check for a defective flasher unit and replace as necessary.

2. Turn signals or hazard lights do not function on either side

a. Check the fuse and replace, if defective.

b. Check the flasher unit by substituting a known good flasher unit.

c. Check the turn signal electrical system for a defective component, open circuit, short circuit or poor ground.

3. Turn signals or hazard lights only work on one side

a. Check for failed bulbs and replace as necessary.

b. Check for poor grounds in both housings and repair as necessary.

4. One signal light does not work

a. Check for a failed bulb and replace as necessary.

b. Check for corrosion in the bulb socket, and clean and repair as necessary.

c. Check for a poor ground at the bulb socket, and clean and repair as necessary.

5. Turn signals flash too slowly

a. Check signal bulb(s) wattage and replace with lower wattage bulb(s).

6. Turn signals flash too fast

a. Check signal bulb(s) wattage and replace with higher wattage bulb(s).

b. Check for installation of the correct flasher unit and replace if incorrect.

7. Four-way hazard flasher indicator light inoperative

a. Verify that the exterior lights are functioning and, if so, replace indicator bulb.

b. Check the operation of the warning flasher switch and replace if defective.

8. Turn signal indicator light(s) do not work in either direction

a. Verify that the exterior lights are functioning and, if so, replace indicator bulb(s).

b. Check for a defective flasher unit by substituting a known good unit.

9. One turn signal indicator light does not work

a. Check for a defective bulb and replace as necessary.

b. Check for a defective flasher unit by substituting a known good unit.

5-G. Horn

1. Horn does not operate

a. Check for a defective fuse and replace as necessary.

b. Check for battery voltage and ground at horn electrical connections when pressing the horn switch. If voltage is present, replace the horn assembly. If voltage or ground is not present, refer to Chassis Electrical coverage for additional troubleshooting techniques and circuit information.

2. Horn has an unusual tone

a. On single horn systems, replace the horn.

b. On dual horn systems, check the operation of the second horn. Dual horn systems have a high and low pitched horn. Unplug one horn at a time and recheck operation. Replace the horn which does not function.

c. Check for debris or condensation build-up in horn and verify the horn positioning. If the horn has a single opening, adjust the opening downward to allow for adequate drainage and to prevent debris build-up.

5-H. Windshield Wipers

1. Windshield wipers do not operate

a. Check fuse and replace as necessary.

b. Check switch operation and repair or replace as necessary.

c. Check for corroded, loose, disconnected or broken wires and clean or repair as necessary.

d. Check the ground circuit for the wiper switch or motor and repair as necessary.

2. Windshield wiper motor makes a humming noise, gets hot or blows fuses

a. Wiper motor damaged internally; replace the wiper motor.

b. Wiper linkage bent, damaged or seized. Repair or replace wiper linkage as necessary.

3. Windshield wiper motor operates, but one or both wipers fail to move

a. Windshield wiper motor linkage loose or disconnected. Repair or replace linkage as necessary.

b. Windshield wiper arms loose on wiper pivots. Secure wiper arm to pivot or replace both the wiper arm and pivot assembly.

4. Windshield wipers will not park

a. Check the wiper switch operation and verify that the switch properly interrupts the power supplied to the wiper motor.

b. If the wiper switch is functioning properly, the wiper motor parking circuit has failed. Replace the wiper motor assembly. Operate the wiper motor at least one time before installing the arms and blades to ensure correct positioning, then recheck using the highest wiper speed on a wet windshield to make sure the arms and blades do not contact the windshield trim.

6. INSTRUMENTS AND GAUGES

6-A. Speedometer (Cable Operated)

1. Speedometer does not work

a. Check and verify that the speedometer cable is properly seated into the speedometer assembly and the speedometer drive gear.

b. Check the speedometer cable for breakage or rounded-off cable ends where the cable seats into the speedometer drive gear and into the speedometer assembly. If damaged, broken or the cable ends are rounded off, replace the cable.

c. Check speedometer drive gear condition and replace as necessary.

d. Install a known good speedometer to test for proper operation. If the substituted speedometer functions properly, replace the speedometer assembly.

2. Speedometer needle fluctuates when driving at steady speeds.

a. Check speedometer cable routing or sheathing for sharp bends or kinks. Route cable to minimize sharp bends or kinks. If the sheathing has been damaged, replace the cable assembly.

b. Check the speedometer cable for adequate lubrication. Remove the cable, inspect for damage, clean, lubricate and reinstall. If the cable has been damaged, replace the cable.

3. Speedometer works intermittently

a. Check the cable and verify that the cable is fully installed and the fasteners are secure.

b. Check the cable ends for wear and rounding, and replace as necessary.

6-B. Speedometer (Electronically Operated)

1. Speedometer does not work

a. Check the speed sensor pickup and replace as necessary.

b. Check the wiring between the speed sensor and the speedometer for corroded terminals, loose connections or broken wires and clean or repair as necessary.

c. Install a known good speedometer to test for proper operation. If the substituted speedometer functions properly, replace the speedometer assembly.

2. Speedometer works intermittently

a. Check the wiring between the speed sensor and the speedometer for corroded terminals, loose connections or broken wires and clean or repair as necessary.

b. Check the speed sensor pickup and replace as necessary.

6-C. Fuel, Temperature and Oil Pressure Gauges

1. Gauge does not register

a. Check for a missing or blown fuse and replace as necessary.

b. Check for an open circuit in the gauge wiring. Repair wiring as necessary.

c. Gauge sending unit defective. Replace gauge sending unit.

d. Gauge or sending unit improperly installed. Verify installation and wiring, and repair as necessary.

2. Gauge operates erratically

a. Check for loose, shorted, damaged or corroded electrical connections or wiring and repair as necessary.

b. Check gauge sending units and replace as necessary.

3. Gauge operates fully pegged

a. Sending unit-to-gauge wire shorted to ground.

b. Sending unit defective; replace sending unit.

c. Gauge or sending unit not properly grounded.

d. Gauge or sending unit improperly installed. Verify installation and wiring, and repair as necessary.

7. CLIMATE CONTROL

7-A. Air Conditioner

1. No air coming from air conditioner vents

a. Check the air conditioner fuse and replace as necessary.

b. Air conditioner system discharged. Have the system evacuated, charged and leak tested by an MVAC certified technician, utilizing approved recovery/recycling equipment. Repair as necessary.

c. Air conditioner low pressure switch defective. Replace switch.

d. Air conditioner fan resistor pack defective. Replace resistor pack.

e. Loose connection, broken wiring or defective air conditioner relay in air conditioning electrical circuit. Repair wiring or replace relay as necessary.

2. Air conditioner blows warm air

a. Air conditioner system is discharged. Have the system evacuated, charged and leak tested by an MVAC certified technician, utilizing approved recovery/recycling equipment. Repair as necessary.

b. Air conditioner compressor clutch not engaging. Check compressor clutch wiring, electrical connections and compressor clutch, and repair or replace as necessary.

3. Water collects on the interior floor when the air conditioner is used

a. Air conditioner evaporator drain hose is blocked. Clear the drain hose where it exits the passenger compartment.

b. Air conditioner evaporator drain hose is disconnected. Secure the drain hose to the evaporator drainage tray under the dashboard.

4. Air conditioner has a moldy odor when used

a. The air conditioner evaporator drain hose is blocked or partially restricted, allowing condensation to build up around the evaporator and drainage tray. Clear the drain hose where it exits the passenger compartment.

7-B. Heater

1. Blower motor does not operate
a. Check blower motor fuse and replace as necessary.
b. Check blower motor wiring for loose, damaged or corroded contacts and repair as necessary.
c. Check blower motor switch and resistor pack for open circuits, and repair or replace as necessary.
d. Check blower motor for internal damage and repair or replace as necessary.

2. Heater blows cool air
a. Check the engine coolant level. If the coolant level is low, top off and bleed the air from the cooling system as necessary and check for coolant leaks.
b. Check engine coolant operating temperature. If coolant temperature is below specification, check for a damaged or stuck thermostat.
c. Check the heater control valve operation. Check the heater control valve cable or vacuum hose for proper installation. Move the heater temperature control from hot to cold several times and verify the operation of the heater control valve. With the engine at normal operating temperature and the heater temperature control in the full hot position, carefully feel the heater hose going into and exiting the control valve. If one heater hose is hot and the other is much cooler, replace the control valve.

3. Heater steams the windshield when used
a. Check for a loose cooling system hose clamp or leaking coolant hose near the engine firewall or under the dash area, and repair as necessary.
b. Check for the existence of a sweet odor and fluid dripping from the heater floor vents, indicating a failed or damaged heater core. Pressure test the cooling system with the heater set to the fully warm position and check for fluid leakage from the floor vents. If leakage is verified, remove and replace the heater core assembly.

NOTE: On some vehicles, the dashboard must be disassembled and removed to access the heater core.

GLOSSARY

AIR/FUEL RATIO: The ratio of air-to-gasoline by weight in the fuel mixture drawn into the engine.

AIR INJECTION: One method of reducing harmful exhaust emissions by injecting air into each of the exhaust ports of an engine. The fresh air entering the hot exhaust manifold causes any remaining fuel to be burned before it can exit the tailpipe.

ALTERNATOR: A device used for converting mechanical energy into electrical energy.

AMMETER: An instrument, calibrated in amperes, used to measure the flow of an electrical current in a circuit. Ammeters are always connected in series with the circuit being tested.

AMPERE: The rate of flow of electrical current present when one volt of electrical pressure is applied against one ohm of electrical resistance.

ANALOG COMPUTER: Any microprocessor that uses similar (analogous) electrical signals to make its calculations.

ARMATURE: A laminated, soft iron core wrapped by a wire that converts electrical energy to mechanical energy as in a motor or relay. When rotated in a magnetic field, it changes mechanical energy into electrical energy as in a generator.

ATMOSPHERIC PRESSURE: The pressure on the Earth's surface caused by the weight of the air in the atmosphere. At sea level, this pressure is 14.7 psi at 32°F (101 kPa at 0°C).

ATOMIZATION: The breaking down of a liquid into a fine mist that can be suspended in air.

AXIAL PLAY: Movement parallel to a shaft or bearing bore.

BACKFIRE: The sudden combustion of gases in the intake or exhaust system that results in a loud explosion.

BACKLASH: The clearance or play between two parts, such as meshed gears.

BACKPRESSURE: Restrictions in the exhaust system that slow the exit of exhaust gases from the combustion chamber.

BAKELITE: A heat resistant, plastic insulator material commonly used in printed circuit boards and transistorized components.

BALL BEARING: A bearing made up of hardened inner and outer races between which hardened steel balls roll.

BALLAST RESISTOR: A resistor in the primary ignition circuit that lowers voltage after the engine is started to reduce wear on ignition components.

BEARING: A friction reducing, supportive device usually located between a stationary part and a moving part.

BIMETAL TEMPERATURE SENSOR: Any sensor or switch made of two dissimilar types of metal that bend when heated or cooled due to the different expansion rates of the alloys. These types of sensors usually function as an on/off switch.

BLOWBY: Combustion gases, composed of water vapor and unburned fuel, that leak past the piston rings into the crankcase during normal engine operation. These gases are removed by the PCV system to prevent the buildup of harmful acids in the crankcase.

BRAKE PAD: A brake shoe and lining assembly used with disc brakes.

BRAKE SHOE: The backing for the brake lining. The term is, however, usually applied to the assembly of the brake backing and lining.

BUSHING: A liner, usually removable, for a bearing; an anti-friction liner used in place of a bearing.

CALIPER: A hydraulically activated device in a disc brake system, which is mounted straddling the brake rotor (disc). The caliper contains at least one piston and two brake pads. Hydraulic pressure on the piston(s) forces the pads against the rotor.

CAMSHAFT: A shaft in the engine on which are the lobes (cams) which operate the valves. The camshaft is driven by the crankshaft, via a belt, chain or gears, at one half the crankshaft speed.

CAPACITOR: A device which stores an electrical charge.

CARBON MONOXIDE (CO): A colorless, odorless gas given off as a normal byproduct of combustion. It is poisonous and extremely dangerous in confined areas, building up slowly to toxic levels without warning if adequate ventilation is not available.

CARBURETOR: A device, usually mounted on the intake manifold of an engine, which mixes the air and fuel in the proper proportion to allow even combustion.

CATALYTIC CONVERTER: A device installed in the exhaust system, like a muffler, that converts harmful byproducts of combustion into carbon dioxide and water vapor by means of a heat-producing chemical reaction.

CENTRIFUGAL ADVANCE: A mechanical method of advancing the spark timing by using flyweights in the distributor that react to centrifugal force generated by the distributor shaft rotation.

CHECK VALVE: Any one-way valve installed to permit the flow of air, fuel or vacuum in one direction only.

CHOKE: A device, usually a moveable valve, placed in the intake path of a carburetor to restrict the flow of air.

CIRCUIT: Any unbroken path through which an electrical current can flow. Also used to describe fuel flow in some instances.

CIRCUIT BREAKER: A switch which protects an electrical circuit from overload by opening the circuit when the current flow exceeds a predetermined level. Some circuit breakers must be reset manually, while most reset automatically.

COIL (IGNITION): A transformer in the ignition circuit which steps up the voltage provided to the spark plugs.

COMBINATION MANIFOLD: An assembly which includes both the intake and exhaust manifolds in one casting.

COMBINATION VALVE: A device used in some fuel systems that routes fuel vapors to a charcoal storage canister instead of venting them into the atmosphere. The valve relieves fuel tank pressure and allows fresh air into the tank as the fuel level drops to prevent a vapor lock situation.

COMPRESSION RATIO: The comparison of the total volume of the cylinder and combustion chamber with the piston at BDC and the piston at TDC.

CONDENSER: 1. An electrical device which acts to store an electrical charge, preventing voltage surges. 2. A radiator-like device in the air conditioning system in which refrigerant gas condenses into a liquid, giving off heat.

CONDUCTOR: Any material through which an electrical current can be transmitted easily.

CONTINUITY: Continuous or complete circuit. Can be checked with an ohmmeter.

COUNTERSHAFT: An intermediate shaft which is rotated by a mainshaft and transmits, in turn, that rotation to a working part.

CRANKCASE: The lower part of an engine in which the crankshaft and related parts operate.

CRANKSHAFT: The main driving shaft of an engine which receives reciprocating motion from the pistons and converts it to rotary motion.

CYLINDER: In an engine, the round hole in the engine block in which the piston(s) ride.

CYLINDER BLOCK: The main structural member of an engine in which is found the cylinders, crankshaft and other principal parts.

CYLINDER HEAD: The detachable portion of the engine, usually fastened to the top of the cylinder block and containing all or most of the combustion chambers. On overhead valve engines, it contains the valves and their operating parts. On overhead cam engines, it contains the camshaft as well.

DEAD CENTER: The extreme top or bottom of the piston stroke.

DETONATION: An unwanted explosion of the air/fuel mixture in the combustion chamber caused by excess heat and compression, advanced timing, or an overly lean mixture. Also referred to as "ping".

DIAPHRAGM: A thin, flexible wall separating two cavities, such as in a vacuum advance unit.

DIESELING: A condition in which hot spots in the combustion chamber cause the engine to run on after the key is turned off.

DIFFERENTIAL: A geared assembly which allows the transmission of motion between drive axles, giving one axle the ability to turn faster than the other.

DIODE: An electrical device that will allow current to flow in one direction only.

DISC BRAKE: A hydraulic braking assembly consisting of a brake disc, or rotor, mounted on an axle, and a caliper assembly containing, usually two brake pads which are activated by hydraulic pressure. The pads are forced against the sides of the disc, creating friction which slows the vehicle.

DISTRIBUTOR: A mechanically driven device on an engine which is responsible for electrically firing the spark plug at a predetermined point of the piston stroke.

DOWEL PIN: A pin, inserted in mating holes in two different parts allowing those parts to maintain a fixed relationship.

DRUM BRAKE: A braking system which consists of two brake shoes and one or two wheel cylinders, mounted on a fixed backing plate, and a brake drum, mounted on an axle, which revolves around the assembly.

DWELL: The rate, measured in degrees of shaft rotation, at which an electrical circuit cycles on and off.

ELECTRONIC CONTROL UNIT (ECU): Ignition module, module, amplifier or igniter. See Module for definition.

ELECTRONIC IGNITION: A system in which the timing and firing of the spark plugs is controlled by an electronic control unit, usually called a module. These systems have no points or condenser.

END-PLAY: The measured amount of axial movement in a shaft.

ENGINE: A device that converts heat into mechanical energy.

EXHAUST MANIFOLD: A set of cast passages or pipes which conduct exhaust gases from the engine.

FEELER GAUGE: A blade, usually metal, or precisely predetermined thickness, used to measure the clearance between two parts.

FIRING ORDER: The order in which combustion occurs in the cylinders of an engine. Also the order in which spark is distributed to the plugs by the distributor.

FLOODING: The presence of too much fuel in the intake manifold and combustion chamber which prevents the air/fuel mixture from firing, thereby causing a no-start situation.

FLYWHEEL: A disc shaped part bolted to the rear end of the crankshaft. Around the outer perimeter is affixed the ring gear. The starter drive engages the ring gear, turning the flywheel, which rotates the crankshaft, imparting the initial starting motion to the engine.

FOOT POUND (ft. lbs. or sometimes, ft.lb.): The amount of energy or work needed to raise an item weighing one pound, a distance of one foot.

FUSE: A protective device in a circuit which prevents circuit overload by breaking the circuit when a specific amperage is present. The device is constructed around a strip or wire of a lower amperage rating than the circuit it is designed to protect. When an amperage higher than that stamped on the fuse is present in the circuit, the strip or wire melts, opening the circuit.

GEAR RATIO: The ratio between the number of teeth on meshing gears.

GENERATOR: A device which converts mechanical energy into electrical energy.

HEAT RANGE: The measure of a spark plug's ability to dissipate heat from its firing end. The higher the heat range, the hotter the plug fires.

HUB: The center part of a wheel or gear.

HYDROCARBON (HC): Any chemical compound made up of hydrogen and carbon. A major pollutant formed by the engine as a byproduct of combustion.

HYDROMETER: An instrument used to measure the specific gravity of a solution.

INCH POUND (inch lbs.; sometimes in.lb. or in. lbs.): One twelfth of a foot pound.

INDUCTION: A means of transferring electrical energy in the form of a magnetic field. Principle used in the ignition coil to increase voltage.

INJECTOR: A device which receives metered fuel under relatively low pressure and is activated to inject the fuel into the engine under relatively high pressure at a predetermined time.

INPUT SHAFT: The shaft to which torque is applied, usually carrying the driving gear or gears.

INTAKE MANIFOLD: A casting of passages or pipes used to conduct air or a fuel/air mixture to the cylinders.

JOURNAL: The bearing surface within which a shaft operates.

KEY: A small block usually fitted in a notch between a shaft and a hub to prevent slippage of the two parts.

MANIFOLD: A casting of passages or set of pipes which connect the cylinders to an inlet or outlet source.

MANIFOLD VACUUM: Low pressure in an engine intake manifold formed just below the throttle plates. Manifold vacuum is highest at idle and drops under acceleration.

MASTER CYLINDER: The primary fluid pressurizing device in a hydraulic system. In automotive use, it is found in brake and hydraulic clutch systems and is pedal activated, either directly or, in a power brake system, through the power booster.

MODULE: Electronic control unit, amplifier or igniter of solid state or integrated design which controls the current flow in the ignition primary circuit based on input from the pick-up coil. When the module opens the primary circuit, high secondary voltage is induced in the coil.

NEEDLE BEARING: A bearing which consists of a number (usually a large number) of long, thin rollers.

OHM: (Ω) The unit used to measure the resistance of conductor-to-electrical flow. One ohm is the amount of resistance that limits current flow to one ampere in a circuit with one volt of pressure.

OHMMETER: An instrument used for measuring the resistance, in ohms, in an electrical circuit.

OUTPUT SHAFT: The shaft which transmits torque from a device, such as a transmission.

OVERDRIVE: A gear assembly which produces more shaft revolutions than that transmitted to it.

OVERHEAD CAMSHAFT (OHC): An engine configuration in which the camshaft is mounted on top of the cylinder head and operates the valve either directly or by means of rocker arms.

OVERHEAD VALVE (OHV): An engine configuration in which all of the valves are located in the cylinder head and the camshaft is located in the cylinder block. The camshaft operates the valves via lifters and pushrods.

OXIDES OF NITROGEN (NOx): Chemical compounds of nitrogen produced as a byproduct of combustion. They combine with hydrocarbons to produce smog.

OXYGEN SENSOR: Use with the feedback system to sense the presence of oxygen in the exhaust gas and signal the computer which can reference the voltage signal to an air/fuel ratio.

PINION: The smaller of two meshing gears.

PISTON RING: An open-ended ring with fits into a groove on the outer diameter of the piston. Its chief function is to form a seal between the piston and cylinder wall. Most automotive pistons have three rings: two for compression sealing; one for oil sealing.

PRELOAD: A predetermined load placed on a bearing during assembly or by adjustment.

PRIMARY CIRCUIT: the low voltage side of the ignition system which consists of the ignition switch, ballast resistor or resistance wire, bypass, coil, electronic control unit and pick-up coil as well as the connecting wires and harnesses.

PRESS FIT: The mating of two parts under pressure, due to the inner diameter of one being smaller than the outer diameter of the other, or vice versa; an interference fit.

RACE: The surface on the inner or outer ring of a bearing on which the balls, needles or rollers move.

REGULATOR: A device which maintains the amperage and/or voltage levels of a circuit at predetermined values.

RELAY: A switch which automatically opens and/or closes a circuit.

RESISTANCE: The opposition to the flow of current through a circuit or electrical device, and is measured in ohms. Resistance is equal to the voltage divided by the amperage.

RESISTOR: A device, usually made of wire, which offers a preset amount of resistance in an electrical circuit.

RING GEAR: The name given to a ring-shaped gear attached to a differential case, or affixed to a flywheel or as part of a planetary gear set.

ROLLER BEARING: A bearing made up of hardened inner and outer races between which hardened steel rollers move.

ROTOR: 1. The disc-shaped part of a disc brake assembly, upon which the brake pads bear; also called, brake disc. 2. The device mounted atop the distributor shaft, which passes current to the distributor cap tower contacts.

SECONDARY CIRCUIT: The high voltage side of the ignition system, usually above 20,000 volts. The secondary includes the ignition coil, coil wire, distributor cap and rotor, spark plug wires and spark plugs.

SENDING UNIT: A mechanical, electrical, hydraulic or electro-magnetic device which transmits information to a gauge.

SENSOR: Any device designed to measure engine operating conditions or ambient pressures and temperatures. Usually electronic in nature and designed to send a voltage signal to an on-board computer, some sensors may operate as a simple on/off switch or they may provide a variable voltage signal (like a potentiometer) as conditions or measured parameters change.

SHIM: Spacers of precise, predetermined thickness used between parts to establish a proper working relationship.

SLAVE CYLINDER: In automotive use, a device in the hydraulic clutch system which is activated by hydraulic force, disengaging the clutch.

SOLENOID: A coil used to produce a magnetic field, the effect of which is to produce work.

SPARK PLUG: A device screwed into the combustion chamber of a spark ignition engine. The basic construction is a conductive core inside of a ceramic insulator, mounted in an outer conductive base. An electrical charge from the spark plug wire travels along the conductive core and jumps a preset air gap to a grounding point or points at the end of the conductive base. The resultant spark ignites the fuel/air mixture in the combustion chamber.

SPLINES: Ridges machined or cast onto the outer diameter of a shaft or inner diameter of a bore to enable parts to mate without rotation.

TACHOMETER: A device used to measure the rotary speed of an engine, shaft, gear, etc., usually in rotations per minute.

THERMOSTAT: A valve, located in the cooling system of an engine, which is closed when cold and opens gradually in response to engine heating, controlling the temperature of the coolant and rate of coolant flow.

TOP DEAD CENTER (TDC): The point at which the piston reaches the top of its travel on the compression stroke.

TORQUE: The twisting force applied to an object.

TORQUE CONVERTER: A turbine used to transmit power from a driving member to a driven member via hydraulic action, providing changes in drive ratio and torque. In automotive use, it links the driveplate at the rear of the engine to the automatic transmission.

TRANSDUCER: A device used to change a force into an electrical signal.

TRANSISTOR: A semi-conductor component which can be actuated by a small voltage to perform an electrical switching function.

TUNE-UP: A regular maintenance function, usually associated with the replacement and adjustment of parts and components in the electrical and fuel systems of a vehicle for the purpose of attaining optimum performance.

TURBOCHARGER: An exhaust driven pump which compresses intake air and forces it into the combustion chambers at higher than atmospheric pressures. The increased air pressure allows more fuel to be burned and results in increased horsepower being produced.

VACUUM ADVANCE: A device which advances the ignition timing in response to increased engine vacuum.

VACUUM GAUGE: An instrument used to measure the presence of vacuum in a chamber.

VALVE: A device which control the pressure, direction of flow or rate of flow of a liquid or gas.

VALVE CLEARANCE: The measured gap between the end of the valve stem and the rocker arm, cam lobe or follower that activates the valve.

VISCOSITY: The rating of a liquid's internal resistance to flow.

VOLTMETER: An instrument used for measuring electrical force in units called volts. Voltmeters are always connected parallel with the circuit being tested.

WHEEL CYLINDER: Found in the automotive drum brake assembly, it is a device, actuated by hydraulic pressure, which, through internal pistons, pushes the brake shoes outward against the drums.

MASTER INDEX